KV-510-911

An Advanced Geography of the British Isles

An Advanced Geography of the British Isles

Harold Carter, M.A.(Wales)
Gregynog Professor of Human Geography,
University College of Wales, Aberystwyth

John A. Dawson, M.Phil.(London), Ph.D.(Nottingham)
Lecturer in Geography,
Saint David's University College, Lampeter

Derek R. Diamond, M.A.(Oxon), M.Sc.(Northwestern)
Reader in Geography with special reference to Regional Planning, London School of Economics and Political Science

Kenneth J. Gregory, Ph.D.(London)
Reader in Physical Geography, University of Exeter

James H. Johnson, M.A. (Wisconsin), Ph.D.(London)
Reader in Geography, University College, London

Alan J. Strachan, M.A.(Edinburgh),
M.Sc.(Wisconsin), Ph.D.(Edinburgh)
Lecturer in Geography, University of Leicester

David Thomas, M.A.(Wales), Ph.D.(London) – Editor
Professor of Geography,
Saint David's University College, Lampeter

HULTON EDUCATIONAL PUBLICATIONS

H. Carter
J. A. Dawson
D. R. Diamond
K. J. Gregory
J. H. Johnson
A. J. Strachan
D. Thomas

ISBN 0 7175 0601 0

First published 1974 by Hulton Educational Publications Ltd.,
Raans Road, Amersham, Bucks.

Printed in Great Britain by Netherwood Dalton & Co. Ltd., Huddersfield

Contents

Preface

In 1967 Hulton Educational Publications issued *An Advanced Geography of Northern and Western Europe*. Though the British Isles are an integral part of north-west Europe, they were specifically excluded from that work on the grounds that in a series produced by British geographers, the British Isles warranted more extensive treatment than the single chapter available for each country would allow. A separate volume was then envisaged, which subsequent demand from readers of the book on north-west Europe has now stimulated.

An Advanced Geography of the British Isles may justifiably be regarded as a companion volume to the earlier work. Like the north-west Europe book, it attempts, hopefully with some success, to be 'shorter, more demanding, more selective, original, new and attractive' than some of its predecessors. Like the north-west Europe book, it has been written by university teachers who are intimately familiar with the subjects and areas they treat, and who have spent more than a few years researching and teaching these specialisms. However, the difference in scale between north-west Europe and the British Isles has meant that the approach and outlook of the present book have had to be modified considerably. The geological ordering adopted for north-west Europe did not seem appropriate for a much smaller, and generally more densely peopled area, where economic and land-use planning have achieved such importance. Consequently the framework of this book is built around the Economic Planning Regions of England and Wales, with Scotland, Ireland, and the smaller islands subdivided into comparable regions. Within the regions a very flexible system has been employed. The conventional geographical ordering of discussion, which, on the one hand, is so safe but, on the other, can become so dull if insensitively used, has not been strictly followed. Indeed, in some chapters it has been abandoned almost entirely. Each region of the British Isles is different, each has a different character and experiences different problems; no one method of approach can accommodate these variations and at the same time allow an adequate characterization of the nature of each part of the British Isles. As a whole, the book is problem-oriented, and pays particular attention to the effects of national, regional, and local planning.

Metrication is now sufficiently advanced for all distances, heights, areas, temperatures, and other quantities in the text and maps where possible to be given in metric units. But in order to assist readers in North America, and in other places where metric measurements are not yet widely used, the imperial equivalents are also quoted.

A selected list of references for further reading is appended to each chapter. The list contains only those suggestions for reading which are very relevant, and which at the same time are reasonably accessible to students and teachers.

In addition to these texts the reader should have the use of a good atlas showing relief, place names, and, if possible, other characteristics of the British Isles. An atlas which can be recommended is The Reader's Digest *Complete Atlas of the British Isles*.

Finally, the authors would like to thank all those who have given them assistance in the preparation of this book. To the many secretaries, in various parts of the country, who have converted the drafts, stage by stage, into finished texts for the press; to the cartographers, whose patience and skill in line drawing has done so much to improve the appearance of this volume; and to Hulton's staff, who have seen this book successfully through the press, sincere gratitude is proffered.

D.T.

Acknowledgements

Thanks are due to the following for permission to reproduce photographs: Aerofilms Ltd. (Plates 1–6, 8–21, 24–35, 38–44, 46–53, 55–58, 60–68, 90, 91); Northern Irish Tourist Board (Plates 7, 78, 79, 81, 85, 88); Greater London Council – Dept. of Architecture & Civic Design (Plate 22); Weekend Telegraph (Plate 23); J. Allan Cash (Plates 36, 37, 45, 69, 70, 71, 72, 86, 87); The John Madin Design Group (Plate 54); Turners (Photography) Ltd. (Plate 73); Scottish Field (Plates 74, 75, 76); Central Office of Information (Plate 77); Northern Ireland Ministry of Agriculture (Plate 80); Northern Ireland Ministry of Commerce (Plate 82); R. L. Anderson (Plate 84); Louis Pieterse (Plate 89).

The following photographs are the authors' copyright: Plates 59, 83.

Permission of the Controller of Her Majesty's Stationery Office has been obtained for the climatic figures in Chapter 2.

Maps and Diagrams

Figure		*Page*

Figure *Page*

Figure *Page*

Plates

Introduction

Judged by any standard the British Isles constitute a very small part of the land surface of the globe. As an island group they may compare quite reasonably with the areas of other off-shore islands. They are five times as big as Ceylon, three times the size of Cuba and Iceland, and about the same area as Japan and New Zealand. They even compare favourably in size with such continental European countries as Italy, Norway and Poland. But it is when they are matched against the larger countries of other continents that their size is seen in true perspective. The British Isles could be fitted ten times into India, twenty-five times into the U.S.A., thirty times into the Chinese Republic, and more than sixty-five times into the Soviet Union.

In such a relatively small area as the British Isles the surprising thing is what great diversity of life and landscape exists. There is diversity in the physical attributes of various parts of the islands, there is diversity in the historical evolution of different facets of life in different places, and there is diversity in contemporary response to these bases of the present-day scene. The marked contrasts which emerge provide one of the major themes of the book. It is concerned, to a great extent, in exemplifying and explaining variations in the landscape, and in unravelling some of the complexities which sometimes hinder clear understanding and appreciation.

Britain and the British Seas

The heading of this section, taken from the title of the classic account of the British Isles by H. J. Mackinder and written in the first decade of this century, poses the initial problem. What are the British Isles, how are they associated, and by what major groups of people are they occupied? These are complexities which have to be faced, partly in order to avoid confusion in nomenclature, but also because a difficult terminology, as is often the case, is a reflection of a highly complicated underlying situation.

Some years ago, in a very perceptive book about the British Isles called *God is an Englishman*, an Australian, Donald Horne, pointed out that there is no acceptable singluar noun to describe the inhabitant of the United Kingdom, let alone of the British Isles. 'Briton' is archaic, 'Britisher' is an Americanism and 'Britishman', to equate with 'Englishman', 'Welshman', 'German', or 'Dutchman', has hardly become popular. Little wonder that Australians and New Zealanders have settled for 'Brit', while the English, particularly the southern English, are inclined to avoid the problem by pretending that England has no boundaries to the north and west. An *Englishman's* word is his bond, and his home, his castle. He strives to perpetuate the *English* way of

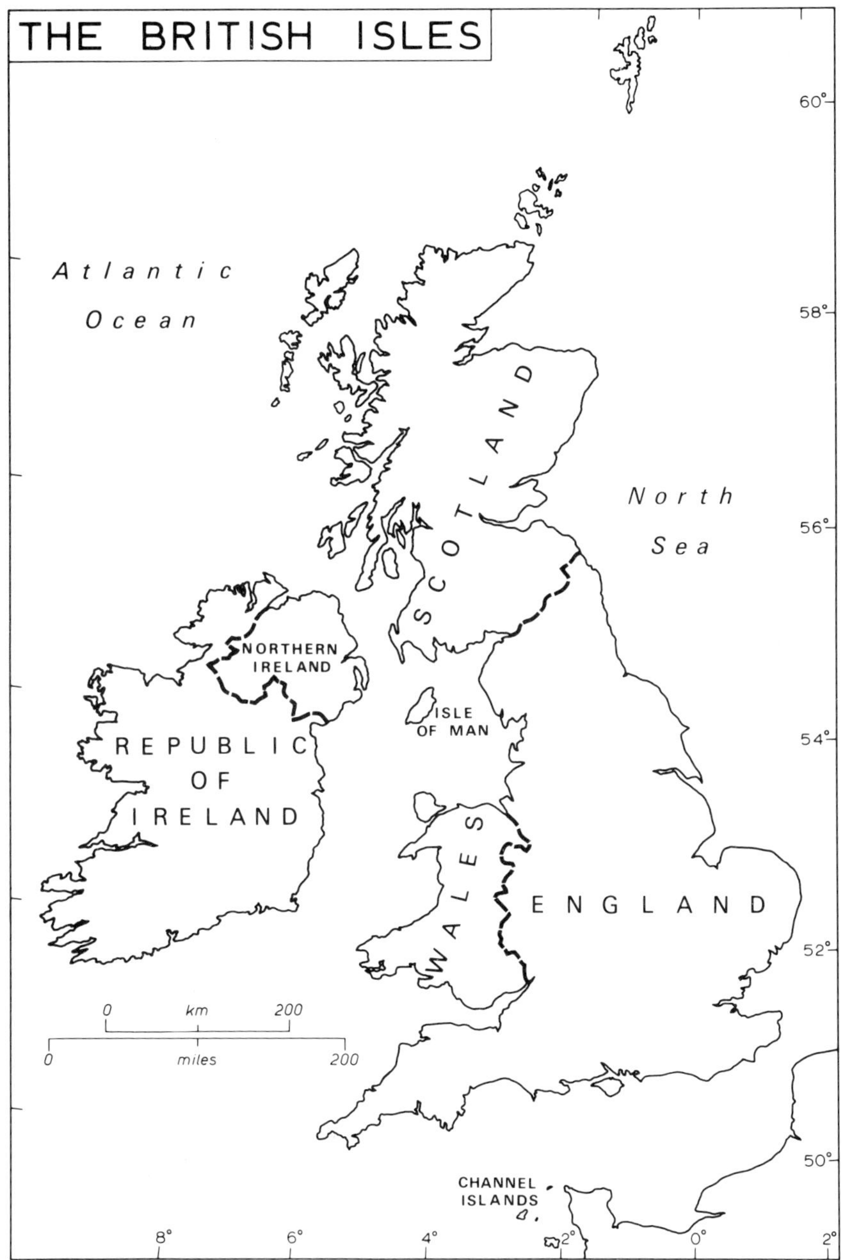

Fig 1 The British Isles
The map shows the constituent areas of the British Isles and their relationships to mainland Europe.

life and aspires to become an *English* gentleman. He is sometimes accused of arrogance by his fellow 'Brits', but in turn may charge them with parochialism and nationalism. It is interesting that though much is written of Scottish or Welsh nationalism, the term 'British nationalism' has received little currency. The fact is that all these peculiarities of the social and political scene arise from the fact that the British Isles, the subject of this book, constitute simply a geographical area, and not a cultural entity. One might justifiably regard the British Isles as being composed of the territories of a number of separate national groups, each group sensing its identity and distinctiveness, but combining, in varying degree at different times, with other groups for political, commercial, cultural, or social purposes.

'British Isles' then, is a geographical term. It includes the United Kingdom of Great Britain and Northern Ireland, the Republic of Ireland, the Isle of Man, and the Channel Islands. The 'United Kingdom' is a political unit including England, Wales, Scotland (with the Orkney and Shetland Islands), and Northern Ireland. 'Great Britain' (sometimes 'Britain') is also a political unit and includes England, Wales, and Scotland alone (Fig. 1).

THE CONSTITUENT AREAS

The largest and most densely peopled of the countries constituting the British Isles is England. It became a unified state in the tenth century, and was conquered and joined with the Duchy of Normandy in 1066. The Duchy revolted in 1204 and eventually became part of France. Since that time England, and particularly its capital, London, has emerged as the centre certainly of governmental, legal, ecclesiastical, and economic life, but to a large extent also as the centre of the social and cultural life of the British Isles. Its influence in these and other fields has extended, in greater or lesser degree, to all the other countries, but most noticeably of all at the moment, of course, to those of the United Kingdom, which operate under the same largely unwritten and customary constitution evolved within England. Under this constitution the hereditary monarch is the head of state and in practice reigns, but does not rule. Political control of England, and of the associated territories of the United Kingdom, is exercised in the name of the Sovereign by His or Her Majesty's Government—a body of Ministers who are leading members of whichever political party the electorate has voted into office, and who are responsible to Parliament. England is thus the pivotal country within a four-nation unitary (not federal) state.

Wales, the country most directly and for longest influenced by England, is an enigma. Although it has long been subjected to outside pressures, it is the only one of the countries of the British Isles which can make any real claims to have maintained its own language. Welsh is spoken by a little over one-quarter of the population, despite the commercial and cultural ascendancy of English. Wales was first brought firmly into the English sphere of influence by the Anglo-Norman incursions of the twelfth century. Military lordships were established, particularly in South Wales and in the present border country, and eventually the conquest was completed by Edward I in the late thirteenth century. English law was extended to Wales under the Acts of Union of 1536 and 1542. The Acts also outlined the boundaries of the modern counties and in so doing delimited the border between England and Wales. The allegiance of Monmouthshire was not clearly defined and this uncertainty has persisted up to the present.

Scotland, by contrast, achieved legislature union with England as late as 1707. The present border was delineated in the thirteenth century and in 1603, when James VI of Scotland became James I of England the two kingdoms became linked, though they were hardly at that time united. The Hebrides were ceded to Alexander III in 1266 by Magnus of Norway, and the Orkney and Shetland Islands fell to the Scottish Crown as a dowry pledge in 1468. Danish suzerainty was formally relinquished in 1590.

The occupation of Ireland by Norman settlers began in the last few decades of the twelfth century. Eventually most of the island was settled and a feudal government established. At later times, particularly in the fourteenth and fifteenth centuries, English control became rather tenuous, and at one stage Royal authority was confined to the 'Pale', a small district around Dublin. Unrest and rebellion were frequent and they led eventually to an Act of Union in 1800. Whatever the hopes, a political union was not followed by integration. A major insurrection in 1916 (the Easter Rising) was crushed, but by the early 1920s the British Government had been forced to partition the northern six counties and place them under a separate Northern Ireland Government (certain legislative and fiscal powers were reserved for the Westminster parliament) while granting the southern twenty-five counties dominion status. The southern counties became the Irish Free State which in 1937 declared full sovereignty. An Act of 1948, which came into force in the following year, changed the name of the state to 'The Republic of Ireland', removed all British control over external affairs, and placed the country outside the British Commonwealth as a completely independent self-governing territory.

The Isle of Man, originally under Norwegian rule, was acquired by the Scottish Crown in 1266. It eventually came under English control and was awarded by Henry V to the Stanley family in 1405. The Stanleys were succeeded by the Dukes of Athol who sold the sovereign rights to the Crown in 1766. The Isle of Man thus became a Crown Colony. It achieved self-government for internal matters in the middle of the last century.

The Channel Islands (the main islands are Jersey, Guernsey, Alderney and Sark) were part of the Duchy of Normandy at the date of the Norman conquest of England. Later, when the Duchy revolted, the islands remained loyal to the Crown and have maintained their special links with Britain ever since, though they have often been under threat from mainland Europe and were in German occupation between 1940 and 1945. The Lieutenant-Governors of the Channel Islands are the personal representatives of the Sovereign and provide the means of communication between the British Government and the local self-governing island legislatures. Though English is the language in daily use within the islands, French and a Norman-French patois are still commonly heard, and are also used on some official occasions.

ADMINISTRATIVE SUB-DIVISIONS

The main sub-divisions of England, Wales, Scotland, and Ireland have traditionally been the geographical counties. These have evolved over more than a thousand years. They originated in the shires of Anglo-Saxon England, and were adopted by the Normans after the conquest, and thereafter, over many centuries, the county system was gradually extended to cover the whole region. In Wales the present county map finally emerged during the Tudor period (the Acts of Union of the sixteenth century have already been mentioned). In Scotland the counties grew out of the nineteenth century Sheriffdoms, which themselves had existed for many centuries. In Ireland the county pattern was established during the reign of Henry II (late twelfth century) but modified later by Cromwell.

As time has gone by, the county system has made certain adjustments to the changing pattern of British life (Fig. 2). The great industrial and population changes of the eighteenth and nineteenth centuries particularly, encouraged alterations, and these were brought about by the Local Government Act of 1888, which undertook a substantial revision of county boundaries in England and Wales and created the administrative counties. It is the administrative counties, with the county boroughs, which came to be responsible for local government services. Similar changes in Scottish boundaries came with Acts of 1889 and 1929.

Boundary revisions have continued to the present. They are now most often caused by the expansion of the major conurbations into the territories of surrounding counties. The most dramatic recent example of this process was in 1965, when a major expansion of the County of London, to create a new administrative area, Greater London, led not only to the annexation of neighbouring counties, but also to the total disappearance of the County of Middlesex. Another frequent feature of economic and population readjustment is the development of more than one county town. In addition to the traditional centre there sometimes arise new economically thriving towns and cities to which the administrative and other county functions tend to transfer.

Each administrative sub-division (counties and county boroughs in England, Wales, and Ireland; counties and burghs in Scotland) has its own elected council—the local authority. This is responsible for providing many of the public services, including health, welfare, education, highways, fire fighting, and town and country planning. In undertaking these duties, local authorities must act with the authority of, and within the limits set by, Parliament. But given this constraint, they are independent bodies with freedom to operate in the best interests of their electorates. They have power to levy local taxes (rates) though normally the product of such a tax covers only about one-third of the cost of local government services. The remainder comes from central government and from a number of miscellaneous sources.

The activity of local government on which most attention will be focused in this book is in town and country planning. In England, Wales, and Scotland compulsory land-use planning was introduced under legislation passed in 1947. (In Ireland, the Isle of Man, and the Channel Islands the introduction of such control has been slower, presumably because the need was not felt to be so pressing.) As a result all counties, county boroughs, and burghs became

Fig 2 Counties of the British Isles
The present county divisions stem from a continuous process of historical, social, and economic development extending over a thousand years or more. Further major changes are imminent.

local-planning authorities, and responsible for the detailed control over the location, size, and character of towns and villages, over the siting of industry, and over the working of minerals. They were also charged with the preservation of the coast and the countryside generally.

Over most of the British Isles planning control is now exercised quite strictly. In England and Wales, for example, a total of some 175 authorities prepare development plans, showing in outline how they consider land ought to be used, and the stages by which development should be carried out. Before building, engineering, or mining can occur, before new outdoor advertising space can be used, or before a material change in the use of land can be made, other than in agriculture or forestry, the approval of the local planning authority is necessary. Activities by the Crown, and certain types of development by the local authorities themselves are exempt. Decisions are made in accordance with the policy expressed in the development plan and subject to right of appeal to the planning minister, who may set up a public enquiry. Nearly half a million planning applications are made each year but around 20% are rejected by the local planning authorities. About a quarter of these lead to appeals. Development carried out without permission may result in prosecution, or even to the serving of an enforcement notice upon the owner or occupier which in extreme cases may require the demolition or complete removal of the development.

THE GROWTH OF REGIONAL PLANNING

Regional organization and administration has not attracted much public attention in the British Isles until quite recently. Planners gradually moved towards regionalism largely because the practical problems presented in many areas of these islands needed solutions on a scale larger than that of the existing local authority areas. For example, substantial areas of the British Isles, mainly those heavily dependent upon the older-established industries associated with the coalfields, have experienced declining prosperity, relative to other areas, as their industrial base stagnates or even contracts. Unemployment is inclined to be above average, and out-migration, particularly of younger people, persistent. Such areas need not only a restructuring of their economic bases, but also a careful programme designed to utilize fully and to renew their social capital. At the other end of the economic scale, prosperous and rapidly expanding areas present substantial problems of organizing growth and minimizing congestion.

While planners, on the whole, have approached regionalism pragmatically, geographers and other scholars have found regional analysis a convenient descriptive and analytical device, and a few have applied these notions to planning and administration in the British Isles. But though much of this work dates from the early part of the inter-war period, and though a certain amount of unco-ordinated decentralization of central government functions took place in the 1930s, it needed the outbreak of war in 1939 to bring about a formal regional arrangement. Civil Defence regions were hastily devised. Scotland, Wales, and Northern Ireland were established as individual regions. England was subdivided into ten regions, each with its own capital. Most government

Fig 3 Economic Planning Regions of the British Isles
In 1965 the United Kingdom government set up a new regional framework within which physical and economic planning could be undertaken. Studies have been made of each of the regions shown and for some there are outline strategic plans which provide guidelines for future development.

departments adopted these when dispersing their activities from London and so, though the Civil Defence regions were far from ideal geographical units, they grew to have some administrative importance. With some small post-war modifications they became the Standard Regions for statistical and other purposes and persisted until 1965.

In order to stimulate the growth of the economy and to spread its benefits more evenly through the United Kingdom, the government decided in 1965 that it was essential to plan on a regional basis for the use and development of physical resources. New economic planning regions were devised (Fig. 3), each with its own economic planning council and board. The councils are composed of individuals selected by the government for their range of knowledge and experience of the region. The boards are composed of senior civil servants, specialists in economic and social affairs, who supply the technical expertise. Together the councils and boards assess the economic potential of each region and make recommendations for integrating their areas into the framework of a national plan. They have no executive authority. Scotland, Wales, and Northern Ireland have a council and board apiece while England is divided into eight regions—the South East, the South West, East Anglia, East Midlands, West Midlands, Yorkshire and Humberside, the North West, and the Northern region. It is these regions which form the basis of the areas treated in Chapter 7 and in the succeeding chapters.

One final development which needs to be mentioned is the attempt made in recent years, to revise the administrative structure of the United Kingdom. This has implications both at the local and at the regional level. Commissions or committees have been at work in each of the four countries. But though they have started with the same premise, that the present system of urban and rural administrative areas is unsatisfactory since it has the effect of cutting off a town or city from its hinterland and therefore breaks a functional unity, each committee has arrived at a separate solution for each country. For England, a system depending upon single all-purpose authorities was proposed, for Scotland a two-tier structure was suggested, while for Wales a mixture of the methods was envisaged.

To take one example: The Redcliffe-Maud Commission on local government in England, the first to report, proposed that the present 45 counties and 79 county boroughs should be replaced by 61 new local government areas covering both town and country. In 58 of these (the unitary areas) a single authority would be responsible for all services. In the three metropolitan areas around Birmingham, Liverpool and Manchester (London had already been the subject of a Royal Commission and so did not fall within Redcliffe-Maud's purview) a two-tier system would operate. At a later stage Southampton-Portsmouth was designated as a metropolitan area (Fig. 4). The Commission proposed that the present economic planning regions should be replaced by eight provinces, composed of groups of the new local government areas. No province is identical with an existing economic planning region. In the south of England there are small discrepancies: in the north, major changes are involved, the present Northern Region being split between three new provinces (compare Figs. 3 and 4).

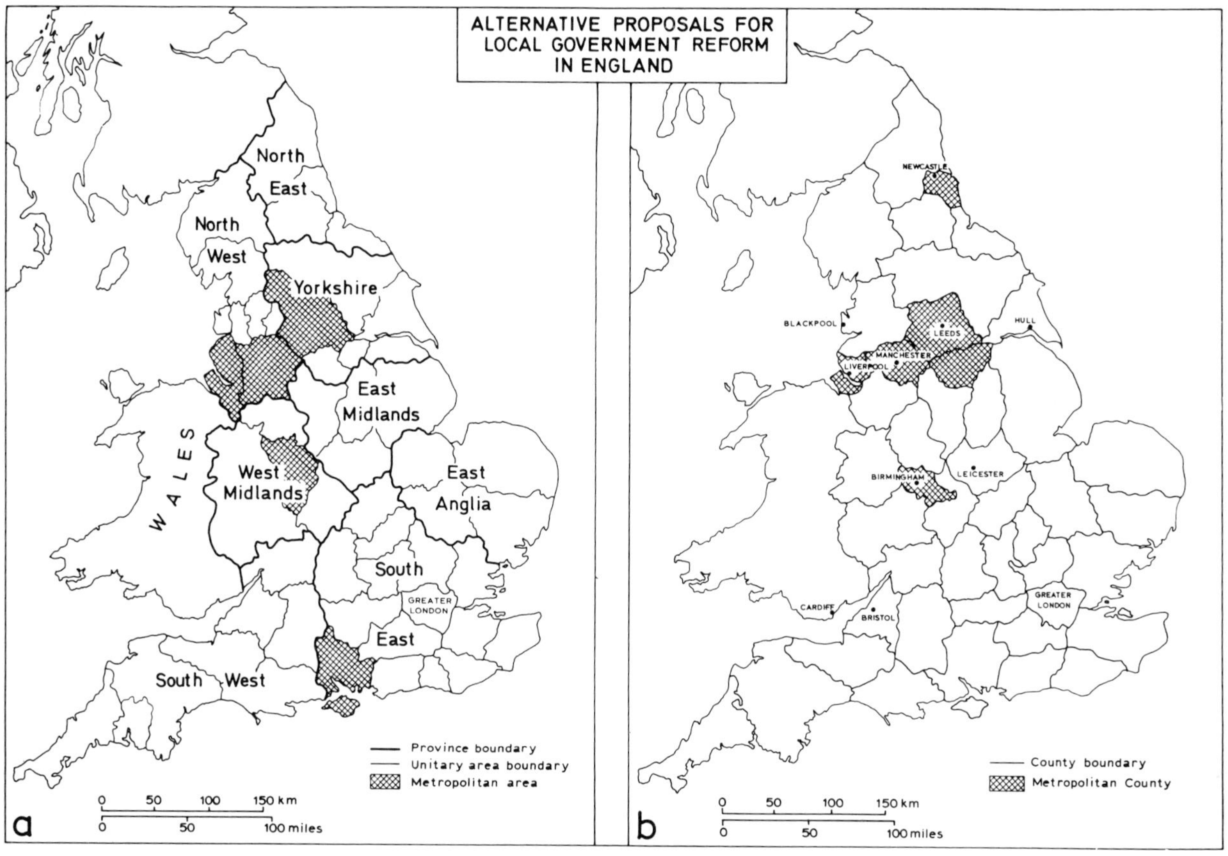

Fig 4 Alternative Proposals for Local Government Reform in England
Section (a) shows the Provincial, Unitary, and Metropolitan areas as they were provisionally agreed following the publication of the Redcliffe–Maud Commission's report on the future of local government, published in 1969. Section (b) shows the County and Metropolitan County proposals introduced by the government in 1971. The latter follow existing administrative boundaries far more closely (compare Fig. 2).

When firm government proposals for England, Scotland, and Wales eventually emerged early in 1971 they were more closely related in concept to the recommendations for Scotland, than to those of the Redcliffe-Maud Commission. The government accepted a two-tier system with counties and districts for England and Wales, regions and districts for Scotland, rather like the present organization though with responsibilities differently apportioned, and this system was to be applied uniformly over the three countries. The two sets of proposals for England are shown together in Figure 4. A comparison with Figure 2 reveals that the present reforms are also far less radical in boundary revision, although the principle of town-country counties has been introduced by amalgamating and reshaping some present counties and by abolishing county boroughs.

The British Isles in a Wider Context

Although this book concentrates on the British Isles *per se*, the implications of its external relations are very great, as will become clear in the following chapters. For example, Great Britain is the world's third largest trading nation (after the U.S.A. and West Germany) and engages in about one-eighth of the total international trade in manufactured goods. It constitutes the largest market in the world for food and agricultural products. For over a hundred years the value of its imports of merchandise has exceeded the value of exports; in many of these years the deficit on visible trade has been more than compensated by net invisible transactions, that is, by receipts from interest, dividends, and overseas investments, and by profits from shipping, insurance and a wide range of financial services. But the balance of payments is a precarious one, and an unfavourable trading year can lead to a draining of gold and exchange reserves and to pressure upon sterling. Such a crisis is commonly met by fiscal measures to reduce consumer and public spending, actions which normally have an effect on the pace of growth of all sectors of the economy. But this is just one aspect of Britain's external linkages. In addition to trade and finance there are many other spheres of influence and interdependence—social, linguistic, and defence (NATO, CENTO, SEATO), for instance.

Some aspects of the developing relations with other countries are treated in the following two sections.

THE BRITISH ISLES AND EUROPE

The attitude of the inhabitants of the British Isles is notoriously ambivalent. Despite strong traditional trading links with the Commonwealth and the U.S.A., over 35 per cent of the total trade of the United Kingdom is with other European countries, while cultural ties, and links through such activities as overseas holiday-making are strong, and are spreading themselves increasingly widely through the population. Yet insularity seems to lead to a sense of individuality and distinctiveness. While the Scots, Irish, and Welsh are very certain of their differences from the English, they are equally clear that, as a group, the 'Brits' are plainly different from other Europeans. Indeed, in everyday speech to cross to the mainland is to 'go to the continent' or even to 'go to Europe', as if to suggest that the British Isles are not part of the continent of Europe. This attitude is well epitomized in the now famous newspaper headline which on one occasion when fog had severely disrupted cross-channel traffic proclaimed that Europe was cut off from Britain. Such are the effects of island living upon a people whose destiny it is to share a land the boundaries of which are more dramatically, more clearly, and certainly more permanently defined than most others in Europe.

But insularity and parochialism are not necessarily combined. During the nineteenth century Britain commanded an empire on which the sun never set. Today that empire has translated itself into a Commonwealth trading group of independent states between which there are also rather tenuous political links. These associations, built upon past events, have a real bearing upon, and add a further dimension to, the problems raised by a desire for a closer association with other European states.

Social, economic, and political difficulties there may be, but in 1957, when the European Economic Community (the Common Market) was formed, the British Isles were already feeling the need for wider, less fettered trading possibilities. Throughout the inter-war period tariff restraints on international trade had increased, culminating in the Ottowa Agreement of 1932 and the setting up of Imperial Preference, under which Commonwealth and Empire countries traded with the United Kingdom on preferential terms. While stimulating trade with the Commonwealth and Empire and giving protection

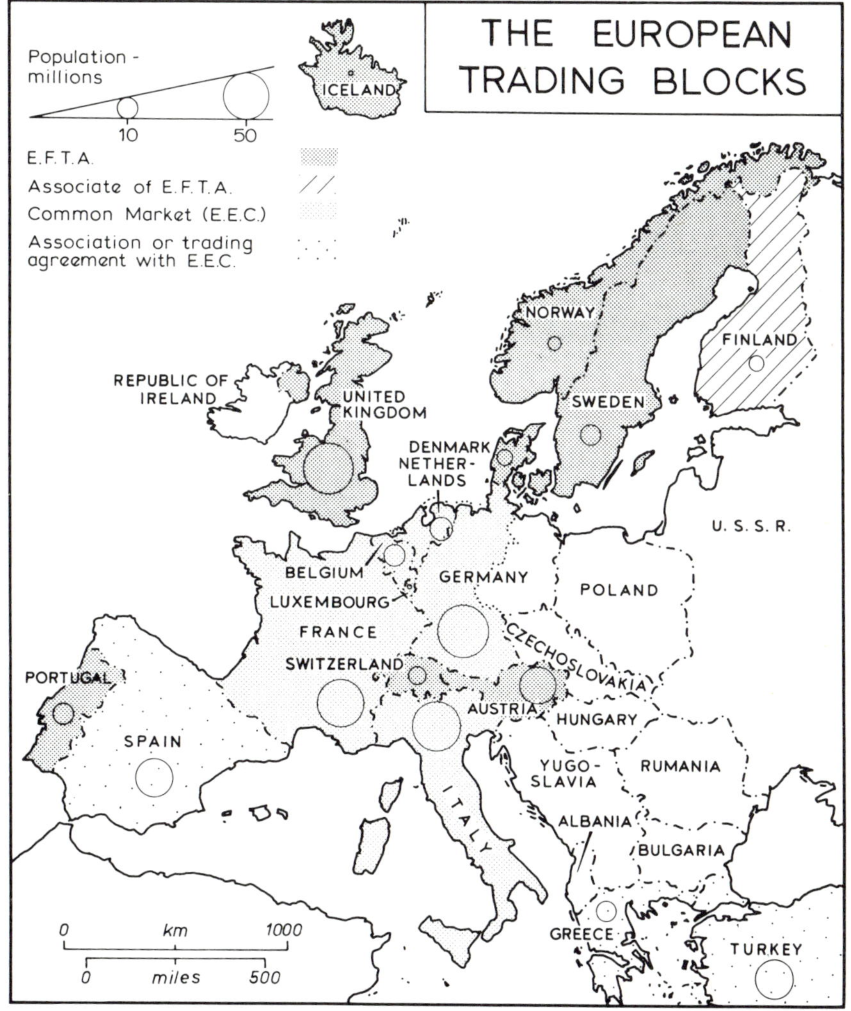

Fig 5 The European Trading Blocks

In the late 1950s the two major western European trading blocks emerged—first, the European Economic Community (Common Market) and then, in response, the European Free Trade Association.

to manufacturers serving the home market, the tariff restrictions greatly limited possibilities of export from the British Isles to Europe and to other parts of the world. Though the immediate effect was beneficial, it was inevitable that in the long run, with an economy so dependent upon expanding overseas markets, that these trade restrictions would not wholly be in the best interests of the United Kingdom. Following the Second World War a gradual re-alignment of trade occurred: the proportion of total trade undertaken with the Commonwealth fell quite sharply, the proportion of total trade undertaken with Europe, despite tariff barriers, increased markedly, while trade with the remainder of the world expanded at a more moderate rate. At the time the Common Market (E.E.C.) was established the United Kingdom was not able to adhere to all the provisions of the Treaty of Rome, which established the trading block, and thus found trading with E.E.C. members (Belgium, France, Italy, Luxembourg, Netherlands, and West Germany) more difficult than before. As a measure of self protection, the United Kingdom and most of the remaining countries of western Europe formed the European Free Trade Association (Fig. 5). Table 1 shows the value of trade between the United Kingdom and the major trading groups a few years before the establishment of the E.E.C. and E.F.T.A., and at two more recent dates. It is interesting to note that despite the very real financial disincentives against trade with Common Market countries, the combined value of imports and exports with this group has expanded fastest of all. The entry of the United Kingdom into the E.E.C. will undoubtedly further encourage this trend.

TABLE 1

FOREIGN TRADE OF THE UNITED KINGDOM

Per cent of total value of imports plus exports

	1955	*1960*	*1970*
Commonwealth	46	46	23
EEC	13	13	21
EFTA	10	11	16
Rest of World	31	36	40

BRITAIN AND THE WORLD

It is clear from what has already been written about Europe that the seas which divide may also unite. Over the last three and a half centuries trade links with the rest of the world have developed strongly, but on other planes associations have emerged which are even more obvious and direct than those observable within Europe. Many of these stem from the period of Britain's colonial expansion. Not only did the British Isles export manufactured goods in return for the raw and semi-processed materials derived from its colonial territories, it also exported people, and with them a language (now the major medium of international communication in the world), sports and pastimes, a particular type of education, new technologies, forms of administration, a method of government, and ultimately, a life-style to many other parts of the world. In return the inhabitants of these overseas territories have developed a special relationship with, and attitude towards, the British Isles which they still regard in some sense as the homeland. While this book concentrates on the British Isles, the implications of these two-way processes can never be far from mind.

Following this introductory note the book opens with six chapters which set the general background against which the detailed development of individual regions may be studied. Two chapters deal with the physical basis of land and air, including man's influence upon the physical characteristics of the countryside and upon such important sustainers of life as water supply. The four succeeding chapters introduce systematic themes, treating the rural scene, manufacturing, population and urban growth, and communications. The view is largely historical in nature, but leading to a discussion of present day national problems in those particular areas of activity. The remainder of the book (fourteen chapters) is devoted to the study of the regions of the British Isles, the Economic Planning Regions in the case of England and Wales, with comparable regional areas being identified for Scotland, Ireland and the smaller islands. These chapters pick up the themes already established and expound them, where relevant, for each region at the present time. Here planning problems particularly are highlighted. In total the book aims to give a comprehensive yet succinct account of the geography of that diverse group of islands off the north-west coast of mainland Europe which we call the *British Isles*.

FURTHER READING

E. G. Bowen, Le Pays de Galles, *Transactions of the Institute of British Geographers*, 26 (1959), 1–24.

H. C. Darby (ed.), *An Historical Geography of England before A.D. 1800* (Cambridge, 1936).

J. B. Cullingworth, *Town and Country Planning in England and Wales* (London, 1967).

T. W. Freeman, *Ireland* (London, 1950).

R. J. Harrison-Church *et al.*, *An Advanced Geography of Northern and Western Europe* (London, 1967).

W. G. Hoskins, *The Making of the English Landscape* (London, 1955).

W. Smith, *An Economic Geography of Great Britain* (London, 1949).

J. A. Symon, *Scottish Farming Past and Present* (London, 1959).

The Physical Basis: The Land

Contrasts in the Landscape

Density of feature was selected by Henry James as being the greatest single characteristic of English scenery. Although his observation referred to the total landscape, it can be applied equally to the form and character of the physical landscape of the British Isles as a whole. Density of feature applies however within a certain scale (Fig. 6). The extremes of the relief scale are set by the height of the highest mountain, Ben Nevis at 1,343 metres (4,406 feet) and by the depth of the deepest Scottish loch (Morar) which reaches 310 metres (1,017 feet) below sea level. Little more than one fifth of Ireland lies above the 150 metre (492 feet) contour. As their name suggests the British Isles include numerous islands other than the two large ones, and Scotland for example includes 787 of which only sixty exceed in area eight square kilometres (3 square miles). The island character imposes further limitations of

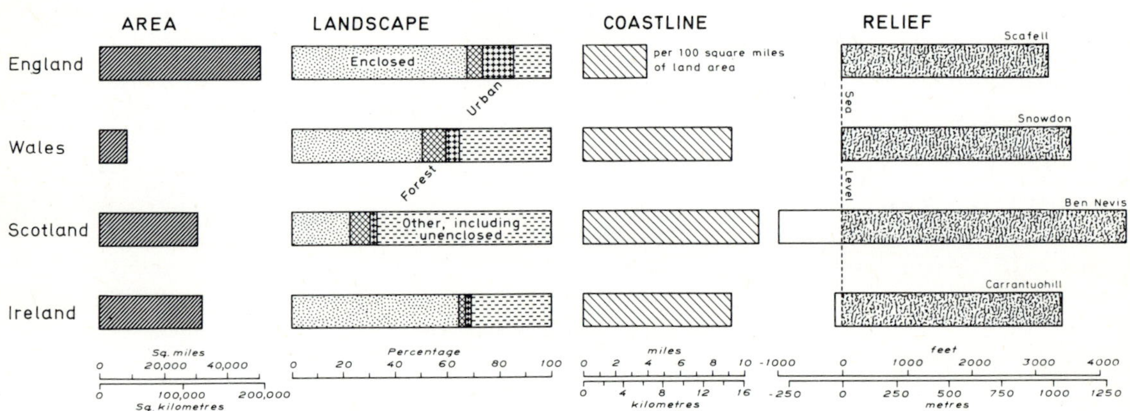

Fig 6 Some Considerations of Scale

The area, percentage of four land-use elements, length of coastline, and amplitude of relief are compared left to right in four divided rectangles. The coastline is shown for comparative purposes as length in kilometres per 259 square kilometres (miles per 100 square miles) of land area.

Fig 7 The Setting and Relief

The two sections are generalized and the 200 metre submarine contour does not correspond precisely with the edge of the continental shelf. In Great Britain the junction of the highland and the lowland zones extends approximately from the mouth of the Tees to the mouth of the Exe.

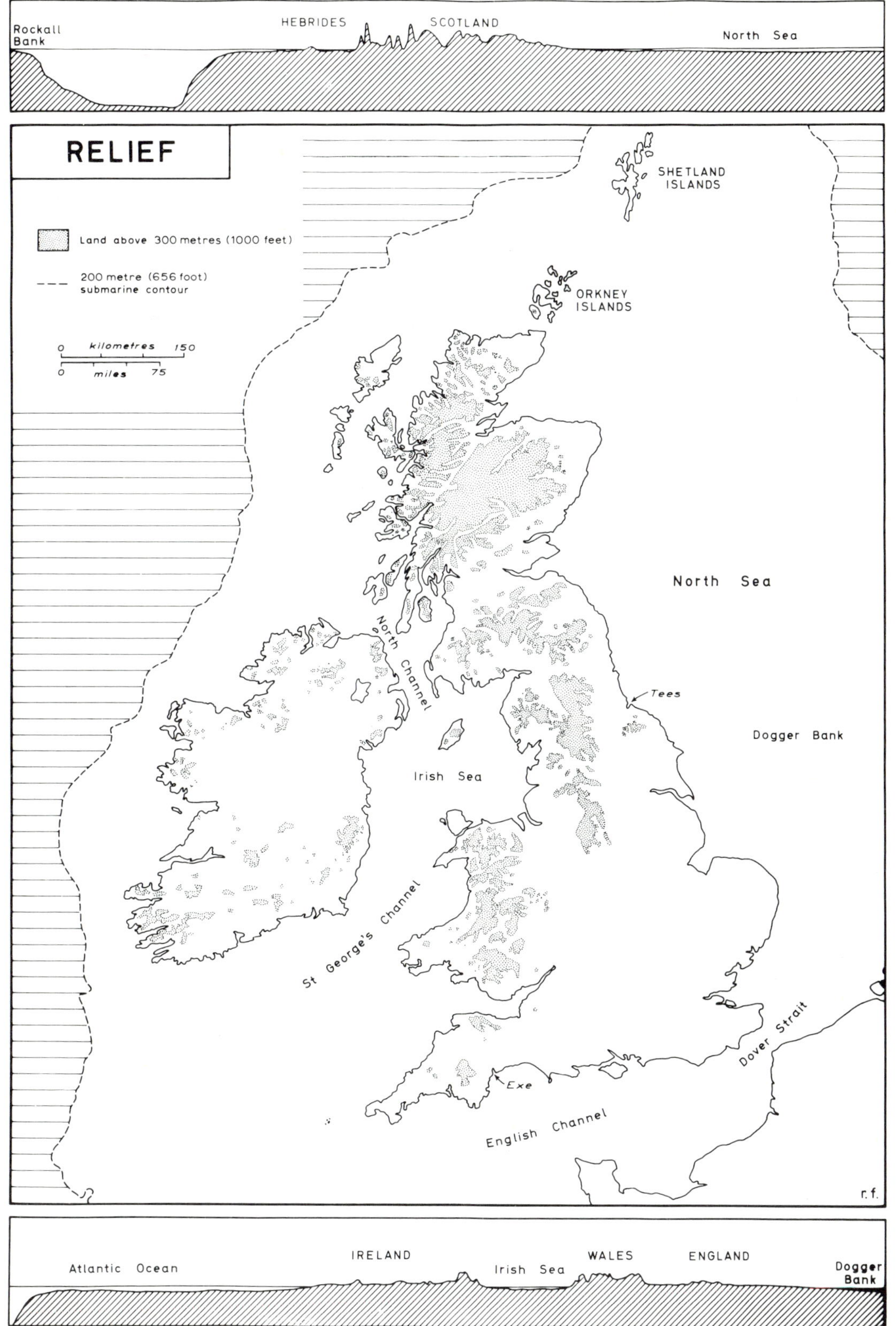
Rockall Bank
HEBRIDES
SCOTLAND
North Sea
RELIEF
Land above 300 metres (1000 feet)
200 metre (656 foot) submarine contour
0 kilometres 150
0 miles 75
SHETLAND ISLANDS
ORKNEY ISLANDS
North Sea
North Channel
Tees
Dogger Bank
Irish Sea
St George's Channel
Dover Strait
Exe
English Channel
r.f.
Atlantic Ocean
IRELAND
Irish Sea
WALES
ENGLAND
Dogger Bank

scale in that few areas are very distant from the sea, few places in Scotland are more than 65 kilometres (40 miles) beyond the margin of the indented coastline, and the ratio of coastline to land area is high (Fig. 6). The scale consideration is further emphasized by the location of the British Isles (Fig. 7) on the continental shelf which is only locally deeper than 90 metres (295 feet); maximum depths below sea level are of the order of 180 metres (590 feet) in the Irish Sea and 150 metres (492 feet) in the North Sea (Fig. 7). Lesser depths are common around the shores of the British Isles, but 50 kilometres (31 miles) west of Ireland and the Outer Hebrides the continental shelf ends and the sea bed plunges to depths of 2,400 metres (7,874 feet) and more in the eastern Atlantic.

Within these limitations of scale however there is ample scope for density of feature and for scenic contrasts. An early response among geographers in Britain was to recognize a highland and a lowland zone (Fig. 7); a contrast depending mainly upon relief, and one which in large measure echoes the difference between older and younger rocks, and which, in turn, is reflected in the broad pattern of climate, soils and land use. An alternative contrast may be drawn between the glaciated north and the unglaciated south. Contained within this two-fold division exist further contrasts, such as that between the deeply-dissected western part of Scotland and the hill masses of eastern Scotland, or between the scattered uplands of Ireland and the lake-strewn boggy plateau which they embrace. Perhaps the most striking contrast is between the enclosed lands and the unenclosed mountain and moorland, for although man's influence is imprinted over all areas, it is most patently apparent in the field boundaries of the enclosed areas, which extend over some three-quarters of England and over one-quarter of Scotland.

The Geological Foundation

The products of geological time are well-represented in the British Isles and the complete range of sediments from Pre-Cambrian to the present finds a place on the geological map (Fig. 8). This map is necessarily very detailed and the claim that the rapid changes in rock type are as great in Britain as anywhere in the world is to some extent a reflection of the attention which has been concentrated upon mapping. The names for many periods in the Geological Column (Fig. 8) are derived from the British Isles.

The Pre-Cambrian, the Lower Palaeozoic and the Devonian and Carboniferous rocks (Fig. 8) are those that underly the highland zone, whereas the area south and east of the Tees-Exe line is founded principally upon younger, less-resistant, and often less folded strata. In the lowland zone the most recurrent pattern of topography is that of the scarp, dip slope and vale, and this pattern occurs not only at the scale of the North and South Downs, the Chilterns and the Cotswolds, separated by intervening clay vales, but it occurs also on the smaller scale of minor cuestas, which add further diversity to the landscape of the lowland zone. The highland zone is generally more elevated as a result of the presence of the more intensely-folded and harder

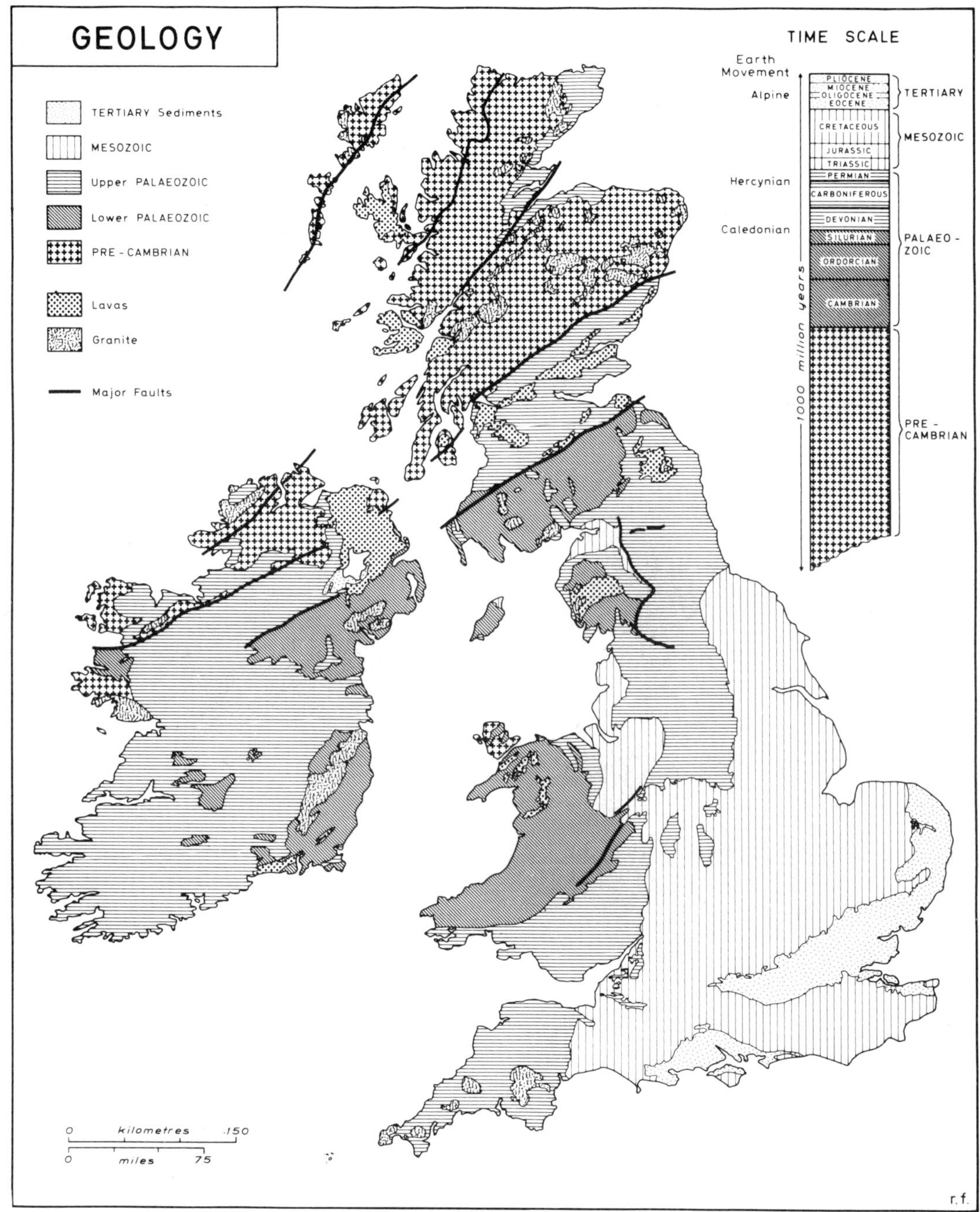

Fig 8 The Geological Basis

A generalized map designed to show the broad geological background. The time scale is drawn approximately to scale and shows the Periods in relation to the shading employed on the map. The Quaternary (Pleistocene and Holocene) cannot be shown at this scale and Pre-Cambrian phases of mountain building or earth movement are not included.

lithologies, which have rendered the zone less susceptible to denudation. Within this two-fold division of Britain are numerous contrasts which frequently reflect variations in rock type and result in areas each possessing a particular distinctive character. Many such areas are referred to by long-established regional names such as Dartmoor, the Malverns and the Ochil hills.

Plate 1 Wenlock Edge (Shropshire)
The pattern of scarp, dip slope and vale is a frequently recurring feature of the English landscape and it gives rise to rapid variations in soils and land use. From left to right the lowland is underlain by Wenlock shales overlain by till, the first scarp is developed on the Wenlock limestone, the clay vale (Hope Dale) is underlain by Lower Ludlow shales and the scarp of the second cuesta (Aymestry ridge) is formed by Aymestry limestone. Variations in soil type have been detected according to the three landscape facets of scarp (rendzina or brown calcareous soil on pure limestone, leached brown soils or shallow acid brown soils where the scarp is formed of silty calcareous shales or siltstones respectively), dip slope (leached brown soils on higher parts but acid brown soils on siltstones and leached brown soils with gleying on silty shales) and vales (leached brown soils with gleying and surface water gley soils on depressed sites).

The Pre-Cambrian rocks, frequently represented by schists and by a variety of well-folded rocks including some igneous and many metamorphic, are extensive in the Highlands of Scotland and in north-west Ireland. In some areas the varying resistances and structural weaknesses have been picked out by glacial erosion as in the case of the Outer Hebrides. Elsewhere in restricted outcrops the Pre-Cambrian rocks impart a distinctive character, as in Charnwood Forest, where colourful slates appear from beneath the Trias of the Midlands. The Lower Palaeozoic rocks are usually slates, shales and sandstones. They underly much of south-west Wales, the southern Uplands of Scotland and eastern Ireland (Fig. 8), and they are revealed, for example, in the large slate quarries of North Wales and the Lake District. The Old Red Sandstones of Devonian age are found in north and south Devon and in areas adjacent to and including south-east Wales. The Carboniferous rocks (Fig. 8), notable for their vertical and horizontal variety of lithology, include limestones, sandstones and not least the Coal Measures. The Coal Measures have exercised a major influence on the industrial evolution of Britain, and this is paralleled by the effect of the massive Carboniferous limestones on the scenery of, for example, the Pennines, the Mendips and North Wales. The New Red Sandstones of the Permian and the Trias include lithologies which, being easily eroded, provide the lowlands or the vales of Eden, York and the Midlands, and generally surround the older rocks mentioned above. Although this group includes scarp-forming lithologies such as the Magnesian limestone, east of the Pennines, the main scarp-formers are provided by the Mesozoic succession, which includes alternations of limestones underlying the most elevated areas, and clays and shales which floor the vales intervening between the cuestas. The scarp-lands of eastern England, dominated by the Jurassic outcrop which extends from Dorset to Yorkshire, are followed to the south east by the Oxford clay vale and then by the Cretaceous limestone or Chalk, which underlies a large area extending south from the Yorkshire Wolds, through East Anglia to the Chilterns and to the chalk-lands of south and south-eastern England. The Tertiary sedimentary rocks are found mainly in basins with surfaces which are low-lying, as in the Hampshire and London basins, but the Tertiary period was also represented in some areas by great outpourings of lava. These horizontal lava flows make their distinctive contribution to the landscapes of areas like the basalt Antrim Plateau of north-east Ireland. The general pattern of rock types, portrayed in Figure 8, is further diversified by numerous areas of igneous rocks, the largest of which are found in the granite batholith of the Wicklow Mountains in south-east Ireland, in the Highlands of Scotland and in most of the hill masses of south-west England. The pattern of outcrops is complemented by broad structural trends. In the lower Palaeozoic rocks the Caledonian trend is clearly shown in the general south-west to north-east alignment of the rock types of south-west Wales and southern Scotland. In southern Ireland and the south-west of England a later Hercynian or Variscan trend is responsible for the broad west to east lineation of the relief. Structural trends are vividly apparent in Scotland, where the lines of the Highland Boundary fault and the Southern uplands fault bound the

Plate 2 Scoraig (Ross and Cromarty)
The north west side of Little Loch Broom, which is a typical fjord basin of the western coast of Scotland, here developed over Pre-Cambrian Torridonian sandstone. The platform, on which the enclosed land occurs, is a typical element around the coastal margins of the highland zone. In some cases numerous platform levels have been identified but in this area three may be observed. The upper two occur below the 50 metre contour and are Pleistocene whereas the third is the post-glacial shoreline. Recent research has shown the extent to which all such shorelines in Scotland are tilted as a result of isostatic recovery of the land.

central lowlands, and also in north-east Ireland. The Highlands of Scotland are further subdivided by the Great Glen fault line, which has been exploited by rivers and ice to form the distinctive linear feature containing lochs such as Loch Ness (Fig. 8).

The Evolving Outlines

Despite the way in which the rocks, through their lithologies and structure, are often responsible for the broad outlines of the British landscape, and despite the fact that they are equally significant in accounting for the detailed variations of slope on many valley sides, and in contributing to the human landscape in the form of diverse building materials and in the fabric of field boundaries, there are many instances in which the structure is ignored by the form of the ground surface and by drainage patterns, and in which the solid foundation is masked by superficial deposits—the products of Quaternary time. These anomalies attracted early attention and the evolution of British scenery has been studied in great detail, not only where the structure has no apparent influence, but also where it is sympathetically reflected in the form of the surface.

In the nineteenth century and subsequently, many writers noted instances where the ground surface of the highland zone, as in South Wales, cuts across structures with complete disregard for the geological variety. The drainage pattern is equally independent of structure in many areas. Much of the highland zone of the British Isles is represented by accordant summit areas of low relief. These upland plains are prevalent, and moorland rather than mountain is common. Upland plains, or surfaces of planation, are accompanied by similar but less extensive surfaces at lower levels fringing the margins of the upland areas (Plate 2). The search for an explanation of planation surfaces which have been discerned widely in the northern and western parts of Britain, and of the drainage patterns with which they are associated, has been long and continued. Frequently conscious of the presence of the sea and of the erosional effects which it can have, early explanations tended towards interpretation of these surfaces as extensive marine plains, which were subsequently dissected. Later theories have relied upon the facts that the Cretaceous rocks of the Mesozoic (Fig. 8) were formerly much more extensive, the mid-Tertiary period was characterized by substantial earth movements of folding, faulting and igneous activity, and that after the end of Tertiary time a shoreline feature was produced at a height of 210 metres (690 feet) above present sea level. Subsequently sea level fell but was interrupted by a series of fluctuations in sympathy with the glacial and interglacial ages of Quaternary time. The explanatory sequence now achieved, assisted by the stratigraphic record of south-east England, suggests that the present landscape of the British Isles began to evolve at the end of the Cretaceous. The Cretaceous sediments may have been sufficiently extensive to cover much of what is now the highland zone. In Tertiary time a series of dominantly eastward-flowing drainage systems were the local controls for erosion, and as the drainage pattern was gradually superimposed on to the underlying rocks, the Cretaceous cover was gradually stripped back. Climatic conditions were then sub-tropical in character, and on the surface produced there are remnants of tropical weathering products, instanced by the sarsen stones of the Chalk outcrops of the south.

In this way, one of the level surfaces so characteristic of the uplands of the British Isles was produced. The early Tertiary surface falls generally in height from approximately 900 metres (2,950 feet) in the Grampians, to 600 metres

(1,970 feet) in Wales, 450 metres (1,477 feet) in south-west England and finally extends below sea level in southern Brittany. The earth movements of middle Tertiary time were responsible for the deformation of this surface. Finally, in the late Tertiary, further surfaces of erosion between 230 and 290 metres (755–950 feet) were produced and accompanied in the most elevated areas by similar surfaces, which also are unwarped and transect igneous intrusions dated as mid-Tertiary.

At the end of Tertiary time the landscape of the British Isles was much less deeply-dissected than is the landscape of the present, but the subsequent Quaternary period introduced more dramatic and diversified elements. A general fall of sea level during the last two million years, accompanied by sea-level fluctuations over a range of 90 metres (295 feet), has produced deep dissection in islands where no area is immune from the influence of the sea. During this period valleys have been deepened in stages and the landscape fashioned to its present form. Often gravel-covered river terraces have been created, as in the Thames and Severn valleys, which record sea levels higher than those of today. The Quaternary period was also notable for the several phases of refrigeration that occurred (Fig. 9).

THE GLACIAL IMPRINT

More than a hundred years of detailed study have been devoted to the description of the glacial deposits, to the morphological consequences of glacial erosion and deposition, and to the use of such information in conjunction with datable horizons to erect a chronological sequence. The increasing wealth of evidence accumulated has led to a deeper and more detailed understanding of the vicissitudes of Pleistocene time, but the achievement of this understanding has in turn been retarded by the physical character of the British Isles, where the evidence for the sequence of glaciations in Ireland, Wales and eastern England cannot easily be inter-related. Furthermore the effects of the most recent glaciations largely obscured the evidence for the earlier ones. Complete unanimity of interpretation has not yet been achieved, but the broad chronological picture of the glaciations which affected the British Isles has now been sketched (Fig. 9). The majority of the evidence for the first two glaciations is found in the drift sequences of East Anglia, although traces of equivalent deposits have been reported in west Cornwall and elsewhere. The penultimate glaciation, more extensive than the last glaciation, is recorded in drift deposits which extend from East Anglia through the Midlands to Wales and is evidenced by the Eastern General deposits of Ireland (Fig. 9). The last glaciation is best evidenced by drift deposits, and these extend southwards to what was formerly described as the limit of 'Newer Drift', a line partly demarcated by morainic accumulations in the Vale of York, on the fringes of the south western Pennines, in the Midlands and in South Wales. In Ireland the equivalent limit is marked by moraines, extending from Dublin to County Clare. This was largely the limit of ice which originated actually within the island, whereas ice originating in Scotland had been an element in the penultimate glaciation. A series of moraines, it has been suggested, occur

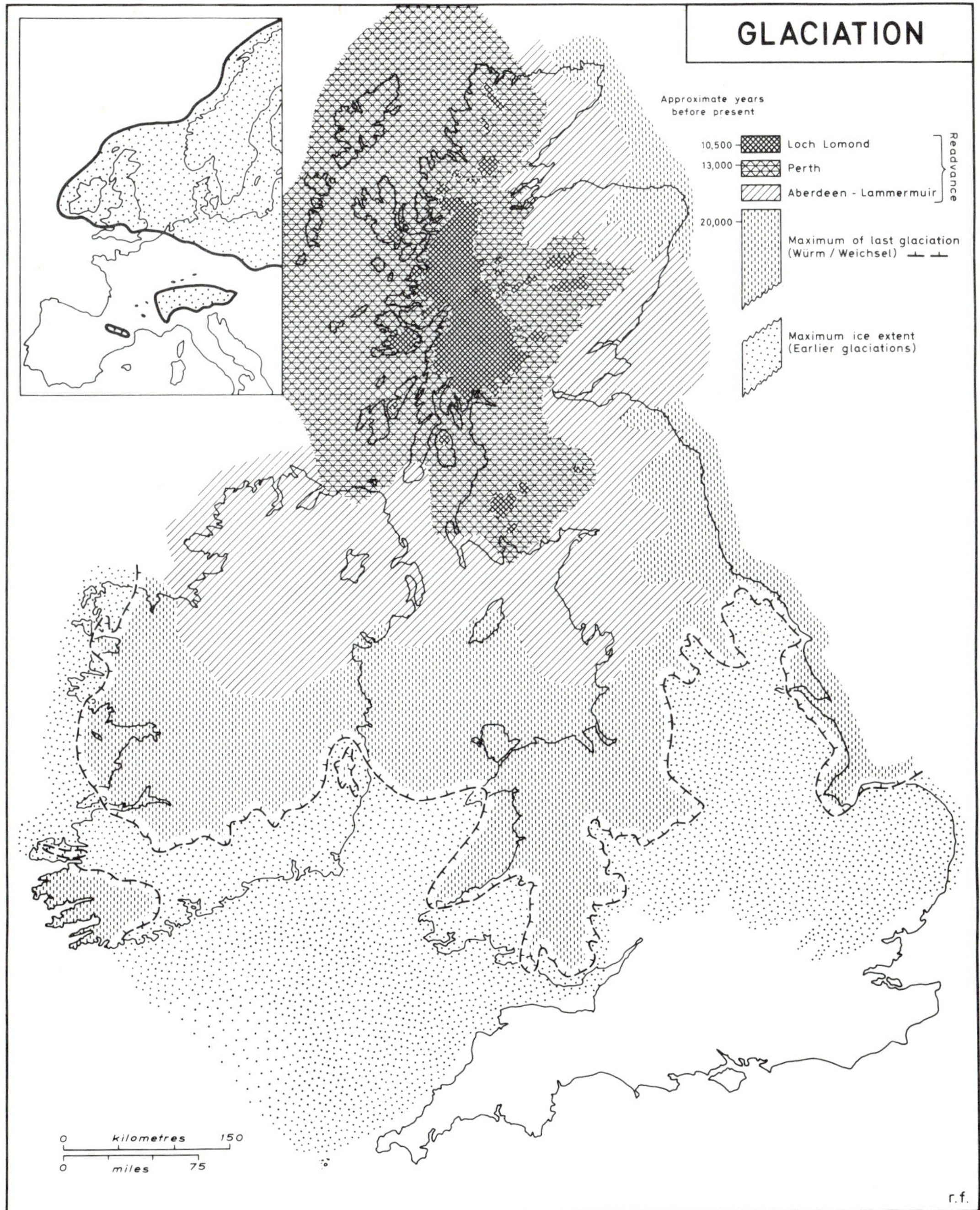

Fig 9 The generalized Pleistocene chronology

The inset map shows the maximum extent of glacier ice and this is indicated approximately on the large map by the southern limit of the shading. Within the limit of the last glaciation ('Newer Drift') the four main stages shown are based largely upon work collated by Dr. J. B. Sissons.

beneath the Irish Sea providing the essential links between the record of Wales and that of Ireland. The last glaciation has gradually been subdivided into four main stages, covering the time period from about 70 to 10 thousand years ago. During this period three important interstadials may have separated the four glacial phases. After the maximum advance of the last glaciation shown in Figure 9 the ice decayed, but there followed a further readvance which covered Scotland, northern Ireland and northern England. The final two readvances were largely confined to Scotland, although the Highland readvance (10,800 to 10,300 years ago) and the earlier Perth readvance may have been accompanied by the extension of small glaciers from corries in areas like the Lake District and North Wales.

The record of these glaciations is the record of a number of phases which profoundly modified the scenery of the British Isles. The glaciations began in areas which included centres in the western highlands of Scotland, the Southern Uplands, the Lake District, Wales and western Ireland, and on each occasion ice spreading from such local centres advanced easily in the North Sea and the Irish Sea basins, and in the lowlands of Scotland, Ireland and around the Pennines in England. These local centres are dominantly within the highland zone—their westerly situation combined with the advantage of altitude encouraged snow accumulation. The consequences, in such areas of the highland zone, include the characteristic imprint of glacial erosion (Plate 3) exemplified by U-shaped glacial troughs extending from corries, and frequently diversified by areas where glacial erosion has moulded, streamlined and exposed the underlying rock. In some areas glacial erosion was not merely responsible for changing the form of the valleys and for introducing new landforms but it could be credited also with the wholesale modification of valley patterns. Glacial over-deepening produced lochs, fjords and small lakes in glacially scoured basins in western Scotland, and the lakes of Cumberland and Westmorland. In some areas watersheds were breached and eroded by ice so that radiating valleys were produced, for example, in the Lake District and in the southwestern Highlands of Scotland including Loch Lomond.

Ice moving from these areas conveyed with it many erratics indicating its source, and these are frequently embedded in a matrix of clay—the boulder clay or till. The matrix of the tills often indicates that erosion must have taken place in lowland areas too, as is shown by the colour of the till in central Scotland and in North Wales derived from the Triassic rocks. Erosion of the lowlands is not as apparent as the features of glacial deposition. Such deposition does occur in the valleys in the uplands but is most extensive in the lowlands. Although the areas of 'Older Drift' such as East Anglia possess few distinctive landforms, elsewhere the last glaciation has left a characteristic imprint, including great spreads of drumlins. Drumlin is a term derived from druim, a Gaelic word for mound or rounded hill, and so appropriate to one of the greatest drumlin concentrations in the world which extends from eastern Down to Donegal Bay in Ireland (Plate 4). Drumlins occur less extensively in the Tweed basin of the Southern Uplands, in the Vale of Eden and in Pennine dales, but perhaps they are most distinctive where they have been partially submerged, as in the inis of Clew Bay, Donegal Bay and Lough Erne in

Plate 3 Wastwater (Cumberland)
One of the radiating lakes of the English Lake District which occurs in a glacially-shaped trough. The maximum depth of the lake is 79 metres (258 feet) and the sides of the trough, scree-covered in their lower parts and with numerous rock outcrops at higher levels, rise to heights of approximately 600 metres (2,000 feet). This area lies within the 2,500 mm (98·4 inch) annual isohyet and the Lake District is a source of water supply for Manchester and other areas. Increase in the supply of water may conflict with local or amenity interests; 2,240 square kilometres (866 square miles) of the Lake District were designated a National Park in 1951.

Ireland. Deposition as well as erosion could produce a lake landscape and the numerous lakes of central Ireland are the depositional counterpart of the basins produced by erosion in the uplands. Throughout all parts of glaciated Britain it has been increasingly appreciated that the decay of the vast ice sheets had a considerable impact on the features of the landscape. These include channels and large valleys cut by meltwater, landforms produced where drainage may have been impounded in the form of ice-dammed lakes, and fluvioglacial deposits in the form of eskers and spreads of gravel, features that have all added further diversity to the legacy of glaciation in the landscape of the British Isles.

Plate 4 Drumlins (County Down)
This area is dominated by drumlins which vary in size but are typically $\frac{3}{4}$ kilometre long and $\frac{1}{3}$ kilometre wide. It has been suggested that there are some tens of thousands of drumlins extending over approximately 12 per cent of Ireland. In this area the drumlins are largely composed of till of the last glaciation (Midland General) and they represent the eastern part of a belt which extends westwards across Ireland to Donegal Bay. The undulations of the surface can be picked-out through the snow cover.

During glaciation sea level was relatively low but high sea levels occurred during the intervening interglacials. The effects of these varying sea levels are recorded in the river terraces and raised shorelines of the British Isles, although in north-east Ireland and in Scotland they have been deformed following the isostatic recovery of the land. The changes of sea level stimulated the increased dissection of the landscape as the Quaternary progressed. Particularly in southern England, beyond the limits of glaciation, early research concentrated upon the effects of sea level change, but the consequences of periglaciation, though not as obvious as those produced by glaciation further north, have subsequently been appreciated as having considerable import. During each phase of glaciation the southern parts of England experienced tundra conditions, in which the mean annual temperature was 7–8°C (13–15°F) lower than at present. The dry valleys of the Chalk landscapes have been interpreted since the nineteenth century as the result of such phases, this interpretation being supplemented by increasingly numerous records of the deposits produced by solifluction, often termed *head* deposits. The legacy of such periglacial conditions is not restricted to the south and there are numerous descriptions of slopes that are mantled by screes now stabilized, or patterned by stone stripes, or punctuated by large landslips now fossilized. The character of much of the landscape of the lowland zone, south of the limit of the last glaciation (Fig. 9), must owe much to the way in which landscape evolution during the interglacial phases combined with the periglacial morphogenesis of the glacial periods. It is increasingly appreciated that during glaciations the parts of the uplands not covered by glacier ice were also modified by periglacial processes.

The Consequences

Fifty million years fashioned the broad outlines, two million years added the final details of the surface and the last 10,000 years have seen the final emergence of the shape of the British Isles as we know it from contemporary maps. During this post-glacial period the climate has changed from tundra through the Climatic Optimum of 6000 to 4000 B.C. to that of the present day, and each post-glacial climate was accompanied by a particular vegetation distribution. The post-glacial rise of sea level that finally severed the south-east of England from Europe and produced the English Channel, also drowned the valleys of southern Ireland and south-west England to produce a ria coast. At its maximum level this Flandrian transgression was responsible for the production of post-glacial shorelines above the present one, and for the deposition of low-level silts and clays subsequently overlain by peat in areas like Morecambe Bay and the Somerset Levels.

THE SOILS

It is largely during this post-glacial period that the soils of the British Isles have developed. The soil profiles reflect the variety of post-glacial climates that were significant in their evolution, the vegetation cover which they supported, and the intrusion of man, manifested primarily through deforestation and later through cultivation of the soils. The soil maps which have been produced for the British Isles necessarily reflect the solid and drift geological maps, but they exceed them in complexity. In the absence of a soil map for the British Isles comparable in detail to that of the geological maps, the broad characteristics of soil distribution are known, but the detailed picture is available only for the areas mapped by the Soil Survey, since 1939 in the case of the Soil Survey of England and Wales.

A simplified version of soil distribution is shown in Figure 10 and it is apparent that at this scale parent material and climate are responsible for the broad differentiation into two main types; podsol profiles dominate in the upland and western areas, and brown earths feature prominently in the south and east.

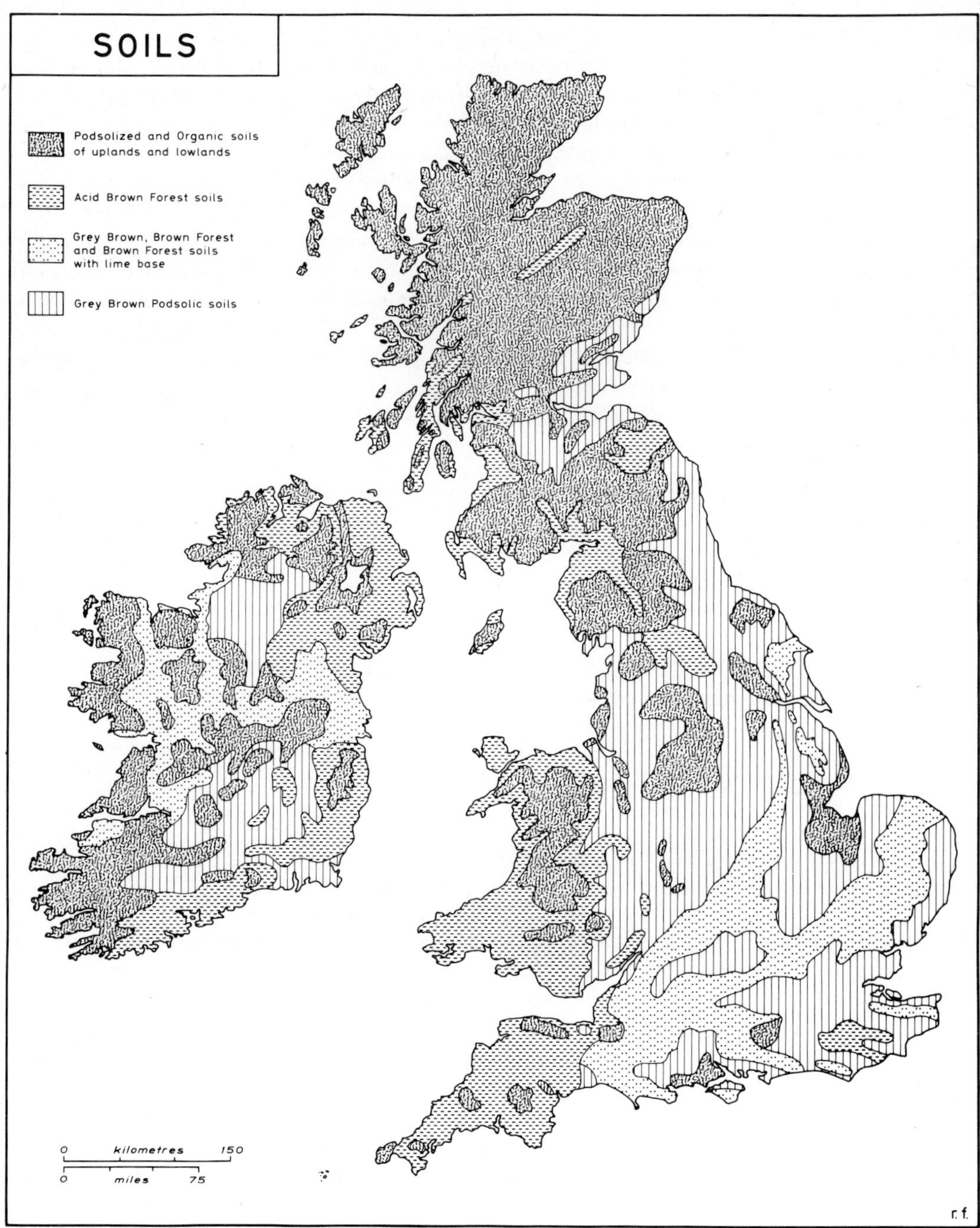

Fig 10 An Outline Map of Soils

The simplified distribution shown is based partly upon a map in *The Atlas of Britain* (Oxford, 1963). The podsolized and organic soils include profiles encountered in uplands and lowlands and those developed on blanket peat; the Grey Brown Podsolic soils are sometimes referred to as leached brown soils and these often include areas of grey soils.

Organic soils occur extensively in Ireland on blanket peat, which is usually found on uplands above 300 metres (984 feet), and on basin peat, which occurs in depressions, between drumlins for example. Blanket peat also provides the basis for soil profiles in the Highlands and the Southern Uplands of Scotland, and on the summits of other elevated areas including the Pennines, Wales and Dartmoor. The climatic considerations which favour the occurrence of organic soils in the uplands are equally important for the development of leached, podsolized soil profiles, and these occur especially on the hill masses of south-west and north-west Ireland, and on other upland areas above 135 metres (443 feet), such as the Wicklow Mountains. The remaining areas of Scotland, and uplands receiving more than 1,500 millimetres (60 inches) rainfall per year, are the domain of a range of types of podsolized soils. Elsewhere in upland areas and on their margins, where annual rainfall totals are not so great, Acid Brown Forest soils are dominant and these are more easily utilized for farming and forestry. Some of them show the characteristics of early development as brown earths, but were later modified by podsolization as a result of deforestation.

The soils of the lowlands present an equally diverse pattern which reflects climate, parent material and the influence of man, in addition to the factor of topography which is responsible for many local variations. The influence of climate on the soils of the lowlands is demonstrated in the case of Ireland, where gleys and peat gleys are frequent on wet sites, and is emphasized by the large amount of clayey, glacial till which comprises a large proportion of the parent materials available. Podsolized soil profiles are found in north-east Scotland and in areas of well-drained parent materials such as the New Forest, and Grey Brown Podsolic soils are generally prevalent over the Midlands of England, areas west and east of the Pennines, and the central lowlands of Scotland (Fig. 10). The effect of parent material is shown clearly on the limestone outcrops which extend over a considerable proportion of the English landscape especially in the southern Pennines, in the Jurassic scarplands and in the Cretaceous scarplands of south-east England. These areas support black or grey soils, including Brown Forest soils, some with lime base, and rendzinas. The pattern produced by these soils is further diversified by the presence of Grey Brown Podsolic soils. The extent of human interference is shown particularly well in tracts of lowland alluvium and peat, in areas like the Somerset levels and the Fens; in the latter area the problem of drainage was seriously tackled from the seventeenth century onwards and has produced one of the most important arable farming districts of Britain. The study of the soils of the British Isles has hitherto been characterized largely by an approach based upon soil genesis, as the names cited above illustrate, and this is justified by the great range of soil variety. The evaluation of the soils however has to be set against the changing methods and technology of the last 800 years. These changes have revalued the significance of particular areas such as the light soils of eastern England, which figured late in the history of improvement, and the marginal lands of the uplands, over which improvement and reversion fluctuated in accord with the value of returns from farming.

Responses to the Landscape

The British Isles afford an environment in which interpretation of the landscape should necessarily be concentrated along evolutionary lines. The wealth of stratigraphic evidence and the results of a variety of geomorphological processes which operated in the past and which are still evidenced in the present landscape have naturally led to an emphasis upon historical evolution in landscape analysis. However the changing 'mental climate' of recent years, accompanied by an increased appreciation of the effect of man upon the landscape, has necessitated a broader approach to the study of the physique of these islands in which 7 per cent of their area is urbanized, 55 per cent is enclosed farmland and approximately 0·29 per cent of England is derelict land. Not only is attention directed increasingly towards the effect of human interference in the landscape of the past, but also towards the study of contemporary processes, in the hope that an understanding of the way in which

Plate 5 Spurn Head (Yorkshire)
An example of a sand and shingle spit which is 5½ kilometres (3½ miles) long and trends south-westwards across the mouth of the Humber from a wedge-shaped boulder–clay area supporting the villages of Kilnsea (right) and Easington (left). Historical evidence has been assembled by de Boer to show that the spit has passed through a course of development involving extension and reduction three times since the Norman Conquest.

the present landscape is changing will indicate broad future possibilities. In an island environment attention was first naturally directed towards the coast where the measurement of contemporary processes could be related to the numerous classic landforms such as Chesil Beach, Dungeness, Blakeney Point and Scolt Head Island (Plate 5). However, inland landscapes also are being scrutinized. The clearing of the summer deciduous forest, which would have otherwise covered many areas up to 450 metres (1,500 feet), occurred intermittently from Neolithic times (*circa* 2000 B.C.) and accelerated in the twelfth and thirteenth centuries. This clearing has had implications for the rivers which drain these deforested areas. Increased erosion gave increased sedimentation in the larger valleys of South Wales, for example; gulleys were initiated in the Southern Uplands and Wales following the change in land use, and their development was assisted by overgrazing and burning; and the flood hazard, indicated by the magnitude and frequency of floods, also increased. These changes, started some 4,000 years ago, have been encouraged and intensified not only by increased enclosure, but also following the improvement in such agricultural practices as land drainage which has occurred over the last three centuries. Such indirect consequences of man's activities may be further illustrated by reference to the extractive industries where surface subsidence due to mining on the coalfields and to the extraction of salt in Cheshire has scarred wide areas. Man's direct influence is shown in large quarries which figure prominently in some landscapes and include the pits of Bedfordshire, which were excavated for clay for brickmaking, and the numerous workings in the Thames valley gravels. It is apparent also on the Norfolk Broads, which are now interpreted as the flooded relics of mediaeval peat diggings. Efforts to restrain the effects of direct interference with the environment may have produced repercussions elsewhere, as in the case of coast protection schemes which possibly have initiated change or modification in adjacent unprotected stretches of coast. 26·5 per cent of the coastline of England and 21 per cent of that of Wales has been developed for built-up areas, and for industrial, commercial and camping purposes, and so recently the protection of Britain's coast, taking a synoptic view of the coastline as a whole, has been advocated. A similar theme is apparent in the rationalization of the enclosure pattern of the British Isles through the removal of hedgerows in some areas, including eastern England and the Midlands (Plate 6). This has prompted estimates that at least 1,600 kilometres (1,000 miles) of hedgerow are being removed from the landscape of Britain each year. The consequences have been to make the upper soil horizons more vulnerable to wind erosion, to change the ecology of the landscape by removing established habitats, and to modify the overall character of the British scene.

Response to recent changes has been manifested in the attitude and increasing breadth of geographic research, and this has been paralleled by an increasing general awareness of the environment. These attitudes have been conceived in the realization that the physical landscape is dynamic rather than static and that the landscape in certain parts of the country is experiencing erosion of its inherited character. Recent action was initiated by the National Parks and Access to the Countryside Act of 1949, which led to the institution

Plate 6 Wicken (Cambridge)
The village of Wicken is sited on a ridge slightly elevated by about 6 metres (20 feet) above the lowlands of eastern England here underlain by Gault clay. This area of fen in the basin of the river Cam has been drained and improved except for patches like Wicken Fen in the foreground. With an area of 283 hectares (700 acres) it represents one of the last remaining stretches of uncultivated fen in the vicinity of Cambridge. It was donated to the National Trust in 1899, and is now the best documented nature reserve in Britain.

of the National Parks Commission for England and Wales and of the Nature Conservancy. The legislation was extended in 1966 by the designation of the Countryside Commission to continue the functions of the National Parks Commission and in addition to promote public enjoyment of the countryside of England and Wales generally. Since 1949 ten National Parks have been designated to cover 9 per cent of the area of England and Wales (Fig. 11) and these are usually in the highland zone. A Planning Board or Committee responsible for each park controls development to ensure that it is in the interests of the character of the particular area. No national parks have been designated in Scotland although several have been proposed but a County Park of 227 hectares (560 acres) was announced in 1970 and several National Forest Parks which include leisure facilities have been developed by the

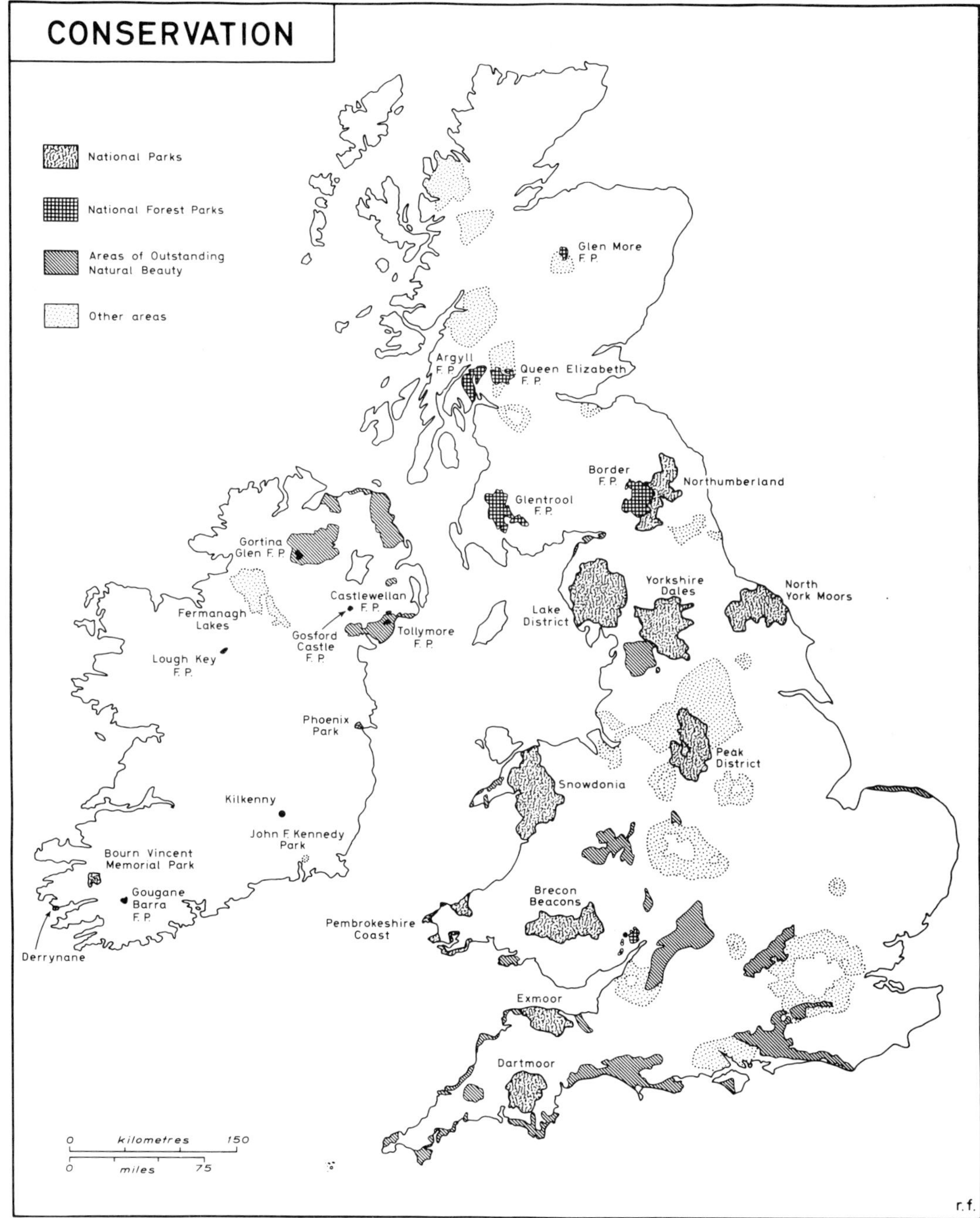

Fig 11 Conserved Areas in the British Isles, 1970
Areas of green belt are grouped with areas of proposed National Parks in Scotland and collectively shown as Other Areas. Information for the Irish Republic was supplied by Dr. D. Cabot (The National Institute for Physical Planning and Construction Research, Dublin). Further National Parks are under consideration in the Irish Republic.

Forestry Commission (Fig. 11). In Ireland four forest parks punctuate the map of northern Ireland, and in the south there are two forest parks and three national parks (Fig. 11).

Areas of Outstanding Natural Beauty, although broadly similar in character to National Parks, are not usually as extensive and do not contain as much unenclosed land or opportunities for outdoor recreation. Areas of Outstanding Natural Beauty, which cover 8 per cent of the area of England and Wales, are found mainly in the south and west, exemplified by the Chilterns and by the North and South Downs, and they occur also in Ireland (Fig. 11). The national picture is further expanded by other areas (Fig. 11) of great landscape value, designated by local rather than national planning authorities, and by Green Belts, designed to discourage urban growth around many cities. Nature Reserves, including the 120 National Nature Reserves in Britain in 1967, Sites of Special Scientific Interest, and the properties of the National Trust, which initiated 'Enterprise Neptune' in 1965 to acquire or protect as much as possible of the remaining unspoilt coastline, complete the picture.

These two responses to, or appreciations of, the environment, dictated by the need to measure the changes and also to exercise some control over them, were recognized by the creation of the Natural Environment Research Council (NERC) in 1965. NERC co-ordinates institutions like the Nature Conservancy, the Institute of Geological Sciences and many others concerned with the land, atmosphere and waters of Britain. It supports research in physical and biological sciences in islands where the rocks cover a time span of more than 500 million years, and where the broad physical outlines have been the consequence of the last 50 million years. The varied environment which has resulted now has to withstand the present demands of an increasing population with expanding leisure time. These demands must be visualized as a basis for further development of conserved areas (Fig. 11).

FURTHER READING

R. Arvill, *Man and Environment* (Penguin Books, 1967).

E. H. Brown, *The Relief and Drainage of Wales* (Cardiff, 1960).

J. K. Charlesworth, *The Historical Geology of Ireland* (Edinburgh, 1963).

C. P. Burnham, The regional pattern of soil formation in Great Britain, *Scottish Geographical Magazine*, 86 (1970), 25–34.

Clarendon Press, *The Atlas of Britain* (Oxford, 1963).

D. Mackney and C. P. Burnham, *The Soils of the West Midlands*, Soil Survey of England and Wales, Bulletin No. 2 (Harpenden, 1964).

W. M. Pearsall, *Mountains and Moorlands* (London, 1950).

J. B. Sissons, *The Evolution of Scottish Scenery* (Edinburgh, 1968).

J. A. Steers, *The Coastline of England and Wales* (Cambridge, 1948).

L. D. Stamp, *Britain's Structure and Scenery* (London, 1946).

A. G. Tansley, *The British Islands and their Vegetation* (Cambridge, 1949).

A. E. Trueman, *Geology and Scenery of England and Wales* (Penguin Books, 1972) revised by J. B. Whittow and J. R. Hardy.

S. W. Wooldridge and D. L. Linton, *Structure, Surface and Drainage in South-East England* (London, 1955).

The Physical Basis: The Air Above

The Character

The density of feature characteristic of the landscape of the British Isles is paralleled on a reduced scale by the diversity of climate. Diversity occurs in space because of the latitudinal extent of the islands, the Shetlands being nearer to Iceland than to London, and diversity occurs in time because of the numerous controls which can be exercised at any time of the year and which can vary from one year to another. Some writers have asserted that the British Isles do not experience a climate but only weather, and other views expressed range from that of Tacitus, who described the climate as 'objectionable with frequent rains and mists, but there is no extreme cold', to that of Charles II who viewed the English climate as the best in the world where 'man can enjoy outdoor exercise on all but five days of the year'. The location of the British Isles, off the north-west coast of Europe, places them in the path of the Gulf Stream and of its extension, the North Atlantic Drift, giving sea temperatures to the north-west Britain of 8°C (46°F) in winter and 12°C (54°F) in summer. This exercises a warming influence and results in an average annual temperature of 11°C (52°F) in the Isles of Scilly and 10°C (50°F) in London, which compare favourably with the annual average of 8·4°C (47°F) in Berlin and 1·7°C (35°F) in Winnipeg, at the same latitude. More generally, the average annual temperature of 10°C (50°F) for the British Isles is the same as the world average for some five degrees further south, at the latitude of southern France.

A location off the coast of mainland Europe places the British Isles in the path of cyclonic and anticyclonic systems which occur within the extra-tropical westerlies. The location results in influence by air streams from a variety of sources, and within this broad pattern further variety is introduced by the pattern of topography. The highland zone receives the full effect of westerly influence and may shelter the lowland zone, which is in turn more prone to influences from the north-east and from the continent. The variety of weather experienced within the limits set by a west coast cool-temperature climate, particularly the variation from south to north and that from west to east, has prompted many attempts to measure the magnitude of the elements through which the weather and climate are expressed. The sustained interest is reflected in observations made as early as the fourteenth century, in the founding of the Royal Meteorological Society in the mid-nineteenth century, in the longest officially established record from 1851 at Greenwich, and in several thousand volunteer observers who have maintained records of rainfall. Such interest has provided the data necessary for the gradual elucidation of the climatic elements (Figs. 12, 13, 14, 15), for the analysis of recent variations and for some speculations on the course and nature of long-term trends.

The Controls

Variation of climate over the surface of the British Isles is exceeded by the variety of the weather which may occur within the year and from year to year. This variety reflects the number of air masses which are liable to exercise an influence, and at least six varieties may be recognized. Tropical, Polar and Arctic air masses, each represented by maritime and continental types, influence the weather experienced. These air masses not only possess the characteristics of their source areas but they are also influenced by the changes brought about during their tracks towards the British Isles (Fig. 12).

Polar maritime air is the most frequent of the air masses affecting the British Isles. After its passage southwards over the warmer sea it is rendered unstable and moist, and the turbulence is responsible for gusty winds, broken cloud, and heavy showers alternating with sunny intervals at all seasons. Polar maritime air may occasion temperatures below average in summer but the degree of instability developed depends upon the length and course of its track. When it approaches from the south-west (Fig. 12), as returning polar maritime, it is rendered more stable by cooling on its final path north-eastwards. Arctic maritime air also is unstable and may be reflected in the sharp snow and hail showers of the winter months in the east from Caithness to east Kent. After its short sea track Arctic maritime air can produce strong north winds on exposed coasts, accompanied by very low winter temperatures. Maritime Arctic air is not as frequent as the Polar continental which also approaches from the east and south-east, largely in the period December to February. The narrow Straits of Dover do not allow instability to develop and so Polar continental can be responsible for the most severe winter weather when conditions are often cloudy but dry. Arctic continental air similarly is associated with very low temperatures but may be unstable after crossing the North Sea and so induce snow showers on the east coast. By contrast Tropical maritime air is stable and has a high relative humidity giving frontal rain in a depression, or orographic rainfall after it reaches elevated coasts. In winter it may bring mild temperature conditions associated with poor visibility, and cloud which thickens inland, whereas in summer, cloud thins inland from the coast. Tropical continental air is rare but reaches southern Britain on average on one day each month during the summer, and is usually associated with high temperatures, sometimes over 32°C (90°F).

Weather conditions on some ten to twelve per cent of the days of the year may be explained by the passage of depressions formed at the junction of two air masses. Such depressions travel at greatly varying rates but may average between 300 and 500 kilometres (187–311 miles) per day, and they may follow a variety of courses. Many, especially lows which develop as secondaries to a primary centred north of Scotland, move along the south coast of Ireland and up the English Channel. The passage of a depression gives characteristic weather conditions, especially in winter when the depressions are most deeply developed. The weather can range from the steady rain of the warm front to the bright periods and showers associated with the cold front which, in its passage, may see a fall of temperature of as much as 4–5·5°C (7–10°F). More stable weather conditions prevail when anticyclones affect the British Isles. The fine, settled weather of summer, with days which are warm and sunny

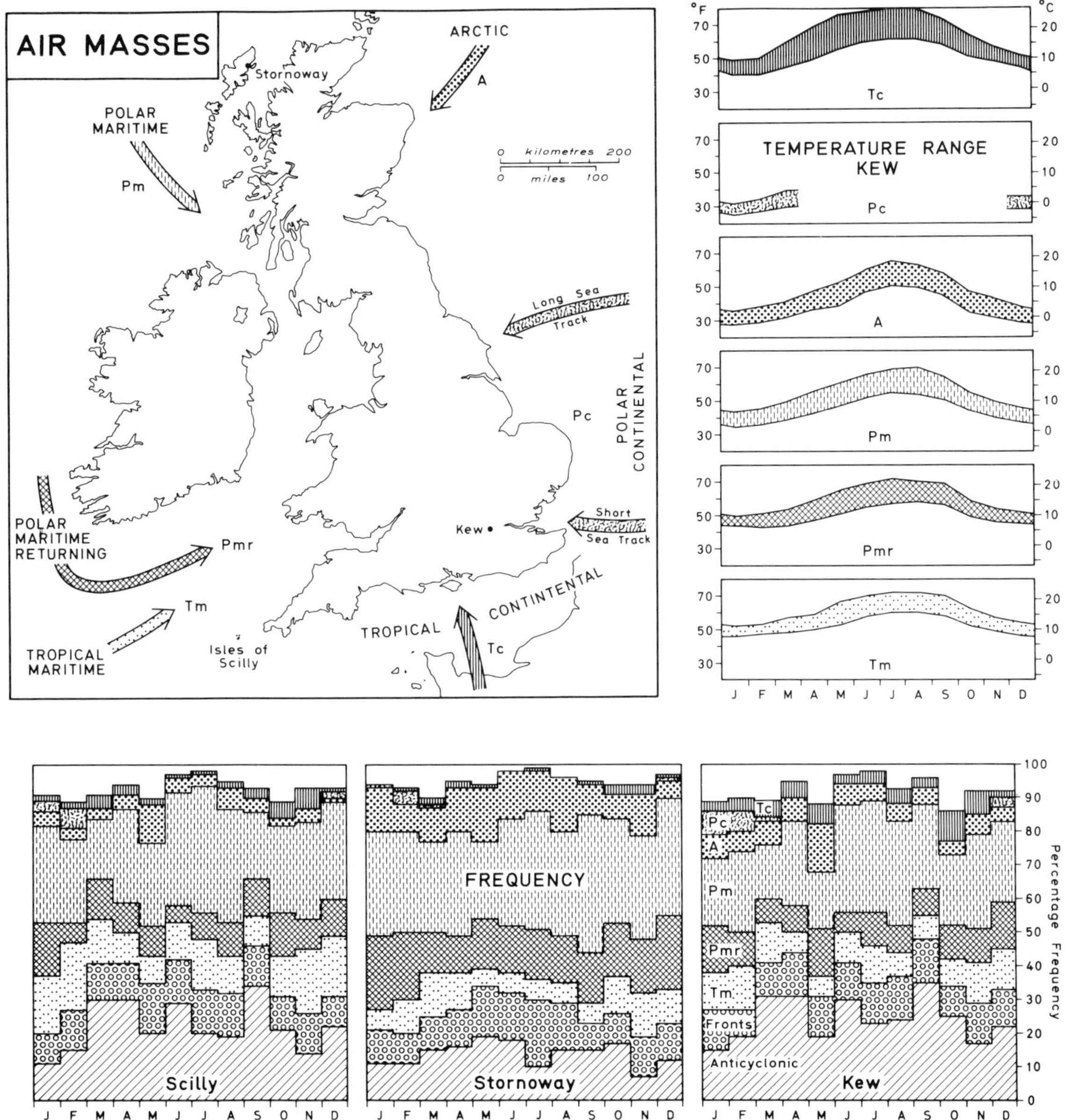

Fig 12 Air Masses Affecting the British Isles
The average frequency at three stations based on one observation each day in the period 1938–1949 and the average temperature range associated with each air mass at Kew is based upon J. E. Belasco, *Characteristics of air masses over the British Isles* (H.M.S.O., 1952).

followed by clear cool nights, is most frequently experienced during anticyclonic conditions. In winter such conditions are frequently marked by overcast skies, and the stable air may encourage the development of radiation fog, which in urban and industrialized areas can produce smoke-fog or smog persisting for several days.

On one occasion on each day in the period 1938–1949 the incidence of each of these classes of air at the surface was noted by the stations at Kew, Stornoway and in the Isles of Scilly (Fig. 12), and this affords some indication of their relative importance and frequency. The annual frequency of Tropical maritime air is twice as great at the Isles of Scilly as at Stornoway, and such air is generally more frequent between October and March than at other times of the year. Tropical continental air is much less common, especially in the north, but Polar maritime air accounts for 59 per cent of recorded air masses at Stornoway, and for 42 per cent at the other two stations during the eleven year period. The anticyclonic category is most important at Kew and the Isles of Scilly in September, at Stornoway in May and least significant at all three stations in November. For one of the three stations (Kew) the average temperature characteristics for each of the types of air are illustrated in Figure 12.

The Average Experience

The irregular incidence of these air-mass types combined with the numerous instances of variation introduced by maritime and topographic controls is responsible for considerable divergence from the average experience.

TEMPERATURE

Annual temperature range is generally well-confined within the range set by the extreme records of 38°C (100°F) and –9·5°C (–17°F). Average monthly temperatures for the British Isles as a whole are usually lowest in January–February at 5°C (41°F) and highest at 15°C (59°F) in July–August. In winter the isotherms run broadly north to south, reflecting the fact that the average monthly temperatures are greater than 6·7°C (44°F) in south-west Ireland and south-west England in January–February, but decrease towards the east coast where they are below 4·5°C (40°F). In spring the pattern of the isotherms changes so that by summer they run east-west reflecting the average July–August monthly average of 15·5°C (60°F) over much of southern Britain, in contrast with averages of less than 13°C (55°F) in northern Scotland. The annual trend is illustrated by average monthly temperatures plotted for six stations in Figure 13. These demonstrate that the lowest temperatures are recorded in January or February in the west, that July is usually the warmest month, and that the annual, like the diurnal, temperature ranges are greater at inland sites than at coastal localities, especially those of the west.

The character of annual temperature over the British Isles can be expressed by a map constructed by plotting the number of months possessing a mean annual temperature greater than 6°C (42·8°F) (Fig. 13). The temperature of 6°C (42·8°F) is one index of the lower limit of growth and so variations in the

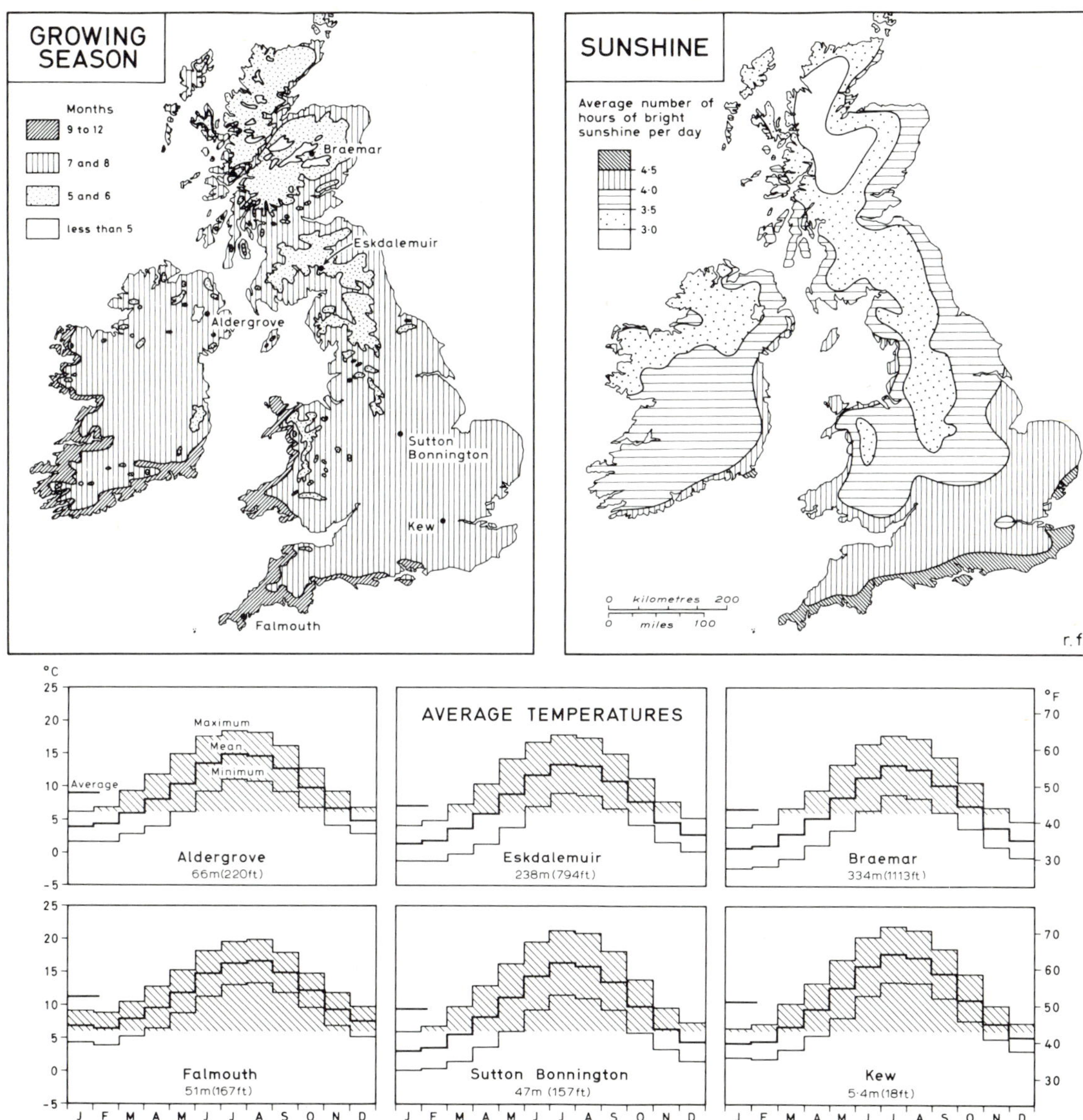

Fig 13 Variation in Temperature and Sunshine

The map showing the average number of months growing season (mean temperature greater than 6°C) is based upon a map compiled by S. Gregory. (In J. Wreford Watson and J. B. Sissons (eds.), *The British Isles: a systematic geography* (London, 1964).) The average number of hours of bright sunshine per day (maximum 12 hours per day) follows the *Climatological atlas of the British Isles* (H.M.S.O., 1952). Average temperatures in the period 1921–50 are plotted for the six stations shown on the map and the shading above 6°C in the six lower diagrams indicates the length of the growing season.

length of the growing season may be demonstrated (Fig. 13). On this basis the extreme south-western coasts of Cornwall, Ireland and Wales may have at least eleven months growing season, and a broad band of between nine and twelve months growing season has been mapped adjacent to these areas (Fig. 13). Much of the British Isles has a growing season which lasts between seven and eight months, but the duration is notably less, five to six months, in the most elevated areas of Wales, the Lake District and the Pennines. The effect of altitude is further illustrated by the growing season of four months in the Highlands of Scotland. The incidence of frost may also be emphasized by the pattern of topography. The frost-free period is usually mid March to mid December on the south-western coasts of England and Wales, early April to early December on the coasts of Ireland, and is of shorter duration, from early May to the end of October, inland in Ireland and in the Midlands of England.

The advantage of the south coast is also indicated by the average annual daily duration of bright sunshine (Fig. 13). This is greatest, nearly five hours, in the south, but decreases inland, northwards, with altitude, and in some urban areas to less than three hours per day. This range expresses a scale from some 40 per cent of the possible sunshine in the south to 20 per cent in the north, but variation during the year is substantial. In December and January few areas receive sunshine for more than 20 per cent of the possible time but from May to August much of southern England, South Wales and occasionally south-east Ireland may receive more than 40 per cent, corresponding to an average of six hours per day.

PRECIPITATION Average precipitation records necessarily obscure greater contrasts. The average annual totals of 831 millimetres (32·7 inches) for England, 1,356 millimetres (53·4 inches) for Wales, 1,420 millimetres (55·9 inches) for Scotland and 1,080 millimetres (42·5 inches) for the whole of Ireland indicate the broad orographic influence but disguise the facts that the highest parts of Wales, the Lake District, the Scottish Highlands and isolated elevated areas of western Ireland receive 2,500 millimetres (98·4 inches) or more each year, and that parts of eastern England annually receive an average of less than 635 millimetres (25 inches) per year. Although the 3,810 millimetre (150 inch) isohyet appears in western Scotland and the 508 millimetre (20 inch) isohyet isolates the Essex coast, more than 80 per cent of England averages between 635 and 1,270 millimetres (25 and 50 inches) and 80 per cent of Ireland averages between 762 and 1,270 millimetres (30 and 50 inches) per year (Fig. 14). In Scotland the central Lowlands and the eastern coastal areas average between 760 and 1,020 millimetres (30 and 40 inches) but the 1,250 millimetre (49 inch) isohyet surrounds the Highlands, the Southern Uplands, much of the Lake District and Wales, and it also picks out the uplands of Ireland and those of the south-west of England.

Variation around these averages is expressed in the distribution during the year, in variation from one year to another, and in the frequency of intense rainfalls. There are few clear seasonal patterns in rainfall distribution over the

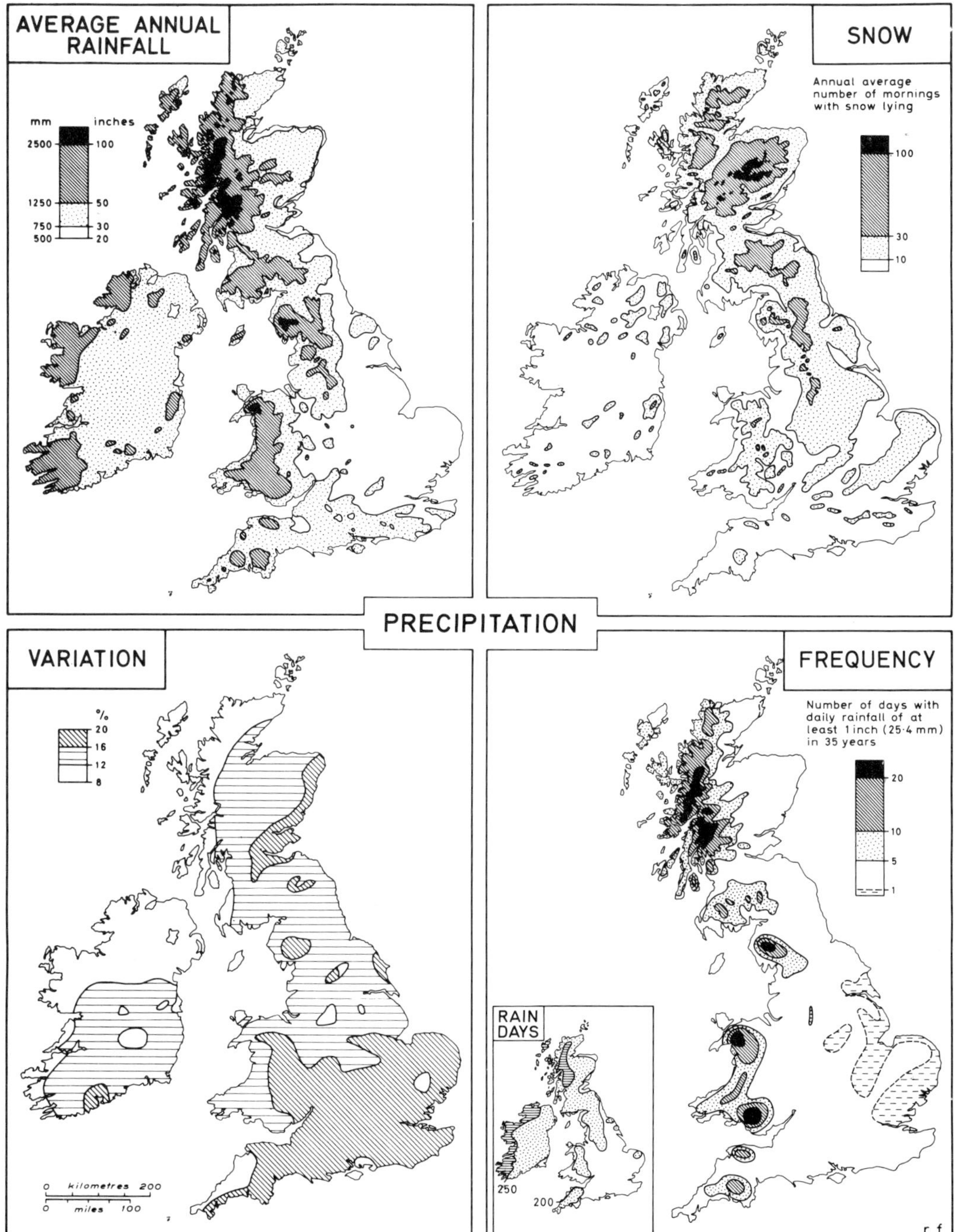

Fig 14 The Character of Precipitation Distribution

Average annual rainfall refers to the period 1931–60 and follows the 1:625,000 map of Great Britain, the annual average number of mornings with some snow lying in the period 1912–38 and the map of the average number of rain days 1901–30 are based upon the *Climatological atlas of the British Isles* (H.M.S.O., 1952). The variation in annual average rainfall indicated by the coefficient of variation of annual rainfall totals 1921–50 is based upon work by S. Gregory. (In J. Wreford Watson and J. B. Sissons (eds.), *The British Isles: a systematic geography* (London, 1964).) An indication of precipitation intensity is afforded by the map showing the number of days with daily rainfall of at least 25·4 mm (1 inch) in 35 years, based upon *Frequency maps of daily rainfall*, Meteorological Office, Hydrological Memoranda No. 25).

British Isles and there are few parts of the country where droughts have lasted more than 30 to 40 days. Absolute droughts of more than 40 days are known only locally in east, central and south-east England. Much of Wales, south-west England, and western Scotland have 60 per cent of their annual rainfall in the winter half of the year, but in central and south eastern districts the continental influence introduces a weak summer maximum. Elsewhere the second half of the year, July–December, is usually the wetter. The number of rain days each year averages between 175 and 200 in the south, but over 250 days in western Ireland and north-west Scotland (Fig. 14).

Generally the average rainfall for a particular station may express a range of annual totals from 60 per cent below in the driest year to 150 per cent above in the wettest year. Variation expressed by the coefficient of variation of annual rainfall totals (Fig. 14) distinguishes the northern and western areas as the ones with the least variation, while the eastern and southern areas are the most variable and also receive the lowest annual amounts (Fig. 14). Rainfall over the British Isles also includes occasional storms of high intensity. The 35 year frequency of daily rainfalls of at least 25·4 millimetres (one inch) demonstrates (Fig. 14) that whereas falls of this magnitude may occur more than five, and occasionally more than 20, times each year over the western uplands, such falls are much less frequent in the east and south. On a longer time scale the western uplands can expect a fall greater than 127 millimetres (5 inches) in one day once within a hundred years and the extreme daily rainfalls recorded include one of over 280 millimetres (11 inches) at Martinstown, Dorset and another of over 230 millimetres (9 inches) on Exmoor.

The proportion of the annual precipitation which falls as snow or sleet depends upon the incidence of air streams of Arctic or continental origin, and upon the surface air being sufficiently cold. Frontal snowfalls can lead to greater accumulations on windward slopes and thus greater falls are experienced on the Yorkshire side of the Pennines than on the western side. The orographic effect is demonstrated by the fact that Dartmoor and the Cleveland Hills can receive much more snow than the adjacent coastlands, and Ben Nevis maintains an average maximum depth of two metres (7 feet) for 215 days from early November to the end of May. The incidence of snow is illustrated by the average number of mornings with snow lying (Fig. 14) although this may not correspond precisely with the frequency of snow falling, especially in the south and east. The pattern of the uplands appears in this distribution (Fig. 14) accompanied by an eastern element reflecting the significance of incursions of Arctic or Polar continental air. Many areas of the British Isles experience a substantial variation from year to year but recent memory often includes at least one deep fall. At Balmoral the number of days with snow lying varies from 21 to 116 and at Durham from 2 to 81.

Plate 7 Red Bay (County Antrim)
This bay lies at the mouth of a glacial trough, Glenariff, in north-eastern Ireland. It has been developed along the line of the Highland Boundary fault and north of Red Bay has exposed upper Palaeozoic rocks beneath the Tertiary basalt which caps the plateau of north-east Ireland. Annual rainfall is generally between 1,150 and 1,270 mm (45–50 inches) per year and a very small proportion falls as snow, usually between 5 and 15 days per year at the lowest levels, but between 30 and 50 days may have snowfall on the highest areas above 360 metres.

The Pattern

The record of the average facts demonstrates the broad distinction between the western elevated areas with their higher rainfall totals, lower temperature range, and more frequent intense rainfalls, and the lowland areas where, particularly in the south and east, continental influences are more prevalent, annual rainfall expectation is much lower with a tendency towards a summer maximum, and a greater range of temperature occurs throughout the year. In addition to this broad topographic influence there are numerous instances where significant variations occur over short distances, illustrated by differences of 250 millimetres (10 inches) in annual rainfall totals within 16 kilometres (10 miles) in the Weald. Wind speeds are greatest on exposed western coasts, such as parts of the Outer Hebrides, where the wind exceeds gale force for more than half of January, but they are also modified by the detail of topography, illustrated by the Helm wind which blows over Cross Fell and the neighbouring slopes of the Pennines and which is indicated by a characteristic cloud formation above the Pennine summits. In coastal areas the contrast between the thermal characteristics of land and sea gives rise to the sea breezes of day and the land breezes of night. These are most evident where the coastal plain is succeeded inland by a belt of low hills, as in the case of the east coast of England. The most bracing conditions are perceived on the north-east

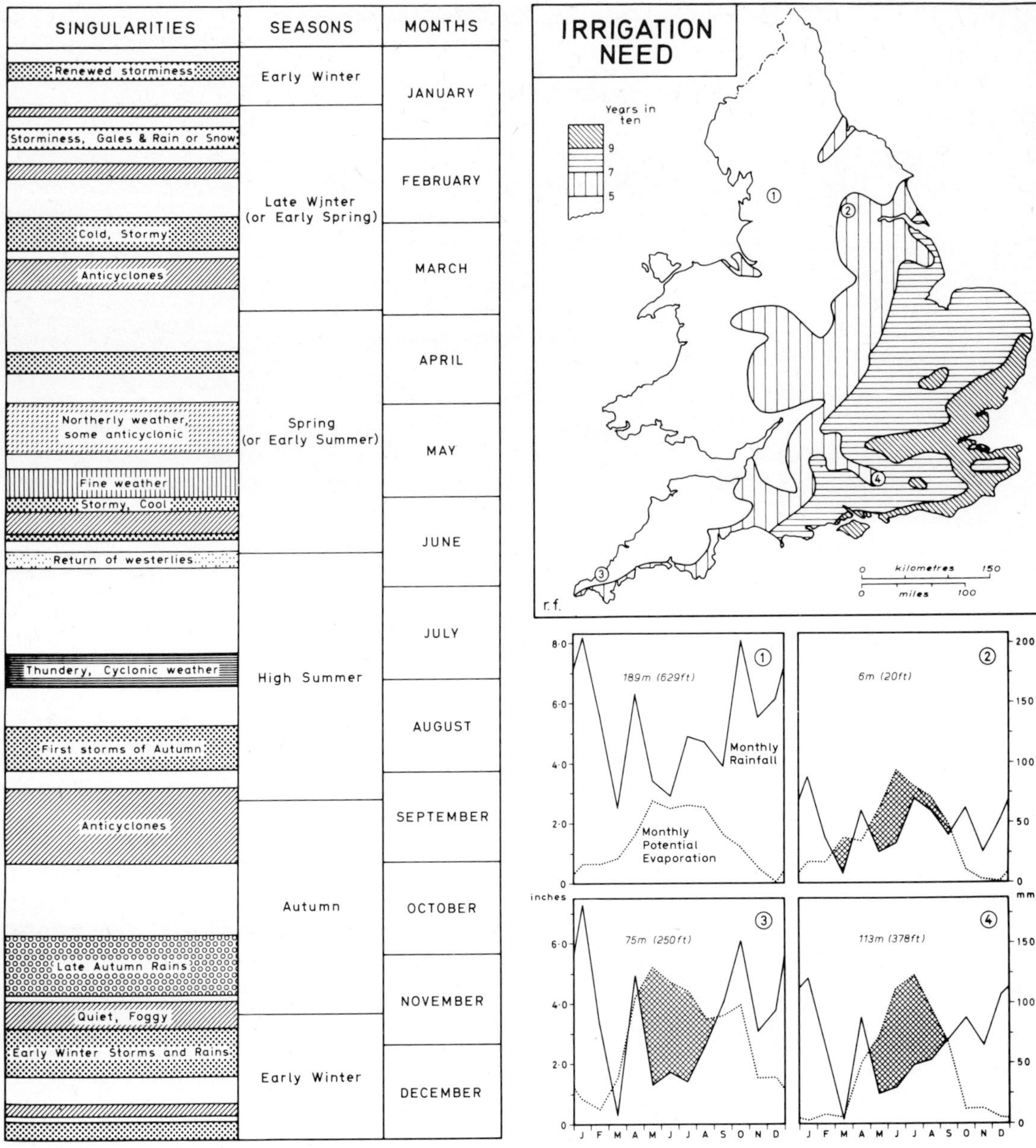

Fig 15 Some Considerations of the Impact of Climate in Space and Time

The relationship between monthly rainfall and monthly potential evaporation at four contrasted stations located on the map is plotted for 1961 to emphasize the contrast between the highland and lowland zones. The map of irrigation need shows the number of years in a ten year period when actual summer rainfall is unlikely to remedy water expenditure, assuming that 76 mm (3 inches) of water could be extracted from the soil by a crop. Crops will continue to live on smaller moisture supplies but are unlikely to maintain maximum growth (*The calculation of irrigation need* (H.M.S.O., 1954). Variation in time is indicated by a diagram showing the singularities and seasons of the year based upon analysis of records 1898–1947 (H. H. Lamb, Types and spells of weather in the British Isles, *Quarterly Journal Royal Meteorological Society*, 76 (1950), 393–429.)

coast of England and to a lesser degree on the western coasts of England and Wales. Also according to the frequency of weather changes, relative humidity and wind strengths, relaxing climates have been perceived in the lee of the Welsh mountains, in portions of central England, and in some sheltered parts of the south coast.

SEASONS AND SINGULARITIES

Although there are a great number of local climates, regional climates are difficult to isolate and it is equally difficult to discern the conditions expected at particular times of the year. Analysis of the records has been used to show that five broad seasons may be detected (Fig. 15). These five seasons, which are more evident in some years than others, were isolated from fifty years of daily weather maps (1898–1947) from which outstandingly long spells of weather were picked out according to the incidence of seven weather types. The description of January–March as late winter or early spring (Fig. 15) illustrates the extent to which spring, and also autumn to a lesser degree, have the greatest variation from year to year. Within these five seasons it is apparent that not all types of weather are equally probable on a particular day. The existence of shorter spells or episodes of weather, termed 'singularities', long known in folklore by terms like 'April showers', are evidenced by the facts that over most of the country February–April tends to be drier than the months on either side, July and August tend to be wet, with September rather drier, before the onset of wet conditions again in October. Anticyclonic conditions with associated fog and frost are often experienced in mid-November, and early December is frequently marked by mild wet weather associated with the passage of Atlantic depressions. H. H. Lamb was able to detect 22 such singularities and these are illustrated in Figure 15. Now that sufficient records are available it is also possible, using mean monthly temperature anomalies, to search for analogues as a basis for long-range 30 day forecasts.

Variability occurs not only during each year and within days of the year, when the changing patterns of light have provided the subjects captured by many landscape painters, but also on the historic time scale when variability is experienced over decades or centuries. The climate of Roman times has been suggested to have been little different from that of today, but in the fourth century conditions were wetter. From 1100 to 1300 milder winters and higher summer temperatures characterized two centuries when vines were grown in southern Britain and tillage was found on more elevated positions than today. The period from the mid-sixteenth century to the eighteenth century was typified by dry but snowy winters, cooler, wetter summers, and included the period sometimes described as the Little Ice Age. With increasing instrumentation and more frequent records it has been shown that since 1850 there has been a general trend towards milder winters, and especially in the early part of this century temperatures were apparently higher than the average for historic times. The implications of these changes must be considered in relation to variations in the length of the growing season, especially on upland margins, in relation to the increase of precipitation and cloud cover which may retard the ripening and harvesting of crops, and, in a modern industrial area such as the British Isles, in relation to the increasing demands for water, and to the fact that in a severe and prolonged winter the fuel demand for heating purposes can be some 40 per cent above the average.

The Impact of the Climate

The limited range of the British climate does not preclude hazards of regular occurrence. A severe winter can cause disruption of transport systems locally within the British Isles, a very dry summer can impose severe local water supply deficiencies, and an intense rainfall can produce flooding, though such occurrences have not been intensively studied until recently. The impact of the climate is illustrated by crop needs for irrigation, by the availability of water for domestic, power and industrial use, and by the flood hazard. These considerations are all related to variation within the year and require consideration of the probability of occurrence of events of a particular magnitude.

EVAPORATION

Average annual evaporation and transpiration over the British Isles generally ranges between 300 and 600 millimetres (12–24 inches). These losses must therefore be considered in relation to the distribution of average annual precipitation (Fig. 14). In the areas receiving the greatest precipitation, where evaporation is at the lower end of the range, there is no serious deficit. In much of Ireland for example, with annual rainfall totals between 760 and 1,270 millimetres (30–50 inches) over 80 per cent of the area and evaporation between 300 and 450 millimetres (12–18 inches) each year, there is a water surplus at all seasons in the arable farming areas, but during the driest season from March to May a deficiency can arise. The monthly values from one year's record at four stations (Fig. 15) substantiate the fact that, viewed in terms of monthly average values, there is a water surplus at stations in the Highland zone and in Ireland, but a deficiency in the south and east of England during the summer months. The average seasonal water deficit has been shown to be 76 millimetres (3 inches) or more on the south coast, in south-east England, East Anglia, Lincolnshire, the West Midlands and the Cheshire plain. Peripheral areas may have a deficit approaching 76 millimetres (3 inches) in summer. However the use of average monthly figures can obscure variation within the months and also from year to year. One map produced to express the irrigation need indicates the number of years in ten during which the actual summer rainfall is unlikely to satisfy the expenditure of water, assuming that 76 millimetres (3 inches) of water is extracted from the soil by a crop (Fig. 15). The map makes allowance for variation in rainfall from year to year and gives an indication of the water needed to satisfy maximum growth during the summer season. In 1967 approximately 100,000 hectares (250,000 acres) could be irrigated in a dry season in England and Wales, and it has been estimated that an area six times larger could theoretically benefit from supplemental irrigation. Locally water supply for irrigation may already constitute a problem, as in the Great Ouse basin, but limited rather than full irrigation will probably be developed more in the future.

WATER SUPPLY

The need for irrigation and for more water for modern stock-producing systems combine with other demands on public water supply. The increased domestic demand for water is shown by the rise in water consumption which averaged eighteen litres (4 gallons) per head per day (lhd) in 1830 and has increased to nearer 225 lhd (50 ghd) in 1960. One estimate puts the average at 300 lhd (65 ghd) in 2001. The availability of water over the British Isles is as uneven as the demand, which unfortunately is greatest where the availability is least. In the past a large number of small water undertakings have been responsible for supply but these have now been rationalized and, in central Scotland for example, seven regional water authorities have replaced the 73 local water undertakings of the fifties. The essence of the national picture is that the north and west has a surplus whereas a deficiency exists in the south and east, but everywhere the needs experienced in dry years must be anticipated by regulated river flow and supply. An approach to the problem was initiated in 1963 by the Water Resources Act and by the creation of the Water Resources Board, which has among other responsibilities that for the 29 river authorities of England and Wales, each concerned with land drainage, conservation, fisheries, prevention of pollution, and flood control, as well as with water supplies. Similar progress was made in Scotland by an Act of 1965.

In Scotland an average annual rainfall of 1,320 millimetres (52 inches) accompanied by an average runoff of approximately 914 millimetres (36 inches) with a population one tenth of that south of the border indicates that a serious overall water shortage is unlikely. Similarly in Ireland the resources afforded by the adequate rainfall amounts and the storage in lakes (Fig. 16) indicates a similar overall adequacy. However in both cases where river water is used for supply, the flow needs to be regulated to cope with the demands of occasional rainless periods. The situation in England and Wales is quite different. It has been estimated that the average annual precipitation is 914 millimetres (36 inches) and that about half of this is lost by evapotranspiration. The total quantity of water flowing over the ground and in underground strata in a dry year is equivalent to about two-thirds of what may be required by the end of the present century. This outlines the magnitude of the problem and although national resources are adequate for envisaged demands, local deficiences can be avoided only by a national approach.

Water supply over the surface of England and Wales has developed against the background of the character of the underlying rocks. In the highland zone surface supplies from rivers and from surface storage are paramount, but the existence of aquifers in the lowland zone supplements surface supply from ground water sources (Fig. 16). Whereas approximately 40 per cent of the total demands of England and Wales are satisfied from ground water sources these are responsible for only 10 per cent of the supplies of Scotland and Northern Ireland. The early pattern of water resource development was achieved against this background and many areas could meet demands from locally available resources. Major urban industrial areas provided the exceptions and when their demands increased they were often able to obtain water collected in neighbouring uplands, in the case of Manchester from the Pennines and the Lake District (Plate 3). Whereas water was formerly often

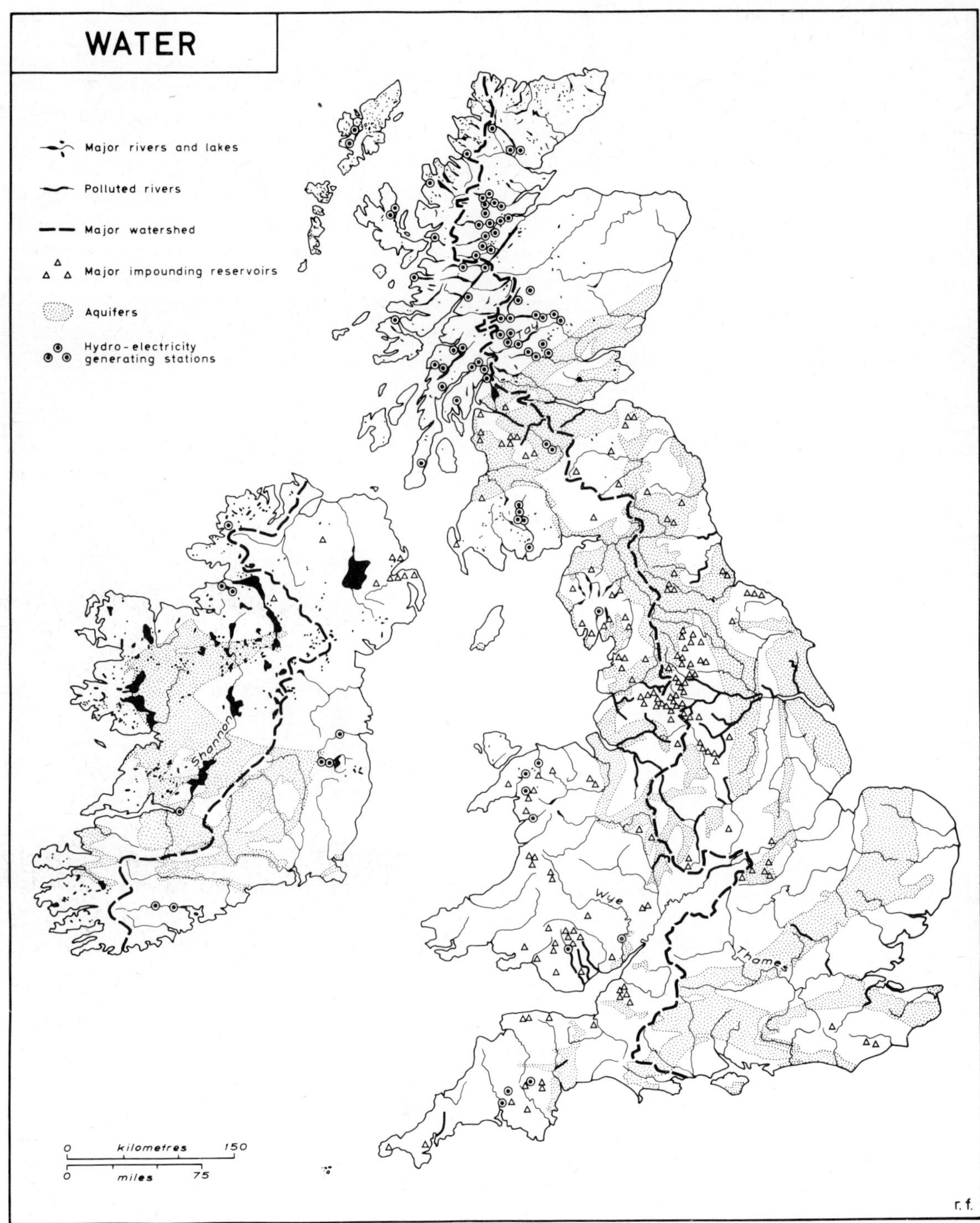

Fig 16 The Distribution and Utilization of Water

Against the generalized background of major rivers, lakes and outcrops of aquifers the location of major impounding reservoirs and hydro-electricity generation stations is shown. Polluted rivers are shown for 1956/57 based upon *The Atlas of Britain* (Oxford, 1963).

piped from impounding reservoirs to Birmingham, Glasgow and Belfast, for example, a more recent solution for such areas has been to use regulating reservoirs in an upland catchment to regulate the flow of the river which conveys water to abstraction points. More recently the potential for future water supplies in the major problem areas of Teesside, South Wales, the West Midlands, south-west and south-east England has been investigated. In the last-named area, where the problem is most acute, it was estimated in 1966 that existing water resources were adequate until 1971, if they could be distributed over the area according to need. In the 49,210 square kilometres (19,000 square miles) of the South East Study area runoff averages 230 millimetres (9 inches) per year but this ranges from as little as 100 millimetres (4

Plate 8 Mole Valley (Surrey)
The photograph shows flooding of the river Mole flowing on Weald Clay south-east of Betchworth (Surrey) in 1968.

Plate 9 Halifax (Yorkshire)
This photograph, taken in 1950, shows pollution of the atmosphere by industrial and domestic smoke. The amount of atmospheric pollution has now been reduced particularly since the Clean Air Act of 1956.

inches) in Essex to 500 millimetres (20 inches) in parts of Dorset, and the predicted population expansion indicates a potential deficiency of some 5,000 million litres (1,100 million gallons) per day by the end of the present century. The immediate solution to this problem is advocated as development of the two main existing sources of supply, namely exploitation of ground water resources especially in the Chalk by direct abstraction or by pumping to augment river flows, and by surface storage in reservoirs. Other methods being considered include the possibilities of importing water from areas outside the south-east, such as from the Severn, of constructing estuarial barrages across the Wash, for example, of artificial recharge of aquifers, and of desalinization, particularly with the utilization of nuclear power. These possible solutions will in the future be relevant to other areas, and over the whole country the increasing demand for water will have to be set against demands for other land and water uses, including the increased need for outdoor recreation.

Increased regulation of river flow is also important for maintaining low levels of pollution in major rivers. The use of water for the electrical supply industry, for the chemical, steel and paper industries together with effluent disposal explains the distribution of the heavily used rivers (Fig. 16). In the future several cycles of use for river water are anticipated and the reduction of pollution levels will make more water available.

Whereas the water supply of Britain focuses attention upon areas deficient in water, the converse is true of the distribution of hydro-electricity generating stations. These occur on a small scale in North Wales, the Lake District, the Southern Uplands and south-west England, but they have been developed on a larger scale in Ireland, and in the Highlands of Scotland since 1896, particularly following an Act of 1943 which set up a public authority for the development of hydro-electricity (Fig. 16). The Highlands now include over 50 power stations varying greatly in size, and in the Republic of Ireland nine stations are responsible for approximately 17 per cent of electricity output (Fig. 16). The largest, at Ardnacrusha on the river Shannon, has a catchment area of 10,400 square kilometres (4,015 square miles) and utilises an artificial fall of 30 metres (100 feet).

The impact of the climate is also apparent in the flood hazard. The effect of occasional intense storms, or of snow melt, is intensified by improved agricultural practices within drainage basins and by river regulation. Certain areas (Plate 8) have experienced a flood hazard which may have increased in magnitude in recent years and the experience of recent floods including those on the flood plains of the Severn and its tributaries, led to the announcement in 1968 of a short-term investigation into the magnitude and frequency of flooding in the United Kingdom.

In these various ways the climate has stimulated a response in the planning of water resources, in the utilization of hydro-electric power potential and in the perception of the effects of flooding, but there are also instances where man has had a direct impact on certain elements of the climate. This appears notably in the character of urban climates and particularly in that of London. Warm air characteristically rests within and above London and gives a heat island which varies diurnally and annually, and accounts for detectable temperature differences between the city centre, the suburbs and the surrounding districts. The nature of urban areas may also be reflected in an increased precipitation at certain times of the year. The most striking urban effect is atmospheric pollution from industry, vehicles and domestic fires (Plate 9), with its attendant repercussions on visibility and sunshine totals (Fig. 13). It has been estimated that London may be coated each year with over 100,000 metric tons of soot and dust. Progress towards the reduction of atmospheric pollution has been made since the Clean Air Act of 1956. The delimitation of 'smokeless zones' has allowed some control to be exercised over this harmful effect of man upon climate.

FURTHER READING

J. E. Belasco, *Characteristics of Air Masses over the British Isles* (H.M.S.O., 1952).

E. G. Bilham, *The Climate of the British Isles* (London, 1938).

T. J. Chandler, *The Climate of London* (London, 1965).

S. Gregory, Climate, in J. Wreford Watson with J. B. Sissons (eds.), *The British Isles: a Systematic Geography* (London, 1964), 53–73.

R. Kay Gresswell, *The Weather and Climate of the British Isles* (London, 1960).

H. H. Lamb, Types and Spells of Weather in the British Isles, *Quarterly Journal Royal Meteorological Society*, 76 (1950), 393–429.

H. H. Lamb, *The English Climate* (London, 1964).

G. Manley, *Climate and the British Scene* (London, 1952).

Meteorological Office, *Climatological Atlas of the British Isles* (London, 1952).

Ministry of Agriculture, Fisheries and Food, *Irrigation*, Bulletin No. 138 (London, 1962).

J. A. Taylor and R. A. Yates, *British Weather in Maps* (London, 1958)

Water Resources Board, *Water Supplies in South-East England* (London, 1966).

The Changing Rural Scene

Contrasts in the Rural Landscape

The British Isles are generally thought of, and quite correctly, as a densely populated, heavily industrialized area. Over 56 million people occupy a little over 30 million hectares (almost 77 million acres), there is less than half a hectare of agricultural land per head, and below 5 per cent of the working population is engaged in agriculture. But when the major land uses of the British Isles are examined in detail, it becomes clear that the urban-industrial areas are relatively compact and are localized in limited parts of the lowlands. In fact, only about 7 per cent of the British Isles is developed for building, industry, and transportation, though in England, the most urbanized of the constituent countries, the proportion of land developed for these purposes is as high as 12 per cent. Over 80 per cent of the British Isles is under farmland and over 6 per cent under woodland.

It is plain that undeveloped land predominates. Because this open land is also exceedingly diverse (see Chapter 1), varying greatly from one part of the British Isles to another, it follows that it bestows character and distinction upon particular areas. This feature may be observed not only on a broad regional scale, but frequently also at a very local and detailed level, within a distance of a few kilometres. As an example, the land-use characteristics of a small part of north Leicestershire are illustrated in Figure 17. The diagram documents the changes that take place eastwards from the urbanized Leicestershire coalfield near Coalville, through Charnwood Forest and the Soar Valley to the Leicestershire Wolds. Note, for instance, the differences revealed between the proportion of land in each region devoted to settlement, open space, grassland, arable, and woodland. Here land use is simply an index of the many landscape differences between the areas which may be observed in the field. The diagram also points to one of the major sets of factors which lie behind the marked differences in landscape response from place to place, namely, the physical characteristics of the land itself.

THE PHYSICAL BASIS

The attributes of land and air have already been outlined in Chapters 1 and 2. It can be readily appreciated that the considerable variations in altitude, bedrock, drift cover, soils, local climate, and hydrological conditions that exist in the British Isles can lead to widely differing rural scenery and very varied agricultural practice. While most farming areas are 'mixed' in the sense that they rely upon a number of different farming enterprises, marked regional specialization occurs (Fig. 18). For example, western Britain, with high rain-

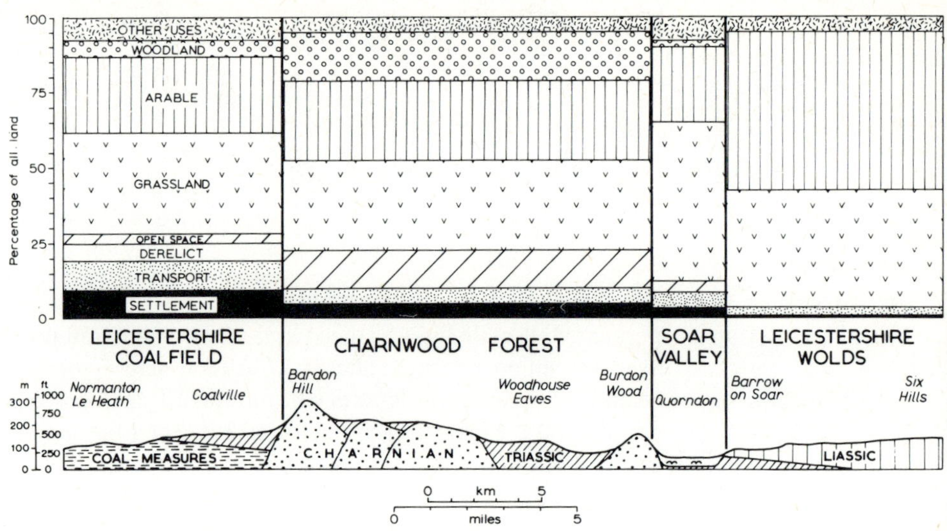

Fig 17 An East-West Transect of Part of North Leicestershire
Note the differing proportions of land devoted to the various uses in each of the four regions shown.

fall, heavy soils, and cool summers, has a natural advantage in grass production and concentrates upon livestock farming. In the higher, more exposed, and even rainier areas of Scotland, Wales, and south-west England, the rearing of livestock becomes more important, and in extreme conditions, predominates. In eastern England, by contrast, where the land is flatter, the growing season longer, the rainfall less intense, and the soils lighter, arable farming is the dominant agricultural enterprise. Where soils of particular quality occur, such as in the Fenland, then horticulture may become important. There is some evidence to suggest that regional specialization is continuing to intensify, a trend which has been evident for a century or more as the means of transporting agricultural goods to their markets have improved, and as new methods of processing and preserving foodstuffs have been perfected. Regions need no longer produce a wide range of agricultural goods for their own needs. It is unnecessary, for example, for market garden produce to be grown on the fringe of London. Soft fruits, vegetables, and flowers can be produced distant from the metropolitan market in the Hampshire basin, in south-west England, and elsewhere in areas of natural advantage, and still arrive in a fresh and acceptable condition. Field vegetables can be frozen, quick-dried, or canned, and marketed when and where required. Fertility is maintained increasingly by artificial means—livestock are not now essential in arable areas—and the more sophisticated and less versatile modern equipment must be fully employed in order to justify its cost. Both these factors have contributed to more specialized cropping.

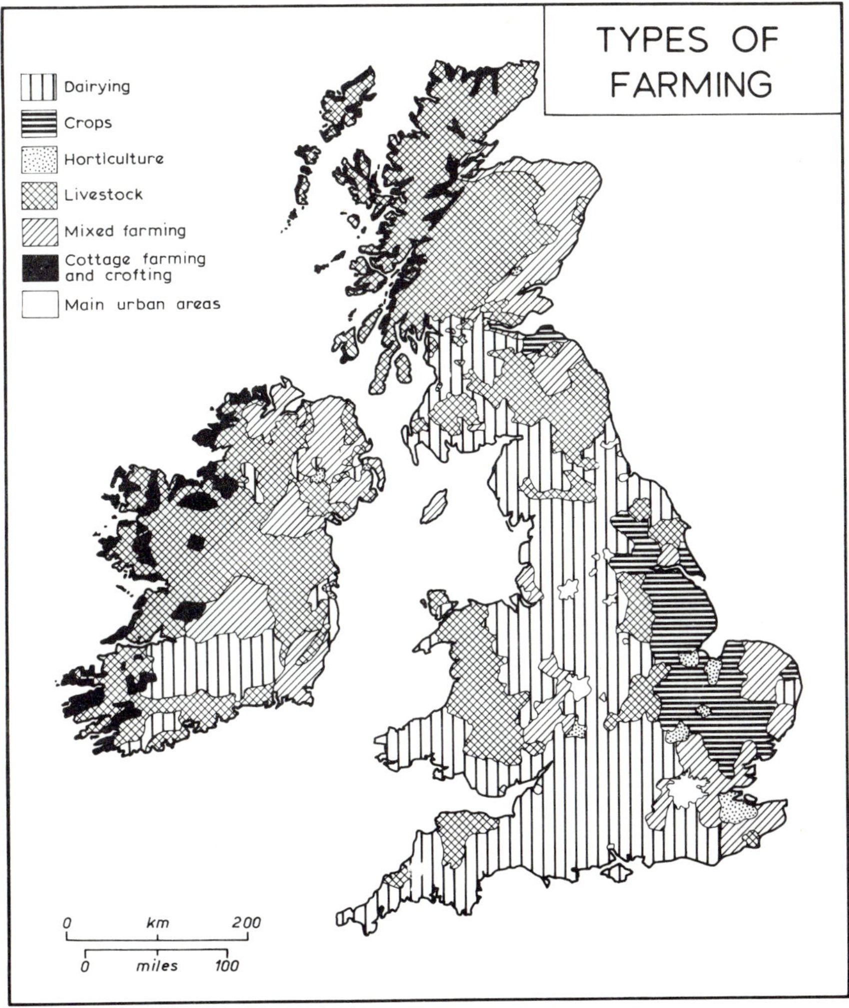

Fig 18 Predominant Types of Farming
Although most farming areas contain a mixture of different types of agricultural activity, marked regional specialization does occur. The map shows some of the major farming specialisms and emphasizes particularly the contrast between the lowland east, and the upland and isolated north and west.

Physical conditions, of course, lead to differences in agriculture other than those of farming enterprise. For example, levels of regional prosperity vary greatly. Farm income per hectare is four to five times higher in eastern England than it is in central Wales. Even so, such is the degree of mechanization (the Republic of Ireland excepted), output overall is among the highest in the world. Farmers of the British Isles now produce about half the food required by the home population. Roughly four-fifths of the value of agricultural output is derived from livestock farming and there is virtual self-sufficiency in eggs, milk, pork and poultry, meat and potatoes.

But it is equally clear that all contrasts in the rural landscape cannot be explained purely in terms of the physical attributes of land and air. Physical conditions are perhaps the most obvious, and perhaps the most stable, of the factors influencing the undeveloped countryside, but they are certainly not the only factors. There is a wide range of contemporary forces bearing upon rural land, but before these are considered it is well to examine the socio-historic background of the open countryside. In rural areas changes often take place very slowly. To compare today's map of any rural area uninfluenced by direct urban expansion, with that of a hundred years ago, is sufficient to reveal how little farmsteads, field boundaries, country roads and tracks, woodland, and even villages have altered in that time. The events of the past are therefore integral to an understanding of the present appearance and functioning of rural areas.

Socio-Economic Antecedents

THE MEDIAEVAL SYSTEMS

Historical geographers and other scholars have grappled for many years with the complexities of the various agricultural systems of mediaeval times. As yet we have a far from full understanding of the origins and operation of these systems, and it is not even possible to draw a definitive map showing the distribution of the different types. However, in a general way it is known that stretching from Yorkshire in the north through the Midlands of England to Dorset and Hampshire in the south there operated an open field type of agriculture based upon a two- or three-field system. This has become known as the 'Midland System'. To the west and north lay the Celtic Systems. To the east and south-east lay the East Anglian, lower Thames Basin, and Kentish Systems (Fig. 19). It is not possible to examine all these types in detail, but the variety of agricultural methods employed, and of the landscape patterns which resulted, may be gauged from a brief account of two highly contrasted, and areally closely-juxtaposed systems: the Midland system, and the Celtic system of Wales.

The open-field system of Midland England was essentially a method of co-operative farming, focused upon a compact village. The arable patch of each settlement was divided into two or three large fields within which the unfenced holdings of the individual farmers lay. The unenclosed parcels belonging to each farmer—usually they were in the form of narrow strips—were scattered more or less evenly about the open fields and ensured holders of a roughly equal share of the best and of the poorest land. All strips in a field grew the same crops in any year. Under the three-field system, one field was normally under winter-sown corn (perhaps wheat or rye), a second was under spring-sown corn (barley or oats), while the third field would remain fallow. Crops rotated, and each field lay fallow one year in three in order to maintain the fertility of the arable patch. Under a two-field system, one field was cropped and the other lay fallow each year. Common cultivation, or co-aration, frequently took place, since a heavy plough often needed a team of eight oxen, particularly in heavy-soil areas. Such a team was usually beyond the means of an individual. Though arable cultivation was the chief objective of the system all strip holders also possessed rights of depasturing stock on the waste land, on the fallow, and upon whatever meadow might exist. It was at one time believed that the open field system was imported into lowland England by the Anglo-Saxons in the fifth and sixth centuries. More recent work, particularly in Germany, has suggested that the system did not arrive as a ready-made and complete practice, but that it evolved slowly and may not have matured until the thirteenth century.

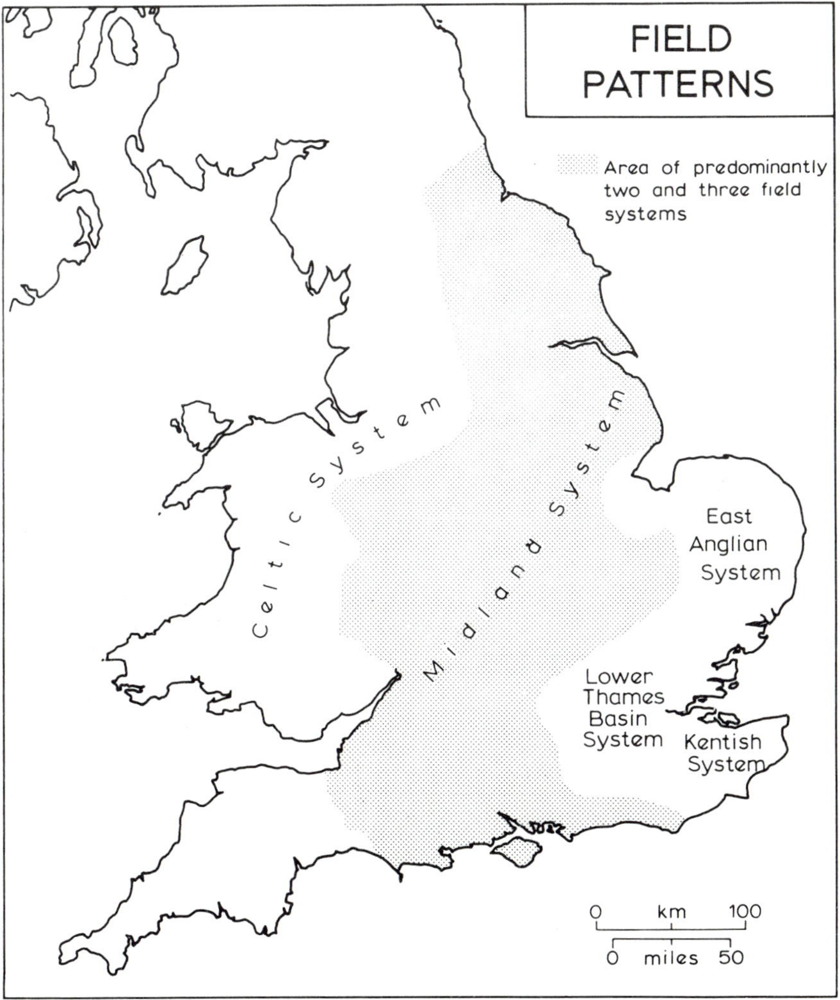

Fig 19 Medieval Field Systems in England and Wales
The map shows the approximate distribution of the medieval systems, as far as they can be adduced from documentary and field evidence. They are important because they had a decided bearing upon later agricultural developments. (After H. L. Grey.)

The system described is the model, from which in practice there are many deviations. The important point here is that the system persisted, and the enclosure of these open arable fields generally came late, typically in the eighteenth and nineteenth centuries. Earlier piecemeal enclosure sometimes fossilized the strip patterns where hedgerows followed the lines of the strip boundaries, but Parliamentary enclosure more usually created compact holdings with large rectangular fields, broad access lanes, and new farmsteads within the farm plot. In essence the Enclosure Awards completely reorganized the farming system, and the farming landscape, something which was only possible because the open fields had survived to provide the Enclosure Commissioners, who were responsible for laying out the new enclosures and plots, with a more or less free hand. Few vestiges of the open arable fields now exist in the enclosed and hedged landscape of the Midlands. One of the most

Plate 10 Ridge and Furrow, Napton (Warwickshire)
The picture was taken with the sun low in the sky. The shadows reveal quite clearly the ridges created by the continuous ploughing of strips in former open fields. Note the discordance, in a number of instances, with present-day hedge lines.

noticeable is the ridge-and-furrow patterning which sometimes persists in the now largely grassland areas, and which marks the strips of former open fields (Plate 10). Ridges are frequently discordant with present-day hedge lines and result from continuous ploughing of open-field strips in a consistent manner, thus causing soil to be piled into the centre of the strip. Field observers must be warned that ridge-and-furrow may arise from other processes and cannot be accepted automatically as indicative of open-field agriculture.

The Celtic System of Wales should not be regarded as typical of all the agricultural systems of the west and north. It is simply one of many related systems between and within which there was a high degree of flexibility. An interpretation of the Welsh system itself has been clouded by the effects of the Anglo-Norman conquest, and the semi-manorialization which followed it. On the south and north Wales coastal plains particularly, but also in the valleys opening out into the border country, Anglo-Norman feudalism became established, and along with it there developed some of the agricultural practices already described in the Midlands. But it is far from clear if a full open-field organization was ever fully or widely adopted in these Englishries, or what precise impact it had on traditional tenurial methods of the Welshries. Nonetheless, the Celtic system as it emerged was sufficiently distinct from the Midland system to produce not only a clear cultural and tenurial divide in the Middle Ages, but also a sharp contrast in the rural landscape today.

The Celtic system originated in a tribal society of semi-nomadic pastoralists. As life became more settled arable cultivation developed, and consequently the tenure of land and dwellings became an important feature. Society was composed of the free, and of those in bond. A free tribesman, while pastoral activities might remain his major concern, was able to appropriate suitable land within his township for arable working. He would enjoy individual ownership of this land and might enclose it, but he would continue to hold grazing rights on the common pasture. Seasonal transhumance might still persist, though it would be focused upon a permanent dwelling near the arable patch. On the death of the holder, the arable land was divided equally between his sons according to the gavelkind practice. One son would occupy the old homestead while the remainder would build new houses at points convenient to their arable holdings. Repetition through successive generations led to a scatter of homesteads in and around the arable area, and highly fragmented arable fields and holdings, the result of continuous parcellation. Inevitably a time was reached when further subdivision became impossible. At this point the next generation would be forced to make a new arable appropriation from the common, and so the process would begin again.

Bond tribesmen were primarily cultivators. Their conditions of tenure varied greatly but there appear to have been two main forms of organization. In the first, bondmen inherited their land holdings in much the same way as in the free system. In the second, land was not inherited but allocated by the lord. This land seems to have been cultivated in open fields and based upon dwellings clustered in a nucleated settlement. In practice it must have appeared very like the Midland system though, of course, its origins and organizations were quite different.

Eventually all those mainly lowland areas suitable for arable working were occupied, the remaining areas being used for common grazing. In the course of time the English legal system came to apply to the whole of Wales. Gavelkind was displaced, farms gradually became consolidated, and the bond status disappeared. The result was an enclosed, relatively stable, small-farm rural landscape containing few primary nucleated settlements. The upland wastes remained under common grazing until the land hunger of the eighteenth and nineteenth centuries. At this time encroachment or 'squatting' upon the common became frequent, and in some areas has left a dense zone of moorland-edge settlement which can still be observed today. Continued encroachment was eventually curtailed by the great enclosure movement which reached its peak in Wales during the Napoleonic Wars (1793–1815). During this period much of the remaining upland common was brought into private ownership, though enclosure did not lead to widespread agricultural improvement, as it often did in the lowland open fields.

THE NEW HUSBANDRY

It is clear from the foregoing account that the rural landscape has always been subject to gradual modification. There have been periods, however, when the rate of change has been more rapid, and one of these occurred in the eighteenth and nineteenth centuries in a period which has come to be known as that of the Agrarian Revolution. It is an important period, not only because the rate of change accelerated, but also because as well as technical innovations, there were profound geographical consequences at a relatively recent stage in the development of the rural landscape.

The new farming techniques, or the new husbandry as it came to be called, which led to the Agrarian Revolution involved both land devoted to cropping and that under stock. The novel arable methods that evolved through the eighteenth century had spread gradually to most parts of the country by the early part of the nineteenth century and caused a profound change in the distribution of arable working. The first principle of the new arable husbandry was constant tillage of the soil. This followed from the horse-hoeing husbandry advocated by Jethro Tull (1674–1741), in which it became necessary to sow seeds in drills rather than broadcast, and to work the soil continuously, before, during, and after seeding. Constant working was clearly better employed in light, freely-tilled soils than on heavy land. A second feature of the new husbandry was that it introduced new crops into rotations and hence greatly diversified the rotations available for use in particular circumstances. The medieval farmer had been preoccupied with grain cropping. Now it became possible and desirable to produce other crops, like turnips, potatoes, temporary grass, clover, which might provide food either for humans or for stock. At the same time, farmers were able to dispense with a fallow year in the rotation, since many of the new crops aided the recuperation of the soil after grain cropping. Turnips were particularly popular, and turnip husbandry, or the Norfolk four-course as it was known (winter wheat, followed by turnips, spring sown barley, and grass ley), diffused widely from its place of origin in East Anglia. The use of turnips, which are essentially a light-land crop, emphasized the effects of constant tillage and directed arable working away from the heavier soils. A third important characteristic of the new husbandry was the close association which grew up between cropping and livestock rearing. Winter fodder was now more plentiful than ever before and therefore stock could be maintained through the winter months instead of being slaughtered in large numbers in the autumn. Turnips were either lifted and fed to cattle in stall or yard, or they might be fed to stock while still in the ground. Sheep were usually folded on the turnip field, the fold being moved progressively until all the crop was eaten. Not only was the crop systematically consumed, but the land was evenly manured and very light soils consolidated by sheep treading.

Associated closely with improvements in arable farming were the innovations in livestock rearing. Since the autumn slaughter of cattle was no longer obligatory, careful selection and breeding became possible. Under the leadership of men like Robert Bakewell (1725–95) new breeds of mutton sheep—they had previously been used largely to produce wool alone—and of beef cattle developed. The success was obvious and readily demonstrated by increases in animal weight, and the methods were applied to the numerous regional breeds of sheep and cattle. It was these developments which laid the basis for the great impact which British regional livestock had upon the world at large in the nineteenth and twentieth centuries. Leicester, Cheviot, Southdown, and Romney Marsh sheep became widely known on many continents, while beef cattle, such as the Aberdeen Angus and the Hereford breeds, and dairy cattle, such as the Ayrshire and Channel Island breeds, were adopted particularly in Australia, New Zealand and in the Americas, but in other places too where quality stock was required. Similar developments can be traced in other types of livestock, for example, pigs, chickens and horses.

The period of the Agrarian Revolution was a time of great excitement in many rural parts of the British Isles. Agricultural societies sprang up with the aim of encouraging improvements in husbandry; at the very end of the eighteenth century the Board of Agriculture and Internal Improvement was established by the government; a rather special and very vigorous brand of propagandist for the new husbandry arose, notably Sir John Sinclair, Arthur Young—first chairman and secretary respectively of the Board of Agriculture—and William Marshall; and a welter of reports, surveys, and prize essays were written extolling those who practised the new approved methods and chiding those who did not. The improved rotations, the scientific breeding, the more advanced farm machinery, the better systems of drainage, and the new fertilizers, all helped to increase output, but they also lowered production costs. Every incentive thus existed for farmers to adopt the improved methods, particularly in periods when the prices of agricultural goods were as inflated as they were during the Napoleonic Wars, though it is possible that the ease with which profits could be made had the opposite effect upon some, however much this was contrary to the spirit of the time.

The new and improved methods could only be employed successfully upon enclosed land. This was a powerful arguement for the enclosure of any open fields remaining in communal use and to a large extent accounts for the rapid

Plate 11 Dairy Farming near Beeston (Cheshire)
The photograph shows a typical dairy farm in the drift-covered Cheshire Plain. Grassland predominates, but there are clear signs of recent tillage in the near and middle distance. The cattle are Friesians.

disappearance of the Midland system, already described. However, the Midland clays, which had been the chief corn-producing soils in the Middle Ages were no longer well-adapted to that purpose and were for the most part put down to grassland for dairying and stock rearing. The stiff clayland which remained under arable tended to follow traditional medieval, rather than the new, rotations, even when it had been enclosed. Arable working under the new system increased sharply on the lighter soils of the Chalk outcrops and in the light-land areas of East Anglia and the Hampshire Basin. It was these areas which were the real beneficiaries of the new arable husbandry.

The Agrarian Revolution therefore brought with it a restructuring of the rural landscape, particularly in lowland areas of England. In the areas where the Celtic system had dominated, there were often profound changes of method, but here the major constituents of the rural landscape were already in being and although land usage and land management might change, the fabric of the landscape persisted. In lowland England, and especially in the Midlands, there were sweeping changes not only in land usage and agricultural practice, but also in many other rural features. New hedges, walls, farmsteads, tracks, and roads emerged as the landscape that exists today evolved under the hands of the Enclosure Commissioners. The Agrarian Revolution brought one further change, the long term effects of which were eventually to be felt throughout the land. Linked with concomitant improvements in transportation it led to the final breakdown of local agricultural self-sufficiency. It paved the way, in fact, for the development of the regional specialization already described in the early part of this chapter.

DEVELOPMENTS TO THE PRESENT

The movement away from local agricultural self-sufficiency brought with it many benefits to large numbers of farmers. Regions developed the types of agriculture in which they possessed greatest comparative advantage, production took place at greater scale, mechanization increased, costs were reduced, and links with the growing urban-industrial markets were forged. But the economic benefits were tempered with some disadvantages, especially those which stemmed from the necessity to dispose of goods in increasingly competitive markets. While subsistence farming still dominated, price fluctuations had limited significance. Once farming became a fully commercial activity, price movements had a major impact upon the economic marginality of land, upon the types of enterprise which were most attractive, and upon the quality of life for all in rural areas. The disadvantages were compounded by the fact that price changes were only partially affected by seasons of plenty and seasons of scarcity within the British Isles. Any self-regulating market mechanism which might have developed was upset by the need to import foodstuffs, particularly bread-corn, as the urban-based population expanded. The difficulties increased in intensity through the nineteenth century and into the twentieth century as self-sufficiency declined, as the demands of the urban population increased, and as the ability of overseas competititors to satisfy these demands improved enormously.

Following the sharp inflation in the prices of agricultural goods during the Napoleonic Wars—the years 1801 and 1812 provided the price peaks—markets steadied at a level reasonably satisfactory to farmers, if not always to their field labourers. Partly responsible for this was the complicated body of legislation known as the Corn Laws, which were introduced to encourage the growth of home-produced grain and to curtail imports when prices on the home market were low. A sliding scale of duties, geared to the market price at home, was imposed on imported grain; when the price at home was low, the duty was heavy, and when the price was high, the duty was nominal. A corn bounty was also paid on exported grain when prices in the British Isles were low. This, in effect, prevented the glutting of the home market with surplus grain. Anti Corn Law agitation, not only on the part of the manufacturers,

Plate 12 Cropland Farming near Peterborough (within Northamptonshire)
The scene is set in the heart of arable, eastern England. There is virtually no grassland, and certainly no permanent pasture to be seen. Note the size and shape of the fields. Compare the hedgerows with those in photographs of other farming areas in the chapter.

who wished to push down food prices as low as possible in order that their own wage bills should be minimized, but very much more widely in the urban community, grew in strength, notably after the new Corn Law of 1815. For a generation or more, until the repeal of the Corn Laws in 1846, the question of agricultural protection divided the country and gave a political focus to the differentiations which were rapidly emerging in other spheres of life between town and country.

In the fifties, sixties, and seventies of the nineteenth century prices of foodstuffs, though slightly lower than before the repeal of the Corn Laws, continued to maintain a reasonable level. But the end of the years of agricultural prosperity, such as they had been, was in sight. During the 1860s the acreage under wheat had already begun to contract, and with increasing imports in the last two decades of the century, the process continued. The imports came not from Europe, which had been the main supplier of grain earlier in the century, but from North America, where lands of the middle and far west were being opened up for commercial farming on an extensive scale as the railways pushed westward, and as steamship eased the transfer of the produce to western Europe. The price of grains in Britain, and especially of wheat, fell dramatically after 1880 and did not recover until shortages arose during the First World War. In grassland farming the depression was not so severe, particularly where the produce was fresh liquid milk. Urban demands for milk were expanding rapidly and there was no competition from overseas to upset prices. Railways played an important part in the marketing of milk and there was a substantial swing from arable to grassland husbandry. Arable land, which had occupied nearly 60 per cent of the agricultural acreage in England and Wales in 1870, by the mid 1930s took less than 40 per cent of a much reduced agricultural area.

The depression in agricultural prices continued in the interwar period and was intensified by a world economic crisis. Lack of resources led to a widespread neglect of farmland and farm buildings, and output continued to fall. At one time, less than one-third of home food consumption was being produced within the British Isles. The United Kingdom government eventually began to intervene, through import duties, quotas, and subsidies. These tentative moves away from free trade in agricultural produce and in the direction of a protected home industry were confirmed during the Second World War when a wide-ranging set of financial controls and subsidies was introduced. Some of the wartime measures have since been abandoned, and new means of support introduced. But their aim has remained the same—to encourage higher productivity. Some subsidies are designed specifically to promote land improvement or desirable practices. Others, like the price guarantees for all the major products of British farming, contribute in a more general way by creating a stable economic climate in which agriculture can flourish. At the moment the farm subsidy bill of the United Kingdom amounts to roughly £250 million and represents a quarter of net farm income. Government decisions about farming aid must therefore be regarded as one of the important determinants of agriculture at the moment.

The Rural Landscape Today

THE STRUCTURE OF MODERN FARMING

Such is the diversity of the background to farming in the British Isles that almost any generalization about its present day structure is in some way inadequate. Size, ownership and tenure, degree of mechanization, and the marketing systems of farms are as varied as the land-use and farm enterprise contrasts already outlined. Though changes are currently underway, the physical basis of farming and its historical evolution have produced patterns which are remarkably persistent.

Farm size provides a good example. Though in England and Wales the acreage occupied by large farms has been increasing significantly for some while, holdings of 400 hectares (1,000 acres) and over are still limited in number and are confined largely to the eastern half of England, mainly in East Anglia and upon the chalk-land of the south. Holdings of under 20 hectares (50 acres), on the other hand, are most prevelant in western counties, the only important exceptions being the market gardening areas of the Fenland, and around London. The most prominent single group of farms, accounting for over 40 per cent of the total agricultural area of England and Wales, is that in the range 40–120 hectares (100–300 acres). Only six counties in England and Wales have less than 30 per cent of their agricultural area occupied by farms of this size. Farm size varies not only by regions, but is also closely related to the kind of enterprise pursued. The smaller holdings are likely to be more intensive than the large ones and to concentrate upon those activities which demand higher inputs per unit area, like poultry, pigs, dairying, and vegetable production. For instance, while the holdings of under 40 hectares (100 acres) occupy about 30 per cent of the agricultural area of England and Wales, they produce 66 per cent of the poultry, 52 per cent of the pigs, and 46 per cent of the dairy goods.

Conditions of land ownership and tenure are also distinctive. Enclosure, particularly when it occurred in recent historical time, as in the Midlands, resulted in the extinction of common rights over the land enclosed and often led to the disappearance of the small land-holder, simply because he could not afford the costs of enclosure and could not survive the loss of common rights. Where this occurred the characteristic type of land holding came to be one in which large landowners rented land to individual, sometimes even substantial, tenant farmers. The landowner provided the land and the buildings, the tenant provided his working capital. In areas where enclosure was earlier, there emerged a higher proportion of owner-operated holdings. In the Republic of Ireland, where a hundred years ago land was owned by large, often absentee, landlords and rented to small tenant farmers, the activities of the Land Commission in redistributing land to owner-occupiers has virtually eliminated tenant farming. Despite a number of strong factors contributing to a swing to owner-occupation—heavy death duties, the increasing importance of farming by business and professional men, and the difficulties of acquiring a farm, except by purchase—nearly half the farmers of Britain are still tenants. In England over 50 per cent of the agricultural land is rented, though in the south-east hobby and part-time farmers increase the proportion owner-operated. In Wales 42 per cent of the agricultural land is rented, in Scotland 41 per cent, in Northern Ireland 10 per cent, and in the Irish Republic almost none. Owner occupation tends to be most frequent in the largest and smallest holdings; the medium-sized holdings being more usually rented.

No change in British farming has been as dramatic in recent years as that in the degree of mechanization. But even here there are wide differences between areas, and not only between the United Kingdom, where mechanization, on the whole, is well developed, and the Republic of Ireland, where it is not, but also between different regions in England and Wales. Before the Second World

War there were barely 50,000 tractors in England and Wales. Now there are half a million. They are most numerous in eastern counties, particularly in areas of intensive arable farming, but in nearly all counties of England and Wales there is more than one tractor per 40 hectares (100 acres) of farmland. Combine harvesters occur most frequently in East Anglia. They are mainly self-propelled machines and contrast with the smaller tractor-drawn machines which are more useful in the smaller fields and rough terrain of the western

Plate 13 Horticulture near Yalding (Kent)
Fruit cropping, particularly of tree fruits, is widely distributed in this part of south-east England. Hop fields, containing posts ready to support the fully grown hop plants, are seen in the middle distance. The farm in the left foreground has five oast houses (circular buildings with conical rooves). These formerly served as hop-drying kilns.

counties. Binders, mowers, and milking machines are used mainly in the grassland west; corndrills, potato planters, potato harvesters, and canning and freezing plant are in demand largely in the arable east.

Finally, the marketing of agricultural produce exhibits contrasts, if not inconsistencies. These, however, stem not so much from the nature of the land, or from the historical development of farming, as from the seemingly haphazard development of marketing systems. In the Irish Republic marketing is fairly straightforward. Livestock are marketed through fairs and marts, milk through creameries, and arable produce through dealers. There is a little contract marketing, but it is important only for malting barley and sugar beet. The unique feature of the Republic's agricultural marketing is that, of all the countries of western Europe, it is the most dependent on farming exports, and it is certainly the only one which is tied almost exclusively to a single national market. The United Kingdom takes three-quarters of all exports and almost all the agricultural export. Within the United Kingdom marketing is complex, with a price-support mechanism and a large number of marketing boards which may be empowered to buy all produce offered for sale, or may have control over the quantity of a commodity produced, or over its purchase price. Livestock, sold by auction at one of the many cattle markets, by private treaty, or direct to meat dealers, may fall within the Fatstock Guarantee Scheme. About half the cattle, but most of the sheep and pigs, are eligible for price support. All milk must be sold through the Milk Marketing Board and most fleece-wool and eggs are also marketed through a board. Poultry on the other hand is handled through normal commercial outlets. Most crops reach the market through the agency of agricultural merchants, but potatoes and hops are exceptions, these crops having marketing boards, and also sugar beet, all of which must be sold to the British Sugar Corporation. Fruit and vegetables are not covered by guarantee, or by a marketing board, and they reach the consumer through large wholesale markets, like Covent Garden in London. Contract marketing is increasing rapidly, particularly for horticultural produce. Co-operative marketing, on the other hand, has developed little when compared with some other European countries.

URBAN INFLUENCES

The point has already been made that the British Isles is a thickly peopled and, in parts, a heavily industrialized area. The developments in manufacturing, and the growth and redistribution of population and settlement in recent historic times are the subjects of following chapters (Chapters 4 and 5). Here it is sufficient to note that rural areas are heavily modified by urban-based influences and attitudes. Although the land used specifically for urban purposes outside the urbanized areas may still be quite limited, the social and economic effects of urban man upon the countryside are widespread. The forces of modification are strongest close to the conurbations and major urban areas, and they decrease with distance from them. But it is doubtful if any part of the British Isles today, with the possible exception of the most westerly parts of Scotland and Ireland, where not even city-based television programmes reach, can be regarded as wholly rural and in no sense urban-influenced.

Plate 14 Livestock Farming in and around the Tanat Valley (Montgomeryshire)
The photograph looks eastwards down Cwm Llech into the Tanat Valley, which runs from left to right across the plate, and beyond to the foothills of the Berwyn range. Fields are small, irregular in shape, and almost everywhere under grassland. Here the valley floor is 200 metres above sea level and the moorland edge is at about 300 metres. The open hill slopes are grazed by sheep at very low density.

Perhaps the single most important factor leading to the introduction of urban influences into rural areas is the attitude of many urban dwellers in the British Isles to the countryside. As time has gone by, and as a swiftly increasing proportion of the population has become urbanized, so the sentimental attachment to the open countryside appears to have strengthened. For some, these feelings are manifested quite positively in the desire to live among fields and trees, even though work places must remain distant in town or city. For others it is sufficient that rural areas of charm should be preserved from harmful development, and that, where possible, they should be accessible to the town and city dweller so that, periodically, he too may share in a green and refreshing countryside. It is not the call of the wilderness—which is what seems to excite so many North Americans—but a call to an idealized rural calm. It is paradoxical that the urban dweller, who often regards so highly the solace which the countryside can provide, is the one who is largely responsible, directly or indirectly, for putting at risk what he treasures most.

Land-use competition, stemming from urban-based pressures, is one of the major characteristics of rural areas, and particularly, of course, of those rural areas nearby the major urban centres. Agriculture is a relatively poor competitor for land and the farmer has everything to gain financially by succumbing to urban demands. As population has increased, and also become more affluent and more mobile, persistent pressures for building land outside present urban limits have been created. City centre and inner suburban redevelopment has contributed further to this overspill. But there have been pressures from

Plate 15 The Pressure of Urban Man upon the Countryside, Haydock (Lancashire)
Despite planning control, the pressures exerted upon the countryside by urban forms of land use is still great. A few of the most important consumers of farmland are shown here—housing, manufacturing, extractive industry, recreation.

other land-use competitors which, though they may not have consumed as much rural land as housing, have certainly contributed to the urbanization of the countryside, retailing development associated with housing, manufacturing industry, extractive industry, transport, public services, recreation, schools, and hospitals. The two most avaricious of these uses have been recreation, the pressures from which are likely to continue increasing, and the extractive mineral industries, which not only provided, largely in the past, the basis for the manufacturing growth in the British Isles, but have supplied more recently the sand, gravel, and limestone materials which have been the raw materials of urban expansion. Though all these competitors for rural land occupy a relatively small proportion of the total land area, their influence through proximity is profound (Plate 15).

Such was the concern felt about the lack of control over urban-based developments, and about what was feared might be the consequent despoilation of the countryside, that in the period immediately after the Second World War a number of important institutional measures were adopted in the United Kingdom to regulate land-use change. In 1946 the New Towns Act was passed to give greater direction to population overspill from the conurbations, in 1947 the Town and Country Planning Act introduced wide-ranging powers for the control of new development in both urban and rural areas, and finally in 1949 the National Parks and Access to the Countryside Act set up the National Park system and also created a mechanism for overseeing all rural activities. All these major pieces of legislation have subsequently been modified and their provisions often strengthened. They are important because they set up in broad outline the mechanisms of land-use regulation which operate in the United Kingdom today, and which have contributed so much to keeping town and country physically if not functionally distinct; they are important also because they provided for, or led to, the establishment of the protected rural areas, such as National Parks, Areas of Outstanding Natural Beauty, Areas of Great Landscape Value, and green belts, which have already been mentioned in Chapter 1 (see Fig. 11).

The general land-use controls together with the special preservation areas have certainly restricted urban sprawl. The rate of acquisition of rural land has fallen dramatically. In the first sixty years of this century the urban area of England and Wales doubled. Now the rate of conversion of rural land is little more than half that in the inter-war period and urban expansion is taking up roughly 1 per cent of the land surface of England and Wales every decade. At this rate about 16 per cent of England and Wales will be developed by the year 2000. These figures compare quite favourably with the position in West Germany and Holland. But while there is no cause for immediate concern at the present rate of urbanization in the countryside, in particularly densely populated and heavily developed regions there are pressing problems of regional organization. It is these and other problems which are explored in greater detail in the following chapters.

FURTHER READING

A. R. H. Baker, Co-operative Farming in Medieval England, *Geographical Magazine*, 42 (1970), 496–505.

R. H. Best, *The Major Land Uses of Great Britain* (Wye College, Ashford, 1959).

R. H. Best and J. T. Coppock, *The Changing Use of Land in Britain* (London, 1962).

J. T. Coppock, *An Agricultural Atlas of England and Wales* (London, 1964).

J. T. Coppock, Ireland, United Kingdom, in *World Atlas of Agriculture: Vol. 1 Europe, U.S.S.R., Asia Minor* (Instituto Geografico de Agostini, Novara, 1969), 227–240, 438–475.

R. Gasson, *The Influence of Urbanization on Farm Ownership and Practice* (Wye College, Ashford, 1966).

W. R. Mead, Ridge and Furrow in Buckinghamshire, *Geographical Journal*, 120 (1954), 34–42.

W. Smith, *An Historical Introduction to the Economic Geography of Great Britain* (London, 1968).

L. D. Stamp, *The Land of Britain, its Use and Misuse* (London, 1962).

D. Thomas, Statutory Preservation of the Countryside in England and Wales, *Zeitschrift für Wirtschaftsgeographie*, 6 (1962), 34–38.

J. G. Thomas, Rural Settlement, in E. G. Bowen (ed.), *Wales, a Physical, Historical and Regional Geography* (London, 1957).

J. Weller, *Modern Agriculture and Rural Planning* (London, 1967).

G. P. Wibberley, *Agriculture and Urban Growth* (London, 1959).

Developments in Manufacturing

To a large extent manufacturing activity in medieval Britain was an urban characteristic and, at a time when communications were severely restricted, regional specialization was but little developed since each part of the country produced its own essential goods. When in the post-medieval period regional specialization developed it largely did so in a non-urban context. To some extent this was a clear reaction to the restrictive conditions of the urban guilds, but it was also linked with exploitation of dispersed resources, particularly water and wood, the prime power supplies. One writer on England in the eighteenth century records that 'to a large extent, industry was rural rather than urban. In some cases, notably in that of the woollen textiles, production had moved from the old corporate towns in search of freer habitats elsewhere; in other cases, for example in those of iron and coal, industry had been traditionally located in the country; finally, in the case of the cotton industry, of relatively recent development, the various processes of manufacture were conducted for the most part outside the towns'. Even so a marked localization of industry was hardly apparent. The woollen industry, which may be taken as an example, was widely spread throughout the country, although three areas of relative importance were evident. These were the West Country, East Anglia and the West Riding of Yorkshire. To a large extent, though by no means simply and exclusively so, these areas emerged by virtue of the local supplies of wool, together with possibilities of import, and the availability of water supplies. In the period prior to rapid industrialization, therefore, although regional specialization was apparent it was associated with rurality and a lack of concentration, a diffuseness which to some extent echoed earlier characteristics.

The period in the late eighteenth and early nineteenth centuries, which is usually termed 'The Industrial Revolution', transformed this earlier situation and laid the foundations of the pattern of manufacturing which was to last until the severe economic depression of the period between the two World Wars. Two major controls were operative during the process of transformation. The first was the importance of fixed resources, particularly of power resources. Part of the revolution in industry was the replacement of dependence upon water power by reliance upon steam generated by coal fired engines. The result was the creation of a dominance in manufacturing industry by the large coalfields of Britain, coalfield and industrial region became co-terminous. Alongside this process of concentration went an advancing regional specialization. Lancashire became firmly associated with cotton textiles, Yorkshire with woollens and South Wales with iron, steel and tinplate. It is true that these industries generated others closely linked to them, and external economies made for the growth of great industrial complexes, but even so the one group of industries remained dominant and indeed specialization was so marked that even in 1949 the late Professor Wilfred Smith could produce a map (dated 1936) which clearly demonstrated the classic intra-regional contrast between cotton spinning mills and weaving sheds in south-west Lancashire. This situation is usually explained as a product of organization, where a horizontal structuring of the industry so that spinning and weaving were entirely separate, produced geographically a segmented expression.

The foregoing brief discussion on the developments within manufacturing emphasize three trends which need further comment, and these trends will be considered rather than a regional description of industrial development. They are agglomeration or coalfield concentration, specialization, and the development of industrial complexes due to the incidence of external economies.

The first of these is best illustrated from that area where the coking of coal was first developed, the Coalbrookdale Coalfield. Prior to the eighteenth century the iron industry was closely associated with timber resources since charcoal was the prime fuel used for smelting iron ore and a serious depletion of eastern resources had become evident. The iron industry had migrated, therefore, north and west to Shropshire, Worcestershire, Warwickshire, Staffordshire, Cheshire and South Yorkshire and into Wales. But since it was still reliant on wood and on a head of water power it was essentially dispersed; the 'tyranny of wood and water' held sway. In the Severn Valley, 'though the industry was relatively small it severely taxed the local timber resources, insomuch that furnaces and forges spread up and down the valley away from the Severn Gorge, though this involved the transport of iron ore. Water power to work bellows and hammers was obtained from streams tributary to the Severn'. The result was a scatter both of furnaces and forges which bore no relation to the small coalfield. By the end of the eighteenth century two major advances had been made in technical development. Abram Darby had developed the process of coking coal so that the impurities which produced a brittle iron were released, and the steam engine not only undermined the dependence on sites where direct water power was available, but increased reliability and capacity (Plate 16). The result was the migration of the furnaces onto the coalfield, though at the forges charcoal continued to be used. The result was a two fold division at the turn of the century, for the furnaces had become concentrated whereas the forges were still as widely dispersed as Shrewsbury and Stourport. By the late nineteenth century, however, the forges too followed partly in response to newer technical developments and also to the organization of fewer, larger companies so that a pattern emerges of integrated late nineteenth century iron works exclusively related to coalfield sites. The three maps reproduced (Fig. 20) emphasize the changing spatial relations and depict the process of concentration which was affecting all the coalfields of Britain.

The aspect of specialization is not so easily understood and, indeed, presents many complexities. One which emerged was the dominance of cotton and cotton textile manufacture by Lancashire, yet there is no evidence why of the

Plate 16 Coalbrookdale (Shropshire)
This is a pre-World War II photograph indicating the general features of the Iron Works. Darby's furnace where coked coal was used was near the stack in the middle distance. The incised valley where water power could be exploited is typical of early locations.

three west coast coalfields, South Wales, Lancashire and the Scottish Ayrshire and Lanarkshire fields, one should have become so exclusively dominant. Any rehearsal of the traditional locational factors in the cotton industry would apply equally to all the western coasts; humidity, soft water, coal supplies and water power are fairly universal as indeed was a basic textile tradition based on wool. In particular it can be argued that Strathclyde was admirably equipped. There were supplies of soft water and water power to be generated in the southern uplands. It had both wool and coal at hand. Even further it possessed trans Atlantic contacts in its trade and was at no disad-

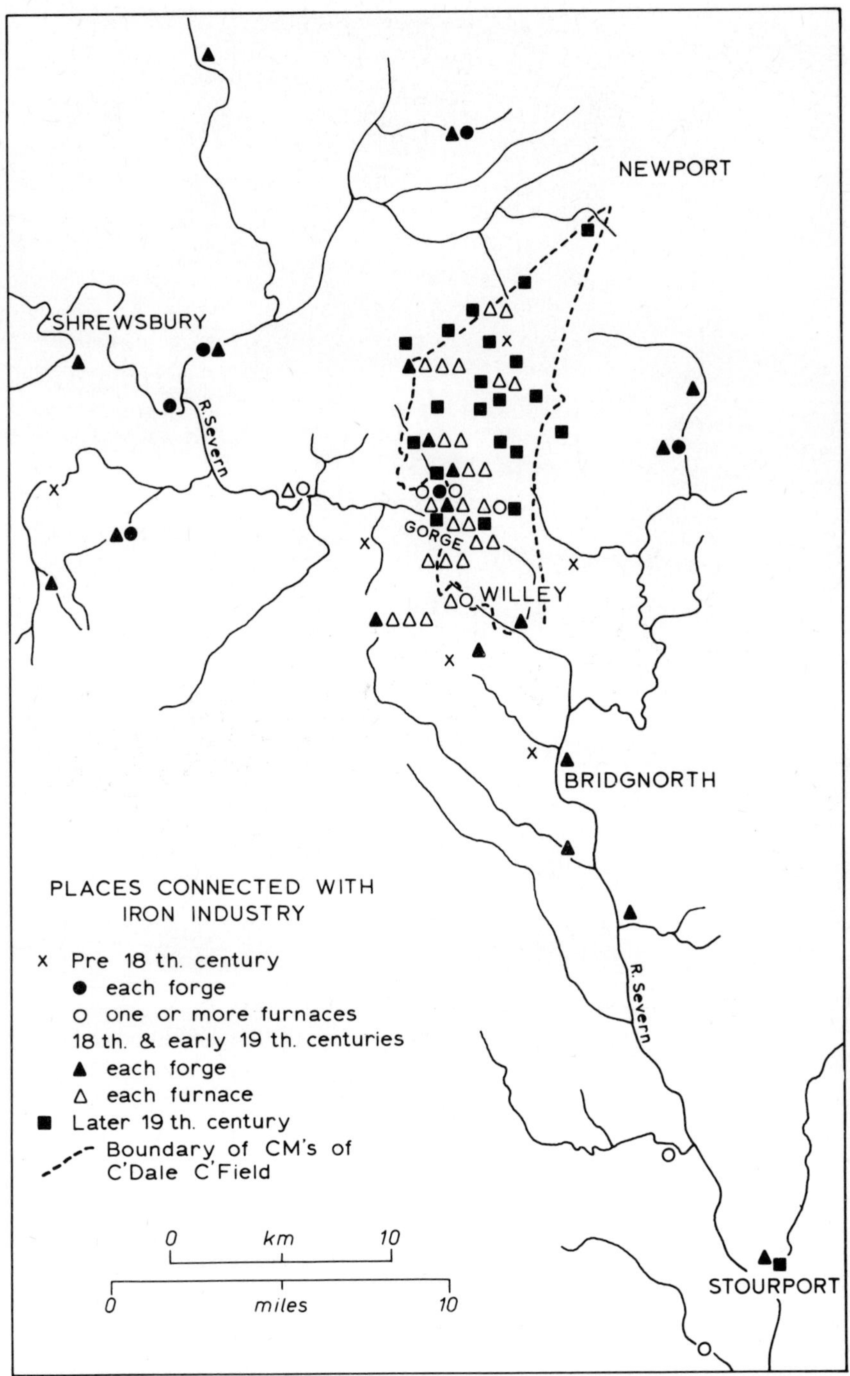

Fig 20 The Coalbrookdale Coalfield
The map shows growth of the iron industry. (After T. W. Birch.)

vantage compared with Liverpool. Indeed it did develop special skills in linen and silk manufacture, and also textile industries at Paisley. The carpets of Paisley and Kilmarnock and the production of knitting wool at Ayr became widely known but there was never that dominance which characterized cotton in Lancashire or wool in Yorkshire. W. Smith could record that in 1936 96·7 per cent of the firms spinning or weaving cotton were in Lancashire and neighbouring areas, but only 1·3 per cent in Scotland and 2 per cent elsewhere.

Chisholm has attempted to elucidate these problems. He considers the traditional interpretation that the demise of the Scottish cotton manufacturing was due to a concentration on high quality goods rather than cheaper products for the growing mass market and that the cotton famine in the 1860s, coincident with the American Civil War, caused industrialists to turn to the metal trades. But he finds it difficult to accept these propositions. Why was it easier for Scottish entrepreneurs to turn from high class textiles to metals rather than to low quality textiles? Was not Lancashire affected by the cotton famine? Chisholm suggests that the answer lies in comparative advantages. Scotland possessed good coking coals and iron ore, and the rather doubtful fact is added of an advantage in the Clyde for shipbuilding. The Clyde possessed real alternatives whereas Lancashire did not. Again Chisholm argues, rather more vaguely, that 'the opportunities favoured the copper and iron trades and the export of coal'. The 'opportunities' need more specification, but it is certainly true that the rapid growth of metallurgy inhibited any development of cotton textiles. It was in the manner, therefore, that contemporary entrepreneurs *perceived* relative advantages that eventually resulted in the distinctive and characteristic specializations of the industrial period.

Into this context must be placed those specializations which were intensifications of existing industries. One of the best examples of this is the cutlery making industry at Sheffield. This has existed from pre-industrial times based on charcoal smelted iron. It is significant that its early start can be associated with Flemish immigrants encouraged by the Tudors to develop their skills in the production of swords. The momentum generated by the industrial period transformed this industry and deepened its specialism even though local raw materials became less important. To a large extent the concern with stainless steel after 1914 and with special steels is derived from this background and part of the Sheffield steel industry is characteristically associated with high quality products and short run orders.

The third element in the growth of the manufacturing areas was the emergence of industrial complexes. This can be illustrated in relation to the Midland Valley of Scotland. In the early phases the Scottish coalfields developed iron industries based on the ores available in the Coal Measure series. The earliest developments were at Carron, north of Falkirk on the navigable estuary of the Forth. In terms of diffusion studies it is worth noting that these works were established by a Sheffield iron master. In subsequent times the exhaustion of local ores meant the necessity of import and here the navigable estuaries were vital. Integrated iron and steel works developed at Carron and also on the Clyde at Glasgow and Coatbridge. The integration of

Plate 17 Glasgow
An assemblage of elements of the older manufacturing areas of Britain. Port development and shipbuilding both in decline together with clearing of the older terraces surrounding.

iron and steel production with other derived industries is epitomised by shipbuilding which underlay the great developments on the Clyde at Coatbridge, Glasgow, Motherwell and Wishaw, and which left the Carron works as an isolated island.

The west coast had long specialized in ocean going sailing ships and in 1812 John Wood launched the Comet as a steam ship for the West African trade in which Glasgow had specialized. The Clyde estuary was not particularly suited but dredging enabled the development of the ship building industry along some twenty miles of river front from Glasgow to Govan. Clearly part of this complex were the engineering industries which rapidly developed specializations in locomotive building, closely associated with the boilermaking part of shipbuilding. Other specialisms were in machine tools, which were closely

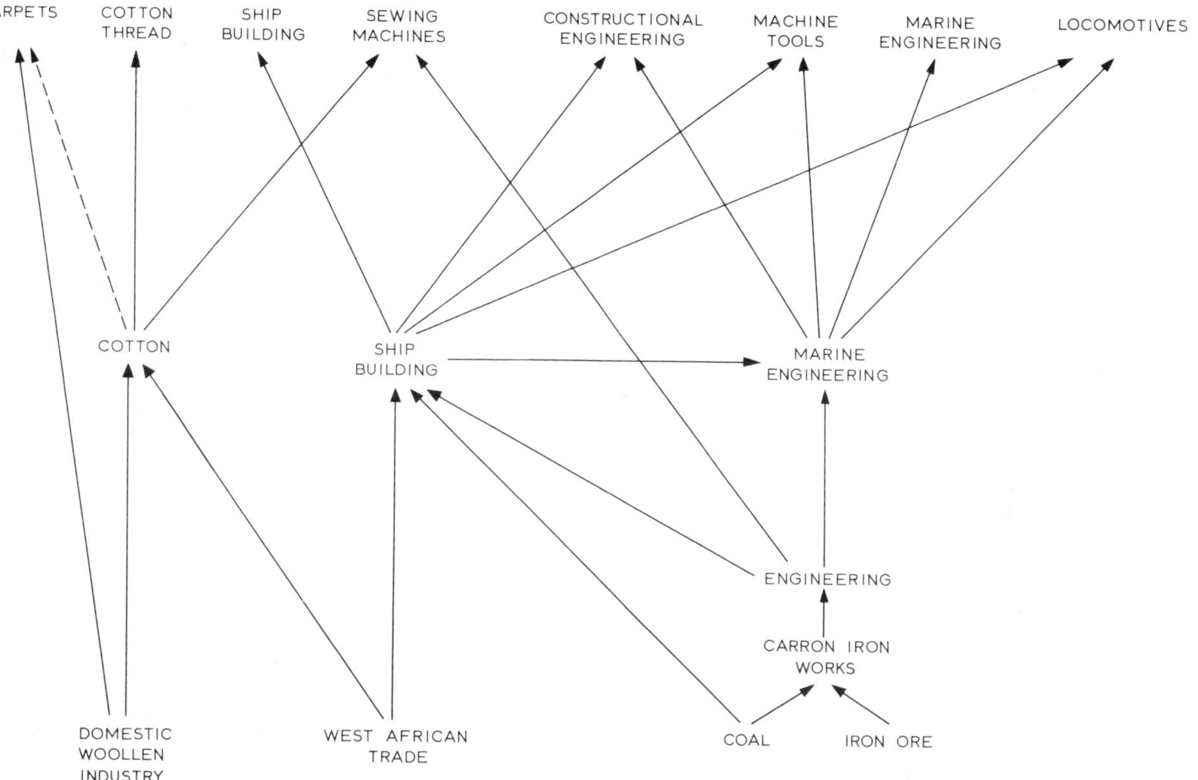

Fig 21 The Development of the Central Valley of Scotland Industrial Complex
Note the wide development of metallurgical and engineering industries which restricted the growth of textiles.

related to the shipbuilding and locomotive industries as well as to textiles and indeed to the mechanization of coal mining; in textile machinery especially linked to its specialization in thread cotton and the production of sewing machines; in constructional engineering again linked to shipbuilding.

To this complex must be added the textile industries which, as has already been seen, were 'headed off' by the rapidly growing metallurgical and engineering industries and remained only as highly specialized survivals.

It is now possible to construct a diagram (Fig. 21) which, if only in crude form, indicates the complex interlocking of industries which characterized the coalfields during and immediately after the so-called industrial revolution. Whether these be related to 'external economies' or 'agglomeration economies' the net result was the same, the emergence of highly distinctive industrial regions on the coalfields whose names became intimately linked with particular products, as Lancashire with cotton, the West Riding with wool, Sheffield with high quality steels, Tyneside with shipbuilding, South Wales with tin-plate and the one where region and product gained the same name, the Potteries. A map of industrial distributions between 1850 and 1930 is essentially a map of the coalfields.

The main changes which have taken place since the 1930s have in general been the antithesis of those which were in operation in the period already reviewed. The coalfields have become increasingly less important as elements controlling the distribution of industry, and not only has there been a contraction in mining but also in nearly all the industries characteristically associated with the coalfields. Along with this has gone an increasing trend to diversification so that regional specialization has been diminished. Moreover, changes in the organization of industry have led in the same direction as horizontal organization has progressively been replaced by a vertical structuring. But the major reasons behind industrial change are related to changes in the basic control of location put forward above, primarily the decline of coal as the major power resource. The widespread use of electrical power freed industry from its excessive dependence on the coalfields and as generation of electricity by oil or nuclear sources also developed, the role of coal as a location factor has become progressively smaller. Added to this has been a diminution in demand for coal overseas so that the coal mining industry has been in a process of severe contraction. The peak in employment figures and output was reached as early as 1913 with some 1·1 million employment and an output of 293 million metric tons (287 million long tons). By the outbreak of the Second World War employment had fallen to 782,000 and output to 230 million metric tons (226 million long tons). By 1968–9 employment was but 318,695 and output 164 million metric tons (161 million long tons) of which about 4 per cent came from opencast sites.

TABLE 2

COAL PRODUCTION IN BRITAIN. 1947–69

Date	*Producing Collieries*	*Deep Mined Total*		*Output per Man*		*Mechanized Output*
	Number	*Long tons*	*Metric tons*	*Long tons*	*Metric tons*	*Per cent*
1947	958	184	187	262	266	2·4
1957	822	207	210	295	300	23·0
1967	438	165	168	390	396	85·7
1969	317	153	155	454	461	91·8

Table 2 summarizes the basic statistics and indicates the continuation of closures of uneconomic mines together with a decrease in total production. Set against this there has been a substantial increase in output per man linked to a complete transformation of method based on mechanization. The resultant, however, is a decline in employment. In the year 1968–9 the total reduction in man power was 46,146, a decrease of 12·6 per cent, the highest percentage rate of rundown since nationalization. This severe contraction epitomises the problems of the coalfield where redundancies from mining are aggravated by the lack of alternative employment.

As manufacturing has become loosened from its close ties with the coalfields so it has gravitated towards the markets, and the great market in Britain has always been in the south-east around the capital. Closely allied to the attraction of the market has been a draw towards those areas where transport is most quick and effective. Again policies of closure of provincial railways and a concentration on inter-city routes, together with the whole concept of motor-way building to provide a system radiating from London, have meant

Plate 18 Brentford (Greater London)
An assemblage of elements of the later twentieth century industrial development of Britain. Here along the Great West Road in the outer suburbs of London, light industry, such as food and drink in the near foreground, is located with good access to roads and markets.

that maximum attraction has been exerted to the South East and the so-called axial belt of industry and population which extends from London, through the Midlands, to Manchester. Into this axial belt much of the industry generated in the inter-war years was attracted. A further set of factors has accentuated this process for as industries become more complex so they become based on the assembly of raw materials or components. Good communications are further emphasized while the advantages of external economies now militate against the older marginal areas. The result of all these influences is the accentuation of the apparent movement of manufacturing away from the older provincial centres and its concentration in southern England and those areas in most immediate access.

The word 'movement' is qualified by the adjective 'apparent' in the sentence above since it is misleading to give the impression of physical shift. There has been a decline in employment in the older, heavy industries while new investment has concentrated in south-east England. This is related to fundamental changes in the technological bases of industry as well as the type of industry.

Fig 22 The Distribution of the Iron, Steel and Tinplate Industry in the Swansea Region, 1940–70 (After G. Humphreys.)

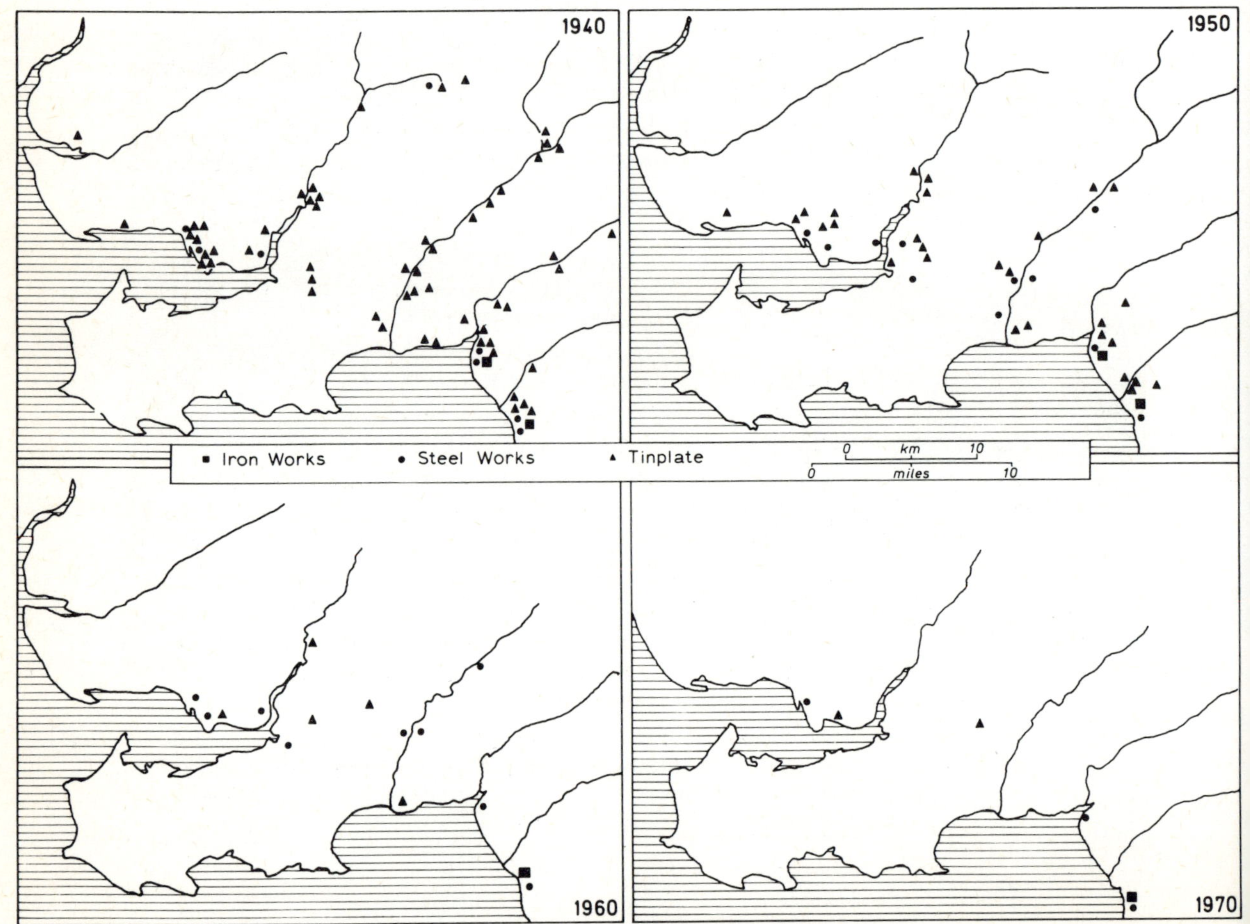

Figure 22 shows the distribution of tin plate works in South Wales in 1933 and the modern strip mills of 1970. The older, scattered plants have been replaced by massive strip mills at coastal locations, whilst heavy investment in automated equipment has meant progressively smaller labour demands. The change from a labour intensive characteristic to a capital intensive one has produced a marked effect on employment. A further example in the cotton manufacturing areas of Lancashire will indicate the forces at work. By the late 1950s the industry was near extinction and indeed by 1958–9 cheap imports of cotton cloth from Asiatic sources exceeded the yardage of exports. The result was government intervention and an attempt to rationalize the industry through the Cotton Industry Act which was designed partly to reduce the industry in size by scrapping surplus machinery and closing redundant mills in return for compensatory payments, partly to provide subsidies for re-equipment so that the process of modernization could be hastened. The result was that, as Rodgers comments, the industry made such indecorous haste to liquidate itself that 49 per cent of the spindles and 40 per cent of the looms were abandoned. The result of this process has been the relative decline of coal and cotton so that they no longer dominate the North West, indeed engineering is now equal to textiles as an employer of labour and much more important as an employer of male labour.

It is apparent from the above that part of the problem facing British industry is the loss of the lead that it once had in many spheres and exhaustion of the natural resources upon which it relied in the early phases of industrial development. It has to survive by the skills of management, the quality of labour, and by innovation and development in the more highly skilled branches of manufacturing. Here again all the advantages lie in the metropolitan area which has developed about London and the regional imbalance in industry is widened. (See Chapter 7.)

This imbalance has been the major factor in government attempts to control the distribution of industry and to prevent excessive regional concentration. Control has been exercised by means of a number of devices:—

(a) Industrial Development Certificates (I.D.C.'s). These were introduced in 1948 and are issued by the Board of Trade. They are required to support all planning applications for industrial buildings over a certain size. The main consequence is that the refusal of an I.D.C. for the building of a factory in the London area can make the company look elsewhere, that is, it acts negatively for areas which are deemed not to be in need.

(b) Direct Assistance to Industry in Development Areas. This is provided by Regional Development Grants for new factory buildings or the adaptation of existing buildings.

(c) Regional Employment Premiums (now being phased out) were payable per employee in the Development Areas and the total benefit per head to the employer was estimated at £1.75.

The Development Areas referred to in the context of assistance to industry and employment premiums were established in 1966 (Fig. 23) in place of a

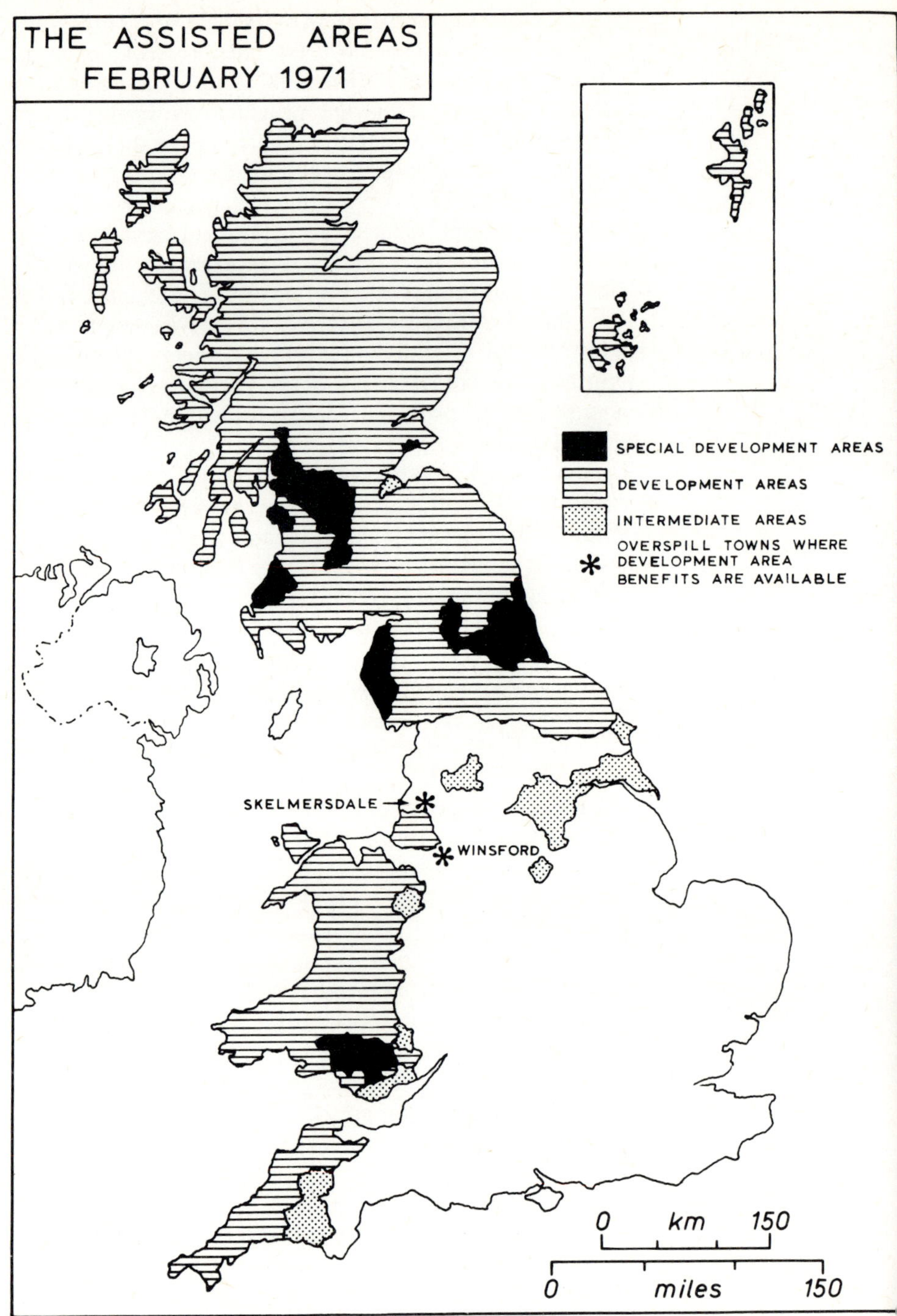

Fig 23 The Assisted Areas in Britain, 1971
(From *Trade and Industry*, February 24th 1971.)

TABLE 3

PRINCIPAL MOVEMENT FLOWS, BY PERIOD WHEN MOVE TOOK PLACE

employment in thousands at end–1966

ORIGIN	DESTINATION				
	Peripheral Areas	*South East and East Anglia*	*West Midlands Region*	*Rest of England*	*United Kingdom*
(*a*) Moves taking place in 1945–51 lower limit for inclusion: emp. of 8,000)					
North West ex Merseyside	18				22
Yorkshire and Humberside	24			11	36
East Midlands	14			9	23
West Midlands Conurbation	17		13		36
rest of West Midlands	18				22
Greater London	65	53			124
rest of South East Region	19			8	34
East Anglia					8
Abroad	41				45
All origins (inc. others not detailed above)	237	67	16	53	373
(*b*) Moves taking place in 1952–59 (lower limit for inclusion: emp. of 6,000)					
North West ex Merseyside	6				13
South West ex Devon and Cornwall	9				12
Yorkshire and Humberside				7	11
East Midlands				6	10
West Midlands Conurbation	7		8		17
rest of West Midlands					11
Greater London	15	92		7	115
rest of South East Region	6	11		9	27
Abroad	18	12		10	41
All Origins (inc. others not detailed above)	79	123	16	56	274
(*c*) Moves taking place in 1960–65 (lower limit for inclusion: emp. of 4,000)					
North West ex Merseyside	5				8
Yorkshire and Humberside	5				8
East Midlands					6
West Midlands Conurbation	15		4		24
rest of West Midlands	8				13
Greater London	35	49		5	89
rest of South East Region	26	7		4	37
Abroad	17	4			23
All Origins (inc. others not detailed above)	122	65	6	30	223

series of more scattered development districts. But the simple encouragement of industry to move to these areas has not been a consistent policy, at least not in its consequences, since the end of the Second World War. A Board of Trade Survey of 'The Movement of Manufacturing Industry in the United Kingdom, 1945–1965' established three phases:

1. The Immediate Post War Period. During this time movement to the Development Areas dominated.
2. The Decade of the Fifties. The immediate needs of the Development Areas had apparently been met and this was the period when the first generation of new towns was being established in London. This meant that the South-East Region was not at such a disadvantage in the attraction of industry.
3. After 1960. The threat of unemployment in Development Areas appeared again and there have been renewed attempts to attract industry away from investment in the prosperous parts of the country.

These three periods can be clearly identified in the data for movement of establishments (including the opening of new branches) between 1945 and 1965.

From Table 3 the dominance of the peripheral areas (mainly though not identical with the Development Areas in 1968) in the first period is clear, whereas this is changed to the South East and East Anglia in the second. In the third more recent period there has been a reversal to the former situation. As a result of this some 30 per cent of all employment in manufacturing in Wales is attributed to moves into the country during the 21 year period 1945–1966, about 20 per cent in Northern Ireland and 12 per cent in Scotland.

In spite of these efforts, however, the underlying trends have continued to operate as indicated in Table 4.

TABLE 4
(after D. M. Smith)

Region	*Regional Share of Increase in Insured Employees 1951–61 per cent*	
London	18·3	
South Eastern	9·0	
Eastern	15·1	
Southern	13·1	
South East England		55·5
South Western	6·9	
Midland	12·7	
North Midland	9·0	
Midlands and South West		28·6
Wales	3·3	
East and West Riding	3·6	
North Western	2·6	
Northern	3·6	
Scotland	2·8	
Wales and the North		15·9
	100	100

Table 4 reveals 'a fundamental geographical distinction between south-eastern England on the one hand and Wales, Scotland and northern England on the other, with the Midlands and South West occupying an intermediate position'.

An attempt has been made by D. M. Smith to identify those industries which can be classed as growth industries or expanding industries and those which are declining. If his identification of these manufacturing industries is accepted then ranked by total increase or decrease in actual employment they are:—

Increase (Growth Industries)	*Decrease (Declining Industries)*
Electrical Goods	Cotton, Linen, Man Made Fibres
Mechanical Engineering	Coal mining
Motors, Cycles and Aircraft	Garments
Paper and Board	Railway Engineering
Precision Instruments	Ship building and Marine Engineering

Again the characteristic relationship of declining industries with the north and west is apparent while the growth industries are essentially those linked with the Midlands and the South East.

Three industries might be taken to illustrate the present trends in industrial location. The iron and steel industry still shows the traditional nineteenth century links with the coalfields. The distribution of blast furnaces is closely associated with steelworks in integrated complexes. These are found in six major groups—in the Middlesbrough area, the southern part of the York, Nottingham and Derby coalfield, South Wales, Clydeside, in the East Midlands at Corby and at Scunthorpe. Three controls operate, the coalfields, the Jurassic ore resources and tidal water to provide easy assembly. The latter tends to become more dominant for even the large Spencer Works at Newport is not on a coalfield site but one where the assemblage of raw materials is most convenient. The general trend is towards larger, massive integrated plants. As this occurs so the more immediate controls of raw materials become less sensitive. This has been confirmed by the Ten Year Development Strategy of the British Steel Corporation published in 1973 which, noting the use of rich foreign ores transported in large bulk carriers, of large modern blast furnaces and of large-scale steel plant employing the basic oxygen (BOS) process, all of which offer major savings, proposes five major steelworks: Port Talbot, Llanwern (near Newport, Mon.), Scunthorpe, Lackenby (on Teesside) and Ravenscraig (near Motherwell). Special steels will still be concentrated at Sheffield–Rotherham and steel making will continue at Corby. Working against these economic trends is regional policy, as indicated above, as well as strong industrial tradition. Steel making at Ebbw Vale in South Wales is perhaps the best example where social reasons have been foremost in retaining an inland site with few locational advantages in contemporary economic terms.

The motor vehicle industry in Britain can be taken as a second industry and

Plate 19 Halewood (Liverpool)

The Ford plant on Merseyside which was part of the 1960–63 expansion. This characterizes the attempt to extend growth industries into areas of high unemployment, but to locations where accessibility is retained with the necessity of assembly. Engines and transmissions were shipped from Dagenham.

one which is also classed as a growth industry. The traditional location of the beginnings of the industry was Coventry where it developed from cycle manufacture. Associated with this was the widely varied industries which were adapted to component manufacture. 'The West Midlands, especially Coventry and Birmingham, took the lead partly because of historical accident, mainly because of the diversified nature of the areas' industrial life. In the local brass, screw-nut and bolt, paint, pressed steel, tube, iron-foundry, leather, spring and plating trades, there were a multitude of independent producers who could adapt themselves to the manufacture of motor parts.' Since the assembly of a wide variety of parts was so characteristic, the industry developed in the 'axial belt' in the inter-war years and particularly in that part between Birmingham and London where by 1935 over 85 per cent of the productive facilities were located. The post war period saw very rapid expansion of these facilities, at first largely in the original areas of concentration, but after 1960 government policy began to play a major role. The result was that the companies chose sites in three areas. Ford, Vauxhall, British Leyland built at Merseyside (Halewood, Ellesmere, Kirkby and Speke) whilst British Leyland, Chrysler, U.K. and Pressed Steel developed in Central Scotland (Bathgate and Linwood). Further British Leyland agreed to extend their existing facilities in South Wales (Llanelli and Cardiff). 'Viewed in terms of the established pattern of company organization almost all these locations appeared to be in defiance of the normal linkages of these companies.' The total pattern of the industry now demonstrates a characteristic link with materials and markets which aligns strongly along the London–S. Lancashire axis but with a series of outliers which must be interpreted as primarily the consequence of government policy pressures.

A third industry which can be briefly noted is that of precision instruments. If the increase in the employment in this industry during the decade 1951–61 is examined then 38,000 out of the 50,000 or so jobs created were in the Eastern, London and South-Eastern regions. This is an industry which is clearly dominated by resources of skilled labour and by the location of the markets it serves and here the dominance of the south and east is complete.

In this context it is worth considering a new type of industrial complex which has already emerged in the U.S.A. This is the scientific complex which contains three elements—science-based industry with related research and development laboratories; government research centres; universities and polytechnics with postgraduate and business training facilities. John Hall has attempted to identify these emergent complexes and there is a concentration around London and Hertfordshire, Buckinghamshire, Berkshire, Surrey and Hampshire. All these counties offer rapid access to London ministries, libraries and institutions. This growth area in the economy can hardly be called 'manufacturing', but manufacturing employs a progressively smaller number of the total work force and the emphasis is moving to the tertiary sector (trades, services and professions) and to what is called the quaternary sector (research, education and communication based activities). As this emphasis develops so the industries it generates will increase in importance and the sorts of developments in precision instruments noted in this paragraph characterize locational trends which are associated.

In reviewing the most recent changes in manufacturing location it is apparent that two major points emerge for comment. The first of these is the apparent advantages of the south-east of England as seen in terms of comparative costs. The implication is made that although distances in Britain are very small by continental standards nevertheless these make perceptible differences in terms of profitability to industry. When congestion costs are taken into account this argument is not immediately convincing but there are very few studies and little evidence upon which a firm conclusion can be based. It may be that habit and prejudice favour the south and east more than the hard facts of finance. The second major point, however, is one which may well increase differentially the advantages of the South East and exacerbate regional contrasts in Britain. This is the British membership of the European Economic Community (Common Market) together with the construction of a channel tunnel. Under these conditions the stress on location near the channel coast might well be emphasized and the location of manufacturing in Britain become orientated still further away from the older areas of the north and west. This chapter has demonstrated, perhaps, an incidental phase in British development which occurred between 1750 and 1920 where owing to the location of industrial raw materials the balance of advantage was temporarily switched from lowland, southern England. Although industry created during that phase will remain characteristic of the coalfields there are no signs that anything but a continuous trend away can be foreseen in the future.

FURTHER READING

R. C. Estall and R. O. Buchanan, *Industrial Activity and Economic Geography* (London, 1966).

J. Hunt, *The Intermediate Areas* (H.M.S.O., 1969).

R. S. Howard, *The Movement of Manufacturing Industry in the United Kingdom* (H.M.S.O., 1968).

H. Rees, *The Industries of Britain: a Geography of Manufacturing and Power, together with Farming, Forestry and Fishing* (London, 1970).

D. M. Smith, *Industrial Location: an Economic Geographical Analysis* (New York, 1971).

W. Smith, *An Historical Introduction to the Economic Geography of Great Britain* (London, 1969).

Population and Urban Growth

Two notable features characterized the population of the British Isles at the beginning of the nineteenth century. Probably most striking to modern eyes was the small total population compared with that found today. In 1801 there were just over 10 million people in Great Britain; and although no census had been taken in Ireland at that date it has been quite reliably estimated that the total Irish population was about 5 million. This total of 15 million in the British Isles provides a startling contrast with the 56·7 million counted in 1966. The present situation also shows a remarkable difference in relative importance, since, instead of providing a home for a third of the population of the British Isles, all of Ireland now contains 4·4 million people, less than 8 per cent of the total.

The second outstanding feature of the population at the beginning of the nineteenth century was its rapid rate of increase. There has been much debate about the demographic factors lying behind population growth at this time, possibly because of the different situations found in various regions. A general view, however, is that in Great Britain a reduction in the death rate was the principal cause of the growing population, which increased by 40 per cent between 1750 and 1801. But there is still discussion about whether the medical changes introduced by the beginning of the nineteenth century were capable of producing any significant reduction in mortality or whether some other factors were responsible for the change. In Ireland, where population increased from about 4 million in 1780 to 8·2 million at the census of 1841, it is thought that a high birth rate, associated with an early average age of marriage, was the single most important cause of population growth, but again there is debate about the details. There is evidence, for example, of some reduction in the death rate in the first decades of the nineteenth century, and there were also forces at work at this time which probably were reducing the birth rate in some parts of the country as well. In fact, during this period before the official registration of vital statistics, the precise balance between birth and death rates is unclear in many parts of the British Isles. Yet, for whatever combination of reasons, everywhere the birth rate substantially exceeded the death rate.

Population Growth After 1800

In Great Britain the resulting high rate of natural increase continued throughout the nineteenth century, producing a rapid growth in population (Table 5 and Fig. 24). Between 1801 and 1831 the total population of Britain increased by nearly 55 per cent. From 1831 to 1861 the increase was just over 42 per cent; and from 1861 to 1891 population rose by nearly 43 per cent. The first hint of a new situation appeared during the next thirty-year period, as smaller families became more common, first among the more prosperous and better-educated in the community and then progressively among other sections of British society. As a result the population of Britain increased by the reduced rate of 24·5 per cent from 1891 to 1921. These demographic changes were confirmed during the next thirty-year period, from 1921 to 1951, when the rate

TABLE 5
POPULATION CHANGE IN THE BRITISH ISLES, 1801–1966
Per Cent Change

	1801–1831	*1831–1861*	*1861–1891*	*1861–1921*	*1921–1951*	*1951–1966†*
England	+56	+45	+45	+29	+17	+8
Wales	+54	+42	+38	+50	—2	+2
Scotland	+47	+30	+31	+21	+4	+1
Ireland	+55*	—25	—19	—7	—1	+1

* estimate † 15 year period

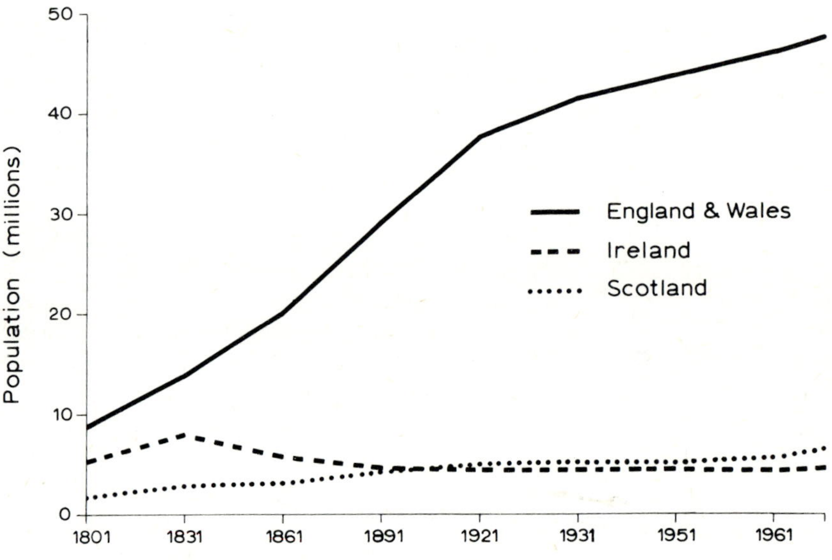

Fig 24 Population Growth, 1801–1966
The total population of the British Isles grew rapidly during the nineteenth century; but there were internal contrasts in the rate of growth, which changed the relative importance of different parts of the country when conditions at the beginning and end of the nineteenth century are compared. The rate of growth slowed considerably in the twentieth century, particularly after 1921, but the rate of expansion in England and Wales still remained higher than in the rest of the British Isles.

of increase in Great Britain fell still lower to 14 per cent. Since then another 7 per cent has been added to the population of Britain between 1951 and 1966. The sharp reduction in the birth rate in the twentieth century has not brought as great a check to population growth as perhaps might be expected, since the death rate has also continued to fall. Figures of total population in fact hide some of the natural increase which took place, since they do not include those people who emigrated. It is estimated that since 1800 some 3 million people who were born in Great Britain left the country permanently. Nevertheless the population that remained showed an increase of over 500 per cent since 1801.

Ireland presents a sharply contrasting pattern of development, reflecting the different social and economic contexts of the two countries. Irish population at the beginning of the nineteenth century was increasing at a rate similar to that in Britain, but nearly all the extra numbers were concentrated in rural rather than in urban areas. Then in 1845 the potato crop, the staple food of many rural dwellers, failed throughout the country and this disaster was repeated at the next two harvests. After such a traumatic experience the total population of Ireland declined for the rest of the nineteenth century. The fall in numbers was checked in the twentieth century, although the total population continued to fall until 1961.

Running parallel with this declining population in Ireland was a falling rate of natural increase, which also dated from the middle of the nineteenth century. This reduction was produced by a decline in the crude birth rate, which began earlier than in Britain and was caused by different factors, since the fertility of married women of child-bearing age was not reduced. Partly the reduced birth rate in Ireland was the result of the selective removal of the young and active in the population by emigration; but it was also influenced by increased celibacy and by a later age of marriage among those who remained. In all Irish counties, however, the birth rate remained higher than the death rate, although the margin between the two rates steadily narrowed. The basic cause of population decline was emigration, usually to urban areas in Britain and North America. The ability of emigration to produce a smaller population, however, was steadily increased by the falling crude birth rate. In the twentieth century a reduced rate of emigration has just about cancelled out natural increase, giving much more stable population totals.

Changes in Population Distribution

The population of the British Isles has not only increased dramatically in numbers since the beginning of the nineteenth century, but in addition its distribution and density have also been radically altered (Figs. 25 and 26). Two processes lay behind these changes. One was rural depopulation, the result of emigration from the countryside. The other was urbanization, caused by the great expansion in the number of jobs of various kinds that found their best location in towns and cities. Both processes in fact represented two sides of the same coin, as they were associated with the economic changes during the nineteenth century that stimulated considerable variations in the number of jobs and level of wages in different parts of the British Isles.

RURAL DEPOPULATION Local and regional contrasts in jobs and wages encouraged a large amount of population movement, in particular the migration of people from rural to urban areas. This movement went on for some time before it produced an actual decrease in rural population. In fact rural depopulation only became apparent in different parts of the British Isles between the censuses of 1821 and 1861. Although smaller areas showed depopulation earlier, Wiltshire was the first English county to exhibit a decline in its total population, a feature which became apparent between the censuses of 1841 and 1851. During this same

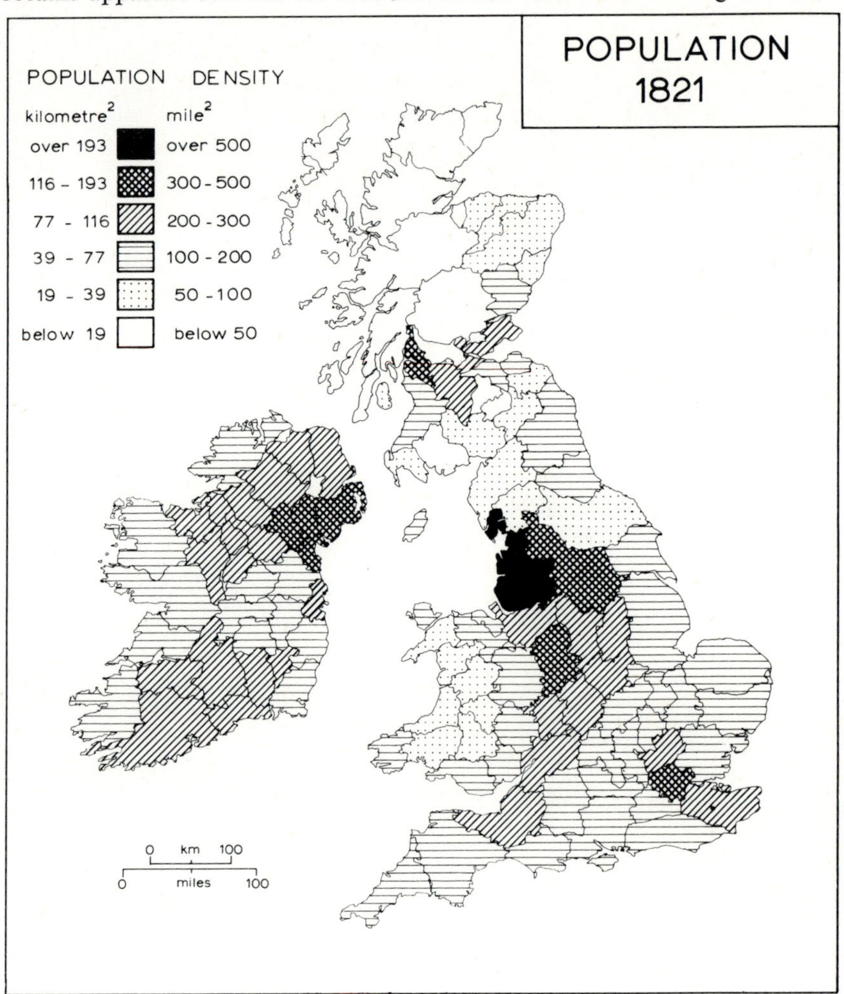

Fig 25 Population Density, 1821

High densities of rural population in Ireland were a notable feature in 1821. Concentrations in the growing industrial regions like Lancashire and the West Midlands were already noticeable. London was an important centre of population, but the south-east did not dominate the map of the British Isles. (After H. C. Darby.)

decade three counties in Wales and every county in Ireland recorded a decrease. In Scotland the decrease of population in some parts of the country was visible even earlier: eight counties had a declining population between 1831 and 1841. In detail, of course, the picture was much more complicated, but it can be said that most purely rural parishes throughout the British Isles attained their peak population sometime between 1821 and 1851 and thereafter showed a decline.

Although the timing of the rural-urban movement may have been different in the various regions of the British Isles and the motivations of the different

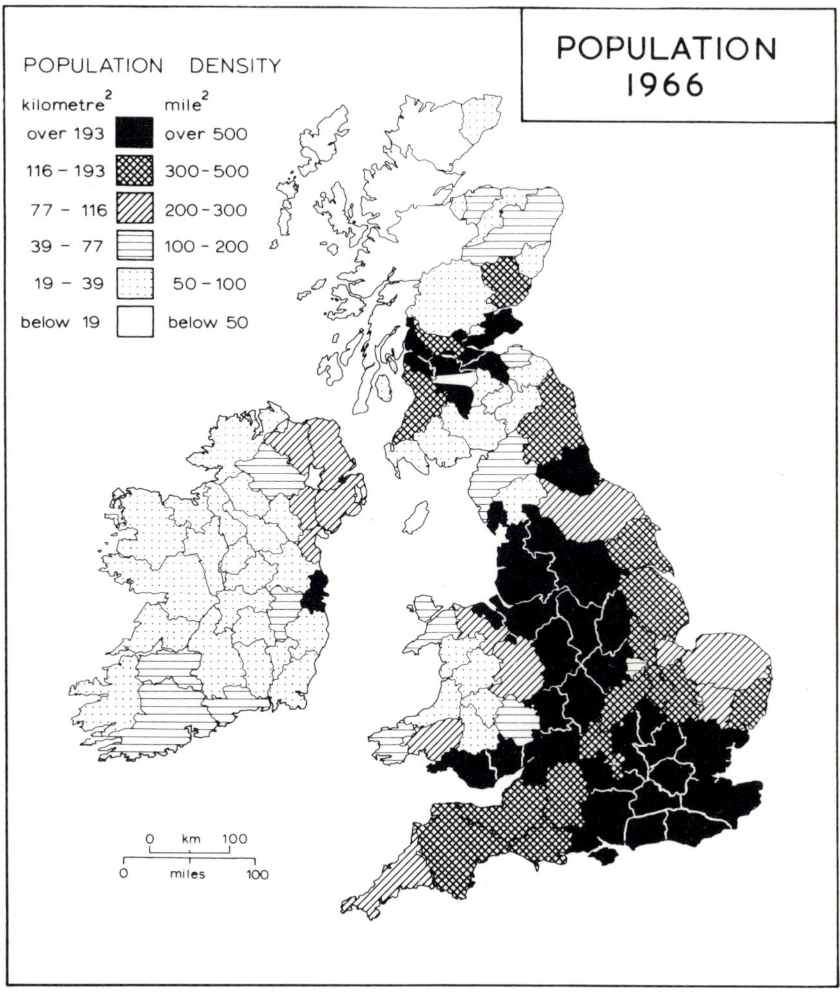

Fig 26 Population Density, 1966

The modern density map shows a dramatic contrast with the situation in the early nineteenth century. The reduction in population densities in Ireland, apart from urban concentrations around Dublin and Belfast, is a notable feature. Concentrations in the Midland Valley of Scotland, South Wales and the north-east of England, formerly early in the nineteenth century, still remain; but population concentrations in the south-east of England and the west Midlands are now of the greatest importance. A comparison of Figures 25 and 26 provides a most impressive summary of the changing human geography of the British Isles over the past century and a half.

social groups involved may have varied in detail, certain general features are clear. The growth of urban manufacturing and service industries was producing a new distribution of employment opportunities, which attracted population from rural areas (see Chapter 4). This 'pull' was further emphasized by the fact that many growing cities were areas of natural decrease until well into the second half of the nineteenth century, largely because the urban environment of the growing industrial cities was a good breeding ground for infectious diseases until medical advances and the development of sanitary engineering were able to redress the balance. Until the last quarter of the nineteenth century even the maintenance of the population of many cities demanded some rural-urban movement to compensate for death rates that were higher than birth rates. Social factors also played a part, since in the long run urban areas offered better facilities for education and recreation to an increasing number of people, and this formed an intangible, but real, attraction for many rural people.

Plate 20 Devil's Reef Tub (Dumfries)

In marginal lands like this, with the hill-grazing of sheep and the cultivation of restricted areas of better land, farmers have required increasingly large holdings in order to provide an acceptable standard of living. As a result rural depopulation has been particularly severe. In spite of government subsidies to hill farmers, rural depopulation still continues, although in some upland areas afforestation is increasing the number of people which these agriculturally marginal lands can support.

At the same time the countryside itself was providing a 'push' to outward movement. Fundamental were the great changes taking place in agriculture, often linked with the conversion of a largely subsistence farming system to one aimed almost entirely at production for sale (see Chapter 3). This process had been taking place in Britain in one form or another from early in the seventeenth century, but it was after the middle of the eighteenth century and particularly in the nineteenth century that its effects were most profound. Improved crops and animals were introduced, new implements were devised and, eventually, mechanical power was applied to driving them. As a result the output of the individual agricultural worker was increased. Greater productivity and the need for a farmer who was engaged in competitive commercial production to count the cost of his labourers led to a great reduction in the number of workers employed in agriculture.

Once established, the rural exodus proved to be a long-continuing movement, since it progressively affected layer after layer of rural society. First agricultural labourers were most affected; and although the demand for labour at harvest-time was not reduced until near the end of the nineteenth century, it was possible to reduce the permanent rural labour force because of the rise in importance of migratory agricultural workers, often drawn from Ireland and the Scottish Highlands. Rural craftsmen also joined the flow of population to the towns, as factory-produced goods—perhaps aesthetically less attractive, but certainly cheaper and more competitive—steadily penetrated rural markets. Then small farmers were attracted to urban life, as they found that their holdings were unable to support the standard of living which their rising expectations demanded. More and more farmers felt this influence, as rural expectations rose to match the growing standard of living actually being achieved by urban workers.

Those rural people who left their homes for jobs in the town were often young adults, with the result that the fertility of the population was reduced, thus making the outward movement from the countryside more effective in reducing numbers and in increasing the proportion of old people among those who remained. This process had more than a demographic effect. The presence of fewer young people impoverished social life and provided a further stimulus to outward migration. Similarly, the smaller total population in rural areas and, in particular, the reduction in the number of economically-active people made the improvement of public services much more difficult. The resulting lack of amenities encouraged further out-migration, particularly as increased literacy (and in the twentieth century, other means of communication) encouraged rural people to expect educational and other facilities at an urban standard. Indeed, continuing rural depopulation in some parts of the British Isles has made it a considerable problem even to maintain rural services at their existing standard.

These social factors have perhaps grown in relative importance in the twentieth century, since in the nineteenth century the economic conditions encouraging movement were more clear-cut and dominant. Even so, social factors must always have been important. In Ireland, for example, the movement from the countryside during the second half of the nineteenth century, triggered off by the Great Famine of the mid-1840s, can only be partially explained on economic grounds. The suffering during the Great Famine produced deep and long-standing dissatisfaction with peasant life among many rural people, thus establishing emigration to urban areas in Britain and North America as a normal feature of Irish social life, as well as the usual strategy for solving personal economic difficulties. In passing, it is important to note that the declining Irish population of the nineteenth century was a special case of the rural depopulation common throughout Great Britain during the same period. It was a special phenomenon in Ireland because rural depopulation dominated population totals for the whole country, because it was such a widespread feature, and because it influenced nearly every aspect of Irish rural life.

URBANIZATION

Running parallel with the movement from the countryside was the growth of population in urban areas. Given a rapidly rising total population, urban areas would have been likely to grow in any case; but the absolute increase in urban population was even more remarkable than the rise in total population, since, in addition, 'urbanization' also increased steadily. The amount of urbanization in a country is usually measured by the percentage of the total population which lives in urban areas. Assessed in this way, urbanization began to increase in Great Britain about the middle of the eighteenth century, and the process was complete by the beginning of the First World War, making Great Britain the most heavily urbanized country in the world. Since this time certain cities have grown more than others, but the proportion of the population recorded by the census as living in urban areas has not risen substantially, although the absolute number of people living in towns and cities has continued to expand.

It is difficult to convert these general comments into precise statements of urban population change, since there are considerable practical problems for census takers in distinguishing rural from urban population and in presenting statistics that can be compared over a long period of time. For England and Wales, however, the census statistics have been corrected to give the best possible comparison of the size of the urban population at various dates during the nineteenth century (Fig. 27). In 1801 nearly 34 per cent of the total population of England and Wales lived in urban areas and this figure had risen to nearly 79 per cent by 1911. In fact the actual total urban population was a mere 3 million in 1801, compared with the 28 million people who lived in towns and cities by 1911.

The population of Ireland also exhibited the same phenomenon, but in a very different demographic context. Dublin was the second largest city in the British Empire at the end of the eighteenth century, but its growth had not contributed much to the urbanization of Ireland because it was matched by the parallel expansion of the rural population. During the nineteenth century rapid urban growth was concentrated in north-east Ireland, particularly in and around Belfast, while Dublin continued to expand more decorously. Taking Ireland as a whole, however, the number of people living in urban areas only rose from 1,215,000 in 1841 to 1,416,000 in 1901, not a great increase by British standards. But as the total population of the country was falling during this period, the degree of urbanization increased much more than might have been expected, from less than 15 per cent in 1841 to 31 per cent in 1901. In contrast with Great Britain, continued urban growth, coupled with a virtually

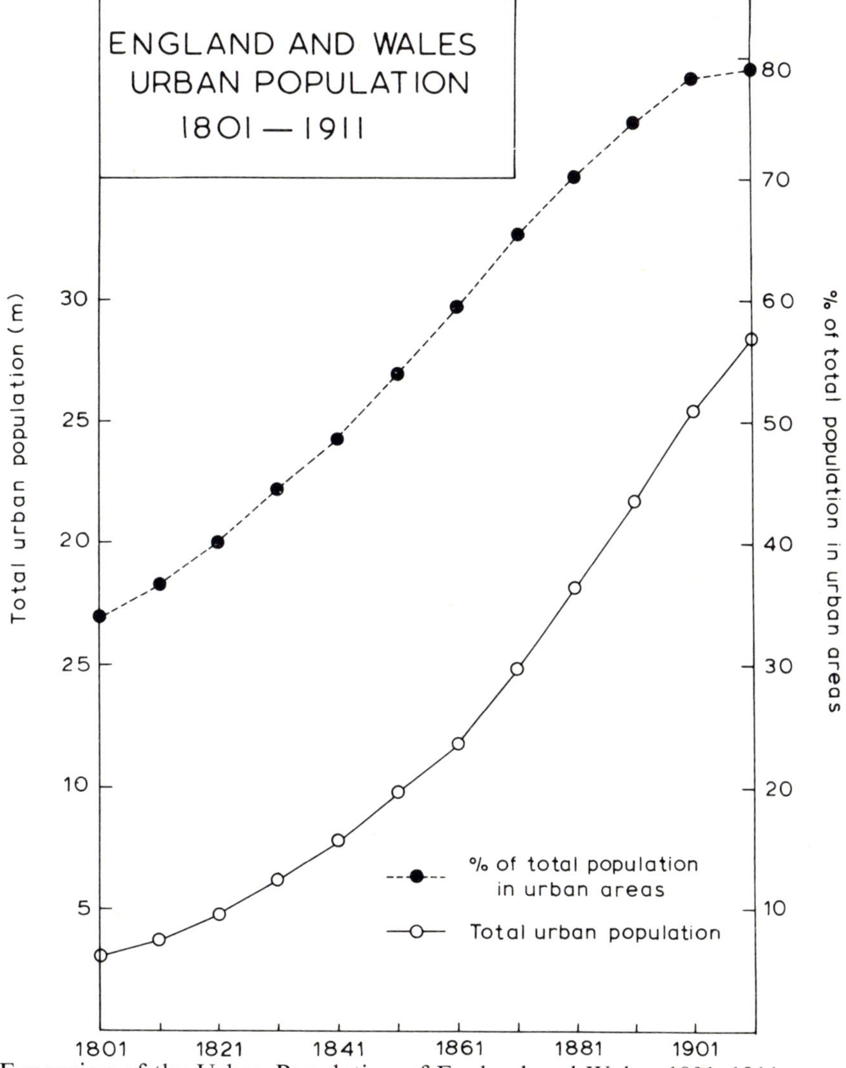

Fig 27 Expansion of the Urban Population of England and Wales, 1801–1911

Not only did the urban population of England and Wales increase very rapidly during the nineteenth century, but the proportion of the total population living in towns and cities also expanded greatly, making this the most highly urbanized country in the world. In the first decade of the twentieth century the rate of urbanization decreased quite suddenly, but this probably shows a deficiency in the statistics rather than any real check to urban growth. By the end of the nineteenth century cities were often spreading out over their legal boundaries, leading to an underestimate of urban population and an overstatement of rural population. The statistics used in the construction of this graph are after C. M. Law.

Plate 21 Bye-Law Housing (Burnley)
The expanding population of the nineteenth century moved into rapidly growing urban areas. In the second half of the nineteenth century legislation attempted to bring order and minimum standards of accommodation to the urban environment: local authority bye-laws were progressively introduced, controlling such matters as street width and the provision of rear access to houses. It can hardly be said that the resulting urban landscape, which owed more to the ruler of the borough surveyor than to aesthetic or functional considerations, produced an attractive urban landscape.

stable total population, has produced a considerable rise in urbanization during the twentieth century, so that by 1951 nearly 48 per cent of the Irish population was classified as urban by the census.

During the nineteenth century the expansion of the urban population, associated with the process of urbanization, was concentrated in London and in those other regions where industry was expanding. Although the growth of urban employment was in tertiary occupations as well as in manufacturing, often these growth areas were on or near a coalfield, since coal had become the major source of industrial energy and could usually be harnessed most economically close to the area where it was mined. In addition coal had a further attraction for employment in that it was also an important raw material for some chemical industries and for the iron and steel industry. As a result, concentrations of dense urban population, directly or indirectly associated with manufacturing industry, developed in south Lancashire, in the West Riding of Yorkshire, in the west Midlands, in the north-east of England, in south Wales and in the Midland Valley of Scotland (see Chapter 4). The date of most rapid urbanization varied according to the fortunes of the dominant industries in the different regions. In Lancashire, for example, a substantial concentration of urban population was already present in the early decades of the nineteenth century, and urban growth in this area was faster in the first half of the century than in the second, although the absolute increase was in fact greater after 1850. In south Wales, on the other hand, the most rapid growth in urban population took place in the second half of the nineteenth century.

In Ireland there were no easily worked coal deposits, but manufacturing developed in north-east Ireland, particularly around the mouth of the Lagan Valley. Here the Industrial Revolution managed to establish a coastal toe-hold, in a location where coal and other raw materials could be easily imported. Here, too, most rapid urban growth was in the second half of the century, after the mechanization of the linen industry and the expansion in the market for steam-driven iron ships.

London is also an exceptional case. Both in 1861 and 1931 manufacturing formed as important a part of employment in Greater London as in the country as a whole, so the importance of London as a manufacturing region is no new feature and its relative importance has been maintained. London's industries were different in that they were more often small-scale, and were much less dependent on fuel. To this must be added the employment associated in one way or another with London's expanding role as the capital of a nation and an empire. As a result the population of the conurbation expanded from 2·2 million in 1841 to 6·5 million in 1901.

New Population Trends in the Twentieth Century

In the twentieth century there have been some alterations to this pattern of urban growth. Some of the major concentrations of industrial population underwent profound economic and demographic changes between the two World Wars. Many well-established industries (like iron and steel, shipbuilding and heavy engineering, coal-mining and cotton textiles) declined or stagnated, so that in some areas of nineteenth century urban growth population now declined and in others there was insufficient new employment to absorb natural increase.

THE DRIFT SOUTH

As a result the most noticeable movements of population during this period tended to be between existing urban areas, rather than from the countryside to the town: those cities with twentieth-century growth industries attracted population from the less fortunate urban areas. The resulting population movement has been characterized as a 'Drift South', although in fact various, more detailed, adjustments to population distribution were taking place within regions, as well as the general tendency for the south of England to gain population at the expense of the rest of the British Isles. Nevertheless it seems as though most of the flows of population from the north of England and from Scotland during the twentieth century tended to by-pass the Midlands on their way to destinations in and about London. The redistribution of population in the Midlands was more of a local process, although people were also attracted to this area from Ireland.

As in the past young adults were principally involved in population movements, rather than the population at large. Because of this age structure among the migrant population, natural increase was also important in redistributing population. Between 1921 and 1931, for example, natural increase was responsible for over 60 per cent of the total rise in the population of Greater London, and this fact should be set alongside the usual view that interwar population growth in south-east England was the direct result of movement into the area.

In the period after 1918, then, urbanization became relatively more important in the Midlands of England, where cities like Birmingham, Nottingham and Leicester possessed a diversity of industries, some little affected by the Depression, others actively expanding in the context of interwar industrial production. Similarly the attraction of south-east England widened. The continuous built-up area of London grew outwards at unprecedented speed. Detached from the conurbation itself, but within its ambit, the population of dormitory, manufacturing and market towns was also expanding rapidly during the interwar period; and this process has continued since 1945, although the outward spread of the continuous built-up area of London has been largely halted.

Measures taken before 1939 to relieve conditions in the economically depressed areas and, even more important, the impact of the Second World War tended to arrest the differential growth of London and its surroundings at the expense of the rest of the country. Since the war even more wholehearted attempts have been made by successive governments to encourage economic growth away from south-east England. But when population statistics are considered, the modest success of this policy is revealed. The statistics show that since 1951 the south-east has had a rate of growth twice the average for Great Britain as a whole.

REDISTRIBUTION WITHIN CITIES

At a more detailed level there was further redistribution of population in the twentieth century, affecting all the large cities of the British Isles. Many inner residential areas were becoming obsolete: around the fringes of city centres residential areas were frequently colonized by commercial land uses, and elsewhere a slow start was being made with their renewal. When renewal came it was often in the form of local authority flats. These changes produced lower densities of urban population in the inner residential areas, either because of the introduction of non-residential uses or because all the existing population could not be rehoused at modern standards of comfort in new dwellings.

Plate 22 Bloomsbury (London)
Around the centre of large British cities formerly residential areas have been colonized by other land uses, and this process has provided a stimulus to the redistribution of population within cities. Here in Bloomsbury, close to the centre of London, the process of replacement can be seen. In the left centre of the picture the University of London has occupied former residential squares. In the foreground shops, offices and small factories have also replaced residences, some of which still survive.

At the same time residential suburbs were expanding rapidly around the edges of cities, producing urban densities lower than had been previously experienced and contributing to the redistribution of population within cities. In part this suburban expansion reflected both changing fashions in housing and also the functional advantages of low density houses for family living. The expansion was also associated with the nature of the growing population of large cities. Not only was the urban population larger, but it also tended to be made up of smaller families, thus creating an even greater demand for new, smaller houses. More dwelling units were required to house even the same total population and older houses were less appropriate for the new family sizes that were becoming common.

This demand was converted into reality in the urban landscape of inter-war Britain by the activity of speculative builders (particularly in the more prosperous parts of the country). Running parallel was the work of local authorities, which between the World Wars began to provide subsidized 'cottage' estates, built at relatively low densities, for many of those who could not afford to buy new houses of their own. The relocation of population increased

Plate 23 Residential Suburbs (Weybridge)
A notable feature of the twentieth century has been the rapid expansion of residential suburbs. This picture illustrates an extreme example of the low densities at which urban dwellers can now live, with perhaps one house to the acre. This tendency towards suburban living has been imitated by much less prosperous, but more numerous, social groups than those housed here. Although more tightly controlled by planning legislation, residential growth has continued to take place around the periphery of the largest cities, as the suburban home has become the ultimate goal of an increasingly large number of people.

the importance of the daily journey to work in British urban areas; but not as greatly as might be expected, since employment in manufacturing industry was also expanding around the fringes of cities.

Since the Second World War the redistribution of urban population has continued, but in the context of changing planning attitudes. The urban sprawl of the 1930s encouraged the development of planning proposals designed to restrict the outward spread of urban areas. This policy was followed most actively around London by the institution of the well-known green belt (see Chapter 1), but in effect similar restrictions to free urban development applied around all the large cities of the United Kingdom, although not always enshrined in formal statements of policy. As a result higher densities were encouraged in new suburban housing estates, infilling took place in gaps between existing developments, and in those older suburbs where there were upper-middle-class houses residential densities were increased by the building of new individual houses in the large gardens of the existing properties.

Meanwhile, urban redevelopment in the inner residential areas has continued at an increased rate, particularly after about 1960, so that the surplus population has had to be rehoused elsewhere. As a result the outward spread of cities has continued, although at densities somewhat above those common on new housing estates between the Wars. Overspill population has also been decanted to new towns and to existing satellite towns around the major conurbations. In other words, redistribution of population has continued, although in a tidier form than that commonly found before 1939.

RURAL CHANGES

Rural as well as urban population changes have continued in the twentieth century, but they, too, show somewhat different emphases. In Britain, rural depopulation has been particularly noticeable in certain core areas, where depopulation has been a consistent feature, either because of the remoteness of these areas, or because their farming has not easily adapted to milk production or to intensive cropping. As a result extensive areas in the Southern Uplands and Highlands of Scotland, the Pennines, central Wales, Exmoor and parts of East Anglia have regularly shown population decline in twentieth century Britain. Although the relative amount of population decrease in many of these areas has been high, the absolute decrease has been small, since most of the surplus population from the days of subsistence farming had already been removed and lower birth rates have been producing a smaller natural increase to be absorbed elsewhere. The rural component in population change in Britain has been much less than in the previous century.

In Ireland, on the other hand, rural depopulation has continued to be important, both relatively and absolutely. In particular, the small farm belt, north of a line between Galway and Dundalk, has been notable for its declining population at census after census. In Northern Ireland, although it lies within the area of small farms, this decline has been less important than in similar areas on the other side of the Irish border, probably a result of higher agricultural subsidies of various kinds, of greater social security payments and of more intensive agriculture (producing higher incomes for small farmers). Elsewhere in rural Ireland depopulation has been a common feature, but it has been less consistent and at a lower average rate.

Not all rural areas in the British Isles have experienced population decline in the twentieth century. But the rural districts with an increase in population more often than not indicate the difficulty of distinguishing between 'rural' and 'urban' in the modern world, rather than provide evidence of any genuine rise in the agricultural population of these areas. Twentieth century rural population increase is the result of two forces. One is the increased diffusion of people who make their living in urban areas to homes in the countryside, unconnected with any clearly-defined urban settlement. In Britain this change has often taken place in spite of planning restrictions, as formerly agricultural villages become occupied by non-agricultural workers, who use motor cars to get to their urban places of work. As a result, rural districts around many of the large cities of the British Isles show population increase, a direct reflection of longer journeys to work and the greater penetration of rural areas made possible by the rising importance of privately-owned means of transport. Population has also increased in those rural districts which are particularly attractive for retirement. In Britain, many rural areas in the south and south-west of the country have acquired a rising 'adventitious' population of retired people, which masks the decline in the agricultural population of these regions.

Features of the Present Population Map

These, then, are the processes which lie behind the present distribution of population in the British Isles. It is clear that the population map is produced by a complex amalgam of past and present economies, and set in the context of underlying demographic conditions. Perhaps the most remarkable feature of the modern map is the great range of population densities which are recorded within this group of small islands (Fig. 28). Present trends appear to be increasing this contrast between areas of high and low density, rather than reducing it.

For example, if present trends are continued there are likely to be further expansions of the extensive areas of dense population focused on London and the Midlands. This zone of essentially urban population has been described in various ways: 'Dumb-bells', 'hour-glasses', 'backbones' and even 'coffins' have been seen in its outline, analogies which perhaps owe as much to the eye of the beholder as to the actual geographical distribution itself. It is almost inevitable that further concentration of people in this heartland of England will take place, if only because of the natural increase that can be expected in an area with a large existing population and with higher than average economic growth. It is not too fanciful to expect that the dense populations centred on the conurbations of Lancashire and Yorkshire will eventually be joined to the areas of urban population further south, although it is impossible to predict the future outline of this urbanized zone, since much will depend on future government planning decisions.

The concentrations of urban population in central Scotland, and around Dublin and Belfast in Ireland, will, of course, remain independent. Their further extension is perhaps a matter of more doubt, since this will depend on the health of the Scottish and Irish economies, which have always been more fragile than that of south-east England. Nevertheless current social policy in the United Kingdom attempts to take jobs to population and the areas of Scotland and Northern Ireland into which new employment can be most easily introduced are those which are already notable for their dense urban populations. Similarly in the Republic of Ireland, in spite of Irish government efforts to develop the west, most new jobs have been located in and around Dublin, where there are important economic advantages for industrial growth.

Intermediate population densities are found in the agricultural lowlands of the British Isles. By international comparison these densities are moderately high for areas of commercial agriculture—a feature which reflects the intensive nature of farming in the more accessible parts of Great Britain, but also indicates the presence of a large adventitious population, since only 5 per cent of the total occupied population of Great Britain is employed in agriculture. The effect of one element in the farming pattern is more clearly seen in Ireland, where the complication provided by urbanization is less important. In the

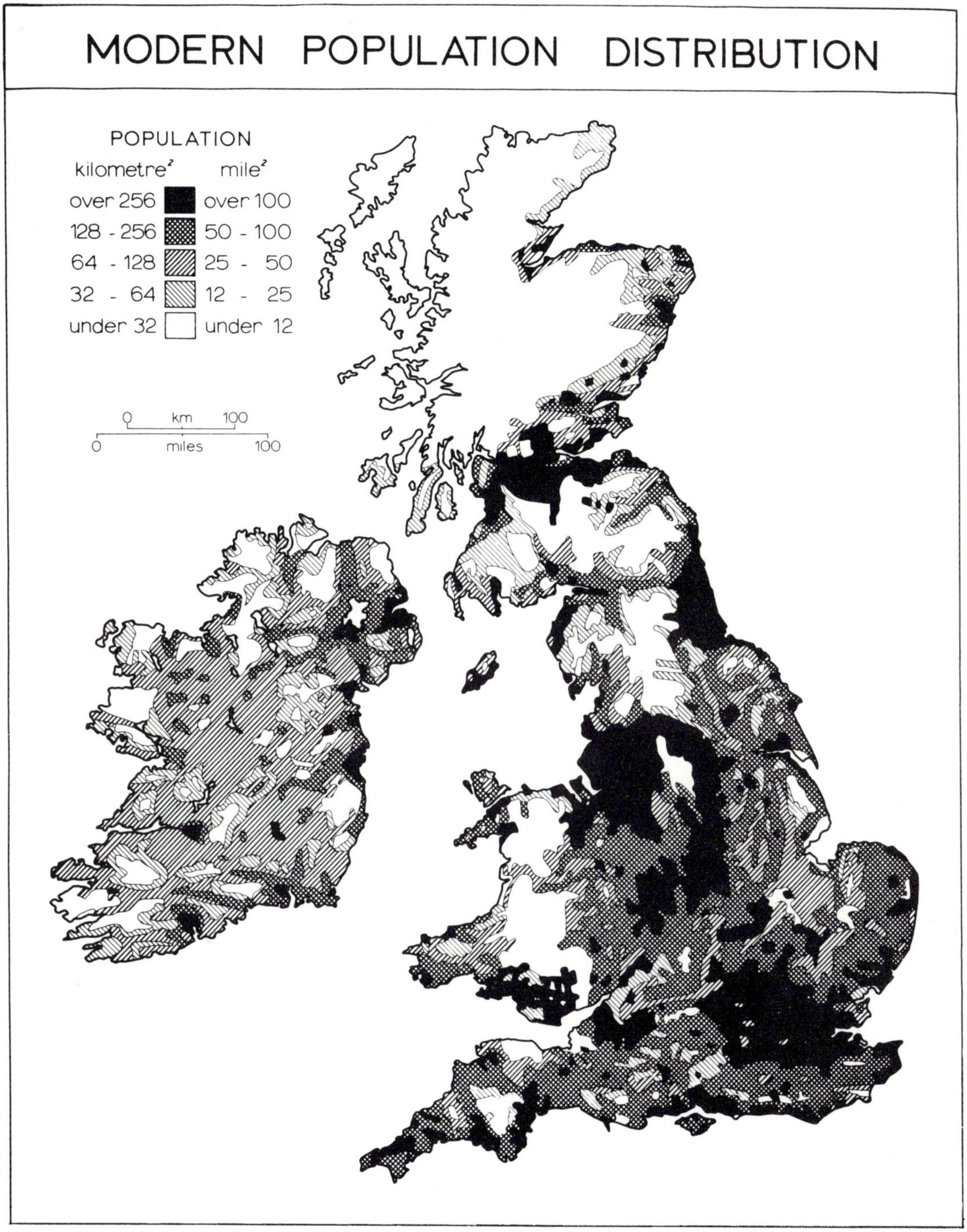

MODERN POPULATION DISTRIBUTION

POPULATION

kilometre²		mile²
over 256		over 100
128 - 256		50 - 100
64 - 128		25 - 50
32 - 64		12 - 25
under 32		under 12

0 km 100

0 miles 100

Fig 28 Modern Population Distribution

Population distributions can be studied at a number of different scales and this map only gives a general impression of contrasting densities in different parts of the British Isles. It is almost inevitable that the concentrations of people in south-eastern and midland England will be further extended, although the precise distribution of population will be shaped by planning decisions. At the same time most areas of low population density are becoming emptier of people.

small farm belt of the north and west, densities are higher than elsewhere. Densities are lowest in the cattle fattening area of Meath, where the average size of farm is the highest found in Ireland. It is notable that this contrast is being reduced, since it partly reflects the underemployment of agricultural labour in the area of smallest farms.

Finally there are the 'empty' areas which characterize the highland parts of the British Isles. These are most dramatically found in the Highlands of Scotland, but are also common in areas like central Wales, the Pennines and much of Connacht. In detail, of course, there are patches of denser population within these areas; and in some favoured spots tourism and retirement have reversed population trends. But generally these areas of low population density are becoming emptier as their traditional occupations become less viable in the modern world.

In detail the population map is actively changing, particularly in the areas where urban growth is spilling over from the conurbations or where small farms dominate the agricultural scene. Over a long period the population map can alter radically, as the evaluation of different areas changes. Nevertheless, it seems at the moment that the major population contrasts within the British Isles are quite stable. Overall urban densities may fall as the residential population in the inner parts of cities is reduced, but most population growth will take place in those regions which are already heavily urbanized. The rate of population decline will be highest in the areas of low density. In the prosperous agricultural areas, however, massive population decline can no longer be expected, provided that the present economic background to farming is maintained.

FURTHER READING

K. H. Connell, *The Population of Ireland, 1750–1845* (Oxford, 1950).

D. Friedlander and R. J. Roshier, A Study of Internal Migration in England and Wales, Part I, *Population Studies*, 19 (1965–66), 239–279; Part II, *Ibid.*, 10 (1966–67), 45–59.

J. H. Johnson, Population Changes in Ireland, 1951–61, *Geographical Journal*, 129 (1963), 167–174.

J. T. Krause, Changes in English Fertility and Mortality, 1781–1850, *Economic History Review* (second series), 11 (1958–59), 52–70.

C. M. Law, The Growth of Urban Population in England and Wales, 1801–1911, *Transactions Institute of British Geographers*, 41 (1967), 125–143.

T. McKeown and R. G. Brown, Medical Evidence Relation to English Population Changes in the Eighteenth Century, *Population Studies*, 9 (1955–56), 119–141.

R. H. Osborne, The Movements of People in Scotland, 1851–1951, *Scottish Studies*, 2 (1958), 1–46.

R. H. Osborne, Population, in J. Wreford Watson and J. B. Sissons (eds.), *The British Isles: a Systematic Geography* (Edinburgh, 1964), 331–357.

J. Saville, *Rural Depopulation in England and Wales, 1851–1951* (London, 1957).

E. C. Willatts and M. G. C. Newson, The Geographical Pattern of Population Changes in England and Wales, 1921–1951, *Geographical Journal*, 119 (1953), 431–454.

The Communication System

The purpose of the communication system of the British Isles as elsewhere is to provide the facilities that enable people, goods and messages to alter their location by moving across physical space. In an advanced industrial society like the United Kingdom there is today an almost incomprehensible volume and diversity of demand for movement, and it appears to be continuing to grow. Total passenger travel in Great Britain, for example, has risen from 180,000 million kilometres (112,000 million miles) in 1952 to 409,000 million kilometres (254,000 million miles) by 1970—an increase of 127 per cent! To satisfy this enormous but diverse demand for mobility a remarkably complex communication system has developed over time, inextricably bound up with the growth of settlement throughout the British Isles.

Although important and marked variations in the communication system exist within the British Isles (notably the low railway and the high road distances per head in Ireland compared to Great Britain) by comparison with most of the world it displays three outstanding characteristics, two of them fundamentally geographical. First is the sheer density of the various networks that exist as road patterns, railway lines, electricity grid lines, air traffic corridors, pipeline networks and so on. Secondly, this dense and on a world scale intensively used system of networks contains a multitude of connection points, usually in the form of purpose-built terminal facilities, both within each system, and between the different types of system. To maintain and operate these communication systems there exists today a bewildering collection of agencies which if not quasi-governmental themselves, in fact have their operations closely supervised and controlled by legislation. This third characteristic, of massive public intervention in the operation of the communication system, only underlines the significance modern society attaches to them, a significance which would equally well be measured in employment or investment terms.

The relatively small size of Britain and Ireland, their reasonably compact shape, the absence of great physical barriers and the location of the British Isles off the north-west coast of Europe, straddling the great circle routes to land-falls in North America between the St. Lawrence River and the Panama Canal, have all contributed opportunities to develop a dense and complex communications network. And while it is obvious that the long settlement history of the British Isles may have helped to create the great complexity of the present day system, it is nevertheless true that these major geographical features of the British Isles—size, shape and location—have exerted their

Plate 24 The Forth Bridges
The photograph taken in 1969 looking south from North Queensferry (Fife) shows how such estuaries as the Firth of Forth provide sheltered harbours but at the same time impede landward routes, thus requiring large investments to be made to overcome their barrier effects.

influence throughout the development of different transport technologies in a surprisingly consistent fashion.

Successive transport networks appear to pass through similar cycles and produce similar patterns. As the railways succeeded the canals, so the motorway network of the present shows a striking resemblance to the railway network before the great proliferation of the 1840s, and the latest government proposals show an expanding network of primary roads not dissimilar from the later railway network.

This is not so surprising when it is remembered that these same basic geographical conditions have had an immense if less direct influence on the settlement pattern too. Thus our island nature astride major world trade routes has for centuries given great significance to the sheltered estuaries with good landward connections. From the time that trade began to develop as a significant economic activity there has been a constant tension in the settlement pattern created by the need of seaward links to be near to the ocean, and the need of landward links to be secure and readily accessible to river or estuary crossing points. Thus the inland settlement at an early feasible water crossing was often subsequently forced to develop an outport downstream, as in the case of Tilbury for London or Port Glasgow for Glasgow as early as the seventeenth century. This tension presents itself today in the need to construct tunnels and bridges to overcome the barrier effects of river or estuary, while paradoxically the port functions continue to migrate to deeper water as a consequence of other changes in transport technology (Plate 24).

Because our coastline has almost always been our national frontier it is possible to trace the way in which each transport technology has helped to create coastal settlements whose growth has been closely related to the transhipment function. The new canal ports of the end of the eighteenth century such as Grangemouth were rapidly converted to railway operation and supplemented by many new rail ports in the nineteenth century, among them —Folkestone, Grimsby, Middlesbrough, Southampton, Ardrossan, and Fleetwood. The growth and development of London from the time of the Roman bridge and harbour to the recent choice of a site for its third international airport shows how consistently these background influences have worked in perpetuating its gateway function, despite dramatic technological change.

Just how significant the location of a connection on the communications system, whether a terminal or a junction, has been for the growth of settlement is revealed by the example of the Watford Gap. Here, midway between Coventry and Northampton a small valley carved by the headwaters of the River Nene, is occupied by the A5 trunk road on the line of the Roman Watling Street, the Grand Union Canal between Birmingham and London, the main line railway with the greatest volume of passenger traffic, a second railway line, and the M.1 motorway with its link to Coventry, the M.45. Despite this concentration of major inland transport facilities no settlement has emerged in the absence of a connection between them.

TABLE 6

Transport in Great Britain

A. Passenger: thousand million passenger – kilometres (miles)

	*Air**			*Rail*			*Road (private)*			*Road (public)*			*Total*	
			%			%			%			%		
1950	—	—	—	36·9	(23·9)	22	51·0	(31·7)	30	80·8	(50·2)	48	168·7	(105·8)
1955	0·3	(0·2)	—	38·3	(23·8)	19	87·2	(54·2)	42	80·2	(49·8)	39	205·9	(128·0)
1960	0·8	(0·5)	—	39·9	(24·8)	16	143·9	(89·4)	56	70·7	(43·9)	28	255·3	(158·6)
1965	1·6	(1·0)	0·5	35·1	(21·8)	11	233·3	(144·7)	70	63·1	(39·2)	19	333·1	(206·7)
1970	1·9	(1·2)	0·5	35·7	(22·2)	9	315·4	(196·2)	77	54·9	(34·1)	14	407·9	(253·7)

* includes Northern Ireland and Channel Islands

B. Freight: thousand million metric ton – kilometres (ton – miles)

	Coastal Shipping	%	*Inland Waterways*	%	*Pipelines*	%	*Rail*	%	*Road*	%	*Total*
1950	? ?	—	? ?	—	? ?	—	37·2 (23·1)	—	28·2 (17·5)	—	? ?
1955	14·5 (9·0)	20	0·3 (0·2)	—	0·2 (0·1)	—	34·0 (21·1)	40	34·0 (21·1)	40	83·0 (51·5)
1960	19·2 (11·9)	20	0·3 (0·2)	—	0·3 (0·2)	—	28·5 (18·7)	31	48·5 (30·1)	49	96·8 (61·1)
1965	24·6 (15·3)	21	0·2 (0·1)	—	1·3 (0·8)	1	24·6 (15·4)	21	67·8 (42·1)	57	118·5 (73·7)
1970	22·9 (14·2)	17	0·2 (0·1)	—	2·9 (1·8)	2	26·4 (16·4)	20	81·6 (59·8)	61	134·0 (83·3)

Inland Movement

CANALS

The first major improvement in the internal movement of freight began with the improvement of rivers for navigation and then the development of canals in the mid eighteenth century, and although the network expanded to include 6,400 kilometres (4,000 miles) by 1830, at the time of nationalization in 1948 the network was only slightly in excess of 3,200 kilometres (2,000 miles). In 1965 the British Waterways Board proposed that only four separate parts of the English system which had previously linked together the estuaries of the Thames, Humber, Severn and Mersey in an 'hour-glass' pattern, should be retained for commercial use. In the 130 years from their heyday, their original advantages in speed and bulk movement have been completely superseded first by rail, then by road, and since 1960 increasingly by pipeline transport. In 1970 only 0·1 per cent of inland freight, judged by weight, travelled by inland waterways. Their modern role is that of a potentially very important recreational facility and of a substantial water-grid for industrial use. It remains to be seen whether the West Midlands, Lancashire and Yorkshire which contain almost all of the canal networks still in existence, whether commercially used or not, can in fact breathe life into this transport mode.

RAILWAYS

Like canals the dominating characteristic of the railway network in recent years has been contraction—a reduction in network length, a decline in the freight and passengers carried, and a reduction in the labour force. By 1970 less than 19,500 kilometres (12,000 miles) remained of a network which in 1948 at the time of nationalization exceeded 31,000 kilometres (19,000 miles) and passenger services were operated over only 75 per cent of this network. Although some lines were closed before 1948, mainly as a result of company amalgamations or because the original coal-carrying function of the line was no longer possible due to the exhaustion of the coal seam, by far the greatest lengths of lines closed to traffic have occurred since nationalization, especially during the 1960s, as a consequence of competition from road and even air transport. In their report on the future of the railway system (the Beeching Report) the British Railways Board recommended, 'eliminating only those services which, by their very nature, railways are ill suited to provide'. This in fact amounted to approximately half the existing network. However, the 1968 Transport Act provides for annual subsidies from the exchequer for 'socially desirable but unremunerative passenger services'. While this has meant continued existence for many semi-fast stopping services which have served the rural areas between the main conurbations, the primary beneficiary has been the suburban commuting lines within the conurbations as the figures in Table 7 show.

TABLE 7
REGIONAL DISTRIBUTION OF GRANTS FOR UNREMUNERATIVE RAILWAY PASSENGER SERVICES — 1969

Economic Planning Region	*Services wholly within Region* £ million	*Total* * £ million
Scotland	9·6	10·2
Northern	3·6	6·3
North Western	10·6	22·6
Yorkshire and Humberside	3·2	6·1
West Midlands	3·5	8·3
East Midlands	0·8	2·7
East Anglia	1·3	2·1
South East	18·8	19·8
South West	1·9	2·2
Wales	1·8	3·5

* Included in the total are grants in respect of services which appear under more than one region and have not been apportioned.

It is in the peripheral rural areas that the impact of closures has been most noticed, as in Wales, where total route length has halved in recent years, and the 730 stations open in 1965 were reduced by 1970 to under 200.

By concentrating on 'developing to the full those parts of the system and those services which can be made to meet traffic requirements more efficiently and satisfactorily than any other available form of transport' the British Railways Board hoped to stem the contraction in the network and the decline in its use. Two main strategies were proposed—one, a series of fast non-stopping trains with increased frequencies between the major cities to be known as the inter-city network (Fig. 29). The Beeching Report had suggested that stopping passenger services could not be regarded as economic below a density of about 10,000 passengers per week. Thus 30 trains run each way each day between London and Bristol with a journey time of 100 minutes, while 48 trains run each way each day to Birmingham, one every half-hour and taking 90 minutes for the journey. The soon to be completed electrification scheme from Manchester to Glasgow is a further part of this strategy to concentrate resources on fast, frequent inter-city passenger travel, which has successfully competed with the air services on the London to Manchester and Liverpool routes, so that only on the Anglo-Scottish services has the impact of domestic air services been really significant.

The second strategy was to operate in a similar fashion for freight, by offering specialized services (e.g. block trains making merry-go-round journeys) for such bulk movements as coal to the power stations, oil, limestone, iron ore, chemicals and even cars. General traffic was to be carried in containerized loads on the freightliner network, with was to consist of trunk hauls between major centres along routes without intermediate traffic facilities. It was hoped

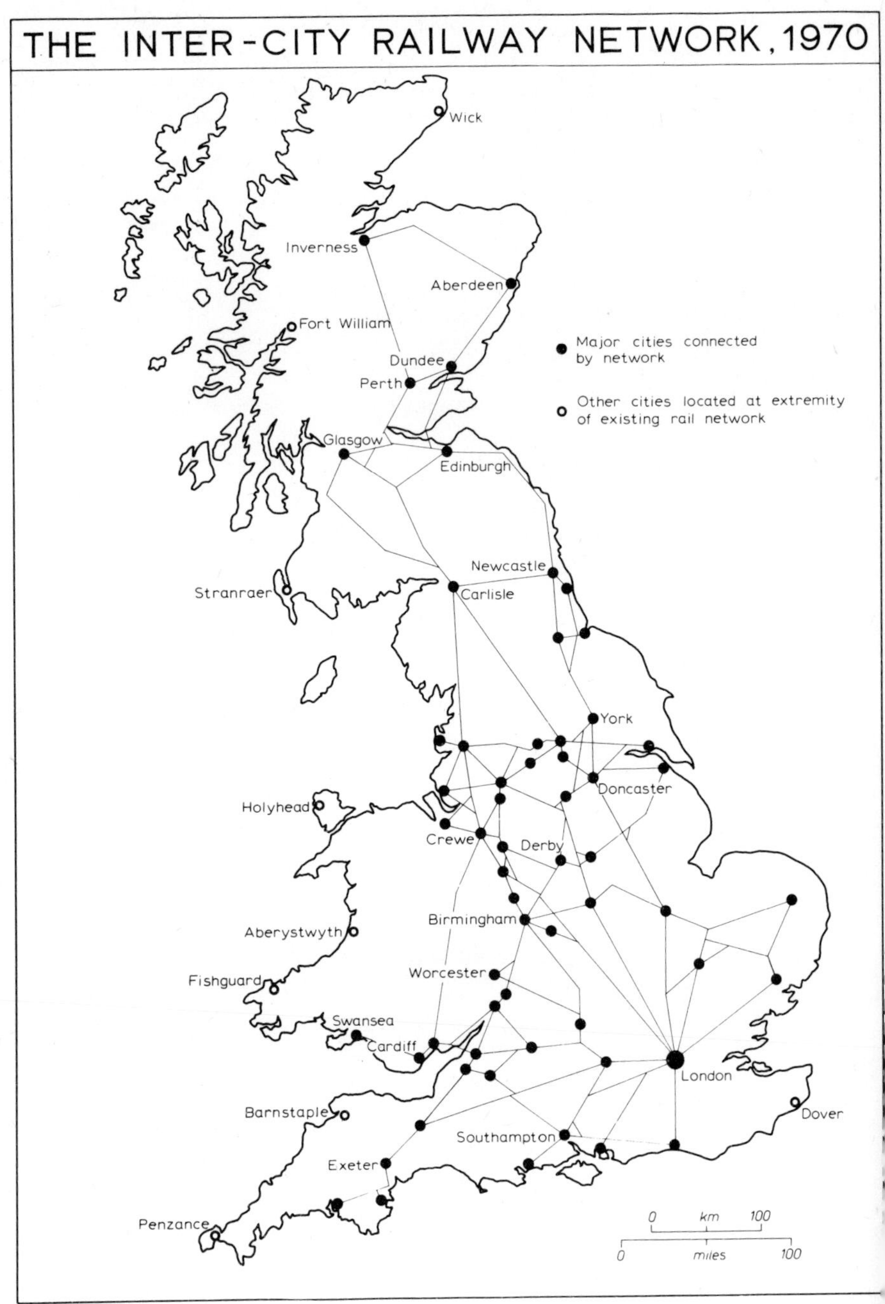

Fig 29 The Inter-City Railway Network, 1970
(Source: British Rail.)

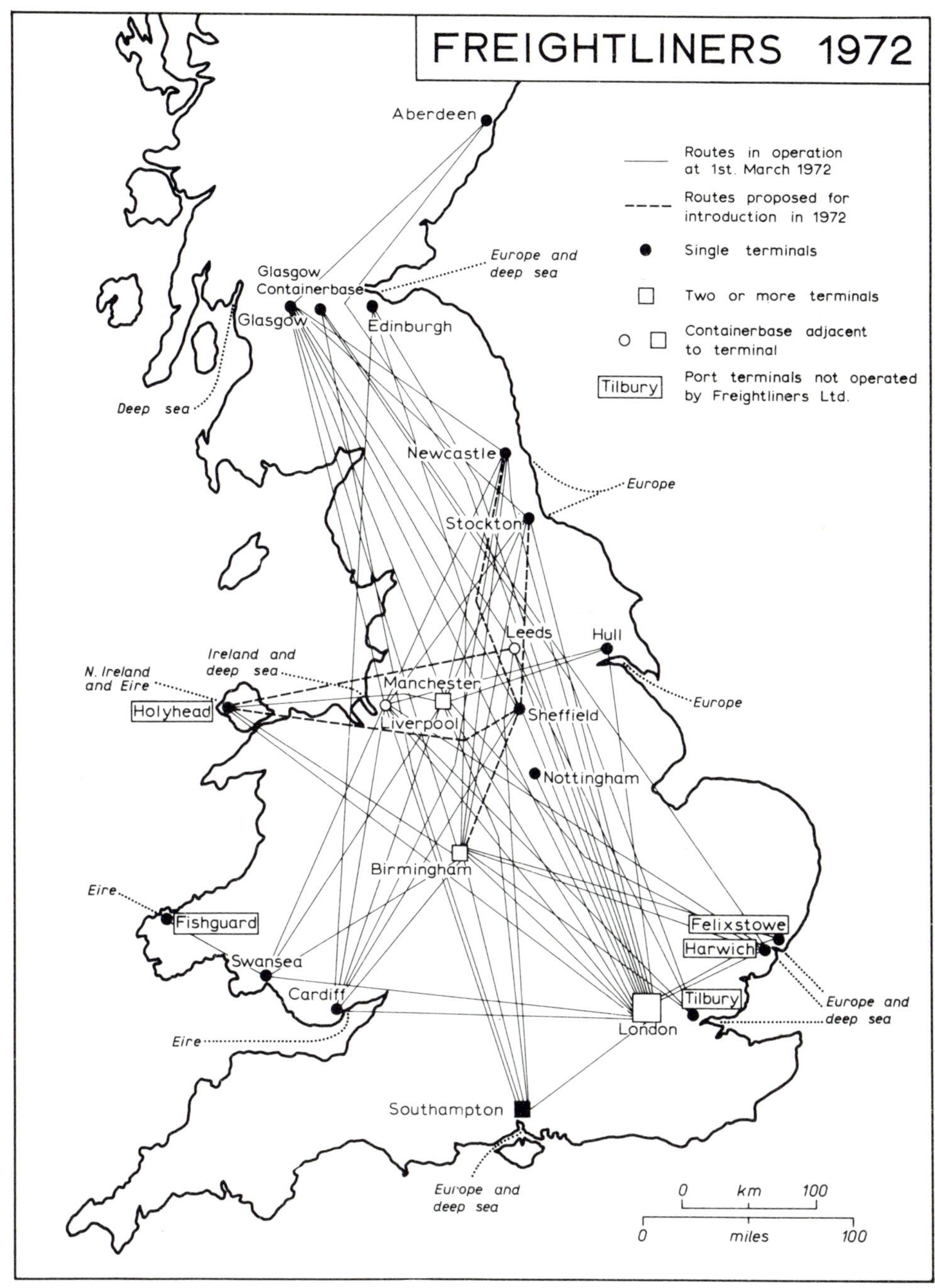

Fig 30 The Freightliner Network, March 1972
(Source: National Freight Corporation.)

in the 1963 report that such a service would be fully competitive with road transport over distances in excess of 160 kilometres (100 miles). The first terminals were opened in Glasgow and London in 1965 and by 1970 the network was practically complete (Fig. 30). Since 1969 when this service was taken over by the National Freight Corporation, established by the 1968 Transport Act, the emphasis has been placed on using the freightliners to feed the maritime container terminals for overseas trade. By 1971 one third of the half million containers carried by freightliners were arriving or departing with overseas trade. These innovations together with the expanding motor-rail services taking tourists' cars on the sleeper trains between north and south have clearly slowed the decline in the railways' share of internal freight movement (see Table 6).

These recent adaptations of the railway network have concentrated frequent passenger and freight services on fewer and fewer urban centres, especially on those in the upper echelons of the urban hierarchy, and have continued the impressive centrality which London established as early as the 1840s. Before the Second World War freight constituted two-thirds of the revenue, today it is a half, and as the average length of haul continues to decline (from 125 kilometres (77 miles) in 1962 to 108 kilometres (67 miles) in 1970) this trend can be expected to continue. The introduction of the Advanced Passenger Train in the late 1970s with its cruising speed of 250 k.p.h. (155 m.p.h.) will further reinforce the importance of passenger revenues and the concentration of services on a limited number of large towns. The opening in 1972 of a new inter-city station at Bristol Parkway, near the M.4 and M.5 intersection with massive car parking facilities may well foreshadow a trend to a new kind of connection between motorways and railways at selected suburban or edge-of-city sites with important implications for the future role of city centres.

TABLE 8

ROAD LENGTHS BY REGIONS 1968

Region	*Route kilometres (miles) (000's)*		*Per cent Share of U.K. Total*	
			Route length	*Area*
Scotland	46·7	(29·0)	13	32
North	24·8	(15·4)	7	8
North-West	22·9	(14·1)	6	3
Yorkshire and Humberside	25·4	(15·8)	7	6
West Midlands	26·6	(16·5)	8	5
East Midlands	22·2	(13·8)	6	5
East Anglia	18·7	(11·6)	5	5
South East	63·1	(39·2)	18	11
South West	44·9	(27·9)	13	10
Wales	33·0	(20·5)	9	9
N. Ireland	22·5	(14·0)	6	6
Total U.K.	350·8	(218·0)	98	100
Eire	82·6	(51·3)		

ROADS However it is measured the growth in traffic on the roads is an outstanding feature of change in the use of communications within the British Isles since 1945. By 1970 as Table 6 shows 90 per cent of all passenger travel and 61 per cent of all freight were carried by road. However, there has since 1950 been a continuous and steady decline in the passenger travel by public service vehicles and a continuous rapid rise in the use of private car (and taxi). It is estimated that the average private motorist covers 13,900 kilometres (8,600 miles) each year, and that 53 per cent of the households in Britain had regular use of a car in 1970.

The real increase in mobility indicated by these figures can only be fully comprehended when the density and ubiquity of the network is realized. Table 8 shows the regional distribution of this network of roads and gives some indication of the variations in density contained in it; but it is the high level of connectivity which is also significant since this manifestly gives accessibility to almost every acre of the British Isles (Plate 25). Thus although the enormous

Plate 25 Graveley Hill (Birmingham)
This intersection of the M.6 and M.38 motorways only 4 kilometres (2·5 miles) from the city centre of Birmingham shows the complex engineering required to 'squeeze' the new primary network through urban and industrial areas. Note how the canal passes underneath the three-level structure which opened in 1972 and completed the linking-up of the M.1, M.5, and M.6 motorways.

growth in vehicular traffic has led to the development of an entirely new transport network, purpose built for the motor-age (the motorways), all the existing roads constitute an important secondary network to which freight and passenger movements have equal access. But increase in mobility and accessibility are increasingly being matched by congestion, accidental death, and loss of amenity in town and country. Britain's roads are claimed to be among the most crowded in the world with 39 vehicles per kilometre of road (63 per mile), while Holland has 36 (57), Italy 35 (56), and Germany 34 (55).

In an urban context the response to growing demand was first to provide more road space and recently to give careful consideration to a large number of related ideas known collectively as 'traffic management'. By restricting parking, reserving one lane for buses only, installing computer controlled traffic lights, arranging one-way street systems and the like, the aim has been to speed the flow of traffic and deter drivers from making unnecessary journeys by private transport. The provision of more road space has often taken the form of massive new investment in bridges or tunnels to reduce congested bottlenecks and in the major conurbations plans for some form of inner ring road and radials of motorway standard are in the process being implemented. More generally there can be no doubt that the form and function of towns are being substantially modified by the increased use of vehicles for such regular journeys as those to work, to shop, and to school and consequently a more dispersed pattern of traffic-intensive land-uses is being recommended by the city planners. In the proposed new cities, such as Milton Keynes and Central Lancashire, the entire urban form has been designed around a network of primary roads which it is hoped will provide for the unrestricted use of private cars by their future populations.

On the inter-urban scale the government planners have drawn up a strategic road pattern (Fig. 31), which consists of motorways and roads of near motorway standard, that will ensure by the middle 1980s, when the 2,700 kilometres (2,000 miles) are complete, that the following six aims are fulfilled:—

1. to achieve environmental improvements by diverting long distance traffic, and particularly heavy goods vehicles, from a large number of towns and villages, so as to relieve them of the noise, dirt and danger which they suffer at present;
2. to complete by the early 1980s a comprehensive network of strategic trunk routes to promote economic growth;
3. to link the more remote and less prosperous regions with this new national network;
4. to ensure that every major city and town with a population of more than 250,000 will be directly connected to the strategic network and that all with a population of more than 80,000 will be within about 16 kilometres (10 miles) of it;
5. to design the network so that it serves all major ports and airports, including the new Third London Airport at Foulness; and
6. to relieve as many historic towns as possible of through trunk traffic.

The door-to-door ability of commercial vehicles coupled with the extensive

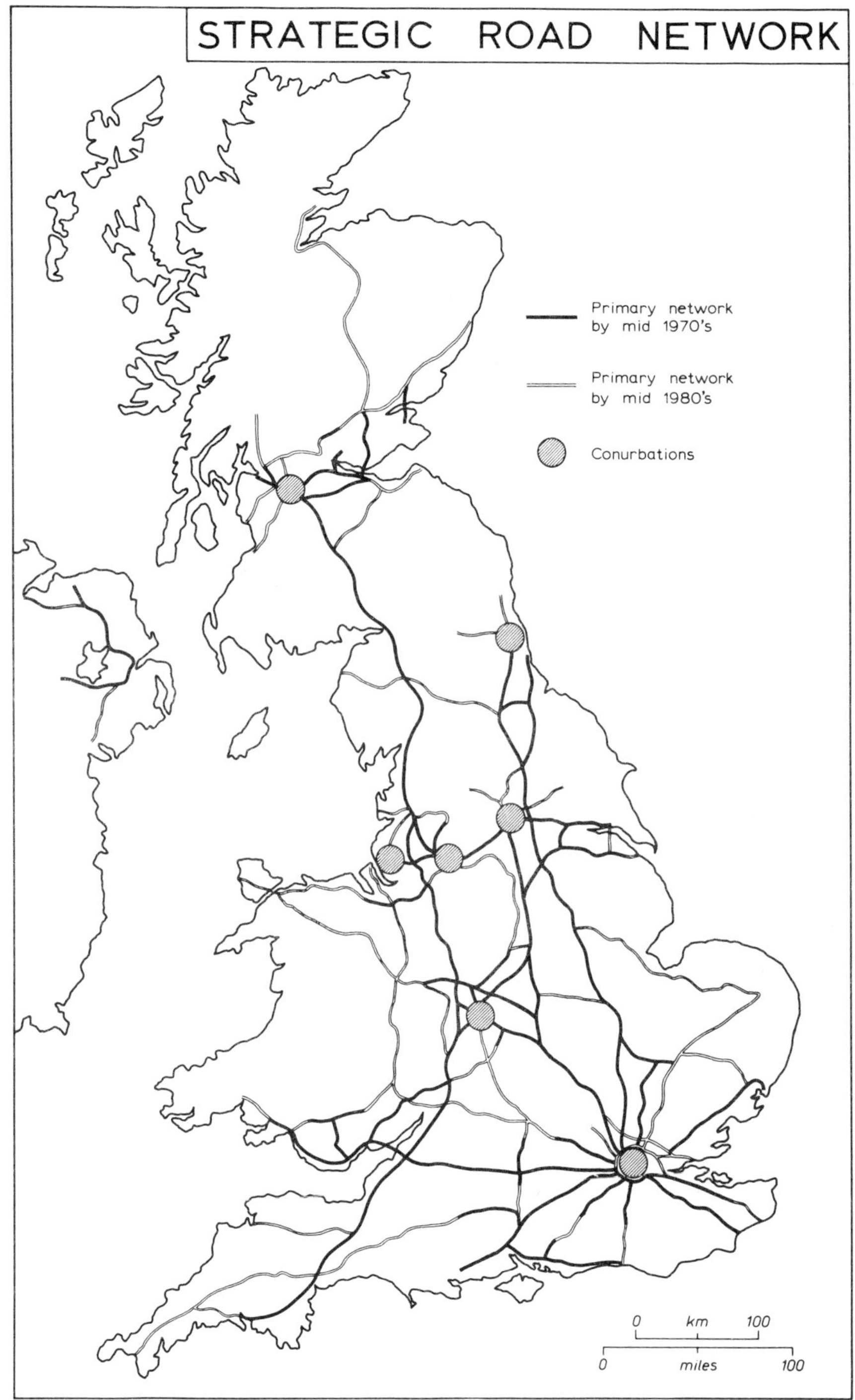

Fig 31 The Strategic Road Network

nature of the road network have been the main reasons behind the rapid growth of road freight movements. In terms of the weight of goods carried by all forms of inland transport in Great Britain in 1968, road movement accounted for 85 per cent. Of the total carried, 18 per cent was food, drink and tobacco, 15 per cent building materials, 4 per cent iron and steel products and 5 per cent other metals and machinery.

By contrast the volume of public road transport between 1950 and 1970 has declined from 80,000 million passenger-kilometres (50,000 million passenger-miles) to 55,000 million (34,000 million), and while both urban and rural areas have been affected it is in the rural areas that the consequences are most notable, as with the railway closures. Consequently car ownership has risen steeply and in several surveys more people were found to travel to work by lifts from friends than on regular bus services. The problem that arises from this situation, even with local authorities subsidizing a minimum bus service at peak hours and on market days, is that of coping with the needs of a small population, too dispersed to justify conventional bus services, and often only requiring public transport for special journeys such as visiting friends in hospital. The government have agreed to examine legislation that, 'will make it possible to devise ways of putting the car to better use to meet the individual, fragmented and often irregular needs' of rural people without cars.

The growth of car ownership has changed many of the patterns of social and economic life and has done so everywhere because of the extensiveness of the road network. No more dramatic example exists than in the day-trip for recreation in the countryside. The reduction in car travelling time created by the motorways has made the national parks accessible to large urban populations for the first time since their designation twenty years ago.

Before turning to the communications that link Britain with overseas, it is necessary to mention (but not to discuss in detail) the rapidly growing networks for sending messages by various forms of telecommunication. Wireless is now supplemented by telephone, teleprinter, telegraph, television and document transmission by wire. Undoubtedly these facilities have developed to serve new needs in the society but just as television may be seen as a replacement for the cinema and consequently causing a reduction in personal travel so perhaps in business will electronic communications develop to the extent that personal travel needs will be lessened. Freight flows too could be affected. Between 1960 and 1970 letters posted increased by 10 per cent while trunk telephone calls increased by 250 per cent.

Overseas Links

Although from the middle of the 1960s the flow of passengers to and from overseas has been greater by air than sea, reaching approximately 70 per cent of the total in 1970, overseas freight movements remain overwhelmingly dominated by ports handling seaborne traffic.

PORTS

Table 9 shows that one-third of the traffic in British ports is to or from other British ports, and that 55 per cent arises from foreign imports. Although the imbalance between foreign imports and exports is magnified by the use of weight rather than value as a measure of trade, the figures reflect the fact that 61 per cent of foreign imports were accounted for by petroleum, and another 20 per cent by basic materials. Manufactured goods which account for 40 per cent of the total volume of exports, and only 8 per cent of the volume of imports, are approximately half the total overseas trade when measured by value. The principal bulk (non-fuel) cargoes imported in 1969 were ores and scrap, cereals, wood, fertilizers and minerals, wood-pulp and waste paper, and sugar.

TABLE 9

TRADE OF BRITISH PORTS 1965 AND 1969

million metric tons (long tons)

	Foreign			*Coastwise*			*Grand*
	Imports	*Exports*	*Total*	*Imports*	*Exports*	*Total*	*Total*
1965	153 (151)	36 (35)	189 (186)	54 (53)	60 (59)	115 (113)	304 (299)
1969	186 (183)	44 (43)	230 (225)	52 (51)	57 (56)	109 (107)	339 (332)

It is the changing composition and direction of trade together with technological development which influences the growth and decline of ports. In recent years an increasing concentration of trade, increasing specialization of trade, and more trading with Europe rather than with the Commonwealth have combined to produce considerable changes in the function and appearance of many British ports. The consequential cost of modernizing old ports and even developing new ones has increased to the level where it is a major national economic consideration justifying overall management by a body established for the purpose—the National Ports Council. Capital expenditure on port facilities between 1965 and 1969 amounted to £206 million in Great Britain, of which London used almost a quarter, Liverpool 13 per cent and Port Talbot and Grangemouth another 7 per cent each.

The main technological developments being catered for in this capital investment programme are the increasing size of vessel, especially bulk carriers to take advantage of the economies of scale, the need to reconstruct quaysides to handle the growing volume of general cargo being shipped in containers, and the need to construct new berths for the great growth in drive-on/drive-off facilities. Containers and the other forms of standardized unit loads (unitization), which in 1969 accounted for four times the volume of trade by these methods in 1964, are expanding rapidly because they shorten journey time (Plate 26). Because travel on land is faster than by sea (especially with freightliners and motorways) the present tendency is for short-sea general cargo to travel by routes that involve long inland hauls but short sea crossings, instead of moving to the nearest port to minimize the cost of the journey. The minimization of journey time is also helping to concentrate deep-sea general cargo on a small number of large ports where there are frequent sailings to many destinations. Deep sea container traffic which is expected to expand rapidly in the future accounted for only 10 per cent of unitized trade in 1969, while 40 per cent of unit traffic was across the Irish Sea, with twice as much going to and from Northern Ireland as the Irish Republic.

Plate 26 Port of Southampton

The photograph, taken in 1970, shows in the foreground the first stage of Southampton's ocean container terminal consisting of a 300 metre (330 yard) berth and 8 hectare (20 acre) container marshalling area. In the background, the traditional quayside sheds with cruise liners and general cargo boats. Stage two of the ocean container terminal came into operation in 1972 when British Rail's freightliner trains operated six times daily to collect and deliver cargoes from and for the Far East.

TABLE 10

MAJOR PORTS IN BRITAIN 1969

	A. *Foreign Goods Traffic (by weight)*	B. *Net Registered Weight of Vessels Cleared*	
		Foreign	*Coastwise*
1.	London	London	London
2.	Milford Haven	Southampton	Belfast
3.	Liverpool	Liverpool	Southampton
4.	Medway	Dover and Folkestone	Cowes (I of W)
5.	Southampton	Milford Haven	Liverpool
6.	Teesside	Harwich	Milford Haven
7.	Clyde	Glasgow	Portsmouth
8.	Manchester	Hull	Tyne ports
9.	Immingham	Manchester	Bristol

These trends reveal themselves in Table 10, and Figure 32. Milford Haven, the deep-water petroleum port, now handles a cargo weight greater than Liverpool, and the oil terminal on Whiddy Island in Bantry Bay in south-west Eire is an even more extreme example of the way in which increasing tanker size has made the search for a suitable harbour more important than the

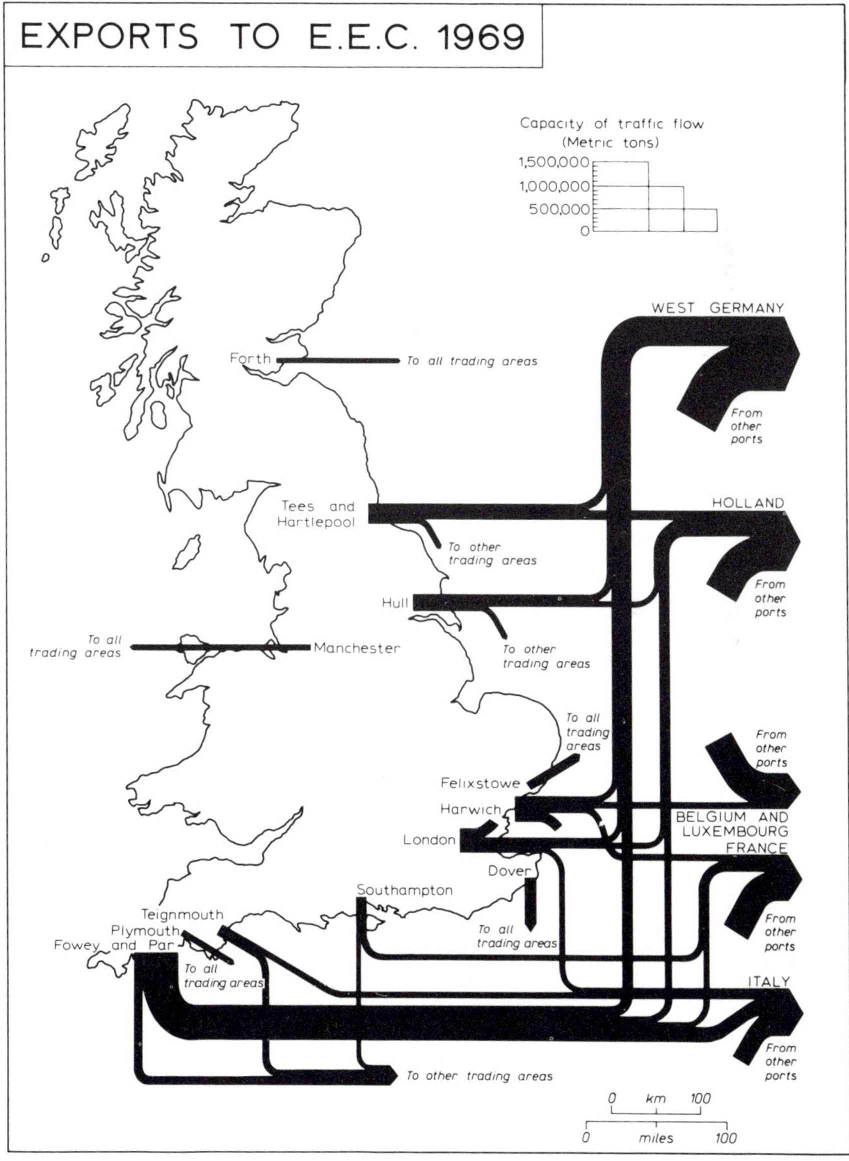

Fig 32 Exports, other than Fuels, to the European Economic Community, 1969
Traffic flows are shown for all ports of Great Britain with non-fuel exports exceeding 100,000 metric tons. (Source: National Ports Council.)

concern for proximity to an hinterland. The importance of Dover and Folkestone and the ports of the Stour and Orwell estuary (Harwich and Felixstowe) reflect the use of the short-sea crossing by roll on–roll off unitized trade. As trade with Europe particularly in manufactured goods and tourist traffic continues to grow these and other specialized ports such as Ramsgate in Kent, where all Volkswagen cars are imported, will expand, and port hinterlands which in Britain have always overlapped to a considerable degree will become even more extensive. It is also an inescapable consequence of concentration and specialization in port facilities that the quality of the connection to inland transport networks is becoming increasingly crucial, whether it involves motorway access, freightliner depots or pipeline terminals.

AIRPORTS

Air traffic between the United Kingdom and abroad (including Ireland) increased from 6 million passengers in 1960 to 22 million in 1970, while domestic travel increased from 2·8 million to 5·4 million passengers over the same period. Apart from its rapid rise to importance as a method of passenger travel, the outstanding feature of the pattern of air traffic in Britain is the domination of the South-East region and in particular the volume and frequency of traffic through London's Heathrow Airport. Located 24 kilometres (15 miles) from the city centre on the west side of the metropolis, and occupying 1,100 hectares (2,700 acres), creating employment for over 40,000 workers, and with over 13 million passengers each year, this airport has almost 10 million international passengers annually making it the largest airport in the western world for international traffic. Air cargo, mainly in perishable goods and those where time is at a premium, such as spare parts for machinery, has also grown, to the point where Heathrow now ranks as Britain's third port in terms of the value of goods handled. This airport, with its motorway and underground railway links, is a remarkable testimony to the importance of London as a gateway city astride the most intensively used global routeways (Plate 27). On a less dramatic scale Prestwick in Ayrshire and Shannon in County Clare, Ireland are further examples of the same locational influence.

Although Figure 33 shows a distribution of airports that embraces all the regions of the British Isles only London serves a wide number of destinations with reasonable frequency in both summer and winter. Manchester, Prestwick, Dublin and Shannon have intercontinental flights, and serve inter-European routes. Although 19 other United Kingdom airports have European flights the number of destinations served is small, the frequency low, and the winter services are only 30 per cent of the summer schedules, reflecting the impact of holiday traffic. Domestic services also reflect the domination of London. London to Belfast, Glasgow and Edinburgh are the busiest all year routes, reflecting the distances involved, while the Scilly Isles, Channel Islands, and Isle of Man constitute almost half of the destinations in a typical summer week. Glasgow airport serves as the base for services to the islands to the north (Orkney and Shetland) and west (Outer and Inner Hebrides) where an annual government subsidy underlines the important social function these routes perform in overcoming isolation.

It is clear in retrospect that thc 1960s were a major watershed in transport technology symbolized by the withdrawal of the last steam locomotive from service, the opening of the first stretch of motorway, the arrival of the first jumbo-jet (Boeing 747) and super-tanker, and the 1968 Transport Act. All of the significance of these and related events are not yet established beyond doubt and the 1970s seem certain to contain further developments in the technology and opportunity for increased communications. In addition to further electronic innovations, the advanced passenger train will increase the distance from London over which rail will be quicker than air, the Concorde

Plate 27 London Airport (Heathrow)
The photograph taken in the summer of 1969 looking north-east, showing 'island' terminal buildings and access to the M.4 motorway via a tunnel under the northern east–west runway.

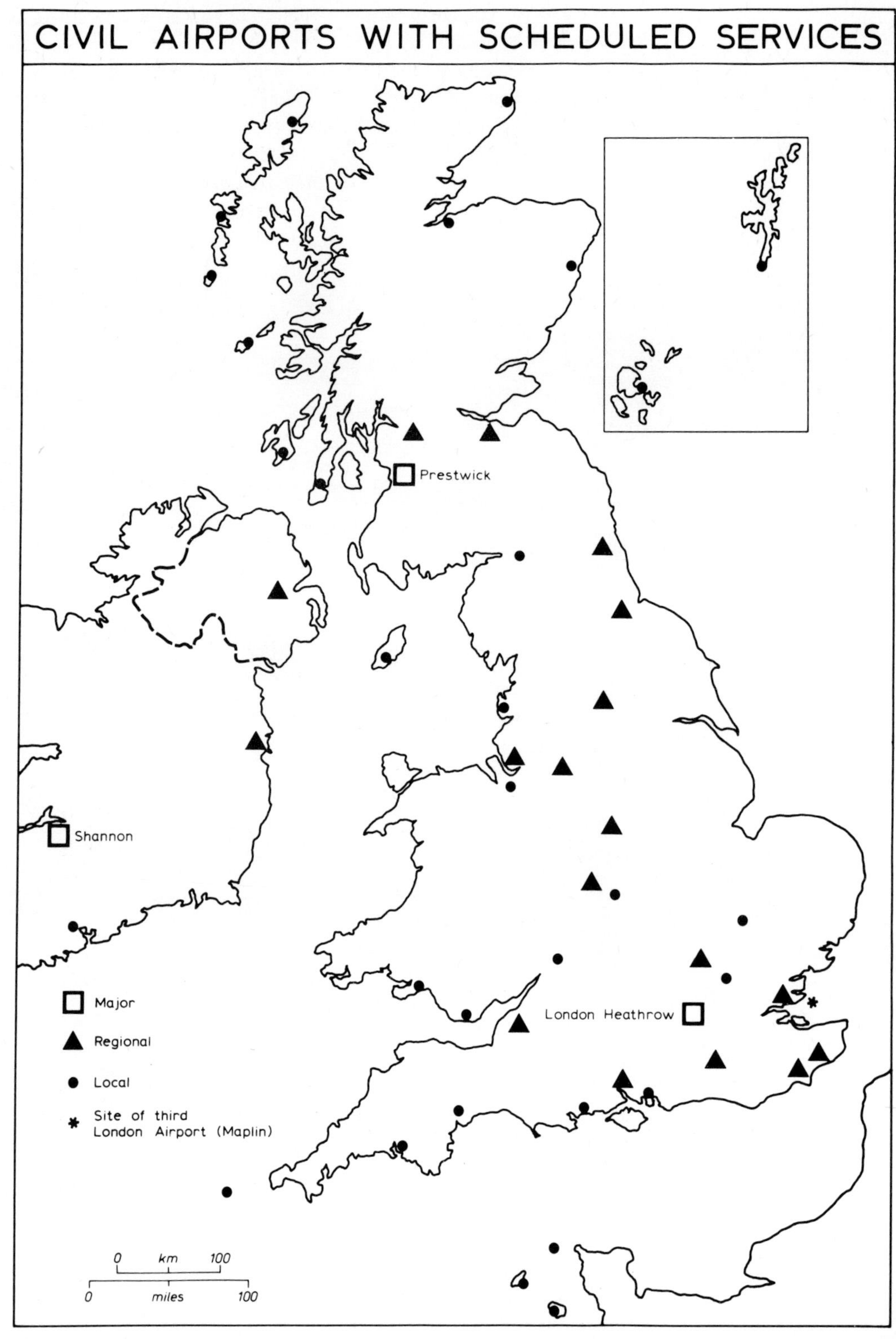
CIVIL AIRPORTS WITH SCHEDULED SERVICES
Prestwick
Shannon
London Heathrow
Major
Regional
Local
Site of third
London Airport (Maplin)
0 km 100
0 miles 100

will make new demands for airport services and the Channel Tunnel raises many questions about the form of our growing connections with Europe.

The potential impact of such developments on the settlement pattern and way of life is considerable and there seems little doubt that society will attempt to influence the rate and direction of the changes. In particular the need to integrate the changes in one mode of travel with changes in the others and the need to plan ahead will mean the continuation of strong Government agencies, and even the creation of new ones, like the Passenger Transport Authorities established in each conurbation with responsibility for all local rail and road services. Perhaps even a national communications strategy will emerge to resolve the growing conflicts between increased communications to support economic growth, and the quality of life impaired by growing congestion, loss of amenity, and pollution of air and beaches.

FURTHER READING

J. H. Appleton, *The Geography of Communications in Great Britain* (London, 1962).

J. Bird, *The Major Seaports of the United Kingdom* (London, 1963).

J. Bird, Traffic Flows to and from British Seaports, *Geography*, 54 (1969), 284–302.

British Railways Board, *The Reshaping of British Railways* (H.M.S.O., 1963).

P. Cowan, Communications, *Urban Studies*, 6 (1969), 436–446.

N. R. Elliott, Hinterland and Foreland as Illustrated by the Port of the Tyne, *Transactions Institute of British Geographers*, 47 (1969), 153–170.

R. Hall, *The Transport Needs of Great Britain in the Next Twenty Years* (H.M.S.O., 1963).

K. R. Sealy, The Siting and Development of British Airports, *Geographical Journal*, 133 (1967), 148–177.

H. D. Watts, The Inland Waterways of the United Kingdom in the 1960s, *Economic Geography*, 43 (1967), 303–313.

M. J. Wise, The Impact of the Channel Tunnel on the Planning of S.E. England, *Geographical Journal*, 131 (1965), 167–185.

British Air Transport in the Seventies, Report of the Committee of Enquiry in Civil Air Transport (Edwards Committee), Cmnd 4018 (H.M.S.O., 1969).

Traffic in Towns, Report of the Steering Group and Working Group (C. D. Buchanan) (H.M.S.O., 1963)

Fig 33 Civil Airports with Scheduled Services

Major airports: those with large long-haul capacity:—London Heathrow, Prestwick, Shannon. *Regional airports:* those with a major domestic role and European connections:—Belfast, Birmingham, Bristol, Dublin, East Midlands (Derby), Edinburgh, Ferryfield (Lympne, Kent), Glasgow, Leeds–Bradford, London–Gatwick, Liverpool, Luton, Lydd, Manchester, Newcastle, Southampton, Southend, Teesside. *Local airports:* those serving as feeders:—Aberdeen, Barra, Benbecula, Blackpool, Bournemouth, Cambridge, Campbeltown, Carlisle, Channel Islands (Alderney, Guernsey, Jersey), Chester, Cork, Coventry, Exeter, Gloucester, Inverness, Isle of Man, Islay, Kirkwall, Penzance, Plymouth, Portsmouth, Scilly Isles, Stansted, Stornoway, Swansea, Tiree, Wick.

The South East

The South East region has many, though of course far from exclusive, claims to primacy in the attention of students of the British Isles. It is the largest of the Economic Planning Regions of England and Wales covering over 26,000 square kilometres (10,000 square miles), that is, it occupies roughly 17 per cent of the total area. It contains more than 17 million people, or about 35 per cent of the population of England and Wales, and houses at its centre the nation's capital. While the region employs only 13 per cent of those engaged in the primary industries in England and Wales, it occupies 32 per cent of the workforce in manufacturing industry, and nearly 43 per cent of those employed in the service and construction industries. Well over half the workforce of the South East finds its employment within the London conurbation, some workers travelling considerable distances from the outer fringes of the region. While this chapter is concerned with giving a balanced picture of the region as a whole, it is inevitable, when present day social and economic activities are considered, that a large proportion of the comment should refer directly or indirectly to London, which, by its size, employment opportunities, and population pressures, has come to dominate the region.

Physical Setting

RELIEF ELEMENTS

The South East region, because of its underlying lithology and structure, is formed of a number of diverse physical components. At a superficial glance it may seem that urban and industrial expansion has proceeded with little regard for these varied circumstances and possibilities. In fact, in detail, the form and nature of the ground surface has exercised substantial control over the growth and timing of development within the region, and therefore a brief review of its physical elements is an essential introduction to a consideration of the South East. It is convenient to begin at the centre of the region and work towards its periphery.

London itself, at the geographical centre of the region (Fig. 34), lies wholly within the London Basin—a large synclinal depression defined by the Chiltern Hills to the north and the North Downs to the south. The Thames, which drains the basin, occupies an asymmetrical position as a result of a post-glacial southward migration, and London, which straddles the Thames, has similarly achieved an offset location. The axis of the basin is formed by the Thames floodplain and this is flanked by flights of gravel terraces, extensive to the north, but pinched out against the Downs in the south. Where they remain undeveloped, the gravels are much favoured for market gardening—

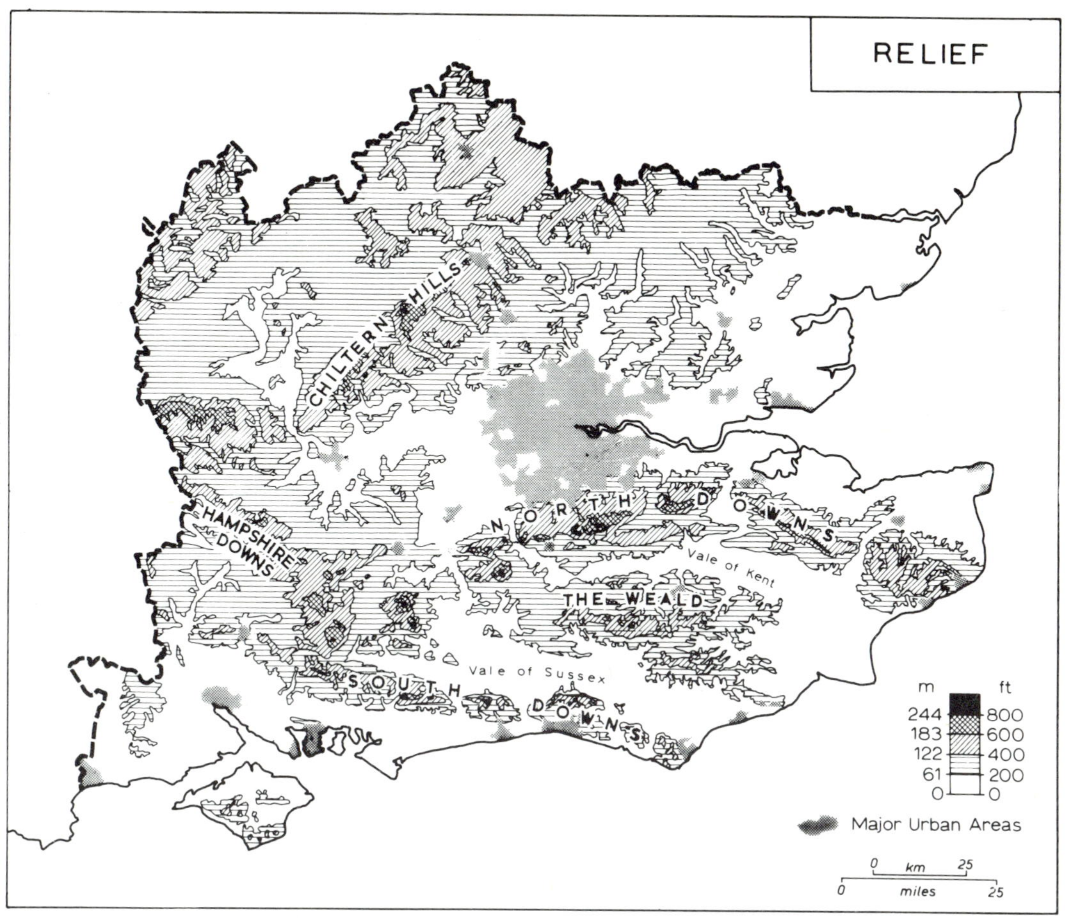

Fig 34 South East—Relief
The region is one of appreciable relief, the main upland features the Chilterns, the North, South and Hampshire Downs, being formed by the chalk.

particularly where they have a covering of brick-earth. Tongues of terrace gravels extend along tributaries of the Thames, especially in the Lea Valley, in the north-eastern quadrant of London, and in the Colne Valley and the Vale of St. Albans to the north-west. The remainder of the basin is floored by extensive deposits of poorly-drained London Clay, much of it now built over, but there are also substantial areas of coarse sands and gravels in the western part, around Camberley and Aldershot, which have traditionally served for recreation and military training.

To both north and south the low lying areas of the London Basin give way to chalk upland (Fig. 34). In the north the Chiltern Hills form a substantial feature of sufficient elevation for the gaps to have proved vital controlling factors in deciding the routes of main road, canal, and rail links into the Basin from the north and west of the country. Basically a chalk cuesta with a north-western facing scarp, the surface is much influenced by an extensive clay-with-flints superficial covering. In the western Chilterns the land is deeply dissected, with a high proportion of woodland which gives the area high scenic value. Further east the relief is more subdued and soils are of better quality. At the extreme north-eastern end, and at the northern boundary of the region, the Chilterns merge into the drift-covered East Anglian Plateau, an area of exten-

Plate 28 Grand Union Canal, Berkhamsted (Hertfordshire)
The canal, linking London with the Midlands, here employs the major gap through the Chiltern Hills between Hemel Hempstead and Aylesbury. The same gap is also used by a minor trunk road (A.41) and main railway line, also connecting London with the midland counties and the north-west of England.

sive arable working. North-west of the Chiltern scarp edge lies the Vale of Aylesbury and beyond it, in the far north-west of the region, the beginnings of the Jurassic Cotswold Hills. These are both areas of dominantly agricultural activity and are largely outside the influence of London.

The southern edge of the London Basin is defined by the chalk North Downs. They have some affinity with the Chilterns, but there is greater internal contrast. West of London the dip of the chalk increases, the outcrop narrows, and in places a hog's back ridge is produced. East of London the Downs broaden and provide good agricultural land, much of it under fruit and vegetables. The country to the south of the North Downs is more varied still, with clay vales and sandy or limestone ridges interspersed. In broad terms the Weald is a structural dome within which erosion has revealed beds older than the Chalk, and in the central area has penetrated to the Hastings Sands. The High Weald, sandy and infertile in nature, contains much rough heath and woodland. It stands in direct contrast with the Low Weald, composed mainly of the broad Weald Clay vales to north and south (Vales of Kent and Sussex) which, though poorly drained and not of good quality, carry agricultural land. South of the Vale of Sussex lies the open chalkland of the South Downs and the coastal plain of the English Channel. Unlike the area beyond the Chiltern Hills, the Weald and the south coast have long been strongly influenced by London. They have provided not only precious areas of open land for recreation purposes, but they have also yielded space in which generally high-value commuters' settlements have been located. Much of this part of the region, lying immediately south of London, contributes over 5 per cent, and often more, of its residential workforce to the conurbation daily. The fact that the chalk rim and the ridges within the Weald are breached by northward and southward flowing streams has greatly assisted movement to and from London.

The Wealden Dome pitches westwards and the outcrops of the north and south swing concentrically around the western end. Here large areas of chalkland again occur in the Hampshire Downs, but these tracts of open farmland give way in the extreme south-west of the region to another Tertiary basin. The Hampshire Basin, though smaller, and facing south instead of east, in many ways resembles the London Basin. The southern edge however is broken by the sea to form the Isle of Wight. Another major difference is that it is floored by a far higher proportion of coarse sandy beds. These are especially important in the south-west of the basin, where the New Forest is established in one of the main sandy areas. Sharply folded rocks in the Isle of Wight give rise to varied scenery, cliffs, and beaches, and contribute to the highly diversified shoreline of the region, which ranges from the featureless esturine flats of Essex, to the high chalk cliffs that occur where the North and South Downs meet the sea in the area of Dover and Beachy Head.

As already suggested, the physical character of the South East region has greatly influenced the detail and timing of the development of the man-made landscape. For example, London itself, in its early growth, was to a large degree restricted first to the Flood Plain and Taplow terraces, on which The City and West End now stand, and later to other well-drained gravel terraces which provided not only good building and agricultural land, but contained also supplies of drinking water for the urban population. Better methods of drainage and rapidly improving building technique led, as time went on, to less constrained development, and by the period of London's great expansion, that between the two great wars, extensive building was taking place on the wet, low-lying London Clay. Beyond the boundaries of the conurbation similar controls are evident. Here, housing, industry, agriculture, and communications have often appropriated the most desirable land. Land which was too wet, too stony, too infertile, too steep, or too inaccessible for these uses remained in woodland, or was left in a rough, unworked condition. These areas, once unwanted, have now come to acquire an enhanced value as recreation space for the urban dweller, and over the last half century or so have acted increasingly as magnets for settlement, rather than as repellents to it.

CLIMATIC CONTRASTS

The South East is climatically the most 'continental' of the regions of the British Isles. July temperatures are the highest in the British Isles, January temperatures among the lowest (the major exception is provided by the Scottish uplands), and rainfall, though generally low, has a high thunderstorm component. However, general climatic patterns in the British Isles have already been treated (see Chapter 2) and the contrasts between different areas highlighted. It remains here to explore some of the pronounced intra-regional variations in climate which in this area often resolve themselves into contrasts between town and country.

Just as London, and the other major urban areas of the South East, have been influenced in their development by the physical setting, so they, in turn, have become an element in the general physical environment experienced by urban man. As towns and cities grow, they replace arable, grassland, woodland, and heath with bricks, mortar, concrete and macadam. They also create sources of heat and pollution which are then released into the atmosphere and influence urban climate.

The most obvious of these climatic abnormalities are the pollutants, most of which are the products of combustion in one form or another. Domestic heating, power plants, factories, road traffic, and trains all release smoke and harmful gases, and these are most concentrated near the centres of large urban areas, particularly London. Smoke control regulations have done much to ease the health and other problems created. For example, smoke emissions in London are now only a quarter of what they were before the Clean Air Act of 1956. But these regulations deal mainly with the visible forms of pollution, and little control has been applied to the invisible and often more damaging gases, such as sulphur dioxide and carbon dioxide, which are released into the urban atmosphere.

It is not surprising to find that though fogs are now less frequent, and true smogs are rare, sunshine amounts are still reduced in polluted central areas of cities such as London. But this is not the only, nor the most marked, modification induced by the city on its climate. One of the more noticeable and interesting is the variation in air temperature which occurs between central London and the cooler surrounding countryside. The differences throughout the year in average minimum temperature are of the order of 1°C (1·8°F), but on still nights in summer and autumn the difference between city centre and rural surround may be as high as 9°C (16°F). The densely packed buildings of inner London conserve the sun's heat and also the heat of artificial combustion in their fabric and release it at night, so producing higher temperatures. Pollution haze contributes to the effect by reducing the amount of outgoing night time radiation over the city.

In modifying temperature, and also other relevant meteorological factors, such as humidity and windspeed, both of which are generally lower in city centres than in the fringing rural areas, the builders of London have substantially altered the climate of the centre of the Thames Basin. In the middle of London snow melts more quickly in winter, and spring flowers appear sooner than in the adjacent countryside. Though fogs may cause difficulties for transport, and for those of the population with chest conditions, housewives' washing dries more quickly and savings in domestic fuel costs may be as high as 20 per cent. The modifications to climate are accidental and unplanned, but they are changes which introduce important and varying influences into the lives of the population of London and its surrounding region.

Population and Economic Expansion

To a large degree the growth in population and in employment in the South East region is closely linked with the expansion of London itself, and with the impact of that expansion throughout the area. It is logical and convenient to begin with London, and then to move outwards towards the peripheries of the region.

URBAN GROWTH

London originated at the city of Londinium, the largest settlement of Roman Britain. Medieval London seems to have been not much larger than the Roman city, but in the seventeenth and eighteenth centuries bridge building across the Thames, and the development by city merchants of spacious houses, and elegant estates, particularly after the Great Fire of 1666, led first to the linking of the original nuclei, the City of London and Westminster, and then to a more general expansion of the urban area.

Growth quickened with the coming of the railways after 1836. Main line termini were located at what was then the edge of the built-up area, but to begin with, many railway companies were more concerned with long-distance traffic than with conveying local passengers. At this stage, trains and horse-drawn omnibuses were the main means of travel to work, and since they allowed people to live at some distance from their work-places in the city centre, they contributed greatly to the growth of London. As the network of suburban railway lines grew, trains increased their share of the commuter traffic. At first, the more prosperous professional workers moved outwards, but they were quickly followed, particularly in the 1880s and after, by other workers making use of cheap workman's fares. Suburban railway stations thus became, and have since continued to be, settlement growth points. The extension of the underground railways system at the end of the nineteenth century stimulated suburban dwelling further. Along roads and railways at this period strips of development stretch into the countryside surrounding London. By the outbreak of the First World War London occupied a circle of radius 10–13 kilometres (6–8 miles) from Charing Cross.

In the interwar period the area of built-up London doubled while its population increased by a little under one-fifth—the density of development

Plate 29 Central London (Westminster)
The photograph covers the core of the London conurbation and shows the parts of the Flood Plain and Taplow terraces stretching from the Houses of Parliament, in the right foreground to The City in the distance (top right). Many of the buildings are, of course, relatively recent, but here and there older buildings, such as Westminster Abbey (centre foreground), indicate the antiquity of this part of London.

was very low. Improved bus services, and the rise of private car ownership had a great influence on the distance and flexibility of road journeys to work. The electrification of suburban railway lines, especially to the south of London, greatly increased the speed of rail transport and hence either reduced journey times or made longer journeys more acceptable. The result was that beyond the yellow-bricked and slate-roofed suburbs of the late nineteenth and early twentieth centuries, new speculative housing estates sprang up with house exteriors characteristically of red brick or rough-cast, and with tile roofs. The contrast in the landscape is most marked and is easily observed. But in other ways there was little change. Building still centred on surface or underground railway stations and ribbon development alongside roads continued. By 1939

Plate 30 Brighton (Sussex)
Many seaside towns in the South East region developed first as holiday resorts, and later became important also as commuters' settlements. The pier, substantial sea-front buildings, and elegant square represent the first function; evidence of the second is seen in the rows of smaller houses in the distance.

London had grown to occupy a circle of radius 20 kilometres (12·5 miles) from Charing Cross.

Beyond the edge of London older settlements were growing rapidly over the same period. Most of these were directly influenced by London. Some served as dormitory towns for part of London's workforce, others grew because the goods and services they provided found an expanding market in the rapidly expanding city. Yet others possessed natural or acquired advantages which gave them a particularly pronounced growth potential. For example, Brighton (Plate 30), Southend-on-Sea, and many other seaside towns, grew in response to the demands of the holiday industries; Dover received stimulus from its role as a packet station and ferry-port; Luton, Watford, and other towns to

Plate 31 Southampton Docks (Hampshire)
The port of Southampton is one of the most important in the country. It has been developed largely because of its sheltered position and favourable tide range. In addition to the conventional facilities, such as the traditional dock-side gantries on the left of the photograph, and the motor car storage depot in the foreground, it has, like many other ports recently acquired new equipment to cope with containerized traffic. This picture is a differently-angled close-up of part of Plate 26.

the north-west of London greatly benefited from their position astride road and rail routes between London and the Midlands and North in marketing their engineering and other light-industrial goods; Oxford attracted population and a certain amount of industry as a result of its university; and finally Southampton, because of its distinct natural advantages of sheltered harbour and tide (Plate 31), grew to become one of the country's major ports, and one of the most important cities of the region.

Since the Second World War a tight control has been exercised over new building both in and around London. But despite building restriction, development has continued. In central London, war-damaged buildings have been replaced, and there has also been a pronounced tendency to replace older commercial buildings nearing the ends of their useful lives by taller, more

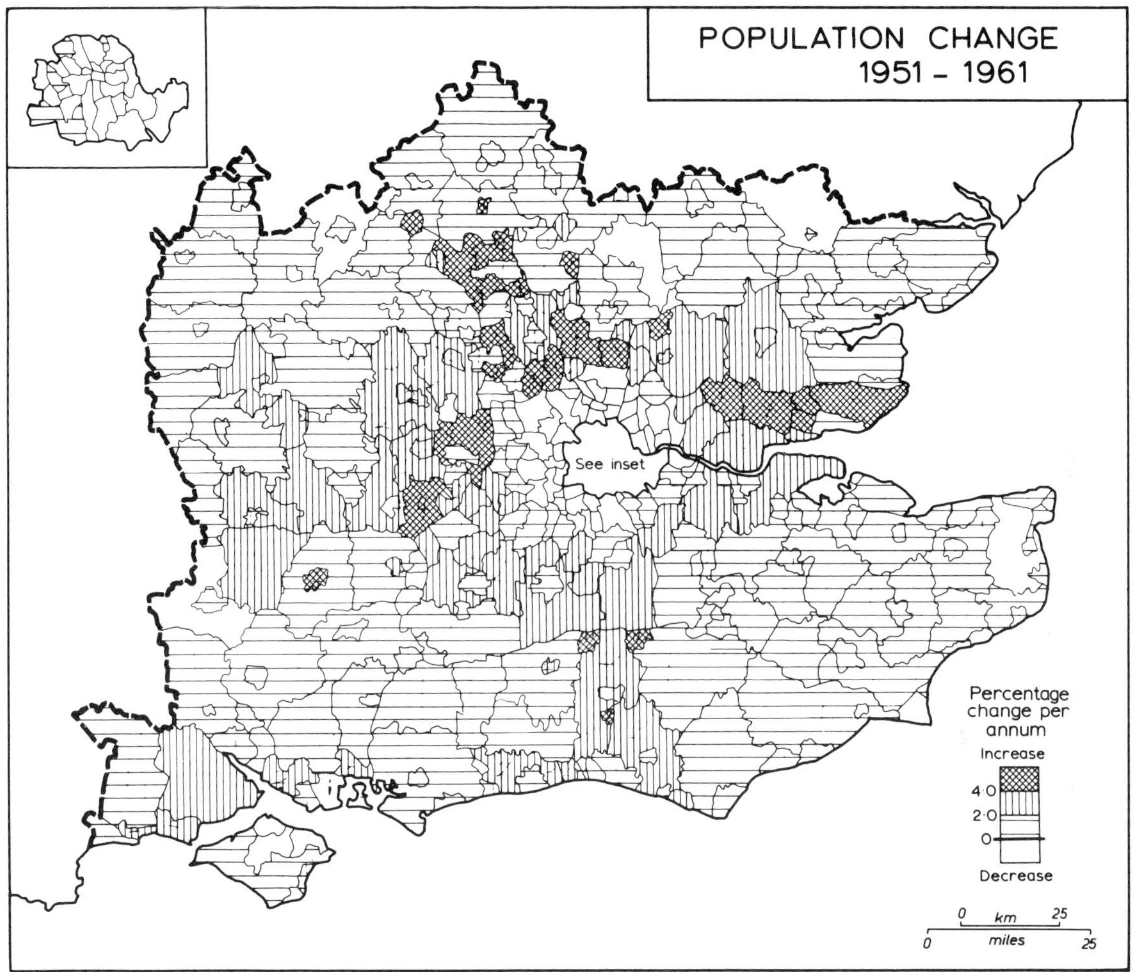

Fig 35 South East—Population Change 1951–1961
London is losing population while the areas outside the conurbation are gaining. Sharpest population increases are in the zone immediately beyond the conurbation limits, where natural increase is high and migration gains considerable.

compact office blocks which make more intensive use of land. In suburban areas spaces previously left undeveloped have been used for building and the orchards and gardens of existing dwellings in the lower density areas have provided additional building land. Outside London similar processes have been underway, but here, of course, greenfield sites have also been employed extensively for building.

Over the last 150 years London has grown from a city of a little over 1 million people to a continuous urban area containing nearly 8 millions. The conurbation is now the centre of a region holding another 9 million people.

While permanent residential population in central London reached its peak in 1901, and has since declined as a result of administrative, commercial, and industrial developments, that of outer London did not reach its maximum until 1951. In aggregate, the conurbation achieved a peak population in 1939, since when numbers have been decreasing slowly. The areas of the region outside London, however, have continued to gain population at a rapid rate, a result of overspill population movements from London, migration gain from other regions, and a high natural population increase. The parts which have experienced the sharpest increase in population lie close to the conurbation, particularly in an arc to the north, where gains recently have been running at a rate in excess of 4 per cent per annum (Fig. 35). In a very broad zone around London, and in radial corridors to the east, west, and south, annual increases have been in excess of 2 per cent, while very few administrative areas in any part of the region outside Greater London have actually suffered population decreases.

EMPLOYMENT OPPORTUNITIES

Without doubt, London has for many centuries been the major focus of both manufacturing and service industry employment in the British Isles. The Industrial Revolution may have increased the rate of employment expansion in coalfield areas for a century or more (see Chapter 4), but, though challenged, London never ceased to be the single most important employment centre. The basis of London's employment strength was craft manufacturing and administration.

Up to the twentieth century London's manufacturing rested firmly upon small-scale, highly skilled, workshop production. Gradually however industries were attracted to the waterside locations along the Thames and lighter, often consumer goods, factory industries were located where sites were available in the expanding outer suburbs, and where communication links with materials, workers, and markets were adequate. It was the development of these last industries that coincided with, and contributed most to, the rapid inter-war growth of London. The Lea, Wandle and other low-lying valley areas provided some of the sites, but the main growth-zone was in north-west London. Sometimes, as at Park Royal (Plate 32), compact estates were established and occupied by many firms. Sometimes plants were disposed along main roads, like Western Avenue, the North Circular Road, and Edgware Road, or less frequently along main railway lines, as at Southall. Some of the industries, wishing to expand, had moved from more congested sites nearer the city centre where often they had craft origins; others, freed by electricity from a coalfield site, were attracted by London's positive locational advantages—its mass market, its substantial labour force, the possibility of contacts with other manufacturers in the same or related fields, and a location at the hub of the country's road and rail system (see Chapter 4).

While manufacturing developments in the interwar period were dispersed in the suburbs, the equally important growth in service employment was drawn to urban nodes. A growing population needed services of all kinds and these were provided in the central retail districts, or in their suburban equivalents, but it was perhaps the increase in jobs in office administration which was most characteristic of the period. Office employment was confined largely to central London. Here it could reap the benefits of proximity to financial and governmental institutions, contact with other administrative offices, and the prestige of a reputable site and address. It was the growth of central office employment, more than any other type, which led to the purely residential suburbs of interwar London.

Since 1945 industrial building within London has been greatly constrained

Plate 32 Park Royal (Brent/Ealing)
The industrial estate at Park Royal was established during the interwar growth of London upon a site first occupied by the Royal Agricultural Society and later, during the First World War, by munitions factories. It is an extremely compact estate, but because of its piecemeal development it contains widely assorted industries and factory styles. The food and drink industries, the paper and book trades, and general or electrical engineering are typical. Note the close juxtaposition of residential and institutional uses of land.

by lack of space and by local authority action. Outside the conurbation, however, there has been more space and less restriction, and in the new towns and in the other settlements through much of the region, there has been substantial manufacturing growth. There has similarly been an enormous expansion in the service industries, and the distinction in location patterns between the two has persisted. Industrial growth has been widespread, but service industries have become even more concentrated than between the wars. This trend has been particularly evident in office building, which more than ever before has been attracted to prestigious central-area sites. Like so many other capitals, London became a 'paper metropolis'. In recent years considerable official efforts have been made to persuade those responsible for office development to decentralize their activities. Some success has been achieved. Croydon, an old-established office centre on the edge of the conurbation, has developed its office potential to the full, while more distant centres within the region, such as Harlow, Horsham, Reading, and Southend, have benefited by office moves from London.

Problems of Growth

Growth in the South East region has brought great economic benefits. It has also presented some formidable problems to the economic and land-use planners whose task it has been to so control economic and social forces that an efficient economic system and an acceptable living environment results. In this section attention will be focused upon the difficulties produced by rapid urban expansion; in the final section of this chapter attention will turn to the positive actions and plans which have been designed to cope with the problems.

PROBLEMS OF EMPLOYMENT

At the root of most of the South East's difficulties, as the previous section hinted, has been its command of attractive employment opportunities, and the disproportionate speed with which that employment has grown in recent decades. This trend had already been identified in the interwar period by the Barlow Commission, set up to examine the distribution of industrial population. Although the Commission to some extent misjudged the rate of employment increase in the South East, its conclusion that the London region was gaining nearly twice its share of industrial development proved to be substantially correct. The swift expansion in employment in the manufacturing and service industries stemmed immediately from the fact that industries with the greatest growth potential tended to be concentrated in the region. Manufacturing industries, such as engineering, vehicle construction, and food processing, were growing rapidly, while services such as building, distribution, administration, and professional activities, expanded as never before. On the other hand, the declining industries, like agriculture, mining, and textile manufacture, were not strongly represented in the London area and so employment gains were not offset, as they were in the depressed coalfield-industrial regions.

The facts led the Barlow Commission to recommend, among other things, that industrial growth in London and the surrounding counties should be decentralized to areas of high unemployment. This recommendation was adopted in the period after 1945 and in essence has continued as public policy up to the present. Though powers were given to the Board of Trade and to local authorities to enable them to implement a decentralization strategy, in practice the task was more difficult than it had seemed. Existing manufacturing and service establishments continued to possess a great growth potential and this was expressed in increasingly strident demands for space for expansion within the South East; London Airport, and other airfields within the region saw a great increase in traffic and made substantial additions to their labour force; the Ports of London, and Southampton grew, and the estuaries on which they were located became nascent industrial regions as waterside locations were demanded by a number of developing industries, particularly in the field of petrochemicals; and finally the eight new towns of the region took not only employment overspill from London but also employment migrating from what had become, in the minds of manufacturers and providers of services, the less desirable regions.

The pace of employment growth in the South East region has caused great pressures upon land. Offices and manufacturing plants needed space for development and in purely economic terms, provided formidable competitors in the scramble for developable land. But the greatest pressure has been exerted indirectly. Employment growth has added in a major way to natural population growth within the region by attracting in people from other parts of the country and from abroad, all of whom need living space. Until 1964 the migration flows into the South East were substantial, but since, the influx has fallen away sharply.

PROBLEMS OF POPULATION AND HOUSING

The scale and rate of population change in the region has already been studied. In brief, London is losing people from its centre and, though there is a certain thickening-up underway in the outer suburbs, the population of the conurbation as a whole is declining. The overspill population, together with natural increase and net migration gain, is accommodated mainly in the parts of the region outside the conurbation. Generally speaking, the rate of population growth varies inversely with distance from Greater London, but with one important exception. Since it is considered that London is already too large for the wellbeing and economic efficiency of its inhabitants, a green belt has been established, some 16 kilometres (10 miles) wide, to prevent the continuous spread of the conurbation, and to provide an inviolable rural hinterland where agriculture, recreation, and other activities requiring little building development may take place. Since it was created in the immediate post-war period, certain extensions have been proposed to the approved green belt, though most of these have never formally been agreed (Fig. 36). In effect, the green belt causes overspill population to leap-frog deeper into the region.

The complement to the restrictive green belt was a positive programme of new, fully planned communities, and this led to the construction of eight new

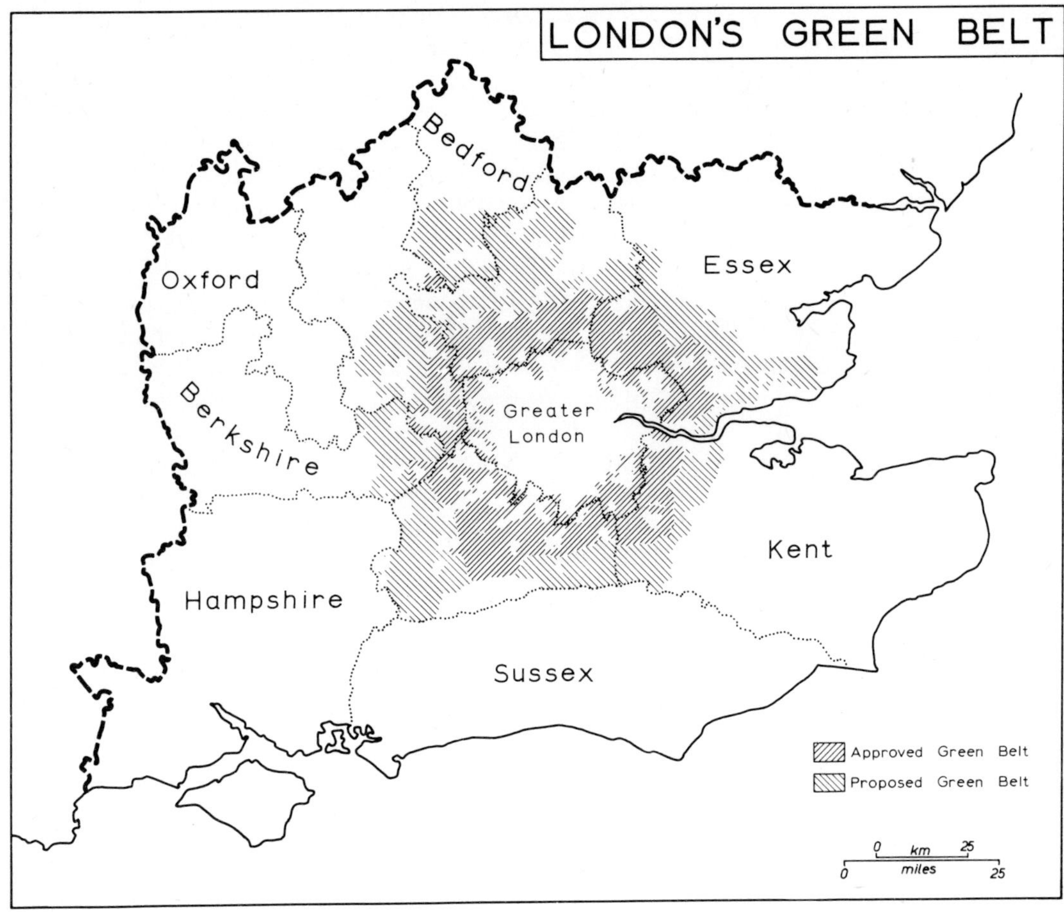

Fig 36 South East—London's Green Belt
The green belt provides an inviolable rural surround to the conurbation where agriculture, recreation and other activities requiring little building development may be pursued. The inner section is firmly approved while the outer section has not yet been finally accepted.

towns on the outer edge of the approved green belt (Fig. 37). At one time it was believed that these would be sufficient to accommodate London's overspill, but this proved a forlorn hope. Population pressure was far greater than anticipated. In London alone by 1951 households exceeded dwellings by about 350,000, and although redevelopment of war damaged areas, and of slums and other property helped to reduce the housing deficit, new building within the conurbation could not rehouse the existing population, let alone cope with natural increase and migration. It has been estimated that between 1952 and 1958 355,000 people moved out of London into the remainder of the region, mainly beyond the green belt. About half moved privately; about half under

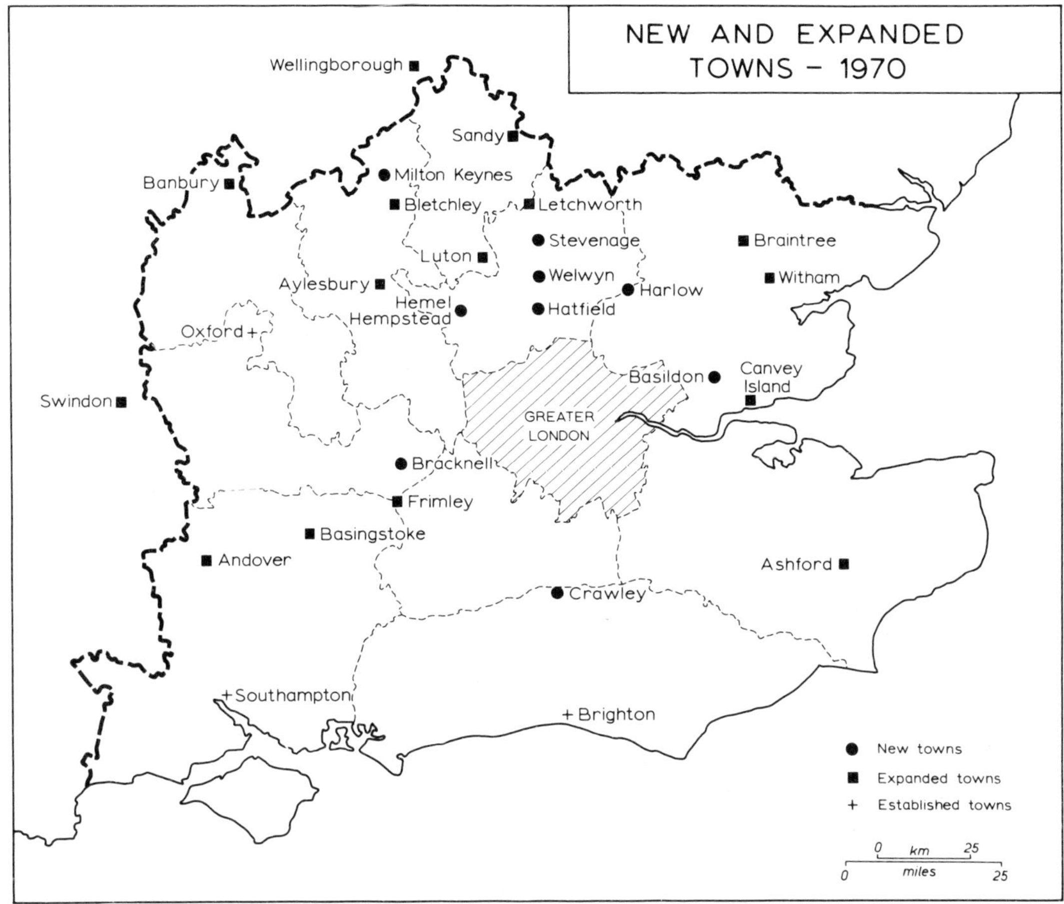

Fig 37 South East—New and Expanded Towns, 1970
New and expanded towns are designed to accommodate part of London's overspill population. They have not, as originally intended, developed as separate and individual entities. Such is the influence of London that, like towns which have expanded naturally, they have considerable economic, cultural and social linkages with the conurbation.

planned overspill schemes. In addition to the new towns, which took the bulk of those involved in planned schemes in the 1950s, others were accommodated in town expansion schemes, particularly in the 1960s, and in 'quasi-satellites' created by the London County Council (Fig. 37).

In the new and expanded towns every effort was made to match the growth of housing and employment, in an attempt to prevent excessive journeying to work. But in settlement growth elsewhere, though local authorities exerted general control and supervision, pressure has been so intense that jobs and people, and therefore workplaces and homes, are often imbalanced. The work journey patterns which result are usually very complicated. Large numbers travel to work in central London from all over the region, the remainder engage in intricate radial and cross trips in outer London, and in and between the other major employment centres of the region (see Chapter 5).

PROBLEMS OF TRANSPORT

So dense is the population, so vigorous is the economic life, and so rapid has been the recent expansion in the South East, that it is almost inevitable that there should arise problems of transportation. These are almost exclusively the result of an expanding demand for transportation unmatched by improve-

Plate 33 Stevenage New Town (Hertfordshire)
The photograph shows construction underway at the edge of the new town. The town centre lies in the distance beyond old Stevenage. Note the planned forms of both settlement and roads and especially the way in which main, local, and pedestrian traffic is segregated (see roundabout, upper centre, for example). It is almost always possible to undertake a journey to work or to the central shopping precinct without crossing a main road.

ments in the means of communication. The congestion of traffic arteries is felt widely throughout the region at most times of the day, and sometimes the night, but there are two particular problems which generate most concern. First, there is the problem of the journey to work which, though general, is most acutely experienced in journeys into central London. Second, there is the problem of city-centre traffic congestion. The two are closely related and, of course, in large part stem from the same causes.

Figure 38, showing the main communication arteries of South East England, gives an immediate impression of the seemingly lavish provision of main roads and railways. But it also points to the heart of the problem—the focusing of almost all of these traffic lines upon London. Along the road and rail routes about a million and a quarter people travel daily into central London to work. About 10 per cent of the commuters travel from outside the conurbation altogether, making journeys morning and evening in excess of 20–24 kilo-

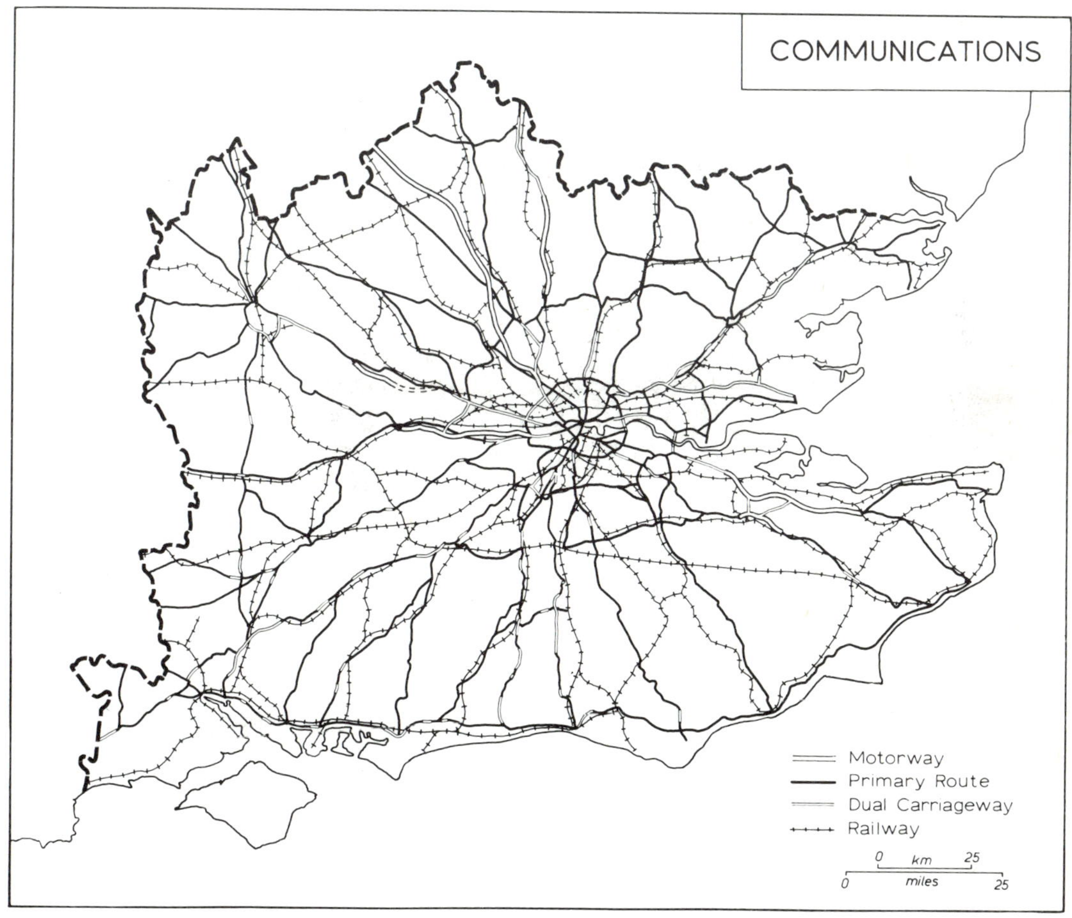

Fig 38 South East—Communications
Note the strong focusing of roads and railways upon London.

metres (12·5–15 miles). Places as distant as Southend and Sevenoaks contribute over 10 per cent of their resident workforce to central London, while many extra-metropolitan urban and rural areas, for example, Berkhamsted, Egham, and Gravesend, lose over 5 per cent of their resident workers daily to the central business district. Though many factors have led to these circumstances, the most important are clearly the growth of the urban area itself, the outward movement of population from the central areas of the conurbation unaccompanied by a commensurate outward movement of employment, and the marked tendency towards the centralization of business administration.

It is easy to see why heavy congestion results when commuter traffic is added to the already substantial quantities of commercial, pleasure, and other traffic passing through and journeying within central London. Most recent pressure has been experienced upon the roads, many of which were designed to carry far lighter traffic at far slower speeds. The problem should not be over-emphasized, however, since traffic has far from ground to a halt. Traffic-light control, parking restrictions, one-way flow systems, and minor road improvement have all contributed to continued traffic movement, which in fact flows more freely than in many other large cities of the world. But clearly, superficial reorganization of road use cannot continue to accommodate increasing traffic. Hence proposals for major road reconstruction, like the Inner Motorway Box. Such developments have the effect of displacing other land uses. They contribute to and reinforce the trend of outward moving population from the metropolitan centre.

PROBLEMS OF LAND

The problems of land, and of land allocation, are the sum of the employment, population, housing, and transport problems outlined above. The South East has the most rapidly expanding workforce in the British Isles. Its population is more densely distributed than elsewhere and, with the exception of central London, is increasing at a rate well above the national average. London's housing deficit is large and this, together with other social forces, has led to population overspill into the villages, towns and cities across the green belt. The increasing divorce of dwelling and workplace has encouraged a lengthening of work journeys, and this, in turn, has promoted traffic congestion, the relief of which will create pressure upon space in other parts of the region. All these are problems which produce an acute demand for land, and an intense competition between different uses of land.

In an attempt to solve some of these formidable problems, and in order to ensure that the strongest competitors are not always the winners in the battle for developable land (economically weak demands also deserve fair consideration) proposals for land-use control and for regional planning have evolved in the South East. They have been motivated by ideas of social justice and are based on the assumption that by organizing and planning land usage, a landscape will emerge more satisfying, and more efficient in meeting the needs of the greatest number, than one produced by chance, or by economic pressures alone. A survey of the major regional plans is contained in the following section.

Planning the Future

Ideas for planning the South East are not new. As London has grown, so increasing concern has been felt about the problems of central area congestion, of fringe development, and of the organization of the region as a whole. Towards the end of the last century a number of public figures, most of whom had a close association with the newly created London County Council, made concrete planning proposals for public recreation areas and for additional transport provision on London's fringe. Ebenezer Howard's garden city movement was also a great stimulus, since an integral part of the garden city concept was the balanced development of adjacent settlements in a comprehensive city-region system. Later in the 1920s and 1930s the continued growth of London and the loss of potential recreation land caused deep misgivings, and after several suggestions for remedy had been rejected, or simply 'shelved', an advisory local authority regional planning committee was established. The committee had the good fortune to appoint Sir Raymond Unwin as its technical adviser and he proceeded to prepare what, in effect, was the first wide-ranging, though outline, plan for London and its region. This contained proposals, among other things, for a more or less continuous parkland belt around London which was in principle, eventually adopted by the London County Council and safeguarded by an act of parliament.

But it was the general thinking behind Unwin's plan, rather than its detailed proposals, that had more lasting effect. Unwin's strategy was adopted by Sir Patrick Abercrombie when he, in turn, came to draw up an advisory plan for London in the 1940s, and it is from the Abercrombie plan that most of the planning ideas on the London region have been derived up to quite recently. Abercrombie viewed London and its region as composed of a number of concentric zones. The inner ring was badly congested and in need to redevelopment. From this area population would have to move outwards for resettlement under better conditions. The suburban ring, which covered the outer parts of the conurbation, would remain virtually static. Beyond it lay the green belt ring, a zone in which land was substantially undeveloped, and in which communities still maintained some semblance of individuality. Most distant from London was the outer country ring, where greatest provision was to be made to accommodate overspill from the conurbation. It was here that the new towns and expanded towns were to be built.

Abercrombie's plan became the basis of post-war local authority planning in the South East, or for all but the outer sections of the present region. As time passed it became clear that some of the estimates on which the plan was founded were less than fully accurate and meanwhile new factors and trends arose which Abercrombie could not have foreseen. The increasing pressure upon land which resulted led eventually to a comprehensive rethinking of regional policy for the South East.

It began with the *South East Study 1961–1981*, a broadly-based investigation into the problems of the South East carried out by the planning ministry in the early 1960s. The report is essentially orthodox in its approach. In many ways it is the Abercrombie plan on a larger scale. It recognizes and defines the population pressure in the region and proposes to accommodate the projected increases partly by normal additions to existing settlements, controlled by the usual planning processes, partly also by creating a second generation of new and expanded towns, conceived on a much larger scale and sited further from London than the new towns of the late 1940s. It was hoped that the new settlements would act as counter-magnets to London and draw away both population and economic activity from the overcrowded and overcentralized conurbation.

Early in 1965 new economic planning regions were defined. Within each region the Secretary of State for Economic Affairs appointed an economic planning council the duty of which was to act as an advisory body to the government upon economic and physical planning. In the South East region the Council was both swift and radical. It was the first to produce a long term physical plan for its area; a plan which was remarkable because in a number of respects it suggested major departures from earlier thinking.

Instead of the series of scattered overspill centres, large and small, proposed by the planning ministry, the Council envisaged a pattern of development based upon sectors following the main radial routes out of London. Substantial growth corridors led urban and industrial deveolpment towards the major expansion areas of Ashford–East Kent, Ipswich–Colchester, Northampton –Milton Keynes, and Southampton–Portsmouth. Minor corridors stretched in the direction of Brighton, Hitchin, and Southend. The existing green belt, it was suggested, should be retained and the physical extension of London restricted. Green 'buffers' were recommended between the growth sectors and also between individual urban agglomerations within the sectors, and a number of largely rural areas were proposed as Main Country Zones. In choosing a corridor plan the Council clearly indicated its feeling that a different strategy was required. It was a change of emphasis designed to bring the development of the London region very much closer to that planned for Copenhagen, Hamburg, Paris, Stockholm, and Washington D.C., than to the model outlined by Abercrombie and his predecessors.

Shortly after the publication of the Economic Planning Council's proposals a planning team was set up to review the relative merits of the alternative strategies, and to produce a new regional plan for the South East. The report appeared early in 1970, and followed neither of the earlier recommendations closely. It deliberately set out to create a highly flexible system in which growth points of varying size and at varying distances from London, were envisaged in most sectors of the region outside the green belt. At the growth points expansion was to be sharply focused so that a maximum of undeveloped land could be maintained.

The new outline plan is still subject to further revision. But whatever the outcome, it is too much to expect that all the planning problems of London and its surrounding region will finally be solved. At best a new plan wi impose a fresh order, will reduce land-use conflict, and will go some way t maximizing the personal welfare of the population of the region. In an are where such dynamic social, economic, and geographical forces interplay th would be achievement indeed.

FURTHER READING

J. T. Coppock and H. C. Prince, *Greater London* (London, 1964).
T. J. Chandler, *The Climate of London* (London, 1965).
D. L. Foley, *Controlling London's Growth* (Berkeley, 1963).
P. Hall, *London 2000* (London, 1963); *The World Cities* (London, 1966).
J. E. Martin, *Greater London: an Industrial Geography* (London, 1966).
Ministry of Housing and Local Government, *The Green Belts* (H.M.S.O., 1962); *The South East Study* (H.M.S.O., 1964).
South East Economic Planning Council, *A Strategy for the South East* (H.M.S.O., 1967).
South East Joint Planning Team, *Strategic Plan for the South East* (H.M.S.O., 1970).
D. Thomas, *London's Green Belt* (London, 1970).

The South West

The South West region is not only the second largest of the English Economic Planning regions, with an area larger than that of Wales, but it is also a long region, extending at least 328 kilometres (205 miles) from north-east to south-west. There are 177 kilometres (110 miles) between Gloucester and Exeter, and another 180 kilometres (112 miles) between Exeter and Penzance. These distances arise from its peninsular nature which provides also a coastline of 1,126 kilometres (700 miles) including two-thirds of the best coastline scenery of England and Wales (Plate 34). The location of the peninsula in the south-

Plate 34 Bude (Cornwall)

The cliffs up to 45 metres (148 feet) high expose the underlying Culm Measures shales which are clearly planed by the coastal plateau between 30 and 45 metres (100–148 feet) in the foreground and at approximately 120 metres (393 feet) in the distance. The crenulate coast enclosing bays of sand and shingle and sharply incised valleys are characteristic of much of the peninsula. The large valley of the Stra provided the site for the development of the holiday industry of Bude (Bude-Stratton; 5629) and some of the twentieth century hotels are evident on the clif tops on the margin of the town.

west of England dictates that it is climatically mild, that it includes areas with a 9–12 months growing season (Fig. 13), and that it is in part exposed to the Atlantic. The variety of the coastline, including deep sheltered harbours, provided a rich maritime history and a formerly well-distributed fishing industry. Although minerals were available for exploitation inland, the region is notable for the absence of the heavy industry that emerged in other parts of nineteenth century Britain. The manifest influence of the sea coupled with the absence of heavy industry in this climatically-favoured part of England provides a region where the holiday industry has prospered, so that today some 25 per cent of its land area is covered by National Parks or Areas of Outstand-

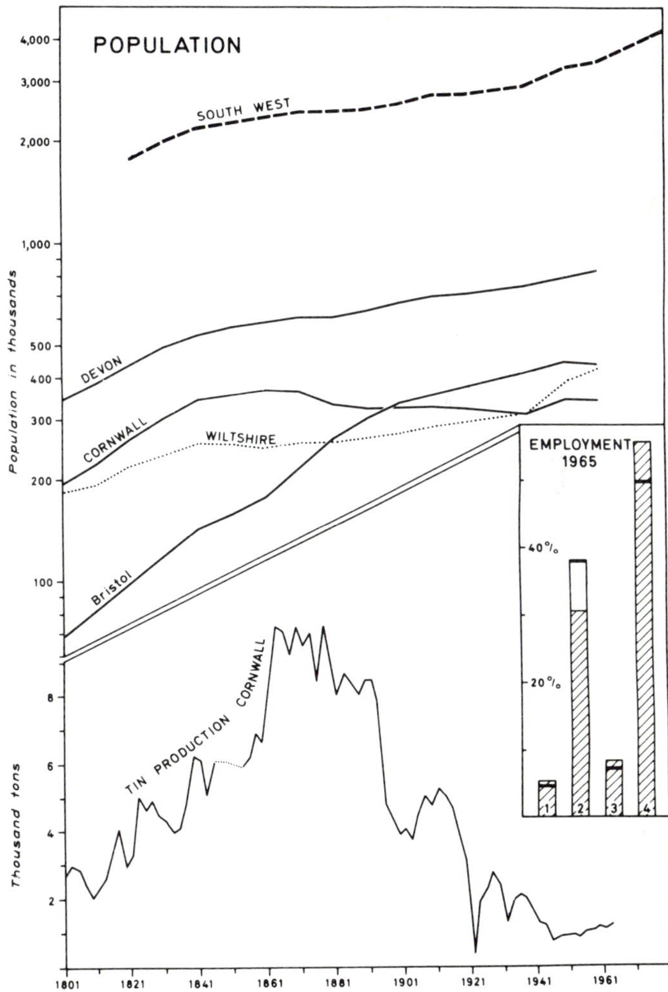

Fig 39 Trends Relevant to Parts of the South West
Employment (1965) compares the region (shaded) with the average for Great Britain (heavy line). Key to numbers: 1—Extractive industries (agriculture, forestry, fishing, mining, quarrying), 2—Manufacturing industries, 3—Construction, 4—Service industries.

ing Natural Beauty, and within it about 20 per cent of the holidays of British people are spent, mostly focused upon the coast. These broad characteristics of the region are reflected in the present population density (153 per square kilometre; 402 per square mile) which is lower than the average for England and Wales (Table 11). In 1821 the region contained 14·6 per cent of the population of England and Wales, until 1931 growth was lower than the national rate and in some areas such as Cornwall population declined (Fig. 39). After 1939 population increased at nearly double the national rate and in 1964 the region included 7·6 per cent of the population of England and Wales. This recent trend is paralleled by employment increase, but unemployment rates still exceed the national average. Employment is less in manufacturing industries than elsewhere in Great Britain, but it is greater in the other three categories (Fig. 39) despite the high proportion of elderly people in a region adopted as a retirement area. There are few large towns, and only Bristol (425,203; 1971) and Plymouth (239,452; 1971) substantially exceed 100,000 population, but smaller towns are numerous especially in the east.

TABLE 11
SOUTH WEST

	South West Peninsula (Counties of Cornwall, Devon and W. Somerset)	*West* (Wiltshire, Dorset, Gloucestershire, parts of Somerset)	*South West*	*England and Wales*
South West Economic Planning Council Sub-Regions 1967	Western, Southern	Northern, Central	—	—
Area, per cent	46	54	100	—
Population 1965	1,212,500	2,444,200	100	—
(per cent)	(33·2)	(66·8)		
Average Population				
Density, per sq. km.	107	207	158	316
(per sq. mile)	(279)	(538)	(409)	(818)
Percentage of population (1964) 65 and over (males) 60 and over (females)	19·8	16·1	17·4	*Great Britain* 15·1
Employment 1965, Percentage				
Agriculture and Quarrying	8·4	4·3	5·4	4·8
Manufacturing Industry	19·2	34·8	30·3	38·2
Construction	8·9	8·3	8·5	7·2
Services	63·5	52·6	55·8	49·8
Agricultural Land use 1964, Percentage				
Grassland	62·6	66·1	64·5	50·5
Tillage	19·3	26·5	23·3	32·9
Rough Grazing	19·1	7·3	12·2	16·6

Despite these general features, the region embraces two personalities. The 'West Country' has been variously perceived, usually including the counties of Cornwall and Devon, but less frequently, the counties of Somerset, Dorset and Wiltshire. Gloucestershire is seldom included. The distinction between peninsular south-west 'set in silver', and the remainder of the region was incorporated in 1967 in the four sub-regions devised by the South West Economic Planning Council (Table 11). A northern sub-region included Bristol–Severnside, Swindon and Gloucester–Cheltenham, and a central sub-region extended over predominantly rural parts of Dorset, Somerset and Wiltshire. Together these two regions are distinct in many ways from the western sub-region embracing the northern part of the peninsula from west Cornwall to Bridgwater Bay, and from the southern sub-region which includes Plymouth, Torbay and Exeter. The differences between the west and the peninsular south-west are long established, and have intensified recently as Bristol–Bath and Gloucester–Cheltenham have become more closely linked with the West Midlands (M.5) and with South Wales (M.4). In the south-east centres such as Poole look to Bournemouth and Southampton, reflecting their former inclu-

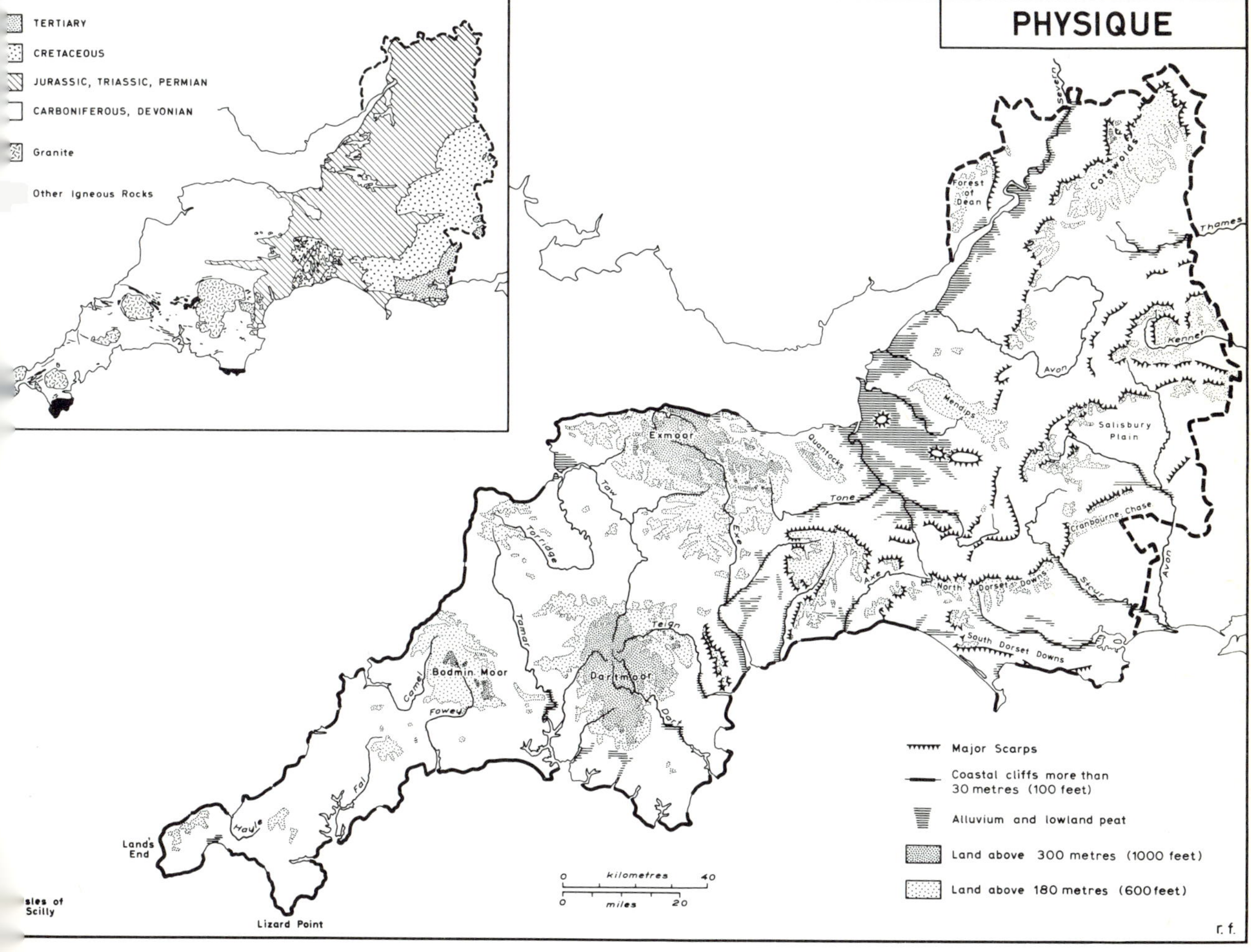

Fig 40 South West—Physique

sion within Wessex. Whereas the west has divided loyalties, the south-west peninsula is united anomalously by its greater isolation, which will hardly be changed by the planned extension of the M.5 to Exeter. The south-west peninsula is characterised by a smaller share of the total population, and so by a lower population density, by a larger proportion of elderly people, by fewer manufacturing industries, and by greater employment in services (Table 11).

Environments and their Evolution

The reality of the two parts of the south-west region is long acknowledged by the traditional boundary of the highland and lowland zones of Britain, which reaches the south coast at Exeter. West of Exeter Palaeozoic rocks provide a cliff-bounded plateau landscape contrasting with the scarplands predominant on the younger rock outcrops to the east (Fig. 40). Small distinctive regions occur throughout, but those of the scarplands frequently echo themes apparent in central and southern England, whereas the components of the peninsula are more individual.

THE WEST

This area may, for convenience, be regarded as extending east of Exmoor and of east Devon, over the counties of Gloucestershire, Wiltshire and Dorset and over much of Somerset. Here the Jurassic scarplands and the Cretaceous cuestas are closer than in other parts of England and a transect from the Bristol channel to the south coast includes three notable elements: the Severn valley and the Bristol channel margins, the Jurassic scarplands of the Cotswolds, and the Chalk downlands. The pattern of escarpments (Fig. 40) is more complex than this simple division suggests, but the scarps usually face north-west and the dip slopes decline in height south-eastwards to clay vales. Areas with well-developed characters diversify the broad picture, not only as a result of the intricate pattern of rock outcrops, but also because of their drainage patterns; for example, the drainage of the Severn to the Bristol channel with its north-west flowing rivers, the eastward drainage of the Thames and Kennet, and the southward-draining rivers such as the Salisbury Avon and Stour (Fig. 40).

The River Severn flows in a broad valley of low relief notable for the extensive gravels which frequently mask the Liassic and Triassic clays of the vale of Gloucester. Close to the margin of the Bristol Channel, the Vales of Berkeley and Sodbury continue the character of this vale and are all typically the domain of dairy farms, pasture land and orchards. The rock valley floor of the Severn decreases to a height of —18 metres (—60 feet) below present sea level. The valley was drowned by the post-glacial rise of sea level which also inundated adjacent areas now mapped as areas of alluvium and lowland peat (Fig. 40). Notable among such areas are the Somerset Levels, which are seldom more than 3 metres (10 feet) above high tide, are underlain by marine clays, peat and alluvial deposits, and are only occasionally diversified by willow-lined channels or broken by protuberances of the solid geology of the Lias which appears at Glastonbury Tor, Brent Knoll and the Polden Hills. The present land use, largely grass for dairy and beef cattle, is a testimony to continued attempts to drain the levels. Such attempts were intensified after 1770, and since 1939 work has enabled the extent of seasonal flooding to be reduced.

Beyond the low-lying margins of the Bristol Channel a number of small distinctive areas diversify the area west of the Cotswold scarp. West of the Severn is the Forest of Dean extending eastwards from the incised meanders of the Wye valley and including several prominent north-south trending ridges developed on Old Red Sandstone conglomerates which are frequently wooded. Woodland, which includes hardwoods as well as the more recent coniferous plantations, is still prominent in the landscape, and the area has been a National Forest Park since 1938. Soils are thin, farms are often small, and the Carboniferous rocks provided an exposed coalfield which was exploited from the thirteenth century until the last mine closed in 1965. These rocks also included pockets of iron ore which were exploited in the nineteenth century. Recreation in the area is now a fourth ingredient of the interwoven pattern of timber production, farming and the legacy of mining within the landscape. Varied relief near Bristol is also partly underlain by Carboniferous coal measures. These outcrop in several areas and gave rise to the Bristol coalfield north of the river Avon, which produced 541,000 metric tons (532,000 long tons) in 1870 but subsequently declined, and to the Somerset coalfield centred on Radstock and Midsomer Norton, which reached a peak production of 1,227,000 metric tons (1,208,000 long tons) in 1910, and declined until 1950 when some production stabilized after modernization. The direct impact of coal-mining upon the landscape is surprisingly small partly because the coal-field did not attract associated heavy industry. Carboniferous rocks also underly the Mendips where the building materials, the scars and the disused lead and zinc workings betray the underlying limestone. Sheep farming, originally dominant, has been complemented more recently by mixed and dairy farming, and limestone is still reflected in the quarrying activities producing some 7·8 million metric tons (7·7 million long tons) annually, in water supply, and in recreation in the area which focuses particularly upon Cheddar and its gorge. The Quantocks provide a further prominent area which rises to a maximum of 384 metres (1,261 feet) comparable with the summit of the Mendips at 325 metres (1,067 feet), but the Quantocks are composed of Devonian rocks, are bounded by steep, heavily-wooded slopes and are not crossed by any major roads.

The Forest of Dean, the Bristol area, the Mendips and the Quantocks introduce elements which diversify the lowlands largely underlain by Keuper Marl and Lias clays, and which extend from the low-lying fringes of the Bristol Channel to the west-facing Cotswold scarp. This scarp is often a prominent feature, reaching a maximum height of 326 metres (1,070 feet) at Cleeve Hill. In the north it is formed by the Inferior Oolite and in the south, near Bath, by the Great Oolite. The dip slope of the Cotswold cuesta is bleak in the most elevated parts, possesses thin stony soils, and was originally the domain of sheep and barley, but cereals are now dominant. Local limestone provided the material and the Cotswold woollen industry provided one of the reasons to utilize that material for the buildings which impart such a distinctive character to the settlements, for example, Cirencester, Dursley and Minchinhampton. These developed particularly in the fourteenth to sixteenth centuries when the woollen industry took advantage of local wool production and of the fast-flowing Cotswold streams. The industry declined in competition with Yorkshire but several concerns survive near Stroud. The development of spa towns included Cheltenham, which increased in population from 3,000 to 13,000 in the first twenty years of the nineteenth century, and Bath with fine Regency crescents of buildings of local Cotswold (Bath) stone which have, according to J. B. Priestley, discovered 'the trick of keeping the lost sunlight of centuries glimmering upon them'. Between the Inferior and Great Oolite limestones are beds of Fullers Earth which were exploited for cleansing wool cloth by the woollen industry, and are still worked today for use in chemical and textile industries. South of the Mendips the Cotswold escarpment is continued by two scarps or bench-like features. Yeovil occurs at the foot of the first scarp, which is succeeded by the Fullers Earth Clay vale and then by a higher scarp of Forest Marble, the upper part of the Great Oolite Series.

Beyond the landscapes of the Oolite Series lie the several portions of the Oxford Clay vale outcrop. In the south, immediately north of the North Dorset Downs (Fig. 40) is the Vale of Blackmore, which is the heavy clay land described by Thomas Hardy in *Tess of the d'Urbervilles*. This portion of the vale is drained south by the Stour, whereas, to the north, the vale near Chippenham and Melksham is drained by the Bristol Avon and further northwards still, by the headwaters of the Thames. East of the low-lying claylands there is often a tract of varied relief before the Chalklands are reached and this may include a small discontinuous cuesta developed on Corallian limestones, as between Calne and Westbury and across the Vale of Wardour, which is followed by a further clay vale floored by Kimmeridge Clay. Swindon, a town which has grown substantially (32 per cent increase in population 1951 to 1961) during the last twenty years, is located on the Kimmeridge clay near the junction with the Corallian cuesta.

Chalk downlands are perhaps the most distinctive of English scarpland landscapes, and the smooth rounded slopes with grey-white soils and occasional splashes of white Chalk exposed, have prompted its description as 'frozen sea' (Plate 35). Despite its early settlement, evidenced at Avebury and Stonehenge, the Chalklands were enclosed late and now have large fenced fields on the thin rendzina soils. Settlements are usually located near scarp-foot springs or in valley floor sites. Cheese was traditionally produced on the farms of the clay vales to the west and the contrast of those areas with the Chalk prompted the Wiltshire saying 'as different as Chalk and cheese'. Some of the most extensive tracts of Chalkland in England are represented by Marlborough Downs, Salisbury Plain, Cranbourne Chase, and the North and South Dorset Downs. Although smooth rounded outlines are common to each, diversity is introduced in several ways. The escarpment bordering the chalklands, locally as much as 165 metres (541 feet) above the clay vale, is sometimes broken into two scarps (Fig. 40) by the Lower and Upper Chalk

Plate 35 The Downs (Wiltshire)
The widely-recognized rounded outlines of the chalk landscape are evident in this photograph. Large farms, large fields with barley crops and leys (carrying cattle) are typical.

Superficial deposits of clay-with-flints sometimes provide areas of heavier soils. Anticlinal folds within the Chalk have sometimes been breached to give further variety in vales, such as those of Wardour, Warminster and Pewsey, with steep, inward-facing escarpments which confront one another across the intervening clay vale. The Chalk and Cretaceous rocks overstepped the underlying older rocks unconformably and so in east Devon the Chalk is now absent and the east Devon plateau is composed of Upper Greensand. Where erosion has succeeded in cutting through the Cretaceous rocks, Liassic clays may be exposed and may produce distinctive flat-floored valleys or distinctive areas such as the Vale of Marshwood.

Thomas Hardy in his regional novels characterized the landscapes of the clay lands, of the chalk lands and also of the heathlands. These heathlands occur south-east of the North Dorset Downs (Fig. 40) where poor soils on the sands, gravels and clays of the Tertiary rocks fringing the Hampshire basin have produced a landscape of unenclosed heathland, afforestation and some farming, relieved only by the more luxuriant valleys of the Piddle, Frome and Stour lined by water meadows. The South Dorset Downs give way southwards to an area where Jurassic rocks arranged in east to west outcrops give belted topography with a similar trend. Two islands figure in the southernmost part of this area. The 'Isle of Purbeck' is an island only in so far as its outcrop of Portland and Purbeck beds are separated from the Tertiary heaths to the north by a Chalk ridge, whereas the Island of Portland which has quarried outcrops of Portland Stone is linked to the mainland by a tombolo which continues Chesil Beach. The differential resistance of the rocks apparent in the belted topography inland is even more vividly expressed in the coast, particularly at Lulworth Cove and at Worbarrow Bay.

Plate 36 Falmouth (Cornwall)
Falmouth is located on the side of an arm of the Fal ria and the docks are an important element in the town economy, which is centred upon marine activities, including ship repairing and engineering, and upon the holiday trade.

THE SOUTH-WEST PENINSULA

The length of coastline and the variety of cliff, beach and ria which it contains are a concomitant of the peninsular character of Devon and Cornwall. Much of the coastline is cliffed, some 86 per cent of the coast of Cornwall being represented by cliffs more than 16 metres (50 feet) high, but the cliffs vary in height and are separated by numerous bays and coves, diversified by beaches of sand or shingle and by valleys which may be drowned as rias, such as the Fal, Tamar and Dart, important for the growth of Falmouth (Plate 36), of Plymouth and of Dartmouth. Inland valleys are typically steep-sided and often flat-floored; the name Devon is derived from a British word meaning deep valleys. The trend of the valleys is dominantly north-west to south-east across the peninsula and at right angles to the predominant direction of population movement. Whereas scarpland is the key theme in much of the area to the east,

Plate 37 Hay Tor, Dartmoor (Devon)

This large tor is located on the 320–410 metre (1,050–1,345 feet) planation surface. In the background on the lower areas there occurs an example of the basin and interfluve morphology so typical of granite outcrops.

Plate 38 Exmoor (Somerset)

The headwaters of the Exe. The planation surface between 320 and 350 metres (1,050–1,150 feet) is snow-covered and bounded by the coniferous plantations in the steep valley side slopes which give way to gentler slopes of the valley floors. The field shapes and their pattern reflect the late enclosure of parts of Exmoor. Unenclosed land still provides a significant area of the National Park as indicated in the top right hand corner.

in this peninsula region, plateau is dominant. Immediately inland from the coast are areas of coastal plateau (Plate 34) usually between 60 and 140 metres (197–460 feet) in height and planed indiscriminately across resistant rocks in areas like the Lizard peninsula and the South Hams, south of Dartmoor. On the higher areas uniform summits recording Tertiary planation surfaces are extensively apparent, at levels between 230 and 290 metres (755–951 feet) and between 305 and 400 metres (1,000–1,312 feet) on the higher areas. Although deep valleys, varied coastline and plateau surfaces are common to most parts of the peninsula, there are contrasts such as that between the exposed windswept landscape of Cornwall and the softer more rounded outlines of Devon, and, like Brittany far to the south, there is often a contrast between the coast and the inland areas. Other contrasts are geologically inspired and arise from the fact that younger rocks in east Devon contrast with the older and more resistant ones further west, and that six areas rise above the general plateau levels of the peninsula.

The first of these, Exmoor, is underlain by a variety of Devonian grits, shales and sandstones and is a tableland on which several distinct planation surfaces have been recognized. From many viewpoints the deep dissection by valleys is not always evident. South of the highest parts of the moor at 520 metres (1,705 feet) drainage is southwards to the Exe basin, and a consequence of this is that the northern coast terminates in impressive cliffs as much as 150 metres (483 feet) high, and the northward-draining valleys such as the Lyn and the Heddon are very deeply incised and often have well-wooded slopes. The early enclosure of the valleys has produced fields which contrast with the larger more regular fields (Plate 38) enclosed in the early nineteenth century after the sale of 'Exmoor Forest' had allowed enclosure to encroach upon the unenclosed heart of the moor. The Exmoor landscape of deep dissection, enclosed and heath-covered plateau was designated a National Park in 1954.

Dartmoor is similarly elevated above the general level of the peninsula, reaching a maximum elevation of 621 metres (2,038 feet). It is characterized by remnants of three planation surfaces but unlike Exmoor it is underlain by granite. This dictates a different surface expression and typically Dartmoor is composed of an alternation of shallow basins and tor-crowned interfluves (Plate 37), the steepest slopes often occurring on the surrounding metamorphosed rocks where the radiating rivers leave the moor in deep gorges. Like Exmoor, Dartmoor is well-endowed with precipitation and receives between 1,220 and 2,160 millimetres (48–85 inches) each year. It has a landscape of afforestation, of reservoirs, of quarries and of unenclosed land and was designated a National Park in 1951. Unlike Exmoor the fringes of Dartmoor possessed reserves of tin and copper which until the nineteenth century contributed to the growth of the surrounding towns, such as Ashburton, Chagford and Tavistock. The Bovey Basin, adjacent to Dartmoor, is infilled by lignites and clays of Tertiary age (Fig. 40) which support woodland, heath or poor pasture and provide ball clays which are exploited for use in making earthenware, sanitary ware and tiles (Fig. 41). In the south-west of Dartmoor itself are large quantities of china-clay (kaolin) which are exploited, largely for export, and locally employ some 800 men. The remaining four prominent areas of the peninsula are Bodmin Moor, St. Austell Moor (Hensbarrow),

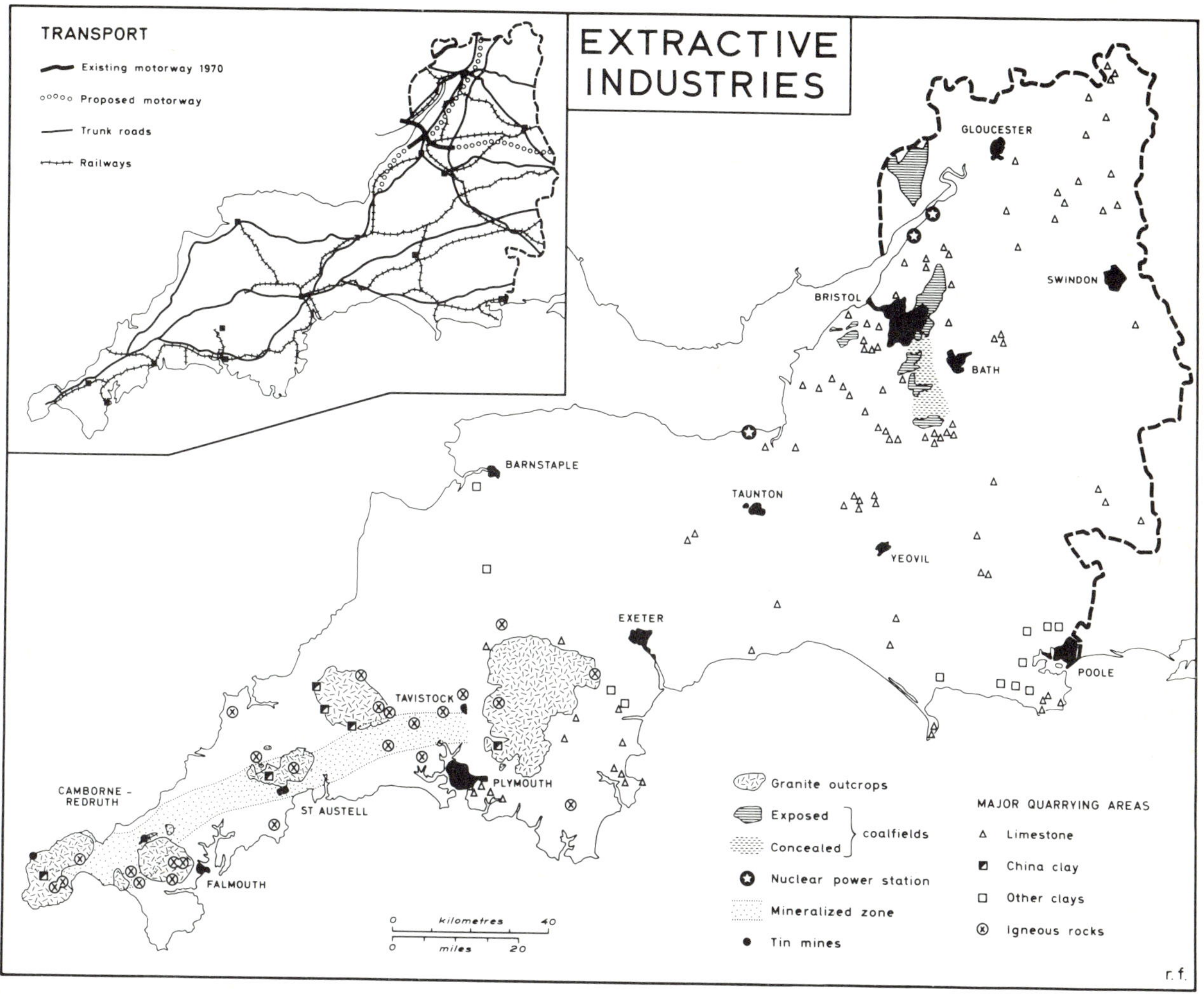

Fig 41 South-West—Major Extractive Industries and Transport
The position of major extractive industries working in 1970 is shown. The mineralized zone in Cornwall was the location for many former mining enterprises. Two existing tin mines are indicated but other trial works are not included. Settlements are indicated as squares on the transport map and these correspond to the centres named on the larger map. The motorway south-west of Bristol is now proposed to be extended to a point immediately west of Exeter.

Carnmenellis and the Land's End peninsula. Each of these areas is underlain by granite, they echo some of the landscape and land use themes presented by Dartmoor, but they become progressively lower in elevation westwards.

Bodmin Moor presents a landscape partly unenclosed and punctuated by tors, which is used largely for pastoral farming and for water supply, and includes granite quarries and china clay pits. In the surrounding areas, especially on the south and east, former tin streaming and mining is evidenced. Past mining and the contemporary extraction of china clay dominate the landscape of St. Austell Moor (Hensbarrow), and are represented visually by the numerous open pits, the mounds of waste and the buildings associated with refining and drying the china clay. Associated with the paper-making and the pottery industries, this extractive industry has not only imparted a distinctive contribution to the landscape of the granite area, but its influence has extended to the coast in the ports of Par, Charlestown and Fowey, and to the recent growth of St. Austell (25,074; 1961). Carnmenellis rises to 256 metres (825 feet) and its adjacent granite outcrops of Tregonning Hill and Carn Brea have unenclosed summits, but it was in the surrounding area of the mineralized zone (Fig. 41) that the ores of tin and copper were exploited, especially in the nineteenth century (Fig. 39), and prompted growth of associated industries in the area between Camborne and Redruth. Mining was also formerly important in the sixth area, the Land's End granite outcrop. The legacy of nineteenth century mining now presents a problem in the form of the reclamation of derelict land, and 16 per cent of the officially declared derelict land of England and Wales lies in west and north Cornwall. The decline in production continued from 1880 to 1920 when colonial sources of tin led to a fall in world tin prices, but recently the high price of tin has encouraged renewed prospecting to supplement the output of the two mines which still exist at Geevor and South Crofty (Fig. 41). The six areas, five of them founded upon granite, are prominent above the plateau of the peninsula, and to them a seventh area may be added, namely the Isles of Scilly, 45 kilometres (28 miles) west of Land's End. They include five inhabited islands and exemplify an island group where chemical weathering was directed by joint spacing, and this followed by erosion between the islands. The landscape of the islands is given character by the growing of early flowers in fields enclosed by hedges of pittosporum or escallonia, and this activity of the early part of the year is complemented by the holiday industry from March to October.

Much of the remainder of Cornwall is a plateau landscape characteristically between 60 and 140 metres (197–460 feet) which is dissected by steep-sided valleys, such as the Fowey, which drain to the drowned estuaries of the coast. Formerly the inland farming landscape was diversified by mining and quarrying and the coast possessed numerous fishing settlements, but these have been superseded by the tourist industry which has extended inland to some extent. Much of lowland Cornwall is underlain by Devonian rocks, some extracted as, for example, the slates between Delabole and Tintagel, but the area of central Devon between Exmoor and Dartmoor is underlain by Culm Measures of Carboniferous age which include shales, some sandstones and some grits. The shales support heavy-textured soils which are difficult to drain and equally difficult to farm for dairy and beef cattle. Some of the area remains in heathland while forestry is important locally, and Tertiary deposits of sand, lignite and ball clay in the Petrockstow basin provide workings reminiscent of those at Bovey Tracey. Two further landscapes are represented in Devon. Outcrops of New Red Sandstone south of Tiverton and embracing the lower Exe basin are betrayed by the soil colour of 'Red Devon' giving some of the best farmland of the county and including the settlement of Exeter and those of Tiverton, Cullompton, Crediton and Honiton, formerly associated with the

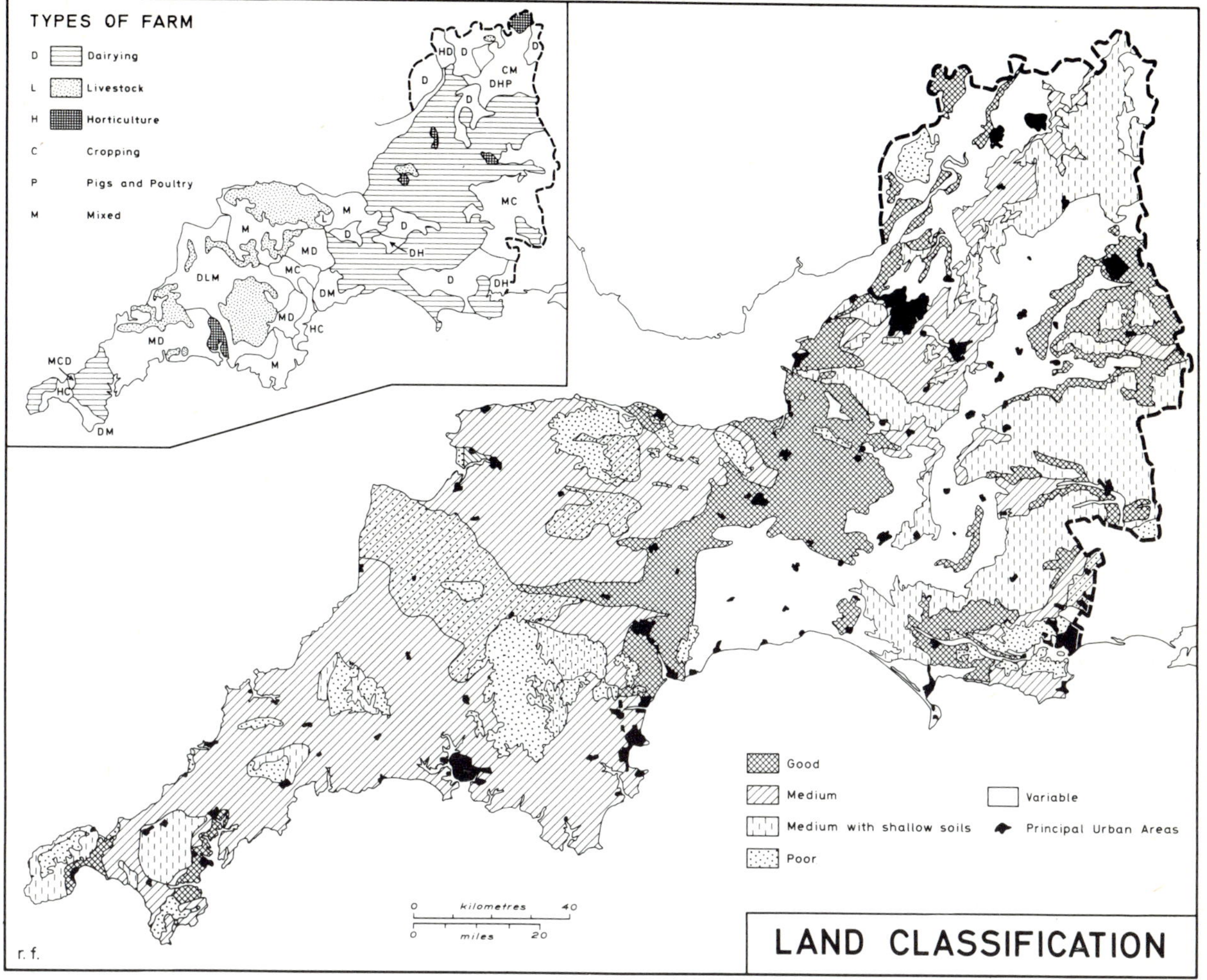

Fig 42 South-West—Land Classification and Types of Farm
Land classification is based upon the 1:625,000 Land Classification map of Great Britain. The category designated as *variable* includes some good land but changes are too frequent to allow detailed divisions to be shown. The types of farm according to dominant enterprise are based upon *A region with a future*, South West Economic Planning Council (H.M.S.O., 1967), p. 34. The map was based upon standard man days in 1964 for farms with labour requirements greater than 275 man days. Areas are shaded where one type of farm is dominant and in unshaded areas the most frequent types of farm are indicated by letters.

woollen industry which survived until the nineteenth century. Eastwards Red Devon gives way to the clay-with-flints covered east Devon plateau, which presents a landscape of heathland, forest and some farming, and is gradually replaced further eastwards by Chalk landscapes.

Occupations and the Present

Several themes emerge from the variety presented by the component landscapes of the South-West, notably the contrasts between east and west, the differences between coast and inland, and the paucity of heavy industry. These themes underly some facets of the character and distribution of farming, of manufacturing industry, and of population. The geographical patterns of the South-West can therefore be visualized in terms of residuals, positive and negative, from the pattern of past development.

The potential for agriculture is indicated by the land classification map (Fig. 42) which isolates the better quality land of Red Devon, of central Somerset and of parts of Gloucestershire, from that of much of the peninsula. The scarplands usually possess medium-quality land or are variable when alternations of land character are rapid in sympathy with soil type. The poorest quality land is found on the heaths of Dorset, in the Forest of Dean, on the heavy clays of central Devon and on parts of the granite uplands of the peninsula. The climatic advantages of mild winters, above average sunshine amounts and a reliably high rainfall give a long season for grass growth and so some 64 per cent of agricultural land is under grass. Dairying dominates on three-quarters of Dorset farms and on more than half of the farms in Somerset and Wiltshire. The 23·3 per cent of farmland under cultivation is unevenly distributed throughout the region and exceeds this percentage in Gloucestershire and on the Chalk of Wiltshire. Peninsular Devon and Cornwall have a pattern of land use faithfully reflecting the included terrain types but livestock farming dominates over an area noted for dairy products. Areas of specialization in horticulture are found on the Isles of Scilly, in west Cornwall, in the lower Tamar valley (Fig. 42) and also elsewhere in Gloucestershire and near urban centres such as Bristol. Fishing, for pilchards, mackerel and herring and its related industries, was until the nineteenth century an important activity of many of the coastal settlements of Cornwall and Devon. It is now much less widely distributed, but is still important in and near Newlyn and at Brixham which together account for half the landings of fish in the region. The contraction of the fishing industry is matched by a shrinkage in the distribution of the varied extractive industries (Fig. 41). Of the many rocks and minerals exploited in the past, China Clay, Ball Clay and limestone are still important and the future prospects for tin in Cornwall are being reconsidered at some localities.

The absence of heavy industry in the region combined with the presence of a long varied coastline and equally attractive inland scenery affording opportunities for bathing, walking and sailing, promoted the development of the holiday industry in the region. This was initiated in the eighteenth century, increased when visits to the continent were impossible, and was often located in settlements in which fishing was beginning to decline. After the mid-nineteenth century the industry expanded and was stimulated by the advent of the railways; the population of Torquay trebled between 1841 and 1871. By the mid-twentieth century the holiday industry was concentrated on the coasts of Cornwall and Devon, to a lesser degree on the coasts of Somerset and Dorset and at inland centres such as Bath and others in the Cotswolds. Since 1950 the source of holiday-makers has widened, the types of holiday and of accommodation available (Fig. 43) have diversified. It was estimated in 1965 that 20 per cent of the main holidays of the people of Great Britain were taken in this region and of those, nearly 90 per cent involved a stay in coastal resorts

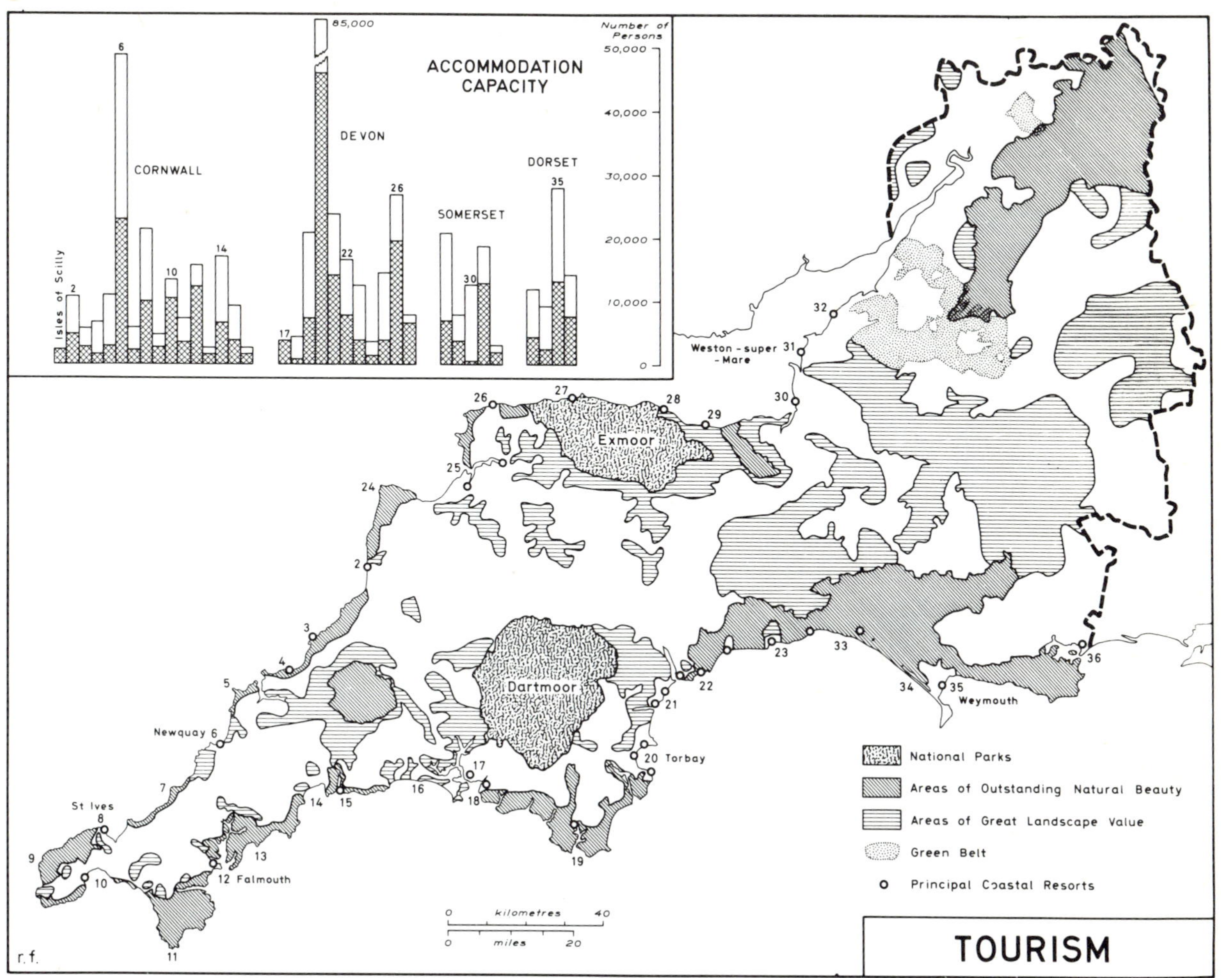

Fig 43 South-West—Tourism

Areas of Great Landscape Value are delineated by County Councils whereas National Parks and Areas of Outstanding Natural Beauty are nationally designated. The accommodation capacity of the coastal resorts is based upon *South West Tourist Study* (British Travel Association, 1969). Traditional accommodation including hotels is shaded, other forms of accommodation including holiday camps, self-catering forms, and caravans are unshaded. The resorts and areas are 2 – Bude, 3 – Tintagel, 4 – Port Isaac, 5 – Trevose Head, 6 – Newquay, 7 – St. Agnes Head, 8 – St. Ives, 9 – Land's End, 10 – Mounts Bay including Penzance, 11 – Lizard, 12 – Falmouth Bay, 13 – Nare Head, 14 – St. Austell Bay, 15 – Looe, 16 – Whitesand Bay, 17 – Plymouth, 18 – Plymstock, 19 – Kingsbridge, 20 – Torbay including Brixham, Paignton, Torquay, 21 – Teignmouth and Dawlish, 22 – Exmouth, Budleigh Salterton, 23 – Seaton, 24 – Hartland, 25 – Bideford, Barnstaple, 26 – Ilfracombe, 27 – Lynton, Lynmouth, 28 – Minehead, 29 – Watchet, 30 – Burnham-on-Sea, 31 – Weston-super-Mare, 32 – Clevedon, 33 – Lyme Regis, Bridport, 34 – Chesil Beach, 35 – Weymouth, 36 – Poole.

such as those of Weymouth, Torbay, Newquay and Ilfracombe (Fig. 43). East of the Exe estuary there are 833 visitors each year per kilometre of coastline (1,340 per mile) and between the Exe and Dart estuaries there are 2,816 per kilometre (4,530 per mile). Problems arising from the holiday industry include the facts that some 90 per cent of the holiday visitors travel by road and only 10 per cent by train, that there is a large accommodation surplus except for the peak period from mid-June to mid-September, and that within this period the volume of traffic reaches a sharp maximum level on Saturdays. Solutions advocated to the problems include improvements in accommodation and in amenities, diversification of the types of holiday to supplement traditional beach and sunshine holidays, and improvements in the capacity of the road network. The significance of the holiday industry is underlined by the fact that holiday expenditure in Devon and Cornwall each year (excluding travel) is approximately equal to the manufacturing output of the two counties.

The absence of extensive nineteenth century industrial development is a negative residual of past development and is a reason for continuing adjustments throughout the South-West region. The present distribution of industry reflects the resources of the region and the woollen industry survives in the textile manufacturing of centres such as Stroud and Tiverton. The sea stimulated the marine engineering industries of Falmouth and Plymouth, and the tropical manufactures of Bristol (Plate 39). Agriculture provided the basis for food-processing industries such as those of Calne; mining in west Cornwall prompted engineering at Camborne, for example; and the railway junction of Swindon provided the basis for railway engineering. The pattern of survivals was later augmented in the twentieth century by the development of the aircraft industry in Bristol, by the expansion after 1945 of aerospace and engineering industries in Bristol, Cheltenham, Gloucester and in other parts of Gloucestershire, and by the growth of electrical and electronic engineering industries in Swindon since the London overspill agreement. Small industries figure throughout the region but more need to be attracted, particularly to the peninsula, to broaden the range of employment, to arrest the movement of young people out of the region and to alleviate the seasonal unemployment problem. Incentives for this are provided by the development area status given to the western part of the region (Fig. 44) but this positive influence has to balance the negative influence of the absence of reserves of skilled labour and of good communications.

Prospects and the Future

Recent trends in population change (Fig. 44) are likely to be continued in the immediate future. Recent population increase has been greatest in the northern and eastern parts of the region, focused for example upon Taunton, Bridgwater, Bristol, Bath, Chippenham, Swindon and upon Poole and Salisbury, as well as in smaller areas around Yeovil, Exeter, Barnstaple and Plymouth-Torbay. These areas of increase have been complemented by areas of decrease in west and eastern Cornwall and in central Devon. The general

Plate 39 Bristol

The site of Bristol (425,203; 1971) and the Avon gorge where the river cuts through the Carboniferous Limestone and is crossed by the Clifton suspension bridge. The docks, 13 kilometres (8 miles) from the sea, are a significant reminder of the early importance (1500–1750) of overseas trade particularly across the Atlantic which gave rise to the industries processing tobacco, chocolate and sugar. By 1400 Bristol was the second greatest seaport in England and the city was the third richest in England by 1790. The port declined in the early nineteenth century, but deepwater facilities were subsequently afforded by Avonmouth (1877) and Portishead (1879). Today imports of grain, oil, ores, timber and tobacco are much more important than exports.

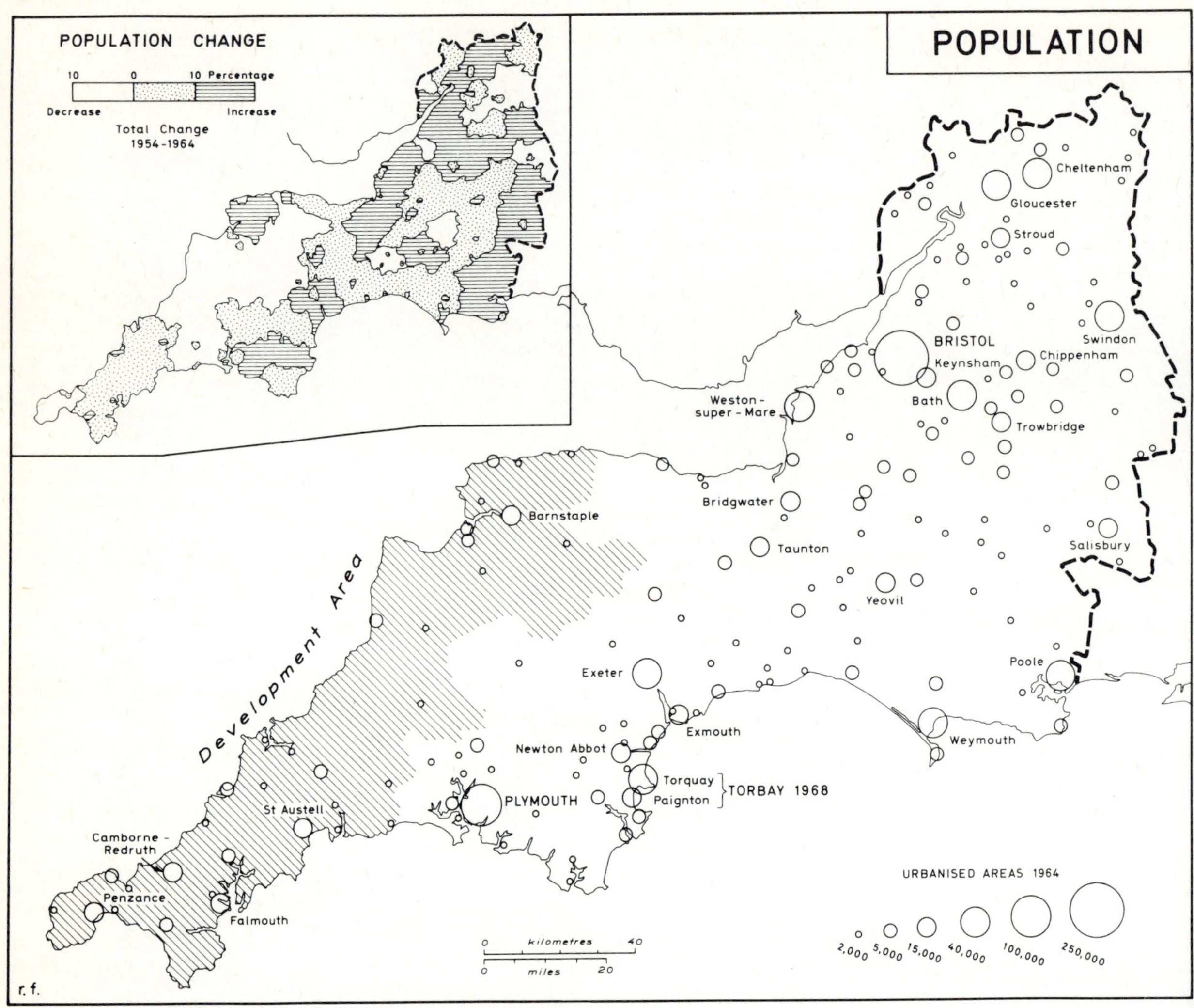

Fig 44 South-West—Population
Urbanized areas are shown in six categories according to their population in 1964. The map of population change is based upon a map in *A region with a future*, South West Economic Planning Council (H.M.S.O., 1967).

contrast between the peninsula and the remainder of the region is emphasized by the map of population changes (Fig. 44) and this contrast is likely to be sustained in the future. The transport network (Fig. 41) which substantially affects the potential of the region, has recently been improved so that Bristol is now linked with the West Midlands by the M.5 motorway, with South Wales by the M.4 (Severn Bridge) and with London by the M.4 eastwards. This should encourage appreciable growth on Severnside. Opportunity for future development is provided by the accessibility of Severnside to the South-East region and to the West Midlands, and is emphasized because Severnside is one of the few remaining estuarine locations available for development in Great Britain, and which has flat land available on the margin of the estuary. The estuary itself could furnish port facilities and ample water for cooling purposes. Expansion of this area could continue the rapid growth in population and employment which has occurred since the early 1950s and it has been estimated (1971) that whereas the area of Severnside would, according to recent trends, increase from its present population of 1,650,000 to 2,300,000 by 2001, no major problems would arise in accommodating 2,650,000 by 2001. Such an accelerated growth could be achieved by development based upon the large centres of Bristol, Gloucester, and Newport, each forming an urban sub-region embraced within a new and substantial green belt system. The necessary expansion could take place to the north-east of Bristol, to the north of Newport, and to the west of Gloucester which would possibly employ a new town organization.

The south-eastern parts of the region including Poole may be expected to prosper in the light of development in Southampton and in the South-East. Elsewhere in the region it is necessary to improve the present position of agriculture, by amalgamation of holdings and by the increased productivity of hill farms, and to develop the holiday industry by offering a wider range of amenities inland as well as on the coast and by appreciating the fact that as leisure time increases, the area may increasingly be used for second, as well as for main, holidays. A further improved transport network is required to achieve these ends, and is even more relevant to attracting new industries and employment to supplement the present situation. The diversification of the employment structure, in Plymouth, for example, where 20 per cent reliance was placed upon the naval dockyard, and the reduction in the number of young people leaving the area could be achieved by attracting new industry to an area which offers a pleasant environment and adequate land. These inducements will probably be most attractive to light industries which are least affected by transport costs. The M.5 motorway is proposed to reach Exeter in 1975; the A.38 to Plymouth and its continuation to Penzance is being improved, but a new spine road is advocated as a necessary long-term solution to the problems of the present transport network. This must be accompanied by improved road links east of Exeter to London and the South-East. Perhaps the great resource of this region is a negative one—that the population (Fig. 44) is distributed less densely than in other southern parts of Britain. Various schemes have been suggested to introduce population to areas including Camborne, Bodmin, Launceston, Swindon, Shaftesbury, and and the Exeter–Tiverton–Taunton area. Such population expansion, in the absence of problems related to water and energy supplies, but in the presence of an improved transport network, could eventually justify the South-West Economic Planning Council's appellation in 1967 of this *Region with a Future*.

FURTHER READING

W. G. V. Balchin, *Cornwall; The Making of the English Landscape* (London, 1954).

F. Barlow (ed.), *Exeter and its Region* (Exeter, 1969).

J. N. H. Britton, *Regional Analysis and Economic Geography: A Case Study of Manufacturing in the Bristol Region* (London, 1967).

Central Unit for Environmental Planning, *Severnside: A Feasibility Study* (H.M.S.O., 1971).

H. C. Darby, The Regional Geography of Thomas Hardy's Wessex, *Geographical Review*, 38 (1948), 426–443.

E. A. Edmonds, M. C. McKeown and M. Williams, *South-West England* (British Regional Geology, H.M.S.O., 1969).

H. P. R. Finberg, *Gloucestershire: The Making of the English Landscape* (London, 1955).

K. J. Gregory and W. L. D. Ravenhill (eds.), *Exeter Essays in Geography* (Exeter, 1971).

G. A. Kellaway and F. B. A. Welch, *Bristol and Gloucester District* (British Regional Geology, H.M.S.O., 1948).

F. M. M. Lewes, A. J. Culyer and G. A. Brady, *The Holiday Industry of Devon and Cornwall* (H.M.S.O., 1970).

A. H. Shorter, W. L. D. Ravenhill and K. J. Gregory, *South-West England* (London, 1969).

South-West Economic Planning Council, *A Region with a Future* (H.M.S.O., 1967).

F. Walker, Economic Growth on Severnside, *Transactions Institute of British Geographers*, 37 (1965), 1–13.

East Anglia

The East Anglian economic planning region possesses two major, yet diametrically opposed characteristics. On the one hand it may be regarded in many ways as a northwards appendage of the South East region, on the other hand it has plainly acquired a distinctive identity and landscape assemblage all of its own. The split personality of the region is reflected even in the formal designation of its boundaries.

In 1939, immediately before the outbreak of war, a set of standard regions had been adopted for civil defence, but which later came to be used for other purposes, including planning. When *The South-East Study 1961–1981* (see Chapter 7) was in preparation in the early 1960s its study area was defined by three of these regions, namely Eastern (broadly the present East Anglia stretched southwards to the northern limits of the London conurbation), London and South-Eastern, and Southern, together with that part of Dorset lying within the South-Western standard region. The area, roughly that south-east of a line drawn from King's Lynn to Lyme Regis, was one considered sufficient to include all those parts of the country strongly under the influence of London.

In the middle 1960s, when the economic planning regions were created to replace the old standard regions, the area of *The South East Study* was retained, with a few minor boundary changes. At a later stage the individual character of East Anglia was recognized, and the South East region was divided into two. The administrative counties of Cambridge, Isle of Ely, Huntingdon, Norfolk, Soke of Peterborough, East Suffolk, and West Suffolk were detached to form the new region of East Anglia.

Physical Setting

Physical geography, no less than human development and planning, shares in creating the dual character of East Anglia. In terms of much of its solid geology the region is closely akin to the London Basin and its related structures. The backbone of East Anglia is provided by the Chalk, an extension northwards of the formation which creates the northern rim of the London Basin. But here the Chalk gives rise to minor relief only in the East Anglian Heights, near the southern boundary of the region, and in the low cuesta on the eastern flank of the Fens (Fig. 45). Unlike the Chilterns to the south, which rise to over 245 metres (800 feet), or the Lincolnshire and Yorkshire Wolds to the north, which achieve a maximum height of 230 metres (750 feet) where the same formation reappears beyond The Wash, there are few chalk

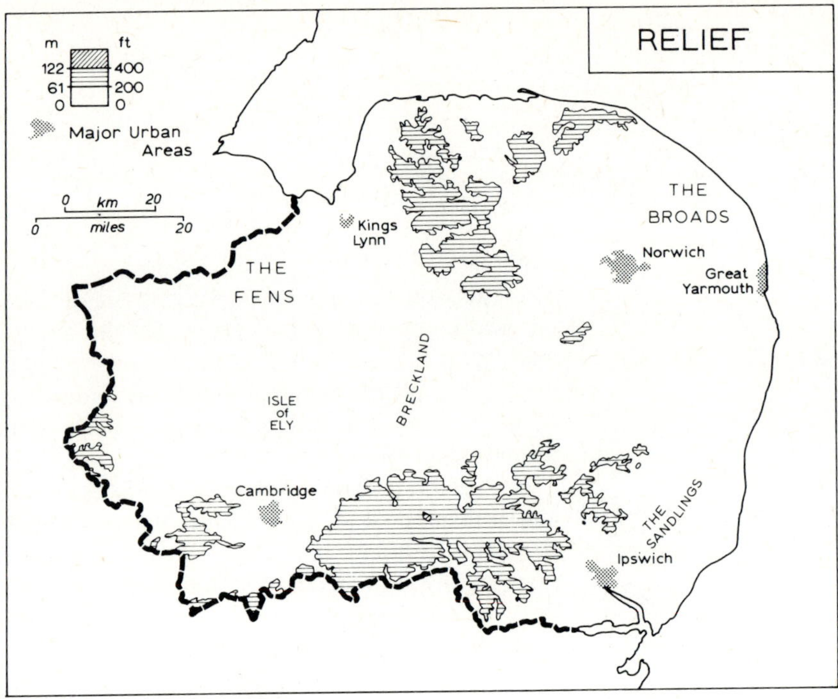

Fig 45 East Anglia—Relief
The region is one of subdued relief in which superficial deposits are important in producing sub-regional distinctiveness.

hills in East Anglia exceeding 120 metres (400 feet). The low-lying western part of the region is floored by lower Jurassic beds which, further south, form the Vale of Aylesbury. In the east, the coastal zone of the region is underlain by beds younger than the Chalk, though here they are of Quarternary date, much more recent than the lower Tertiary rocks which floor the London Basin.

But to discuss solid geology alone is to mislead. East Anglia is a low undulating plain, often virtually flat over many miles. The real character and internal diversity is provided not by major changes in elevation, but by the nature of the glacial and other surface deposits. A few examples of the most distinctive areas will suffice to support this contention.

The Fenland, as already noted above, is a north-eastern continuation of the Jurassic clay lowland of south-central England. However, the Fens share none of the characteristics of that lowland, except its elevation. The shallow embayment inland from The Wash has been infilled with clay, silt, and peat deposits which have completely transformed the area physically, and hence its utility for agricultural and other purposes. The distribution of these superficial deposits is as complex as their mode of creation, but broadly the silts and clays lie near the coast, while landward, and generally at a slightly lower elevation, lies the peat fen. Drainage of the peaty areas has lowered the

Plate 40 The Fenland (Norfolk)
The photograph shows an area of peaty fen to the south of Downham Market. Note the pattern of drainage ditches and also the exclusively arable nature of the farming.

surface level and cultivation has allowed wind erosion to denude the peat, contributing further to the fall of land level. This has accentuated old river channel and levée deposits, which now stand out above the general surface level, and has also aggravated the already difficult problems of land drainage. But the area provides rich arable land, and the grain, roots, market gardening, and fruit production are in marked contrast with the grassland farming which dominates the remainder of the Jurassic vales (Plate 40). Apart from the raised banks of river deposits, which have provided sites for dwellings, farms and roads, only the occasional residual hills, such as in the Isle of Ely, offer elevated sites for urban development.

Over much of the remainder of East Anglia diversity and distinction are bestowed by differences in the character of glacial drift deposits. In the north, an end moraine forms a feature of over 60 metres (200 feet) in elevation, the Cromer Ridge (Fig. 45), but elsewhere, it is the role of drift in soil formation which has had greatest impact on farming and settlement. Medium to heavy boulder clays are the basis of grain production in the central part of the region, but it is perhaps the lighter, sandy soils which have given rise to the most distinctive areas. In the north and north-west, in a part sometimes known as the 'Good Sand Region', light, easily-worked soils have developed on sandy and gravelly drift, and upon outwash material. It is an area which achieved a countrywide reputation as the origin of the many developments in agrarian practice in the seventeenth and eighteenth centuries which led eventually to the agricultural revolution in the British Isles (see Chapter 3). In the south-east of the region, glacial sands and gravels overlying Crag have produced the light sandy, and frequently podsolized, soils which have given character to the area known as 'The Sandlings'. Here, though the land is less fertile than elsewhere in the region, its freely draining nature has encouraged arable working, particularly for barley, wheat, oats, sugar beet, and vegetables. In the centre of the region lies the largest of the unreclaimed dry heaths of East Anglia, that of the Breckland, which forms an outstanding sub-region. Its fine sandy textured surface, often blowing and occasionally forming dunes, its heathland vegetation, its meres, and its vast areas of coniferous forest contributed by the Forestry Commission, produce a landscape which is so obviously different from most other parts of the region.

A final example of an area equally as distinctive as the Breck, but owing its origin more to man's utilization of superficial deposits, than to the nature of the deposits themselves, is afforded by The Broads in the north-eastern part of the region. In the middle basins of the rivers Bure, Waveney, and Yare intensive peat working in medieval times created shallow, but quite extensive hollows which were eventually flooded in the fourteenth and fifteenth centuries. The wide lakes thus formed, together with the linking stretches of river and canal, grew to be a centre of navigation, fishing, fowling, and reed-collecting, but in modern times the area has become devoted to the pleasure industries, and fishing, sailing, and cruising are now the major preoccupations.

Agriculture

Originally the majority of the East Anglia region was extremely isolated. To the north and east was the sea, to the south the thickly forested lowlands of what is now Essex provided a barrier to movement, and to the west lay the impassable marshes of the Fenlands. Only the low Chalk upland provided a route into the region. As time went on the marshes were drained, the woodland was cleared, and traffic by sea became more frequent and more reliable. The former isolation disappeared and East Anglia, partly because of its geographical position within the country and in relation to the remainder of Europe, developed external linkages which other regions of the country could hardly match. Particularly over the last four centuries the region has received stimuli from without, and in return has contributed technically, as well as in kind, to other parts of the country and to the world. Of no field is this generalization more true than of agriculture.

THE BACKGROUND TO AGRICULTURE

It is plain from what has already been written that the present-day rural landscape of East Anglia is far from natural. Man has brought about major changes and created conditions which are essential for the types of agriculture practised in many parts of the region today This is particularly evident in the Fenlands.

Of the two major divisions of the Fens, the silt fen around the margins of The Wash, and the peat fen further inland, it was the first which proved easier to reclaim from sea and marsh. Here, serious reclamation began at an early date. By the twelfth century, the villages of the silt fen were among the richest in Norfolk and new settlement was vigorously pushing seaward, using sea banks and drainage ditches. Generally, the newly reclaimed land was put under arable while the inland marshes provided grazing for cattle and sheep. By 1700 substantial areas of The Wash had been recovered, and since that time reclamation and enclosure has continued, particularly in the estuaries of the rivers Nene and Ouse, between Wisbech and King's Lynn.

A certain amount of piecemeal, and largely peripheral, reclamation had also occurred in the peat fen in medieval times and after. Villages on the margins of the peat pushed their arable land into the fen to a limited extent, and grew large and prosperous as a result of the process. But most of the larger scale attempts at reclamation up to 1600, including those organized by local monasteries, were unsuccessful. They lacked technical knowledge, capital, but most important of all, the overall co-ordination and planning necessary in such a large area, lower-lying than the intervening land towards the coast. It was not until the Duke of Bedford provided capital, and introduced Dutch engineers in the seventeenth century, principally Cornelius Vermuyden, that a real start was made in converting a district of swamp and rushes, of wild-fowling and fishing, and of turf cutting and summer grazing, into one of the most important and productive arable areas of the British Isles today.

The drainage system is based upon straight cuts to shorten the course of water to the sea, and hence to increase the outfall. Some of these cuts are as much as 35 kilometres (22 miles) in length. A network of subsidiary drainage ditches feed the main drains and, where necessary, water is raised to a level from which it can flow freely to the sea by pumping. Sluices control water flow in the main channels; regulation is particularly important in times of flood, or when tides are high in The Wash. Technical difficulties have more than once almost caused the system to break down. More often than not the trouble has arisen from the shrinkage and wastage of the drying peat, producing a land surface increasingly further below the level of the streams flowing across it, and over large areas, below sea level. Respite has been gained by digging further drainage cuts, and also by improving pumping. Wind driven pumps were replaced by steam pumps in the nineteenth century. Today electricity and the petrol engine have brought further technical improvement, and increased the speed of response to changing water levels.

The consequence of all this improvement is a man-made landscape of rich farming and prosperous settlement. The intrinsic qualities of the soil have been released and the already flourishing towns and villages of fen islands and peat margin have grown more wealthy still. A vivid indication of their continuing prosperity is seen in the size and elaboration of the churches and cathedrals of the area, for example, the magnificent cathedral at Ely, an

Urban District of only 10,000 population.

Quite a different form of modification had less dramatic, but certainly more widespread, effect than Fenland drainage. It resulted from the practice of marling, that is, the process of digging material from below the land surface, and spreading it upon the surface soil to correct its acidity, or to improve its texture. The light soils of East Anglia were particularly responsive to this treatment. Their excessively acid and friable nature was easily corrected, and their value quickly improved by heavy marling with calcareous material derived from the solid Chalk. On the heavy lands, sandy material was often excavated to assist in breaking down the stiff clays, hence allowing them to be worked more easily in arable rotations.

Marling has been employed in East Anglia certainly since 1252, when the practice is recorded in north Norfolk. It was very widely used in the same area by the seventeenth century. In the Breckland there are records of marling as early as the fourteenth century. Long use of the practice, together with the fact that bulky dressings were needed, has meant that a considerable amount of material has been excavated over the years. The cost of carting and spreading the marl is considerable. To minimize costs and to reduce the length of haul, marl pits were sited virtually in every field, often in the middle or at the tops of slopes so that loaded carts could run downhill. Since much of East Anglia is flat and under the plough, the characteristic small, steep-sided symmetrical hollows, most overgrown with shrubs and trees and often remote from villages, farms, and roads, constitute a marked feature of the landscape. There are approaching 30,000 of them in Norfolk alone. In addition to the physical expression of the hollows and their vegetation, marling, of course, also resulted in a widespread improvement in soil composition and texture. Its impact on farming, therefore, though less obvious at the present time, is even more important than its role in creating the more evident pits and ponds.

Shallow pits and depressions in the land surface of East Anglia have also arisen from other causes. Some are known to be the result of mineral working, others have a geomorphological origin. For example, it has been suggested that some may be swallow holes, some may be kettle holes and thaw sinks. It is possible that marl workers utilized these natural depressions where they existed. But whether or not marl pits were dug in existing hollows, the actions of man in modifying nature are hardly less profound.

AGRICULTURE TODAY

The climate of East Anglia (cold winters, warm summers, relatively dry, but the only region of the British Isles to experience a rainfall regime with a summer maximum) combined with its currently easily worked and fertile soils, has created a situation in which the cash cropping of cereals, root crops, and horticultural products, maximizes farm incomes over wide areas. Even in periods, such as that between the wars, when crop production was generally economically unattractive, the region retained substantial proportions of land in arable. Today, 10 per cent of the work force is occupied by agriculture, a figure substantially above the national average.

Over most of the western part of the region large farms with large fields are

Plate 41 Swaffham (Norfolk)
The photograph illustrates one of the small but prosperous market centres of the western part of East Anglia. The market area in the middle of the town has now been partially built over.

typical. Barley, grown for fodder as well as for malting, is universally the most important cereal, occupying over one-quarter of the farmland, and is favoured particularly on the lighter land. On heavier soil, wheat is preferred, and it achieves about one-sixth of the agricultural area. The leading rootcrop is no longer turnips, once an essential ingredient of the Norfolk four-course rotation (with wheat, barley, and clover), but sugar beet, which is carefully controlled by government policy to supply the demands of the local sugar beet refineries. Sheep, also once closely connected with the Norfolk system, are now no longer prevalent. Livestock are not commonplace. A quarter of all livestock are pigs. Poultry is also important. (See Plate 41.)

On the silt and peat fens cropping becomes much more intensive. Farms are inclined to be smaller and are almost exclusively devoted to arable. Cash cropping and horticulture (that is, where crops are grown mainly for sale and consumption without processing) are the principal types of farming, almost to the exclusion of all others. Wheat, sugar beet, potatoes and other vegetables, are the staple crops. These are either marketed fresh, or increasingly in the case of vegetables such as peas and beans, grown under contract for local canning or quick-freezing factories. Some small areas specialize in particular crops. One of the more important of these is the zone near Wisbech, where apples and small fruits, especially gooseberries, raspberries, and strawberries, are produced. Here again there is a close link with local processing plant, in this instance, of the jam industry. Livestock farming in the Fenland is limited, except for pigs and poultry.

In the eastern half of the region agriculture is much more mixed in character. Farms tend to be smaller than is general in the arable western half of the region, fields are also smaller and hedgerow timber more common. Dairying, and also the fattening of beef cattle, is quite important and together they provide a substantial proportion of farm income in many areas. Permanent pasture, though not abundant, is certainly not as uncommon as it would be to the west. As in most of East Anglia, pigs and poultry are a familiar part of the rural scene, with turkeys a speciality.

Population and Settlement

In complete contrast with its neighbour, the South East economic planning region, which, as Chapter 7 has shown, is thickly peopled, densely urbanized, and heavily industrialized, East Anglia is lightly populated, with widely spaced urban centres and a relatively low incidence of manufacturing industry. It has the smallest population and lowest gross population density of any region in Great Britain. While it occupies well over 8 per cent of the surface area of England and Wales, it contains only 3·3 per cent of the population. Its largest settlement is Norwich, with a population of little above 160,000 and only three other centres have populations exceeding 100,000, namely, Ipswich, Great Yarmouth–Lowestoft, and Cambridge. It is ironic, but perhaps understandable, that East Anglia, a relatively weakly urbanized region, but one with a simply structured settlement pattern, should have attracted some attention from urban theorists. The geometrical disposition and the hierarchical relationship of towns and cities closely approximate the postulates of central place studies. This was first identified in the 1930s, but the similarity of reality and theory has been the subject of comment many times since.

But East Anglia is not likely long to remain so undeveloped. The comparatively empty spaces are attracting overspill from other economic planning regions, particularly from the South East, and a below average regional population growth rate, which has persisted since 1801 and which was particularly low between 1851 and 1941, has now been translated into the fastest regional growth rate in the whole country. The region will not, of course, quickly regain the dominant position it held in the population map of the British Isles from Domesday times through to 1750, when industrialization elsewhere changed the population density balance (see Chapter 5). Since population density is now comparatively low, the absolute gains are unimpressive when set against increases in numbers in nearby regions. In the remainder of this section an attempt is made to summarize the new demographic situation in East Anglia by identifying the characteristics of population change and town expansion.

Plate 42 Cambridge (Cambridgeshire)
King's College Chapel in the centre of Cambridge.

PRESENT POPULATION TRENDS

The population structure of the region deviates in two important respects from the norm. First, because of the large number of United Kingdom and United States Service bases within East Anglia, and because of the existence of the large Universities at Cambridge (Plate 42) and Norwich, there is a disproportionately high number of males in the age-group 15–44 years. Secondly, the region has a somewhat higher than average proportion of old people. Until fairly recently it has been an area of persistent outward migration, and this has tended to create an ageing resident population, but the fact that the north and east have more old people than elsewhere in the region suggests that the coast and The Broads have attracted retirement population which has augmented the numbers in older age-groups. A high incidence of young males, outside family groups, and of old people leads to a low natural birth rate.

Since the regional population total is now increasing faster than that of any other region, it is plain that net migration gains are substantial. East Anglia first appeared as the fastest growing region in 1951 and since then continued in-migration has further speeded growth in the region. In the five year period 1961–66 population in England and Wales increased by 4 per cent; in East Anglia it rose by 6·2 per cent. In absolute numbers this represents a gain of nearly 93,000 people, and well over half of this was contributed by net migration increase. Broadly speaking, it was the south and east of the region which experienced greatest growth in both relative and absolute terms, and the north and west which attracted least.

In detail, recent population changes within East Anglia have been extremely complex, as Figure 46 indicates, but some broad trends do appear. The most consistent areas of increase are either in those parts of the region accessible to the South East region (from which many of the migrants have come) or they are adjacent to the large towns of the region, such as Norwich or King's Lynn, which have generated overspill as a result of natural increase as well as by migration from elsewhere. Where large towns lie in accessible areas, such as in the south of the region in a belt from Huntingdon in the west through to Cambridge, Bury St. Edmunds, and Ipswich in the east, growth is particularly heavy. But in the rural heart of East Anglia and also along the north coast, where holiday resorts have not expanded nearly so dramatically as those on the east coast closer to London, substantial areas have continued to experience declining population. In a number of areas the annual rates of decrease are quite high, but since these are all sparsely populated rural districts, the absolute losses are quite small.

TOWN GROWTH

The towns are clearly the growth points of East Anglia. In common with towns and cities elsewhere in the British Isles they have often lost population at their centres, or gained population less swiftly than the surrounding areas, as a result of central area redevelopment, but they have grown rapidly by peripheral expansion and have greatly stimulated the development of adjacent towns and villages. The five major settlements of the region, Norwich, Ipswich, Great Yarmouth/Lowestoft, Cambridge, and Peterborough contain 38 per cent of the population; all settlements over 10,000 population contain together 50 per cent of the population, with a further 25 per cent in the small market towns and large villages with populations in excess of 1,000. Although these figures do not match those of the heavily industrialized regions, they represent substantial urbanization when compared with the position even a few decades ago.

Up to the middle 1950s urban growth was based largely upon what has been called 'voluntary' migrations, that is, largely unplanned and unorganized movements of people attracted by job opportunities or by residential advantages. Since that time organized movement to specially planned new or expanded towns has become increasingly important and over the next decade is likely to dominate as a factor in town growth. Most of the new comers to the planned schemes have come, and will continue to come, from London, but a minority come from other regions and from other places within the region. Migrants are generally young people with families. In time they will transform the population age structure and also correct the present low birthrate of the region.

Town expansions (see Fig. 47), stemming from the Town Development Act of 1952, though planned as urban entities, are also haphazard in the sense that the overall distribution of such towns is a product of more or less independent

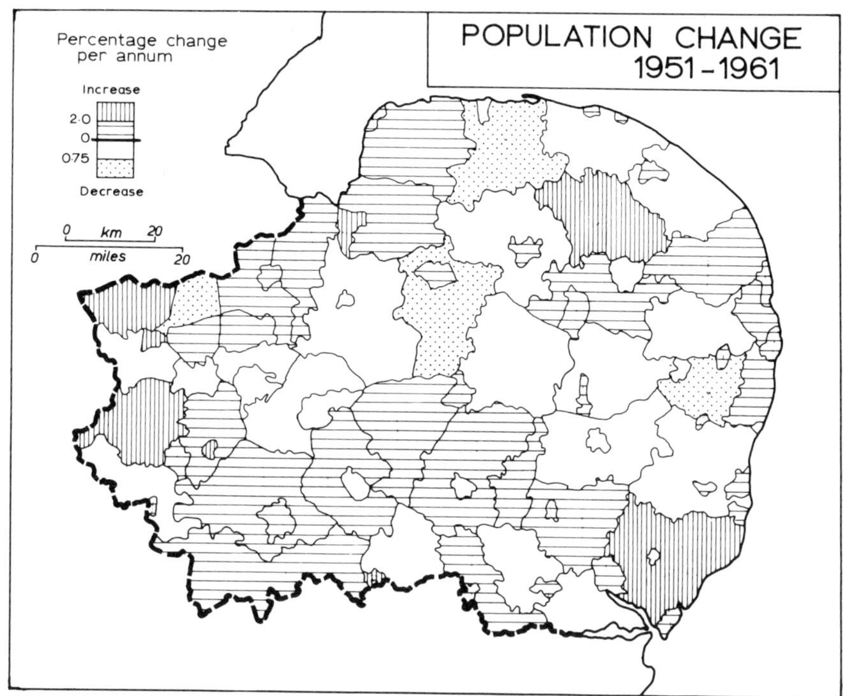

Fig 46 East Anglia—Population Change 1951–1961

The areas of most substantial increase lie on the southern boundary of the region, adjacent to the South East region. The centre and north are areas of slow increase or decline in population.

Fig 47 East Anglia—New and Expanded Towns, 1970

The towns for which expansions have been agreed tend to lie close to the border with the South East region. The only new town so far approved is distant from the South East region partly in order to ensure that the town will have an independent life of its own and that it will generate maximum economic benefit to East Anglia.

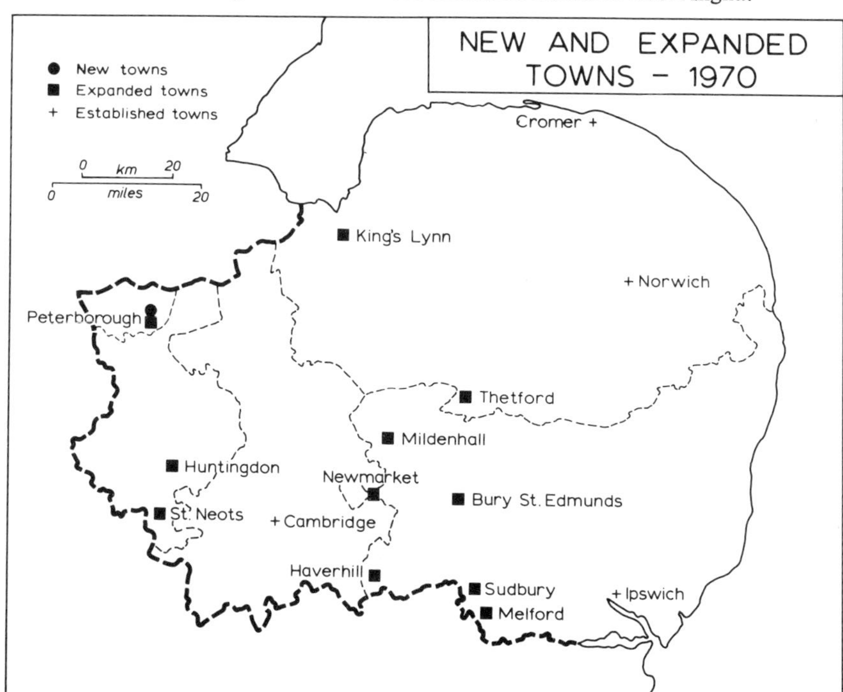

decisions by a large number of local authorities. They have tended to cluster in the southern part of the region and have, of course, already greatly contributed to population increases in that area. Overspill agreements already concluded provide for 22,000 new homes, sufficient for 75,000 people, before 1981. It is likely that major extensions of present schemes will be forthcoming and that new town expansions will be agreed further to the north, to take advantage of the even emptier land of central and north Norfolk, where population at the moment is declining.

By far the most impressive schemes were conceived by the government within the framework of the New Towns Act. In 1965 it announced its intention of designating two new towns, one at Peterborough and another at Ipswich. A draft designation order was published for Ipswich, but at a later stage it was decided not to proceed with the new town in its envisaged form. At Peterborough progress was swifter and surer. The new town was formally designated on 1st August 1967, following studies by town planning consultants, and since then growth in population has been rapid. At the date of designation it contained nearly 83,000 people, by the end of 1970 it was approaching a population of 89,000, and its proposed target population is nearly 188,000. The hope has been expressed by the regional economic planning council that the new town is sufficiently distant from London to ensure that the expanding community will have an independent life of its own, and that it will make an effective contribution to the future prosperity of the region.

The Future

Plainly the future of the region is relatively bright. It has high population growth and plenty of space in which to develop new centres of employment, new residential land, and new means of communication to facilitate internal and external economic and social linkages. But there are certain difficulties apparent already, which, if not resolved, will inhibit growth. Perhaps the most obvious of these lies in the present road and rail system (Fig. 48). Although apparently giving a good coverage of the region it will be noted that many passenger and freight rail services have been curtailed, and some withdrawn, while the traffic which once went by rail now goes by road. Here it has been augmented by new traffic which has stemmed from greatly improving living standards, and also from population and employment expansion. A system which was adequate enough in time of economic stagnation is now badly stretched. East Anglia has relatively little modernized highway (note the sparse stretches of dual carriageway) and unlike most other regions it has no direct access to the national motorway network.

But not only are there difficulties, there are also uncertainties. To a large degree these arise from the fact that the present employment structure of East Anglia in some major respects is quite unlike that of the country at large, and the future depends upon whether these dissimilarities persist, or whether East Anglia becomes more like the remainder of England and Wales. For example, in East Anglia, employment in agriculture, forestry and fishing is five times that in England and Wales generally, while the proportions of workers engaged in the food, drink, and tobacco trades, and in construction greatly exceed those for the country as a whole. Conversely, the metal, vehicle, textile, engineering, and electrical industries are substantially under-represented. But though it is extremely difficult to arrive at reliable estimates of the future economic performance of the major enterprises of the region, it seems likely that the current expansion in the manufacturing sector, particularly in the new and expanding towns, will continue to narrow the differences between East Anglia and other regions. At the moment East Anglia has a lower proportion of its labour engaged in manufacturing than any other region in Great Britain except the South-West. Manufacturing industry accounts for 31 per cent of the employed labour force, compared with 38 per cent in England and Wales.

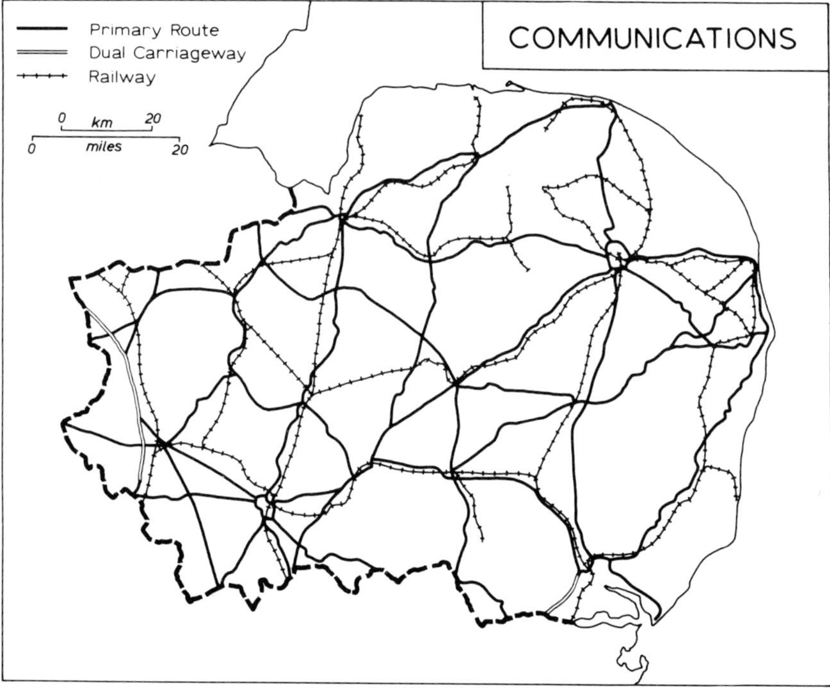

Fig 48 East Anglia—Communications
The region is well-covered by roads and railways, but with increased traffic and railway closures the system is becoming badly stretched.

Much more certain is the future of tourism and recreation within the region. The leisure and holiday industries have for long been well-established in East Anglia. The region has a distinctive combination of advantages for such activities. It has a dry and bracing climate, a long and attractive coastline with many sandy beaches (Plate 43), long inland waterways—the Broads (Plate 44)

Plate 43 Near Overstrand (Norfolk)
The sandy beaches and fine coastline of East Anglia provide one of the bases of its flourishing tourist industry. Note where the beach material comes from.

Plate 44 Wroxham (Norfolk)
This small settlement on the Broads is the major centre for sailing and cruising in East Anglia. Note the boat yards, sheds and basins which occupy so much of the centre of the town.

alone have 195 kilometres (120 miles) of navigable water, and the Great Ouse complex even more, while Grafham Water Reservoir in the Diddington Valley, near Huntingdon, has a surface area of 600 hectares (1,500 acres) available for water sports—quiet rural areas of charm and often of great landscape interest, and many buildings, villages, and towns of considerable historical and architectural value. Increasing leisure time, incomes, and mobility have stimulated participation in recreation, particularly in such pursuits as driving for pleasure, sightseeing, picnicking, walking, swimming, boating, and cultural activities, the very range of leisure pursuits that East Anglia is best able to provide. The region may therefore confidently expect a great increase in the demand placed upon its recreation resources both from within the region, and from without.

Such demands, however, like almost all demands upon land, involve certain conflicts of interest. The land most desirable for recreation is also that, by and large, which is of greatest interest to urban developers, and both uses must expand at the expense of agriculture, at present employing 10 per cent of the region's labour force and working land nearly 80 per cent of which is classified as good or very good (the average for England and Wales is below 50 per cent). The more recreational facilities are developed, the more they are likely to attract population, for both short duration trips and for longer period holidays, from neighbouring regions which are deficient in recreational opportunities; and so the greater the chance that local amenity will be lost and inconvenience caused by the over-use of finite resources. Even in one of the most promising and most predictable facets of the life of the region, formidable problems are presented to the regional planner.

FURTHER READING

H. C. Darby, *The Draining of the Fens* (Cambridge, 1939).

H. C. Darby, *The Medieval Fenland* (Cambridge, 1940).

East Anglia Consultative Committee, *East Anglia: A Regional Appraisal* (Bury St. Edmunds, 1969).

East Anglia Economic Planning Council, *East Anglia: A Study* (H.M.S.O., 1968).

J. M. Lambert, *et al.*, *The Making of the Broads* (London, 1960).

H. C. Prince, Pits and Ponds in Norfolk, *Erdkunde*, 16 (1962), 10–31.

H. C. Prince, The Origin of Pits and Depressions in Norfolk, *Geography*, 49 (1964), 15–32.

CHAPTER TEN

The East Midlands

Diversity, prosperity and opportunity are recurrent themes in the East Midlands. Although the Midland Plain underlain by Triassic rocks is the dominant element in many conceptions of the area, this plain contains substantial variety, and peripheral areas provide further variations in physical landscape and in agricultural and industrial utilization of the land. The river Trent, which rises beyond the region in the West Midlands and reaches the sea beyond the region in Humberside, provides a long established artery, and the middle Trent basin was the focus of the Midland kingdom of Mercia in the fifth century A.D. Subsequently, after the Danish invasion, the five towns of Derby, Leicester, Lincoln, Nottingham and Stamford became leading centres of the territory known as Danelaw. Diversity of physique is exceeded by diversity of resources, which notably include high quality agricultural land and reserves of water, coal, iron ore and other bases for extractive industries. Such varied resources were the basis of early prosperity founded upon diversity of activity. A wide spectrum of industries including heavy industries, textile industries, hosiery, lace, leather and footwear manufacture, against a varied and prosperous agricultural background provide the clues to the characteristically broad-based East Midlands economy. This broad base must be seen not only spatially, but also temporally. Working on the exposed coalfield was followed by exploitation of the concealed field; the Coal Measure iron ores, soon exhausted, were succeeded by the Jurassic ores of Leicestershire and Northamptonshire; and the rurally-based industries were replaced by the concentration of textile, hosiery and footwear manufacture in areas more concentrated but sprinkled over the area of the East Midlands.

Opportunity, a key theme isolated by the East Midlands Economic Planning Council in their 1969 report, emerges, partly because of this diversity in the spatial distribution of resources variously utilized against the background of the technological advance of the last two centuries, but also for several other reasons. In the mid-twentieth century there are a number of urban and industrial centres in the East Midlands, but no one centre completely dominates the area. Therefore although the Derby-Nottingham area may be approaching a conurbation in character it is not as well-developed as the other six which have emerged in England. This concentration of population is detached from the concentration around Leicester, which is in turn separated from the towns more proximate to the South East, such as Northampton. The presence of a large number of independent towns provides opportunity for appreciable future development within the East Midlands, and this is emphasized by the average population distribution in 1965 of 268 per square kilometre (695 per square mile) which compares favourably with the average of 382 per square kilometre (990 per square mile) in the West Midlands and with 316 per square kilometre (818 per square mile) in England and Wales as a whole. Yet the main industrial centres are sufficiently close to afford some of the advantages of industrial concentration. The setting of the East Midlands, near to the South East, but not yet seriously affected by its problems, and equally close to the older industrial areas of the West Midlands, south-east Lancashire, and west Yorkshire, provides another facet of the available opportunity. The realization of this opportunity of position is dependent upon good communications, and the Midland and east coast rail routes, the A.1 and more recently and significantly the M.1, have enabled the advantages of position to be realized. The diverse employment pattern includes the growth industries of engineering and electronics, and location is also favourable with respect to the methane and natural gas grids and to water supplies, at least in the immediate future. Opportunity is further encouraged by the varied environment which includes a portion of the Peak District National Park and other potential recreation areas such as Charnwood Forest and Sherwood Forest.

Varied Environments and Resources

There is lack of agreement on the definition of the extent of the East Midlands. Although, on the west, Hinckley has closer associations with Leicester than does Nuneaton, on the north the boundary between the East Midlands and west Yorkshire is purely administrative and on the east the boundary is not a convincing one. In the south certain centres have a closer affinity with London and the South-East than with the Nottingham–Derby–Leicester area which in many respects represents the core of the East Midlands. Four sub-regions have been recognized by the Economic Planning Council and these, indicated in Figure 52, are a suitable basis for a description of the varied landscapes.

NOTTINGHAMSHIRE–DERBYSHIRE SUB-REGION

In 1967 this area, which extends southwards and eastwards from the southern Pennines to the river Trent, accounted for nearly 54 per cent of the population of the East Midlands. Geologically, a breached dome of Carboniferous rocks is margined to the south and east by Permo-Triassic rocks (Fig. 49). The oldest rocks, Carboniferous limestone, are exposed in the centre of the dome in the Peak District, and further east a series of cuesta-landscapes reflects the succession of rock types. The physical contrasts within the sub-region are probably greatest therefore in the west-east transect (Fig. 49) from the Peak District to the river Trent.

The centre of the dome, in the north-west of the sub-region, is dominated by the limestone plateau of the Peak District. This plateau, representing a Tertiary planation surface, is undulating in character and usually lies between 300 and 360 metres (984–1,181 feet). Limestone outcrops do not figure in this landscape as prominently as in comparable areas of the central Pennines—a contrast ascribed to lack of ice cover over the southern Pennines during the last glaciation. The limestone is often mantled with silty drift, perhaps of

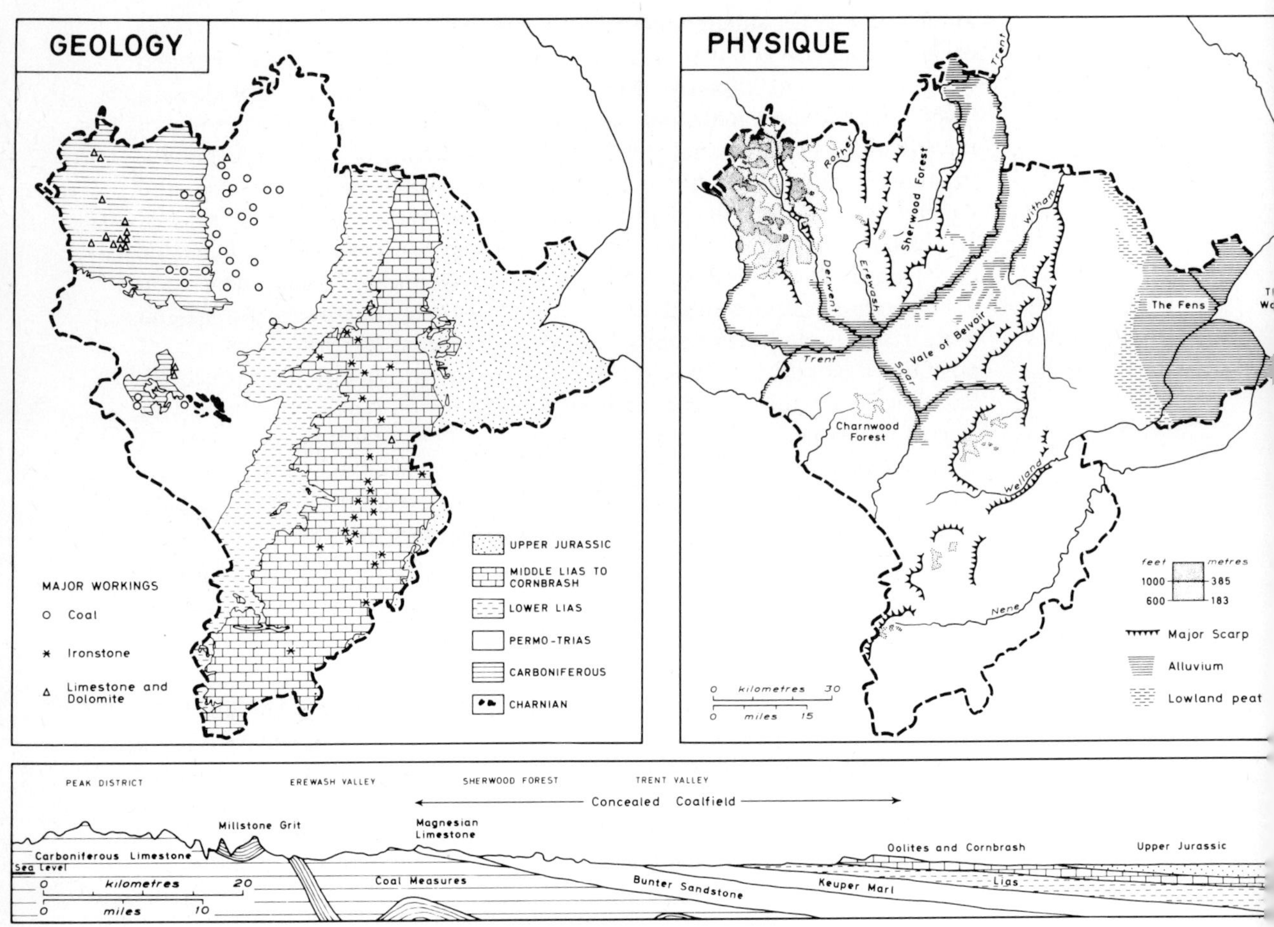

Fig 49 East Midlands—Geology and Physique
The generalized section is drawn from the Southern Pennines (Peak District) to the Wash.

aeolian origin, which provides the parent material for the rendzinas, brown calcareous soils and brown earth soils which are most frequently encountered. The character of the underlying limestone rock is shown where valleys or dales are sharply incised into the plateau surface, and it is equally apparent in the fabric of the dry limestone walls, in the building materials, and in the numerous abandoned quarry faces. Quarrying survives at certain locations, such as Wirksworth, and limestone formerly utilized for lime burning is now used mainly in cement manufacture. Intrusions in the limestone are quarried also and minerals which occur in veins include lead, zinc and fluorspar. Exploitation of lead was important in Roman times, it continued up to the nineteenth century and increased dramatically in the early part of the twentieth century but a mere vestige survives to the present time. The limestone plateau forms the heart of the Peak District National Park (Fig. 54) created in 1950. Just beyond its margins are towns like Matlock and the spa of Matlock Bath, and

Plate 45 Southern Pennines (Derbyshire)
The Kinder Scout Hills from across the Edale valley. The harder measures of the Millstone Grit provide the dramatic upland scenery of the High Peak.

within the Park, market towns such as Bakewell act as centres for a National Park the boundary of which is within 80 kilometres (50 miles) of nearly half of the population of England. Preservation and enhancement of the landscape includes not only the removal of unsuitable buildings but also tree-planting and the improvement of derelict land; the utilization of the landscape is encouraged by information services, by facilitating public access and by developing accommodation and car parks.

Eastwards from the limestone outcrop the National Park extends to the cuesta-like Millstone Grit country (Plate 45). A series of west-facing scarps or edges, often tree-covered or unenclosed, provide harsher outlines punctuating a plateau landscape which is dissected by steep-sided valleys such as the Derwent. Soils are usually poorer than those of the limestone country because the sandy rocks support acid, freely-drained soils. Strips of improved land may occur on the included shales, although elsewhere these shales, and also the areas mantled by glacial drift, support imperfectly-drained podsols and gleyed soils.

The pattern of scarp, dip slope and vale encountered on the Millstone Grit outcrop is imitated in a more subdued form on the Coal Measures outcrop to the east. These Measures generally consist of a rhythmic alternation of coal, mudstones, sandy mudstone or sandstone, and seatearth. This sequence may be repeated within a thickness of 10 metres (33 feet), and some 25 coal seams, representing less than 5 per cent of the total thickness, occur within the

Measures which are between 900 and 1,500 metres (3,000–5,000 feet) in thickness. The Coal Measures are subdivided into Lower, Middle and Upper (unproductive), and the coal seams outcrop progressively from the oldest Belper-Lawn in the west, through the Kilburn and Black Shale seams to the High Main coal further east. The seams were generally first exploited in the west and the exposed coalfield extends east of a north-south line through Ripley embracing the Rother valley in the north and centres such as Chesterfield, Clay Cross and Alfreton, with the towns of Heanor, Eastwood and Ilkeston in the Erewash valley further south. By 1870 131 mines were recorded in Derbyshire and before 1880, facilitated by the growth of the railway and of the canal networks, coal mining was the leading occupation of the county. The coalfield produced good steam coal for industrial purposes and high quality domestic coal. Good coking coal was restricted to the area between Mansfield and Chesterfield. The consequence of increased coal production in the nineteenth century was a landscape dotted with mining settlements rather than a great industrial-urban complex. High productivity from the coalfield was favoured by the geological conditions, was achieved by a high proportion of well-equipped mines, and was continued by a high degree of mechanization. By the early twentieth century the balance of mining activity had extended eastwards to the concealed field. After this eastward movement, centres of iron industry survived on the exposed field; these centres were originally based on the Coal Measure iron ores first exploited particularly in the early nineteenth century. The eastward movement had also left in its wake a landscape exhibiting the impact of the coal-mining which no longer exists to sustain the area. This is particularly apparent in the Erewash valley, literally characterized by D. H. Lawrence, and this area, together with the area north of Alfreton and the area extending west to Ripley, was designated an Intermediate Area in 1969. The 23 collieries in the area in 1958 had been reduced to 8 by 1969. Since 1945 the practice of obtaining coal by surface opencast methods has, after subsequent restoration, produced a landscape of more regular field shapes lacking the hedgerows of the older-established enclosures. The essentially man-made soils of such disturbed areas complement the gleyed profiles which are generally characteristic of the soils of the Coal Measures country.

Further eastwards a contrasting landscape is introduced by the outcrop of Magnesian Limestone. This outcrop is sometimes marked by a sharp west-facing escarpment, often wooded, as near Bolsover, and succeeded by a dip slope with freely-drained, sandy-loam textured calcareous soils which classically support arable cultivation although the deeper mines of the concealed field have intruded into this essentially agricultural landscape. Succeeding the Magnesian limestone is a further discontinuous escarpment between Nottingham and Worksop developed on the Bunter sandstone and Pebble Beds. A variety of soil types on this cuesta ranges from brown earths to humus-iron podsols and there is an equal variety of landscape and of land use. North of Nottingham is Sherwood Forest, much of which was scrub or heath in the late eighteenth century, and near Worksop the area known as the Dukeries was originally dominated by large estates and mansions. The modern developments in this area are the large coniferous plantations, the hospitals which have replaced the mansions, the increasing use of water from boreholes in the Bunter aquifer, and more recently, the increased recreational activity (the area is adjacent to Nottingham and to the industrial area to the east). Eastwards the Keuper Marl is often recorded by a cuesta (Fig. 49) stimulated by the fine-grained basal sandstones. The Marl outcrop spreads in a broad arc, fringing the landscapes described above, west and north of the river Trent. Relief is characteristically low, of the order of 50 metres (164 feet) and the landscape is often mantled by glacial drift and by gravels of the terraces of the Trent. Three horizons of Gypsum are included within the Keuper Marl succession and this is extracted at Chellaston near Derby, at Newark, at several places between Nottingham and Leicester, and at East Leake in the Leicestershire sub-region to the south. The deposits of gypsum represent the largest workable deposits in the country and now account for more than 50 per cent of the national output, much of which is used in the building trade for plaster, plasterboard and cement, whereas a massive variety of gypsum was formerly the basis of the Alabaster industry.

The river Trent forms the southern and eastern border of the sub-region. It flows in a broad flood plain up to 3 kilometres (1·9 miles) wide above Nottingham, whereas below that city it flows in a broad trench in which the modern river is underfit. The valley provided an early routeway between the West and East Midlands and it is now significant for the location of major power stations (Fig. 52) along the river, and for the extraction of gravels from the flood plain and from the low terraces. Present gravel workings will be more extensive in the future and they intrude into the predominantly grass land agriculture developed upon a complex association of acid brown soils with gleys. The river Trent receives effluent and sewage from the Black Country via the Tame, and from the Potteries, and so it has high pollution levels as it enters the region. These levels are increased further at Burton-on-Trent, by the Derwent from Derby and by the Soar from Leicester. At Trent Bridge, Nottingham it has been estimated that the dry weather flow of 3,400 million litres per day (748 million gallons per day) already contains 1,350 million litres per day (297 million gallons per day) of sewage and of industrial effluent; and that at the present rate of increase this could rise to 3,100 million litres per day (682 million gallons per day) by the year 2000. Work is in progress to reduce the level of this effluent particularly as the Trent may eventually be required as a source of water supply and also because it has been suggested that the Trent valley from the Dove confluence to Newark could become a regional park in which recreation would be a major activity.

THE EASTERN LOWLANDS

Alternation of scarp, dip slope and vale is continued on a more reduced scale and in a more attenuated fashion east of the Trent. The Keuper Marl is succeeded by the low-lying Lower Lias outcrop and these clays, mantled in part by boulder clay, underly distinctive lowlands such as the Vale of Belvoir (Fig. 49) and further north what is aptly termed the Western Clay Lowland. Rhaetic rocks, between the Keuper Marl and the Lower Lias, produce an

Plate 46 Boston (Lincolnshire)
Boston (25,995; 1971) has developed astride the river Witham. The picture is taken looking south-eastwards towards the Wash over reclaimed fenland now intensely cultivated, but seldom higher than 3 metres (10 feet). Boston was an important port in the twelfth to fourteenth centuries; port activity still continues, and engineering, canning and brewing industries are found in the town.

escarpment in some areas, and limestones in the Lower Lias also produce a distinctive relief element, and on the east an escarpment is developed by the iron-bearing Marlstone of the Middle Lias. This area continues under the boulder-clay covered high ground south-east of Nottingham, termed the Nottinghamshire Wolds, and to the south in the Leicestershire Wolds. A significant feature known as the Cliff or the Edge 60 metres (197 feet) high in the north and 90 metres (295 feet) in the south extends for 80 kilometres (50 miles) south from Lincoln (Fig. 49) and is produced by the Inferior Oolite. Two gaps marking former courses of the Trent break the line of this escarpment at Lincoln (followed by the river Witham) and at Ancaster. The northern part of the dip slope is known as Lincoln Heath and is a landscape which possesses shallow soils, was improved in the nineteenth century, and now has large fields often bounded by walls of local stone. South of Grantham the Oolitic rocks are nearly horizontal and, increasingly covered by boulder clay, produce the plateau character of Kesteven and Rutland rising to 180 metres (590 feet). But drift obscures the solid geology and no scarp is visible. Upper Jurassic clays succeed the Oolitic limestone outcrop and underly the Mid Clay vale of Lincolnshire interposed between Lincoln Heath and the Cretaceous Lincoln Wolds beyond the region to the east.

To the south the Mid Clay vale broadens to the Fenland where recent sediments rest on glacial deposits overlying Cretaceous and Jurassic rocks and provide one of the most distinctive areas of Britain, the largest extent of low-lying land, and the largest area of productive and highly-cultivated land (see also Chapter 9). The landscape is largely a reflection of reclamation (Plate 46) by man and there are few contrasts. The siltlands near the Wash are characterized by light silts up to 4 metres (13 feet) deep which support sandy, well-drained soils which warm up easily. This zone has been raised by marine and estuarine silts to higher levels than those of the inland peat fen, which frequently lie at or below mean sea level and have soils darker in colour, heavier in texture and sometimes more difficult to work. Reclamation dates from the seventeenth century, and drainage schemes have had to contend with the facts that the level of the inner peatlands is now lower than the areas peripheral to the Wash, that the rivers draining large watersheds occasionally have high flood discharges, and that the rivers and drains are often at levels higher than the fields. Reclamation continues today and the reclaimed areas are usually incorporated into the existing, often large, farms. The Wash has been considered as the area for a barrage to augment future water supplies and more recently (1970) as the site for a group of four adjacent reservoirs restrained by banks built to 9 metres (30 feet) above sea level. These pumped storage reservoirs would begin about 1·5 kilometres (1 mile) away from the present coastline leaving an intermediate strip available for further reclamation for agricultural or recreational purposes.

LEICESTER SUB-REGION

Carboniferous rocks underly the hill country rising to 171 metres (561 feet) in the Swadlingcote area (Fig. 49). These rocks include Coal Measures and, as an anticlinal fold strikes from north-west to south-east through Ashby de la Zouch, the unproductive Lower Coal Measures outcrop in the centre of the South Derbyshire–Leicestershire coalfield, flanked by two areas underlain by the productive Middle Coal Measures centred on Swadlingcote (west) and Coalville (east). The impact of coal mining on the landscape is reflected in spoil heaps, derelict buildings and mining subsidence, and these features are supplemented by clay pits, as the Coal Measure clays have been the basis of a long-established clay industry. Surrounding the Carboniferous rocks is a continuation of the Midland Plain underlain by Keuper Marl, occasionally diversified by small isolated hills such as the Carboniferous Limestone Breedon Hill, which is scarred by a large quarry. A more distinctive variation is provided by Charnwood Forest (Fig. 49), where four narrow uplands trending north-west to south-east are founded upon Pre-Cambrian slates, grits, quartzites and volcanic ash exhumed from beneath the Triassic rocks which persist in the intervening depressions. Farming in the vales contrasts with the conifers, dry oakwood, grassland and bracken which clothe the thin soils of the ridges which rise to a maximum of 278 metres (912 feet). The Charnian rocks were formerly quarried extensively but the area is now notable for amenity, for reservoirs which supply Loughborough and Leicester, and for the site of a proposed (1969) Country Park (see also Fig. 17).

East and south of Charnwood Forest the characteristics of the Trent valley are echoed by the valleys of the Soar and of its tributaries which drain an area underlain by Triassic and Lower Liassic rocks. These extend to where the Jurassic cuestas provide the Leicestershire Wolds or 'High Leicestershire' which continue the terrain southwards from the Eastern Lowlands sub-region. Middle Lias Marlstone provides the first escarpment and with an average iron content of 32 per cent the rock is the basis for an iron ore extractive industry centred on Melton Mowbray.

NORTHAMPTON-SHIRE SUB-REGION

Jurassic scarplands are a distinctive element in this sub-region, and east of the Lower Lias outcrop the Marlstone scarp is well-defined, occasionally reaches over 200 metres (656 feet) and is succeeded by a dip slope giving way to well-dissected hill country. Inferior Oolite provides the next scarp. This is discontinuous south of Market Harborough but straight and continuous south-east of the Welland valley (Fig. 49). The Inferior Oolite and Great Oolite cap the Northamptonshire Plateau, and sharply-incised meandering valleys with numerous tributary dry valleys occur between the broad, flat divides which support a wide range of soil types, many of which are light, freely worked and widely-cultivated although they may tend to scorch in hot weather. The Northampton Sands at the base of the Inferior Oolite, best developed north-east of Northampton, are worked around Wellingborough, Kettering and Corby (Plate 47) for the ironstones which average two to six metres (6–20 feet) in thickness and give an ore with 28–35 per cent iron content. Extraction has taken place since the nineteenth century and present working (Plate 47), north-east of the older fields, entails the removal of up to 30 metres (100 feet) of overburden by walking draglines, and the 'hill and dale' landscape, sometimes forested, contrasts with the barbed wire enclosures on land more recently reclaimed. A small area of the Upper Jurassic Clays occurs east of the river Nene but this is a small fragment of the much larger clay vale which fringes the East Midlands and is developed in the South-East and in East Anglia.

The East Midlands therefore include a variety of landscapes which possess a variety of resources utilized at various times during the last two centuries. The rates of increase in coal production and in iron ore production are sketched in Figure 50 and the general relevance of the geological background is expressed in Table 12. Since 1951 population growth in this area has been greater than in the country as a whole and the salient characteristics of the employment structure are that employment in agriculture and forestry (Fig. 50, No. 1), in extractive industry (2), metal manufacture (5), textiles (10), and in clothing

Plate 47 Corby (Northamptonshire)
The picture shows surface working of Northampton Sands, which yield about 32% iron, on the margin of Corby (47,761; 1971). Opencast extraction of iron ore provides more than is needed locally for iron and steel production although the New Town of Corby has one iron and steel works which produces one-third of the national output of tubes.

and footwear industries (12), are substantially greater than the average for Great Britain. Therefore despite the absence of a high concentration of population, the area is highly industrialized and has some 43·5 per cent of its employees engaged in manufacturing industry.

Agriculture

Agriculture necessarily varies between the four sub-regions (Fig. 52) and is most significant as a source of employment in the Eastern Lowlands. The major contrasts are between intensive arable production in the east and north-east, the mixed arable and livestock dominant on the heavier soils of Leicestershire and Northamptonshire, and the dairy farms in the north-west, including the grassed hill country of Derbyshire. Overall, approximately three-quarters of the land of the region is agricultural, representing 10 per cent of the agricultural land of England and Wales. The region accounts for 15 per cent of the acreage of England and Wales under wheat, potatoes, sugar beet and green vegetables, for about 7 per cent of the dairy calves and heifers, and for about 9 per cent of other cattle and calves. Government policy has influenced the detail of farming throughout the region but the major contrasts of Land

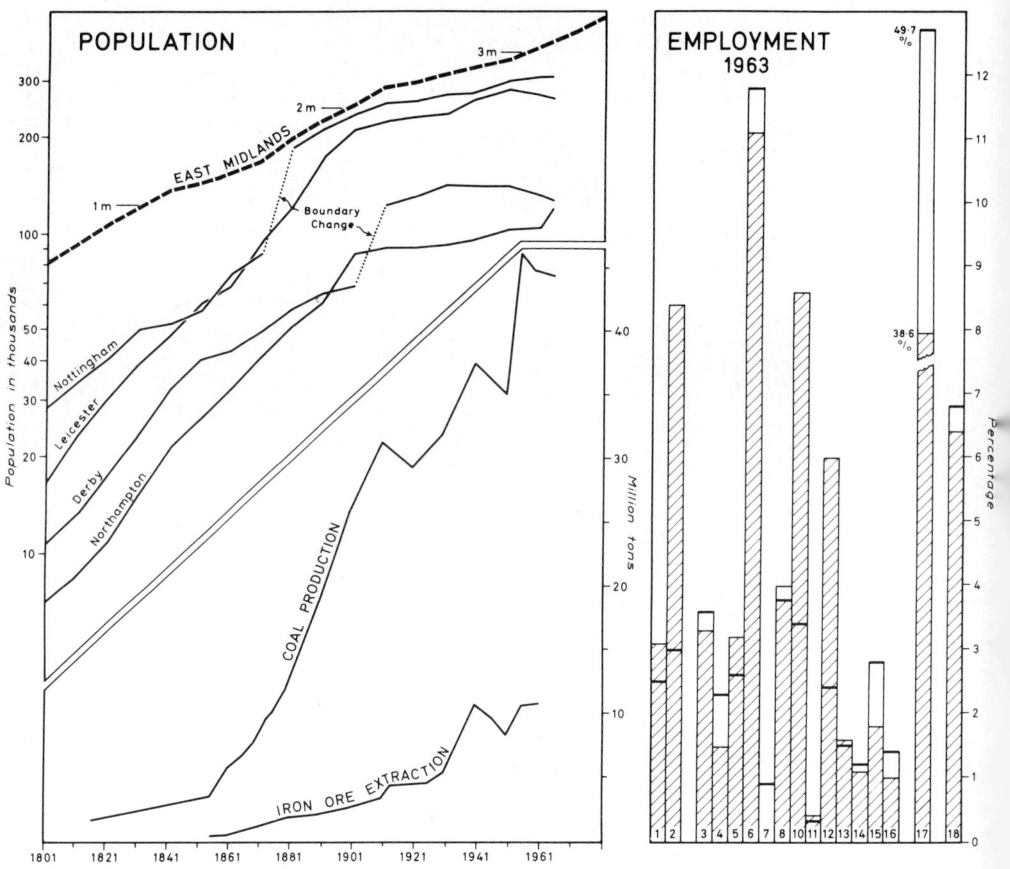

Fig 50 East Midlands—Trends in Employment
The shaded portions of the employment diagram represent the percentage employment in the East Midlands and the thicker lines in each category refer to the average for Great Britain. The numbers refer to employment in 1 – Agriculture, forestry and fishing, 2 – Mining and quarrying, 3 – Food, drink and tobacco, 4 – Chemicals and allied industries, 5 – Metal manufacture and metal goods, 6 – Engineering and electrical goods, 7 – Shipbuilding and marine engineering, 8 – Vehicles, 10 – Textiles, 11 – Leather, leathergoods and fur, 12 – Clothing and footwear, 13 – Bricks, pottery, glass, cement, etc., 14 – Timber, furniture etc., 15 – Paper, printing, publishing, 16 – Other manufacturing industries, 17 – Service industries, 18 – Construction.

Classification are indicated by the map based upon the Land Use Survey of the 1930s (Fig. 51). This map isolates the fertile soils of the Eastern Lowlands, it suggests the good quality land existing over much of the Midland Plain, and over the Jurassic and Magnesian Limestone dip slopes, and it separates the poorer land on the thin soils of the Bunter outcrop (Sherwood Forest), of the Millstone Grit, of Charnwood Forest and of parts of the Coal Measures. The response to this broad picture is generalized in the map of farming enterprise combinations (Fig. 51) which shows the dominance of cash crops in the

TABLE 12

THE GEOLOGICAL SUCCESSION AND ITS UTILIZATION IN THE EAST MIDLANDS

System	*Rock Type and Lithology*	*Products* (Past and Present)
QUATERNARY	Pleistocene and Recent gravels, clays	Gravel
MESOZOIC	JURASSIC – Kimmeridge clay	Brick-making
	Ampthill clay	
	Oxford clay	
	Kellaways Beds	
	Great Oolite Series – include limestones, clays	Cement, Roadstone, Building stone
	Inferior Oolite Series – include limestones, clays, shales, ironstone	Iron ore, Building stone
	Lias – Upper – Clays	Brick-making
	Middle – Marlstone, clays	Iron ore, Building stone
	Lower – argillaceous limestones, shales, clays	Limestone for cement
	Rhaetic – Black shales, calcareous siltstones	
	TRIASSIC – Keuper – Red marls, skerries, fine sandstones,	Marls for brick-making
	gypsum	Gypsum for Alabaster
	Bunter – Sandstones, pebble beds	Gravels and building sands moulding sands.
PALAEOZOIC	PERMIAN – Magnesian Limestone – Marls, dolomites, sandstones	Building stone, Lime Marls for bricks and pottery
	CARBONIFEROUS – Coal Measures	30 workable coal seams clays for pottery and pipes Oil in basal Coal Measures
	Millstone Grit	Building stone
	Carboniferous limestone + Igneous rocks	Lime, road stone Ochre, Lead + zinc, Fluorspar, Barytes, Calcite
PRE-CAMBRIAN	Volcanic and Intrusive rocks	Road metal, artificial stone

north-east, of sheep and of beef cattle on the Jurassic uplands, and of dairy cattle over the Midland Plain and in the Peak District.

In the east a mean annual precipitation of less than 630 millimetres (25 inches), high sunshine averages and a freedom from air frost from early May to October favour intensive crop production. Three-quarters of Lincolnshire is under arable and of this approximately 70 per cent is under wheat (Mid Clay vale), barley (lighter soils), potatoes and sugar beet. High outputs of cash crops, including a controlled acreage of sugar beet to ensure a certain proportion of home-produced sugar, are achieved by intensive use of labour against a background of high rents and drainage rates. Diversity is introduced by numerous small holdings producing flowers, vegetables and fruit, and by certain localized areas of specialization. These include bulb growing and flower

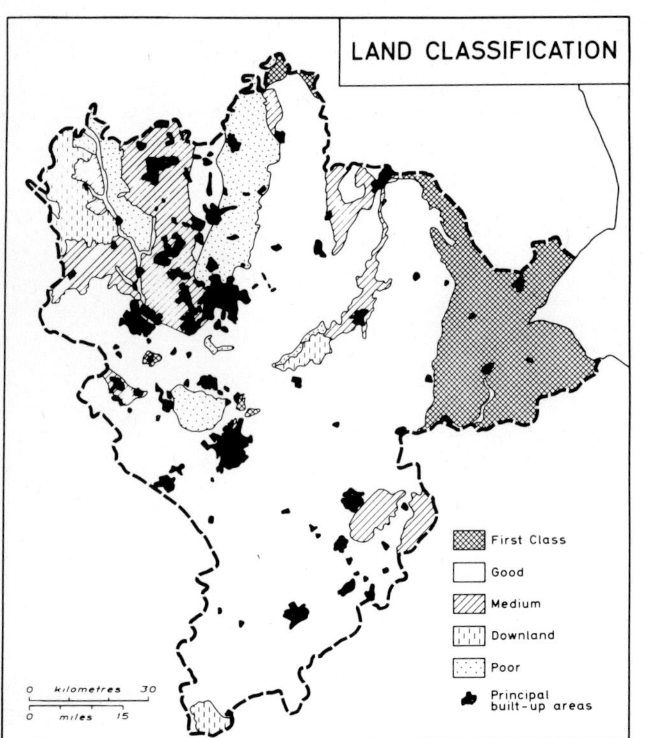

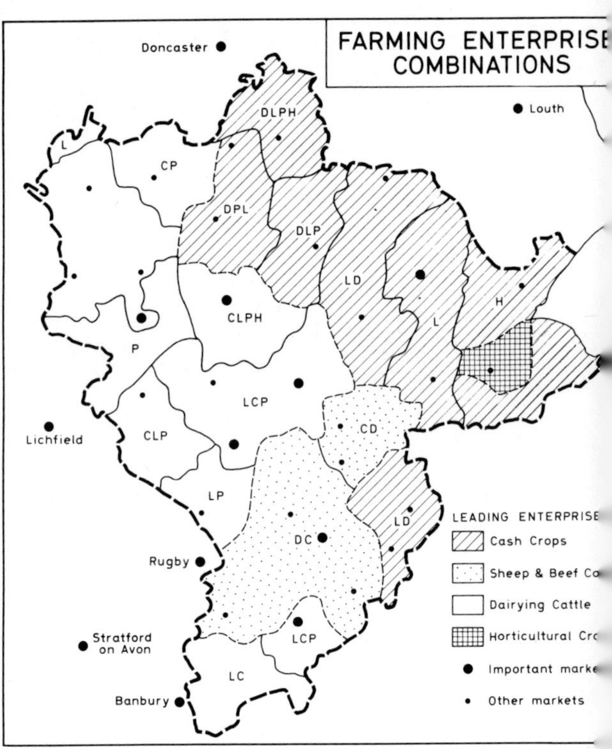

Fig 51 East Midlands—Land Classification and Farming Enterprise Combinations
Land classification is based upon the 1:625,000 Land Classification map of Great Britain. Farming enterprise combinations are based upon 1958 data according to the proportion of man days attributed to five enterprises. Letters indicate the second, third, fourth and fifth enterprise in rank order. Letters represent C – cash crops, P – pigs and poultry, H – horticultural crops, D – dairy cattle, L – sheep and beef cattle. The farming enterprise combinations are based upon J. T. Coppock, *An Agricultural Atlas of England and Wales* (London, 1964).

growing on the light soils near Spalding and eastwards to Sutton Bridge and north to Kirton, sugar beet grown within 16 kilometres (10 miles) of the factories in Spalding, and early potatoes grown north-east of the Witham near Boston. Crops of cereals, potatoes, and sugar beet are predominant on the large farms of the Keuper Marl and Bunter Sandstone areas, although numbers of hens and pigs have increased recently (Fig. 51) and horticulture increases immediately north of Nottingham. There are other localized specializations such as the production of carrots in four parishes north of the important market of Newark. Permanent pastures along the Trent are utilized for the summer grazing of beef cattle, particularly between Newark and Gainsborough. Yields in the eastern areas are subject to drought and some crops, such as main crop potatoes, sugar beet and intensively-managed grassland justify expenditure on irrigation systems.

Farms in the north-west of the dairying area are smaller in size, and in Derbyshire there were, in 1964, 11·3 dairy cows for every beef cow. Whereas Lincolnshire and Nottinghamshire have high percentages of their farmland under arable (82 per cent and 71 per cent respectively) the percentage is lower in Leicestershire (53 per cent) and in Derbyshire (31 per cent). The dairying enterprises in the north-west are frequently accompanied by poultry production, and Nottinghamshire is already the leading poultry producer in the Midlands. In south Nottinghamshire and north Leicestershire is an area noted for the production of blue and white Stilton cheeses. Although not now dependent upon local milk supplies fifteen dairies, twelve in the Vale of Belvoir, are still operative. Further south, beef cattle fattening is established in south and east Leicestershire and in north Northamptonshire. The latter county with 60 per cent of its farmland under arable includes the Jurassic Uplands, a continuation of the Cotswolds from the South-West region. These uplands are bleak and cold in winter and so the winter housing of cattle and sheep is becoming common.

Local areas of specialization diversify the general pattern of land use in western areas and Melbourne, 10 kilometres (6 miles) south of Derby, has some 40 per cent of its parish devoted to horticultural crops. Nurseries figure on the medium-light Keuper soils near Borrowash, and rose cultivation, which originated more than 100 years ago as a spare-time occupation, is notable near Bamford and at six localities south and west of Nottingham on the Keuper Marl soils. A natural concomitant of the pattern of land use is the existence of agricultural industries and these include canning of peas and other vegetables at Boston (Plate 46), canning and freezing at Wisbech, and the manufacture of potato crisps at Lincoln, in addition to the presence of five sugar beet factories in the region.

Industry

Perhaps the most striking characteristic of industry in the region is its variety This variety has resulted first from the diverse raw materials. Although coal production and the number of miners employed has decreased slightly in the mid-twentieth century this decrease has been less than elsewhere. As late as 1965 a new deep and fully automated colliery was opened at Bevercotes near Retford, and Cotgrave colliery, 8 kilometres (5 miles) south-east of Nottingham, was inaugurated in 1964 and employs about 1,600 men. The region accounts for a quarter of the national coal output and achieves high output per man shift. In 1966 71 mines operated on the Notts-Derby coalfield which now extends from Chesterfield–Derby in the west to Worksop, Ollerton and Nottingham in the east. Reserves are substantial and six major seams each have 400–500 million metric tons (900–1,160 million long tons), the reserves of others having yet to be assessed. At present the large quantities of small-sized industrial fuel produced are very suitable for automatic stoking and about half the output is consumed by power stations. The second most valuable mineral produced is iron ore which is largely obtained by open cast working. It was initiated in the mid-nineteenth century, and reserves are now estimated to

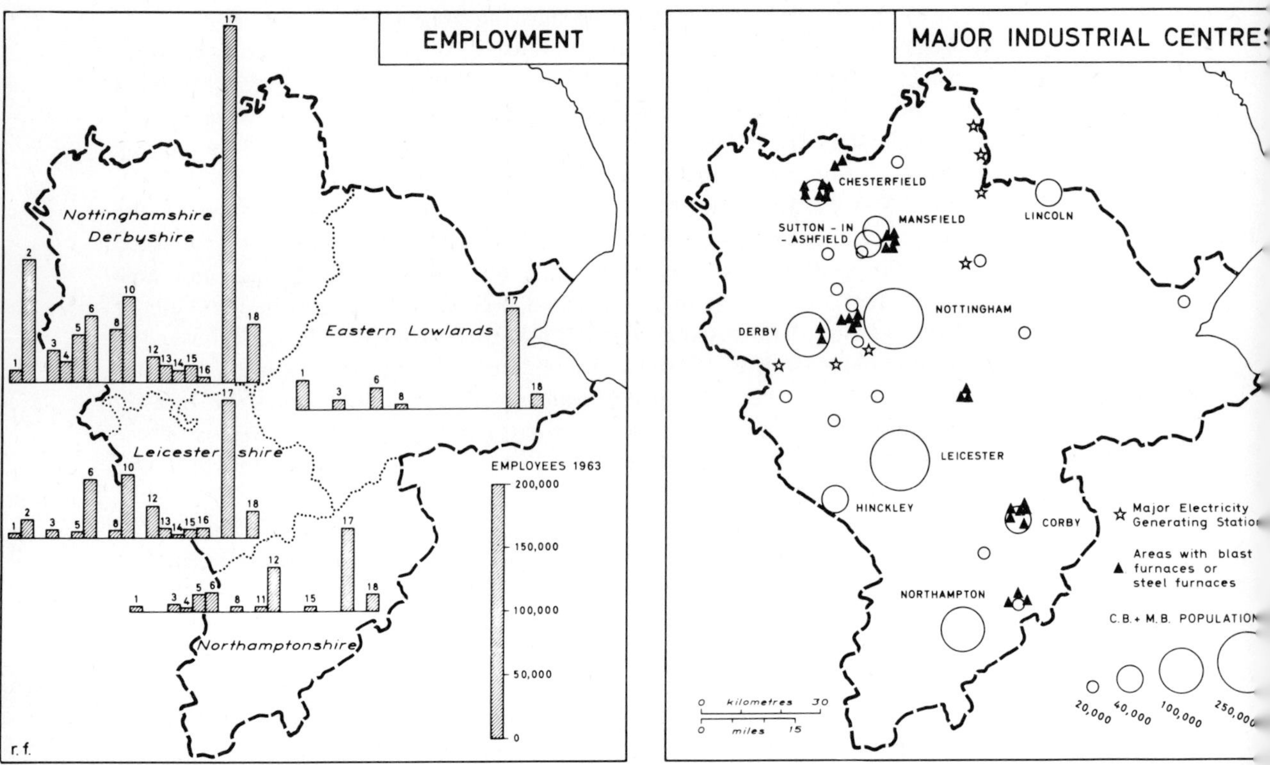

Fig 52 East Midlands—Employment and Major Industrial Centres
Employment is shown for the four sub-regions and the key to numbers is given below Figure 50. Population categories were based upon 1965 population estimates.

be sufficient for the next 160 years. Much of the iron ore is used within the region although some is sent to the North-East, Scunthorpe, the West Midlands, Sheffield, Lancashire and Cheshire. The early growth of the iron industry upon the exposed coalfield, in the Rother and Erewash valleys for example, accounts for the presence of centres such as Stanton and Staveley, which have survived the exhaustion of the local iron ore and the movement of the centre of gravity of coal mining towards the concealed field. Twentieth century development of iron and steel industry has been marked in Northamptonshire, and despite some reduction in the number of blast furnaces (Fig. 52) Corby, which had two blast furnaces in 1914 when its population was 1,350, was designated a New Town in 1950. By 1966 it had a population of 45,000 and the Stewart and Lloyds iron and steel works, producing tubes, accounted for a third of the national output. Industries utilizing metal are widely dispersed and they include the manufacture of mining machinery on the Notts-Derby coalfield, of agricultural equipment at Lincoln, Derby and Hucknall, and of constructional machinery at Lincoln, Grantham and Leicester. Other extractive industries include the output of sand and gravel, especially in the Trent valley (some 10 per cent of the England and Wales total), limestone in the Pennines, Leicestershire, Lincolnshire and Northamptonshire, Igneous rocks, and fireclay, which gives rise to 25 per cent of the national output of sanitary ware and salt-glazed pipes at Swadlingcote.

Several other industries further diversify the present industrial structure. Leather manufacture expanded in the early nineteenth century in the vicinity of Northampton and subsequently in Leicester, so that the two counties are now responsible for one-third and one-quarter respectively of the national output of footwear. This is especially significant for employment in Northampton and for centres in the Nene and Ise valleys. Further north textile manufacture, usually by small- or medium-sized firms, is now concentrated in a belt bordered by Matlock, Mansfield, Hinckley and Leicester and arose from diverse antecedents. The hosiery industry, now with some two-thirds of the country's hosiery workers, was concentrated in the East Midlands by the eighteenth century. It was associated with the cotton industry of the Derwent valley, Mansfield and the Nottingham district, and grew in association with the lace industry centred on Nottingham and the silk industry focused on Derby. The modern picture includes the production of artificial fibres at Spondon, south of Derby, and knitted garments in Leicester. The two established industries of iron and of textile manufacture combine in the manufacture of textile and footwear machinery in Leicestershire and Northamptonshire. Further variety is introduced by electrical engineering, which is expanding rapidly in Loughborough, Towcester, Beeston, Leicester, Lincoln and Corby, by the manufacture in Leicester of parts for vehicles assembled in the West Midlands, by the aircraft industry in Derby, by the production of 85 per cent of Britain's bicycles in Nottingham, and by pharmaceutical and cigarette manufacture—the latter industry being one of the largest employers within the city of Nottingham.

The broad-based industrial structure is opportune for future development in a region where 13 electricity power generating stations at present produce 15 per cent of the Central Electricity Board's output representing more than twice the requirements of the region. Three further Super stations are planned along the Trent and the region is also well placed with respect to North Sea gas, and some firms in Chesterfield are making machinery in response to the new demand. The present employment structure is illustrated for the sub-regions in Figure 52, which demonstrates the significance of mining and quarrying (2), textiles (10), engineering and electrical goods (6), vehicles (8) and metal manufacture (5) in the Nottinghamshire–Derbyshire sub-region. Textiles, engineering and electrical goods, and clothing and footwear (12) occupy the leading positions among manufacturing industries in Leicestershire, and clothing and footwear assume greater importance in Northamptonshire, where they are associated with engineering, electrical goods and metal manufacture. In the Eastern Lowlands agriculture is paramount, but engineering and electrical goods are important in centres such as Lincoln, and agricultural industries (3) also make a substantial contribution. Throughout the East Midlands service industries (17) account for a smaller proportion of employment (38·6 per cent) than in the nation as a whole (49·7 per cent).

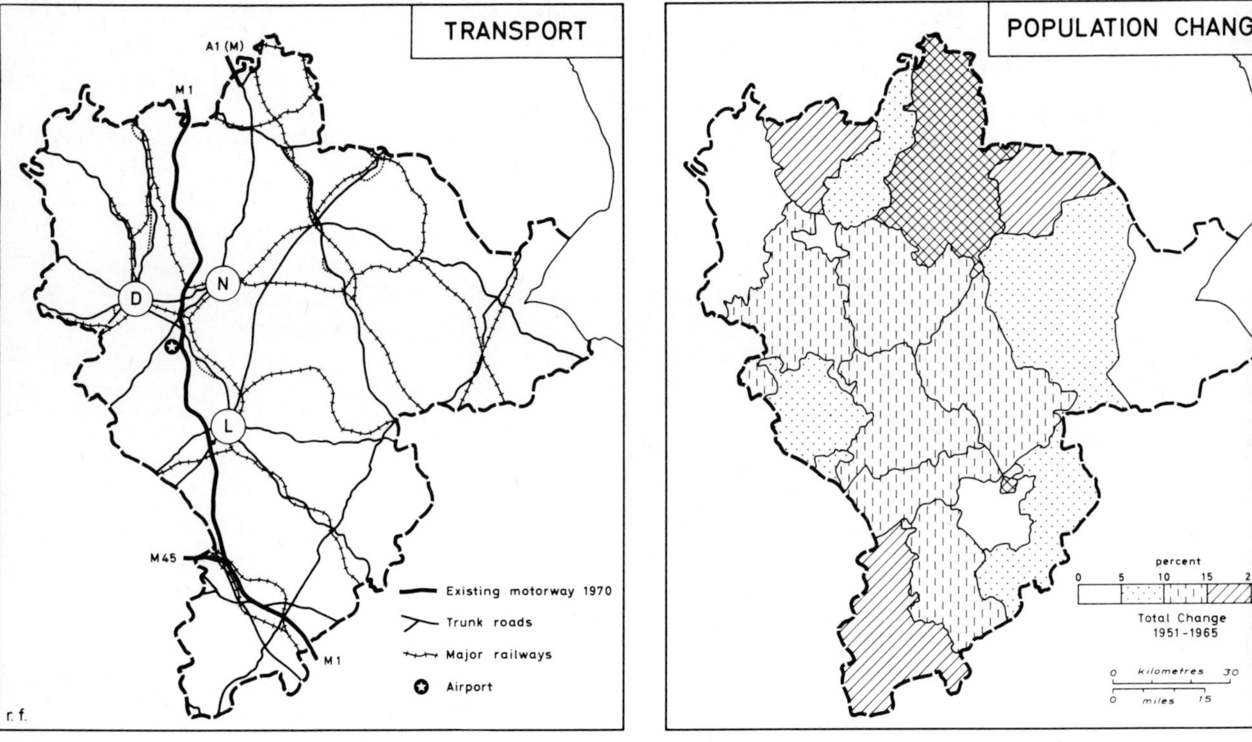

Fig 53 East Midlands—Transport and Population Change
Derby (D), Nottingham (N) and Leicester (L) are shown. Data on population change was obtained from East Midlands Economic Planning Council, *The East Midlands Study* (H.M.S.O., 1966).

Employment in service industries is increasing as is employment in food, drink and tobacco (especially in Leicestershire and Northamptonshire), in chemical industries (Nottinghamshire–Derbyshire), in metal manufacture (Nottinghamshire–Derbyshire, Northamptonshire), in bricks, pottery, glass and cement (13), and also in the construction industry. Recent decreases in employment have been apparent in agriculture (1), in mining and quarrying especially on the Nottinghamshire–Derbyshire and on the South Derbyshire–Leicestershire coalfields, and in the clothing and footwear industries, especially in Leicester, but this city is showing increased output, with innovations in manufacture, despite a reduced labour force.

Population and Prospects

In this region, where unemployment has been below the national average since 1951, the population is concentrated in the north and south. Since 1951, population change has tended to be greater in these areas than in the predominantly agricultural areas (Fig. 53) and this trend may be continued

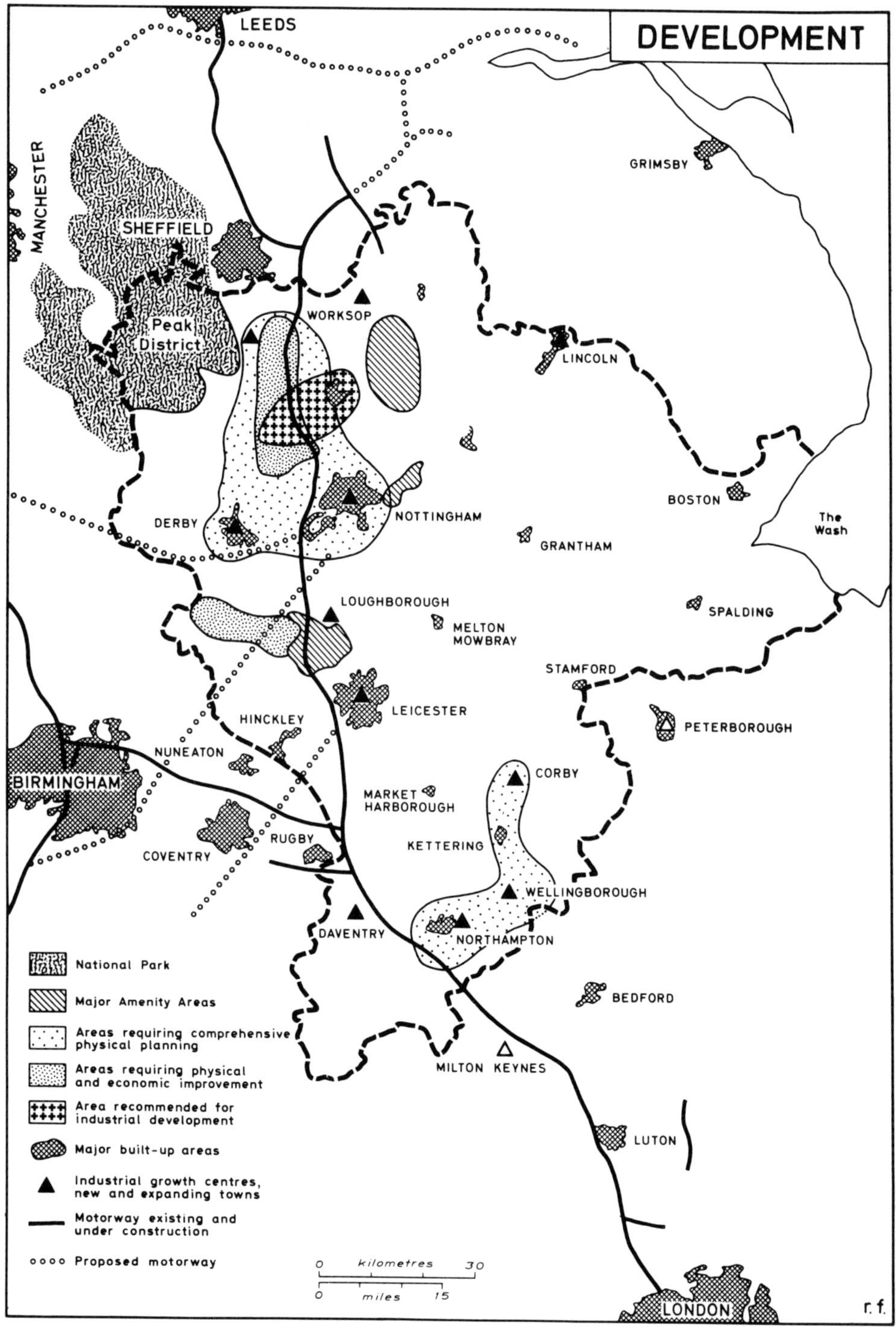

Fig 54 East Midlands—Potential for Development
Shaded areas are generalized and the map is based upon one in East Midland Economic Planning Council, *Opportunity in the East Midlands* (H.M.S.O., 1969).

because overspill from the South East to the new town of Northampton, and from the West Midlands to Daventry, could affect the south, while the expansion of Sheffield may have an effect upon the size of Chesterfield. The north and the extreme south are thus the two areas most favoured for future industrial expansion and this could be facilitated by the present transport network (Fig. 53). The M.1 affords an axis for both of these areas and links them with the South East and with West Yorkshire. The M.45 already provides a link between the southern area and the West Midlands, and the improvement of the A.38, and subsequently the addition of a motorway, will strengthen communication between the Nottingham–Derby area and the West Midlands (Fig. 54). The railway network is dominated by three main lines to the South East region, and one to the south-west, and the East Midlands airport was opened in 1965 as a co-operative venture by the County Councils of Derby, Leicestershire and Nottinghamshire with the Corporations of Derby and Nottingham (Fig. 53). Eventually, when an M.1–M.5 motorway link is developed, this airport may encourage industrial development at Loughborough and other adjacent centres.

Opportunity for future development therefore exists within the East Midlands and not least in the Nottinghamshire–Derbyshire sub-region where potential urban growth is less inhibited than in the South East and in the West Midlands, which has comparable locational advantages. Such urban growth could be achieved by expanding Nottingham as a regional capital, by developing Derby as a centre of industrial technology and services, by encouraging employment in centres like Worksop and Chesterfield, and by developing a major industrial growth zone centred on Mansfield–Alfreton. Such developments would meet the problems of the declining industries in the coalfield area where there is a need to regenerate old towns, to attract new industries, and to improve the character of the Erewash valley by physical and economic improvement (Fig. 54). The south Derbyshire–Leicestershire coalfield similarly requires physical replanning and the development of new forms of employment, and to the south-east the expansion of Greater Leicester (Plate 48) could be achieved, avoiding the best land, by two extensions, one to the north-west and one to the south-west, both related to an improved road network. Physical planning and employment diversification is also required in an area extending from Northampton to Corby (Fig. 54) which has some 40–60 per cent of its insured population dependent upon iron and steel.

The comparatively low population density and its distribution are therefore favourable for expansion without occasioning excessive and continuously built-up areas. One suggestion is that a new circular road, 25 kilometres (15·5 miles) in diameter centred upon Loughborough and touching the fringes of Derby, Nottingham and Leicester, is a potential mechanism available for future urban expansion, but however this expansion is achieved there is ample scope for a planned physical environment. The control of water quality, by reducing the pollution levels in the Trent (some 30 per cent of dry weather flow) and its tributaries the Soar (40 per cent) and the Erewash (50 per cent), is a necessary development, particularly as the river may be required as a source of water supply by 1980. Water supply in Northamptonshire is covered by

Plate 48 Leicester
The air photograph looks north-westwards across Leicester (283,549; 1971) to the Soar flood plain. The early site of the city was on the eastern bank of the Soar on a low terrace, it grew as a market centre and as a focus of the wool trade, and expanded rapidly eastwards in the nineteenth century (Fig. 53), and later on the western side of the Soar (in the distance). In addition to hosiery and footwear, contemporary industries include engineering, often of a specialised nature.

existing schemes into the early 1970s but subsequent consideration must be given to additional sources, such as the recharging of underground supplies and the development of a barrage or of pumped storage reservoirs in the Wash. Equally important is the development of amenity areas (Fig. 54) to complement the existing Peak District National Park. The establishment of Country or Regional Parks for Charnwood Forest, for the area between Leicester and Market Harborough, for Sherwood Forest, the Trent valley and the area around Matlock possibly complemented by the preservation of 'greenways' between the major towns and linking the regional parks are suggestions which have been offered to this end. In 1970 the East Midlands is therefore a region of anomaly where the coal and iron resources are no longer as significant as they were in the nineteenth and early twentieth centuries, but the landscapes and their labour supplies inherited from this phase are poised for development in the latter part of the twentieth century against the background of location and accessibility.

FURTHER READING

B. A. Hains and A. Horton, *Central England* (H.M.S.O., 1969).

G. H. Dury, *The East Midlands and the Peak* (London, 1963).

East Midlands Economic Planning Council, *The East Midlands Study* (H.M.S.O., 1966); *Opportunity in the East Midlands* (H.M.S.O., 1969);

East Midland Geographer, especially Special issue in honour of K. C. Edwards, 5 (1970), Numbers 33, 34 (Department of Geography, University of Nottingham, 1954–).

K. C. Edwards (ed.), *Nottingham and its Region* (Nottingham, 1966).

Leicester City Council and Leicestershire County Council, *Leicester and Leicestershire Sub-Regional Planning Study* (Leicester, 1969).

Nottinghamshire County Council, Derbyshire County Council, Nottingham City Council, Derby County Borough Council, *Nottinghamshire and Derbyshire Sub-Regional Study* (Loughborough, 1969).

D. M. Smith, *The Industrial Archaeology of the East Midlands* (Dawlish, 1965).

S. Williams, *Farming in the Midlands* (London, 1967).

The West Midlands

The West Midland Region consists of the counties of Shropshire, Staffordshire, Warwickshire, Worcestershire and Herefordshire, an area about 128 kilometres (80 miles) square. The region lacks a popular image; it has no Ilkley Moor or Brighton Pier. It has a motor car industry, however, which colours many views not just of the region but also of the country, for rates of economic growth in Britain depend to a considerable extent on the current state of the engineering industries in the West Midlands. Although forming the heartland of Britain, both in situation and in its regulation of the British economy, it is a between-land, with Northerners considering it part of the South and Southerners visualizing it as part of the northern 'nether lands'. In some respects the region compromises between northern and southern attitudes and customs. Take the cooking of green vegetables for example. Market research has shown that Midlanders place their vegetables in warm water, in the North cooking is started from cold while in the South green vegetables are put into boiling water. In other customs West Midlanders side with the South, for example in their passion for dining room tables, but in other respects, such as the consumption of malt bread, affinities are with the North. A split personality is present even within the region with a dichotomy between on the one hand the Birmingham Conurbation, The Potteries, and Coventry, and on the other hand the rural west. This division means that in many respects the region lacks cohesion and frequently the attitude of Birmingham is the one to carry the day. This lack of unity coupled with the central position engenders an outward looking attitude in people and industry alike. Here the Bristol–Humber axis crosses the Thames–Mersey axis, and with recent motorway connections the land-locked West Midlands is now within easy reach of more major ports than any other region of the country. As an area dependent on inter-regional and inter-national trade the West Midlands has a particularly strategic position in Britain.

The Physical Background

The physical structure of the West Midland Region is complex, with inter-penetrating lowland, scarp and vale, plateaux, platforms and highland areas. Many of these areas are parts of major structural units within west and central Britain; sections of the Severn lowlands, the English scarplands, the Pennines and the Welsh Mountains lie in the West Midlands. Even a simple division of the physical landscape must consider at least 12 very definite geomorphological sub-regions. Four of these sub-regions are essentially highland areas above

Fig 55 West Midlands

250 metres (800 feet), four are lowlands generally below 90 metres (300 feet) and four are plateaux and platforms between these two heights. (Fig. 55).

In the north-east of the region lies part of the Pennines. The interbedding of bluish grey shale with hard sandstones produces a landscape of infinite variety. A rounded subdued landscape has developed on the shales, while the sandstones have proved much more resistant to erosion. Stream density is particularly high on the shales and over wide areas acid wet soils predominate. The River Trent falls 250 metres (800 feet) in only 20 kilometres (12 miles) as it drains the moors north of Leek and then acts as an open drain for parts of the Potteries. Successful efforts have been made in recent years to control the amount of industrial and domestic waste entering the river and life is now returning to previously dead stretches of river. The second highland area is drained by another major English river, the Severn. The Long Mynd and Stiperstones masses rise to 520 metres (1,700 feet). The northern edge of these uplands drains directly into the Severn while the southern parts drain into the Onny, which eventually joins the Severn at Worcester. On the east the Long Mynd falls sharply to the Church Stretton rift and to the east again the Precambrian rocks continue in the hog's back igneous ridges of Caer Caradoc. The Wrekin (Plate 49) forms a north-eastward extension of these ridges. The flat, heathy, tops of the Long Mynd with podsolized acid brown soils contrast

Plate 49 The Wrekin (Shropshire)
422 metres (1,385 feet). There is a strong contrast between the stoney, well drained, acid brown soils on the ridges and the surrounding low land with its reddish-brown clays and sandy clays developed on sub-glacial parent material.

sharply with the craggy outlines of the Stiperstones where shallow stoney soils have formed on resistant quartzites. In contrast again are the Silurian and Old Red Sandstone landscapes to the south in the Clun Forest. This is the third highland mass; a much dissected plateau with summits between 300 and 425 metres (1,000 and 1,400 feet) but over the county and national boundary in Radnorshire the highland is both more extensive and higher. The rivers Clun and Teme flow in deep steep-sided valleys. In the area generally the surface deposits are particularly disturbed often by landslipping. The final highland area is also intimately connected with the Welsh mountain system. A part of the Black Mountains lies in the West Midland region. In Herefordshire the horizontal Old Red Sandstone beds have a complex lithology of marls and sandstones, and as in Clun are much dissected; only remnants of former extensive erosional and depositional surfaces are seen in the present day landscape.

The lowlands together form a giant T shape drained by the Severn and the Trent, with additionally in the south-east, the Avon valley, and in the south-west, the Wye. The Trent lowlands are characterized by a fleet of low, wide, gravel terraces, and a frequently flooded flood plain, with its alluvium over a mile wide at several places, for example at Kings Bromley. A major tributary is the Tame which drains the higher land of the Birmingham plateau south of the main Trent valley. The Severn lowlands can be divided into those of North Shropshire—upstream of the gorge at Ironbridge (Plate 50)—and those of Worcestershire. The Shropshire lowlands are developed on Bunter sandstones and Keuper marls but more important in the formation of the physical landscape are the glacial sands and gravels which cover the area. The gentle slopes, broad valleys, marshes, and mires result in a landscape similar to that of the Trent valley. Typical mires are Baggy Moor and Boggy Moor east of Oswestry. The peaty soils provide fine permanent grassland. South of Ironbridge the lowland of the Stour and Severn lies in a syncline of Triassic sandstone, slopes are somewhat steeper than in the upstream portion, and generally there is greater relative relief in the dissected landscape. The Severn lowlands continue into Worcestershire where problems of soil drainage on the lowest parts are produced by the presence of underlying Keuper marl. The Avon joins the Severn on the southern boundary of the region; the Avon valley forms a third lowland area. Development of the present form of the Avon valley is almost certainly wholly post-glacial for previously the river was part of the Trent drainage basin. Along considerable stretches of the valley there are five levels of extensive river terraces, frequently up to a kilometre (0·6 miles) wide above a narrow flood plain. A particularly important terrace occurs at approximately 10 metres (33 feet) above the present river level and on this terrace the light well drained soils have been used for agriculture with considerable economic success. The fourth lowland is the Wye valley and this is very different from the three others in its gently rolling relief developed on red marls. Occasional hills rise from the overall low area, for example Wormsley Hill rising to 294 metres (963 feet). The fairly gentle slopes, coupled with a mild dry climate, means that much of the land must be classified as first class in any system of agricultural land classification.

Plate 50 The Severn Gorge at Ironbridge (Shropshire)
Note the iron bridge itself, built by Abraham Darby III and opened in 1781.

The third group of physical landscapes are the plateaux, platforms and scarplands. In the south-east and joining the region to the scarplands of southern England is Feldon. Here a Lower Lias plateau at about 90 metres (300 feet) grades into the scarps of the Middle Lias. The clay lands of the plateau were originally heavily wooded, but were cleared very early in the history of human occupance of the region and so have been used for agriculture for many centuries. In the west of the region there are more impressive scarp features. East of the Caradoc Hills are a series of scarps developed in Silurian rocks. Wenlock Edge, in Silurian limestone, is an example. The scarps, although broken in places, can be traced into north-west Herefordshire to the Kington district. The shale lowlands generally are cultivated but the uplands are of little agricultural value. South-east of the Silurian scarps there are Old Red Sandstones and on these the Clee Hill Platform has developed. Lying between 150 and 250 metres (500 and 800 feet), this is a broken upland, and is particularly dissected in the south around Bromyard. Above the plateaux a few isolated hills rise sharply—Titterstone Clee rises to over 520 metres (1,700 feet) and its presence is partly due to a capping of hard dolerite which has slowed down the processes of erosion. The final plateau area is the Birmingham Plateau on which stands much of the West Midlands Conurbation. The Birmingham Plateau is subdivided into two parts by the north to south valleys of the Tame and Blyth, these plateaux are the South Staffordshire Plateau and the East Warwickshire Plateau which lie between 90 and 250 metres (300 and 800 feet). Somewhat higher land is found around the margin, for instance in the south-west the Clents rise above 300 metres (1,000 feet) in small areas. While the eastern part of the Birmingham plateau is developed on middle and upper Coal Measures, the western part consists of a series of plateaux, separated by steep bluffs; the Cannock High Plateau is developed on Bunter Pebble Beds; the Harborne Plateau forms much of the site of Birmingham; that city's southern suburbs are on the Solihull Plateau at about 130 metres (425 feet).

The diversity of the physical landscape in the West Midlands region has far reaching effects. The existence of highlands, particularly around the edge of the region, means that movements out or into the region are funnelled through breaks in this rim. From the agricultural point of view the variety of land types in the region means a considerable range of possible agricultural specialisms. The physical variety allows freedom for variation in social as well as economic decision making. A family from the West Midlands Conurbation has within 80 kilometres (50 miles) a variety of recreational areas greater than that around any other major centre of population in Britain.

Altitude influences climate to a considerable extent in the West Midlands. The mean annual temperature at Birmingham is 9°C (48°F) but 7°C (45°F) is more common at heights of 300 metres (1,000 feet). In the lowlands below 250 metres (800 feet) rainfall amounts to between 610 and 890 millimetres (24 and 35 inches) but in the Avon valley, and districts around Shrewsbury and Tamworth, amounts are less than 635 millimetres (25 inches). Above 250 metres (800 feet) rainfall increases sharply and isohyets and contours are coincident, with the 300 metres (1,000 feet) contour being equivalent to the 890 millimetres (35 inches) isohyet in west Shropshire and to the 1,140 millimetres (45 inches) isohyet in the south-west Pennines. Evaporation in the upland areas, with their lower temperature, higher relative humidity and greater cloud cover is about 350 millimetres (15 inches) per year, while in the lower areas 500 millimetres (20 inches) is not uncommon. Effective rainfall here can therefore be quite low, 100 millimetres (4 inches) for Shrewsbury with 580 millimetres (23 inches) of rain, 480 millimetres (19 inches) of which are evaporated. Agricultural spraying and irrigation channels are not unusual sights in the region.

Agriculture

The diversity of the physical landscape provides a basis for variety in the agricultural economy of the region. Land, however, is only one of the determinants of the agricultural type; considerations of market, labour and capital are equally important to the farmer in making his decision on what to grow and how to grow it.

The impact of the market can be seen in the behaviour of farmers in the Lichfield and Bromsgrove areas. In these districts market gardens are commonplace. The Bunter and Keuper sandstones have produced lightish soils eminently suitable to vegetable production but the proximity of the West Midlands Conurbation is an overiding influence. In the Vale of Evesham considerations of labour availability are important in the farmers' decision making processes. Again suitable soils and nearby markets play a part, but the smallness of holdings often leads to hand cultivated, specialized crops such as asparagus, for which the district is famous. Capital availability on the larger farms of east Shropshire, Feldon, and north Worcestershire is partly reflected in the dominance of arable crops with their mechanized methods of cultivation. The sugar beet processing factory in Kidderminster provides a market and the system of price guarantees helps towards the high capital inputs necessary on the sugar beet farms, for example around Hartlebury.

The influences of land quality are apparent in the livestock farming areas in the region. Much of Staffordshire has soils formed on boulder clays or heavy Keuper marls and although the land was under the plough during the war, it has since been returned to pasture for dairy cattle. The towns of the Potteries undoubtedly provide a market but the quality of land has been important in the decision to grow grass rather than vegetables, or some other market orientated product. Agriculture in the hill lands of the west and Herefordshire is dominated by livestock enterprises. The Clun breed of sheep and the Hereford cattle are famed throughout the world. A combination of the character of the land, remoteness from markets, and the relatively small number of the rural labour force affect decisions made by the farmer and so result in a fairly extensive agricultural system.

The general decline in the needs for, and in the supply of, agricultural labour is seen in the West Midland region for on average over recent years two farm workers have left agricultural employment every day. Over the region as a whole less than 2 per cent of the employed population is classified as being engaged in agriculture, but locally in the west of the region the figure rises to over 30 per cent. The increase in mechanization of so many types of farming coupled with the increase in the size of holdings has meant that on an acreage basis, fewer workers are required to maintain the same or even increased levels of production.

Although no longer a major employer the agricultural industry has important new functions. The increase in mechanization has meant that the industries making farm machinery have had a considerable boost, while all industries dependent on agriculture have improved their levels of output and productivity in recent years. With the increased capitalization of farming practices on the one hand and the increase in the processing of farm products on the other the farmer becomes not just the tiller of the land, but a unit in a chain of linked industries joining the tractor factory to the canning factory. Thus although the population directly dependent on agriculture has declined drastically during the last decade the total number of people connected in some way with agriculture has increased.

Population and Housing

The central district, the Birmingham conurbation and immediately surrounding areas, dominates any consideration of patterns and problems of population and housing in the West Midlands. In this sub-region there are almost 2½ million people, many of whom live in property over 100 years old. Nineteenth century and twentieth century development exist side by side with industry and housing, forming a pepperpot of land uses. Only with the introduction of effective planning controls after 1947 have land uses become segregated. A similar but smaller problem exists in North Staffordshire where

Plate 51 Great Malvern (Worcestershire)
The east face of the Malvern Hills is a fault scarp, at the foot of which there developed low density Victorian–Gothic housing, reflecting the popularity of spas in the mid-nineteenth century.

pits and pots dominated the economy and urban scene for so long. About one million people live in the Potteries in a series of contiguous towns. In these towns there is considerable urban renewal as the older obsolescent houses are replaced both by estates in the main body of the towns and by fresh building on the fringe of the urban region. The rural west—west of the Severn—has approximately 320,000 population. Shrewsbury and Hereford form the major centres and around each of these is a circle of smaller towns, for example, Oswestry, Whitchurch and Wellington. Problems of redevelopment very different from those of the conurbation are associated with some of the western towns. Malvern, with its very low density of housing per acre (Plate 51), presents particular problems. The New Town of Telford in the Wellington, Dawley, Oakengates area will distort this relatively simple pattern and in the future the triangle enclosed by Birmingham, Telford and the Potteries could take on a new significance and become particularly attractive to residential development.

Within the central part of the region, and within the Birmingham conurbation especially, population growth has been considerable in recent years. The population increase is greatest for any of the conurbations of Britain and natural increase accounts for much of the growth in numbers. Migration during recent years has been far less important than natural increase, but this is a new phenomenon; in the decade 1954–64 over 100,000 more people entered this sub-region than left it. Many of these immigrants to the area were in the younger age groups and many were from the West Indies, Pakistan, or Ireland. Such younger immigrants were attracted by the job opportunities while increasing numbers of emigrants were older people moving away to retirement areas. The Commonwealth Immigration Act of 1962 resulted in a decrease in the inflow to the conurbation, but the numbers leaving the area continued to increase. That the area has not declined in absolute population numbers is the result of the high rate of natural increase due to both high birth rate, concomitant on the inflow of young people, and the low death rate due to the outflow of older people.

The increase in the number of households, particularly in the 1950s, together with the large areas of potential slum property resulted in a housing problem of serious proportions, and if this problem is to be solved there will have to be a major redistribution of the present population. Within the conurbation over 200,000 houses are over 100 years old and there are additionally many slums which are far younger. In the 20 years from 1945, over a quarter of a million people were involved in overspill projects. The 50,000 people now living in Chelmsley Wood are an example of the results of this overspill policy. With a regional population in 1981 forecast at 5·7 million however, it is estimated that in the 15 years after 1965 at least 20 times as many people will have to be rehoused as were rehoused in the previous two decades. With much of the population increase occurring in the conurbation the bulk of the rehousing programme will be tied to replacing sub-standard property in the Birmingham area.

The scale of the need for new building to rehouse the present population can be seen from Table 13 showing the age of housing in the conurbation. The smallest problem is with the housing owned by the local authorities, while the largest problem is with privately rented property. To help eradicate substandard property almost 20,000 new houses were built in the region in 1969—a figure of almost 400 per week. This creditable result has been achieved largely by the use of industrialized building methods. Of the new houses in 1969, 52 per cent were built by such methods, while in England and Wales as a whole the corresponding figure was 38 per cent. Completed houses in 1969 were 7·3 per thousand population and only in East Anglia was this figure exceeded. But if the public sector only is considered then the figure of 4·1 for the West Midlands is exceeded in no other region. The local authorities in the region are thus making a considerable effort to improve housing standards within the region.

The rapid expansion in the numbers of houses is not without difficulties, for the conurbation is an area of already densely developed land. Least land is available in just the places where it is needed most. Many of the slum areas are at a very high density of population per acre and redevelopment has to take place at a lower density, thus making it necessary to find additional housing land. The under-provision of schools, roads and open space in the slum areas means that on redevelopment not all land previously used for housing may be used again. Some land thus changes use. The mixture of land uses in the conurbation means that industry and housing developed side by side. Some land formerly in industrial uses is now derelict or only part used. Often accessibility, or the location of this land restricts its use for housing purposes. A conscious policy of limiting peripheral development by a green belt has further kept housing land in short supply and there has been little release of land beyond the green belt. Part of the problem has been overcome by the use of high-rise blocks, but even so, service and open space provision is needed in proportion to the population housed.

TABLE 13

AGE OF HOUSING IN THE WEST MIDLAND CONURBATION

	percentages of:			
Period	*All Houses*	*Private Houses*	*Local Authority Houses*	*Others inc. Private Rented*
pre 1919	28	28	13	65
1919–1944	37	42	37	24
post 1944	35	30	50	11

NEW HOUSES BUILT IN 1969

Sub Region	*Percentage in Public Sector*	*Percentage in Private Sector*
Conurbation	62	38
Coventry area	38	62
North Staffordshire	30	70
Rural West	41	59

The major shortages of land are associated with the Birmingham–Wolverhampton area. The same problems but on a much smaller, and more manageable scale, occur in the Potteries and Coventry. Land problems in the west are very different, for here the problem is the protection of good agricultural land around the towns. New development tends to be more often by private developers than by local government authorities. The movements of population in the west have been, and promise to be, on a much smaller scale than in the conurbation, but in terms of the size of the community affected, the movements can have equal effect. A private estate of 25 houses in a community of 500 people can affect the community just as drastically as several thousand new houses built in a large city.

Industry

The relocation of population cannot be divorced from changes in the pattern of jobs in the West Midlands. Movement of population without a commensurate movement of jobs means an increase in commuting. Much industry is firmly rooted to its present location, in which it has been settled for perhaps 50 years or more, despite changing locational requirements. But population growth of recent years has been paralleled by an increase in job opportunities. Expansion of the number and variety of industrial jobs has occurred over the whole of the West Midlands Conurbation and the central part of the region; in the Potteries employment growth has lagged behind that of the rest of the region and in the rural west new employment has been concentrated in a few towns, especially Shrewsbury and Hereford. Over the region as a whole there has been a high level of business activity during the 1960s, unemployment levels have been low and activity rates high. While this situation is not an absolute indication of economic health or efficiency, none the less it suggests a prosperity not apparent in some of the other industrial regions of Britain.

The outstanding feature of the industrial structure of the West Midlands is the importance of manufacturing industry to the regional economy. Over 50 per cent of the region's jobs are in the manufacturing sector compared with less than 40 per cent for Great Britain. Primary industries account for about 1 in 25 of the workforce, which is not very different from the national average, so the large percentage of manufacturing jobs occurs at the expense of the service trades.

The dominance of manufacturing is no new phenomenon in the region. In Tudor times certain of the market towns of the region were already developing specialized industries. In Birmingham and Coventry textiles were important and at Walsall there was a concentration of tanners and leather workers. The glass industry at Stourbridge not only made that town wealthy but also produced a notable regional export. By the sixteenth century the ironstones in the Black Country were being worked and provided one of the raw materials for the production of nails, needles, locks and agricultural implements such as scythes. As skills developed and innovations in manufacturing technique were accepted, so more advanced products were made in the region and sold throughout the country, thus accentuating specialisms of towns or parts of the region. The needs for ever increasingly sophisticated weapons made defence spending an important part of baronial expenditures in this period and the production of guns in the towns that today make up the conurbation, provided the basis for the growth of a large group of industries relying on defence contracts. By the end of the seventeenth century there existed a well-defined group of industries heavily dependent for their success on technological know how and the individual ability of craftsmen.

During the seventeenth century a somewhat similar process was occurring in the north of the region where slipware, a form of rough pottery, was being produced. Technological advance was rapid and McLuhan's dictum that if it works it's obsolete was as relevant then as now with the ever-present search to improve the product, or to produce more for a lower price. In the eighteenth century the production of pottery was the cynosure of manufacturers in the North Staffordshire towns. By the middle of the century methods for the production of porcelain were being tested at such factories as Longton Hall. The manufacture of porcelain from the Worcester works must be seen as a related technology at this time. The production methods frequently were closely guarded secrets and key individuals were vitally important in the success or otherwise of a particular enterprise. Similarly with the decoration and painting of the porcelains; as skilled men moved from factory to factory so the competitive standing of the different factories changed. However, the role of the individual declined rapidly in the early years of the nineteenth century after the Spode factory began the mass production of china.

The influence of the individual on industrial patterns is seen in a rather different way in the metal manufacturing towns. At Coalbrookdale in 1709 Abraham Darby successfully smelted iron by using coke, instead of the more usual charcoal (see Chapter 4). This individual technological achievement heralded a new era for the factories of the burgeoning towns of the Black Country. The successful use of a steam engine by Boulton and Watt at the Soho Works in Birmingham enhanced further the possibilities of larger factories, which in turn meant specialization of product and production methods. The industrial inheritance of the West Midlands meant that by 1800 there were employees already partly conditioned to accept the changes of the industrial revolution, and the industries benefited to the full in the great surge of markets that opened up during the nineteenth century.

The long tradition of working in metal placed firms in a strong position to exploit the changed market conditions which became apparent after 1918 with the increase in demand for vehicles and electrical goods. The development of the town of Stafford after 1900 may be related to the growth of a market for electrical goods of all kinds. Similarly the increase in defence spending apparent over the last 50 years has provided a stimulus not just to armament producers, but also to the electrical engineering industries. Birmingham and the Black Country remain dominant in industrial production, but growth in the Nuneaton, Rugby, Coventry belt with the manufacture of sewing machines, cycles, electrical goods, aircraft, machine tools, cars, and man-made fibres have produced another national industrial region. Elsewhere in the region new manufacturing industries have been located in towns such as Hereford, Shrewsbury and Leamington Spa to complement their traditional industries.

With this long history of dependence on metal manufacturing industries it is hardly surprising that in the region in 1970, employment in the 'metal and engineering industry groups' was 10 times greater than in its nearest rival—

brick and pottery—with 83,000 employees. Three older major industrial groups each employed more than 25,000 employees; these were first, food industries, including chocolate at Bournville and brewing at Burton-on-Trent (about 75,000 employees); second, textiles, including carpet production at Kidderminster (about 35,000) and third, chemicals (about 25,000).

To view the industries in the region grouped into classes based on the goods produced is only a partial interpretation of the industrial structure of the region for there are strong and vital linkages among industries; change in one industry can have wide ranging effects over a whole range of other industries. Linkages of three types are usually recognized. First, there are vertical linkages, for example, between non-ferrous metal refining and non-ferrous goods production. Vertical integration can occur in a firm when the technical processes are extended, so that a metal refining firm goes into the production of metal goods. A feature of the industry in the West Midlands is a lack of this type of vertical integration. Rather, vertical disintegration is notable and various processes which normally take place in one factory are divided among specialist firms. Secondly there are convergent or horizontal linkages, for example the manufacture of bolts, tyres, electrical equipment, and bodies, all for motor vehicles. Thirdly, there are those linkages which act as a service for several local industries, for example jobbing foundries and construction engineers. This specialized service type of linkage is particularly common in the West Midlands' industrial structure. In their inter-relations the firms compose an industrial system in which a change in technology may affect the strength and direction of particular links and in turn affect production patterns and ultimately the type of industrial land use.

Related to this idea of linkages among industries, it is possible to define groups of enterprises which function in similar ways. Studies have suggested that in the West Midlands there are four such major classes of enterprises in the metal and engineering industries. Firms which carry out particular processes on metal either in its raw or semi-finished state form a first class. Examples of such processes are tinning, enamelling, and general iron founding. Firms carrying out these and similar processes are particularly important in Tamworth and Droitwich. Other firms specialize in creating finished and semi-finished components for direct use by other firms producing finished manufactured articles. These firms constitute a second group and typical are those making taps or gauges for incorporation into further production processes. Other than in the conurbation itself the towns where these industries are concentrated are Cannock, Hereford, Bedworth, and Lichfield. A third group of firms are those producing components for final assembly into complete articles. Towns in which these firms predominate form a swathe of places around the southern edge of the conurbation. Notable are Nuneaton, Leamington, Bromsgrove, and Redditch. Lastly, there are the firms which perform the final assembly; often these firms do little if any manufacturing. Many motor vehicle and electrical machinery firms are of this type. Stafford, Rugby, Burton-on-Trent, and Rugeley are towns where this type of firm predominate. The present day industrial structure of the region is firmly based on the metal and engineering industries which together form a strong indus-

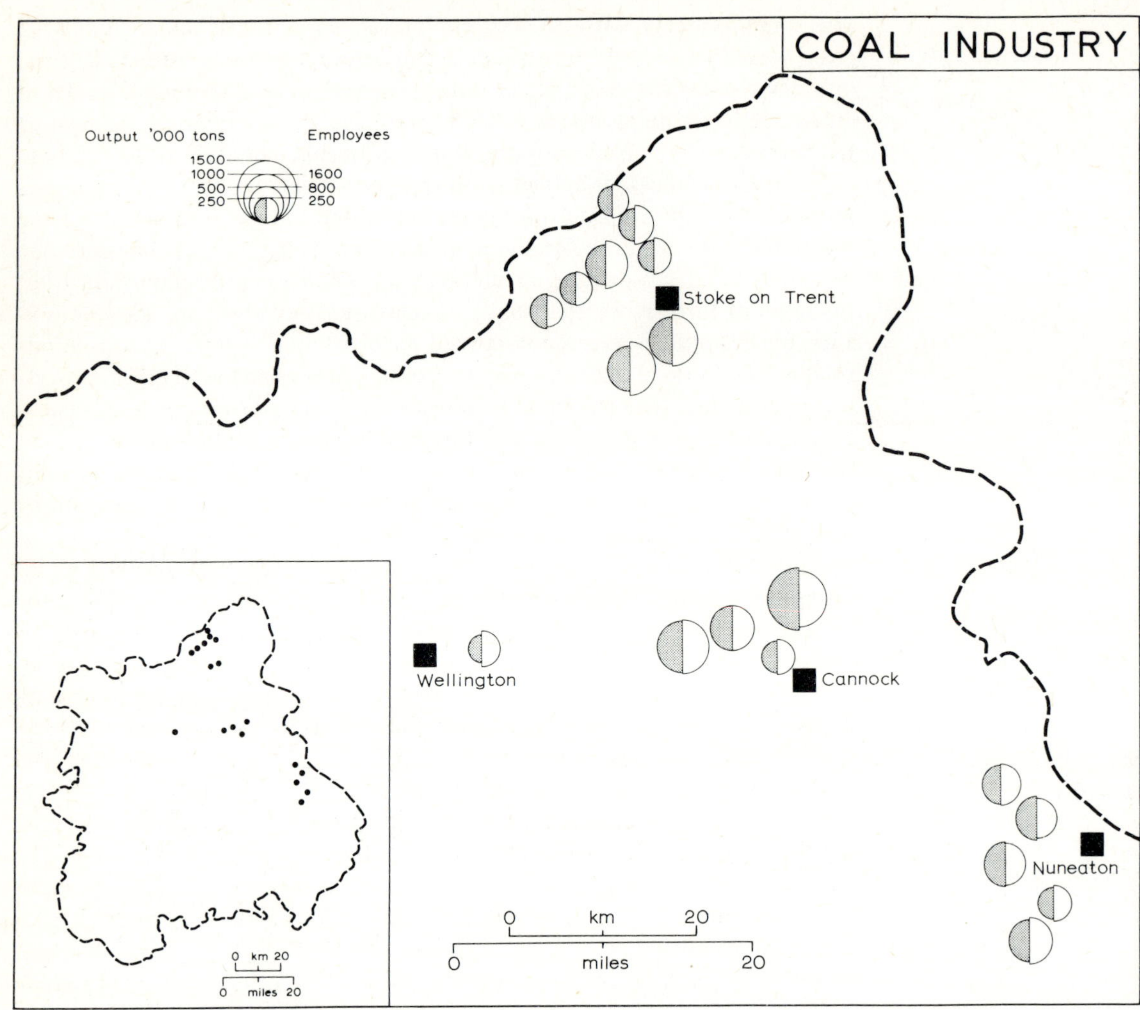

Fig 56 West Midlands—The Output and Employment in Coal Mines, 1970

trial system.

While the manufacturing industries account for the majority of the work-force, nonetheless there is a thriving series of primary industries apart from agriculture. Building materials are particularly important to a region in which construction of both domestic and industrial buildings is so vital. The gravel deposits of both Severn and Trent valleys provide valuable sources of raw materials. Possibly even more important than the gravel are the coal deposits under the Potteries, Cannock Chase, the Coventry industrial belt and Shropshire. Reserves are considerable, Lea Hall Mine produces $1\frac{1}{2}$ million tons annually, and although a relatively small amount of employment is generated by the mines, productivity is high. The size of the pits in the region is shown in Figure 56. One of the problems associated with some of the older mines is that of derelict and waste land (Plate 52). Much of this is in the Potteries where already drabness often pervades the urban scene. It is mainly in or near these same areas that derelict land forms a problem. In many instances the reclamation of derelict land would not only help to improve visual amenity but would provide valuable land for urban redevelopment and thus save virgin land elsewhere.

Transport

The combination of the inland position of the West Midlands and the heavy dependence of its industry on markets outside the region and indeed outside Britain, means that efficient transport facilities are essential to the regional economy. A reflection of the importance of transport to the industries of the region can be seen in the early and intense development of canals. The physical features of the plateau area on which Birmingham developed

Plate 52 Newcastle-under-Lyme (Staffordshire)
A mine on the Staffordshire coalfield.

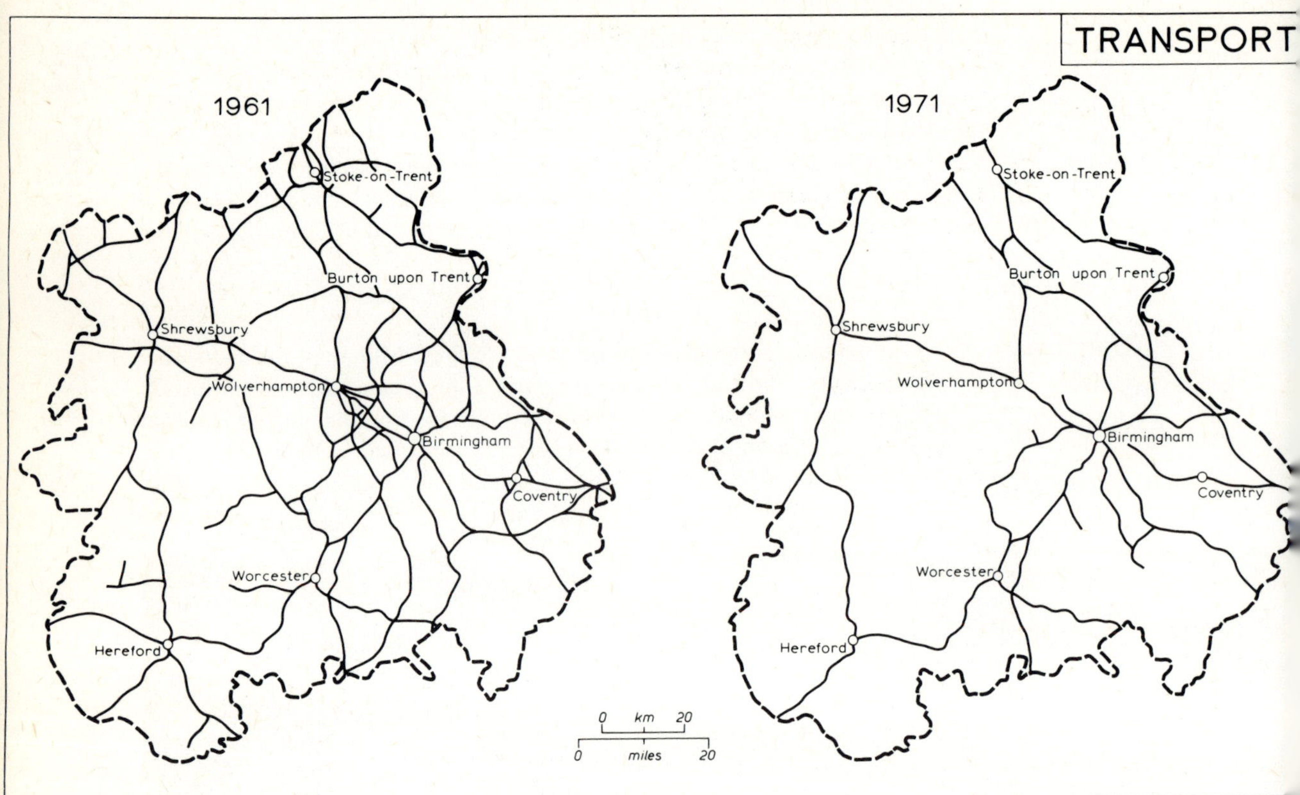

Fig 57 West Midlands—The Railway Routes open for Passenger Traffic in 1961 and 1971

provide obstacles to canal building, but the demand for the cheap transport was such as to stimulate eighteenth century engineers to considerable feats of technology in their designs for fleets of locks and tunnels. Transport costs are equally important today, and the heavy export trade of West Midland industry means that developments in freight handling at ports, especially Liverpool and Bristol, influence the economics of many firms. The provision of container services, both by rail and road, to the ports is but one change in transport techniques that is affecting the West Midlands. Another development outside the region which has affected travel patterns within the region is the increasing mobility of London's commuters (see Chapter 7). Long distance commuting into London from homes in the West Midlands is a response partly to the faster rail connection consequent on electrification of the London to Birmingham line, and partly to the differential in house prices between the South East and West Midland regions.

Changes in transport patterns have also occurred within the region due to influences from inside the West Midlands, and from within the conurbation particularly. The concentration of the region's population in the conurbation

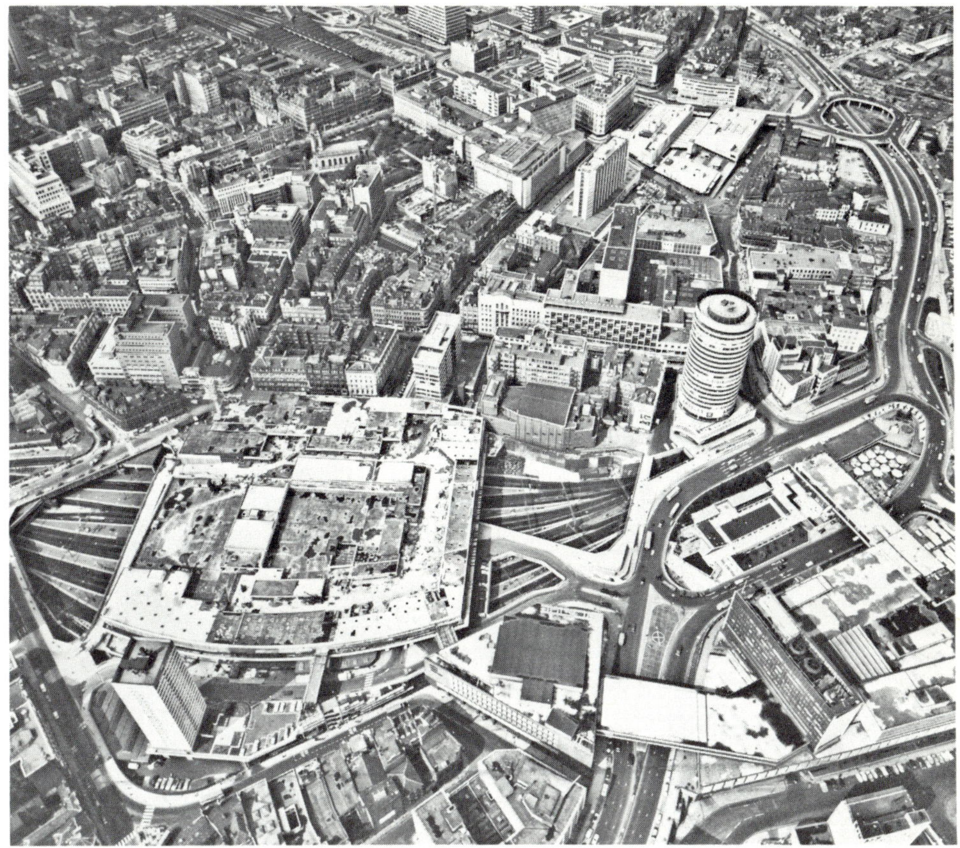

Plate 53 Central Birmingham

means that traffic flows along routes joining home to work are particularly heavy. Some capital investments have been made, though as yet these are inadequate. The improvement of the A.38 trunk road from Birmingham to Derby undoubtedly has solved some problems, particularly by allowing improved communication with south Yorkshire and Nottinghamshire. Additionally improvements to the Oxford road have shortened, in turn, journey times to Southampton. The motorways have perhaps been the most important recent addition to the road network, with Birmingham at the hub of spokes to London, Bristol and the North West.

Electrification of the main rail links to London and the North West also has brought home markets for West Midlands' industrial goods within easier reach of production points. While the closure of some rail routes has taken place, for example Figure 57 shows the extent of passenger route closures in the 1961–71 period, major investment schemes have occurred in the region. The rebuilding of Birmingham New Street Station (Plate 53) is one such scheme. With rationalization of passenger and freight handling facilities as well as routes, the railways and transport industries, in general, represent a smaller slice of the employment cake than they did a decade ago.

Service Industries

The service sector in the West Midlands, in terms of the number of jobs at least, is less developed than in most other major regions of Britain. This situation is unlikely to last long as the regional growth rate of service industries is even greater than the high national growth rate for these activities. Service industries are inextricably linked with patterns of population, and with the redistribution of population in the region there have been related changes in the pattern of service employment and in the structure of the service economy.

Movements of households mean movements of purchasing power, changes in the sales characteristics of shopping centres, and perhaps even the building of new shopping centres. Such new developments are also initiated by urban renewal and redevelopment schemes. With city-centre renewal it becomes possible to replace outmoded service facilities and to provide not just new shops, but new administrative offices, fire stations, schools and other services. It is perhaps in the provision of new shopping centres that most progress has been made, for the economic return here is potentially very high.

The demand for better and more shopping provision stems from two factors: it results first, from the relatively high wages paid in the region and secondly from the rapid growth of wage levels in the industries which are

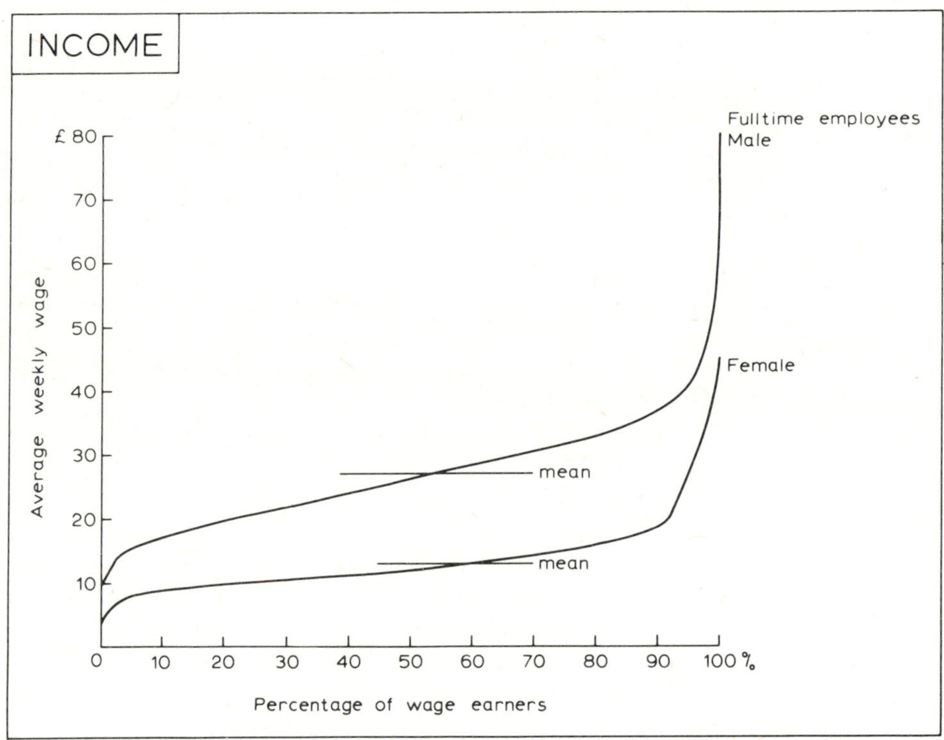

Fig 58 West Midlands—
The percentage distribution of weekly earnings of full-time employees, 1969.

concentrated in the region. The average weekly manufacturing wage for a full-time male employee in the region in 1969 was £25 and for females just less than half this figure. These average figures disguise the very wide spread of wages as shown in Figure 58. Average weekly household income in the West Midlands is some 4 per cent above the average for the United Kingdom. This higher income together with individual regional taste preferences leads to a different spending pattern for the region in comparison with the country as a whole (see Statistical Appendix). Expenditure on foods is particularly high, while ownership of consumer durables, other than cars, is notably low. In 1969 56 per cent of the population owned refrigerators, compared with 61 per cent for the whole country, and an equally large differential occurs for telephones. Demand for these consumer goods has been increasing faster than the national average however, so that these differentials will not be apparent for very much longer.

Partly to meet this buoyant demand and partly as a search for a better environment, new shopping centres have been developed in many towns in the last ten years. The Sandwell Centre at West Bromwich is typical of many. Figure 59 and Plate 54 show the centre. Opened in the summer of 1971 it was by Christmas 1971 a thriving shopping precinct of 58 shops. The Sandwell

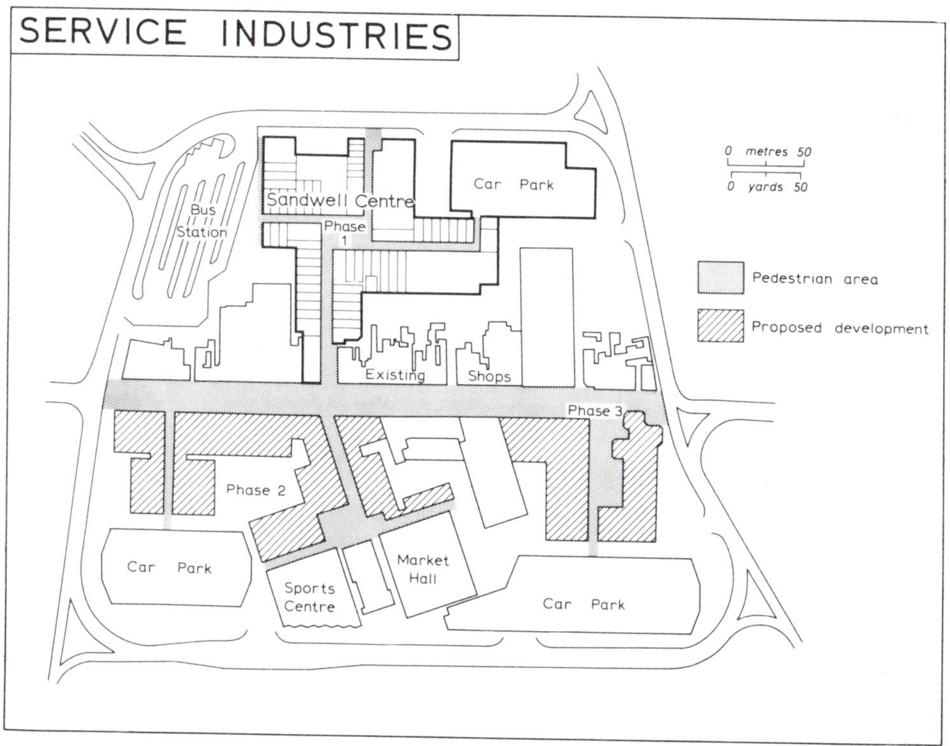

Fig 59 West Midlands—The Plan of the Sandwell Centre at West Bromwich

Centre consists of covered, air conditioned, shopping malls and marks the first phase in a large renewal of the town centre of West Bromwich. The new shops are less than a mile from an interchange on the M.5 and only a few miles from the M.5–M.6 junction, and thus the potential shopping hinterland of the centre stretches far beyond the borough itself. Much of the development has taken place on land cleared of slum dwellings and the site now represents an investment of over £4 million. A second phase to the centre is planned which will house other service facilities, including a recreation centre. The development in the two phases will be joined by the High Street, to be freed from traffic, and it is hoped that in this way the High Street will be revitalized.

Plate 54 West Bromwich (Staffordshire)
The interior of the Sandwell Centre.

Patterns of Future Development

The main problem facing both land use and economic planners in the West Midlands is how to accommodate the massive overspill of people from the central part of the conurbation. In contrast to the majority of the other British regions in 1971 the West Midlands region had no overall plan to guide patterns of growth. One suggestion is to concentrate development along a north-east/south-west axis through the conurbation, while a more general policy of decentralization also has been advocated. New towns are presently under development at Telford and Redditch, and overspill schemes have been agreed or are being considered in the circle of satellite towns around the conurbation. The expansion of existing towns throughout the region is probably the cheapest possible strategy, but strong forces exist for the preservation of the present employment concentration in Birmingham and its environs. Any regional plan is the result of compromises and many will have to be made in the West Midlands before there emerges an acceptable cohesive strategy for development.

FURTHER READING

Department of Economic Affairs, *The West Midlands* (H.M.S.O., 1965).

G. M. Lomas and P. A. Wood, *Employment Location in Regional Economic Planning: A Case Study of the West Midlands* (London, 1970).

K. E. Rosing and P. A. Wood, *Character of a Conurbation: A Computer Atlas of Birmingham and the Black Country* (London, 1971).

West Midlands Economic Planning Council, *The West Midlands: Patterns of Growth* (H.M.S.O., 1967).

M. J. Wise (ed.), *Birmingham and its Regional Setting: A Scientific Survey* (Birmingham, 1950).

Wales (including Monmouthshire)

The area which is at present called 'Wales' has little meaning other than in purely administrative terms, for the boundary line which appears on Figure 60 coincides with the limits of no physical or cultural feature. It is a regional limit, therefore, only in the arbitrary context of government and administration. But before proceeding to consider the internal geographical detail within this area it is essential to sketch the way in which it came into being in its present form.

The present areal extent of Wales is that which, apart from some minor modifications, was determined at the time of the Act of Union with England in 1536. That Act was the culmination of a process long in operation. The formative period in the emergence of the Welsh people was the immediate pre-Roman era, when groups of people of Iron Age B culture moved into western Britain from the continent via the western sea routes. These people built elaborately fortified camps on the hill summits (hill forts) and probably spoke a Celtic language of the Brythonic group, the ancestor of modern Welsh.

The first restriction of the Celtic speaking population of Britain to a purely western distribution was a consequence of the Anglo-Saxon invasions of lowland Britain which followed the collapse of the Roman system. Conventionally the Battle of Chester about 616 is seen as detaching the Welsh of Wales from their fellow Celts in Cumbria, and the Battle of Dyrham (near Bath) in 577 as breaking the link with Devon and Cornwall. One of the most powerful of the Anglo-Saxon kingdoms to emerge was Mercia and between 778 and 796 Offa, King of Mercia, constructed an earthen embankment along the western limit of his territory. This bank, known as Offa's Dyke, ran along the eastern fringes of the Welsh Highlands and has been called the 'boundary line of the Cymry', for it seems to have marked an agreed frontier between the Celt and the Saxon. This is the first physical identification and delimitation of the area now called Wales and 'crossing Offa's Dyke' has remained the symbol of leaving Wales. In this sense it was physically, as it has remained symbolically, a divide between two cultures.

Behind this boundary some form of development towards independent statehood would probably have been achieved but for the fact that beginning in 1080 further invasions from the east took place. These were the incursions of the Norman conquerors following the invasion of England in 1066. The occupation and pacification of this western, highland area, which was a threat to the successful assimulation of England, became an essential part of Anglo-Norman policy. It was, in part, completed by the conquest of Wales by Edward I—the Statute of Rhuddlan in 1284 marks the Edwardian settlement

Plate 55 Caernarvon
A characteristic small Welsh market town which originated as a 'bastide', a planted castle town, in 1282. The restored castle dominates the town which has now expanded well beyond the discernable semi-circular walls. In the middle ground the Arfon lowlands backed by the Snowdonian mountain massif.

of this problem. By the statute Wales was divided into the Principality, which was held by the King's eldest son, the Prince of Wales, and a series of marcher lordships. The Principality was made up of the newly constituted counties of Anglesey, Caernarvon, Merioneth, Flint, Cardigan and Carmarthen, which represented in the main the northern and western areas of substantial Welsh resistance. The Marcher lordships occupied the territories along the English border and in the south.

By the date of the Tudor accession, and after the widespread disturbances of the Wars of the Roses, lawlessness and the continued threat of disruption from the west, which had been epitomized in the Glyndŵr rebellion, made a 'final' solution of the problems of this western country essential to the English throne. This was accomplished by the Acts of 1536, usually known as the Act of Union, and of 1542. By these the lands of the Marcher lordships were divided into counties and the eastern boundary of Wales finally settled along the line which it takes today. One point of contention remained. In 1542 for the purposes of legal administration, Monmouthshire was detached from the

Court of Great Sessions for Wales and was not associated with any one of the four legal circuits which were set up within Wales. It was instead attached to the Oxford circuit and hence achieved an ambivalent status. There is little doubt, however, that in all subsequent legislation it was regarded as a Welsh county, to the extent that 'Welsh' meant anything after an Act of Union which nominally made all the counties one with England.

This historical narrative constitutes an essential prerequisite to the geography of Wales, for it emphasizes that the territory to which the name is applied is the product of history and has little relevance to the geographer who is concerned with landscape. Moreover, it has no more meaning to the cultural geographer. Inroads of English influence occurred continually and the boundary of Welsh speech has been progressively pushed back. In consequence the frontier is at present in no sense a cultural divide. The political area of contemporary Wales, therefore, derives no unity from the conventional bases of regional identity, either physical or cultural. Accordingly it is within the country that these creators of regional variation and identity must be sought.

Regional Variations

Within Wales itself three forces have played major roles in the creation of regional variation and it is their interplay which are the major elements in contemporary problems. These three can be identified as variations in the survival of Welsh culture, variations in relief and associated physical conditions, and variations in the development of industry. They will, in the first instance, be considered separately.

Cultural Divisions in Wales. Many of the characteristics of the human geography of Wales are derived from the distinctive social organization of the Welsh people, particularly as it developed in the formative phase at the time of the Anglo Norman conquest. Most important of these features is the rural settlement pattern. The development of the single isolated farm as the main unit is directly related to the social patterns of tribal Wales. At a very much later date in the eighteenth and nineteenth centuries, the intense nonconformity which was a native Welsh movement, resulted in the building of a large number of simple chapels, often in a neo-classical style. Often these became the points about which small hamlets with biblical names, such as Bethesda, Saron or Nazareth, developed. It follows that there is a contrast between those areas which remained predominantly Welsh, and which are characterized by the single farm and small hamlet, and those areas which were early anglicized during the medieval period, such as the Vale of Glamorgan, Gower and South Pembrokeshire, and where the village is the unit of rural settlement and the church tower the dominant feature. But subsequent anglicization has pushed the language frontier well back beyond these older limits (Fig. 60) and produced a distribution which is essentially northern and western, forming an Atlantic fringe area to the remainder of Wales. The critical point is whether the language can be accepted as the matrix of a distinctive culture and hence diagnostic of a differentiated culture region. Welsh tradition is essentially

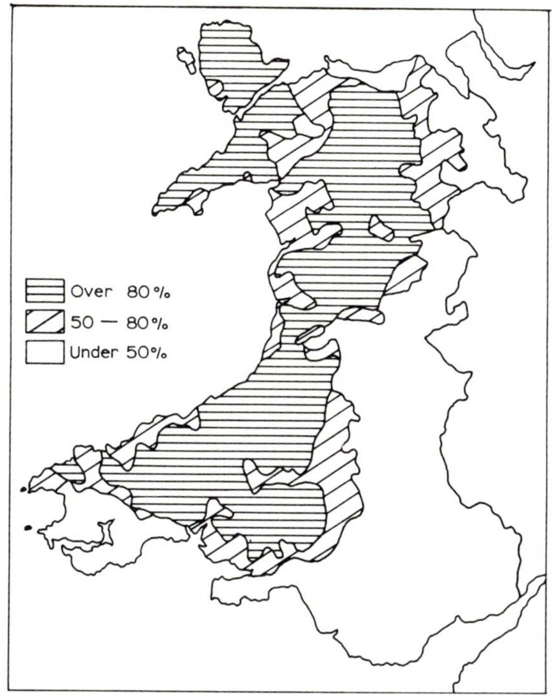

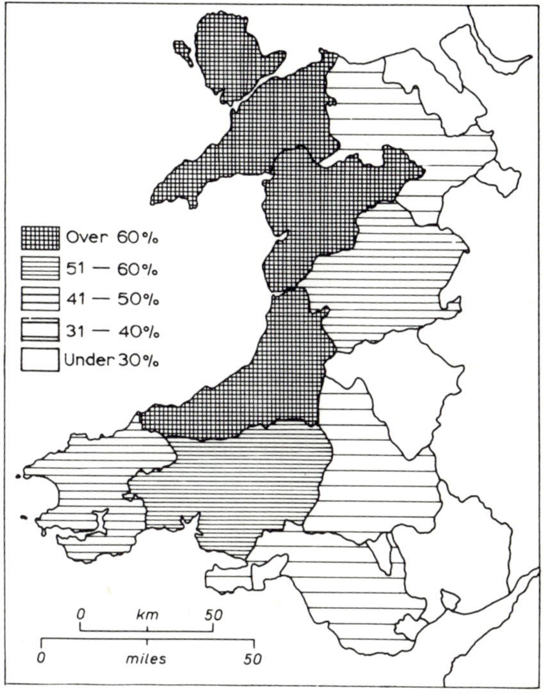

Fig 60 Wales—Language and Culture
The upper figure indicates the proportion of the population over three years old able to speak Welsh in 1961. The lower figure indicates the proportion voting against the opening of licensed premises on Sunday at the 1968 Referendum.

literary and linguistic and hence it can be argued that the language is the effective symbol of the culture. In addition it can be shown that certain attitudes seem to be associated with the language, for example when the referenda on the closing of public houses on Sundays were held in 1961 and 1968 the 'dry area' coincided very clearly with those areas which were predominantly Welsh in speech (Fig. 60). On this basis, therefore, it can be argued that Wales can be divided into two broad cultural areas. The first of these can be called Welsh Wales (*Cymru Cymraeg*) and the other Anglo-Wales (*Cymru di-Gymraeg*) and the division lies roughly along the line which is indicated in Figure 60 marking those areas where more than half of the population is able to speak Welsh.

Physical Divisions in Wales. In terms of relief Wales can be regarded in simplest terms as a highland block characterized by a series of plateau-like erosion surfaces which are regional rather than local in significance. These, as presented by E. H. Brown, are:—

(a) Low Peneplain. 215–335 metres (700–1,100 feet), most frequently 215–275 metres (700–900 feet) and/or 300–335 metres (1,000–1,100 feet).
(b) Middle Peneplain. 365–485 metres (1,200–1,600 feet), most frequently 365–425 metres (1,200–1,400 feet) and/or 460 metres (1,500 feet).
(c) High Plateau. 520–580 metres (1,700–1,900 feet) rising to 610 metres (2,000 feet).
(d) Summit Plain. 640–1,065 metres (2,100–3,500 feet) across the monadnock crests.

There is also a series of less extensive and more fragmentary coastal plateaux, below the level of the low peneplain, which produce identifiable levels at approximately 180 metres (600 feet), 120 metres (400 feet), and 60 metres (200 feet). These are, however, more complex features than simple altitudes suggest.

The incision of drainage systems into these uplifted plains has produced a number of river basins, characterized by polycyclic features. Since Wales is a highland massif the distribution of these river basins is roughly radial, although those opening out to north, south, and west are generally smaller than the eastward draining basins, for example the Severn.

It is now possible to resolve these morphological features into a pattern significant in the creation of regional contrasts.

1. The Monadnock Group or the Summit Plain. This comprises the mountain areas of Wales, which were the centre of Pleistocene glaciation, and glacial landforms dominate. These are the areas of true mountain scenery, with bare rock outcrop and scree in the higher parts—the Snowdon Massif, the Brecon Beacons and Black Mountains, Radnor Forest, Pumlumon, Cader Idris, the Berwyn and Arenig Mountains.
2. Upland Plains. These form the high plateau areas of Wales. Near the coast they form only limited interfluvial spurs, but inland they open out to give extensive moorlands around the mountain cores.
3. Coastal Plateaux and Lowland Basins. These make up a discontinuous

girdle flanking the upland and mountain heartland. The main features in this girdle are, from the south-east, the Vales of Gwent and Glamorgan, Gower, the Tywi valley (Ystrad Tywi), the south Pembrokeshire plateau, The Teifi valley, the coastal plateaux of west Wales, Lleyn and Anglesey (Môn), the Arfon plateau, the Vale of Clwyd and the Dee estuarine lands. Along the eastern margin there is a series of lowland basins, those of the rivers Dee, Severn, Wye, and Usk.

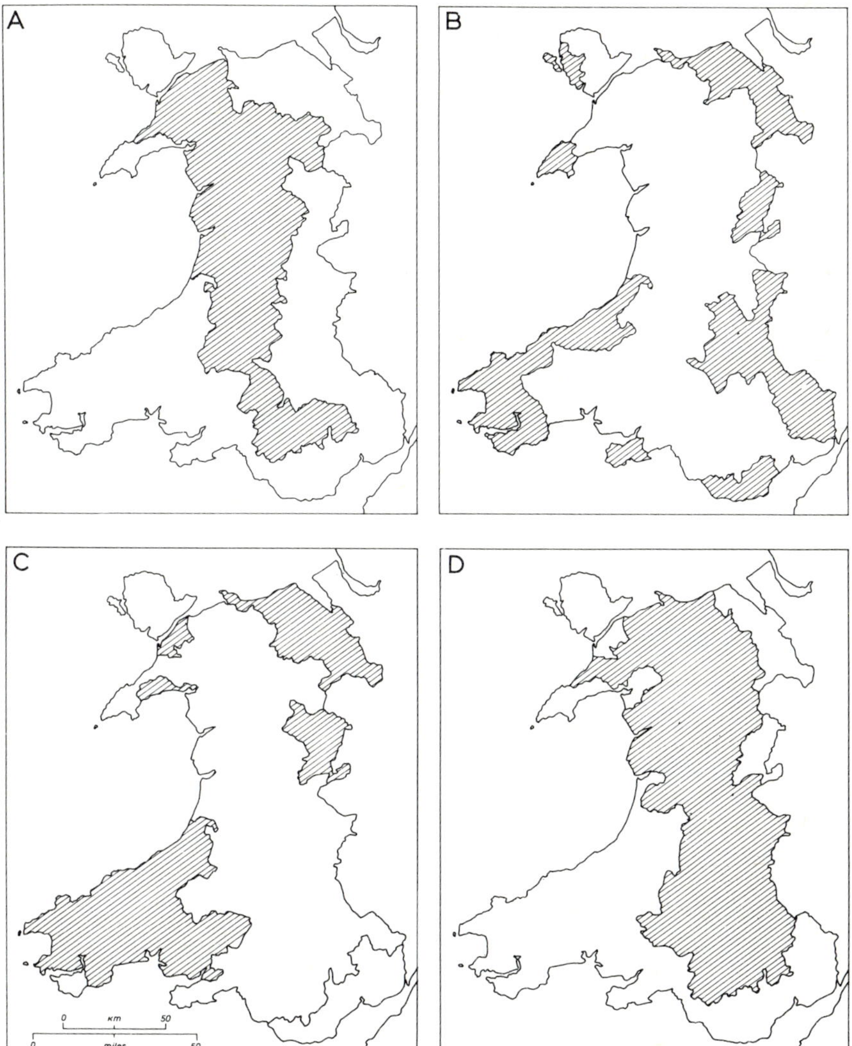

Fig 61 Wales—Agricultural Distributions

A. Rough grazing as a percentage of agricultural land. Areas where this percentage is over 30 are shaded.
B. Tillage as a percentage of agricultural land. Areas where this percentage is over 10 are marked.
C. Livestock units per 100 acres of agricultural land. Areas with over 15 dairy cattle are shaded.
D. Livestock units per 100 acres of agricultural land. Areas with over 15 sheep are shaded.

All maps after J. W. Aitchison, *The farming systems of Wales*.

In general, variations in climate and vegetation are closely associated with those of relief. The mountain areas have more than 1,500 millimetres (60 inches) of rainfall and are characterized by mountain fescue grasses or heather moor and fell. The upland plains receive between 1,150 millimetres (45 inches) and 1,500 millimetres (60 inches) of rain and are covered by molinia-nardus moorlands at their upper limits, although agrostis pastures with a frequent rush admixture are found at the lower edges. The lower coastal plateaux and basins with less than 1,150 millimetres (45 inches) of rainfall are either cropland or under agrostis-ryegrass mixtures. 'The fundamental contrast between upland core and lowland periphery has persisted in both past and present vegetational patterns, all of which show orthodox correlations with climatic, topographic, and edaphic features. These correlations are closest in the higher parts of the upland core where human interference has been least. On the lower plateaux and lowland periphery human interference has been greatest, and the originally thick deciduous forest has been extensively replaced by a man-made agricultural landscape with its patchwork of enclosed grass and arable fields and its vast spread of unfenced rough grazings.'

It follows that it is possible to divide Wales into a mountain core, or heartland, surrounded by a girdle of intermediate uplands and lower discontinuous peripheral plateaux.

Plate 56 Nant Gwynant (Caernarvonshire)
Typical of the mountain areas of Wales with the small area of improved farmland giving way rapidly to unimproved mountain terrain. Note the single farm with its 'long house' structure.

The land use and agricultural patterns closely reflect these physical conditions. Some 42 per cent of the farm land is in permanent grass, 38 per cent in rough grazing and 12 per cent in temporary grass. This means that only 8 per cent of the land is under tillage with grassland and rough grazing totalling 92 per cent. The areas where arable land becomes significant are severely limited to western Pembrokeshire and south coastal Cardiganshire, Gower, the Vale of Glamorgan, eastern Monmouthshire and Breconshire, the Vale of Clwyd and the Flintshire lowlands, the western tip of Lleyn and western Anglesey. In contrast rough grazings occupy all the central areas, while the intermediate areas are essentially under permanent or temporary grassland (Fig. 61). These land use patterns reflect the agricultural enterprises. Sheep farming is dominant over most of upland Wales, whereas along the coastal plateaux and along the valleys, particularly the Tywi, dairying is dominant. Beef production is combined with both the above enterprises in Anglesey, Lleyn and Pembrokeshire, and along the middle borderland country in Radnorshire and Breconshire. Cash cropping and horticulture, which coincide with the tillage areas noted above, are found in areas of distinctive climatic advantage. A characteristic representative is the production of early potatoes in south Pembrokeshire. These general characteristics of Welsh agriculture are summarized in the maps constituting Figure 61.

Contrasts in Industrial Development. The location of two coalfields in Wales (Fig. 62), the one in the south and the other in the north-east, mattered very little in terms of regional diversity until the middle of the eighteenth century and the rapid onset of industrialization. With the discovery of the process of coking coal and its use in the blast furnaces of the iron industry, extensive development took place along the northern outcrop of the South Wales Coalfield mainly after 1750. Here the coal measures outcrop and the raw material was easily accessible. In addition clayband and blackband iron ores were present in the coal measures, while the carboniferous limestone which fringed the coalfield was available for use as a flux in the furnaces. To the west of the Vale of Neath the anthracitic coals were not suitable for the production of coke and development, therefore, was limited to those areas which lay to the east of the river Neath. The growth of the iron industry created a distinctive line of settlement which extended from Hirwaun and Aberdare, through Merthyr Tydfil, Tredegar and Ebbw Vale to Pontypool.

The second phase of development took place in the second half of the nineteenth century, and mainly after 1860, when the mining of coal for export began to dominate as deeper mines in the valleys to the south of the iron towns were sunk. The Rhondda valleys were exploited mainly in the last quarter of the nineteenth century, in a period when South Wales was to lead the world as a coal exporter. Coal production reached its peak in 1913 when some 56 million metric tons (57 million long tons) were mined and some 270,000 people were employed. This phase created the characteristic elongated mining villages and towns which are usually seen as the stereotype of settlement patterns in South Wales.

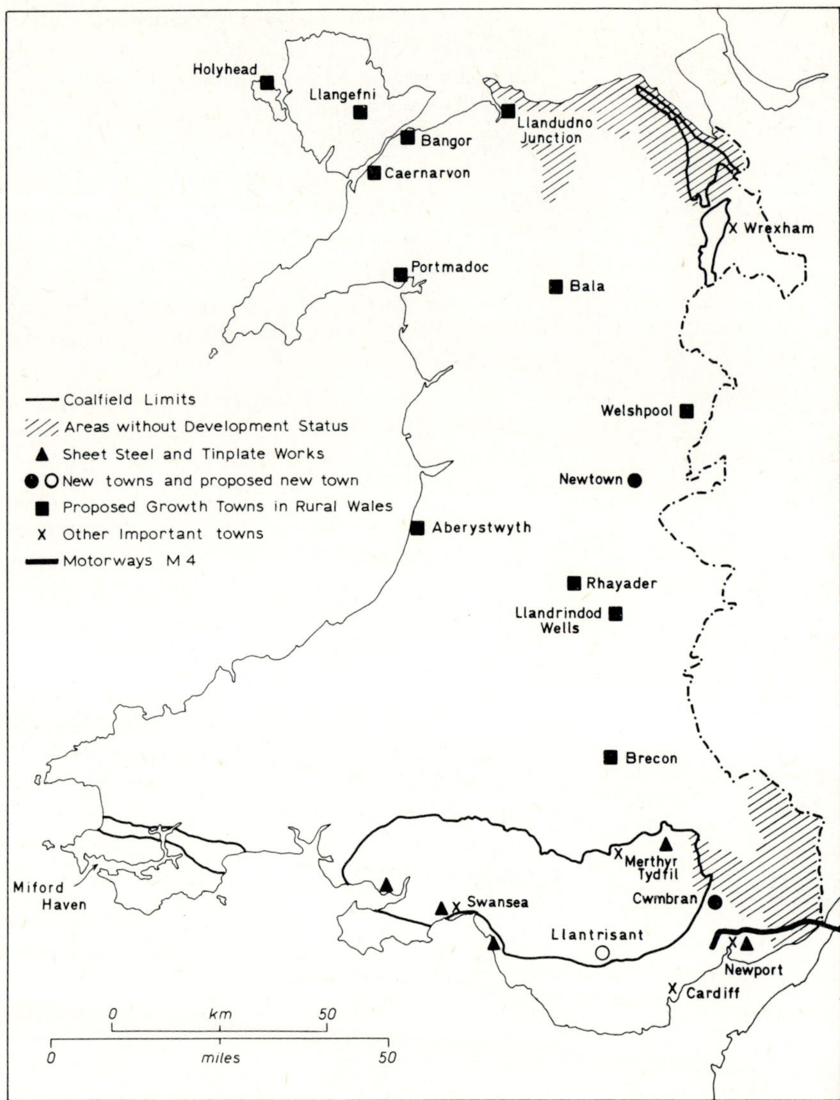

Fig 62 Wales—Some General Economic and Social Features Relevant to Modern Planning

As coalmining moved to its peak so the older metallurgical areas were experiencing a relative decline. The local iron ores were rapidly exhausted and the necessity for import gave coastal locations a particular advantage. The result was that the iron industry of the interior decayed and newer developments, at the turn of the century, took place at Cardiff. At the same time the much older metallurgical traditions of the area about Swansea Bay were revived in a metallurgical complex where the production of tinplate became one of the dominant features.

Plate 57 Trealaw (Rhondda, Glamorgan)
River, railway, road and terraced housing produce the stereotype view of the South Wales coalfield.

In the north-east of Wales a similar pattern had evolved. In the Denbighshire section of the coalfield the iron industry had developed centred on Wrexham, while in the Flintshire section a wide range of metallurgical developments took place about Hollywell, as well as chemical and textile industries.

The result of these mainly nineteenth century developments was radically to alter the economic balance within Wales by creating two concentrated areas of economic development. The result is that the country is characterized by a most unequal distribution of population with some 70 per cent of the total concentrated on or near the two coalfields with the bulk in the south.

It is essential to the comprehension of the patterns of regional variations in Wales that it be understood that the three creators of variations described above do not in any way coincide, but overlap each other. Wales of the High Plateau is not Welsh speaking Wales, although this confusion is sometimes perpetuated by the notion of a highland survival of the language and culture. In fact its survival is essentially western and northern and some of the upland areas of Radnorshire are among the most anglicized parts of Wales. Likewise industrial Wales is not completely part of Anglo Wales, for the area of over 50 per cent Welsh speaking, that is where the language is at least co-dominant, overlaps in east Carmarthenshire with the coal-mining and metallurgical areas of the western part of the coalfield. Even coalmining itself is not exclusively limited in south Wales to the upland area of deeply incised valleys, for the coal measures themselves overlap the relief boundary between the Vale of Glamorgan and the coalfield basin and mining takes place, as for example at Llanharan, in what is conventionally part of the lowland Vale. These patterns of spatial variation which have been analysed in turn, together with the nature of their unequal overlap, are basic to the major regional problems which characterize Wales today. These problems can be considered briefly first of all in relationship to rural Wales and then in relationship to the areas of industrial development.

Rural Wales

The physical characteristics of much of the upland area have already received comment as well as the general character of the agriculture. The severity of the environmental conditions in the physical context has been accentuated by problems inherent in the social environment. The area, as already noted, has been dominated by a pattern of single farms and small hamlets. This situation was accentuated during the early nineteenth century when Parliamentary enclosures resulted in the bulk of the common grazing land being converted into compact farms. This brought about the effective separation of upland and lowland as complementary elements in the farming system, and the creation of a number of purely upland farms. At the same time, farms developed from 'squatter settlement' added to the number. Under present conditions these farms are often no longer viable—they are restricted in size for such locations, lack valley land and are far removed from amenities now regarded as essential. When the Welsh Agricultural Land Sub-Commission made an investigation of mid-Wales in 1955, it estimated that 57 per cent of the farming enterprises were definitely too small to be economic, that a further 31 per cent had be be classified as marginal and only 12 per cent were classified as economic enterprises. In some parishes the uneconomic percentage was as high as eighty (Fig. 63).

As a result of these conditions many holdings have been amalgamated and the farms become derelict. Progressive mechanization has led to a decline in the demand for agricultural workers and these two factors are at the root of depopulation. It was estimated that the reduction in the numbers of insured and self-employed persons engaged in agriculture in the mid-Wales counties between 1951 and 1961 amounted to 29 per cent, representing some 7,000 jobs.

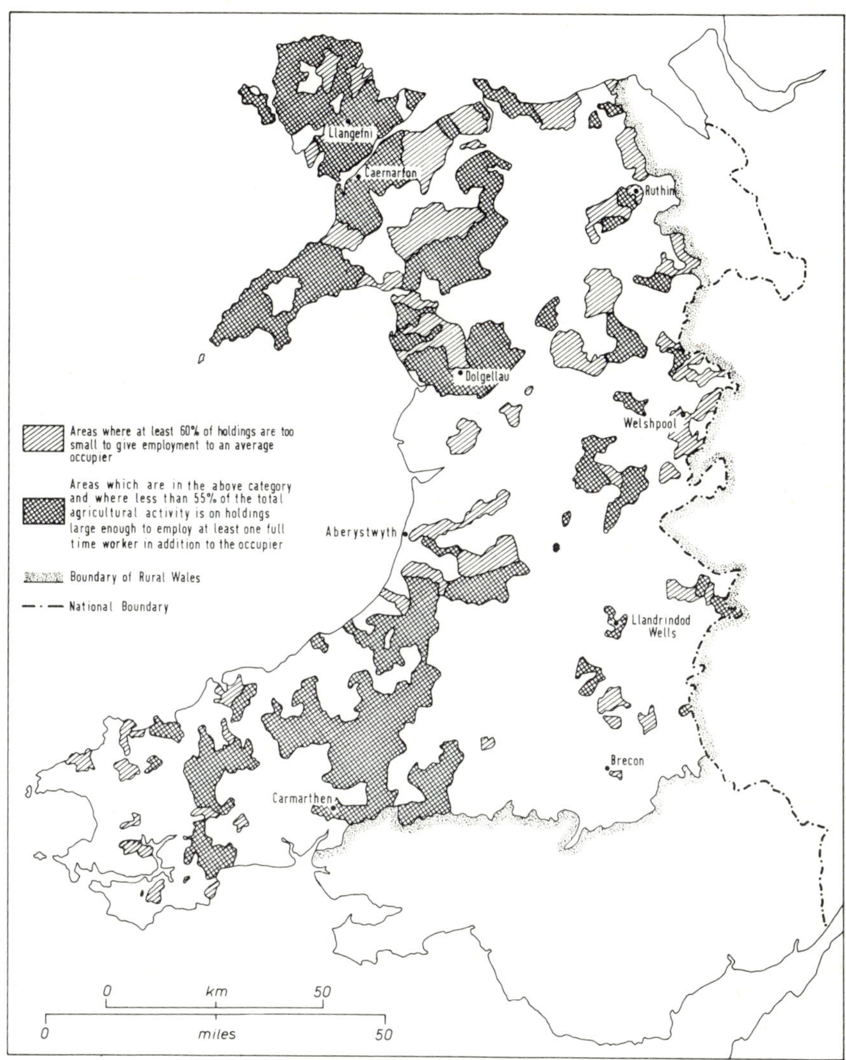

Fig 63 Wales—Size of Farm Businesses in Rural Areas
From Welsh Council, *A strategy for rural Wales* (Cardiff, 1971).

Between 1964 and 1969 employment in agriculture in Wales as a whole fell by some 4,300.

In addition to the limitations on agriculture, the mineral resources of the area are extremely limited and only two have had extensive development, lead and slate. Lead mining reached its peak at the end of the last century and in spite of rising prices, exploitation is unlikely to be resumed on any scale. The 'lodes' are small and fragmentary and cannot provide the basis for modern industry. Likewise the slate industry of Caernarvonshire and Merioneth provides little opportunity for modern extensive development. The derelict rows of miners' cottages and settlements such as the sad, slate village of Corris now give a physical impression of decline to an area where the natural beauty often obscures economic decay. Schemes have been proposed for mineral extraction in the Dyfi estuary and Coed-y-Brenin, a Forestry Commission area in Merioneth, but little progress has been made and there is considerable opposition from conservation interests.

The dominance of the single farm in the area has already been indicated. This is associated with a great number of very small hamlets which, under the conditions of depopulation, are rapidly losing the elementary services they now provide. Schools and chapels are being closed through lack of demand and the social cores of the communities are being eroded away. This means in turn that attempts to provide services such as piped water and electricity are extremely expensive. Perhaps the simplest way to indicate the cost to the country of sustaining services, such as education, in these areas is through the rate deficiency grants (now called 'support grants') and the extent to which local expenditure has to be subsidized from the central exchequer.

TABLE 14

County	*Rate Deficiency Grant Per Cent*	*Government Grants as percentage of Expenditure*
Brecon	50·43	78
Cardigan	58·74	84
Merioneth	55·89	84
Montgomery	75·12*	88*
Radnor	63·57**	84**

* Highest in England and Wales.

** Second highest in England and Wales.

Source: Local Government Commission for Wales, *Report and Proposals for Wales* (H.M.S.O., 1963).

The urban pattern is equally diffuse. This is a classic situation where the lack of a native urban tradition has combined with an absence of intensive economic development and with a situation where the only good agricultural land was a fringing marginal zone about a mountain core. The result is that there are no large towns outside the industrial areas, the regional capitals have only about 10,000 to 15,000 people. In mid-Wales none of the 31 towns (except Aberystwyth) has a population of over 10,000 and most of them have a population in the range 1,000 to 2,500.

The communication network is completely inadequate to hold this diffuse pattern of tiny settlements together. It has been estimated that there are only 10,100 kilometres (6,300 miles) of road in mid-Wales, an area of 7,500 square kilometres (3,000 square miles), and only 8 per cent of that, or some 725 kilometres (450 miles) are trunk roads. But these problems extend right through the scale from inter-town links and external links to the problem of farm access. Again the Land Sub-Commission showed that out of the 1,404 farms surveyed only 161 had access via a good farm road, while 108 had a rough road passable in summer, 194 a cart track and 86 only a footpath.

The railways of rural Wales are mainly single line and suffered severely under the Beeching Plan. For example, the main link to south Wales, from Aberystwyth south to Carmarthen, was closed so that there is now no direct rail link between this area of mid-Wales and the south Wales coalfield. At present the Cambrian Coast line from Machynlleth to Pwllheli is in danger of being closed. All these closures result in a substantial loss of employment.

The net result of all these problems is substantial and continuing depopulation. The population of mid-Wales reached its peak about 1871. Subsequently, the population of the five constituent counties has fallen by nearly 25 per cent. During the decade 1951–61, the population fell by 4 per cent as compared with increases of 1·6 per cent for Wales and 5·3 per cent for England and Wales, while during 1961–71 the population fell by 2·5 per cent. During the decade Merioneth's population fell by some 8 per cent. The whole area has, therefore, been dominated virtually for a century by a process of depopulation. This has had its obvious effects on the age structure and this is now an area of an ageing population, which in Cardiganshire and Merioneth resulted in an intercensal natural decrease as well as a migratory loss.

To offset this situation a whole range of plans and schemes has been suggested which differ widely both in purpose and procedure. They are summarized below in three general groups beginning with the least radical.

THE RATIONALIZATION OF PRESENT TRENDS

The first question which any regional planning scheme poses is the role of the region within the nation. It is inherent in economic growth that transfers of productive resources take place and that regional shifts follow. If this be so, current trends can be accepted as precise reflections of changing economic values and planning is concerned with the guiding of these trends so that their impact is lessened in terms of the disruption created. The main proposals are as follows.

(a) *The encouragement of farm amalgamation.* This is to be carried out so as to build up viable units in terms of present economic conditions. This can be thought of in terms of the creation of large scale sheep ranches in the upland areas, but each having associated valley land. This will not check population decline but it might diminish the heavy cost of subsidies.

(b) *The development of afforestation.* The area under the Forestry Commission increased by 20,000 hectares (50,000 acres) in 1950 to 45,000 hectares (112,900 acres) in 1961, an increase of 125 per cent. There is every possibility that further extensions of the forestry area will take place, for it is estimated that some 180,000 hectares (450,000 acres) are suitable for planting. The ratio of employment to acreage is small and it is evident that only small amounts of labour can be absorbed by forestry. It can provide a second source of income for a farm holding and a valuable addition of population to the small settlements, now that the idea of creating new forestry villages has been abandoned. But it provides no basis for real economic growth and employment in forestry fell in the last half of the decade 1961–71.

(c) *The exploitation of water resources.* There are two aspects to this. First, the supply of water to the industrial areas of the Midlands and Lancashire and second, the generation of electricity. In both cases the product is going out of the area. There are certainly cogent arguments for the rational development of these resources by a Welsh National Water

Authority, rather than by a process of piecemeal exploitation, but even this development offers but little in the way of local employment.

(d) *The development of tourism.* Within the basic idea of the rationalization of present trends, tourism becomes the major possibility of inducing growth, for the demand for outdoor recreational facilities is likely to increase. The ideas of the Council for Wales and Monmouthshire in regard to tourism were certainly not dramatic. 'Holiday making developments there (mid-Wales) which would be compatible with the character and with the known preferences of holidaymakers would not necessarily change the economy dramatically nor would they, necessarily, halt depopulation; but certainly the industry could be developed further, so as to provide some additional strengthening of the economy and perhaps additional employment.' At present a number of speculative schemes for developments along the Cardigan Bay coast have been produced and one major scheme started at Towyn (Bron y Môr). Certainly the coastline of Wales is becoming littered with caravan sites. The Welsh Tourist Board estimates that the income of Wales from tourism is some £80 million and an investigation revealed that generally only Switzerland and Austria earn more per head of population from tourism. It would seem that a much greater contribution could be made to employment and wealth than many people estimate.

(e) *Rationalization of the settlement pattern.* It is now evident that the present pattern of settlement cannot be maintained; systems which were well adapted to the physical, social and economic conditions of former periods are completely inappropriate at the present. The extension of services to minor hamlets is expensive and uneconomic. It is possible to identify a rudimentary hierarchy of smaller settlements in the area—

Sub Towns
Key Villages
Villages
Hamlets

Over a long period, there would be a general running down of the hamlets and some villages, and a concentration of population and services in the selected key villages. This would create a settlement pattern more in keeping with modern needs. This basic policy has general approval, but no scheme has yet been produced treating an actual area of rural Wales in this way.

In conclusion, the whole of the above programme sees rural Wales as an area which should be subject to no major new developments apart from tourism. More and more Britain would crystallize into two parts, the one intensely urbanized and gaining all the advantages from concentration, the other made up of areas preserved as open leisure spaces, and of these, rural Wales would be one.

THE INTRODUCTION OF LIGHT INDUSTRY

This is obviously not in any sense an alternative to the various procedures outlined above, but is an addition to them, a further step in economic diversification which needs separate comment. The general principle is quite clear 'the general strengthening of the basic economy and through the attraction of industry, the provision of more employment, the aim being to retain more people in mid-Wales, to attract in additional population and very gradually build up some of the area's towns'. This has been the aim of the Mid-Wales Industrial Development Association. Because its problem is one of depopulation and not of unemployment, mid-Wales was not initially recognized as a Development Area. Accordingly in the late 1950s, the area began its own efforts to attract industry and by means of purely local initiative in 1957 the Development Association was formed by the five constituent counties. Since its inception it has sponsored many new developments spread over all the counties and located in 20 towns.

The efforts of the Association deserve every praise for local initiative has been successful when none was forthcoming from any central source. But the Association itself realizes that it can do little more than provide a palliative to depopulation. It would be quite unrealistic not to question whether the area's resources in both financial and human terms are sufficient to achieve the speed and scale of development which will be necessary if depopulation is to be stopped. The Mid-Wales Industrial Development Association has said, clearly, many times, that it believes substantial help from the Central Government will be necessary if the population decline of the area is to be reversed and mid-Wales is to be re-invigorated.

The problems associated with this introduction of light industry are simple: the factories are small, the labour supply is limited and because no concentrated labour supply exists expansion is inevitably limited. The mortality rate of these factories is high.

The conclusion is that, when added to the proposals under the rationalization of present trends, this form of industrial development increases diversity, it is only a palliative to the basic problems.

THE INTRODUCTION OF A NEW TOWN

As early as 1959 the Mid-Wales Industrial Development Association considered the possibility of establishing a new town in the area. The reactions from official circles were not encouraging but the idea was revived as part of the Labour Party's programme for Wales.

The theory behind this policy is well known, for the association of economic growth with continued urbanization is close; 'one thing is certain: that economic advancement is related to urbanization and that increasing specialization and continued urban growth go hand in hand'. Again the United Nations Symposium at Moscow in 1964 put the same point in attaching 'importance to comprehensive national and regional planning, including the planning and building of new towns as a means of providing economic development. Such towns would not only accommodate new activities but could encourage and reinforce the incentives for such development, especially in the less developed or depressed regions of a country'.

It is from these generalities that the case for a new town was derived and was initially preferred to the less spectacular building up of the small towns. A new town would provide a large labour pool of its own through which the growth of industry could be sponsored. This would in turn exercise a generative effect upon the whole economy. It would demand transport and other services which the area cannot now warrant and would introduce and command financial and human resources which are not available in mid-Wales. The problems of mid-Wales are closely linked with accessibility and only through such a project as a new town are communications likely to be greatly improved.

There are, however, obvious drawbacks to the proposed new town. It would be an imposed solution and, depending on the location chosen, it might have difficulty in attracting industry and population. Mid-Wales, in this context, is regarded as having the closest regional relations with the West Midlands, but the site usually suggested at Caersws is some 96 kilometres (60 miles) from Birmingham and connected by minimal transport facilities. Moreover, it could well accentuate rural decline and, indeed, by the concentration of effort at one point, lead to comparative neglect of much of the area as a whole. There is a further issue. If this new town is to house overspill population from Birmingham, then the introduction of a large alien population into these areas could as effectively destroy the language and culture as continuing depopulation. The Welsh Nationalist Party (Plaid Cymru), at one time supporters of a Welsh Brazilia, have now turned against it for these very reasons.

The present reaction to these varied policies has been one of compromise. The extreme policies of doing nothing or endeavouring to inaugurate large scale development have both been rejected. Some twelve towns have been nominated as growth centres in mid and north Wales. The general intention is that the population of these small towns will be doubled. Of them Newtown in Montgomeryshire has progressed further under the Mid Wales New Town Development Corporation. This policy is clearly on too small a scale to initiate growth, it can only prevent the continuation of depopulation in an area which, for the reasons already outlined, must remain one of economic difficulty.

The problems of depopulation are all the more critical since these areas constitute largely, though not exclusively, the cultural core of Wales as it has been earlier identified. To some extent an impasse appears in that extensive development means anglicization, whereas no development means *in situ* decay of the most Welsh areas. The present policy is at least a hesitant mid-way course between these extremes.

Industrial Wales

Throughout Europe coalmining and heavy industry in general have undergone considerable contraction, particularly in terms of employment, during the last fifty years. As has already been explained both the coalfields in Wales are based on such heavy industry and, consequently, they have suffered a characteristic decline.

In both coalmining and the metallurgical industries the development of mechanization and automation have considerably diminished the demand for labour but, in addition, the production of coal has actively declined as competition from other sources of power such as oil, hydro electricity and nuclear fuels has developed. In Wales the consequences on coalmining have been extensive and almost catastrophic. Between 1947 and 1966, the major period of rationalization, some 115 collieries were closed. The total number employed in coalmining has fallen from its peak of over a quarter of a million just before the First World War to 91,200 in 1964 and to 57,000 in 1969. The number of underground workers has fallen from 93,000 in 1948 to only 32,000 in 1970. On the other hand productivity has increased for output per manshift has risen from 1·36 metric tons (1·34 long tons) in 1960 to 2·04 metric tons (2·01 long tons) in 1970. In spite of this total production of coal has decreased from 23·71 million metric tons (23·34 million long tons) in 1948 to 16·82 million metric tons (16·55 million long tons) in 1970 in south Wales, and from 2·5 million metric tons (2·47 million long tons) to 1·03 million metric tons (1·01 million long tons) in north Wales. Although these figures show that production has declined it is evident that it has not been nearly in proportion to the very rapid decrease in the labour force.

Such structural changes in industry have affected the iron, steel and tinplate industries. The concentration in terms of location is illustrated in Figure 62. The large number of former small scale installations have been rationalized to produce a limited number of large works. It has been estimated that some 500 hand tinplate mills were closed. The major installations are now the Spencer Works at Llanwern (near Newport), the Ebbw Vale Works, which is the sole survivor of the former Heads of the Valleys area of iron working in the nineteenth century, the Margam and Abbey Works at Port Talbot, and the two tinplate works at Swansea (Velindre) and Llanelli (Trostre). In north Wales there is the Hawarden Bridge Steel Works at Shotton. There are other works producing different steel products, as for example at Cardiff. Wales now produces about one-third, 8·6 million metric tons (8·5 million long tons), of the total crude steel of the United Kingdom and in 1970 1·29 million metric tons (1·27 million long tons) of tinplate, terneplate and blackplate were produced, constituting the bulk of British production.

The decline of coal mining together with the closure of so many of the small scale metallurgical enterprises in the coalfield uplands have led to a major unemployment problem. To offset this, policies for diversification of industrial type and for the introduction of light industry have been developed since before the Second World War. In the immediate pre-war period the Board of Trade sponsored an industrial estate at Treforest near Pontypridd. Subsequently other estates have been developed at Bridgend, Aberdare (Hirwaun), Swansea (Forestfach) in south Wales and at Wrexham (Marchwiel) in north Wales. Indeed most of Wales has benefited from the financial incentives which are available to development areas for at present virtually the whole country is classified under the headings of Special Development Area, Development Area or Intermediate Development Area. Only the coastal fringes of the north-east and the extreme south-east margins do not come under one of these headings. As a result a wide range of industry has developed. Characteristic of this is the spread of sections of the motor vehicle industry into Wales where components are manufactured. Thus British Leyland has factories at Llanelli, Ford at Swansea and Rover at Cardiff. Again the Hoover Company has developed a major installation, on land made derelict by the old iron industry, at Merthyr Tydfil for the production of washing machines. An indication of this sort of development can be seen in the amount of new industrial buildings approved. New floor space has ranged from 200,000 square metres (2·2 million square feet) in 1961 to 750,000 square metres (8·03 million square feet) in 1970. In each year over half of this was in industrial south Wales. In 1970 the estimated additional total employment provided was 14,650 (11,140 of these jobs were for men).

These new developments, however, are only sporadic in their nature and inevitably limited in their impact. They are insufficient to make up for the losses in employment consequent upon the decline of the old heavy industries

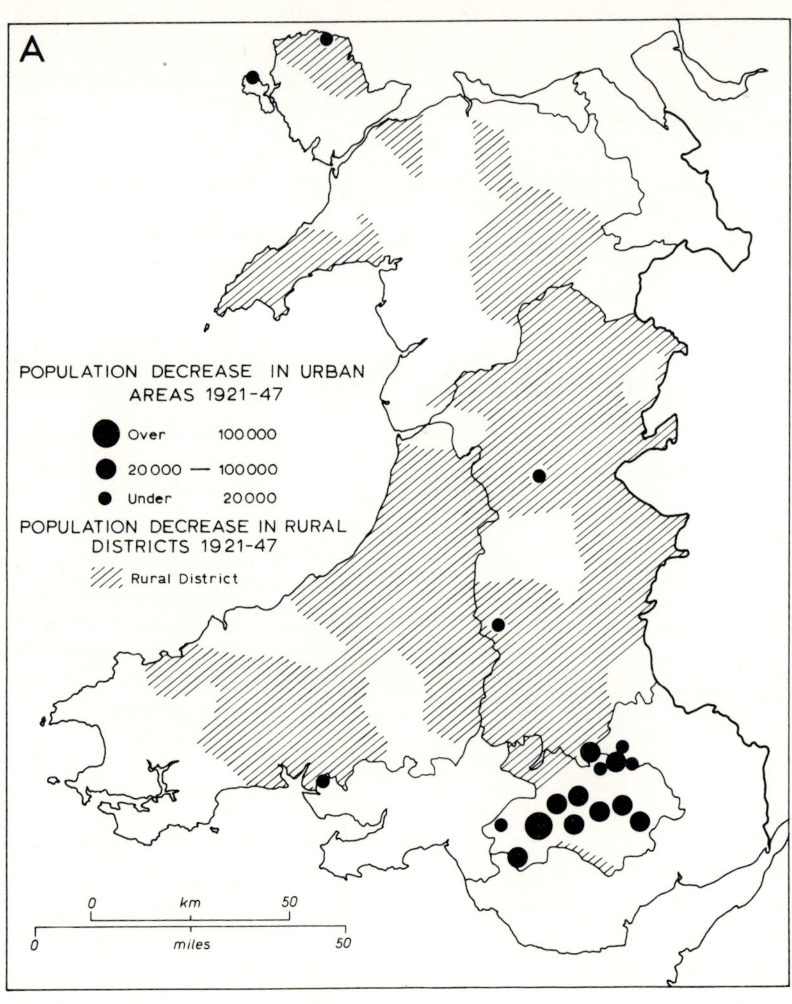

Fig 64 Wales—Areas of Persistent Population Decrease
A. 1921–1947. B. 1951–1966.

and the result has been a continuing and consistent loss of population (Fig. 64). Sample figures from the towns of the coalfield can illustrate this process over the last twenty years.

TABLE 15

Area	*Population*		
	1951	*1961*	*1971*
Aberdare U.D.	40,932	39,155	37,760
Merthyr Tydfil C.B.	61,142	59,039	55,215
Rhondda M.B.	111,389	100,369	88,924

The problems of the south Wales valleys are particularly acute. They are areas which are remote from the major markets of Britain and also removed

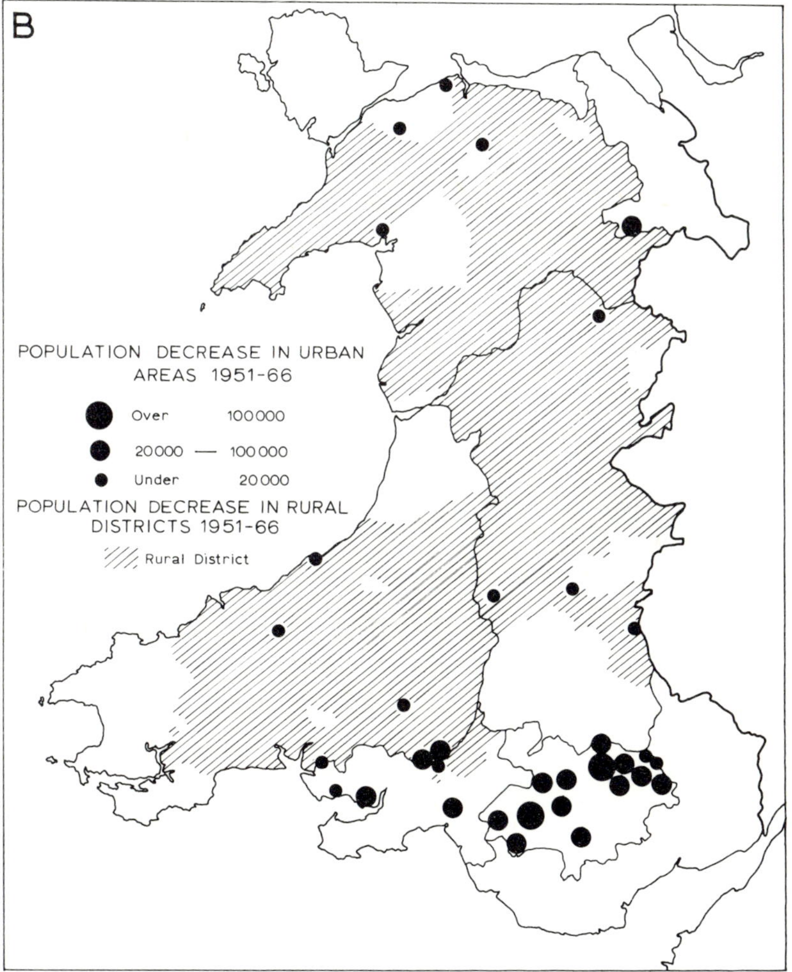

Adapted from *The Intermediate Areas: report of a committee under the chairmanship of Sir Joseph Hunt* (Cmnd 3998, H.M.S.O., 1969).

from the points of easy assembly of raw materials or components on the coast which is a key feature in modern industry. The communication system is old and inadequate for modern and effective movement and inter-valley communication is particularly difficult. It is true that a newly constructed road, the Heads of the Valleys road, along the northern boundary of the coalfield has provided a significant new means of linkage both with the Swansea area and with the Midlands, while a road under construction from Cardiff to Merthyr will provide a major link from this line to the major line of the M.4 through south Wales. But these are but the beginnings of an effective communication system. In addition there are large amounts of poor quality and outmoded housing in unattractive settlements. There are considerable areas of derelict land and the general environment of these upland and colder and wetter areas of south Wales is relatively unattractive, in spite of the easy

Plate 58 Llantrisant (Glamorgan)
The church and castle of the old town, oval in shape, are clearly to be seen marking the border ranges of the coalfield. To the south of this area a new town has been proposed, it is already the location of the Royal Mint.

access to open land and the Brecon Beacons National Park. All these factors explain the continuing drain of population.

In contrast to this pattern of loss on the coalfield, the areas of gain have been those which are peripheral, in particular, in the coastal fringes from the English border through to Newport and Cardiff. In statistical terms between 1951 and 1971 the standard area defined as Industrial South Wales, Central and Eastern Valleys, declined in population by 7·5 per cent. In the same period that area defined as Industrial South Wales, Coastal Belt, increased by 20·3 per cent. This process of development has been aided in the eastern or Monmouthshire section by the development of the new town at Cwmbran. This was originally proposed in order to solve the problem of a shortage of housing in a heavily industrialized area but its development within commuting distance of Newport has meant it has become closely associated with the development of that town. A further new town in south Wales has been proposed at Llantrisant, some 15 kilometres (9 miles) from Cardiff and located in the Vale of Glamorgan. This town has three aims. The first is to provide an overspill for the growth of Cardiff, the second to prevent uncontrolled suburbanization within the Vale of Glamorgan, and the third to provide employment at the southern outlets of the south Wales valleys on to the coastal plain. Already part of the Royal Mint has been located there. If this new town is developed then it must certainly contribute greatly to the further depopulation of the industrial valleys as inevitably people will seek residences more conveniently located to place of work. Moreover, the major growth area in employment at the present day is in the tertiary sector, that is, in office work and in retail and service trades, and this is by no means at present significantly developed in industrial Wales. In the percentage growth in commercial office floor space between 1964 and 1967 Wales was ranked last of all the nine regions of England and Wales, and it was ranked seven out of nine in the growth of shop and restaurant floor space. It is true that some amelioration of this situation is taking place with the deliberate location of offices in Wales, as for example, the Motor Taxation and Driving Licence Office at Swansea, but this is limited in scale and exclusively coastal in its location. If Llantrisant does become the centre of the new Mid-Glamorgan county proposed under local government reform, then the loss of tertiary employment in the valleys will be a most severe blow to the balance of employment in those areas.

It is apparent that present official policy in relation to the industrial interior areas of South Wales is to adopt an attitude which can be described as 'superintended decay'. The process of depopulation is seen as irreversible and to continue, and the areas of growth are considered to be the coastal strip. Here ease of assembly of raw materials and components is speeded through the presence of the south Wales ports, the fast rail connections to London, and the new M.4 motorway. In contrast to the patterns of population loss in the interior these coastal fringes from the English frontier through to the Swansea Bay area display a population gain.

Conclusion

At the outset of this chapter an attempt was made to outline the way in which the present national territory of Wales had evolved. It has been made apparent that this territory is subject to a number of divisive influences. If it is split into Welsh Wales and Anglo Wales in cultural terms, it is also split into north and south. North Wales looks to Liverpool as its capital, south Wales to Cardiff. The development of communication patterns does nothing to offset this north-south division since most proposed developments are concerned with getting people out of Wales easily rather than with enabling rapid transit within Wales. The rural and industrial areas have different problems and in some ways conflicting interests. But above this is the fact that the two major areas of development are peripheral to the country and lie athwart its south-eastern and north-eastern boundaries. These areas are respectively Severnside and Deeside. The proposals for Deeside envisage a barrage across the estuary and an attempt to rationalize the chaos in settlement pattern brought about by earlier periods of development. It is true that the proposals for development are couched in the terms of maintaining a distinctive Welsh character for the area, but even so it is difficult to regard it as anything but a fringe of Merseyside or Greater Liverpool. In the south-east the newly built Severn Bridge and the whole concept of a Severnside development, means that south-east Wales is likely to become more and more involved with its eastern neighbours. If the new M.4 motorway puts Cardiff that much nearer to Bristol and London, in comparative terms it puts it that much further away from Bangor and Llangefni.

To a large extent this chapter has devolved into a discussion of contemporary regional developments in Wales. However much objectivity and quantification is brought into regional analysis, like all other aspects of the social sciences, it cannot hope to remain value free. Thus some of the changes will be seen as simply the necessary adaptations to changing economic conditions and the differential operation of locational advantages. On the other hand, to some people these changes will be seen as erosions of the regional character of Wales. The two major and distinctive characteristic regions of Wales have been its rural core, which is the repository of the language and the culture, and the southern coalfield, which is the cradle of its great radical tradition. Both have been shown to be in decline. It is around the conflict between the decline of these traditional areas, the growth of newer centres on the peripheries of the country, and the policies which have to be adopted in light of these circumstances that much of the controversy over regional development in Wales revolves.

FURTHER READING

E. G. Bowen (ed.), *Wales: A Physical, Historical and Regional Geography* (London, 1966).

E. H. Brown, *The Relief and Drainage of Wales* (Cardiff, 1960).

H. Carter, *The Towns of Wales* (Cardiff, 1966).

E. Davies and A. D. Rees (eds.), *Welsh Rural Communities* (Cardiff, 1960).

M. Davies, *Wales in Maps* (Cardiff, 1958).

F. V. Emery, *Wales. World's Landscapes No. 2* (London, 1969).

G. M. Howe, *Wales from the Air* (Cardiff, 1957).

M. E. Hughes and J. James, *Wales: A Physical, Economic and Social Geography* (London, 1964).

T. M. Thomas, *The Mineral Wealth of Wales and its Exploitation* (Edinburgh, 1961).

Yorkshire and Humberside

The Yorkshire and Humberside Economic Planning Region consists of the East and West Ridings of Yorkshire and of the northern part of Lincolnshire. In many ways this produces a curiously-shaped region for planning purposes, since it includes diverse areas within its relatively small extent, each with its own distinctive problems for its economy and land use. Nor does the region possess any over-riding community of interest, since in many ways Humberside is socially and economically independent of the Leeds conurbation and of Sheffield. Yet this area contains 4·75 million people (8·5 per cent of the total in Great Britain and Ireland), concentrated in an area of 14,300 square kilometres (5,500 square miles), which represents 4·6 per cent of the area of Great Britain and Ireland; and it provides an interesting example of the variety of landscapes and planning problems that are found within quite small areas of the British Isles.

In Yorkshire and Humberside this variety is associated with the topographical sequence across the area from west to east, which in turn closely follows the underlying geological structure (Fig. 65). The highest upland lies in the west, where the Pennines provide a broad boundary to the region. In the north-west of these uplands Carboniferous limestone forms the underlying geology, often rising to form a plateau over 600 metres (2,000 feet) high, covered with moorland and upland pasture. Millstone Grit measures lie to the east and also form the core of the Pennines further south. Here there are considerable plateau areas over 450 metres (1,500 feet), with a landscape that is characterized by heather-covered peats, broken by cliffs of weathered rock, where grits and flags of this series outcrop above softer shales. Throughout the uplands the major rivers are deeply incised, often as much as 90 metres (300 feet) below the general level of the plateau. Lying parallel with the Millstone Grit and extending south from just north of Leeds are the coal measures which provided the natural resource that stimulated the nineteenth-century growth of the west Yorkshire conurbation and also of Sheffield. The coal measures outcrop in the foothill zone of the Pennines, with incised valleys broadening out to the east and the general elevation also falling in the same direction.

Beyond the foothills a broad lowland associated with the lower courses of the Ouse and the Trent is underlain by Triassic sandstones and marls, but these rocks are covered by extensive recent deposits, in particular alluvium, which form flat agricultural land of high quality. South of the Humber the broad alluvial lowland is terminated to the east by a zone of low hills, formed by a series of Jurassic rocks, in particular the Ironstone and Oolite that have provided the basis for the Scunthorpe iron and steel industry. Reflecting the

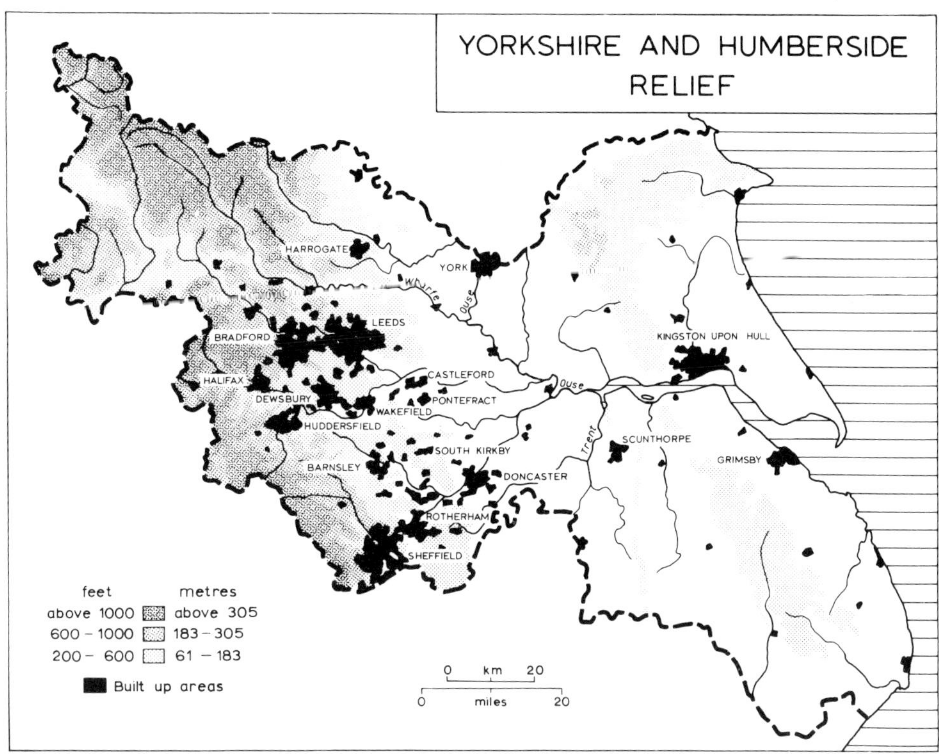

Fig 65 Yorkshire and Humberside—Relief
The topographical sequence across the region closely follows the underlying geological structure. Contrasting problems for both land use and economic development are associated with the major sub-divisions of the Region, which consist of the Pennines, the predominantly urban coalfield area, the richer farmlands to the east, and the urban developments on and close to the Humber estuary.

varying lithology of the Jurassic outcrops, the lines of hills alternate with clay vales, the largest being the central clay lowland of Lincolnshire. These Jurassic rocks narrow in width from south to north, and beyond the Humber they form only a very narrow band of no topographical significance.

Next in sequence to the east, extensive areas of Chalk outcrop both north and south of the Humber. Behind an eastward-facing scarp the Chalk forms the low, broad hills of the Lincolnshire and Yorkshire Wolds, which support wide areas of rolling, prosperous farmland, separated by the industrial developments of Humberside. North of the Humber the Chalk is succeeded by a broad plain covered by glacial deposits. Parts of this area are liable to flood, but along the coast the recent deposits, mostly boulder clay, form easily-eroded low cliffs. The boulder clay plain continues into north Lincolnshire, but here the coast is often lined by marine siltlands which are of high fertility if suitably drained and protected from flooding.

The Rural Landscape

A great variety of soil types is associated with this diverse geological background, and the topographical contrasts within the region also produce considerable variations in local climates. As a result there is a parallel variety in the detailed agricultural pattern of Yorkshire and Humberside, with the major contrast being between the agriculturally-difficult moorland and dale region in the west, where cultivated land is often under grass, and the rich farmlands of the east, where corn and root crops commonly dominate the agricultural scene (Fig. 66). Agricultural differences within the region can most easily be picked out in a traverse across the area from west to east, in which different types of farming appear as elevation falls and as changing soil and drainage conditions make their influence felt.

AGRICULTURE IN THE WEST OF THE REGION

The hill-farms of the western uplands are mainly concerned with stock-rearing and sheep farming, using grazing on the peat, grass and heather which dominate the vegetation of this area. Many farms have some grazing land in the dales, the deep valleys that dissect the plateau; but only some of these

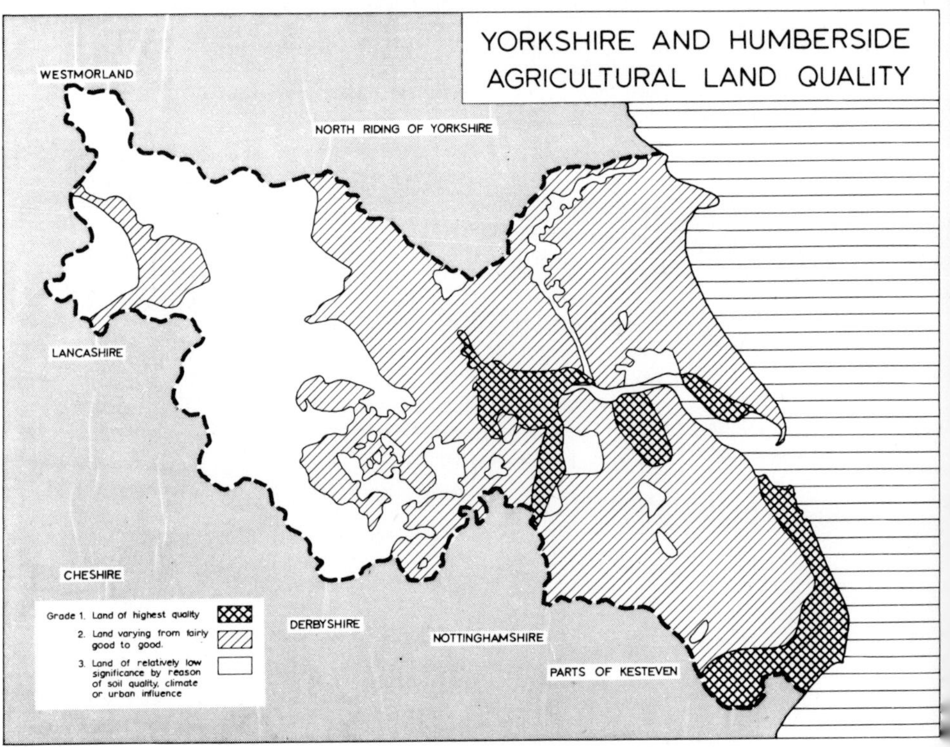

Fig 66 Yorkshire and Humberside—Agricultural Land Quality
Farmland varies widely in type from the difficult environment for cultivation found in the Pennines, where small hill-farms are typical, to areas in the East Riding of Yorkshire and north Lincolnshire, where some of the best agricultural land in the country is worked by large, highly-capitalized farms.

farms are involved in the production of milk for sale, partly because of inaccessibility and also because they are not equipped with the necessary buildings and facilities to make milk production an efficient undertaking. On the better pastures of the Carboniferous limestone area, however, dairying is more common and some milk cows are kept as well as sheep. In response to modern market demands, sheep-rearing in the uplands now focuses on the keeping of hardy ewes, able to withstand the difficult conditions of winter, and each also able to rear a lamb which is normally sold at the beginning of winter.

Current ways of improving agriculture in this area involve adjustments to present practices, rather than any drastic alterations to farming. The larger hill-farmers have been improving their herds of cattle by introducing Galloway stock which produce good beef animals and are hardy enough to winter out-of-doors. Attempts are being made to improve grazing by eliminating bracken, by reseeding and by land reclamation. Farm buildings are also being renovated and adapted, particularly on the smaller, more accessible farms, where increased emphasis on milk production is possible and makes economic sense.

To the east, in the area where coal measures outcrop, an important influence on agriculture has been the nearby presence of urban and industrial land use. Historically, the local urban market encouraged the production of liquid milk and although this is now a less powerful influence in an era of modern motor transport and of large companies undertaking milk distribution, the influence has not died out entirely, particularly in the more accessible upland valleys, where grass is the most logical crop in any case. Competition from urban and industrial land use is at its greatest in the vicinity of the west Yorkshire conurbation and also close to Sheffield, thus causing a reduction in the area available for agriculture. This loss of land is steady rather than spectacular, but it has more impact than might be expected on the relatively small farms of this area, which under modern economic conditions find it difficult to adjust to any reduction in their size. In the coalfield urban belt, too, atmospheric pollution reduced the amount of sunlight received, to the detriment of agricultural yields, although this is a factor of decreasing importance as smoke control legislation begins to make its influence felt. The pollution problem has its most severe expression near Sheffield where, to the north-east of the city, deposits of fluorine from the atmosphere collect in the herbage, making the keeping of cattle impossible in the worst affected areas. Yet in spite of these difficulties, there are agricultural areas, interdigitated between the urban growth, where a considerable amount of good farming is still going on.

As both the height and the amount of easily cultivated land varies across the coalfield zone, there is also a similar gradation in the emphasis of farming. In the western coalfield, in the valleys and on the lower slopes of the Pennines, milk production is the most important farming activity. Farms are often small, particularly near the urban areas, although to the south larger farms of about 40 hectares (100 acres) become more common. On these small farms, in an area where the ripening of grain crops often poses problems in any case, much of the feed for the dairy herd is bought in from outside the farm, and what arable cultivation there is often aims at producing food for stock. On the smaller farms near the towns, pigs and poultry provide important supplements to farmers' incomes. Further east altitudes are lower, rainfall is less and farms tend to be somewhat larger, with 20 to 40 hectares (50 to 100 acres) being a frequent size. As a result, although there is still a substantial emphasis on dairying, arable farming is more important here, farmers tend to be more self-sufficient in the production of feed for their stock, and some cash crops are also produced on the farms, particularly potatoes, wheat and barley. Finally, on the eastern fringe of the west Yorkshire urban belt, farms tend to be larger in size, dairy herds become less common, and more income is derived from store and beef animals and from arable cash crops. Arable cultivation is easier here and competition from urban uses is less serious, both because the total pressure is lower and because the loss of some agricultural land has less important economic implications for the larger farmers found in this area.

AGRICULTURE IN THE EAST OF THE REGION

Lying to the east is the broad lowland, orientated north–south and centred on the rivers Ouse and Trent, which provides a relatively unbroken area of good agricultural land, some of it of the highest quality. Again there is a gradation of farming conditions across the area, here reflecting soil and drainage conditions. First, on soils developed on Magnesian limestone, there is a belt of moderately large farms with big fields, largely concerned with arable farming. At one time sheep were important here, but now the problems of trespass and worrying by untrained dogs, associated with the urban zone immediately to the west, have considerably reduced the number of sheep kept. On these free-draining soils potatoes, sugar beet and, in particular, cereals are the most important cash crops. Immediately adjoining is a zone in which soils are derived from Bunter sandstone and pebble beds, or from outwash sands and gravels. Here rainfall is lower than further west and on these sandy soils a hot dry summer can have severe repercussions, making profits somewhat less reliable. Here again sheep (and the root crops on which they fed) have been replaced by vegetables, grown as a farm crop and sold in the nearby industrial area. Finally, along the Ouse and its main tributaries and, further south, in a broad zone along the Trent, alluvial soils have produced an area in which summer drought is much less of a problem. This is an area of mixed farming, in which farms are smaller but yield is higher. There are problems of subsoil drainage here, but in recent years considerable effort has been invested in improving drainage and increased production is often an important result of this work. Wheat is the main cereal on the alluvium, and potatoes and sugar beet produce high yields; but beef cattle are also everywhere important. The pastures on these soils are easily damaged by treading in wet weather, so that the winter housing of cattle is necessary.

To the east of the Ouse–Trent lowland, scarp and vale topography characterizes east Yorkshire and, in a somewhat more complex manner, north Lincolnshire. In Lincolnshire the central alluvial lowland gives way to the Heath, where the low scarp of the Oolitic limestone provides the western boundary of a narrow area of freely-drained soils, where heath, ferns and gorse, together with some patches of poor grass, dominated land use until the nineteenth century. Then this area was completely changed by agricultural improvement into a landscape dominated by cultivation, with scattered farms and with large fields, surrounded by dry-stone walls. On these large farms, often over 120 hectares (300 acres), cereals and root crops, with arable sheep, are now the most common land use.

In the remainder of north Lincolnshire and in east Yorkshire there are three terrain types, with differing agricultural patterns. One of these is provided by broad alluvial plains, as in the valley of the Hull river in Yorkshire or along the line of the Old River Ancholme in Lincolnshire. These areas were formerly ill-drained, but now they offer fine testimonies to the role of human effort in creating good arable land as a result of drainage works. Drainage work has been underway since medieval times, but in some areas the creation of permanently cultivable land has been completed only very recently. Now they produce high yields of diverse crops, but still depend on careful management of their drainage.

A second type of farming area is associated with the surface outcrop of the Chalk. The western fringe of this area offers rather poorer agricultural land because of the steeper slopes associated with the scarp and the somewhat greater height of this zone, but mostly the area provides good agricultural land. Again this was a landscape that was shaped in the mid-nineteenth century, when enclosure, tree-planting and new modes of farming converted the Wolds into an important arable area. Sheep, folded on turnips, are still found on a few farms, but now temporary grass has become more important for stock feed. Barley and wheat remain the most important cereals.

Finally there are the spreads of boulder clay which form rolling, hummocky plains, particularly along the coast. In Lincolnshire the boulder clay has deposits of marine clay on its outer margin, which, near Grimsby, has supported market gardening; but in general this coastal strip is notable for deep, moist, medium-heavy clay soils, where grain and root crops are important, but where there is as much grass as arable.

In the eastern half of the Yorkshire and Humberside region farming is commercially efficient and dominates broad areas of the landscape. One result of this is that rural depopulation still continues in this area, reflecting the general trend towards a steady and rapid reduction in the agricultural labour force. Away from the industrial developments on the Humber, where residential population is spreading out from the towns into the country, rural populations show a steady decline, associated with the contraction of agricultural employment but without any reduction in agricultural productivity.

THE NATIONAL PARK AREAS

Agriculture is not the only form of rural land use, and the loss of farmland to urban growth is not the only kind of land-use competition in the countryside. Given the highly urban context of this region, the attractive countryside of the Pennines takes on special significance. Here areas of great scenic attractiveness, both in the farmed areas and above the limits of cultivation, are located very close to great centres of urban population on both sides of the uplands, and hence pose special planning problems.

As a result, much of the west of the region has been protected from inappropriate development in various ways. In the north-west the Yorkshire Dales National Park was designated in 1954 and closely adjoins the Forest of Bowland Area of Outstanding Natural Beauty. In the south-west a narrow segment of the Peak District National Park overlaps into the region; this park was established in 1950 and abuts the fringes of Sheffield. In addition, it has been proposed that Nidderdale, immediately to the east of the Yorkshire Dales Park, and the stretch of the Pennines to its south should also be areas given careful protection because of the recreational pressures to which they are likely to be exposed (Fig. 67).

Both the National Parks in the region have problems in common. One is the impact of the motor car, particularly in an area where upland roads are narrow and the nearby urban population usually visits as day-trippers rather than as longer-staying holiday makers. The modifications that would be necessary to cope adequately with the demands of the motorist might well destroy the aesthetic attractiveness of the rural landscape; and although 'attractiveness' is an attribute that is difficult to specify precisely, it certainly does not include dual-carriageway roads leading to conspicuous car and caravan parks. For many, one of the major attractions of these areas is the very absence of population, a quality which is particularly difficult to reconcile with the increased enjoyment of these areas by many more people. There can be no completely satisfactory solution, but one possibility is to choose local centres, around which to organize visits by car-borne day-trippers, with car-parks, picnic areas and the opportunity for taking short walks and playing games. These areas could be within the Parks themselves or at other attractive areas outside: perhaps Fountains Abbey already provides an indication of the kind of facilities that might be appropriate elsewhere (Plate 59).

A policy of this kind should relieve pressure on the more remote areas, where solitude could still be preserved and more energetic means of recreation like rock-climbing and hill-walking could be undertaken, without conflict with the needs and pressures of other visitors. Nonetheless there are potential conflicts, since the present use of much of the uplands as grouse moors would not be compatible with its increased use for other forms of outdoor recreation.

A similar problem of competition is related to the fact that the National Parks are actively used for economic purposes by their permanent inhabitants. In this planning region the Yorkshire Dales Park is the area where this feature is of major importance. Here attempts to maintain the 'attractiveness' of the landscape have sometimes conflicted with the activities of farmers. Difficulties arise when for good commercial reasons it seems appropriate to a farmer to remove field boundaries on his own land, or to use temporary buildings which are cheap to erect but do not fit the romantic image of the appropriate landscape for the Dales. The provision of electricity poses similar problems, both in the open countryside, where major transmission lines fit awkwardly with the relatively subdued topography of the area, and also in villages where electricity supply lines and telephone wires weave a cat's cradle around the houses.

Extractive industries also impinge on the landscape. Lead mining has now

Plate 59 Fountains Abbey, near Ripon (Yorkshire)
The remains of Fountains Abbey, a Cistercian foundation, lies within the grounds of a later landscape garden and seventeenth century hall. It lies outside the boundary of the Yorkshire Dales National Park, but with its car parks and other facilities it provides an attractive destination for day-trips by car from nearby urban areas. Local centres of this kind help to preserve the solitude of the more remote parts of the National Park.

virtually ceased, although in the 1860s 4,000 workers were employed. Paradoxically the remains of the industry, represented by spoil heaps and abandoned mine-workings, take on an attraction for some once they have been softened by decay or have acquired a patina of age. Old limestone quarries also seem to melt into the landscape, but modern quarries are still active and are much larger and obtrusive than their nineteenth-century predecessors. Fortunately this twentieth century development has been in a few restricted areas, for example near Grassington in Wharfedale and between Settle and Horton-in-Ribblesdale. This is a land use which must be located where the limestone deposits are economically workable, but which conflicts with the generally-accepted view of what is appropriate in a National Park.

In the last resort it is almost inescapable that, owing to pressure from nearby urban areas, the National Parks in the Yorkshire and Humberside region will continue to be used for residence, agriculture, quarrying and water catchment, as well as recreation. These various competing uses can only be reconciled with difficulty. Certainly it will require the tactful but energetic use of the relatively limited powers and resources of the various National Park committees involved if what is valuable in the landscape is to be preserved in these areas.

The Urban Landscape of the Coalfield

The major concentration of urban population in the region is located on the coalfield in a central urban belt which runs north–south across the area. In fact there are three subdivisions to this urban complex. First there is the group of towns centred on Leeds and Bradford which forms the west Yorkshire conurbation, with a population of nearly two millions. Then there is a group of towns in the central sector of the urban belt, where coal mining is still an important occupation. Here the main towns are Barnsley and Doncaster and the total population is about three-quarters of a million. Finally there is the city of Sheffield, Rotherham and other settlements nearby, with a total population over 700,000. Each of these groups has certain problems in common; but there are also differences in emphasis between them.

One of the general problems is the highly specialized nature of employment, particularly in the smaller towns. This specialization is often in industries which are no longer expanding and hence there is a general need to attract more diverse forms of employment to this area. Until recently it was without government aid for this purpose, with the result that it found difficulty in competing with the subsidized Development Areas or with the dynamic economies of the Midlands and the South East. Part of the planning region

Plate 60 Hebden Bridge, on the River Calder (Yorkshire)
The Pennine uplands are deeply dissected by the main river valleys and the wool textile industry of west Yorkshire had its earliest location in some of these valleys, attracted by the availability of water-power. The role of the valleys as a routeway for rail and road can also be seen in this picture. The textile industry is declining in these marginal locations, new industry is difficult to attract, and areas like these are likely to experience continued out-migration of population.

has now been designated an Intermediate Area, in which various government inducements to new industry are being granted. Although this aided area does not include Leeds or Sheffield, it embraces many of the smaller towns where the attraction of new industry is most difficult, so that although the economic problems of the central urban belt are far from solved, its future prospects now look brighter.

A second general problem facing the urban areas on the coalfield is the prevention of urban coalescence. This is a desirable goal, since the present loosely-structured built-up area has advantages in making open space available to urban residents. It has been argued, too, that there are good aesthetic and social reasons for keeping communities separate that are physically distinct from one another, although they may be closely bound by economic ties. The solution that has been currently advanced is the designation of a green belt which surrounds the west Yorkshire conurbation and Sheffield. Although this belt has yet to be formally approved by the central government, local authorities are operating a policy of restricting new urban development within its area and their decisions are being supported by the Department of the Environment. It can be argued that this particular battle has already been partly lost, since in the Leeds area, at least, the built-up area seems almost continuous to a casual visitor. But even here there is still open country that is undeveloped between the main roads. Similarly, the Dales area to the west is worth preserving from unrestricted suburban expansion, and the agriculturally-valuable Vale of York, to the east, also is worthy of some protection. To the south the more open pattern of urban development in the direction of Barnsley is also worth maintaining, if only to keep the present separation between the west Yorkshire conurbation and the Sheffield area. If attempts at improving the economy of the central urban belt succeed, then the green belt policy may take on added significance as a means of steering the physical expansion of towns and cities into the most appropriate areas for further growth.

A third general problem of this central urban belt is that of obsolescence and dereliction. The impact of this problem varies from town to town; and some local authorities have been more active than others in improving the environment for living which their towns offer. Yet in many areas the tip heaps and subsidence associated with mining still remain and have produced considerable areas of derelict land; and, despite slum clearance in recent years, the drab urban landscape of many of the smaller towns has stayed relatively unaltered. Not only is there a need to replace old houses and rebuild unattractive town centres in order to improve the day-to-day environment of the population, but improvements of this kind also have the advantage of making the area more attractive to the managers who are essential if new industry is to prosper.

THE WEST YORKSHIRE CONURBATION

The largest concentration of population in the central urban belt is in the west Yorkshire conurbation, which is the home of nearly half the people living in the Yorkshire and Humberside Region. This is one of the most loosely-

Plate 61 Part of Central Leeds
In common with much of the west Yorkshire conurbation there are extensive areas of Leeds in need of redevelopment. The photograph shows the piece-meal fashion in which this is being achieved, as a result of new road building, by the replacement of older residential areas by new blocks of flats, and by the erection of new commercial buildings on cleared sites. To the top of the photograph are some of the buildings of the university, which itself is an important force in changing the townscape of this section of the city.

structured conurbations in Britain, since the physical background of the area, with urban growth concentrated in the valleys and with open farmland and moorland lying between, has produced a relatively low overall density of population and built-up area for such an important urban complex. Socially the conurbation is similarly fragmented, since although Leeds is the dominant city in the economy of the district, local loyalties and shopping are also focused on a number of smaller centres. This loose pattern is reflected in the communications network, which lacks the integration found in a unicentred conurbation (compare Chapters 7 and 11).

The economic prosperity of this area was founded in the nineteenth century on wool textiles, coal, clothing and iron; and 40 per cent of the population continues to depend on the manufacture of textiles and clothing. Traditionally this emphasis has been related to the availability of wool from Pennine sheep, soft water from the Millstone Grit, together with power from upland streams to drive mills and, later, local coal to fire steam engines. It must be said, however, that chance may have had much to do with the development of this particular form of industrial specialization, although once established the close links between the different branches of the textile trade have encouraged its continued location in this area.

Many of the current problems of the area spring from its nineteenth century background. Although unemployment rates do not reach those found in some other parts of the country, there is an unhealthy dependence on a limited range of employment and net emigration is considerable. Although new service industries have been established in Leeds and Bradford, many of the smaller towns, particularly in the western valleys of the conurbation, have not been successful in diversifying. This problem has been emphasized during the 1960s, a period when the wool textile industry has been undergoing two parallel changes. One of these has been the fall in demand for the products of the wool-textile industry as a whole, in particular for woven cloth. The other has been an increase in the consumption of man-made fibres. As a result, new methods of manufacture have had to be adopted, and this development has favoured the larger firms, able to make the necessary investment. Because of this, the number of firms in the industry has fallen; and it is now being transformed from an industry based on, and heavily influenced by, the processing of wool fibre, to one possessing certain distinctive types of machinery and skills, used for the processing of a variety of fibres. Fewer firms with greater productivity and smaller overall demand has brought an accelerated reduction in the number of workers in the industry and this influence is making its influence felt in unemployment figures in the conurbation.

THE COAL-MINING TOWNS OF THE CENTRAL URBAN BELT

To the south-east coal-mining becomes increasingly important, although there is a transition from the activities of the textile area to those of the area where coal-mining is dominant. Ten per cent of the workers in Wakefield, for example, are employed in mining; but this town is also the administrative centre of the West Riding County Council, and textiles, engineering and electrical goods produce a diversified manufacturing sector. Other small towns nearby, in particular Castleford and Pontefract, have a less diversified economy and as much as one-third of the population is employed in mining. Here a contraction in male employment must be expected in coal-mining, but in the small towns and in Wakefield there is some long-term hope that other kinds of employment will expand. Not only is active male labour available, but there is also a good supply of potential industrial sites and recent motorway building has greatly increased the accessibility of this area. A further advantage is that these towns lie within the Intermediate Area where government benefits are available to new industry, giving it an advantage over competing areas in the north-west of the conurbation (Fig. 67).

Still further to the south-east coal-mining is of greater importance in absolute terms, and its economic potential is still relatively high, although its labour force must also be expected to decline to some extent as a result of modernization. Doncaster, for example, is located in one of the richest parts of the Yorkshire coalfield, but also has diverse manufacturing industries. Population growth has been rapid here, because of a high rate of natural increase and because it has been able to avoid loss of population by net emigration. Until recently the economy of this town was buoyant, with the decline in the labour force required for mining being offset by the expansion of manufacturing. At present, however, the expansion of employment has been

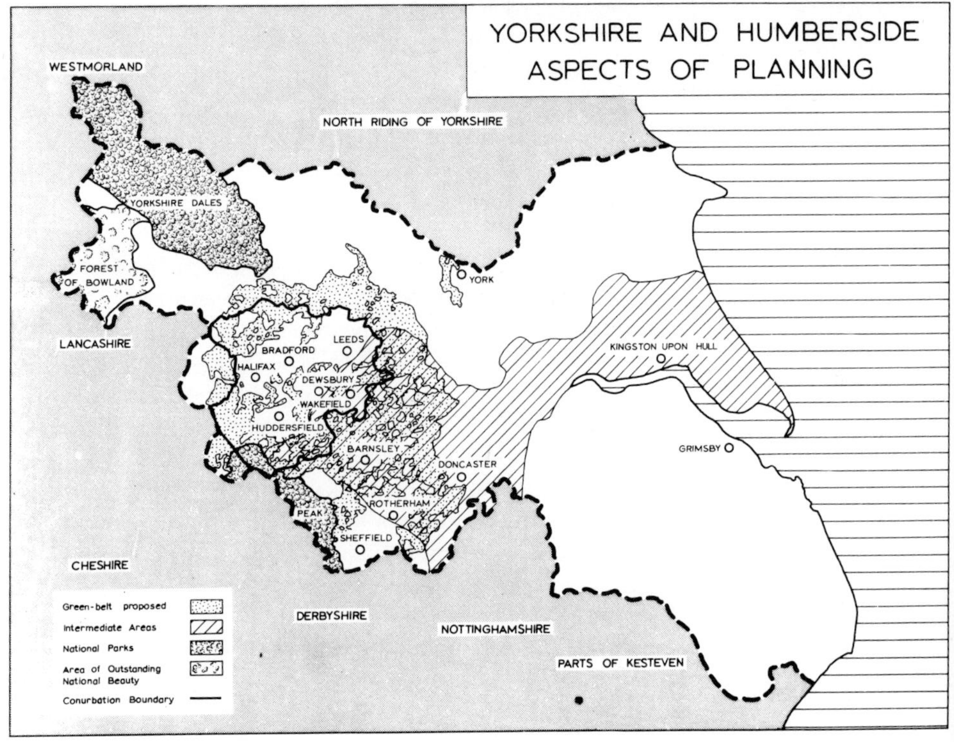

Fig 67 Yorkshire and Humberside—Aspects of Planning
Much of the attractive landscape of the Pennines has been protected by the designation of National Parks and an Area of Outstanding Natural Beauty. Attempts have been made to prevent urban coalescence in the coalfield area by proposing a green belt zone. In parts of the region economic growth has lagged behind that achieved elsewhere in the country, although unemployment has not reached the levels common in the Development Areas; the so-called Intermediate Area is designed to correct this problem by giving government aid to new industry, although not at the level appropriate in some of the areas of greater economic difficulty.

checked, and it is forecast that the demand for male labour will drop further in the near future. Yet, again, renewed expansion is likely in the long run, since this town also lies within the Intermediate Area, it has good communications by road and rail, and cheap sources of power of various kinds are available. Barnsley presents a similar picture, but being a smaller centre with less diversity in its industrial structure, its problems are rather more urgent than those of Doncaster but also open to potential solutions. The smaller coalfield towns in this south-eastern area, however, present a more difficult problem. Hemsworth, South Kirkby and the Dearne valley area are very heavily dependent on coal-mining, and large numbers of people travel long distances to work in other towns because of the lack of local opportunities, particularly for women. These smaller towns have been suffering from the lack of alternative employment for a long time, particularly as the service sector of the economy is only poorly developed. These problems have become more difficult recently, as a result of the continued run-down of the labour force in mining. Unfortunately it is difficult to introduce new industry here, as the labour force lacks diversity of skills, it is not concentrated in any one centre, and these towns have a generally delapidated appearance, unattractive to modern industry.

THE SHEFFIELD AND ROTHERHAM AREA

The central urban belt of the Yorkshire and Humberside region continues further south to include Sheffield and Rotherham. This urban complex is separated from the mining area further north only by a narrow belt of open country, but possesses a contrasting industrial structure since it has acquired an international reputation for its steel, cutlery and tool industries. Its steel production is highly specialized and concentrates on the manufacture of special alloy steels: nearly two-thirds of the British output of this product is made here. In all about one-third of total employment is in metal-using industries of one kind or another, often in small specialized firms dependent on close links with each other.

The seeds of industrial specialization in this area were sprouting in the middle of the eighteenth century, when coal-mining, the manufacture of iron and steel, and the production of tools and cutlery were already being undertaken in Sheffield and its surrounding villages. The fabrication of metal was often being carried out by part-time farmers and shopkeepers; and the demand for steel from the cutlery trade was sufficient to be an important reason for the rise of a local steel industry. Local environmental factors have been quoted as important factors in shaping the nature of specialist industry here. Certainly the presence of water-power and suitable rocks for grindstone must have made some contribution to the cutlery trade, if hardly a decisive one. In the same way, the availability of local coal and iron resources must have encouraged the early iron and steel industry, although in the long run the contribution of individual innovators was more important.

As early as 1740 Joseph Huntsman moved into the area. As a clock-maker he was seeking better materials for springs and pendulums, and his experiments led to the production of a hard steel that could be cast. His process was imitated by others, and towards the end of the eighteenth century there were possibly as many as eleven manufacturers in the district using the process that Huntsman had pioneered. It was in Sheffield, too, that Sir Henry Bessemer opened his own works in 1858, after other manufacturers had been reticent about adopting his revolutionary steel-making process. Again the new technique was progressively adopted by other iron-masters in the district. In the 1860s the greatly expanded industry was not only meeting the needs of the local metal-using trades, but was supplying the demands of the railways. Later, in the 1880s, it was to supply steel plate for ships' hulls.

Although the steel industry is susceptible to cyclical fluctuations, since the Second World War this area has enjoyed consistent industrial prosperity. Employment here increased rapidly in the 1950s; and although in the late 1960s the level of employment has been more static, this can at least be partly explained by a rise in productivity rather than by contraction in demand. Not only is the resulting structure of employment heavily dependent on steel-making and metal-using industries, but employment in the service sector is relatively low for an urban area of this size, when it is recalled that there are nearly one million people in Sheffield and its immediate hinterland. Further declines in employment in coal-mining are certainly likely, and further increases in productivity may check any growth of employment in steel-making and metal fabrication.

Yet, in spite of these difficulties, this remains the most prosperous section of the central urban belt of the Yorkshire and Humberside region. In the immediate future the decisions of the British Steel Corporation will be decisive in controlling the number of jobs in the area; but in spite of its dependence on a limited range of employment at present, Sheffield enjoys certain significant advantages for the future. One important element is the energy with which the local authority has been replacing sub-standard housing, recasting much of the urban landscape of the city in the process. The city also has immediate access to the Peak District National Park, and advances have been made in controlling the atmospheric pollution formerly inescapably associated with its industries. The generally-improved environment for urban living that is being created will make the attraction of new employment a much easier task, given the city's good access to the motorway network and to main railway lines. The size of Sheffield is itself an advantage for future development, since it is large enough to provide a wide range of ancillary services for trade and industry; and improvements to its central shopping area are likely to lead to an increase in the number of jobs in tertiary occupations.

Urban Development in Humberside

If many of the problems of the Leeds conurbation and the Sheffield area are derived from the need to adjust past urban landscapes to new demands, future urban development on and near the Humber estuary will be less inhibited by a legacy from the past. The extensive urban growth typical of the coalfield did not affect Humberside, although the Scunthorpe iron and steel industry, based on the ores of the Oolite, is an isolated example of a typical nineteenth century development in the east of the planning region, and much of the industrial structure of Hull was also established in the nineteenth century. Yet the main effect of nineteenth-century economic developments here was to encourage the growth of ports on the Humber, able to handle imports for the industries of Lancashire and the West Riding. These ports only attracted a limited range of manufacturing industries, often concerned with processing imported raw materials. Similarly the iron and steel industry of Scunthorpe was highly specialized around a local primary resource. As a result industries in the area were not bound together by close local linkages to form a distinctive industrial region; the Humber itself was a positive handicap to any kind of interaction of this kind, as it effectively divided the area in two.

In the twentieth century the urban economy of Humberside has remained relatively remote from the mainstream of economic activity in England. Yet Humberside has potential for future development. Indeed, this potential is increased by the smaller share of industrial expansion that it has enjoyed in the past, since the Humber is one of the major estuaries of eastern Britain, close to the urban areas of the Midlands and the North, with most room for future expansion and with good sea communications to growing markets in Europe. Here there is reasonably deep water to accommodate the bulk-carriers that are becoming much more important in ocean freight. Here, too, the absence of a local industrial hinterland is becoming a less pressing restriction, as plans are evolved for the construction of a bridge across the Humber and as motorways are constructed closer to the area.

Present urban development in Humberside is concentrated in three main areas. The city of Hull and subsidiary settlements close-by dominate urban life north of the Humber. To the south the industrial pattern of the Scunthorpe area is quite distinct from that found in Grimsby and Immingham.

The economy of Hull is dominated by its port function (Plate 62). The deep-sea fishing industry is obviously associated with this, but so too is the city's chemical, food-processing and timber-using industries. Hull also has light and heavy engineering and a branch of the aircraft industry in its industrial structure, yet in recent years the outward migration of population has been high, with younger and more skilled workers being common among the emigrants. Although the major manufacturing industries mainly employ men, male unemployment is higher than female because of the demand for women workers in the expanding tertiary sector of this large city, with over 500,000 people living in and around it.

The basic problem in Hull is that many of its industries are declining, or at least growing only very slowly. The trade of the port can certainly be expected to increase, but in spite of this it is likely that improvements in freight handling will produce a fall in the total labour force employed by the docks. Because of these difficulties the area immediately north of the Humber has been designated an Intermediate Area (Fig. 67), but it will be some time before this will have much effect. At present, housing conditions in the city are the worst found in Humberside, and do not create the kind of environment that is attractive to modern light industry. In spite of plans for improvement, east-west communications are not of the quality which expansion of the city would demand; and close links with other industrial areas remain difficult to establish. This difficulty will be alleviated to some extent when the Humber

Plate 62 Hull (Yorkshire)
The river Hull is on the left of the photograph and represents the old harbour of the city. The large dock in the centre of the picture is Victoria Dock, now too small for much modern traffic. In the top right is Alexandra Dock, which has been extensively reconditioned in recent years and now large ocean-going vessels can use it. Further down the estuary the King George V dock and deep water jetties at Salt End provide a range of terminal facilities for 'roll-on roll-off' and bulk cargoes.

bridge is at last constructed, but the best hope for prosperous economic growth is likely to depend on the exploitation of the deep-water estuary.

The Scunthorpe area presents a contrasting situation because of its extremely specialized economy based on the iron and steel industry. The local ore was first exploited in the 1860s, iron manufacture took place soon after, and steel was first produced in 1890. As a result Scunthorpe has grown, mainly in the twentieth century, from a cluster of villages to a town with a population of over 138,000. Although the growth in the number of jobs for men has attracted considerable inward migration in the twentieth century, the specialized nature of the town has created a shortage of employment for women. Female vacancies exist in Hull, but although Scunthorpe lies within commuting distance as the crow flies, a daily journey to work is not possible using imperfect roads and the present bridging point at Goole.

Even the expansion of the labour force in the iron and steel industry now looks less assured. Paradoxically, plans recently announced by the British Steel Corporation for a massive investment of £130 million in their Scunthorpe plant will result in a decline of over 3,000 in the labour force. The amount of alternative employment that can be expected to develop is problematical. Housing conditions are good, and the Humber bridge will open up jobs for women in Hull and may encourage local opportunities in Scunthorpe by giving access to the ancillary services provided by a large city. On the other hand there are few local industries other than iron and steel to provide a base for the future expansion of manufacturing, and the fact that the town does not have the status of an Intermediate Area may make it difficult for it to compete with the area north of the Humber for new industry coming to the region.

Grimsby and Immingham together have a population slightly larger than that of Scunthorpe. The fishing industry, traditionally associated with Grimsby, continues to flourish and has been modernized rather more swiftly than that of Hull. The preservation of fish and other sea-food by freezing has expanded the range of industries in the town; and as it was a natural step to expand by freezing fresh vegetables as well, in particular peas, this industry has had an impact on agricultural production in the rural area close by. Other industries like paper-making and jam-making have grown up, but the town still largely depends, directly and indirectly, on fishing. Ten kilometres (six miles) further up the estuary Immingham Dock was established in 1912. Although originally intended for the export of coal and the import of timber and iron ore, since the Second World War Immingham has attracted chemical and petro-chemical industries, using flat land for extensive plants and the nearby deep-water channel for access by large bulk-carriers. These two towns, which have now virtually grown together, have a buoyant economy because they have attracted some of the expanding industries in the British industrial scene. Certainly the new chemical industries here involve a large investment of capital for a relatively small permanent increase in the labour force and the economy of the two towns will remain independent from other centres of employment. Yet the space that they possess for further industrial expansion along the coast and the likelihood that their present industries will continue to grow, gives this urban area a positive advantage over the other towns and cities of Humberside.

FURTHER READING

M. W. Beresford and G. R. J. Jones (eds.), *Leeds and its Region* (Leeds, 1967).

P. Lewis and P. N. Jones, *The Humberside Region* (Newton Abbot, 1970).

D. L. Linton (ed.), *Sheffield and its Region* (Sheffield, 1956).

I. G. Simmons (ed.), *Yorkshire Dales: National Park Guide No. 9* (H.M.S.O., 1971).

Yorkshire and Humberside Economic Planning Council, *A Review of Yorkshire and Humberside* (H.M.S.O., 1966).

The North West

With the exception of the industrial revolution, the cultural revolutions of Britain were late in arriving in North West England and slow in becoming absorbed into the society of the region. The Neolithic Revolution, based in the south of Britain ignored, for a long time, the wooded clay plain of the North West. The great cultural revolution introduced by the Romans occurred sporadically through the region but was based on military rather than civil occupance. The changes in eighteenth century British agriculture were slow in penetrating the conservative agricultural economies of the region and only the onset of the feverish activity of the industrial revolution in the nineteenth century spurred agriculture into technological awareness. The region in the late twentieth century is the most intensely industrialized and urbanized planning region in Britain, though the electronics revolution has had less effect so far than in other regions.

Within the region, much of today's economic and social activity is focused on the large lowland belt between the Irish Sea and the three upland areas, the Forests of Bowland and Rossendale, the southern end of the Pennines, and the Furness Fells of the Lake District (Fig. 68). Nineteenth century industrial growth occurred on the lowland and in the foothills of the uplands and was the work of individual industrialists. Today large areas of landscape are still influenced by the activities of these men. Industrial growth and decline in more recent times has been less the prerogative of individuals and more the work of the state, often with a view to reducing the high level of unemployment prevalent in the region for 50 years. In specific terms, governmental intervention in industrial location has resulted in new industries such as the motor-car plant at Halewood, while Government sponsored construction projects, such as the new oil-fired power station at Ellesmere Port, also provide valuable jobs and have had an impact on sub-regional unemployment levels. Although there are considerable changes taking place in the region as agricultural and industrial resources are reassessed, nonetheless large areas of landscape remain as a monument to times long past.

The Physical Basis of Economic Development

Contrasts abound in the physical landscape of the North West, not only between the fault separated lowland and highland, but also within upland and lowland; variety occurs in solid and superficial geology and the particular physical processes have reached separate stages of development. Man's responses to this physical diversity exhibit his role as an active agent in landscape change.

The folded Carboniferous sandstones, gritstones and shales of the Forests of Rossendale and Bowland both rise to over 460 metres (1,500 feet) and trend east-north-east/west-south-west from the main spine of the Pennines. But the wild, and inaccessible slopes of the Forest of Bowland have little in common with the heavily industrialized and urbanized valleys of Rossendale. In Rossendale the Lancastrians' entrepreneurial ability took full benefit from both geological and geomorphological landscape elements. In the northern

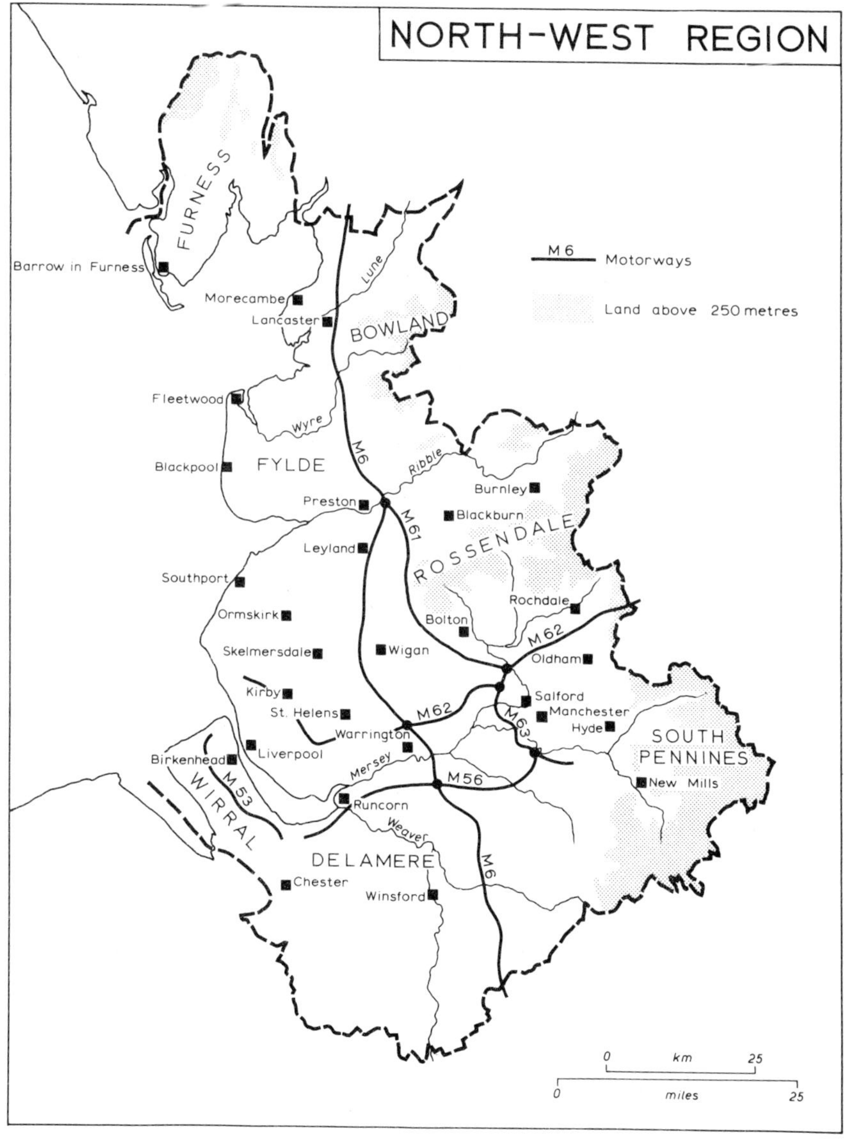

Fig 68 The North West Region

part of the Rossendale Forest the rivers Darwen and Calder lie in a syncline of coal measures which came to be the Burnley coalfield. Faulting, which governs much of the minor relief, introduces lower coal measures strata around the flanks of the upland and produces plateaux and benches—a particularly notable one occurs at 300 metres (1,000 feet). Many of these flatter areas bear heavy scars of industrial and urban use and misuse dating from the industrial boom years of the last century.

The Pennines in the south-east of the region have a strongly folded structure and a well developed cuesta landscape with classic examples in the breached anticline at Todd Bank and the perched syncline at Goytshead. The earth

Plate 63 New Mills (Derbyshire)
A gorge on the river Goyt provided potential power which was exploited in the development of cotton mills. Some more recent development can be seen on the periphery of the town.

movements producing these structures also resulted in a syncline of coal measures in what became the Mid-Goyt valley, and the nineteenth century entrepreneurs of Cheshire and Derbyshire were no less adroit than their counterparts in Lancashire in realizing the potential of such a syncline. Elsewhere in this part of the Pennines glacial alteration to the landscape produced industrial responses before the major exploitation of the coal seams. Drainage diversion and deflection resulted in new river courses in post-glacial time and the irregularly graded streams provided fleets of power points which served some of the earliest cotton mills and around which industrial villages developed. New Mills (Plate 63) and Marple on the Goyt, and Broadbottom on the Ethrow are typical settlements associated with glacial interference in stream patterns. Similar examples may be seen around Rossendale, particularly on the Irwell.

Valley and channel development in the glacial and immediately post-glacial period also influenced the development of transport routes. In many parts of the southern Pennines these routes follow meltwater channels. The Walsden Gorge between Rochdale and Todmorden provided a course for trans-Pennine routes—turnpike, canal, and railway—and also provided a diffusion route into Yorkshire for Lancashire cotton technology. While structure is the dominant factor in the broad physique of this south-eastern area, glacial modification has played a considerable role in the evolution of the present landscape.

The third highland group in the region lies north of Morecambe Bay where the Furness Fells rise to the mountains of the Lake District, which is discussed fully in Chapter 15. In respect of the physical contrasts between highland and lowland, the Furness is a microcosm of the rest of the region. The cover of glacial drift, in some places 15 metres (50 feet) deep buries very effectively the geological structures and smoothes large areas of countryside. As in the other areas glacial channels have been important in affecting economic success in some locations. The straight channel separating Walney Island from the mainland has glacial origins, and provided the sheltered water necessary for the development of the port and shipping town of Barrow in Furness.

The lowland between the Pennines and the sea is a structural lowland; it is over 50 kilometres (30 miles) wide in the south tapering to 10 kilometres (6 miles) in the north and only in a few places does it rise above 60 metres (200 feet). Structure, however, plays little part in the physical landscape to be seen on a journey on the M.6, for a cover of glacial drift obscures most structural elements. The whole area has been planed by a series of erosional cycles and part cycles, but it is not a plain, for there are notable nuances of relief where different textured drift deposits occur and where occasionally bedrock is revealed at the surface. A structural warp for example brings coal measures almost to the suburbs of Liverpool. At the Mersey estuary, limestone with Keuper sandstone provides a plateau of firm foundations for the site of Liverpool. But for the most part a drift cover, sometimes 60 metres (200 feet) thick, of boulder clays, sands, and gravels dominates the landscape, with the clays smoothing the undulations of the lowland and the sands giving rise to a landscape of intricate patterns and slightly ragged in appearance. Superficial deposits on the drift are locally important both geomorphologically and economically. The Shirdley Hill Sands, for example, are wind transported and originate from a sandy coastline, the Hillhouse coastline, well to the east of the present coast. Locally quite thick, these angular sands have filled depressions in the drift cover and their purity has resulted in their commercial working giving rise in turn to the St. Helens' glass industry. Peatmosses, for example, Longton Moss near Preston, developed on drift cover and later deposits alike. These recent natural deposits were both strongly acid and more neutral, depending on particular formation processes. Agricultural improvement in the nineteenth century involved the drainage and reclamation of many of these mosses, but their legacy remains in local soil conditions. The complexities of the glacial and later deposits, which together so dominate the lowland, lead to considerable variation in soils even over quite small areas.

The difference between upland and lowland is firmly apparent in the climate and especially the rainfall. Parts of the Cheshire Plain lie in the rain shadow of the Welsh Hills and rainfall amounts are in places less than 760 millimetres (30 inches) per annum. Over the rest of the lowland around 900 millimetres (35 inches) per annum is commonplace. These amounts increase sharply on the slopes and crests of the uplands with some stations recording over 1,520 millimetres (60 inches) per annum. The higher rainfall on the uplands is paralleled by greater cloud cover and shorter sunshine periods. In some of the lowland areas, however, the degree of air pollution limits the annual sunshine totals reducing values by as much as 200 hours, to the 1,100–1,200 hours of upland stations. The creation of smokeless zones and other curbs to industrial air pollution have reduced the number of serious fogs in south-east Lancashire and many places are now experiencing annual sunshine totals 20 per cent higher than at the turn of the century.

Population

GENERAL COMPARISONS

The bulk of the region's population, of over six and a half million people, is concentrated in a belt of urban development in the south of the region. This belt stretches across the lowland from Liverpool to Manchester and on to Bolton. Well over five million people live in this area. Other concentrations of population are the towns in the Ribble valley and the coastal resorts especially of the Fylde. Despite the concentrated nature of the population, the region as a whole still has a high average density of population. The figure of over 7·5 people per hectare (3 per acre) compares with a corresponding figure of less than 5 per hectare (2 per acre) for South East England. In contrast to the south Lancashire conurbation, areas north of the Ribble and parts of Cheshire have a population barely sufficient to sustain a level of services adequate for twentieth century living. The North West generally has a low net emigration of population and this coupled with a small natural increase means the high average density of population is something of a paradox. The answer, however lies in the nineteenth century period of industrialization and urbanization when rates of natural increase were high and people flooded into the region particularly from Wales and Ireland. The population pressure in the urba areas, due to the rapid growth at this time, resulted in very high densities which have declined only slowly.

In the 1960s there was a net migration loss of people from the region. Out-migration was much lower in the 1960s than in either the previous decade or the depression years between the wars but even so emigration exceeded immigration. With this decline in net out-migration, population appears to be stabilizing, but the net figure obscures considerable movements of population. The estimates of the Ministry of Labour, for example, show in the period 1951–1962 that there was a net migration loss of 45,000 people. This difference is the result of 655,000 people moving into the region and 700,000 leaving the region. In recent years the gross movements of population have increased but the movements are more balanced.

During the 1960s there has been only slight natural increase Death rates are high. This fact may be associated particularly with diseases of the cities, for example, bronchitis and some forms of cancer, rather than any unusual characteristics of the age profile of the population.

POPULATION CHANGE

Heaviest population growth has occurred in the suburban districts and in towns, for example, Preston, Wigan and Warrington, close to the route of the M.6 motorway. Typical of suburbanization in the region is the growth of Altrincham and Macclesfield, both of which have a low natural increase but high rates of immigration especially of young married couples. This predominance of young married migrants will doubtless result in higher rates of natural increase. A somewhat similar process is to be seen in the Wirral and Chester areas and already, high natural increases in these areas has led to even greater population growth. Growth of a very different type has occurred in the Fylde where particular districts are favoured as retirement retreats.

Population decline is apparent in some parts of the region especially in the towns of east and north-east Lancashire, central Manchester and much of the Furness District. In towns in the Blackburn and Burnley areas decrease is due both to net out-migration and a natural population decrease. The decline in central Manchester is characteristic of that in many metropolitan areas which are undergoing major redevelopment (see Chapter 7). The provision of better housing has eased the disruption of social ties of the families moving from central Manchester to new estates, such as those at Middleton to the north and Hattersley to the east.

Conditions in Liverpool differ somewhat from those of Manchester, for although there are major overspill schemes, as at Kirkby, there is only a slight decrease in the population of the core of Merseyside. Out-migration from Liverpool, Birkenhead and Bootle, and some of the adjacent areas has been evident from early this century, but nonetheless there has been little net loss of population. Between 1961 and 1966 there was a net migration loss of 5 per cent but total population stayed much the same. Voluntary rehousing caused much of the out-migration with over 50,000 people moving to Kirkby in the period 1952–60. Many of these constituted part of Merseyside's young Catholic community, and the natural increase in population since 1960 has been

Plate 64 Tarporley (Cheshire)
Although granted a charter for a market in the thirteenth century this agricultural village failed to develop to any extent until the motor car era when it took on a residential function.

considerable. In 1966 56 per cent of Kirkby's population was under 25 years old compared with 41 per cent for Liverpool. The rural districts of Formby, Prescott, and Skelmersdale are similar to Kirkby in having a heavy inflow of migrants who retain their economic and social ties with Merseyside's core. The influence of this core is less in places such as Ormskirk, Runcorn and Southport, but it is still felt and there develop dual and sometimes contradictory forces. They are big enough to act as social and economic centres for their own populations, yet they remain affected by housing policy in Liverpool.

The influence of the conurbations stretches over much of the North Wes and only the deeply rural parishes, for example in the Lune Valley, are littl affected. Over large rural areas there are pressures both from the out migration of population from the conurbations, and from the growth c country towns. The improved communications of the Cheshire towns an their proximity to major markets in both the North West and West Midlanc make them particularly attractive for industrial development. Populatic growth is frequently a concomitant to such development. Villages close these towns have also benefited by change in industrial location patterns (Pla 64). Many of the rural areas are now receiving back the population they se to the urban areas in the nineteenth century. The motives for the return of th population, however, are very different from those which caused the rur exodus in the 1830s and '40s.

Housing

THE DEMANDS FOR NEW HOUSING

Some of the areas of heaviest out-migration of population are those where there are a large number of houses in poor physical state, and in need of replacement. Statistical tests suggest a strong areal association between the rate of out-migration, especially of the younger age groups, and poor housing. The housing market within the North West is very complex, with the population increase in some areas requiring general housing, and in some areas, as in the retirement districts, requiring a particular type of housing. Secondly, there are existing shortages of houses in some parts. These shortages are particularly acute on north Merseyside where, in the district centred on Kirkby and Huyton, there is a current shortage of over 20,000 houses. Thirdly, many thousands of houses in the region are in desperate need of renewal or at least of radical improvement.

The need for houses to meet the increase in households is greatest in south-west Lancashire and in many of the towns of Cheshire, where there have been increases in job opportunities accompanied by a high level of natural increase in population. The increase in households and demand for housing is not apparent in all parts of the region. The effects of migration, for example, in many of the towns to the north and east of Manchester, means that these towns have suffered a net loss of households.

Current shortages of housing are noteworthy in much of south Lancashire and especially north Merseyside. Overcrowding is the natural result of this actual shortage. A commonly used criterion for defining overcrowding is an average of more than 1·0 person per habitable room. The 1961 census statistics revealed that 12 per cent of the population of Liverpool, 19 per cent of the population of Kirkby, and 13 per cent of the population of Huyton were living at a density of more than 1·5 person per room. Similarly, in the whole of Manchester there were 6 per cent of the population living in such grossly overcrowded conditions.

It is mainly in the Lancashire towns which grew so rapidly last century that the needs of housing renewal are greatest. Rateable values of housing, although subject to some local variations of valuation, present a measure of the general quality of housing in an area. Figure 69 is a map of the rateable value of the smaller houses in the urban areas of the region. For the purpose of this map the smaller house has been defined as one having a rateable value of £100 or less. On the map therefore the places with an average rateable value close to £100 are areas where generally the needs of housing renewal are least. On the other hand the places with scores below £50 have a major problem of renewal. From the map it can be seen that it is the area of industrial decline and population decrease, particularly around Burnley and Blackburn, where this renewal problem is greatest.

THE SUPPLY OF NEW HOUSING

The considerable variety of housing needs in the region means that additional housing land is required. While there is a shortage of building land on Merseyside, in general over the region, land is available in the right places for the housing shortage to be solved. In many instances there are greenfield sites where no previous urban development has taken place. Plate 65 of a housing

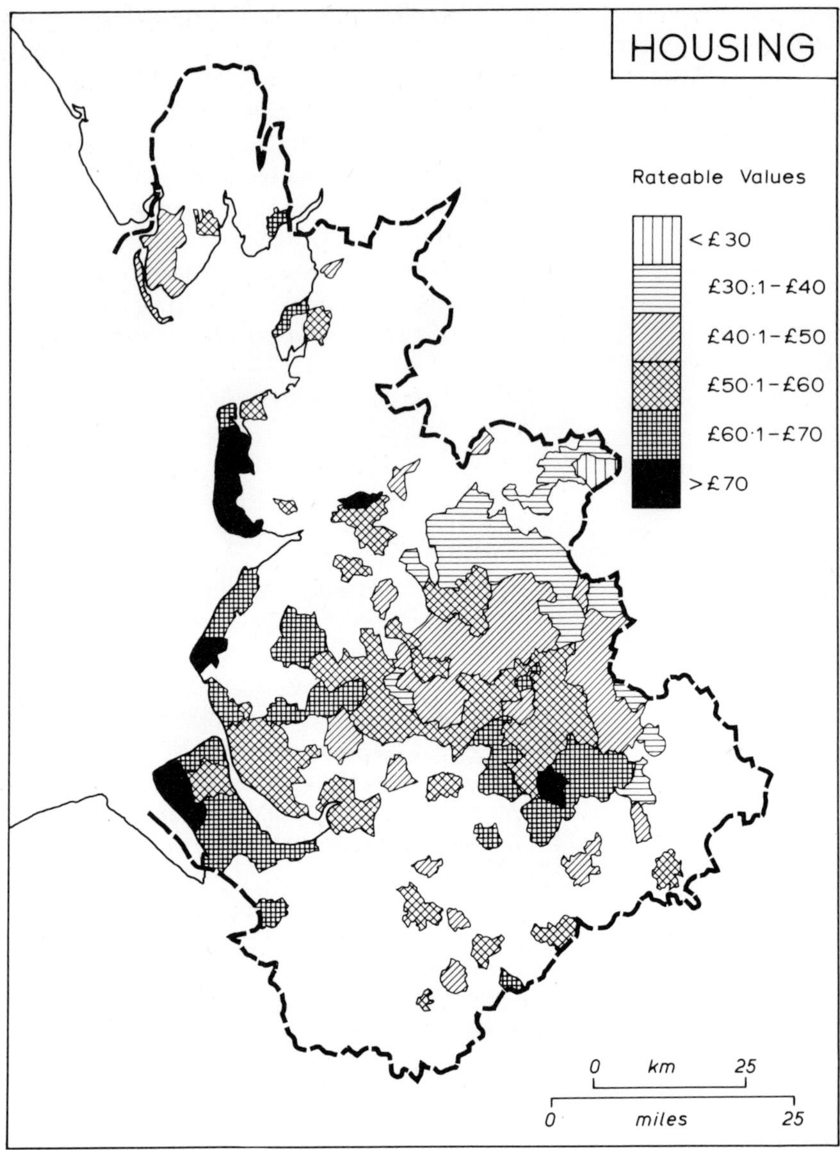

Fig 69 North West—The Rateable Value of the Smaller Houses in the Urban Areas, 1969

scheme near Hyde shows a development on this type of land and the mixture of high and low rise buildings on an estate of relatively low housing densit can be seen. In other areas the available land can be obtained by renewal. Slum clearance releases large tracts of land on which housing estates can be buil sometimes with a higher density than previously. The picture of Salfor

(Plate 66) shows both a new housing scheme on the site of former blighted houses, and also other areas ripe for renewal. The third source of building land to which the planner has looked to solve the housing shortage is reclaimed land. In the North West and particularly in the Lancashire coalfield there are considerable areas of derelict land which in some instances can be restored, and with landscaping can provide a valuable source of building land. Within Lancashire there are between 4,800 and 6,000 hectares (12,000–15,000 acres) of derelict land, and actual figure depends on the criteria used for its definition. In the decade prior to 1971 Lancashire County Council and the County Boroughs restored to economic use more than 1,200 hectares (3,000 acres). A considerable job is being done but much dereliction remains.

Plate 65 Hyde (Cheshire)
An estate under development on the outskirts of the town. The steeper slopes in the foreground show the effects of their use as a children's play area—small gulleys have developed and the processes of erosion have been speeded up considerably.

Plate 66 Salford (Lancashire)
The photograph shows urban renewal underway.

To meet the housing needs of the region there have been, since 1960, several large scale housing projects. These include the four new towns at Skelmersdale, Runcorn, Warrington and Leyland–Chorley. Table 16 shows the proposed and current (January 1972) size of the new towns and some of the major town expansion schemes. The schemes itemized in Table 16 include only those in which central government has played a role. In addition to these there are many local agreements on overspill schemes between the exporting centres of Manchester and Liverpool, and towns such as Middleton and Hyde and Kirby, and Halewood. Some schemes involve only a few hundred houses but they represent in total a major attempt to redistribute the population of the southern part of the region.

The new town at Runcorn is expected to have an ultimate population of 90,000. The estimated capital expenditure to build the new town is £28 million,

TABLE 16

NEW TOWN DEVELOPMENT IN THE NORTH WEST REGION

New Towns	*date of designation*	*population*			*Development since designation to Dec. 1971*		
		initial	*present Dec. 1971*	*proposed*	*Houses*	*factories*	*shops*
Preston/Leyland	1971	250,000	250,000	430,000	—	—	—
Runcorn	1964	30,000	90,000	40,000	4,500	69	115
Skelmersdale	1961	10,000	80,000	30,200	6,334	61	72
Warrington	1968	122,300	202,000	129,600	3,590	6	12

DEVELOPMENT AS A RESULT OF THE TOWN EXPANSION PROGRAMME

Expanded Towns	*Houses*			*Factories completed*
	To be built	*built Dec. 1971*	*under construction Dec. 1971*	*number of firms in occupation Dec. 1971*
Burnley	4,900	87	N.A.	N.A.
Ellesmere Port	5,500	2,325	68	0
Widnes	4,160	532	322	18
Winsford	7,230	3,187	0	36
Crewe	4,000	40	10	0
Macclesfield	1,250	750	0	24
Worsley	4,518	4,518	0	0

N.A. Information not available.

of which about half will go on housing developments. Development so far has been on a small scale with less than 10,000 newcomers in residence in 1971. The plan of the new town however shows some individual features which promise to make it unique among the new towns of Britain. The town has been planned on the assumption that all families will own at least one car. In addition an attempt has been made to provide a public transport system attractive to the majority of people so that peak movements are not unnecessarily demanding on expensive road and carpark construction. The generalized plan is shown in Figure 70. The proposal is to build a rapid transit system, consisting of special buses operating on a reserved track, which forms a spine for the new residential communities. All the population will live within a five minute walk of one of the stops on this bus system. The layout of the bus route is a figure of eight with the new town centre at the intersection. The old town will also be incorporated into the bus route. Loops to the basic system serve industrial areas on the periphery of the town. Additionally, an encircling road of motorway standard will connect with main routes into Liverpool and with the North Cheshire Motorway. In the plan for Runcorn an attempt has been made to provide a realistic balance between public and private transport in which neither obtrudes into home environments.

Industry

As well as the problems of housing people, there are certain problems in the North West of housing industry. In some areas there is a shortage of satisfactory industrial premises with Victorian houses in Salford and Cheetham ending their lives as small factories. A wide variety of industries have adapted

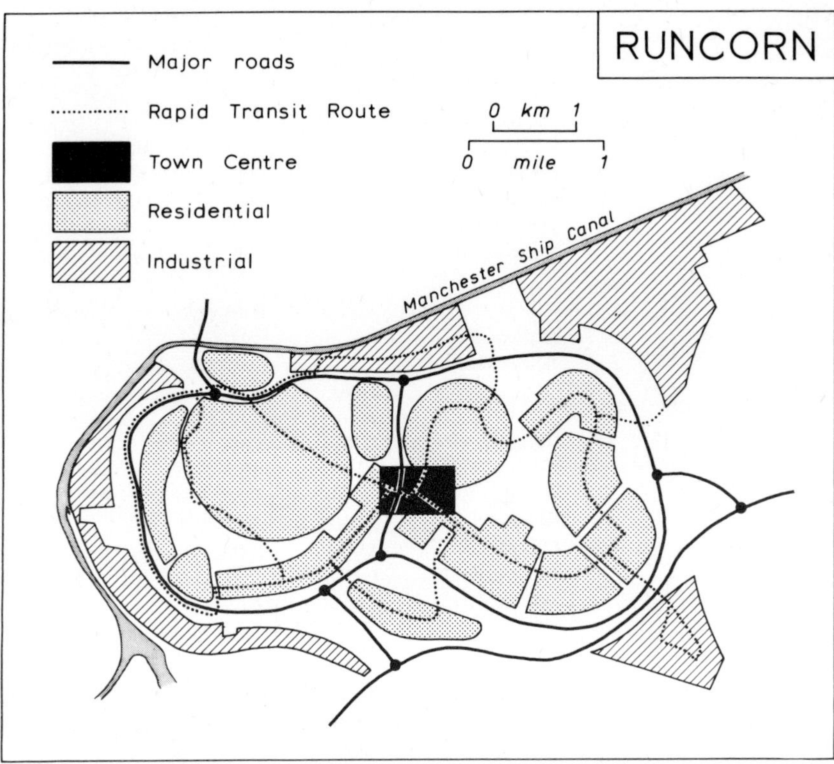

Fig 70 The Plan for Runcorn New Town

cotton mills to their own particular needs. On the other hand, there are certainly custom-built factory estates associated with many towns and some of these estates have had a long and distinguished history. Trafford Park, for example, dates back to the end of the last century and is associated with the development of the Manchester Ship Canal. Newer developed estates have been specially prominent in the attempts by Merseyside towns to attract new industry.

While some new industry has come to the region in recent years, much of the present-day industrial landscape was already present by the end of the nineteenth century, and the expansion of industrial land uses in the last century can be traced in all parts of the region. The growth of Barrow in Furness began in the late 1850s and by the turn of the century it was a thriving community. Much of the present-day landscape of the Furness ore field dates from the second 50 years of the last century when the influence and power of The Ulverston Company stretched beyond the North West, for example, it attempted to win iron ore from Exmoor. Much of the development of heavy industry on the Lancashire coalfields is also at least a century old. By 1900 the two industries of coalmining and textile work dominated the regional economy. They dominated the landscape of the towns as well with the structures of pit and mill (Plate 67) towering above the terraced houses. The physical dereliction surrounding Wigan and which now is being reclaimed slowly has its origins in this period of great economic prosperity for the region.

Although the present industrial landscape has strong connections with the past it is not to say that there has been no recent industrial change in the region. The textile mills in the 1970s are closing at an average of two per month while vehicle manufacture at Halewood and Leyland presents an example of a new industry growing in the region. The decline of the cotton mill began quite early this century so that by 1931 towns heavily dependent on the weaving trades, such as Blackburn, were already in a decline. From 1931 to 1951 Blackburn lost two thirds of its mill employment. Other towns were hit somewhat later so that during the 1950s 87,000 employees left the industry and many left the region altogether. The hardest hit of the weaving towns were Burnley, Blackburn, Nelson, Colne, and Accrington. Conditions in the spin-

Plate 67 Shaw (Lancashire)
Note the buildings of the cotton mill.

ning towns of Bolton and Oldham were only slightly better. The textile industry rationalization scheme of 1959 reduced the number of spindles by 49 per cent and looms by 40 per cent, but it had little real effect for many machines were already idle. The reduction in the present decade is hitting the towns of south-east Lancashire and north Cheshire which were able to weather some of the earlier storms because of a slightly wider industrial base. Towns such as Ashton and Hyde, for example, have a range of engineering industries as well as a share in the cotton trades. The diversification took place early in the southern towns and is now being attempted by many of the towns of Rossendale, but there is fierce competition to attract any industrial enterprise which can be tempted by the cheap industrial premises and large available workforce. In many of the towns diversification has not kept pace with the decline in the cotton industry and rises in the unemployment totals have an inevitability about them which taxes the social fabric of even the most tightly woven Rossendale valley community.

The mass of nineteenth century industry was on the coalfield but the change of emphasis in industrial location has freed the newer industries and allowed growth in Cheshire and Merseyside. The use of electricity as a power source, and above all the greater role of market attraction in the location of many light industries makes sites close to the M.6 and within easy reach of Manchester, Liverpool and the West Midlands conurbation particularly attractive. The popularity of the industrial estate at Winsford (Table 16) is evidence of the change in industrial location values which is remaking the industrial geography of the North West region.

Port Activities

Recent capital investment in the region is nowhere seen more sharply than in the plans for the Mersey Docks. The plan of the National Ports Council of 1965 suggested the development of container handling facilities at Seaforth docks at the northern end of the Liverpool Dock System. In the period 1965–71 over £40 million were spent in capital programmes in Liverpool docks. In 1969 alone while £12·2 million were spent on all the docks and ports in the North West, £10·7 million were spent at Liverpool. Liverpool, however, is but one of the ports of the region: there is the major cargo port at Manchester and more specialized dock systems include the railway-developed dock at Garston, the railway-used dock at Heysham, tanker terminals at Ellesmere Port and fish docks at Fleetwood.

The dock system of Merseyside includes Liverpool, Birkenhead (Plate 68), Garston, and Bromborough. The high tidal range of 9·5 metres (31 feet) in the estuary has resulted in the main docks being impounded with entrances through lock gates. The docks at Liverpool began to grow substantially in the seventeenth century when traders played a particularly important role in the Plantation of Ulster. On a wider horizon the triangular trade route of Britain West Africa, North America developed subsequently and laid the basis for some of the present-day trading patterns of the port. There are considerable imports of food and basic industrial materials from North America and Wes

Plate 68 Birkenhead (Cheshire)
A general view of the docks.

Africa. Metal manufactured goods dominate Liverpool's export trade and destinations in the Far East and Australia are particularly prominent. With the development of containerization at other United Kingdom ports, and especially the Australian service focused on Tilbury, this export trade may decline over the next decade. The Liverpool docks declined in importance during the 1950s relative to most of the major docks of the United Kingdom. The container services at Seaforth could halt this decline particularly if these services prove attractive to shippers and shipping lines concerned with the North American trade.

The other ports of the Merseyside system appear to have a rather less rosy future. Birkenhead (Plate 68), ever since its inception as a town and port in 1843, has been a town of unfulfilled promise. The lack of a city focus means that activities in Liverpool dominate society and economy in the town. The

Garston docks were originally developed by the London and North Western Railway to provide an outlet for coal from the Lancashire coalfield. Now much of the coal shipped from there comes from the East Midlands and the dock trade seems likely to decline. Imports of timber in recent years have served to provide a *raison d'etre* for the port. Recent rationalization in the labour organization of British ports means that for many purposes the ports of the Mersey estuary are considered as a single unit. In this Mersey Dock Unit, Liverpool reigns supreme.

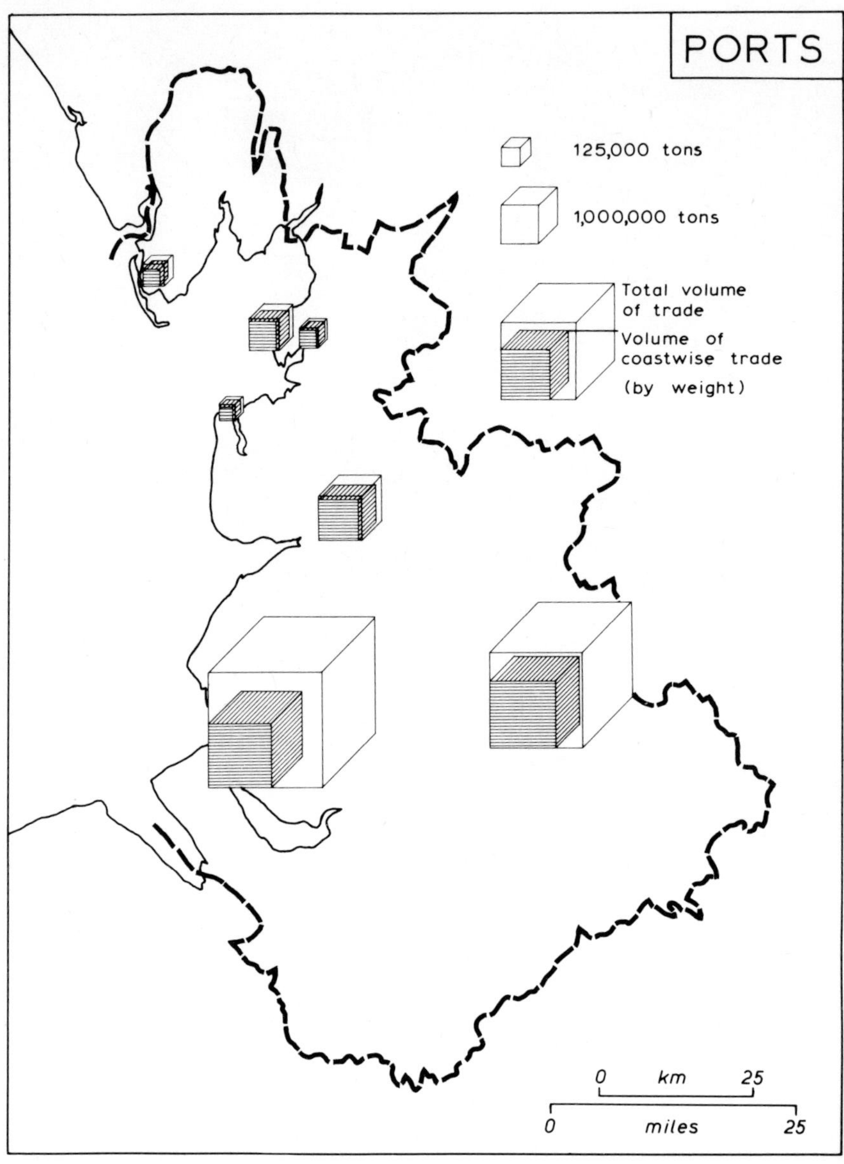

Fig 71 North West—The Tonnage Handled through the Ports, 1969.

The second major cargo port in the region is the inland dock system at Manchester. The port hinterland stretches east of the Pennines and south into the Midlands. Manchester docks include for administration the facilities in central Manchester and also those along the Manchester Ship Canal. In contrast to Liverpool much of the port trade is with the six countries of the original E.E.C., although the Scandinavian timber trade is substantial. The comparative size of Liverpool and Manchester can be been in Figure 71. In this map the tonnages handled include oil. Two thirds of the tonnage of the Manchester system is in oil and much of this sees little of Manchester proper, but is unloaded at tanker terminals along the ship canal. Thus even in recent times, the canal is a strong influence on the location of certain industrial concerns, acting in the same way as it did in earlier decades in attracting industry to the Trafford Park Industrial Estate. The canal was opened in 1894 and the estate, adjoining the canal, in 1896. Port industries, such as wood pulp, thus were able to develop in Manchester due first, to the canal, and secondly to the availability of industrial land in the right location in respect of the canal.

The other ports of the North West fall well below Manchester in any table of cargo handled, labour employed or similar criterion of port importance. Fleetwood with landings of fish valued at £4 million is possibly the most important of the smaller ports (Fig. 71). Other trade through Fleetwood is heavily directed towards the Mediterranean countries, especially the fuel imports (Fig. 72). Lancaster and Heysham both trade very definitely with Ireland, while the basic wood pulps coming into Barrow are Scandinavian in origin. Figure 72 indicates that foreign trade in most of these smaller ports is subservient to coast-wise traffic. The dominance of the Scandinavian trade of Barrow excepts this port from the general pattern, but in Fleetwood, for example, only 30 per cent of trade, by weight, is foreign. Although important to individual urban economies, these smaller ports together employ scarcely 700 workers compared with 1,400 in the Manchester docks and 9,000 in the Liverpool Dock Labour Board District.

Agriculture

In common with industry and urbanization, agriculture must be seen against a backdrop of the nineteenth century economic and social processes in the region. By 1850 there had developed a very considerable diversity in the agricultural economy not just as between upland and lowland but within both upland and lowland areas.

The agrarian revolution was felt first by the farmers close to the towns for the rapid growth of the market could not help but influence agriculture. Thus for example in the upland areas around the burgeoning towns of Rossendale there developed a form of dairy farming geared very closely to the urban demands for milk. Small scale farmer-retailers served small confined neighbourhoods. Many of these small scale enterprises still characterize this area. In the lowlands the growth of demand in the large towns resulted in a concentric zoning of land uses around the town. For example around Liverpool

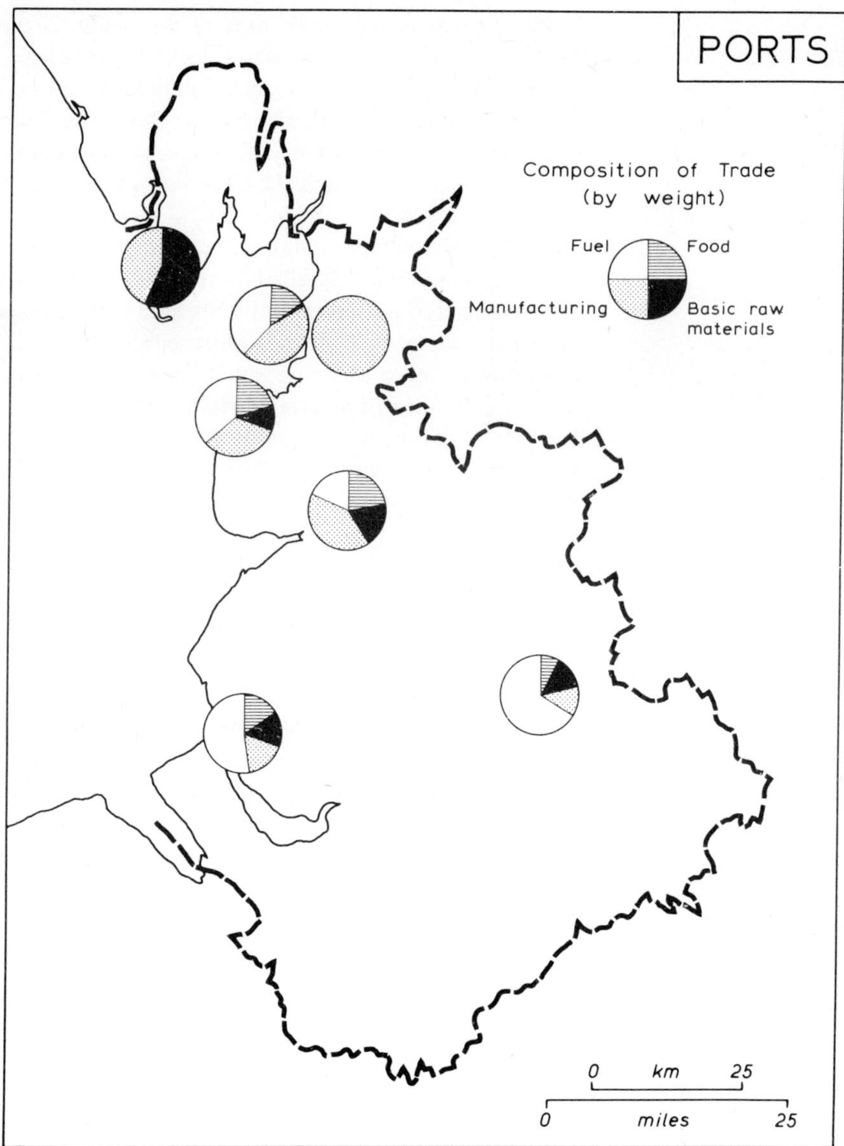

Fig 72 North West—The Composition of Trade passing through the Ports, 1969.

there was a band of market gardens about 5–6·5 kilometres (3–4 miles) from the centre and this merged into grassland for dairying up to about 16 kilometres (10 miles) from the centre.

This zoning began to break down as the railway affected agricultural transport costs and corridors were superimposed on the ring pattern. In the market garden corridors increased specialization of cropping took place in response to local soil conditions and to the individual transport costs of particular crops. For example, carrots were the specialism around Scarisbrick and potatoes around Ormskirk. Elsewhere in the lowland there was reclamation of the peat mosses and they were transformed into fertile arable land. Even by 1850 waste and subsidence in the coalfield was affecting agriculture. Much of Cheshire away from suburban Manchester was under grass with cheese production especially notable in the south. The agriculture of 1850 depended heavily on urban areas both for its market and for the considerable quantities of human waste used as fertilizer in the market gardens.

Agriculture in the North West still depends heavily on the urban markets within the region. The urban influence is felt in the market gardens and dairy farms which cover most of Cheshire. In the south of the county the differences in soil conditions are reflected in the cropping patterns. Soils formed on the glacial clays usually are grass-covered while the soils of fluvioglacial sands are cropped for roots. There has been an increase in the amount of land under the plough since the 1930s. The outbreaks of foot and mouth disease in the late 1960s decimated many dairy herds resulting in increases in arable land. The county is still however very firmly a dairy region for only in the northern parts do the urban influences result in horticulture and nursery cultivation.

The richest lands in the North-West and some of the richest in Britain occur along the coastal belt from south of the Fylde to Merseyside. Farms in this area often have over 90 per cent of their land under the plough. The peats reclaimed in the last century are largely responsible for this prosperous farming belt. Wheat, barley and oats are all cropped and it is unusual for grain farming to be so economically viable in Atlantic Britain. The Fylde is similar physically, but after many decades of arable farming the soils are exhausted for cropping other than grasses, and intensive dairying similar to that found in south Cheshire dominates the agricultural economy. Stock on the farms come from breeders in both Lonsdale and Bowland.

In north Lancashire the fattening and breeding of cattle is common on the lower lands and foothills and sheep dominate the livestock population of the fells. Steers are imported from Ireland and Scotland, fattened and then sold in the market in the south of the region. Thus even in the far north of Lancashire the pervading economic influence of the Lancashire/Cheshire conurbation is still a force to be reckoned with in the region's agricultural system.

Levels of Living

The interplay of the varied processes active in the physical and human environment results in wide disparities in the standards of living in the region. A measure which indicates levels of living is the proportion of dwelling houses on which a rate rebate is claimed. (Figure 73 shows by administrative area the percentage of houses which received such a rate rebate in 1969.) This measure is associated in part with income levels, for the criterion used to determine eligibility of rate relief was an income of £9 per week for a single household and £11 per week for a married couple. Reasons for a low income are numerous including living on a pension or receiving unemployment benefit. In Figure 73, areas where the percentage is highest, in some cases rising to over

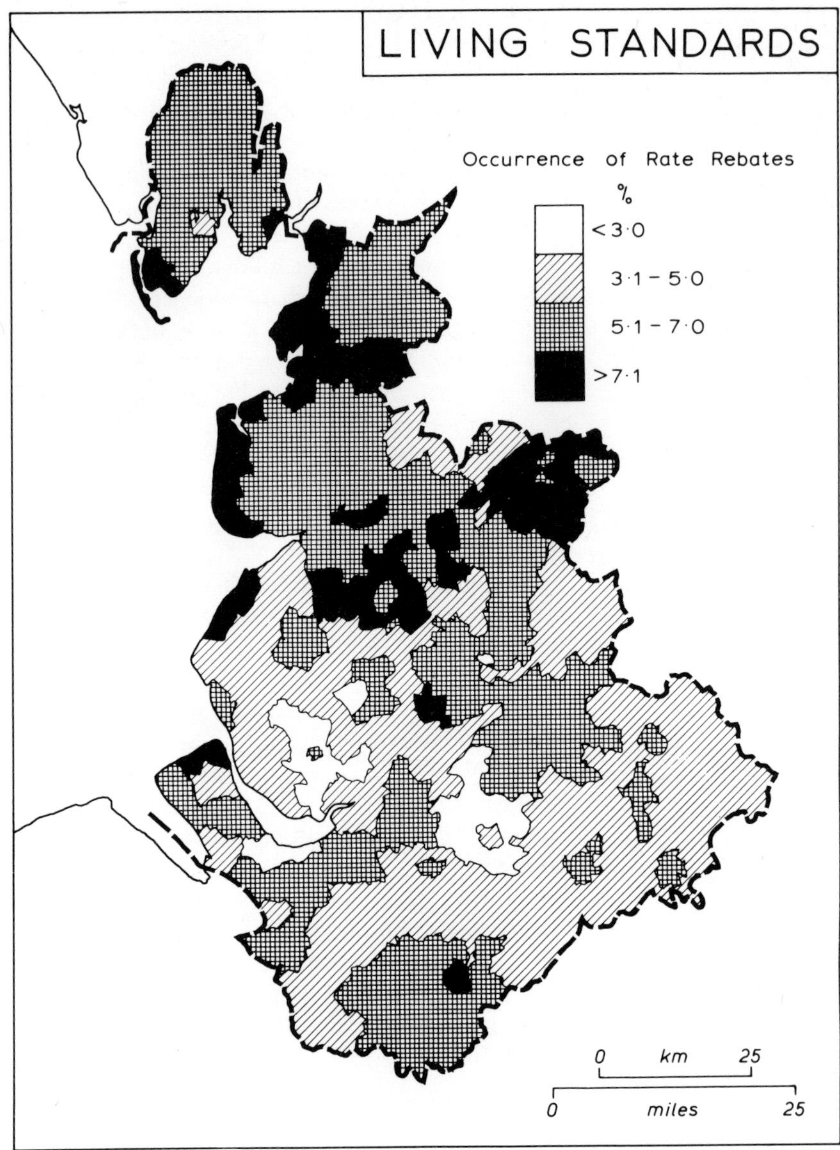

Fig 73 North West—The Percentage of Properties to which a Rate Rebate was Granted, 1969

12 per cent, are those areas where there have been recent influxes of retired population or effluxes of younger working population. The Fylde coast and the Burnley area have, therefore, the largest percentage of houses with rebates. Some northern parts of the coalfield also show high figures and these areas have suffered considerable out-migration leaving a high percentage of pensioners in the population. One of the reasons for the out-migration is the high

level of unemployment and lack of job opportunities, which in turn means a considerable percentage of the population on low incomes. In these areas, therefore, the high level of rate rebate has two causes.

At the other end of the scale, rate rebates are at their lowest in the areas of suburban Manchester and Liverpool where income levels are well above average and commuter societies have taken over village communities. Income levels of the 'original' inhabitants are often low and the 'original' population is often an old population, for the younger married people are unable to pay the house prices in the commuter zone. The map of the percentage of houses having a rate rebate thus mirrors the very wide range of living standards in the area. The spatial disparities in the standard of living both relate to the complexities and interactions of the factors affecting the human environment and serve to summarize much of the geographical individuality within the North-West region.

FURTHER READING

J. Bird, *The Major Seaports of the United Kingdom* (London, 1963).

Department of Economic Affairs, *The North-West—A Regional Study* (H.M.S.O., 1965).

T. W. Freeman, H. B. Rogers, and R. H. Kinvig, *Lancashire, Cheshire and the Isle of Man* (London, 1966).

R. Lawton and C. M. Cunningham (eds.), *Merseyside—Social and Economic Studies* (London, 1970).

North West Economic Planning Council, *Strategy II: the North West of the 1970s* (H.M.S.O., 1968).

D. M. Smith, *Industrial Britain: the North West* (Newton Abbot, 1969).

The Northern Region

North from Lancashire and the industrial heart of Yorkshire is an extensive area on which neither has stamped its personality—the Northern Region. It covers more than 13,000 square kilometres (5,000 square miles) and is currently administered by five county authorities. Despite underlying cultural traits transitional between the Anglo-Saxon English core areas to the south and the more strongly celtic lands of Scotland, the region's image to the outside world is of an area with an avid sense of identity and unity. There are, however, strong sub-cultures and pockets of local consciousness epitomized in local names such as Hexhamshire, Bedlingtonshire or the various Dales of the Pennines, but to those outside the region these local differences are subsumed beneath the regional image. The core of the region and its most populous district lies between the Rivers Tyne and Tees (Fig. 74). Newcastle upon Tyne forms a logical regional focus, even for the western parts of the region. Carlisle, for example, looks naturally along the Tyne gap to Tyneside for shopping as well as football. This provincial consciousness is further fostered by sheer distance from the seat of central government and the relatively narrow contact zone, through the lowland Northallerton corridor, with southern England.

The Physical Basis

The Northern Pennines dominate any consideration of the physical landscapes of Northern England. As a physiographic unit in their own right and as an influence on post-carboniferous geological events they are of immense importance to an understanding of the physique of the region. The main Pennine chain of limestone hills separates the Lake District, with its fringing ironfield and coalfield, from the great coalfield of Northumberland and Durham and ironfield of Cleveland. The highest stretches of the Pennines, for example Cross Fell (893 metres (2,930 feet)), are near the western edge of a tilted, desk-like, structure with limestones dipping to the east, first under the millstone grit and coal measures of the exposed Durham coalfield and subsequently below the west facing Permian scarp of magnesium limestone in east Durham.

The main masses of the Pennines which fall within the region are the Alston Block and Askrigg Block. The more northerly of the two, the Alston Block, is defined on three sides by fault systems. The main Pennine Fault divides it from the Vale of Eden and Lake District to the west. Part of the northern edge is defined by the Stublick Fault of the Tyne Valley, and to the south the east–

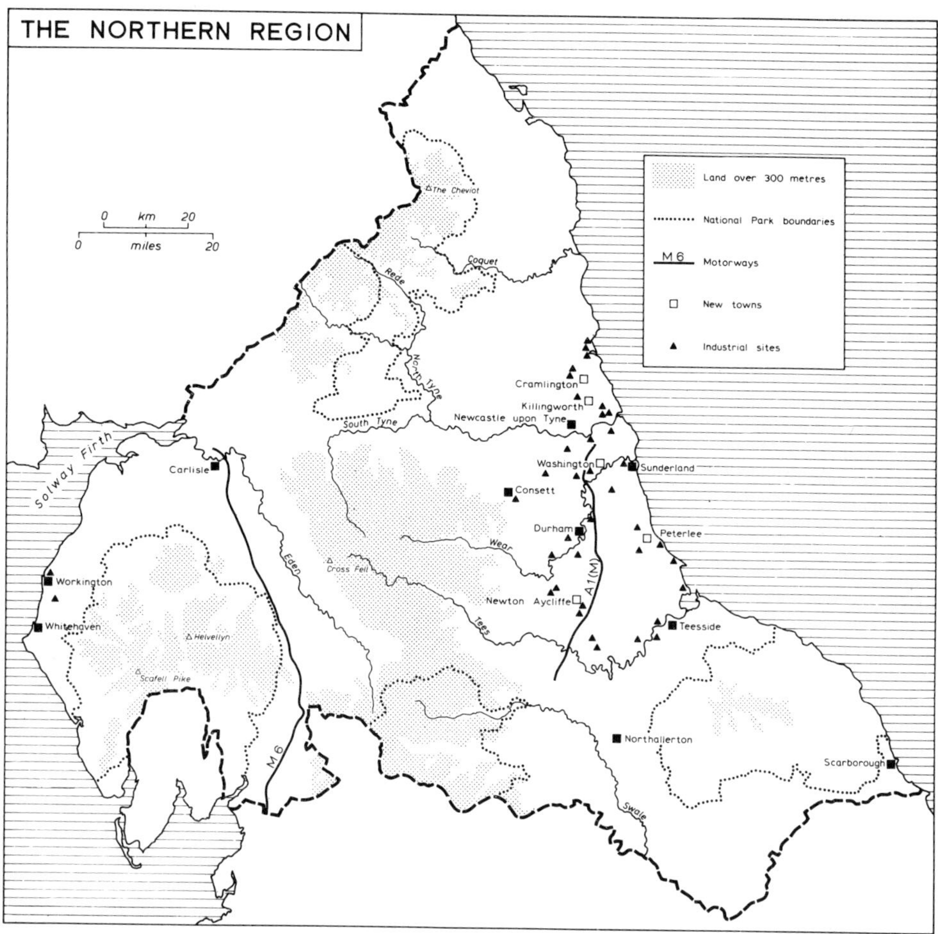

Fig 74 Northern Region

west faults of the Stainmore depression separate the Alston from the Askrigg Block and the Yorkshire Pennines. Many of the landscape details of Alston depend on the occurrence of outcrops of the Great Limestone and coarse gritstones. The latter produces bleak heather moorland with peat and peaty-gley soils. In Askrigg, however, the main hill builder is the thick Great Scar Limestone which is surmounted by the Yoredale series of limestone, shale, sandstone. The major high points of Askrigg, for example, Whernside, Penyghent, and Ingleborough, lie just beyond the regional boundary but the massive limestone with distinctive jointing and bedding stretches into the Northern Region and has been responsible, in part, for the formation of areas of karstic landscape. The Askrigg Block is terminated in the south by the line of the Craven Fault, well into the West Riding. North of the Tyne Gap the Carboniferous cuesta landscape reappears but on a less massive scale as softer sandstones and shales lap against the Cheviot Mass in the upper reaches of rivers North Tyne and Rede.

The Cheviot area consists of the deeply dissected remains of a Devonian volcano, the lavas from which cover some 600 square kilometres (230 square miles). Granite has been intruded into the core of this volcanic mass to form a roughly circular outcrop of about 50 square kilometres (20 square miles). Carboniferous scarplands dip away on all sides of the Cheviot and their quite heavy dissection forms landscapes of undulating drift covered valleys, with interfluves bearing a thinner cover of glacial deposit. In Northumberland the valleys of the Breamish and Coquet are typical. The Fell Sandstones form the small upland of Rothbury Forest—an area of tabular hills and barren moorland—and pass into similar country in the North Tyne Valley. The Cheviot mass and fringing scarps and vales effectively block off the northern end of the Northumberland plain and reduce it to a narrow coastal fringe scarcely 8 kilometres (5 miles) wide north of Alnmouth.

The coastal plain of Northumberland, at around 50 metres (160 feet), and the low plateaux of Durham (100–150 metres (330–500 feet)) flank the eastern side of the Pennines. These lower lands are well covered in heavy glacial drift and the boulder clay has filled hollows in the preglacial landscape, so producing a rather featureless area. Only at the highest points does the bedrock protrude as rocky knolls, for example Shaftoe Crags in south Northumberland. Borings on the Durham coalfield have shown drift deposits up to 60 metres (200 feet) thick which suggests that the magnesium limestone scarp in East Durham rose at least 200 metres (650 feet) above the preglacial landscape. Both the northern and southern end of this drift mantled Carboniferous and Permo-Triassic plain are closed by highland masses. The Cheviot, lies to the north and in the south the stark north facing Jurassic scarp of the Cleveland Hills overlooks the lowland of Bunter sandstone and Keuper Marl at the mouth of the River Tees.

The Cleveland Hills produce abrupt cliffs far higher than any in Durham and Northumberland. The major part of the Cleveland Upland and North Yorkshire Moors is an eastward tilted scarp-edged plateau of Mid-Jurassic sandstones and Lower Jurassic shales flexured and folded into a series of minor domes and basins. The largest dome is the Cleveland Dome which, although heavily eroded, rises to over 400 metres (1,300 feet) at its centre. The Eskdale Dome and Robin Hood's Bay Dome are also eroded; the latter's soft Liassic centre is being removed by the sea.

In the west of the region the Vale of Eden lies below the scarp of the Pennine Fault and forms part of the belt of Permo-Triassic rocks which almost encircle the Lake District. The valley of the Eden, the Solway Lowlands and the West Coast Plain are all covered in glacial deposits of wide variety and only rarely does bedrock appear. Rising steeply above these low plains is the Lake District. Its dome form is probably due to uplifting in tertiary times when a radial drainage pattern was imposed on the older rocks. This pattern is seen today in both river arrangement and lake alignments. The influence of rock type on scenery is strong in the Lake District. The country developed on Silurian rocks in the south, rarely exceeds 275 metres (900 feet) in height and comprises rugged hill landscapes. The most dramatic scenery of crags and scree occurs on the Borrowdale Volcanic Series in the centre of the district. Included here are the highest mountains, namely Scafell Pike (979 metres (3,210 feet)), Scafell (964 metres (3,162 feet)) and Helvellyn (950 metres (3,118 feet)). To the north are friable Skiddaw slates which produce far less rugged scenery with relatively little bare bedrock. Overall these geological types, however, certain common landscape features are present. Major erosional surfaces are present at 130 metres (430 feet), 250 metres (820 feet) and 320 metres (1,050 feet), while numerous other less obvious levels and bevels occur at other heights. The three major surfaces are particularly well developed on the west side with the upper surface especially clear across the Skiddaw Slates and Borrowdale Volcanics.

While the Pennines provide one major key to an understanding of the physical landscapes of this region, consideration of the glacial history of the region provides another. The sequence of glacial advances and retreats affected mountain and lowland with dramatic consequences on landform and drainage. At the height of the main phase of glaciation little of the region was ice free. There is evidence of ice cover at 600 metres (2,000 feet) in the Pennines and at over 500 metres (1,700 feet) on Cheviot. On Cleveland, summits of 300 metres (1,000 feet) were probably ice free but would have been strongly affected by periglacial processes.

The Lakeland landscape shows all the features characteristic of highland glaciation. Straightened and deepened valleys contain lakes radiating from the drainage axis of the Lake District dome. Glacial overdeepening and moraine damming have resulted in 16 major lakes; Wastwater for instance, has a lake floor below sea level. Arêtes, corrie tarns, hanging valleys and the many other features of glacial erosion are present. Although glacial deposition is more typical of lowlands, boulder clay was deposited in the mountain areas. The floors of both Langdale and Borrowdale, for example, are covered in glacial deposits.

Boulder clays are extensive and deep in the lowlands but are not the only form of material left by the glaciers. The drumlins of the Solway Plain and Vale of Eden are of classic proportions and form. The northern end of the Vale of York shows a wide variation of depositional material within a relatively small area. A thick heavy boulder clay is present particularly in the north and additionally a series of terminal moraines, rising over 10 metres (30 feet), swing across the vale. To the south of the moraines lie almost flat areas of melt-water sands and skirting the lowland are clays from glacial lake beds.

One effect of this heavy deposition of glacial debris in the lowland is the disruption of preglacial valley patterns. This is noteworthy with the Wear which rises in the Alston Block and in its upper course flows in a relatively open drift filled but preglacial valley. Its lower course, however, is gorge-like and post-glacial. The preglacial Wear probably joined the Tyne along the line of the present Team valley. This route became blocked by ice and a glacial lake was impounded which first overflowed to the Tees by cutting the Ferryhill Gap. Subsequently on glacial retreat, when a lower col became exposed the Wear cut a second gorge in which it now flows. Even more complicated histories than that of the Wear have been ascribed to most of the rivers of Durham and Northumberland and a complex system of buried river valleys lies below the boulder clay.

The character of the physical landscape differs over quite small areas as geological structure and geomorphological process interplay; correspondingly large local variation is evident in climatic patterns with sharp contrasts in the degree of exposure and in the shadow effects of different small areas. At a broad regional level, rainfall ranges from well over 3,800 millimetres (150 inches) in parts of the Lake District to less than 630 millimetres (25 inches) along the North Sea coast and in the valley of the Lower Tees. At a more local level the east side of the Eden valley has a rainfall ranging from less than 900 millimetres (35 inches) to over 1,500 millimetres (60 inches) within scarcely 8 kilometres (5 miles) from the River Eden to Cross Fell. The smaller cuesta landscapes elsewhere in the Pennines provide even more local rain shadow effects. Temperature differentials distinguish the milder west from the raw east, but altitude is of far more importance than either longitude or the warmth of coastal waters as a determinant of temperatures. In the heart of the Pennines mean January temperatures are barely above freezing point while at coastal stations in Cumberland they are over 4·5°C (40°F). This difference has a significant effect on the growing period for plants, but again very local conditions of temperature and rainfall are probably as important as the sub-

Plate 69 Peel Fell, the Cheviot Hills (Northumberland)
Peat bog and rough grazing are being replaced by Forestry Commission plantations.

regional variations in affecting the length of growing season. Local frost hollows are common in both upland and lowland, often picking out the hollows in the cover of glacial drift. The occurrence of gales can also be of considerable importance in limiting plant growth and in the upper Pennine areas it is not unusual for there to be 120 days per year with gale force winds.

The glacial deposits have a profound effect upon the soils of the region. Almost all lowland soils have glacial parent material and the local variations in parent material mean individual farms can boast several distinctive soil types. The upland massive limestones give rise to thin dry soils while in other upland parts blanket bogs have developed on gentle slopes. Blanket peat varies in depth from about 0·5 metre (1 foot) to over 4·5 metres (15 feet) and covers the highest parts almost irrespective of surface deposits; it develops with equal ease upon coarse sandstones and upon clay loam slope deposits. In recent times peat erosion has been more widespread than deposition. Climatic variations are also vitally important to the soil forming process. Differences in rainfall, for example, mean that many upland soils are intensively leached with podsolization being an important mechanism. Lowland soils have been affected by cultivation and man has become an important soil forming agent. Most lowland soils have a thick brown surface horizon resulting from ploughing. Artificial drainage as well as nutrient additions have changed, over the years, the natural character of lowland soils. The various combinations of physical landscape, climate and soil conditions influence to considerable degree the suitability of areas for agriculture. In the region there are large tracts of land of below average quality for agricultural use and little or no first class quality land. Apart from lower Swaledale, the Derwent valley, and scattered small patches in Edendale there is little land of above average agricultural quality. It is against this rigorous physical background that agricultural activity is carried on.

Agriculture

One third of agricultural land in the Northern Region is rough grazing. For the most part breeding and rearing sheep, hardy Swaledale and Cheviot breeds, dominate the uplands while on the lowland fattening of stock is widespread. Increasingly the sheep fattening is being forced to what were once thought marginal lands as beef fattening takes the lusher pastures. Upland pasture is frequently common land and, where grazing is unrestricted, tracts of hill land are badly overgrazed with consequent loss of stock in bad years. The upland valleys are cropped for hay after lambing ewes have had the early bite until early May. Haymaking therefore is late and drying can present problems when mowing does not take place until August. The field barn is much in evidence and is indispensable in the annual rush to get the hay crop in and under cover. Some hay is fed to sheep on the higher pastures in February and March but much is used for winter feed for small herds of dairy and beef cattle. The improved accessibility of upland Dale farms, together with guaranteed markets for milk, have broken the dairy monopoly of the lowlands and the monthly milk receipts produce a welcome addition to the income of many upland farmers.

Lowland agriculture is truly mixed farming with very few areas of markedly specialized production. Upland sheep are brought to the lowlands for fattening and beef stock is bought in for final fattening before slaughter. Both dairying and meat production are common farm enterprises. The former was originally particularly important to the industrial district between Tyne and Tees, but it has now spread to all lowland areas. Producer-retailers, however, are still in evidence particularly on the Northumberland and Durham coalfield. Almost all lowland farms have some arable land with the proportion of arable to grazing varying in relation to the quality of the drift soils. In the east, for example, the largest arable areas are on the light soils of the sands and gravels south and west of the Cleveland Hills, but even on the heavy clay loams of coastal Northumberland ploughed fields are not an uncommon sight. These heavy lands have been drained, many in the nineteenth century, and the legacy of this drainage is the ridged form of many fields in lowland Northumberland. Barley is an important grain crop and provides feed for the beef herds; the commonest root crop is swedes with most farms also growing a few potatoes.

Agricultural production in the region has increased steadily in recent years despite both a decrease in manpower and the loss of agricultural land for industrial and urban development. In the decade 1955–65 31 per cent of regular farm workers left the industry and some 20,000 hectares (50,000 acres) were lost to agriculture. Often this land is of relatively good quality and its loss is not compensated by improvements to marginal lands in the uplands. Better drainage and more selective use of specialized fertilizers is improving the grazing of some upland areas. A more drastic change in upland land use is the increasing area of woodland. Worked commercial woodlands cover some 130,000 hectares (320,000 acres) of the region with over half of this concentrated in Northumberland, especially in the Border Dales. Some marginal upland farmland was planted with coniferous plantations in the nineteenth century but the major development has occurred since World War I as the Forestry Commission has obtained land and planted it with Sitka Spruce, Norway Spruce and Lodgepole Pine. North Tynedale and Redesdale have reached their current potential as plantable areas, although experiments with planting above 380 metres (1,250 feet) (the considered maximum economic limit) are taking place and, if successful, could mean an even larger planted area. The considerable capital input of the Forestry Commission has not only meant a change of scenery from desolate fell to lush woodland, but perhaps more important has meant more jobs, new roads, new villages such as Kielder and Byrness, and a considerable potential tourist attraction. The change of land use from hill grazing to forestry is not without its critics, but mature managed forests provide, directly, ten times as many jobs as the same area under sheep grazing as well as providing a sound industrial base for secondary production.

While forestry is changing the upland, the restoration of former derelict land is changing landscapes in the lowland coalfield areas. Although problems of subsidence remain, and these can be considerable on the drained heavy claylands, many hindrances to cultivation are being removed. A decline in atmospheric pollution has meant more productive swards where there were once 'industrial pastures'. Restoration of derelict mines and opencast sites is not only removing eyesores but also providing fine farm land. Newer methods of restoration of opencast mining sites have the effect of leaving the surface in better condition than before opencast operation. The restoration process takes above five years, but limited cropping or grazing is possible often after three years. When finally handed back to the owner the reclaimed land has been intensively fertilized, drained, fenced and each enclosure supplied with water. Reclamation is a slow and expensive process affecting only a few hundred hectares per year (800 hectares (2,000 acres) in 1960 costing about £2,500 per hectare (£1,000 per acre)). Local authorities anticipate however that all derelict land justifying treatment will have been reclaimed or be under treatment by the late 1970s. Thus some 8,000 hectares (20,000 acres) of formerly agriculturally useless land will be provided for economic agricultural uses.

Quarrying and Mining

Within the primary economic sector agriculture is not the only industry with a declining work-force. Both quarrying and mining have had drastic decreases in their labour requirements since the mid 1950s. Limestone quarrying is less widespread than formerly but the quarries at Stanhope in Upper Weardale do provide considerable employment with the associated Weardale cement works employing over 400. The small-scale lime burning enterprises, so common when lime was applied to the ill-drained soils, have closed and the plentiful remains of the lime kilns in Pennine Dales and Northumberland are a remnant of this extractive industry of 100 years ago. In the mid-nineteenth century the Dales of Alston were also important as a lead producing area with, during peak years, some 4,000 workmen involved in lead mining and smelting. Competition from overseas in the 1870s and 1880s caused a serious fall in production. In some dales, notably Allendale, the collapse was so serious that population numbers have never recovered from the outflow of miners and their families. Thus it is not just derelict mines and spoil which litter the landscape, but also ruined cottages.

Also producing dereliction of industrial plant and village fabric within the Northern Region are iron ore and coal mining. High grade haematite ores with an iron content of between 42 and 62 per cent and with low phosphorous content are found in the Carboniferous Limestone series of west Cumberland. Mining of these deposits was a thriving industry in the mid-nineteenth century with supplies of ore going not just to the burgeoning iron industry of Furness and west Cumberland, but also to furnaces in South Wales. The ores are mainly worked out but mine sites are not difficult to recognize. Quarries, pits, and spoil heaps abound around Cleator Moor, which was one of the more important mining centres. A second iron ore field is present within the region, in the Cleveland Hills. Mining of these ores ceased in the mid 1960s, over 100 years after their discovery at Eston, near Middlesbrough. High levels of production gradually declined during this century. Both the Cleveland field and the Cumberland field are important not in terms of the quantity of output, but in terms of their formative role in the British iron and steel industry. Both fields produced ores at a time when industrial technology and the prevailing economic climate allowed the addition of important steel and engineering industries to the already present basic industrial infrastructure of the coal-fields of the Northern Region.

On the north-western flanks of the Lakeland Dome lies the Cumberland coalfield, while under much of east Durham and south Northumberland are much larger deposits of workable coal. Seams in both fields stretch under the sea and it is these undersea reserves which currently concern the National Coal Board. There are considerable proved reserves in both areas and additionally a large potential area of reserves, details of which are unproved, under 900 metres (3,000 feet) of the Trias of the Solway Basin. The Northumberland and Durham field is by far the more important both regionally and nationally, with reserves exceeding 5,000 million metric tons (49,30 million long tons). The coalfield forms are broad, shallow triangular basin dipping slightly to the east. There is comparatively little faulting, in contrast to the Cumbrian field, and local domes and basins are quite small structures. Mining activity has moved east off the exposed field into the area where sandstone and magnesian limestone conceal the coal bearing strata.

Mining of the Northumberland and Durham field began in the thirteenth century but did not develop to any extent until the sixteenth century when markets in London and other North Sea cities stimulated mining activity. The need for transport to these markets encouraged development at coastal sites with pits and staithes common along the Lower Tyne. By 1800 some 2·51 million metric tons (2·5 million long tons) of coal were shipped out of the coalfield. The growth of markets during the industrial revolution coupled with technological innovations in the mines, such as steam powered winding gear and more efficient underground working, helped expand the worked area on the exposed field. By about 1840 most of the exposed coalfield north of Durham City was being worked. The early start to mining operations meant that decline had begun by the later decades of the nineteenth century. By 1890 the intensively worked exposed Durham Coalfield had passed its peak. Average output per man from Durham pits began to fall in the early 1880s. Decline of operations continued steadily up to and after nationalization in 1947. Pit closure and reorganization in the 1957–65 period reduced the mining work force by 25,000. The decline has been selective in its intensity with the earliest mines in west Durham and south-east Northumberland hardest hit, while the Ashington area and coastal Durham have been more fortunate. Figure 75 emphasizes the differential pattern in pit closure in County Durham in the 1960s. The acute problem of redundancy in west Durham can be appreciated from this pattern, and while it has been possible to introduce subsidized commuting from west Durham pit villages to east Durham pits the rationalization programme of the National Coal Board has taxed the social fabric of many west Durham communities.

Plate 70 Durham (County Durham)
Some typical nineteenth century industrial housing. The castle and cathedral, in the background, mark the older part of the city.

Plate 71 Whitehaven Haig Pit (Cumberland)
Active coalmining, but more often disused and abandoned pit gear and spoil heaps, scar the landscape of the coalfields of the region.

The effects of mine closures are far reaching and mean not only redundancy for some miners and commuting for others, but uncover more deeply seated labour problems. The abler, younger, and often more skilled men, leave the mining workforce altogether and seek work in engineering industries, so moving away from the mining community. The redundant miners pose a welfare problem to local authorities and their lower incomes in turn mean lower spending capacities in local shops. A downward spiral of the social and economic health of villages can be started quickly under such circumstances and is difficult to stem. The planning problem posed by such conditions has been met with a number of suggested policies ranging from cold and hard attempts to run down certain pit villages and regroup the inhabitants in more viable communities, to ultra-sensitive attempts to provide enough new jobs and retraining to preserve the pit village in a state of social fossilization. The most human policy must lie between these extremes—some population movement as well as considerable new job provision in key villages.

Industry

The association between coal mining and iron production was one of the most important industrial linkages of the industrial revolution in Britain. The intensity of the industrial changes in the Northern Region in the early

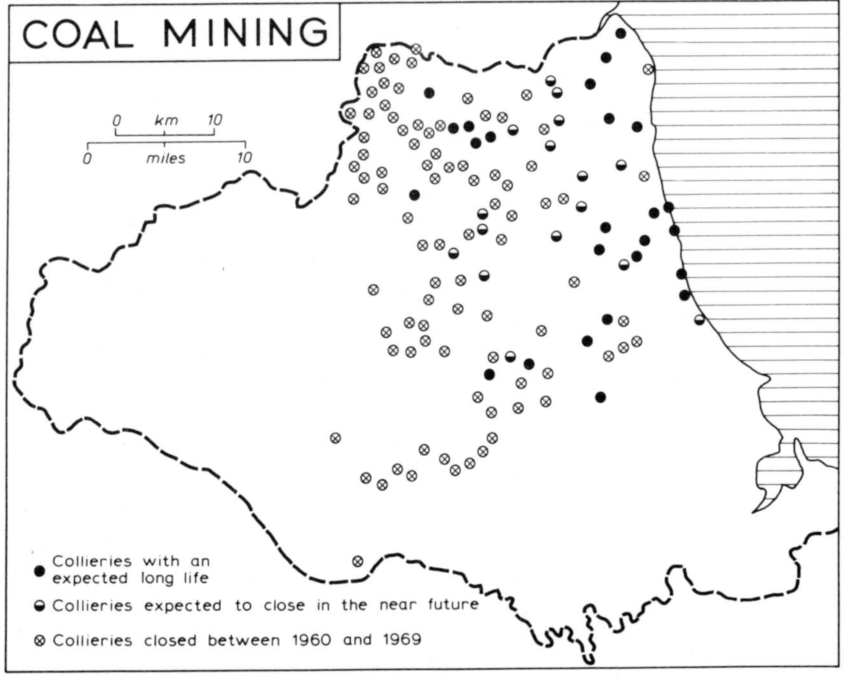

Fig 75 Northern Region – Operating coal mines in 1969 and closures 1960–69, County Durham.

nineteenth century means that this link was particularly strong. On the eastern coalfield the proximity of high quality coking coals in west Durham to deposits of iron ore made the district eminently suitable for pig iron production. By 1850 there were 38 blast furnaces operating in Northumberland and Durham, with more than a third of these at the Derwent Iron Co. at Consett. The generally dispersed pattern of iron production became concentrated as the full economic effects of the industrial revolution began to be felt. The period 1850–80 marks the high point of puddled and wrought iron production in the region. During this era the Cleveland ore field was opened and iron production developed on the Tees, with the works of Bolckow and Vaughan, Bell Brothers and Dorman. Teesside by 1875 had become the centre of British iron production. Increasingly from 1880 onwards steel superseded iron with a greater dependence on the newer technologies of the Gilchrist, Bessemer and open hearth processes. Teesside firms, after some initial opposition to the introduction of steelmaking, added steel producing plant alongside the iron works. Policies of firms differed as to how to obtain the new steel works. Some firms favoured take-overs of existing plant, Dorman Long provide a good example, taking over four Teesside firms in 20 years, while other firms, for example Bolckow and Vaughan, favoured increasing their own site capacity. Thus by 1914 the patterns of production had changed drastically from the dispersed pattern of 1830. Production had become primarily concentrated at Teesside, but with other works in Durham and North Yorkshire. Throughout all the amalgamations and rationalization that resulted in this concentration the large works at Consett remained independent.

The dependence of the iron and steel industry on markets of a notably cyclical nature is reflected in the booms and depressions that have affected the industry in the last 50 years. Production of the Northern steel companies consists primarily of capital goods—plates, rails, and heavy sections for use in ship building and the heavy construction industries. The expanding sector of the steel market in the 1920s and 1930s was in strip and sheet steel for fabricating into consumer goods. Iron and steel production in the Northern Region thus lost ground, relatively, to other steel making centres in the country. Even greater locational rationalization resulted from these changes in the world steel market so that by 1939 with the exception of Consett all the important steel furnaces of the North East were associated with the Teesside complex.

The years since 1945 are marked by a large investment in new plant—some £200 million—producing two large integrated steel works on Teesside in addition to the plant at Consett. A report on the national position of the industry, the *Benson Report* of 1966, foresaw further rationalization of steel making capacity with perhaps before many years the two complexes on Teesside providing the only steel making capacity in the region. Such a view implies the closure of the Consett works, despite its recent heavy capitalization and the serious implications of such closure on employment in the sub-region of north-west Durham and south Northumberland. Whether a policy based on welfare economics or on economy of production finally triumphs will be determined by the mid 1970s. Iron and steel industries have been fundamental to the region's well-being in the past, and now in the age of regional economic and physical planning the industry is likely to play a key role in the overdue economic transformation of the region.

Hand in hand with regroupings in the iron and steel industry, contraction and concentration have occurred in a second heavy industry basic to the regional economy. Shipbuilding on Tyneside, Wearside and Teesside has been transformed within a hundred years from a small-scale craft industry to a large-scale assembly type technological industry. Its full passage through this transformation is not totally completed with important advances currently occurring in technology, management and industrial relations. Characteristics of the early developmental phase of the industry were the indigenous nature of most firms, their localization on one river and their growing integration with the marine engineering industry. The twentieth century has provided a period of very mixed fortunes for shipbuilding in general. The rapid changes in the world market for ships has meant that shipbuilding has been plagued by a sequence of crisis and boom. The diversity of production on the Tyne, which characterizes activities on that river even today, helped alleviate some depressions, while the greater specialization of yards on the Wear resulted in deeper troughs, but higher peaks of economic activity. The depressions in the industry played a part in reducing the number of yards fairly steadily. The *Geddes Report* on the future of British shipbuilding suggested that two major consortia would best serve the needs of the region. The Swan Hunters and Tyne Shipbuilders group is a major step towards this end but the formation of a comparable second group will take longer. With the reduction in the number of operating firms both locational diversification and product diversification has occurred. Whereas particular firms were once closely affiliated to individual rivers, now the firms are of regional nature. Both yards on the Tees, for example, are within the Tyne consortium. Although product diversification was present on a locational and company basis, with particular firms specializing in specific products, this latter diversification has vanished while the former has remained. The Tees seems to be developing as a centre for bulk carrier building; the Wear is employed in building the SD14 standard cargo vessel as a replacement for the Liberty ships; variety still characterizes the Tyne with its range of projects including supertankers, container ships, train ferries, and a guided missile frigate. Despite these attempts to put its own regional house in order, the ultimate future of shipbuilding in the Northern Region depends upon factors beyond regional control—factors both of national economic expansion and of the world market for ships.

Unlike steel and shipbuilding, other industries in the Northern Region are passing through a period of steady and sustained growth. Most notable is the chemical industry. From small beginnings in John Walker's production of 'friction lights' in Stockton in 1827, using schoolboys and almshouse labour, the chemical industry on Teesside has now grown to employ some 35,000 people. It is an industry noted for large output per employee. Paints, drugs, soaps and dyes also form an important part of the industrial mix of Tyneside and, with the exception of the post-war rundown of war materials, have shown continued employment growth since the early 1920s. This growth in employment has been of considerable importance to the total regional employment picture, but growth in the output, volume and work of the chemical industry has depended more on new technologies than on more labour. In west Cumberland industrial chemicals have been important in the somewhat limited post-war diversification of production. Production of sulphuric acid at Whitehaven has utilized local raw materials, particularly anhydrite. Also in Whitehaven is an incipient synthetic fibres industry producing material for fashion garments. But it is on Teesside that the main growth of the chemical industry has occurred with the massive I.C.I. plants at Billingham and Wilton forming a catalyst for a wide variety of developments.

The banks of the Tees now represent the largest petro-chemicals and general chemicals complex outside the U.S.A. Until the First World War chemicals on Teesside were unspectacular with important, but not outstanding, plants producing fertilizers and sulphuric acid. A government decision to produce ammonia on a site near Billingham was fundamental to the upsurge in the investment in chemicals on Teesside. In 1926 the four largest chemical producing firms in Britain formed I.C.I. and immediately became involved in the chemical plant at Billingham. Further development was consequent on the production of organic chemicals in 1928. The linkages within the chemical industry whereby a product is both marketed in its own right and is also used for producing other chemicals, means that once a chemical plant has been established at a particular site it then acts as an attractive force for other chemical based industries. Thus with the increasing demand for petroleum products as feedstock in the petro-chemical processes, it became logical to build oil refineries where the petroleum was needed. Three refineries were built between 1965 and 1968. Two are operated jointly by I.C.I. and Phillips Petroleum Co. and the third is a £25 million Shell project. Despite the fact that massive capital schemes are both underway and forecast over the next 10 years, particularly on reclaimed sites at the mouth of the Tees, employment in the chemical industry will probably remain steady with output increasing as productivity levels reach those presently found in comparable North American chemical complexes.

Industrial growth at the other end of the size spectrum from the chemical plants is provided by a very wide range of small factories which have been attracted to industrial estates within the region. From 1960–66 some 100 new manufacturing firms arrived in the region and almost all of these took sites on industrial estates. Figure 74 shows the locations of the most important of these estates. The Team Valley Estate was one of the earliest forms of this industrial type and subsequently the estate concept has been used extensively in government regional economic policy. Approximately 100,000 of the regional workforce are employed in factories on such estates.

Population, Housing and Settlement

At some stage in the working life of many of the 3·3 million people in the region, absence of employment has presented major personal problems. The regional unemployment rate has been consistently above the national figure for some years. Both industrial and agricultural districts suffer from this economic and social malaise. After a job a second prerequisite to an acceptable level of living is a house. In the provision of this necessity it is the planning authorities of the industrial districts which have the greatest overall problem to solve although on a percentage basis, potential slums are more common in rural areas. Estimates made in the mid 1960s suggest that there were in the region some quarter of a million houses which were either slums or potentially unfit for habitation (Fig. 76). To replace these and to cater for population growth up to 1980 approximately 600 new houses per week are required from 1970 to 1980. It seems unlikely that this will be achieved and so poor housing conditions will remain a feature of life in some industrial towns of the region.

At a regional level an aggravating factor to the problem of physical blight of housing is the high proportion of small dwellings. The percentage of dwellings with three rooms or less is higher than for any other region of England and Wales. These small dwellings are concentrated particularly on Tyneside. In addition, household size in the region is large, particularly so on Tyneside and the coalfields. Gross overcrowding is thus not uncommon. The region also has a high proportion of tied dwellings. Many are owned by the National Coal

Plate 72 Newcastle upon Tyne (Northumberland)
The picture, taken from the Civic Centre, shows an area ripe for urban redevelopment.

Board and British Railways, both of which are pursuing a policy of selling off tied houses, some to individuals and some to local authorities. About 200,000 dwellings in the region have a low rateable value, are over 60 years old and lack basic services such as fixed baths and hot water systems. In the replacement of these substandard buildings it is the private sector which has lagged behind the public sector. Since 1945 the local authorities have consistently built more dwellings per head than their counterparts in other regions. This difference is shown in the tenure figures for 1961 (Table 17). The areas with a

TABLE 17
TYPE OF TENURE OF DWELLINGS 1961

	Owner occupied	*Rented from local authority*	*Privately rented*	*Tied*	*Rented with farm or business*
Northern Region	34	32	25	8	1
England and Wales	42	24	28	5	1

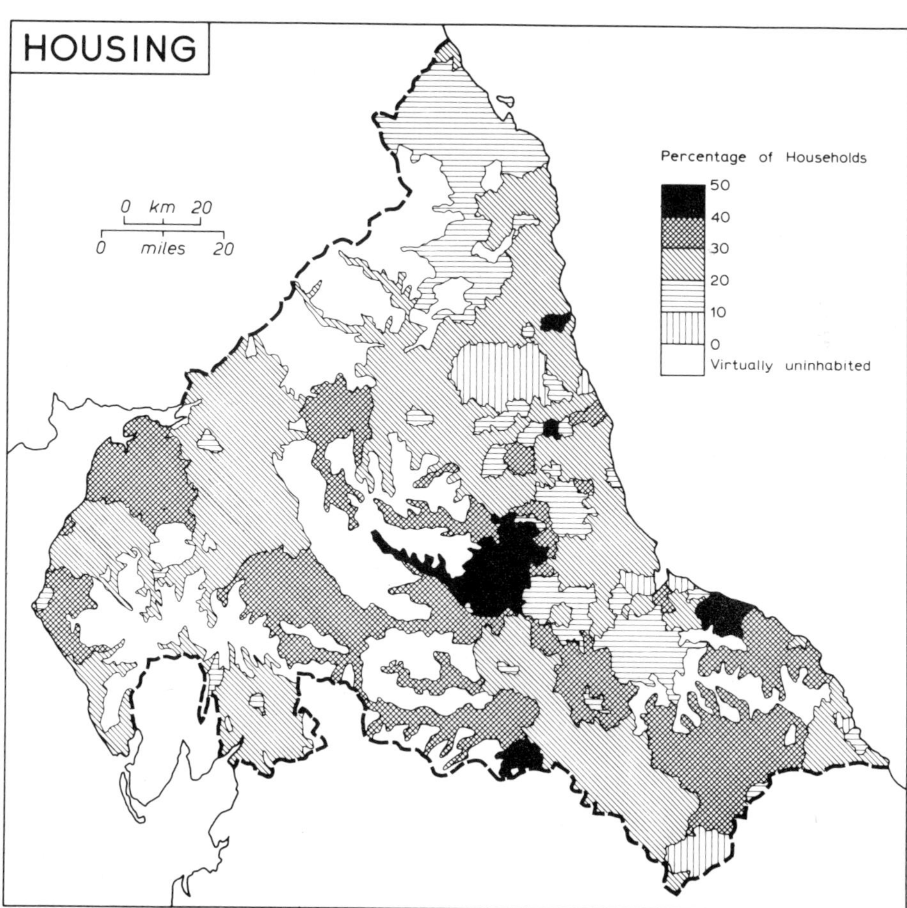

Fig 76 Northern Region—Percentage of households without exclusive use of all four basic household facilities (cold water tap, hot water tap, fixed bath and water closet), 1961.

major housing problem are the urban centres of the coalfields, and it is these areas that are most heavily built up. Land for new housing probably will become available outside the existing built up areas, and it follows that many families will have to move from urban sites to estates in greenfield situations.

As a result of the changes occurring both in industry and in population and housing it is only to be expected that a transformation is taking place in the settlement system of the region. The small agricultural settlements have altered their function and become weekend retreats, or middle class commuter suburbs when accessible to either of the two main conurbations of Tyneside and Teesside. These two urban areas exert considerable nodal influence even over the larger agricultural settlements with, for example, Carlisle looking eastwards to Newcastle upon Tyne and much of Yorkshire's North Riding centring on Darlington. Distinct from this attractive force of the conurbations are processes of decentralization which result in the emergence around each conurbation of a zone which is functionally an integral part of the town, but which has neither the economic nor social characteristics of a totally urban centre. Urban fringe areas are particularly notable to the north and west of Tyneside, where a series of old established settlements, for example Ponteland, have been changed both in form and function by suburban housing development. The low proportion of sub-standard housing in this area (Fig 76) bears witness to the newer residential nature of the district. On south Tyneside the fringe has merged with that around Sunderland and the Wearside urban complex is rapidly becoming part of Greater Tyneside.

A second changing element of the settlement composition of the region is the coal mining settlements. In the extreme west of the Durham coalfield, where very small pits and opencast sites were common, a dispersed settlement pattern grew up. A more nucleated settlement, but of straggling sprawling form, was associated with the small mines in the heart of the exposed coalfield. Houses were built in small groups and the unity of purpose and outlook of the inhabitants gave rise to socially very closely knit communities. It is these settlements which provide the greatest headache for local authority settlement regrouping policies. On the concealed coalfield, with the larger pits and generally more concentrated mining activity, settlements are larger than to the west, with several mining communities of over 7,000 people. Places such as Easington show incipient urban functions. Local authority planning policy particularly that of Durham County Council, has been a major factor in the changes occurring in the mining settlements. With the run down of the coal industry it became clear in the early 1950s that a concerted effort to redesign the settlement pattern was necessary. Villages were classified on the basis of their potential for expansion and a policy related to six types of villages has been devised. The types range from settlements undergoing rapid expansion through settlements where no new development will occur but which will continue in existence for some time, to settlements which are being cleared altogether. This approach provides not only for a positive framework for future housing development, but allows service and shop provision to be seriously planned and thus encourages investment at key centres. The key centres are closely linked to the major urban areas as well as having conside able potential for their own development.

A final feature of the changing settlement pattern is provided by the New Towns of the region. Five are being developed. Three in County Durham were stimulated by central government agencies and two north of Newcastle upon Tyne are being developed by local government authority. Newton Aycliffe, a few miles from Darlington, and Peterlee, close to the Durham coast, are of the former type. The decisions for their designation in the late 1940s involved considerations of the provision of work for employees from the declining coal industry and of the regrouping of mining households. The two towns differ significantly, however, for Newton Aycliffe was initially envisaged as a small centre of 10,000 people, built around a war-time ordnance factory converted to an industrial trading estate. The concept of Newton Aycliffe has changed

Plate 73 Killingworth New Town (Northumberland)
Recently completed blocks of flats with an elevated pedestrian path to the shopping centre in the background. Note the walkway beneath the road in the foreground giving access to the school. When the photograph was taken landscaping was incomplete.

over the years and a population of 45,000 is now being planned for. Peterlee was designed as a larger unit from the outset; 30,000 people were envisaged as resident but, with the surrounding dense village network, central facilities are being provided for 100,000 people. Washington, the third and newest of the Durham New Towns lies on the River Wear, south of Tyneside. The New Town lies within the urban fringe of both Tyneside and Wearside and it is envisaged that there will be heavy outflows of people to work in the two major urban areas. A somewhat similar, though smaller, development north of Tyneside is being sponsored by Northumberland County Council at Killingworth (Plate 73). Lying on the periphery of the conurbation, the town is rehousing overspill population from the redevelopment of the inner parts of Tyneside. Cramlington, 13 kilometres (8 miles) north of Newcastle, is a larger venture with a planned population of 50,000, and also being developed by the local planning authority without the usual massive central government aid for new towns. At Cramlington new employment will be provided to offset the decline in mining activity and the town will also provide a livelier urban environment than currently exists in this part of south-east Northumberland.

Recreation

The Northern Region includes within its boundaries parts of four National Parks. The whole of the North Yorkshire Moors and Northumberland Parks lie in the region together with substantial parts of the Lake District and Yorkshire Dales Parks. Designated recreation areas also include the Northumberland Coast and Solway Coast, which are defined as Areas of Outstanding Natural Beauty, and the Border Forest Park of upper North Tynedale. These areas in combination provide a varied recreational scene for both the regional population and for holiday makers from further afield, whether day-trippers from the West Riding towns or staying visitors at coastal resorts, such as Scarborough and Whitley Bay. In several of the Park areas, attempts have been made to provide activity nodes which do not conflict with the more general wild and undeveloped nature of most of the park area. At Grizedale in the Lake District, albeit the Lancashire section and so strictly in the North-West Region, facilities include camping sites, picnic sites, car parking, all in a large woodland tract adjoining Coniston Water, nature trails and forest walks, a wildlife centre, deer museum and treetop watch towers. Such positive planning for recreation is not unique to the Lake District or indeed the National Parks. The central Pennine areas are now subject to recreational land use planning and the worst landscape features of leisure activities are being minimized.

A considerable part of the region remains remote and undeveloped for tourist activities. Figure 77 shows the areas more than one kilometre (0·6 mile) from metalled roads in the Cheviot district of Northumberland. Even in this small sample district extensive areas remain very difficult of access to any but the most practised of walkers. Large tracts elsewhere in north Northumberland and in the Pennines and Yorkshire Dales are equally remote. In these inaccessible areas land ownership plays an important part in releasing land for public recreation. In north Northumberland vast tracts of open moorland are used as training grounds for the armed services and have at most very limited public access. The opposite situation of free access is provided on land owned by the National Trust. Figure 78 shows land owned by the National Trust in the Lake District National Park. Within the Park the National Trust owns one-sixth of the land. Although some control of numbers of people at particu-

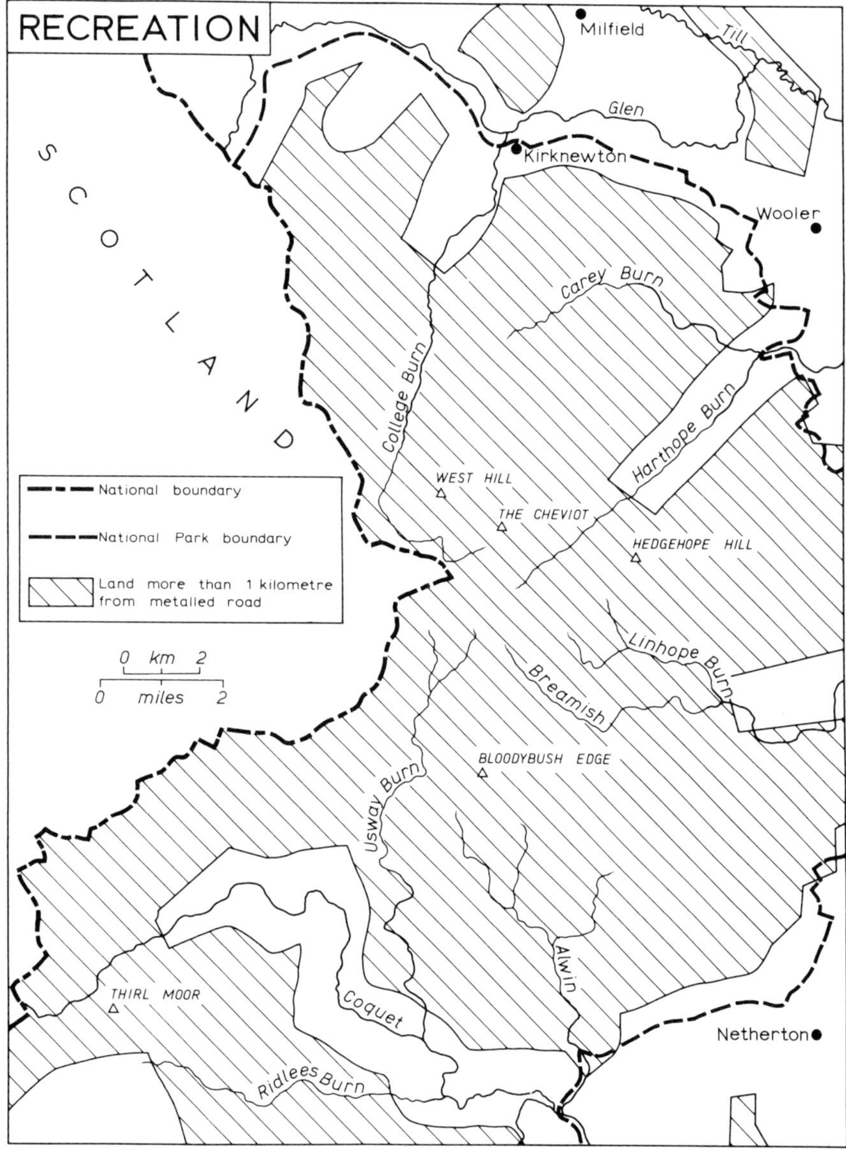

Fig 77 Northern Region—Areas more than 1 kilometre from a metalled road in north Northumberland.

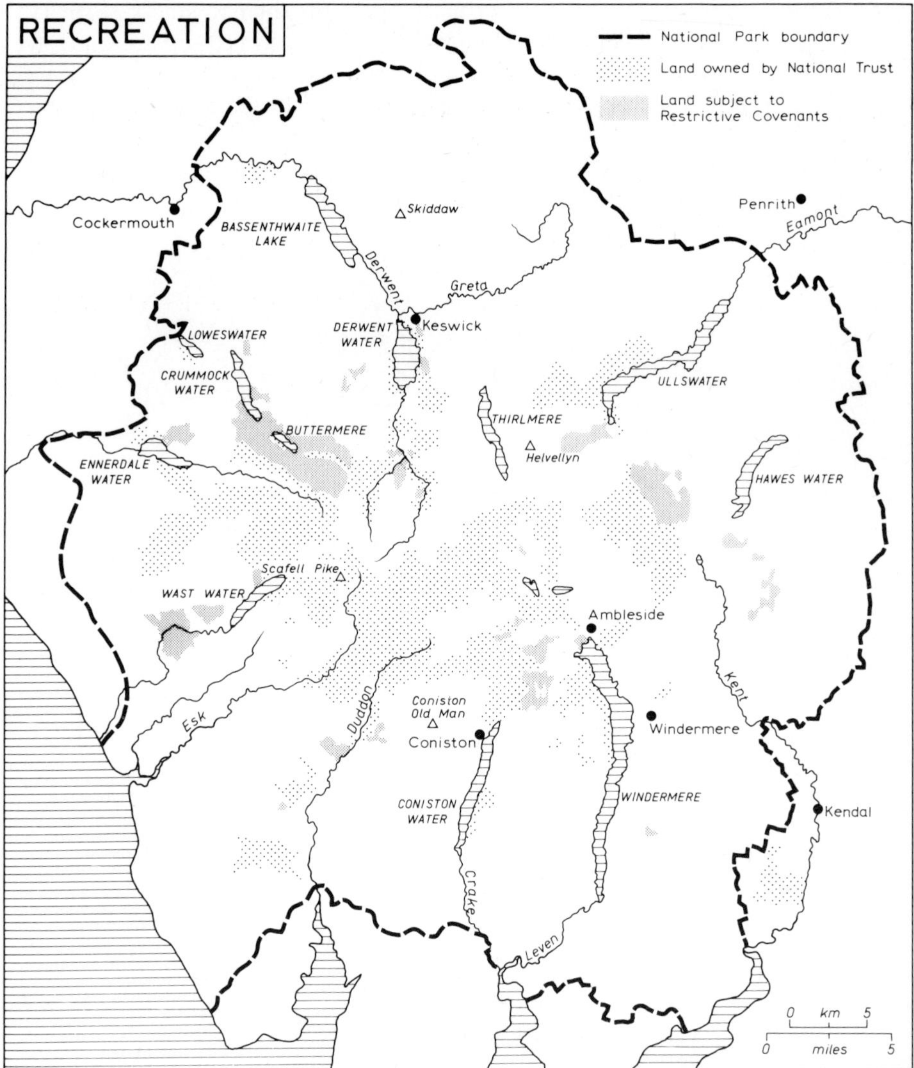

Fig 78 Northern Region—Land under the administration of the National Trust in the Lake District, 1968.

lar points is necessary there are vast open moorland tracts in the centre of the district which provide unrestricted access.

The reasons for many of the North's landscape changes of the last decade lie in the deliberate policy decisions and plans of local and central government. The direction which free enterprise economic and social forces have taken within the region have made it imperative that such forces become controlled and manipulated to the benefit of the region's population. A series of broad scale programmes for regional development and growth have been devised with the growing appreciation of the problems of the region since the early 1960s. The overriding objectives of these plans were the interests of the national and regional economy and the securing of co-ordinated development at a broad regional scale. In the late 1960s the scale of these studies changed with the sub-region rising in prominence. Recent proposals have been put forward for the development of small areas. The Teesside district has been the subject of a special study, as have north Northumberland and west Cumberland. As the policies provided by such detailed studies are put into effect within the context of the regional strategies, so the sub-regional wrinkles on the face of the region will change their character at the hands of the economic and social physicians.

FURTHER READING

J. C. Dewdney (ed.), *Durham County and City with Teesside* (Durham, 1970).

J. W. House, *The North East* (Newton Abbot, 1969).

Ministry of Housing and Local Government, *Teesside Survey and Plan* (London, 1969).

Northern Economic Planning Council, *Challenge of the Changing North* (London, 1966).

Northern Economic Planning Council, *Outline Strategy for the North* (Newcastle upon Tyne, 1969).

A. Smailes, *North England* (London, 1968).

Scotland—Physical Geography: The Central Lowlands

Physical Background

Scotland has a land area of 7·2 million hectares (29,796 square miles) which is slightly over one-third of the total area of Great Britain. It is a country of quite marked extremes. The land rises from sea level to 1,466 metres (4,400 feet), the climate on the west coast is distinctly oceanic while that on the east is slightly more continental and is much drier, soils range from sandy loams on the coastal plains to peat bog and scree slopes on the higher ground, and the natural vegetation types include grass covered coastal beaches, deciduous forest, coniferous forest and high altitude meadows. This diversity results from the interaction of the relief, the geological structure, and the past and present climates of the area.

Structurally Scotland can be divided into three regions which although not completely homogeneous are quite distinct from each other. The differences have been highlighted by subsequent economic and social development.

THE HIGHLANDS AND ISLANDS

North of the 'highland boundary fault' (Helensburgh to Stonehaven) is a mountainous area of schists and gneiss' which dates from Paleozoic times, but which includes an outcrop of more ancient pre-cambrian rocks along the north-west coast. Most of the land, apart from a limited amount of coastal lowland, is over 200 metres (600 feet), with considerable areas over 700 metres (2,100 feet). This mountain area has been subjected to repeated uplift and in consequence has an extremely complex geological structure. Intense folding, accompanied by widespread faulting and metamorphism resulted in the formation of very resistant mountain masses upon which the forces of erosion have subsequently acted.

THE SOUTHERN UPLANDS

This region, lying between the 'southern boundary fault' (Girvan to Dunbar) and the border, is a broad dissected plateau of tightly folded Ordovician and Silurian grits and shales. In contrast to the Highlands it is an area of rolling hills rising to between 500 metres (1,500 feet) and 600 metres (1,800 feet), but with a few peaks of around 900 metres (2,700 feet). The lower Tweed basin, 'The Merse', an area of Carboniferous sandstone, and the eroded Silurian rocks of the Solway basin, from the only extensive lowlands in the region.

THE CENTRAL LOWLANDS

Between the Highlands and the Southern Uplands lies the fault bounded Central Lowlands of Scotland. This is a region of Old Red Sandstone and coal bearing Carboniferous rocks which have been eroded much more rapidly than the resistant rocks of the adjacent hill masses. The name lowland is something of a misnomer, however, since much of the land is over 130 metres (400 feet). Igneous intrusions in the form of dykes, sills and volcanic plugs are found thoughout the area.

Ice Activity

Weakened by the onslaught of wind and water throughout Mesozoic and Tertiary times the whole country was then subjected to intense ice action during the Quaternary era. Ice fields formed over the Highlands and radiated from these over the central and southern parts of the country and merged along the east coast with the much larger Scandinavian ice sheet.

The details of the present landscape are largely the result of ice action and associated processes. In the highlands cirques and cols were formed under the ice fields; the adjacent mountains were severely eroded producing their present rounded form; valleys, particularly those following fault lines, were considerably deepened and the fiord coastline of the west was gouged out as the ice plunged seaward from the adjacent mountains. The softer rocks of the central lowlands were particularly vulnerable to erosion by the south- and east-moving ice from the highlands. Wide valleys punctuated by upstanding remnants of the resistant volcanic intrusions were formed and were subsequently given a covering of till deposits. The southern uplands were also severely eroded giving rise to a smoothly rounded upland area with till and drumlin deposits in the lower Tweed basin.

The changes in sea level which accompanied the glacial activity resulted in the formation of raised beaches at varying heights around the coast. These flat sandy areas have come to play a very important part in the agriculture of the country and in some districts form the only cultivable land.

Climate

Scotland derives great benefit from its location in the path of the North Atlantic Drift and the prevailing south-westerly winds from the Atlantic. This is particularly true on the west coast, which experienced the full effects of the mild and moist oceanic conditions, while the east coast, in the lee of the mountains, has slightly more extreme temperatures and markedly less rainfall.

TEMPERATURE

The ameliorating influence of the ocean is very clearly illustrated by the January temperatures which average 5·5°C (42°F) in the western islands, while on the east coast they are 3·3°C (38°F). Much lower temperatures are, however, recorded in the interior of the Grampian Mountains. During the summer months the temperature gradient is reversed with the sea tending to cool the west coast, particularly the north-west where temperatures range from 12·7°C to 14·4°C (55°F to 58°F), while on the more continental east coast temperatures vary between 14·4°C and 15·5°C (58°F and 60°F).

RAINFALL

Rainfall reaches a maximum in the Fort William area with 4,320 millimetres

(170 inches) falling on Ben Nevis, but totals of over 2,540 millimetres (100 inches) are recorded over the greater part of the counties of Argyll and Inverness. Precipitation totals decline to between 1,270 and 1,525 millimetres (50 and 60 inches) in south-west Scotland. Eastwards, in the lee of the mountains, there is a gradual fall in the amounts of precipitation recorded from 1,525 millimetres (60 inches) in the interior to 640 millimetres (25 inches) on the coastal lowlands. The seasons of maximum rainfall in the Highlands are autumn and winter, while in the south there are summer and autumn maxima.

SOILS AND VEGETATION

The interaction of relief, parent rock and climate has given rise to a wide variety of soil and vegetation types in the area. It should, however, be emphasized that over the years man has done much to change the original vegetation cover of the country and has also attempted to improve the soils with the result that truly 'natural' conditions are rare.

The combined effect of these physical elements, structure, climate, soils and vegetation has had a considerable influence on the value of the land to man, and on the uses to which it has been and could be put.

The Central Lowlands

The low-lying eastern section of the central lowlands emerged at an early date as Scotland's main agricultural area. By the fourteenth century it was by far the most prosperous part of the country and Edinburgh, its main town, had emerged as the national capital. The dominance of the east over the economic and social welfare of Scotland lasted until the eighteenth century when, as a result of the union of the parliaments of England and Scotland and the subsequent expansion of trade with the Americas, Glasgow developed as a trading and manufacturing city. Initially activity concentrated on imported cotton and tobacco: these were quickly supplanted by iron smelting (using local coal and blackband ore) and the manufacture of machinery. The development of metal-hulled ships and steam power during the nineteenth century transformed the local shipbuilding industry making it into the largest in the world. Engineering and a whole multitude of smaller ancillary industries were also established along the River Clyde. The combined effect of all this industrial activity was the transference of the economic focus of Scotland to the west coast; it led to a massive increase in the area's population brought about by migration from less favoured parts of the country coupled with high rates of natural increase.

The present overwhelming concentration of Scotland's population in the central lowlands (75 per cent) is a legacy of the emergence of this area as one of Britain's major industrial regions during the nineteenth century (Fig. 79). Unfortunately, however, the basis of this growth was primary production and heavy engineering, which have subsequently declined in importance. Many of the region's present employment and industrial problems are a result of the inability of its economy to diversify and keep pace with modern technological developments. These problems are aggravated by an outmoded settlement

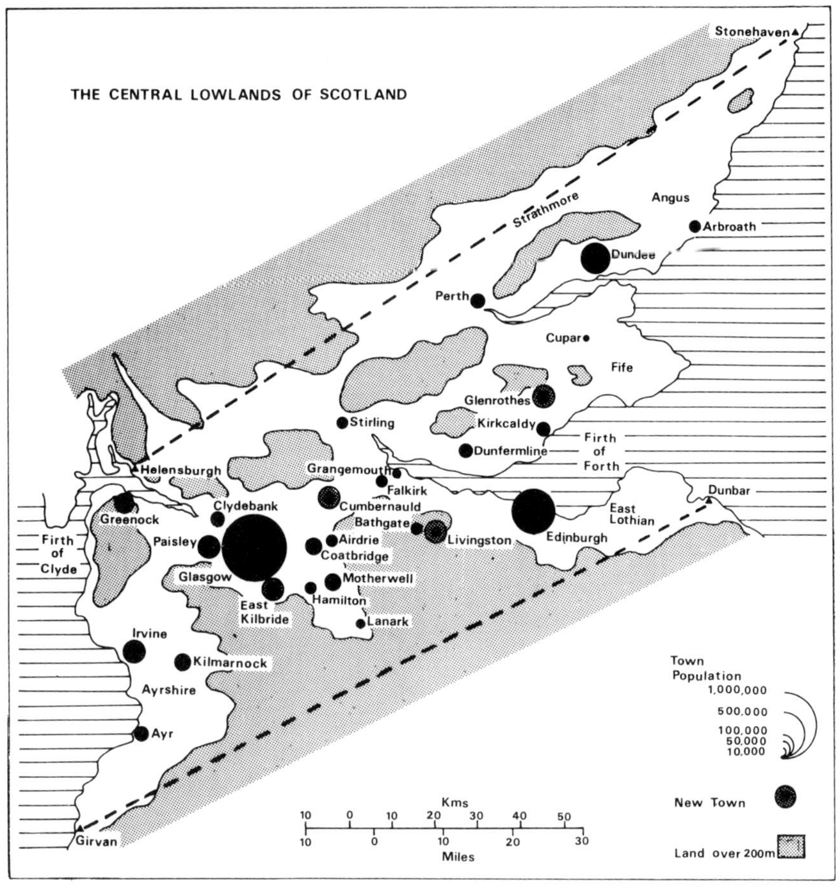

Fig 79 Distribution of Relief and Urban Population in Central Scotland
Particular note should be made of the relatively high proportion of land over 200 metres within the region. The concentration of urban population in the west and the location of the five new towns is clearly illustrated.

pattern and urban fabric which no longer meet the requirements of a modern industrial society.

Industrial Development

TEXTILES

Textile manufacture, originally based on local wool, is one of the oldest industries in the region; linen was also woven from both home grown and imported flax. The woollen industry has continued to be of considerable importance to the Scottish economy, but its focus has subsequently moved south into the Border Counties. Linen, on the other hand, has almost completely disappeared and has been replaced in the Kirkcaldy area by the manufacture of synthetic textiles and linoleum, and in the Dundee area by jute and cotton weaving. This specialization in jute weaving took place during the last quarter of the nineteenth century and gave Dundee a virtual world monopoly. In recent years, however, this dominance has been increasingly undermined as a result of the introduction of the manufacture of the fibre in Bangladesh, where it is grown, and by competition from other manufacturing centres.

With the opening-up of trade with the Americas during the eighteenth century cotton spinning and weaving replaced the woollen industry in the Clyde valley and was for many years the basis, along with tobacco, of Glasgow's prosperity. Increasing competition from Lancashire, however, led to the decline of the industry in the west of Scotland. The manufacture of sewing thread at Paisley and the carpet industry at Kilmarnock are all that remain of this early specialization in textiles.

This reversal of fortune in the Glasgow area proved to be a blessing in disguise since it forced industrialists to look for other more profitable activities; taking advantage of local interest in the manufacture of textile machinery they began to develop the machinery-making and engineering industries. The replacement of wood by metal in these industries led to the establishment of local iron foundries and these set the scene for the future industrial development of the area.

COAL MINING

Coal had been mined in Scotland since the Middle Ages. Initially, however, mining was mainly in the eastern lowlands and was on a small scale controlled by various religious houses and a few large landowners. The coal was mainly for domestic use, but the salt evaporating industry on the Firth of Forth at Prestonpans was also an important consumer. With the development during the eighteenth century of techniques to use coal in smelting iron ore (see Chapter 4), and the growing demand for iron in the expanding industries of the Clyde valley, the Lanarkshire and Ayrshire coalfields soon became the main centres of production. The presence, in these particular fields, of blackband iron ore deposits in the coal seams was of great significance in reducing the cost of iron smelting and this encouraged the local expansion of the metal using industries.

The domestic, industrial and shipping market for coal increased throughout the nineteenth century and reached a peak in 1913 when the central Scottish coalfields produced one-seventh of the United Kingdom total output. Since then, however, their low *per capita* productivity and high mining costs have put them at a disadvantage compared with the more productive English coalfields. The recession in the Scottish industry, intensified by increased competition from other fuels, has been particularly severe in the Ayrshire, Lanarkshire and Stirlingshire coalfields, where narrow discontinuous seams and small output per mine have so increased costs as to make them uneconomic. This has necessitated many closures. Since the establishment of the National Coal Board in 1947 the Scottish coal mining industry has undergone considerable change with emphasis now being placed on the Fife and Midlothian fields where the geological formations make it possible to concentrate activity in a few large mines, such as those at Longannet, Seafield, Bilston Glen and Monktonhall. The introduction of modern techniques and equipment has already increased output per man shift to 1·78 metric tons (35 hundredweights): this is still below the national average, however, and the mining costs are higher. The current output of deep mined coal is almost sufficient to meet the demands of the Scottish market. Modern methods, however, make it possible to produce this coal with fewer and fewer men; the present employment of 40,000 compares with 70,000 in 1960. This loss of employment has not been counterbalanced by expansion in other sectors of industry. High unemployment and hardship has resulted, particularly in the western and central coalfields where the decline has been greatest; high out-migration from central Scotland to other parts of the United Kingdom and abroad may be partly attributable to this recession.

An additional diseconomy results from the fact that the main coal producing areas are now in the east, but the main consumers of coal are still located in the western part of the central lowlands. This means that high transportation costs must be added to the price of coal which is already above the national average.

IRON AND STEEL

The iron and steel industry in the Glasgow area is still of considerable importance, but the era of rapid expansion which brought the towns of Airdrie, Coatbridge, Motherwell and Wishaw into being has long since passed and a period of modernization and rationalization has begun.

As industrial development in the eighteenth and nineteenth centuries gathered momentum supplies of local iron ore soon became inadequate and were increasingly supplemented and then replaced by the import of richer ores from overseas. The substantial investment in plant which had already taken place in the established smelting towns, and the pool of skilled labour within them, however, ensured their continued dominance of the iron (and later the steel) industry. In consequence the imported ore was transported by rail from the river to these centres. This was, and still is, an expensive procedure and has given rise to repeated proposals that the industry be moved to the coast. So far these have been resisted, but a proposal that an integrated plant be located at Hunterston in Ayrshire, where the new ore terminal is being developed, is currently under consideration.

The output of crude steel in 1967 amounted to 2·6 million metric tons (2·56 million long tons) and that of pig iron 1·25 million metric tons (1·23 million long tons) (12 per cent of the British iron and steel production). One of the most important developments in the Scottish iron and steel industry in recent years was the opening in 1964 of a semi-continuous hot strip-mill at Ravenscraig near Motherwell. This complex has an annual production of three-quarters of a million tons of sheet steel which means that for the first time the industry can produce the lighter steel products (such as sheets of light plate) required by the motor vehicle and consumer durable industries. This is of major importance since the traditional markets for steel—shipbuilding, railways, heavy engineering and mining machinery—are declining, and the new consumers require specialized types of steel not previously produced in the area.

The number of people employed in the Scottish iron and steel industry has remained relatively constant at around 30,000 during the 1960s.

Plate 74 Clydebank (Lanarkshire)
Ships and shipbuilding are an essential element of the economic well-being of the central lowlands of Scotland. Here a small tanker is launched and held by many tonnes of drag chains as she enters the constricted and congested river Clyde.

SHIPBUILDING This is undoubtedly the industry for which Glasgow and Clydeside are best known. It had its origins in the wooden vessels built for the colonial trade. The Clyde with its local iron industry was able to take full advantage of the intro-tion of the steam engine and metal hull and for many years the annual tonnage launched exceeded that of any other centre in the world. At one time there were twenty shipbuilding firms along a twenty mile stretch of river down-stream from Glasgow. These yards produced ships of all kinds, but specialized in the building of passenger liners. This specialization was of great importance to the industrial development of the area since in addition to steel and engines these vessels required the products of an almost limitless range of ancillary industries to fit them out ready for service.

The industry prospered on Clydeside until after the Second World War; since then outdated yards, shortage of capital and increased competition have all worked together to undermine its position. The post-war growth in the popularity of air travel brought the era of the ocean liner virtually to an end and although the Queen Elizabeth II was completed on the Clyde as recently as 1969 it will probably be the last vessel of its type to be built anywhere. The area still builds about one-third of the annual tonnage of ships launched in Britain.

Shipbuilding is also found, but on a much smaller scale, at Leith and Dundee on the east coast.

Employment in the industry is at present around 47,000 which is 50 per cent less than it was in 1950. This clearly illustrates the recent decline of shipbuild-ing and indicates the urgent need to both revitalize the industry and provide alternative employment.

The problems facing the industry on Clydeside have been highlighted by the recent closure and collapse of several of the yards, despite repeated capital investments by the government. The answer would seem to lie in amalgama-tion, modernization, increased efficiency and greater adaptability. Attempts have been made within the past few years to rationalize the industry in these ways and it remains to be seen whether or not they can revitalize the industry and bring back a measure of prosperity and security to the shipbuilding towns.

Population

The industrial development of the central lowlands during the nineteenth century resulted in a rapid increase in the region's population from 683,047 in 1801 to 3,425,684 in 1911. From then until 1961, however, growth was much less spectacular, being almost stationary for the period 1939–61 and increasing by only 533,707 to 3,958,391 in the previous 50 year period. This situation is a product of the economic conditions in the area and has been brought about mainly by the decline of the basic heavy industries, particularly since 1945, and the inability of other industries and the service sector to counterbalance this loss of employment. Poor job opportunities have forced people to look else-where for work with the result that out-migration to other parts of the United Kingdom and overseas has been very high. During the 1960s emigration from Scotland averaged around 35,000 people every year (80 to 90 per cent of the country's natural population increase). Consequently, despite a rate of natural increase of 7·1 per cent, which is above the United Kingdom average, there is little or no population growth. With an unemployment rate of 4·3 per cent at the present time this loss of people seems likely to continue. This is a matter for great concern since persistent out-migration, involving as it has done, the younger more able members of the community has resulted in significant demographic and labour supply changes. These have had social and economic implications which have intensified the industrial and housing problems of the area; these problems have in turn influenced the rate of out-migration. If development is to take place in this region it is imperative that this vicious circle be checked by the introduction of new industries, improved infrastructure and better housing standards.

Regional Development Incentives

Faced with these problems the government has introduced several schemes which, it is hoped, will both attract modern industry into the region and improve the living conditions within it. The most recent approach is embodied in the Industrial Development Act 1966 under which all of Scotland, apart from Edinburgh the capital city, was designated a development area. Under this legislation low rents were charged for government financed factories, and loans and grants were made available to attract new and expanding firms to the region. The operation of the Industrial Development Certificate procedure, whereby industrialists wishing to expand their premises, or to build new ones, must receive permission from the Department of Trade and Industry is a further means of helping the area. The Department attempts to steer new developments to those areas in greatest need of industry. The fact that 43 per cent of the money allocated by the government for industrial development between 1960 and 1968 went to Scotland, mainly to the central lowlands, is a measure of the central authority's concern about the need to expand and diversify the Scottish economy.

If new industries are to be attracted and flourish, improved factories, services and transport facilities must be provided. The existing industrial sites within established urban areas are no longer suitable because of expansion, transport and amenity restrictions. This has resulted in the need to develop out of town sites and to group these together to form industrial estates. Estates of this kind had already been established in the Glasgow area before the Second World War, but they have multiplied greatly during the post-war period encouraged by both the national and local authorities. Hillington, Bellshill and Newhouse industrial estates have been joined by many others in the Glasgow area; and others have been established adjacent to Dundee and Edinburgh, as well as in Fife and Stirlingshire. In all there are now 36 government sponsored estates in Scotland, mostly in the central lowlands; in addition many more have been established by local authorities. Industrial estates also form integral parts of the five Scottish new towns.

New Town Development

The new town movement in Scotland arose initially in response to the need to ameliorate Glasgow's housing problem and to bring about a much needed redistribution of people from the overcrowded Clyde Valley towns.

EAST KILBRIDE (65,500—1971)

Designated in 1947 this was the first Scottish new town and to date is by far the most successful. The choice of a site so close to Glasgow (11 kilometres (7 miles)) has meant that it has never been able to develop independently, but has always been overshadowed to a certain extent by the adjacent city. This has not, however, retarded its growth nor has it detracted from its attractiveness to new industries. Rolls Royce, the National Engineering Laboratory, and numerous light engineering and food processing firms have been established there.

The proximity of East Kilbride to Glasgow is, in the light of subsequent experience, a distinct advantage since although it was originally intended that the new town would be economically self-contained no account had been taken of the surprisingly strong local ties exhibited by the Glasgow families. Right from the new town's inception there has been a considerable cross movement of people between it and the city for work, shopping and social visiting, and this has not diminished over the years.

East Kilbride Development Corporation has been given the additional role of building Scotland's sixth new town at Stonehouse about 19 kilometres (12 miles) from East Kilbride. Indications are that Stonehouse will have a designated area of around 2,800 hectares (7,000 acres) of which approximately 280 hectares (700 acres) are likely to be industrial estates situated on the M.74 motorway, the main link between Scotland and England. Preparatory work involving technical studies and surveys have been undertaken pending the designation of the area of the new town.

CUMBERNAULD (34,000—1971)

A similar pattern of interaction soon emerged between Glasgow and Cumbernauld new town which was designated in 1955. This took place despite its greater distance from the city (24 kilometres (15 miles)) and the establishment of numerous industries including office machinery and light engineering in the town. Movement between Cumbernauld and Glasgow has been facilitated by the construction of a motorway link. Studies have shown, however, that the intensity of interaction between Cumbernauld and the city is less than that recorded between East Kilbride and Glasgow. Because of this Cumbernauld has been able to develop its own individuality and identity much more rapidly, but at the same time has not been so far away to prevent the people retaining their established social, shopping and entertainment links with Glasgow.

IRVINE (45,000—1971)

This is the youngest of the Scottish new towns (designated in 1966) and although it is located some 32 kilometres (20 miles) from Glasgow, a fast road link brings it within easy reach of the city. In 1966 Irvine already had a population of nearly 37,000, the only new town in Scotland to have a large established population; few of these people worked in the city. New town status has already begun to attract new industries as well as more people to the town.

The other new towns, Glenrothes and Livingston, are both located in the eastern lowlands and although they were not established specifically to rehouse Glasgow families it was hoped that they would prove attractive to people from the western area and so help in the redistribution of the population within the region.

GLENROTHES (30,000—1971)

This was particularly true in the case of Glenrothes which was to have a very large and modern mine as its focus, thus providing work and new homes for miners from the declining Lanarkshire coalfield as well as for miners displaced by closures in other parts of Fife. Due to unforeseen geological difficulties the mine never became fully operational which necessitated a complete reconsideration of the town's industrial basis. In many ways this was a fortuitous development since the introduction of the electrical industry on a very large scale, in addition to other forms of light engineering, paper making and clothing manufacture, has brought about a much needed diversification and modernization of the local industrial structure.

LIVINGSTON (16,400—1971)

This new town is still in the early stages of development, but it has already attracted a company, employing some 2,000 people, which makes forgings for the aircraft, power and oil industries. In the long term it is planned that this town will become a regional service and shopping centre in addition to its important industrial role. The hope is that Livingston will act as a growth point for both industries and services within an area which has suffered acutely from the closure of the oil shale industry and the decline of coal mining.

OVERSPILL SCHEMES

Although the creation of new towns was undoubtedly the most spectacular policy aimed at improving central Scotland's industrial structure and redistributing the population, other means have also been used to achieve these objectives. Under the Housing and Town Development (Scotland) Act, 1957, statutory embodiment was given to Glasgow's overspill scheme. This enabled Glasgow to enter into agreements, with willing local authorities throughout Scotland, whereby families and industries would move from the city to these reception areas. Many towns sought to take advantage of the scheme, but for the reasons already discussed above, success has most often been achieved in agreements with towns situated close to Glasgow, such as Kirkintilloch and Linwood. Industries and people have both been less willing to move to more distant towns; where such movement has actually taken place the success of the venture has been undermined by a very high turnover of families returning to Glasgow.

The new town and overspill policies have failed to bring about a major change in the distribution of population in the central lowlands, but this was possibly never a feasible proposition. They have, however, been successful in illustrating the ways in which housing standards and layout can be improved and how thriving industrial complexes can be promoted. This example has not gone unnoticed by other towns in the central belt. Most of these have undertaken extensive re-development schemes and transport improvement programmes, as well as promoting industrial development. Urban renewal and industrial diversification are changing the out-dated character of many central lowland towns.

Modernization and Diversification of Industry

The adjustment of several of the traditional industries to the needs of the twentieth century has already been considered, but the introduction of new industries is of even greater significance to the economy as a whole.

ENGINEERING

This continues to be the largest manufacturing activity in central Scotland, but there has been a change in emphasis with radio and other electronic apparatus, office machinery and electrical machinery now dominant. These activities are found throughout the entire area with the largest concentrations in the new towns.

MOTOR VEHICLES

Until 1966, when the British Leyland Motor Corporation started to produce commercial vehicles, tractors and diesel engines at Bathgate, Scotland played no part in the modern British motor industry. This breakthrough was due mainly to government pressure and the provision of large financial inducements; these factors were also responsible for the opening of the Chrysler U.K. plant at Linwood in 1963, the only car producing plant in Scotland. An adjoining factory at Linwood makes car bodies and commercial vehicle cabs for the two plants. Starting from a labour force of zero in 1961 the motor industry now employs nearly 19,000 people.

Although motor vehicle manufacture has only recently been reintroduced into Scotland, the manufacture of aero-engines by Rolls Royce has a much longer history and now employs some 12,000 people mainly in the Glasgow and East Kilbride areas.

OIL REFINING AND CHEMICALS

The mining of oil-shale in West Lothian and its processing into kerosene and lubricants dates back to the middle of the nineteenth century. It was, however, only when the oil-shale reserves became exhausted, and were replaced by imported, and far cheaper, crude oil, that the refining industry began to expand rapidly. The increased dependence on imported oil resulted in the movement of the industry to the shores of the river Forth at Grangemouth. There, the wide tidal mud flats provided ample room for these large plants and for any future expansion. Recent increases in tanker size have meant that the Forth can no longer be used, but this problem has been overcome by the opening of a deep water terminal at Finnart on the west coast just north of Helensburgh, and the construction of a cross-country pipe-line to carry the crude oil to Grangemouth. With a refining capacity of four and one half million tons this is one of Europe's largest oil refining complexes. The chemical industry, using the by-products from the refinery, is also very important in this area and the newest of a whole series of large plants produces acrylonitrile and is the first of its type in Britain.

The only other major chemical manufacturing centre in Scotland is the Imperial Chemical Industries plant at Ardeer in Ayrshire where explosives and artificial fibres are made. A recent addition to this complex has been a nylon polymer plant.

FOOD AND DRINK

The whisky industry is one of the fastest growing in Scotland. In 1967 it employed 20,000 people and produced 550 million proof litres (121·5 million gallons) much of which was destined for the export market. Distilleries are found throughout the country, mainly in the north-eastern Highlands, but by far the greatest proportion of the industry's labour force is employed in blending and bottling which is almost exclusively undertaken in and around Glasgow and Edinburgh.

Other branches of the food and drink industry are to be found in all of the major towns. A few have, however, emerged as specialized centres such as fruit and vegetable canning around Dundee, sugar refining at Greenock, biscuits in Edinburgh and Glasgow and beer in Edinburgh, Glasgow, Falkirk and Alloa.

SERVICE INDUSTRY

Although great emphasis has rightly been placed on the need to attract new industries and expand those already established in the central lowlands, the importance of service industries in the economy of the region should not be overlooked. These account for nearly 50 per cent of the jobs available in the area, a proportion similar to that in the rest of Great Britain; the bulk of this employment is in the central lowlands. Adequate and up-to-date services are important if new industrialists are to be attracted to the area. Their importance is reflected in the steady increase in the number of people employed in service industries such as distributive trades, professional and scientific services, public administration and finance over the past few years. These activities are represented in all communities, but the large towns, particularly Edinburgh and Glasgow, have the highest concentrations.

Agriculture

Farming in the central lowlands is generally of a very high standard and the area ranks among the most productive in Britain. It can be divided areally into three different sections each with its own particular specialization.

THE UPLAND AREA

Land over 133 metres (400 feet) accounts for almost one half of the region and is for the most part unsuitable for arable cultivation. The quality of the grazing is not very high in these upland areas and consequently they have been given over almost exclusively to hill-sheep farming, although at the present time the number of beef cattle is being gradually increased.

THE WESTERN LOWLANDS

West of a line which runs roughly north–south through Grangemouth the mild and moist climatic conditions favour diary farming. The large market for liquid milk generated by the urban concentrations in central Scotland and northern England have encouraged specialization in milk production and this activity now dominates the farm economies of this area.

There are, however, two notable exceptions. The light raised beach soils of the Ayrshire coast have proved ideal for the cultivation of early potatoes and in the Upper Clyde valley around Lanark soft fruit is grown; the glasshouse cultivation of tomatoes and flowers destined mainly for the Glasgow market is also found in the Clyde Valley.

THE EASTERN LOWLANDS

Slightly higher summer temperatures, high sunshine totals and low rainfall account for the extensive arable farming found in the eastern lowlands. Fife and the Lothians are renowned for the high yields of wheat, barley and potatoes produced; further north in Angus, where the climate is a little more rigorous, oats are grown. Sugar beet is also an important crop, but with the proposed closure of the sugar beet factory at Coupar, Fife, the only one in Scotland, the excessive transport costs to the English factories will prohibit its continued cultivation. Despite the high proportion of arable land, however, prime beef is the largest cash product of the farms in the eastern lowlands. In addition to breeding the world famous Aberdeen-Angus cattle which emanate from the north-eastern coastal lowland, cattle are also brought in from the Highlands and Ireland for fattening. Notable specializations are also found in this area as in the western area. Strathmore is a renowned soft fruit growing district (particularly raspberries, used in jam making around Dundee) while in East Lothian the market gardens supply vegetables to much of central Scotland and north-east England.

Agriculture in the central lowlands of Scotland is well adjusted to both climatic and market influences and is efficient and profitable. Employment is, however, declining as increased use is made of machinery, and farm units are enlarged. The surplus labour force thus produced is forced to turn to the urban areas for work.

This is symptomatic of the problem facing the central lowlands at the present time. High unemployment resulting from the decline of the traditional industries. As yet the newer industries have been unable to offer sufficient job opportunities. This situation is aggravated by the out-dated settlement pattern and infrastructure found in the declining areas, making them unattractive to incoming industrialists. Every effort is being made to remedy this through the various redevelopment, new town and overspill schemes already discussed and by the construction of a motorway network both within and between urban areas; the efficiency of the railway is being improved, port facilities are being extended and airports developed. It is felt that only in this way can a social and economic environment conducive to modern industrial expansion be provided. This policy has already begun to have the desired effect, particularly in the new towns, but a much wider application is essential if the problems facing the economy of the central lowlands are to be overcome.

FURTHER READING

British Association, *Dundee and District* (Dundee, 1968).

British Association, *Scientific Survey of South-Eastern Scotland* (Edinburgh, 1951).

British Association, *The Glasgow Region* (Glasgow, 1958).

Scottish Development Department, *Tayside: Potential for Development* (H.M.S.O., Edinburgh, 1970).

The Scottish Economy 1965–1970: A Plan for Expansion Cmnd. 2864 (H.M.S.O., 1966).

Third Statistical Account of Scotland:

County of Ayr (J. Strawhorn and W. Boyd, 1951).

County of Dumbarton (M. S. Dilke and A. A. Templeton, 1959).

East Lothian (C. Snodgrass, 1953).

County of Fife (A. Smith, 1952).

City of Glasgow (J. Cunnison and J. B. Gilfillan, 1958).

County of Lanark (G. Thomson, 1960).

Counties of Renfrew and Bute (H. A. Moisley *et al.*, 1962).

CHAPTER SEVENTEEN

Scotland—The Highlands, Islands, and Southern Uplands

The Highlands and Islands

To most people in Britain the words 'Highlands and Islands' conjure up a picture of an area characterized by its remoteness, its splendid rugged mountain and wild moorland scenery, and its romantic heritage (Fig. 80). Such impressions are superficially true, but they by no means completely sum up the area. Its problems and potentialities and its position in the regional framework of Britain are the realities on which attention should and must be focused. The area's environment and past history help give an insight into many of its present problems, and are also the foundations on which its future must be moulded. They provide the key to understanding the region and therefore form essential elements in any study of the area.

Social Background

Despite the arduous physical conditions prevailing throughout much of the area the Highlands have a history of human settlement which dates back to neolithic times; these early peoples tended to concentrate in a few favourable locations, mostly close to the coast. With the passage of time the population increased and spread inland. The limited potential of the interior, however, particularly for agricultural production, controlled the amount of population which the area could accommodate with the result that settlement away from the low-lying coastal areas was extremely sparse.

Economic life revolved round the 'croft' and the 'income' from this was augmented by fishing and craft industries. The social structure of the area was based on the 'clan' system. Among these closely-knit groups there was great rivalry and a good deal of warfare, but to the outside world they presented a united front. Population growth in the area was therefore solely due to the natural increase of the indigenous peoples and was not augmented in any way by in-migration.

The pacification of the Highlands following the Jacobite Rebellion of 1745 changed this situation. For the first time in its history the area was drawn into the mainstream of British life.

High wool prices in the late eighteenth and early nineteenth centuries resulted in the conversion of confiscated estates and land bought from impoverished clan chiefs to sheep ranges. Commercial farming on the scale practised by the new southern landlords brought many human problems. People were forced to move from the land, since the labour requirements of the new system were much lower than the old crofting one which it replaced in many areas, and had either to resettle in less favoured areas or to emigrate.

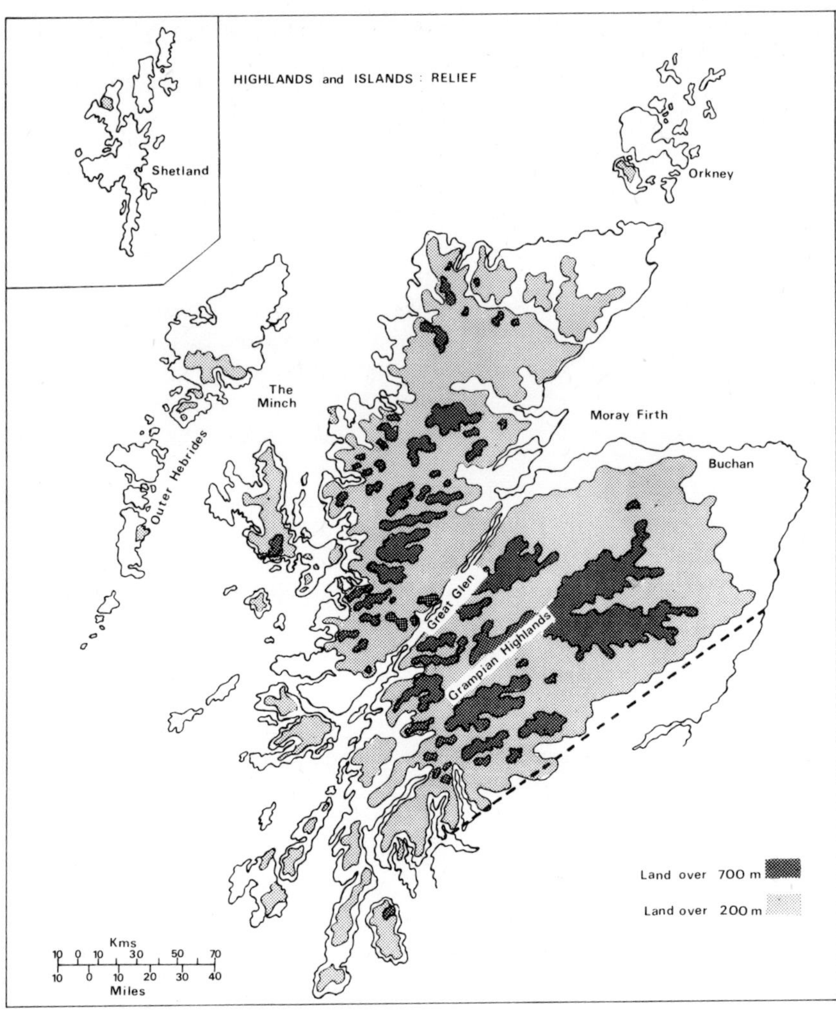

Fig 80 The Highlands and Islands
The restricted area of land below 200 metres is of particular significance especially on the west coast where it is not only limited in extent but also discontinuous.

Population

Emigration, initially as a consequence of the 'Highland Clearances', but later because of poverty and limited local employment potential has been a characteristic of the region since the beginning of the nineteenth century. High rates of natural increase during the early years of the nineteenth century, however, offset these losses, and it is only in the past 100 years, and particularly in the period 1900–30, that the population declined in absolute terms.

Out-migration has persisted over such a long period that it has seriously eroded the social and economic life of the area. The heavy losses in the younger age groups have consistently found expression in low birth rates, and have resulted in a gradual ageing of the population. The economic consequence of this has been a reduction in the size and quality of the labour force, and this in turn has acted against the introduction of new forms of employment. The social consequences have appeared in the form of declining and more costly services, medical provision, education, transport and building maintenance.

Throughout the region depopulation has been greatest in the rural areas (between 10 per cent and 50 per cent in the decade 1961–71). It has been counterbalanced to a very limited extent by a small increase in the numbers in the urban concentrations. The cities of Aberdeen (184,070, 1966) and Inver-

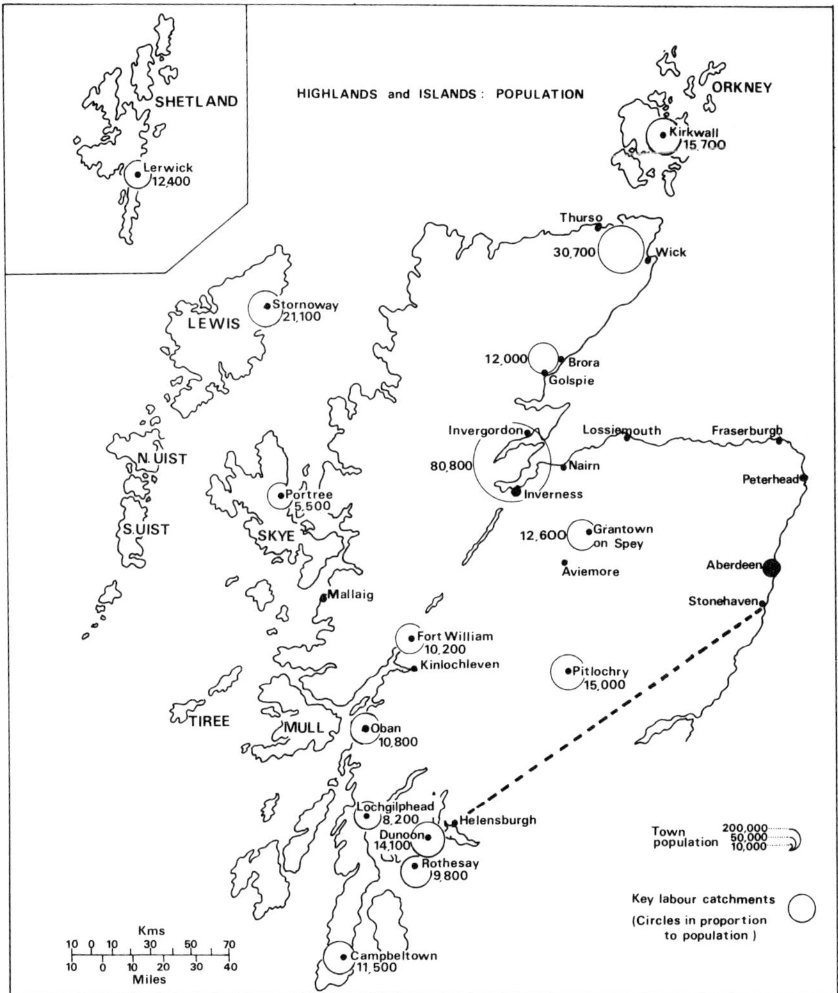

Fig 81 Distribution of Urban Population in the Highlands and Islands
Apart from the cities of Aberdeen and Inverness the towns in the Highland region are both small and dispersed. The labour catchments are shown for those towns selected as being suitable for industrial development.

ness (30,410, 1966), the smaller mainland burghs of Pitlochry, Grantown-on-Spey, Campbeltown, Dunoon, Lochgilphead, Oban, Fort William, Wick and Thurso, and the island burghs of Stornoway (Lewis), Kirkwall (Orkney) and Lerwick (Shetland) have all grown slightly. A proportion of the rural migrants would therefore seem to be attracted to the nearby urbanized communities (Fig. 81).

The population level in the region is, however, extremely low. In 1971, 14 per cent of Scotland's and 1·3 per cent of the British Isles population lived there.

Development Policies

It has long been recognized that from both the social and the economic points of view continued depopulation was a dangerous trend, but it was not until the early 1960s that remedial measures in both the physical and the economic planning sense became matters of urgency.

The peculiar character of the problems experienced by the area led to the appointment of the Highlands and Islands Advisory Panel in 1947 and this was followed in 1949 by the designation of the Moray Firth lowlands as the Highland Development Area. At that time this was the largest rural area to which development area incentives had been applied and it was chosen because it was felt to be one of the few locations in the highlands where growth could be fostered successfully. Despite these high hopes, however, progress was very slow, in part because this type of legislation was best suited to aiding those areas with an established industrial heritage. During the 1950s and early 1960s White Papers highlighting Highland problems were produced, but little was done other than to extend Development Area Status to the whole region in 1960. The ineffectiveness of this policy in the Highland context and the continued deterioration of the social and economic life of the area led to the establishment of the Highlands and Islands Development Board in 1965. This is an executive body with extensive powers, for example to acquire land, erect buildings, set up businesses and give financial assistance by way of grants and loans. This meant that for the first time something positive could be done to help solve some of the problems found in the western and northern counties of Scotland: Shetland, Orkney, Caithness, Ross and Cromarty, Sutherland, Inverness and Argyll. The other counties in the highland area remained under the control of the established regional and local authorities.

In addition, the Forestry Commission, the Department of Agriculture and Fisheries and the Scottish Tourist Board, have each undertaken many schemes, some in co-operation with the Highland Board, to encourage growth and development in the area.

As can be seen there was a marked change in the climate of opinion on regional economic planning during this period away from simple preoccupation with alleviating unemployment and towards a much wider understanding of the basic problems, and from this change the area derived much benefit. Thorough studies of the social and economic development of the region have been made, and ways of alleviating its problems and utilizing its potentialities have been explored.

Present Economy and Future Prospects

AGRICULTURE

Three different types of farm economy can be recognized within the Highlands—the arable and cattle rearing farms of the Moray Firth and Aberdeenshire lowlands, the large sheep and cattle rearing estates of the mainland mountain areas, and the crofting settlements scattered along the west coast and on the islands.

Arable and Livestock Farming

The Old Red Sandstone rocks and the eroded schists of the Buchan Plateau on the southern shore of the Moray Firth form the only extensive lowland area in the Highlands. The soils derived from these parent materials, particularly from the Old Red Sandstone, are quite fertile and this, in conjunction with the long hours of sunshine and low rainfall of the area, has proved ideal for grain and grass cultivation. Barley is grown for the numerous local whisky distilleries while oats are grown mainly for cattle fodder. The rearing of cattle is of great importance in the farm economy in this and the surrounding upland areas. This is the main beef cattle rearing and fattening region in Scotland with over one quarter of the country's total beef livestock. Dairy farming is limited to those districts adjacent to the main urban centres, particularly Aberdeen and Inverness, as is fruit and vegetable farming (apart from the concentration around the processing plant at Fochabers).

Under the prevailing economic conditions livestock farming will continue to be the most profitable specialization in this area, but greater returns could be gained if farm units were enlarged and up-to-date methods more widely applied. Changes of this nature will, however, result in a marked decline in the agricultural labour force; this is already beginning to take place, and must be counterbalanced by increased industrial job opportunities if the out-migration of people from the area is not to become even more serious than it is at present.

Estate Land

Over much of the mainland the large estates created in the eighteenth and early nineteenth centuries still remain and although sheep farming is not as important on these as it was previously it is still the dominant farming activity. Changes are, however, taking place with the re-introduction of cattle on an ever increasing scale in response to the growing demand for beef and to the recognition of the important role cattle can play in improving grazing land. This resurgence of interest in cattle rearing owes much to the establishment in 1944 of the Great Glen Cattle Ranch. In addition to the use of advanced animal husbandry techniques this project also involved the amalgamation of holdings, land improvement and land reclamation. These undertakings necessitated the employment of a large labour force and illustrated the contribution which could be made to the local economy by a landowner with large amounts of capital to invest. Lack of capital on the necessary scale has meant that other estate owners have been unable to emulate this scheme in full, but the methods used have been copied by others working on much smaller areas.

The future prosperity of farming on these large estates depends in part on the expansion of cattle rearing and associated land improvement schemes; it also involves the question of the land-use priorities of the landowners involved. These estates extend over such large areas that farming has got to compete with forestry, deer forests and grouse moors, all of which are of considerable importance in the economic management of each unit. A simple subdivision of the land between these different uses is not possible due to the fact that, depending on the suitability of the land and the likely economic returns, they may be intermixed or in direct competition for the land available.

Deer Forests

The use of a large proportion of Highland land, 1·2 million hectares (2·9 million acres), as deer forest has always been a controversial subject, particularly in the past when participation in the sport of stalking was limited to the landowners and their friends. At the present time, however, deer stalking is much more of a commercial venture. Its economic contribution to the area is twofold: it supplies a growing continental market with venison; and it provides a recreational resource of some significance. As a land-use it has major drawbacks. For effective operation a deer forest has to be very extensive and does not readily mix with other land uses. This, at least, partially, limits the type of multiple use possible over vast tracts of land. For instance, it is not possible to extend commercial forestry into these areas as young trees have to be protected from deer and other animal damage. The close planting characteristic of commercial forestry is not suitable for deer and makes far from ideal stalking country. Sheep and cattle are not, however, precluded from deer forest areas, but their numbers have to be restricted in order to avoid overgrazing of the hill tops. Many of these would in any case be exclusively deer territory as they would be inaccessible to the less agile and less mobile animals.

Grouse Moors

Like deer forests grouse moors are recreational resources of considerable economic importance despite the fact that they are used by a limited section of the population. These extensive areas are located mainly in the eastern highlands, whereas the deer forests are in the west. As the demand for outdoor recreation pursuits increases it is expected that more and more people will come to participate in the sport of grouse shooting; walking will probably continue, however, to be the main use of the open moors. The expansion of commercial forestry onto, or an increase in the numbers of sheep and cattle on, these moors would be in conflict with the need to maintain an environment suitable for grouse breeding and feeding.

If present trends continue there will be more rationalization of the uses to which estates are put. Assessments of the social and economic benefits to be derived from the various possible land uses will have to be made. Careful management will then allow the realization of the potentialities of these areas in terms of agricultural practices and recreational resources and bring about a balance between them.

Crofting

Of the three main agricultural types found in the Highlands crofting is the only one peculiar to that region. It involves an estimated 60,000 people working 20,000 crofts in approximately 700 widely dispersed townships along the western and northern seaboard, in the Outer Hebrides, on Skye and on Orkney and Shetland. The croft is a small parcel of enclosed ground between one-half and two hectares (one and five acres) in size which it was hoped would provide the basis for self-sufficiency in those remote communities. This was possible, at a subsistence level, as long as all the crofts in the community were worked, part-time fishing was actively pursued and the other communal activities such as peat cutting, livestock herding and building were kept up.

Oats and potatoes were, and still are, the basic crops grown on the crofts although other vegetables are becoming increasingly important. These are grown on land which, although divided from the adjacent croft by stone walls, is not internally subdivided. This system is a result of the irregularity and smallness of the patches of cultivable soil available. Together these factors make the unit difficult to work and prohibit the introduction of machinery. The croft remains a hand-worked agricultural unit. In addition to the enclosed area each croft has a defined right of grazing on the adjacent common land which allowed a certain number of sheep and cattle to be kept by each crofter. The arrangement was jealously preserved in the old days, but has subsequently lapsed, resulting in serious overstocking of the common lands and a growing imbalance between sheep and cattle numbers.

Working the land, however, has never been a full-time occupation in these areas; crofters have always depended to some extent on ancillary activities such as fishing and weaving. At the present time very few families are supported by the croft and supplementary activities have grown more and more important. These are no longer only in the traditional occupations, but are mainly in service provision such as shops, in hotels, forestry and the skilled trades.

The future of the crofting counties is not very bright since the prevailing hereditary tenure system mitigates against the amalgamation of holdings. Because of this, one possible solution to the problem of maintaining these communities is lost and the only future for crofting would therefore appear to lie in the production of vegetables and milk for the increasing number of tourists visiting the area. This would provide a steady cash income which would do much to increase the standard of living of the people in these communities.

More radical changes are, however, necessary if the area is to be revitalized. The Highlands and Islands Development Board have sponsored a bulb industry on croft land in North Uist (which followed an earlier unsuccessful private venture in Tiree) whose success indicates one possibility for the future.

FISHING Fishing is traditionally closely associated with the crofting way of life, but has declined markedly in recent years: there are now 900 crofters, mainly from Skye, the Outer Hebrides, Shetland and Orkney actually involved on a part-time basis.

Full-time fishing with processing and other ancillary activities is a basic industry in numerous small towns from Aberdeen to Lossiemouth and in several towns and villages elsewhere along the east coast. On the west coast and in the western islands full-time fishing is carried on from only a few settlements notably Campbeltown, Tarbert, Mallaig and Stornoway. Most of the fish landed at the west coast ports of Kinlochbervie, Lochinver, Ullapool, Gairloch and Oban, however, comes from boats registered in east coast ports. The absence of rapid transport links with southern markets is a major handicap to the expansion of fishing in the north-west. This is also true of the Shetland Islands where fishing and agriculture form the backbone of the economy.

Apart from the Aberdeen fleet Highland fishing is almost exclusively inshore, mainly for herring and smaller amounts of haddock and plaice. Depending on the state of the market these may be filleted, or smoked, or converted into fishmeal. At the present time the industry is barely holding its own due to increasing foreign competition and over-fishing. The need to foster this traditional activity has led the government to provide substantial grants to help buy new boats and equipment since these are essential if fishing is to maintain its important position in the economy of the region.

Aberdeen is the centre of the Scottish trawl fishery, but despite the fact that the port has been modernized to facilitate quick handling and processing of fish for despatch south by train and lorry, it has also encountered problems in recent years. These are due to increased competition from the English trawling ports, the growing number of freezer trawlers now in operation, over-fishing of the northern waters and low fish prices. The cumulative effect of these has been the virtual stagnation of the industry with little prospect of growth in the near future.

FORESTRY At the beginning of the twentieth century little remained of the forest which formerly covered the entire country. A few progressive land-owners, mainly in the Grampian Mountains, had undertaken a limited amount of re-afforestation during the nineteenth century, but this was largely cut over during the First World War.

Forestry Commission

The virtual absence of a native timber supply and the consequent dependence on overseas suppliers prompted the government, in 1919, to establish the Forestry Commission in an attempt to increase the production of home grown timber. Despite the setback during the Second World War when much of the existing timber was felled the state now owns a high proportion of the country's forested area. In the Highlands it owns some 143,200 hectares (358,000 acres): this together with the 108,800 hectares (272,000 acres) under private management accounts for 5·5 per cent of the land area.

Forestry is regarded as possibly the best way to maintain a minimum level of rural population in the region since it provides all the year round employment. The total number of people employed in the industry as forest workers, contractors, haulage workers and sawmill workers is 4,500, and this number will continue to increase as the forested area expands. The Commission buys land which is suitable for tree planting wherever it becomes available and has come to play a very important role in preserving, revitalizing and establishing small communities throughout the Highlands. This side effect of forestry is welcomed by everyone, but in other fields the Commission has not received similar acclaim.

The Forestry Commission naturally prefers to make any single forest as large as possible in order to maximize the return from the capital invested and to provide full employment for the labour force. On this point, however, the Commission has come into conflict with the agriculturalists and sports interests who wish to preserve the seasonal movement of animals between the valleys and the mountain tops. Because of this forest stands are for the most part on a relatively small scale. Criticism has also been encountered from tourist and local amenity organizations who feel that the sombreness of the planted forest is detrimental to scenic beauty and makes poor walking country.

Planting by private individuals is usually on a much smaller scale than that by the Forestry Commission. Because of this they blend more readily into the existing countryside and do not conflict with amenity, sporting and agricultural interests to any great extent.

A recent study of British forestry has, however, pointed to the great tourist potential of these areas, and has indicated that the social benefits to be derived from the development of tourist activities could be considerable.

TRADITIONAL INDUSTRIES

Textile manufacture and whisky distilling are perhaps the two activities most closely associated with the Highlands.

Textiles

The Hebridean 'Harris Tweed' industry is of considerable local importance. It has its focus in Stornoway, but is found on a smaller scale in most settlements in Lewis and Harris. The tweed is protected by its registered trademark and has a world-wide market. Tweed is also produced in Oban while on the east coast textiles are manufactured at Elgin and Keith. The Shetland knitwear industry is not as well protected from competition as the Harris Tweed industry, but nevertheless forms an important cottage industry on these islands.

Whisky

The whisky industry has grown tremendously in response to both national and international demand. Most of the distilleries are located on the Moray Firth lowland in Banffshire and Moray, with a secondary concentration in Skye, but others are to be found scattered throughout the region. The labour force employed in this industry is, however, limited due to the separation of distilling from blending and bottling; the latter employs far more people and is located in the central lowlands of Scotland.

The New Approach

The foregoing account has highlighted the dilemma facing Highland development at the present time. The traditional activities of the area no longer provide an adequate living for the people dependent on them and this is resulting in many, mainly the young who are so vital for the future of the region, leaving in search of a higher standard of living elsewhere in Britain and overseas. The problem facing the authorities, however, is not merely to bring this drift to a halt, but to revitalize the area completely in order that it can effectively contribute to the economic and social well-being of Scotland and the British Isles as a whole. There seems little chance of achieving this goal within the framework of the traditional activities since the introduction of new techniques and increased efficiency would probably throw even more people out of work. A partial answer has been found in the expansion of forestry activities and in a few of the projects sponsored by the Highlands and Islands Development Board, but a more radical solution is required. The provision of a job is not enough, it must be the right kind of job, and it must be backed up with an attractive social environment. Good housing, adequate services and improved accessibility are as important as work. Faced with this problem the various development authorities in the Highlands have decided to follow a policy of urban expansion since new jobs and improved living conditions can be most readily provided in the larger settlements.

FORT WILLIAM

The success of a policy of this kind has already been proven at Fort William and Kinlochleven where, from a very small beginning in 1896, aluminium smelting, using local Hydro Electric Power, provided an industrial base around which thriving communities could develop.

The new pulp mill, opened in 1966 at nearby Corpach, has considerably strengthened the local employment situation. This is a new industry to Scotland and reflects the growing importance of forestry in the Highlands. At the present time, however, much of the raw lumber has to be imported, but as supplies of home-grown wood increase imports will decline.

The major industrial development and several much smaller concerns have been mainly responsible for the 27 per cent increase in Fort William's population during the 1960s and for the much more dramatic growth recorded in the adjacent districts.

THURSO–WICK

Since the opening, in 1954, of the Atomic Reactor Station at Dounreay ther has been a dramatic increase in the population of the surrounding districts. Fo example, between 1951 and 1966 the population of nearby Thurso grew fron 3,249 to 9,360. This influx, mainly of highly paid and highly trained people has necessitated the construction of some 2,000 new houses, the expansion o existing shopping and service facilities, and improved educational facilities Several small firms have been attracted to the district to capitalize on its ne found prosperity and further industrial growth is being actively fostered by th local authorities and the Highlands and Islands Development Board. Thes new industries are very necessary since the community is faced with collaps when the reactor ceases to be operational. There is therefore some doubt abou

Plate 75 Loch Long (Dunbartonshire)
An example of one of the limited number of modern industrial establishments in the Highlands. The picture shows an oil installation on a west coast sea-loch. The complex acts as a terminal supplying Grangemouth on the Forth estuary.

the long-term future of the district especially if a second reactor or some other forms of employment are not forthcoming. The government have, however, made it clear that they are very conscious of the possible consequences of any future policy decisions they may take.

INVERNESS–INVERGORDON

Inverness (30,410—1966), the capital of the Highlands, has long been the recipient of people from the rest of the region. In the past, however, this has often only been an intermediate move before out-migration to other parts of the country; much greater efforts are now being made to retain these people and to attract others back to the city.

In addition to its role as a service, administrative, educational and legal centre, Inverness has woollen mills, distilleries and light engineering firms. More recently there has been much industrial development particularly in the modern and highly sophisticated engineering and electrical goods sectors.

The possibilities of further expansion at Inverness seem very good and also at nearby Invergordon which has good communication facilities, extensive sites suitable for industrial development and a deep anchorage. These assets were of considerable importance in the location there of a new aluminium smelter, opened in 1971, with an annual capacity of 102,000 metric tons (100,000 long tons). This is a very significant industrial development which, it is hoped, will attract other firms to the area. The fact that the anchorage could take tankers of up to 200,000 metric tons (198,000 long tons) has resulted in numerous schemes for the establishment of an oil refinery, but these have as yet been unsuccessful although the recent discovery of large oil reserves under the North Sea could have important repercussions in the district.

ABERDEEN

Despite its regional importance and considerable size, Aberdeen (184,000—1966) has stagnated in recent years. Its long established industries, fishing and fish processing, shipbuilding, papermaking and granite finishing have declined in importance offsetting slight increases in light engineering and port activities. Considerable efforts are being made to attract new industries to the city in an attempt to prevent any further loss of population, but up until the present these have not been very successful. The prospect of new development is, however, offered by the growth of oil exploration in the North Sea. Aberdeen has emerged as the main depot for the northern concessions. This has already given rise to a small increase in employment and could result in a considerable expansion of both service and manufacturing facilities to meet the needs of this new industry.

THE SMALL BURGHS

In addition to these more dramatic growth schemes smaller industrial developments have been fostered in most highland towns—clothing, pottery and printing in Dunoon; clothing in Rothesay and Campbeltown; printing, publishing, seaweed processing and glass making in Oban; glass in Wick; food processing in Elgin, Keith, Huntly, Turriff and Fochabers; boatbuilding in many east coast towns. These represent a blend of traditional and new industries and offer an increasing choice of employment in districts with high unemployment rates.

Future Prospects

Over the past ten years a vigorous attempt has been made to find a solution to the Highland Region's main problem, depopulation. To date the proliferation of small enterprises in the urban communities has been successful in reducing the level of out-migration, but only the major industrial projects, the Atomic Reactor, the pulp mill and the aluminium smelter have attracted people into the region. This is an important pointer to the future since it is industries such as these, particularly those with a strong growth potential, which could put the economy of the region on a much sounder basis.

At the present time the Highlands lack industries of this kind, but with the discovery of an extensive oil field in the North Sea off the north-east coast and off the Shetland Islands, there is the possibility that the refining and chemical industries could be developed. The fact that these are growth industries could be of great significance in attracting people and capital into the region. Aberdeen and the Shetland Islands have already emerged as depots for the drilling operations, but processing is a far more lucrative activity. To secure this part of the industry the Highlands will have to compete with the established centres in other parts of the United Kingdom and Europe. This is the challenge that will have to be met if the regional authorities hope to do more than simply keep the loss of population to a minimum.

Tourism is another industry which the region must exploit to a far greater extent than it does at the present time. An important feature of this industry is that it brings business not only to the settlements, but also to the smaller communities where employment opportunities are even more limited. Hotels and other services required by the tourists provide work for both men and women, but this is often only on a seasonal basis. With the increase in the number of tourists visiting the region much is being done to improve the facilities available, but this has tended to be on a small scale and scattered over a very wide area. Improvement must be intensified and extended; in addition more custom-built centres, such as that at Aviemore, which cater to both summer and winter visitors need to be developed. Centres such as this provide all year round employment for the local people and bring in much needed money. The expansion of the tourist industry could also provide an answer to some of the problems experienced by crofters and other farmers in the region, since the increased market for fresh vegetables and milk could be supplied locally.

It is to be hoped that developments based on these potentials will, during the next few years, alleviate the area's immediate problems and provide a secure foundation for its future economic and social well-being.

The Southern Uplands

The region can be divided into two distinct units, 'The Borders' to the east of Nith Valley and Galloway to the west (Fig. 82). The former has strong histori-

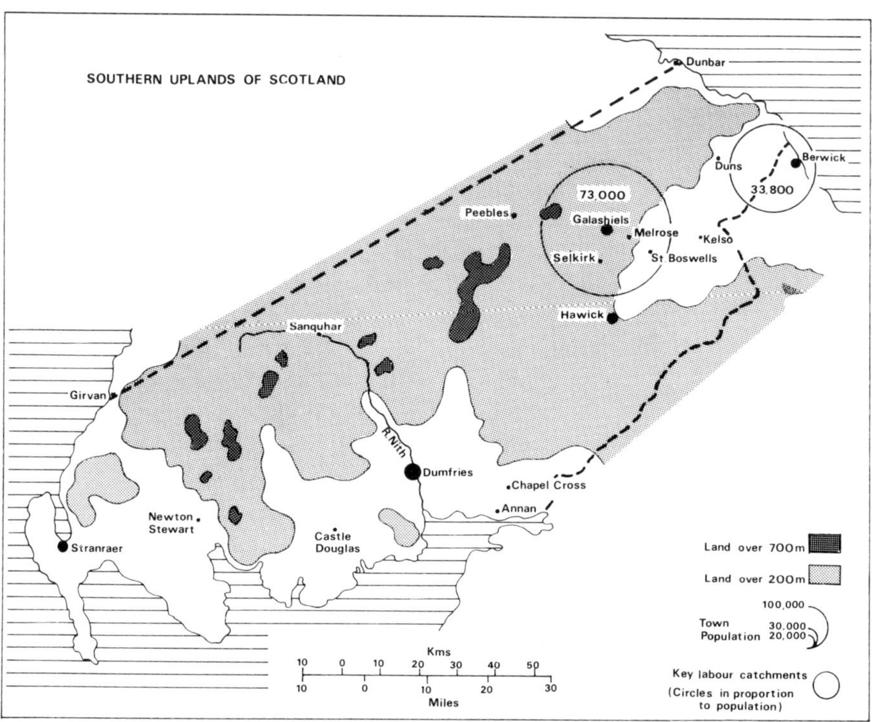

Fig 82 Relief and the Distribution of Urban Population in the Southern Uplands
This map illustrates the dominant upland character of the region and the wide scatter of urban centres where industry could best be established.

cal ties with Edinburgh and the Lothians lying as it does across the shortest route between the Scottish capital and England, whereas the latter, lying away from the early routeways, developed slowly in isolation, but eventually came to have closer links with Glasgow.

The Borders

POPULATION

Depopulation is the main problem facing the area at the present time. This is taking place not only from the rural parts (which contain almost 50 per cent of the total population of 125,000—1961) to the urban communities, but also from these settlements to other parts of the United Kingdom. The special characteristic of the depopulation of the region is that besides thinning out the population of the countryside it has also, to an extent unparalleled elsewhere in Britain, eroded the demographic stability of the main towns. The proportion of young people in the population is well below the Scottish average and the number of married women of child bearing age has fallen so much that if the current levels of migration continue the number of births will soon be insufficient to balance the deaths in the population. The proportion of the population in the older age groups, on the other hand, is well above the national average.

AGRICULTURE

Sheep farming is the dominant activity on the higher ground and gives way on the lower slopes to farm units on which cattle, sheep and crops are equally important. The richest farmland is 'The Merse'—a triangular lowland in the lower valley of the River Tweed. Here as much as 50 per cent of the land is under cereal production, mainly barley for beef fattening; potatoes are also widely grown. Cash cropping, however, is everywhere less important than animal husbandry.

The agricultural development of the area has resulted in large units which are highly mechanized and whose activities complement one another. The farms are among the most heavily stocked in the country. Sheep and cattle are either bred or bought in, fattened, and then sold for final fattening in other parts of the United Kingdom. Improved techniques and a small amount of farm amalgamation is resulting in a slight decline in labour demand; unemployment remains low in this sector of the area's economy, however, due to out-migration.

TEXTILES

The textile industry in the Borders, centred on Galashiels, Hawick and Selkirk, specializes in high quality woollen goods, especially tweeds and knitwear, and provides employment for 12,000 people (or about one-third of the working population of the Borders). Although at the present time the labour force is equally split between the tweed and the hosiery sectors this has not always been the case. Formerly the tweed industry employed far more than hosiery, but it has shown little growth during the past fifteen years, owing mainly to the small scale of the various firms involved. Because of this production costs are high and this has forced firms to concentrate on the manufacture of smal amounts of high quality goods, about 50 per cent of which are exported. Expansion of the industry would require investment beyond the means of the existing firms and an increased labour force to make full use of new machinery. Since workers are already being brought in from outside the area, expansion of this kind is unlikely.

The hosiery industry, on the other hand, has grown slightly during the last decade. It produces medium to high quality garments—dresses, socks and underwear—mainly in wool, and specializes in the use of cashmere. Again almost 50 per cent of the output is exported. This side of the textile industry is more attractive to female labour than the tweed industry. However, further expansion will be hampered by the local shortage of workers.

Future Prospects

At the present time the Borders present a picture of an area with a healthy agricultural base, a stagnating textile industry and a particularly unbalanced demographic structure. Out-migration does not have any detrimental effects on agriculture, but depopulation and industry are caught up in a cause and effect syndrome. The absence of an internal growth point to which both people and industry could be attracted is thought to have been an important factor in producing this situation and in an attempt to reverse population and industrial trends in the area a large urban development between Galashiels and Melrose was proposed in the 1960s and is now under construction. It is hoped that this will provide the Borders with a much needed economic and social focus.

Galloway

Galloway is an area in which the effects of a declining rural population have been largely offset by increases in local urban communities, particularly in Dumfries and in the south Ayrshire towns. The demographic structure is balanced and natural growth steady, which augurs well for the future. The total population of the area in 1961 was 194,976.

AGRICULTURE

This is the most important industry in the region. There is little land suitable for extensive arable cultivation, but the mild climate is ideal for cattle grazing. The long grazing season and the fact that winter feed can be grown locally accounts for the importance of dairy farming. Milk can, therefore, be produced cheaply which means that despite the high transport costs it can be readily marketed throughout northern England and central Scotland. Almost 60 per cent of the farms in the area have a dairy specialization, the remainder, mainly those on higher ground, depend on cattle and sheep rearing, the animals being sold to other parts of the United Kingdom for fattening.

Activities associated with agriculture, such as milk processing, slaughter houses, bacon factories, auction markets, animal feed mills and agricultural engineers are found in towns throughout the south-west.

Food and drink industries are also widely scattered throughout the area making butter, cream, cheese, powdered milk and soft drinks.

INDUSTRY Industrial employment opportunities in Galloway are limited by both the restricted range of firms and their small size.

The textile industry, tweeds and hosiery, employs over 2,000 workers mainly in Dumfries, Cumnock and Newton Stewart. The chemical industry has shown the greatest increase in employment in recent years as a result of the opening of the atomic reactor station at Chapel Cross and developments by Imperial Chemical Industries at Dumfries. Metal using industries are poorly represented in the area, boilermaking is found at Annan, agricultural engineering at Dumfries and Castle Douglas and radiators are made at Dalbeatie.

Local service industries provide the only other sources of employment.

Future Prospects

During the past decade Galloway has attracted the attention of central government agencies who are becoming increasingly aware of the area's incipient industrial/economic problems and the fact that without help these could develop rapidly. As a result great efforts are being made to attract new industries through the provision of factory space and by emphasizing the availability of a plentiful labour supply in the area.

Plate 76 Loch Trool (Kirkcudbrightshire)
Galloway has high tourist potential. New motor routeways are likely to make such fine ice-moulded scenery as this in the Glentrool Forest Park more accessible to the population centres of western Scotland and north-west England.

The tourist industry of the south-west is also receiving greater attention. At the present time this industry is on quite a small scale having suffered in the past because of the area's relative isolation. The completion of the M.6–A.74 motorway will, however, bring it within easy reach of the large population concentrations in western Scotland and north-western England. The holiday and recreation industry of Galloway has a very bright future as society becomes more affluent and has greater amounts of leisure-time (Plate 76). This would provide a much needed boost to Galloway since the development of the area's tourist potential will not only provide employment and bring in much needed capital, it will also provide the necessary incentive for the maintenance and development of services for the rural community.

Galloway is therefore at a cross-roads since without development either in manufacturing industry or tourism, or both, the stability exhibited by the population of the area at the present time will give way to decline. Every effort is being made to prevent this and if successful the future of Galloway will be quite bright.

FURTHER READING

British Association, *The North-East of Scotland* (Aberdeen, 1963).

British Association, *Scientific Survey of South-Eastern Scotland* (Edinburgh, 1951).

Highlands and Islands Development Board: Annual Reports 1966 to 1972 (H.M.S.O., Inverness).

North-East Scotland: A Study of its Development Potential (H.M.S.O., Edinburgh, 1969).

A. C. O'Dell and K. Walton, *The Highlands and Islands of Scotland* (Edinburgh, 1962).

The Scottish Economy 1965–1970: A Plan for Expansion Cmnd. 2864 (H.M.S.O., 1966).

Scottish Development Department, *The Strategy for South-West Scotland* (H.M.S.O., Edinburgh, 1970).

Third Statistical Account of Scotland:

The City of Aberdeen (H. Mackenzie, 1953).

County of Argyll (C. M. Macdonald, 1961).

County of Banff (H. Hamilton, 1961).

County of Dumfries (G. Houston, 1962).

Counties of Moray and Nairn (H. Hamilton, 1965).

Counties of Peebles and Selkirk (J. M. Urquhart, 1964).

D. Turnock, *Patterns of Highland Development* (London, 1971).

Northern Ireland

When the Irish Free State was founded in 1920, six counties in north-eastern Ireland remained part of the United Kingdom. These counties formed Northern Ireland, a province which is partly self-governing, since it has an assembly of its own concerned with local affairs. It also returns 12 members to the House of Commons at Westminster. As a result Northern Ireland represents an early experiment in the regional devolution of government within the United Kingdom, although it was not explicitly established for this reason but more as an attempt at political compromise, given the difficulties of reaching a settlement of the Irish problem.

The Political Distinctiveness of Northern Ireland

A basic question in Irish political geography is why two separate states should have arisen in a small island not marked by any major physical division. Certainly, the frontier between the Irish Republic and Northern Ireland bears little relation to geographical reality. An attempt to draw an acceptable line between those people who wished for a close connection with Great Britain and those who did not, essentially failed. Northern Ireland was produced by the mere grouping together of pre-existing counties, which owed their origins to the sixteenth century rather than to the twentieth. It is not surprising, therefore, that the detailed location of the frontier is artificial in both a physical and human sense, as a study of any atlas map will show. The basin of the river Foyle is split, the outlet of the Lough Erne drainage system is cut off, the zones of influence of the towns of Londonderry and Newry are broken by the border, to cite only a few examples. Neither does the border reflect any exact division of loyalties, since areas with majorities opposed to union with Britain are found within Northern Ireland. Yet the partition of Ireland does symbolize real divergencies of political views; and these, in their turn, are a symptom of the regional consciousness that exists in the northern part of Ireland.

THE PLANTATION OF ULSTER

Regional consciousness is partly an expression of the proximity of north-east Ireland to Scotland. The influence of Scotland can be picked out at a number of times in the early history of Ireland, but the origins of the modern situation date from the beginning of the seventeenth century, when the northern part of Ireland became more vulnerable to rule by the British crown, after the king of Scotland also became king of England. Thus in the first few years of the rule of James I much of Antrim and Down, where settlers from Britain were already

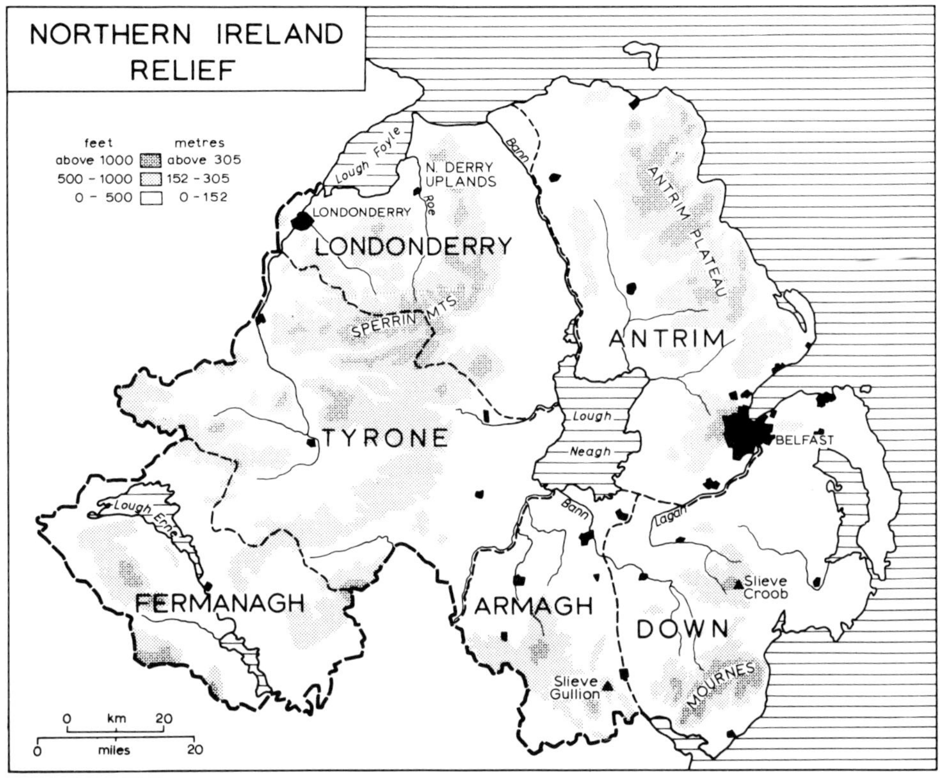

Fig 83 Northern Ireland—Relief and Places mentioned in the Text
Northern Ireland was established in 1920, by the grouping together of six pre-existing counties. The presence of the city of Belfast provided a centre around which this separate province of the United Kingdom could function, although separated from the rest of Ireland.

found, was appropriated by a few influential Scottish and English landlords and the grip of the Crown was tightened on the rest of Ulster. Then in 1607 an extensive, government-organized colonization of the remaining counties of Ulster was commenced, involving the introduction of English and Scottish settlers into Donegal, Londonderry, Cavan, Fermanagh, Tyrone and Armagh.

Not all the native Irish were driven away from these counties, since their labour was needed on the estates of the settlers; but certainly the effectiveness of occupation varied. In Cavan and Donegal, two of the agriculturally-poorest areas settled, the number of colonists was less than elsewhere; and in Monaghan the government-sponsored scheme was not applied. It is not without relevance that these three counties (which form part of the historic province of Ulster) now lie outside Northern Ireland. From the point of view of later political events, the most important result of the Plantation, as the process of occupation was called, lay in the introduction of Protestantism; and since immigrants at all levels of society were brought in, Protestantism became more firmly rooted in the 'planted' counties and in Antrim and Down than elsewhere in Ireland.

The Protestant group was not without its internal divisions: many of the new settlers were Presbyterians from lowland Scotland, whereas those from England were often Anglicans. Historically there were important distinctions between these two groups. The Presbyterians, for example, nursed a sense of grievance against the British government during the eighteenth century because of the religious disabilities which they suffered along with their Catholic neighbours. Or again, the ultra-protestant Orange Order was originally associated with members of the Anglican church and was directed against Presbyterian dissenters as well as Catholics. But during the nineteenth century both Protestant groups became more united in the face of the growth

Plate 77 Part of Central Belfast

This view of a small corner of central Belfast gives an indication of the late nineteenth century prosperity on which much of the growth of the city was based. The modern piece-meal redevelopment also visible here indicates the relative commercial prosperity of this area within Northern Ireland still continues. Indeed, the major planning problem of Northern Ireland is to steer new employment away from Belfast and its immediate zone of influence, where space for further development is now severely constricted.

of Irish nationalism; and in this developing solidarity a common fear of Catholic dominance was a principal motive. Thus in the long run the religious distributions established during the Plantation were of critical importance in the modern political separation of Northern Ireland from the rest of the island. Today adherence to Roman Catholicism usually means sympathy for Irish nationalism, and the support of the Unionist party (which is dedicated to maintaining unity with Britain) comes from the Protestant community.

THE GROWTH OF MANUFACTURING AND OF BELFAST

A further element in the emergence of regional consciousness in north-east Ireland was the coming of the industrial revolution, a process which was almost entirely confined to the north-east. The details of manufacturing industry in Northern Ireland will be discussed later, but in the meantime it is sufficient to record that the nineteenth century industrial background of north-east Ireland coloured the political views of many influential Ulstermen.

The products of Ulster's factories, owing to their specialist nature and to the small market within Ireland, were sold almost entirely outside the country, mainly in Britain but also throughout the world. In addition, nearly all the raw material used by these industries had to be imported. The idea of an industrial north of Ireland complementary to an agricultural south is a myth that dies hard in Irish political folklore, but in fact the nature of industry and its economic orientation made northern businessmen value a close political connection with Great Britain even more highly. A protected Irish market had little attraction for men dealing in exports, and their wishes were made more effective politically by the concentration of manufacturing in the north-east.

The growth of the city of Belfast also contributed to the establishment of Northern Ireland. The great nineteenth-century expansion of this city, when it grew from 50,000 people in 1831 to 350,000 in 1901, was intimately connected with the development of manufacturing industry; but at the same time this rapidly growing settlement attracted functions other than industry (Plate 77). By the end of the century it possessed its own financial institutions, it was a centre of professional life and was the obvious mecca for the Presbyterian community in Ireland. By this time, too, it was the centre of the local network of roads, railways and shipping routes, and it possessed secondary schools, libraries and hospitals, as well as a flourishing university. As a result, when various interests in the north of Ireland wished to disassociate themselves from the newly-formed Irish Free State in 1920, Belfast was available both as a focus for the loyalties of the region and as a large accessible centre around which a separate province could be organized.

Looked at broadly, most of Northern Ireland lies within what might be called the Ulster Basin, centred on Lough Neagh and formed of the drainage system of the river Bann and its tributaries. Historically, access to this basin has been provided through the lower Lagan valley and through gaps in the basalt escarpment to the north of Belfast. It is in this wide region of north-eastern Ireland and on the eastern coast that the strongest cultural links have become established with Great Britain. A narrower strip of the province lies to the west of the Ulster Basin in Fermanagh and in parts of Tyrone and Londonderry; and, significantly, the majority of the population of this western area least values the connection with the United Kingdom, both politically and socially.

Topographical Contrasts within Northern Ireland

In spite of the basically simple topographical arrangement, Northern Ireland contains a remarkable variety of physical landscapes for an area that represents only one-sixth of all Ireland. Some of these regional differences are

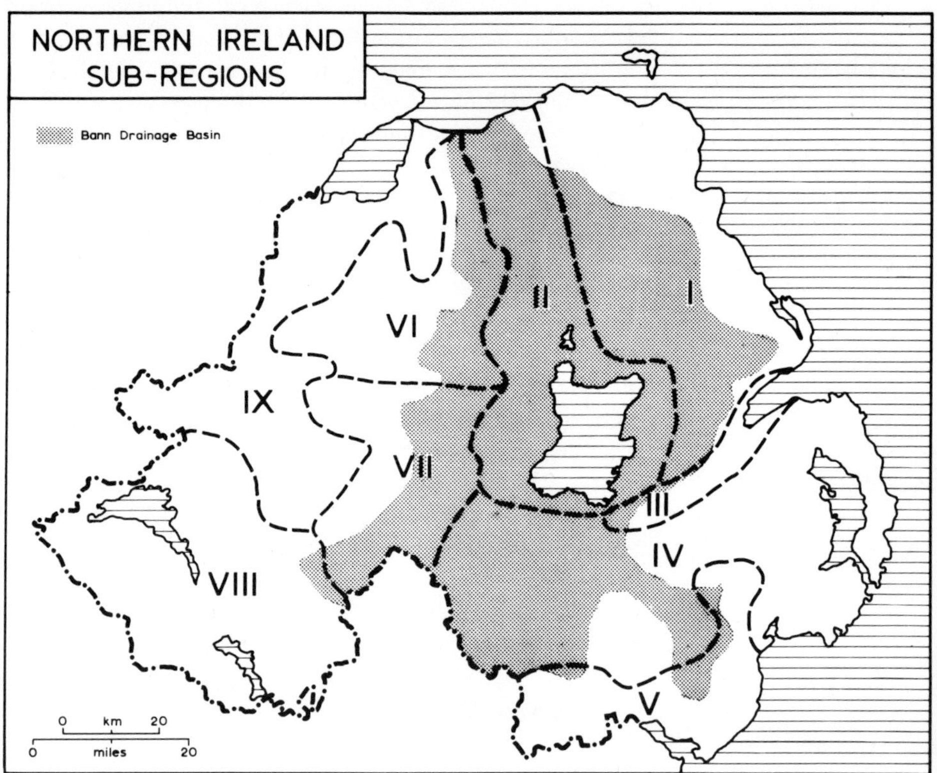

Fig 84 Northern Ireland—Topographical Sub-Regions
- I The Antrim Plateau.
- II The Lower Bann Valley and Lough Neagh Lowlands.
- III The Lagan Corridor.
- IV The Low Hill-Lands of Armagh and Down.
- V The Igneous Uplands of Armagh and Down.
- VI The North Derry Uplands and Sperrin Mountains.
- VII The Mid-Tyrone Plateau.
- VIII The Vale and Plateaux of Fermanagh.
- IX The Foyle Basin.

Most of Northern Ireland lies within what might be called the Ulster Basin, centred on Lough Neagh and formed of the drainage system of the Bann and its tributaries; but in spite of the basically simple topographical arrangement, the province contains remarkable variety in its physical landscapes for an area that is only one-sixth of all Ireland.

summarized in Figure 84, but it should be recalled that within these regions there are many detailed variations which cannot be described here, but which are important in the landscape and life of the countryside.

EASTERN NORTHERN IRELAND

In the north-east of Northern Ireland most of county Antrim is floored by a basalt plateau, with its highest areas lying quite near to the eastern coast (region I). In the north and east of the plateau short streams have bitten deep into the basalt edge; and sombre peat-covered hills dominate the landscape close to this broken coastal escarpment. Further south, at somewhat lower elevations, grassland and rough pasture characterize the agricultural scene of the basalt lands to the north of Belfast, where milk production is the most important agricultural activity. Streams flowing west from the plateau have more gentle profiles; their broad, open valleys form good arable land, particularly where glacial sands alleviate the heavy soils commonly found on the basalt.

To the west of the Antrim Plateau the basalts have sagged to form a long north–south depression, which is occupied by the lower Bann (possibly the only unequivocal consequent stream in Ireland) and by Lough Neagh, the largest lake in the British Isles (region II). In this lowland area glacial deposits again have special significance, providing well-drained agricultural land in a region where a high water-table is commonly present, particularly on the alluvium of the Bann. Along the southern shore of Lough Neagh large peat deposits are particularly characteristic, but many smaller areas of bogland are also found in the lower Bann valley.

The Lough Neagh lowlands are linked with Belfast by the lower Lagan valley, but this corridor region is important in its own right (region III). The Lagan here winds north-eastwards among the glacial sands and gravels that lie on Triassic sandstone and marls. The resulting light and easily-worked soils and the nearby presence of the Belfast market make the Lagan Corridor one of the best agricultural regions in Ireland, with vegetables and early potatoes being particularly important.

To the south the low hills of county Down dominate the landscape and this undulating topography extends into county Armagh (region IV). Geologically this region represents a continuation of the Southern Uplands of Scotland, but although a higher plateau rises above 300 metres (1,000 feet) in south Armagh, the metamorphic rocks have normally been reduced to a low peneplain and have been later covered by glacial deposits, often in the form of drumlins. The bogland which formerly lay in the hollows between drumlins has largely been cut-over and drained; and although the underlying rocks occasionally appear through the drift cover to form bare-rock surfaces, much of the region is good farmland with rather more arable than average. In north Armagh apple orchards are characteristic of the drumlin slopes and the preparation of beef cattle for export is also important. Further east, in county Down, mixed farming is the rule, with market gardening and the production of potatoes, barley and grass-seed diversifying the universal emphasis on dairying.

In south Down and south Armagh igneous intrusions have formed an area of high upland (region V). In county Down craggy uplands centred on Slieve Croob are formed of Devonian granite and associated metamorphic rocks. Here moorland dominates the land use pattern. The Slieve Croob upland links up with the foothills of the Mourne Mountains, which are formed of more recent Tertiary granites. The founded summits of the Mournes are often over 600 metres (2,000 feet) high and these uplands provide extensive sheep pastures. Much more important is their role as a recreation area for the city of Belfast and as a catchment area from which this large urban settlement and a number of smaller towns draw most of their drinking water. On the lower hill-slopes conifers have been planted by the Northern Ireland government; and in the foothills small, intensely-cultivated farms often specialize in the commercial production of potatoes (Plate 78). The area of igneous rocks continues into south Armagh, but here the mass of Slieve Gullion, the highest mountain, consists of an intrusion of gabbro, not granite. Drift has been swept round this resistant core by former ice sheets to form a dramatic example of 'crag and tail'. Surrounding the central upland is a ring of lower but barren hills, often formed of dolerite. Government reafforestation has been undertaken on the slopes of Slieve Gullion, but generally this is a bleak area, with small, poor farms on the lower land. Among the farmers in this region ancient traditions have survived, in an area where, in spite of its location in eastern Ireland, poverty has protected it from change.

Plate 78 The Mourne Mountains (County Down)
The summits of the Mournes rise to over 600 metres (2,000 feet). Small farms dominate the foothill zone, and the granite uplands themselves provide extensive sheep pastures. Even more important is their role as a water catchment and recreation area for the city of Belfast.

WESTERN NORTHERN IRELAND

There are equally diverse regions in west Ulster. Immediately to the west of the lower Bann valley the basàlts of Antrim again reappear in county Londonderry, where they form an upland area to the north of the Glenshane Pass. This area of basalt upland is narrower than the Antrim Plateau and rises more steeply from the Bann lowlands. The land use of these North Derry Uplands is dominated by government forestry plantations, now beginning to become productive. The basalt uplands of north Londonderry form a continuous hill mass with the schists of the Sperrin Mountains further south (region VI). The main body of the Sperrins is characterized by rounded summits often over 600 metres (2,000 feet) high, with heather moor grazed by sheep (Plate 79). On the lower hill-slopes government reafforestation has again been important in a few areas (Plate 80); deep glens provide tenuous patches of cultivated land, where traditional farming practices still survive.

Further south, in county Tyrone, the Sperrins become lower, falling eventually to a well-developed planation surface lying between 180 and 240 metres (600 and 800 feet) above sea-level (region VII). Detailed variety is given to the landscape of mid-Tyrone by a variety of glacial drifts, which include kames, eskers and undulating spreads of boulder clay. Cattle rearing dominates the farm economy, with the result that land-use in mid-Tyrone often consists of bogland intermixed with better grazing on the well-drained glacial deposits.

This emphasis on cattle is even stronger in Fermanagh, where Upper and Lower Lough Erne occupy a central vale and where farmland was often liable to flooding before some improvement was brought about by recent drainage schemes (region VIII). Underlying this south-western area of Northern Ireland are horizontal deposits of sandstones, limestones, shales and grits; south-west of the lakes these strata have been faulted into a series of blocks which form a number of sharply-defined plateaux. This is the most remote and most rural part of Northern Ireland, with much less ploughed land than elsewhere and a strong emphasis on milk-production and stock rearing on the damp pastures of Fermanagh.

North of Fermanagh and to the west of the Sperrins lie the lowlands associated with the basin of the river Foyle and its tributaries (region IX). Particularly around the town of Omagh the river has eroded along lines of weakness in the sandstones and shales to form a broad lowland basin, coated with glacial drift. Here farms are larger than usual in county Tyrone, there is more ploughed land, but cattle rearing and milk production remain the most important agricultural activities. Further north, around the mouth of the Foyle, the flood plain of the Foyle joins with the lowland areas along the shores of Lough Foyle and in the Roe valley. In this coastal lowland a post-glacial raised beach rises in two steps and is then backed by an older 15 metres (50 feet) terrace, which is usually formed of fluvio-glacial sands and gravels. Along the coast there is also an area of reclaimed land, first drained in the nineteenth century and restored again in recent years. Here there is some of the best agricultural land of Northern Ireland where the proportion under crops is high, but where the finishing of cattle for sale as beef animals is also an important activity.

Plate 79 Sperrin Mountains (County Tyrone)
The Sperrin Mountains are characterized by rounded summits, with heather moor grazed by sheep. In this photograph there is evidence that cultivation formerly extended further up the mountain slopes. Traditional farmhouses still survive and the emphasis on these upland farms is on rearing store animals.

Plate 80 Slieve Gullion (County Armagh)
This government-planted forest is part of a Northern Ireland Government scheme for the reafforestation of areas that are marginal for agriculture. This policy is designed to replace trees that were removed as a result of earlier indiscriminate cutting and of heavy demand during the two World Wars; to put marginal land into more productive use; to provide new sources of employment; and eventually to provide raw materials for new industries such as saw mills, pulp mills and the manufacture of chipboard. Note the marginal farm and the unimproved land in the distance.

Some Aspects of Agriculture

THE IMPORTANCE OF THE SMALL FARM

This brief regional description hints at some of the variety in agricultural land use in Northern Ireland, but there are some general features that transcend these detailed observations. The most important factor underlying the agricultural geography of Northern Ireland is the small size of agricultural holdings (Plate 81). If those holdings that have been let to other farmers and those that are so small that they are little more than residential plots are excluded, there remain just over 37,000 farm businesses in Northern Ireland. Of these nearly 33,000 have less than 40 hectares (100 acres) under crops and grass (including 23,000 farms with fewer than 20 hectares (50 acres)).

The demands on labour made by different types of farming vary considerably, and so these acreage figures can be interpreted more meaningfully by calculating the number of man-days required to work a farm. The Northern Ireland government assumes that under local conditions there a 'full-time' farm is one which requires 200 man-days to work it satisfactorily. In 1970 only 19,100 farm businesses came up to this standard of size and, of these, just over 11,800 required less than 450 man-days for their cultivation. Many farms are therefore really part-time holdings and gross figures of the agricultural labour force certainly conceal considerable under-employment. These figures also show that the majority of full-time farms can be worked by one man, aided by some help from his immediate family.

The small family farms of Northern Ireland are part of the historical legacy of Ireland: they form the greater part of a belt of small farms that runs across the whole country, north of a line between Galway Bay and Carlingford Lough. The reasons for this distribution are not clear, although there is an

Plate 81 The Rural Landscape, near Strangford Lough (County Down)
Small family farms are a dominant feature of the agriculture of Northern Ireland; so, too, is the production of livestock. This typical view of lowland County Down, gives an impression of the rural landscape in one of the better farmed and more prosperous areas of Northern Ireland.

interesting similarity between this belt of small farms and the great swarm of drumlins which extends over roughly the same area. It may be that the pattern of small patches of good cultivable land produced by this topography influenced the size of farm that could conveniently be established. Whatever the original cause, an important element in preserving the small farm belt in the eighteenth and early nineteenth century was the supplementary income derived from the domestic linen industry that flourished in the north of Ireland. Within Ulster, landlords found it difficult to remove small farmers from their holdings because of the operation of the so-called 'Ulster Custom' of tenant right, which probably dates from the Plantation and among other things, required that a farmer should be compensated by his landlord if evicted. Owner-occupation of farms became normal at the end of the nineteenth century, because of the operation of various land purchase acts, hence fixing the pattern of holding sizes even more firmly in the agricultural landscape.

As a result, these small farms have survived to the present; and in modern commercial farming it is necessary for them to produce a high profit per acre if they are to provide an acceptable standard of living for their owners. This fact is connected with both the nature of farming in Northern Ireland and also

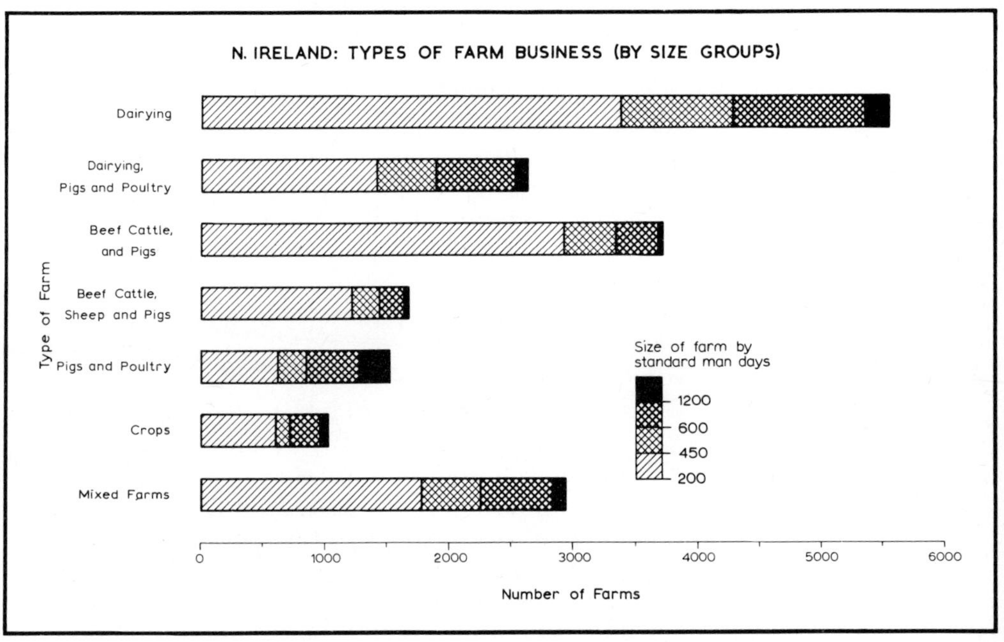

Fig 85 Northern Ireland—Types of Farm Businesses, by Size Groups

The size groups in this diagram are based on the number of man-days that are required to work a particular farm, bearing in mind the types of land use and farm activities that are carried on. As a result this is probably a more meaningful way of assessing size than by area, which could involve land of different quality being used in different ways. A farming 'type' for the purposes of this diagram is defined as an activity from which 60% or more of a farm's income is derived.

with many of its problems. Agriculture in Northern Ireland is dominated by the production of livestock, which represents over 90 per cent of farm income. In fact, this activity includes quite a diversity of types of output: cattle make up about 27 per cent of the total value of livestock and livestock products sold, pigs represent about 25 per cent, eggs and poultry 23 per cent, and milk just over 20 per cent.

These statistics refer to the total farm output, but it is also possible to examine the emphasis of agriculture as it is expressed by types of farm businesses (Fig. 85). If attention is restricted to the 19,100 full-time farm businesses and a farming 'type' is defined as one from which 60 per cent or more of a farm's income is derived, over 5,500 farms depend on dairying, over 2,600 belong to a 'dairying pigs and poultry' type, and nearly 3,800 depend on beef cattle and sheep. (For further details see Figure 85.) In other words, the Northern Ireland farmer depends on four basic commodities: milk, pigs, eggs and beef cattle. These products fit conveniently the demands of the physical and economic environment of agriculture.

THE PHYSICAL AND ECONOMIC ENVIRONMENT OF AGRICULTURE

High levels of humidity, cool summers and relatively limited periods of bright sunshine restrict the ripening period of crops. When the discrepancies produced by relief are discounted, there is a decline in the amount of rainfall from west to east: the lowlands of Fermanagh, Tyrone and much of Londonderry receive over 1,000 millimetres (40 inches) of rain, and similar areas in the east experience less than this amount. As a result the cultivation of grains and greater intensity of cropping are more commonly found in the east; but everywhere grass is the most important crop. Although it is a traditional part of Irish farming 'to take the plough round the farm', only a small proportion of cultivated land is under the plough in any one year.

As a result, enterprises connected with grazing are dominant; but small farmers require ancillary activities in order to bolster their income. Dairying, pigs and poultry represent three agricultural enterprises which are particularly suitable for the small farm economy. With guaranteed prices (a product of the general agricultural policy of the United Kingdom) milk, pigs and eggs provide a regular and relatively valuable income; and, if animal feed is purchased, high outputs can be achieved from small acreages. The rearing of beef cattle is also an important enterprise, and although this represents an extensive use of land for small farmers, in fact the store cattle upon which this type of activity is based are a by-product of dairying, and the fattening of the cattle for market is more often undertaken on larger, specialist farms.

Perhaps surprisingly, individual small farmers in Northern Ireland do not specialize in any one particular activity. A variety of cash products provides some protection against those fluctuations in yields and prices to which a small farmer is especially susceptible. A number of agricultural activities also allows a farmer who is dependent on his own labour, with some assistance from his family, to spread his tasks more evenly through the year. Similarly, the production of poultry and eggs is a job that is traditionally allocated to the farmer's wife, allowing her to make a convenient, but important contribution to the output of the family farm.

As a result there are usually no great regional differences in types of farming, except where the physical environment has imposed particularly severe constraints. For example, sheep are important in the uplands of south Down and south Armagh, in the Sperrins, and in the north-east of the Antrim Plateau. Or again, specialist milk production dominates the ill-drained pastures of Fermanagh and the basalt uplands north of Belfast. Normally, however, differences in emphasis rather than marked agricultural contrasts can be picked out. For example, cattle over two years old (probably being prepared for sale as beef animals) are more common in north-west Londonderry, north Armagh and in the lower Lagan valley. Pig fattening is important in the agricultural lands of Antrim and Down; and poultry has a similar distribution, being most important on small farms in the eastern half of Northern Ireland. Ancillary activities like these are less important among small farmers in the western counties.

Unfortunately it is in the west that the need for these additional sources of farm income is greatest, since here there are fewer possibilities of supplementary urban employment for a farmer's grown-up children; towns are less common and, in any case, urban unemployment is at a relatively high level. Farming is also less intensive, and hence the concealed level of rural underemployment is greater in the west. As a result, the rate of rural emigration from the western counties of Northern Ireland is higher than average, although larger agricultural subsidies and higher social security payments have made these small farms much less susceptible to rural depopulation than equivalent areas in the Irish Republic.

Future prospects offer little encouragement. In those areas where rural depopulation is greatest, there is least chance of intensifying agriculture, partly because of the difficulty of growing successful crops other than grass and because of the remoteness of the western counties from market, in comparison with farmland closer to Belfast. Even in the most accessible parts of rural Ulster, however, it seems clear that the income of most farmers is relatively low. In assessing the profitability of their holdings, Northern Irish farmers often do not compute the value of their own labour very accurately and (as they are owner-occupiers who have bought their farms with cheap mortgages, based on values 60 years ago) they also tend to underestimate the full amount of capital invested in their farms. Even at present the drift from the land would probably be much greater, if it were not for the long-standing difficulties impeding the growth of urban employment in Northern Ireland.

More intensive production only provides a partial solution to the economic problems of the small farms. Higher output would bring in its turn the problems of overproduction of eggs, milk and pigs—a difficulty not unknown elsewhere in western Europe. Solutions involving increased horticulture and more intensive crop production are appropriate only in the environmentally most favoured and most accessible areas in the east. As younger farmers steadily become aware of the commercial implications of their way of life, they are likely either to desert agriculture or to enlarge their holdings. This enlargement of holdings will necessarily be a slow procedure, since those farmers who would most profit from selling out are often loath to surrender their personal independence. Yet sale, amalgamation and depopulation seem to form an inevitable process in most rural areas.

Manufacturing in Northern Ireland

ORIGINS OF MANUFACTURING INDUSTRY

Many of the problems of urban employment in modern Northern Ireland result from the manner in which manufacturing industry developed in north-east Ireland during the nineteenth century. In a sense the very presence of nineteenth century manufacturing industry, let alone its concentration in north-east Ireland, forms somewhat of a problem, since Ireland is devoid of easily worked coal and iron, the traditional 'natural resources' for such a development. In seeking an explanation both the possibility of capital accumulation and the proximity of Scotland are relevant.

The less onerous demands made by landlords as a result of the Ulster Custom on tenant right allowed some farmers to become prosperous, and it was from this class that the small *entrepreneurs* of the domestic linen industry—the bleachers and the merchants—were recruited. As the organization of the domestic industry became more elaborate in the first decades of the nineteenth century, with 'manufacturers' bringing in linen thread spun by machinery in Britain and issuing it to farmer-weavers to make into cloth under contract, the domestic industry became more concentrated in the Lagan valley and the lower Bann valley. The development of the domestic linen industry in the north-east also led to the further accumulation of capital there by people who were willing to invest money in industry. This influence was particularly marked after 1825, when joint-stock banking became possible in Ireland. Significantly enough, the first provincial joint-stock bank was founded in Belfast, and by the middle of the 1830s, although such banks had been diffused throughout Ireland by this time, the numerical concentration in the north-east was still clearly marked.

In fact, cotton and not linen pioneered the introduction of genuine factory industry; and here the close connections between north-eastern Ireland and Scotland were influential, since at least some of the early pioneers knew of conditions in Scotland. For example, the first steam engine used in Ireland was imported from Glasgow in 1790 and installed in a Lisburn cotton mill; by 1811 there were fifteen steam-driven mills in Belfast.

The Irish cotton industry was concentrated in Belfast and in towns immediately around because it depended on imported yarn and fuel, but it was on too small a scale to compete with Lancashire, particularly after protective tariffs were removed in the 1820s. Yet before it died out, it served as a model for the reorganization of the production of linen. The reorganized linen industry was much more firmly based. It could draw workers and techniques from the cotton industry and from an extensive, if decaying, domestic linen industry; as it produced a more expensive fabric than cotton, it could bear the high costs of imported fuel and still be competitive; finally, it had in flax a locally-produced raw material, until the expansion of the industry eventually resulted in demand far exceeding indigenous supplies. Hence existing cotton mills were converted to spinning linen thread, new factories were specially designed, and in the 1850s new power-weaving machinery for producing linen cloth was adopted.

Shipbuilding was firmly added to the industrial structure of the north-east in 1853, but the assured growth of the shipyards came after 1859, when the business was taken over by Edward Harland. Without local coal or iron the expansion of shipbuilding was due to the enterprise and inventiveness of this Scot. Once again a Scottish influence had made its presence felt in the north of Ireland. Indeed in a real sense the shipbuilding industry was a branch of an enterprise that had begun earlier on the Clyde; until as late as the 1880s only the hulls of ships were constructed in Belfast, and engines were imported, mainly from Scotland.

The resulting industrial structure in the north-east was dominated by ships and linen, and by the engineering industry which grew up in association with these two basic industries. Linen weaving had a fairly wide distribution in north-east Ireland, but spinning was more strictly confined to Belfast. Shipbuilding and engineering were even more closely concentrated in this rapidly-growing port and city. Other manufacturing industries also developed here to serve the local concentration of population, but some of these products managed to penetrate British and even overseas markets, in particular cigarettes and tobacco. Manufacturers of ropes and ventilating equipment (both originally linked with shipbuilding) also were able to establish a broader market for their goods. Similarly, the shirt industry of Londonderry had connections with the linen industry and also managed to make progress in the British market.

The industries upon which the wealth of Victorian Belfast was built had a number of things in common. Since the local market in Ireland was a static one, they were dependent on export sales; and imported raw materials also played a dominant role in production. As a result the successful industries were those in which fuel costs, import costs and final delivery costs were low in comparison with the price of the finished product. Unfortunately, the basic industries on which prosperity was based were particularly susceptible to economic fluctuations, since ships and heavy machinery were expensive capital goods and linen was aimed at the luxury end of the consumer market.

MANUFACTURING IN THE TWENTIETH CENTURY

In the twentieth century these fluctuations in demand (and in the level of local industrial employment) became more grave and their solution more intractable. During the great depression of the early 1930s, the demand for linen fell, and although the Second World War brought recovery, post-war competition from man-made fibres became irresistible. In the same way the demand for warships in the late 1930s and early 1940s brought a temporary return of prosperity to the shipyards, but fundamental changes in the technology of transport have meant that the demand for passenger liners, on which the Belfast shipyards made their reputation, has never been re-established.

As a result there have been long-standing attempts by the Northern Ireland government to solve the modern unemployment problem. Government subsidies and guaranteed prices increased the prosperity of agriculture; but, as has already been pointed out, a reduction in rural population is inevitable. Indeed such a reduction is essential if the incomes of individual farmers are to keep pace with their growing expectations. Hence any solution of the unemployment must come from an expansion of the number of jobs in urban areas.

The total population of Northern Ireland has increased slightly since 1937, but a local population of less than 1½ million has meant that any great expansion of the tertiary sector is unlikely, except perhaps in the tourist industry. Government attention has therefore been concentrated on alleviating the problems of existing manufacturing industries, on diversifying the industrial base of the economy and on expanding the total number of jobs available.

Employment in the textile industry has been changed by the conversion of linen-weaving machinery to handle new fibres and by the introduction of suitable alternative industries like carpet manufacturing, warp knitting and the production of various hosiery goods. This broadening of the textile industry

Plate 82 Maydown Works, Londonderry

One of the results of the generous capital grants given to industry by the Northern Ireland Government has been the establishment of six man-made fibre plants in various parts of the Province. This photograph shows a small part of one of the factories established by the firm of Du Pont on the Maydown Industrial Estate outside the city of Londonderry. The 240 hectare (600 acre) industrial estate on which it is located lies on the shores of Lough Foyle and is probably one of the most self-contained estates in the United Kingdom, having its own power station, jetties, water supply and labour training centre.

has been helped by the establishment of six large plants producing man-made fibres of various kinds, located in north Londonderry, Antrim and close to Belfast (Plate 82). Substantial government grants have aided the establishment of these new factories; but although many construction workers are required when the factories are actually being built, once they become operational they employ relatively few people in relation to the amount of capital invested.

Plate 83 Harland and Wolff's Shipyard, Belfast
The Belfast shipbuilding industry now concentrates on the production of bulk carriers, particularly oil tankers. This new building dock has been constructed with government financial assistance; and it is designed to allow huge ships to be floated out, rather than launched by conventional method. To give some idea of scale, the ship in the photograph, the first vessel to be built in the dock, is a 253,000 ton tanker, which is 350 metres (1,150 feet) long, 50 metres (170 feet) wide, and 25 metres (84 feet) deep. In fact the dock is large enough to house a 1,000,000 ton vessel, if it was thought appropriate to construct one.

The shipbuilding industry is also changing and now concentrates on the production of bulk carriers, particularly oil tankers, rather than on passenger or naval vessels. With government assistance a new building dock has been constructed (the largest in the world), so that modern super-tankers can be produced; and production facilities generally have been modernized (Plate 83). Unfortunately these developments mean that a reduced labour force is required, fluctuations in demand will still be likely in the long run, and at present foreign competition is intense and profit margins narrow.

Expansion of employment therefore depends on the introduction of new industries which are expanding and profitable. Government help includes the provision of factories at cheap rents and other financial assistance which is negotiated directly with the particular industrialist involved. A 45 per cent grant can be made towards the cost of new machinery and plant, and various industrial training schemes have been introduced. Since 1950 a total of nearly 70,000 new jobs have been created with government assistance in a diverse range of light industries: new factories connected with electrical and electronic engineering and with food processing using agricultural raw materials have been particularly successful. Unfortunately, as existing employment has been declining at the same time, there has been an increase of only about 20,000 in the total number of jobs available in Northern Ireland. Workers as well as government have taken steps to redress the unemployment figures: from 1951 to 1966 about 130,000 people have left Northern Ireland as emigrants, largely going to Great Britain. Even so unemployment has rarely dropped below 6 per cent of the workforce and has commonly been over 7 per cent. This situation is made even more difficult by the fact that Northern Ireland has the highest rate of natural increase in the British Isles. From 1951 to 1966, for example, natural increase was nearly 250,000; and, as a result, there are a large number of young people now seeking jobs.

SOME CURRENT ECONOMIC DIFFICULTIES

A number of difficulties inherent in the particular context of Northern Ireland have impeded the expansion of employment, in spite of the efforts made by the Westminster and Northern Ireland governments. Civil disturbances have been common since 1968, and although they have seriously affected only limited areas of Belfast and of the city of Londonderry, they have created local tensions that are discouraging overseas industrialists from locating new plants in Northern Ireland. This problem may only be temporary, but more fundamental is the fact that some new industries have not achieved the financial success that was originally expected of them. For example, the manufacture of aircraft was located here during the Second World War, but this industry has remained restricted to one, relatively small, independent firm, which has failed to establish a consistently profitable and expanding *niche* in an international market. Some of the difficulties of this and other firms spring from the relative remoteness of Northern Ireland from the main centres of industrial employment in Britain. The new light industries that have been introduced often have much stronger day-to-day links with businesses in the Midlands and south-east of England than with other firms in Northern Ireland, either

Plate 84 Larne Harbour (County Antrim)
The picture shows part of the port installations at Larne Harbour, County Antrim, the outport of Belfast. Industrialists in Northern Ireland are largely dependent on exports, particularly to Great Britain, and considerable efforts are being made to ease the flow of goods across the Irish Sea. Larne Harbour is now increasingly specializing on container and drive-on lorry service to Stranraer in Scotland and to Preston in England. It also operates an important car-ferry and passenger service to Scotland.

because they are branch factories of larger British companies or because they are dependent on Britain for components.

As a result the policy of attracting new industry has been most successful in Belfast and its immediate surroundings, partly because of the ancillary services available here and also because of the more direct transport connections which this area has with Britain and overseas (Plate 84). But when the economic climate is difficult in Britain even this relatively favoured area has difficulty in maintaining the new jobs that have been created. If a British firm is forced to make economies, branch factories are often the first to be shut down; industrialists using cheap, rented factories perhaps have less commitment to the local area; and the marginal location of Northern Ireland takes on greater significance when the need for a pool of labour to support expansion is less important.

Whatever the general state of the United Kingdom economy, small towns in the west of Northern Ireland have even greater difficulty in attracting and keeping new industries. The facilities and port of Belfast are more remote from this area. The absolute number of workers suitable for new industries is low in comparison with the number available in and around Belfast. Unskilled and older men form a more important segment of the unemployed, and the factories that can be steered to this area commonly employ a preponderance of women. In short, the best that possibly can be hoped for in the western counties of Northern Ireland is a modest expansion of jobs in a limited range of undemanding types of employment.

FURTHER READING

F. W. Boal and B. S. MacAodha, The Milk Industry in Northern Ireland, *Economic Geography*, 37 (1961), 170–180.

British Association, *Belfast in its Regional Setting: A Scientific Survey* (Belfast, 1952).

E. R. R. Green, *The Lagan Valley, 1800–1850* (London, 1949).

K. S. Isles and N. Cuthbert, *An Economic Survey of Northern Ireland* (Belfast, 1957).

J. H. Johnson, The Political Distinctiveness of Northern Ireland, *Geographical Review*, 48 (1958), 554–566.

E. Jones, *A Social Geography of Belfast* (London, 1960).

L. Symons (ed.), *Land Use in Northern Ireland* (London, 1963).

M. D. Thomas, Manufacturing Industry in Belfast, Northern Ireland, *Annals of the Association of American Geographers*, 46 (1956), 175–196.

The Republic of Ireland

Politically the Republic of Ireland is a completely independent, sovereign state, and consists of 26 out of the 32 counties that make up all of Ireland (Fig. 86). These 26 counties represent an area of nearly 70,000 square kilometres (26,000 square miles) five times that of Northern Ireland but containing only twice the population. The Irish Free State (as it was originally named) was established in the early 1920s as the result of a treaty between the United Kingdom and the delegates of the revolutionary Irish republican government. The State took its present name in 1949, when the Irish Republic formally ceased to be part of the British Commonwealth, although it had never sought this association.

Terminology is difficult. As far as Britain is concerned the correct name is the Republic of Ireland. The official Irish view is different: that part of the island governed from Dublin is described simply as 'Ireland' (or 'Éire' in the Irish language), although in official documents it is usually necessary to give some indication that the six north-eastern counties are not included. The term 'The Six Counties' is often used as a euphemism for Northern Ireland, whose existence is not officially recognized in Dublin, although in fact there is some practical co-operation between the two states. Such a terminology may accord with political dogma, but it is awkward to use. Here the terms 'The Republic' and 'Éire' will be used for independent Ireland—although this has no official support it accords with common usage.

The Government of Ireland Act, passed by the British Government in 1948, recognized the complete lack of any formal political association between the United Kingdom and Éire; but political independence should not be allowed to hide the strong economic, social and demographic connections between the two states. Indeed, the most important single factor influencing the human geography of Ireland is the nearby presence of the larger island of Great Britain. Even the physical geography of the country exhibits this link, since many of the structural provinces of Ireland are similar to those found in Britain, so that in a very real sense Ireland is an outpost of the larger island. These structural provinces provide the basis for a summary of the topographical variety of the Republic, since there is a close connection between Irish landforms and structure.

Contrasts in the Physical Landscape

The oldest and hardest rocks in Éire are found in the north-west (Fig. 87). These Pre-Cambrian rocks underwent their most recent folding in Caledonian times, and, as a result, there are two factors which guide the broad outlines of

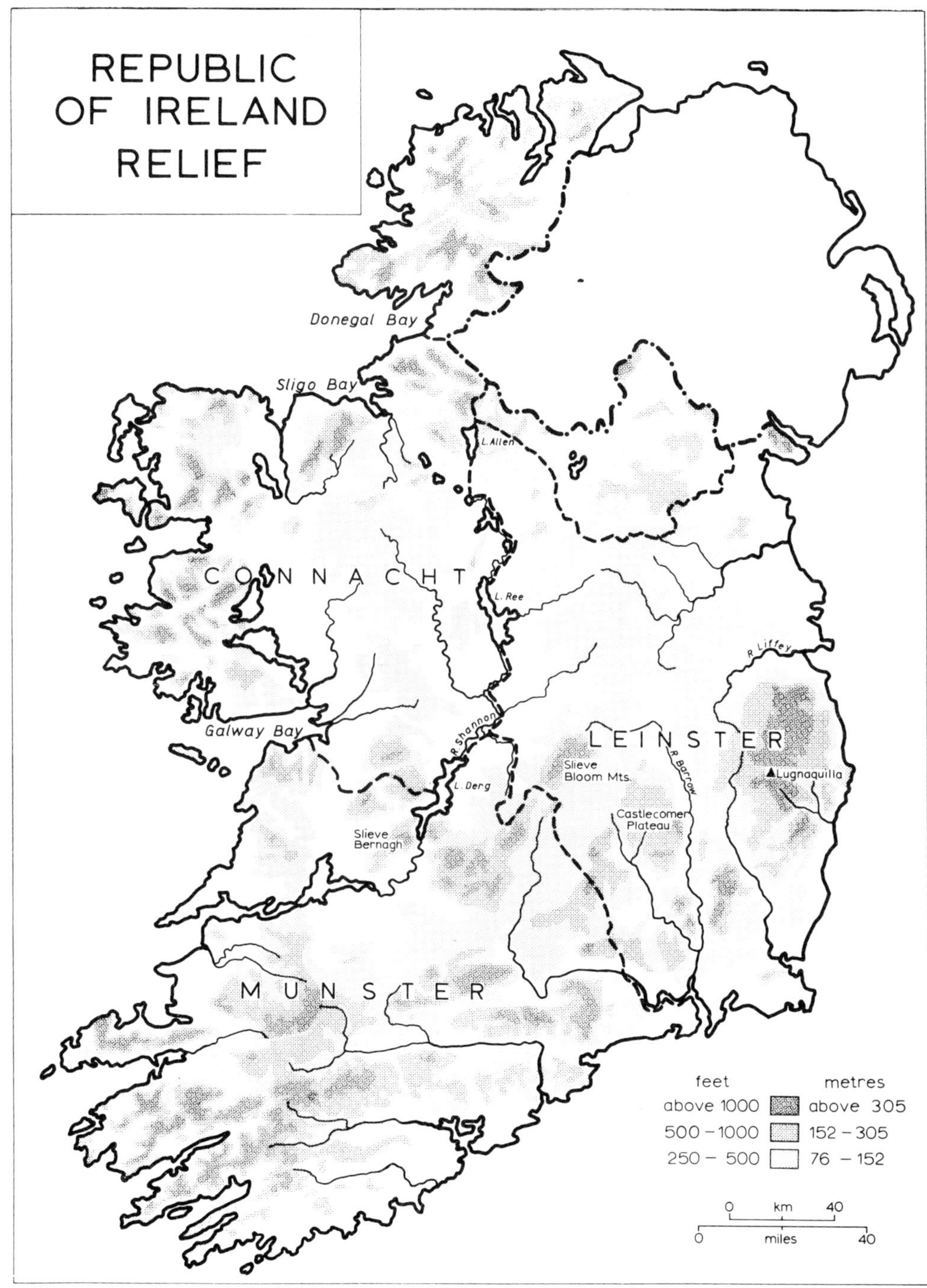

Fig 86 Republic of Ireland—Relief

The Republic of Ireland consists of three of the historic provinces of Ireland, together with three counties of Ulster. The state was established in the early 1920s as a result of a treaty with the United Kingdom. The map shows that the common description of Ireland as having the form of a saucer owes more to the eye of faith than to geographical reality.

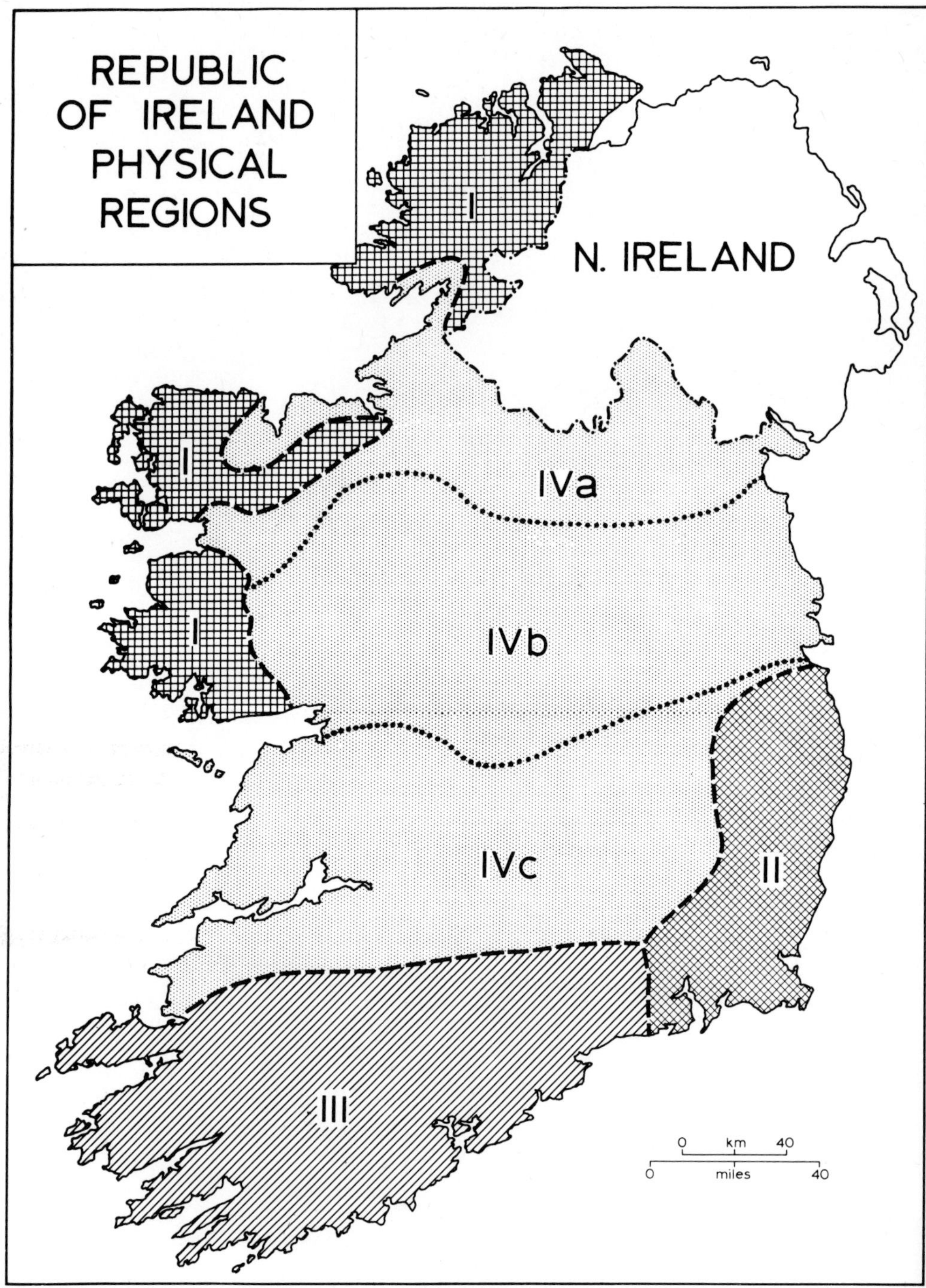

Fig 87 Republic of Ireland—Physical Regions

I The Caledonian Province of the north-west.
II The Leinster Chain.
III The Ridges and Valleys of the south-west.
IV The Central Lowlands
a) the drumlin belt
b) the moraine and bogland sector
c) the hill and vale zone.

THE CALEDONIAN PROVINCES

relief and drainage in the *Caledonian Province of the North-West*. One is the differential resistance of the rocks to erosion, and the other is the tendency for rivers to pick out lines of weakness, which characteristically run in a south-west/north-east direction.

This area of ancient rocks stretches from Malin Head in north Donegal to the shores of Galway Bay in the south; but it is not a continuous zone, as the Caledonian province in Donegal is separated from that in Connacht by the broad embayment formed by Donegal and Sligo Bays, where the Carboniferous limestone of central Ireland extends to the shores of the Atlantic (Fig. 87). The metamorphic rocks and granites of this area form extensive upland areas, with the sharpest peaks being formed of quartzites which protrude above lower planation surfaces, often cut in schists. The area has been intensively glaciated by ice sheets radiating from Donegal and the highest parts of Connacht. This area is notable not so much for its height as for its bleakness, with thin soils, frequent strong winds and very high humidity making agriculture difficult. As a result limited areas of lowland take on particular significance, particularly the coastal raised beaches.

The influence of the Caledonian period of mountain building was not limited to north-west Ireland, since in the east younger rocks were also folded at the same time. In particular, the *Leinster Chain* represents the remains of an anticline formed during the Caledonian orogeny. The granite core of this anticline has been exposed by denudation and forms the largest exposure of granite in the British Isles, some 112 kilometres (70 miles) long from south-west to north-east, but only approximately 24 kilometres (15 miles) wide.

In the north this granite area now forms a rolling upland, which in places reaches a height of 600 metres (2,000 feet), and is often covered by blanket bog. On either side lie Ordovician rocks, mostly shales and slates, which have been metamorphosed into mica-schists at their point of contact with the granites. This narrow contact zone frequently forms a topographic feature, where the valleys of streams crossing it are constricted. To the south of Lugnaquilla, the highest peak, the granite has often been reduced to an extensive undulating plain about 150 metres (500 feet) above sea-level. In this southern section the Leinster Chain becomes a much narrower range of hills, the surface expression of the more resistant rocks around the edge of the granite.

Most of the higher parts of the Chain have been modified by glaciation. Corries are often found on north-east slopes, and the larger valleys are notable for their 'U' shapes and morainic deposits. The present limit of cultivation is roughly about 300 metres (1,000 feet), but above the modern cultivated areas the remains of abandoned farms, last occupied in the early nineteenth century, show that the limits of cultivation had previously been higher. On the steeper hillsides a number of forestry plantations have been established, mostly in the twentieth century. On the more level uplands a hill pasture zone of sheep farms and moorland creates an area of transition between the agricultural lowlands of the valleys and the open rough-pasture and bogland of the highest parts of mountains, grazed only by a few sheep.

THE RIDGES AND VALLEYS OF THE SOUTH-WEST

A final extensive area of high upland is in the south-west, where alternating ridges and valleys characterize relief. In this region Devonian and Carboniferous rocks have been pressed into large, rather simple folds during Armorican times. A dominant feature here is the apparent clarity with which the form of the land has been controlled by the underlying structure: uplands are formed of Devonian mudstones, sandstone and, occasionally, quartzites, which are found in the cores of the anticlines; and Carboniferous limestones, shales and slates are preserved in the synclines that often underlie the dominant east–west valleys of the region. In fact the relationship between surface and structure is less simple than this arrangement would suggest, since the physical landscape of the area is polycyclic in origin, with some elements of the drainage pattern being superimposed. Streams are thought to have originally developed on a cover of later deposits, but as erosion took place these deposits were removed and rivers became progressively more adjusted to the underlying structure. Here and there, however, the rivers have maintained small parts of their original north–south courses, where they transverse the sandstone ridges as superimposed streams. In the south-west, as elsewhere in Ireland, the differential resistance of rocks to erosion has been of considerable importance in shaping the form of the land, since the chance fact that Carboniferous limestone was underlain by more resistant Devonian rocks has been a critical factor in the re-emergence of the cores of the anticlines to form upland ridges in the modern landscape.

In east Cork and west Waterford the east–west valleys are broad and the intervening ridges narrow. Further west the synclinal valleys grow progressively narrower and the intervening ridges form much higher, more continuous and more barren mountains with considerable areas over 600 metres (2,000 feet). Still further west, the east–west valleys widen out again; but here the lowlands have been flooded by the sea to form rias, interpenetrated by bleak sandstone ridges, to form the famous discordant coastline of south-west Ireland. The coastal plain here is very narrow, if present at all; and in this maritime location the surrounding uplands experience some of the heaviest rainfall in Ireland. Although unglaciated areas occur in the nearby lowlands, the mountains of the south-west have been sharpened by numerous corries and in many valleys erosion by ice has added greater drama to a landscape already deeply dissected in pre-glacial times.

THE CENTRAL LOWLANDS

The major upland areas of Ireland lie around the periphery of a lowland, where underlying Carboniferous limestone is often masked by glacial drift and peat deposits. In fact much of central Ireland probably presents the remains of an extensive erosion surface lying between 60 metres (200 feet) and 120 metres (400 feet) above sea-level. Some evidence of this is given by the course of the Shannon, the largest river of Ireland, which dominates the drainage system of the Central Lowlands (Plate 85). For much of its tortuous course this river has only a slight gradient: in over 300 kilometres (190 miles) downstream from Lough Allen it drops only 18 metres (60 feet). Then the low plateau character of the region is indicated by the river's much more rapid fall of 33 metres (110

Plate 85 The River Shannon, near Killaloe (County Clare)
Close to Killaloe the Shannon, after flowing along a remarkably flat course, cuts through the Slieve Bermagh uplands seen on this photograph, and drops more rapidly to tide level. This fall has been used for the famous Shannon Hydro-Electric Power Scheme. The full potential of the Shannon as a tourist attraction has not yet been exploited, but motorists from Britain are discovering the attractions of the relatively empty Irish roads, and tourism is making an important, if seasonal, contribution to the expansion of the Eire economy.

feet) over the 24 kilometres (15 miles) between Lough Derg and tide-level at Limerick. In spite of this disposition of upland and lowland, the common description of Ireland as having the form of a saucer owes more to the eye of faith than to geographical reality. Not only is the mountain rim of the so-called saucer very incomplete and broken by extensive gaps, but the Central Lowland itself contains important internal contrasts. These contrasts owe something to the presence of isolated areas of upland and also to variations in the nature of superficial deposits.

South of a line between Galway Bay and Dublin the Central Lowlands are characterized by isolated, low uplands between 300 metres (1,000 feet) and 600 metres (2,000 feet) in height, with broad fertile vales lying among them. The underlying geological structure of some of these uplands, like Slieve Bernagh, is of Armorican age; others, like Slieve Bloom, show Caledonian elements in their trend. In this area, too, horizontally-bedded Carboniferous rocks have been left upstanding to form higher plateau areas, notably to the west of the river, Barrow (where the Castlecomer Plateau lies at about 300 metres (1,000 feet) and in county Clare (where the enclosed basin at Carran is one of the largest *poljes* in western Europe). The broad, relatively well-drained lowlands of this sub-region form some of the best agricultural land in Ireland, especially in Limerick and Tipperary. Higher land is also found to the north-west of the Central Lowland where (in counties Sligo, Leitrim and Roscommon) the Carboniferous limestone forms rather higher plateaux which reach 600 metres (2,000 feet) in places.

The Central Lowlands are also diversified by their cover of glacial drift. Although west of the Shannon discontinuous patches of bare limestone pavement appear from beneath the drift, glacial deposits are remarkably common throughout the area, but vary in their composition, distribution and thickness. In particular, a belt of country which stretches across Ireland from Sligo Bay to the north-east coast is made distinctive by swarms of drumlins, with patches of bogland between these low hills breaking farmland up into small cultivable patches. To the south the drift is made up of long esker ridges and kame moraine; and in the extensive, ill-drained areas between these deposits, peat in the form of large patches of raised bog has accumulated. The glacial deposits provide lines of easier communication east–west across this area and their well-drained soils provide islands of good grazing and arable land. It is this zone that most closely fits the stereotype commonly attributed to central Ireland of a dull landscape in which brown bogland is interdigitated between low green ridges. Glacial deposits are also found in the hill and vale belt further south. Here rolling end-moraine stretches east from the Shannon estuary and winds its way around the various uplands before reaching the Irish Sea just north of the Leinster Chain.

Agriculture

THE CLIMATIC ENVIRONMENT FOR AGRICULTURE

The contrasting morphological regions of the Republic of Ireland introduce variety into Irish land use, in particular by creating scattered negative areas where commercial farming is greatly impeded. But although detailed contrasts are often the result of local topography, the explanation of major geographical variations in types of farming must be sought in other factors.

One of these is provided by the climatic environment, which has both a general and regional impact on Irish farming (Fig. 88). In comparison with Britain there are more days on which rainfall is recorded, fewer hours of sunshine and higher relative humidity—features which are a product of the maritime location of Ireland to the west of the European mainland. Temperatures are similarly affected. There are fewer days with frost in winter and, as the tourist knows to his dismay, long dry spells of hot weather are rare in summer. As a result grass is everywhere a climatically-favoured crop and there are inherent difficulties in ripening cereals on a reliable and profitable basis.

Within this overall context, however, regional climatic differences encourage variations in the nature of farming and produce clear east–west contrasts as well as less marked north–south ones Measured on any general scale, of course, climatic differences within Éire are limited, but those that occur tend to straddle critical thresholds and thus have a greater influence than might be expected on first inspection. If the upland areas above the limits of cultivation are excluded, rainfall ranges from just less than 750 millimetres (30 inches) per annum in a limited region around Dublin to 1,250 millimetres (50 inches) in

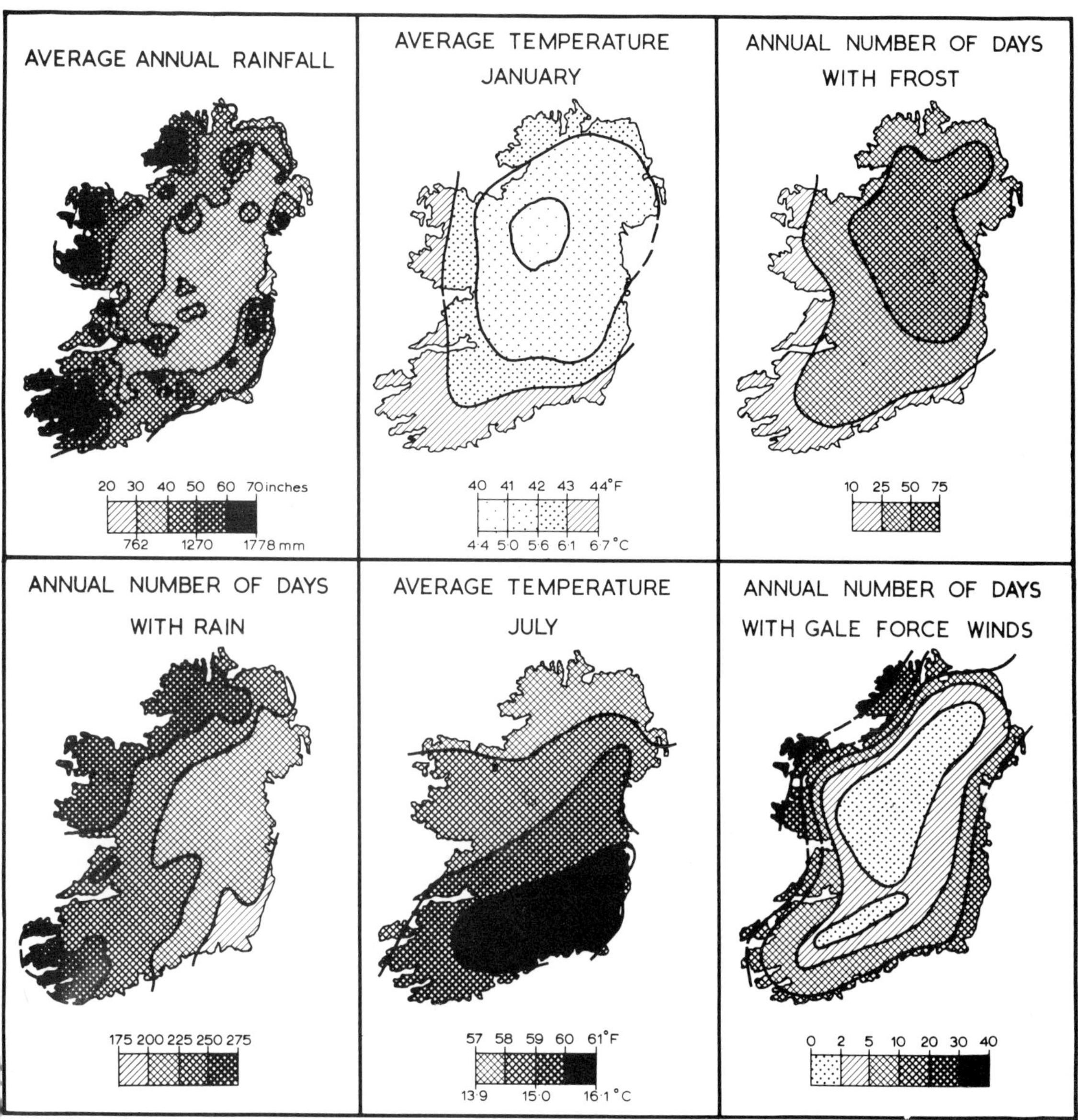

Fig 88 Republic of Ireland—Some Aspects of the Climatic Environment

Generally there are no extreme contrasts in the climatic elements within Ireland. But the differences that do exist are emphasized in importance by the fact that they lie close to critical thresholds for agricultural production.

the western farmlands of the Republic. These amounts are important in that the 1,125 millimetre (45 inch) isohyet marks the effective limit of commercial arable cultivation, with the result that the eastern lowlands present many fewer problems to the arable farmer.

Winter temperatures exert a similar influence on the regional pattern of agriculture. In particular, frosts are relatively uncommon in the south-west and an extensive area in this region of Ireland has an average January temperature of over 5·5°C (42°F). As a result, the growth of grass in winter is merely checked, rather than completely halted. The grass crop is inherently lusher in this area, it is available for grazing during more of the year and milk production is the dominant farming activity. Historical factors have also been important here, since the Cork butter market had a long-standing tradition and, at the end of the nineteenth century, the co-operative creamery movement was important in maintaining milk production during changing market conditions (Plate 86).

Plate 86 A Small Co-operative Creamery (County Kerry)
The continued importance of milk production in south-west Ireland has been encouraged by the development of co-operative creameries at the end of the nineteenth century. These remain a flourishing aspect of agriculture in this area: the creameries not only collect milk and process it, but are also involved in the bulk buying of fertilizers and other requirements of the farmers.

In the south-east sunshine is more prevalent, evaporation is greater and (in comparison with conditions further west) rainfall amounts on the cultivable lands are lower. These conditions, the demands of a famous Dublin brewery, and a more firmly-established tradition of arable farming all encourage the production of cereal crops in this distinctive region, although grass still remains an important crop. Measured by day-degrees of temperature, the northern midlands of Éire have a growing season that is only two-thirds of that commonly found along the south coast. Spring growth in these more northern counties begins several weeks later than further south and the cooler growing season means that the ripening of grains is less reliable, though not impossible in a normal year. This north–south contrast, lying close to the critical threshold for the ripening of cereals, again influences the nature of farming, but in this case the effect of climate is masked by other factors, in particular farm size.

THE ROLE OF FARM SIZE

A second general factor influencing the pattern and emphasis of agriculture is the size of holdings and the nature of land tenure. The break-up of large estates and the transfer of their ownership to the tenant farmers began in the last two decades of the nineteenth century and has continued further since Irish independence. The holdings that were converted from occupation by tenants (often with uncertain tenure) to owner-occupation were usually very small. If anything, the change of tenure has fossilized the size of many farms; agricultural statistics show that half of the farms in the Republic of Ireland are under 12 hectares (30 acres) in size, although there are technical difficulties in assessing the true size of functioning holdings both because of the practice of renting land from other farmers on very short leases (conacre), and because of the continuing use of common grazing above the limits of cultivation. Nevertheless it remains true that, on average, actual farm working units are also very small (Fig. 89).

There are, however, regional contrasts in the average size of holdings, associated with different types of farming and with contrasting densities of rural population. The smallest holdings are found along the west coast; these are often little more than gardens, traditionally devoted to potatoes, but now less intensively cultivated in an era of overseas remittances and government assistance (Plate 87). A zone of small farms, between 12 and 20 hectares (30 and 50 acres) in size, lies north of a line between Galway Bay and Dundalk Bay. Farms over much of the south and east of the Republic are larger, often averaging between 20 and 30 hectares (50 and 75 acres). Finally, near Dublin the largest farms are found, with an average size of over 40 hectares (100 acres), in an area where cattle fattening is a dominant activity.

In the 1930s densities of rural population were closely associated with these contrasts in farm size. In the 'cottage' areas of the west densities as high as 150 per square kilometre (400 per square mile) were found on restricted areas of cultivable land; in the small-farm belt of the north-west densities between 40 and 70 per square kilometre (100 and 180 per square mile) were commonly found; in the best agricultural areas of the south-east densities were between 25 and 40 per square kilometre (60 and 100 per square mile); in Meath (an area of large, cattle-rearing farms) population density was about 20 per square

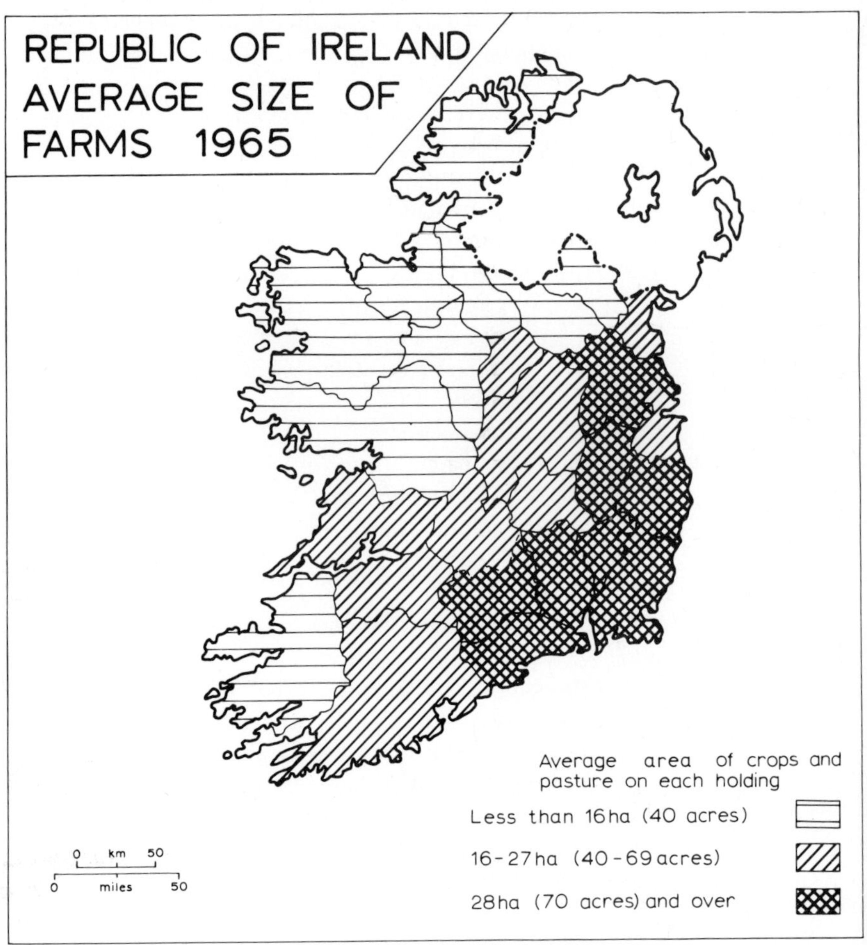

Fig 89 Republic of Ireland—Average Size of Farms, 1965
This map is based on the areas actually cultivated by farmers as working holdings, rather than on the size of farms they legally own. Holdings of less than four hectares (10 acres) have been excluded as being too small to be effective units of agricultural production; then, on a county basis, the remaining number of holdings has been divided into the total acreage of crops and pasture.

kilometre (50 per square mile). Since that time the impact of rural depopulation has been unevenly spread and has been greatest in the north-west and west of the country. As a result regional contrasts in population density have been greatly reduced, but not completely removed.

Curiously, in spite of this removal of surplus population from the area of smallest farms, there have not been comparable increases in the productivity of agriculture in these areas. Improvements in agricultural output have proved difficult to achieve in all parts of the country and the performance of this sector of the Irish economy has tended to fall below expectations; but in Connacht, an area of smaller than average holdings and greater than average depopulation, the growth in agricultural output has been further behind the modest levels achieved elsewhere in the Republic. Similarly, production in the three Ulster counties that remain in the Republic of Ireland (Donegal, Monaghan and Cavan) has lagged behind the growing output of Leinster and Munster.

In theory, perhaps, a declining rural population should have led to an increase in the income of those who remained on the land and, by removing surplus labour, should have made it easier to orientate agriculture more firmly towards commercial production. Paradoxically, the effects of depopulation have been slowest in making this kind of impact in those areas where population decline has been greatest. The farmers who have stayed on their holdings

Plate 87 Farms and Field (County Clare)
In the west of County Clare settlement is concentrated close to the coast and the environment for farming is particularly difficult. Here is one of the most extreme examples of the 'cottage' farming, typical of the west coast of Ireland. Traditional houses still survive here and land-ownership is complex. In spite of a high density of population in relation to the area of cultivable land the intensity of farming is not as high as might be expected, since the average age of the population is high and there is a flow of remittances of various kinds from outside the area to support the population.

have often been older men, now close to retirement. Usually they cannot adapt easily to changing conditions and are unable to run their farms as energetically as might be hoped. The owner-occupation of holdings has also been a positive disadvantage in these areas, since emigrants have not always felt inclined to sell their small farms, so that these holdings have fallen into decay or have been let on short leases under the conacre system, to the detriment of good farming practices. As a result adjustments in farm-size have lagged behind population decrease; and this influence has been greatest in those areas of the Republic with the greatest need for change, where farmers are more likely to underestimate the full commercial potential of their land and often prefer traditional modes of production that are difficult to justify in strict economic logic.

These difficulties are greatest in the areas where small farms are dominant and at least partly explain the fact that on average the output of crops per acre on small farms in Éire is now less than on larger holdings, in spite of the economic pressures on small farmers to squeeze more out of their limited holdings. This tendency is now also becoming apparent in the density of livestock as well as of crops. In spite of government attempts to enlarge holdings and to improve agriculture by focusing attention on carefully chosen 'pilot' areas in the west, it remains true that agricultural investment is greater, the structure of farm holdings is much more satisfactory and the gross rise in output is higher in the already more prosperous south and east of the Republic. It may be, however, that the present situation is ripe for quite rapid change, since many small farms are worked by men close to retirement, often without heirs living on the farm. As a result there may be a relatively early opportunity to bring about amalgamation of holdings, although the need to find capital to purchase owner-occupied farms does restrict the process. The exploitation of this potential for future change remains a challenge for the Irish government, since only if this opportunity is energetically but sensitively handled can it be turned to economic advantage without exacerbating the social problems of the poorer rural areas.

AGRICULTURAL PRODUCTION AND THE BRITISH MARKET

A third important influence on farming is provided by the dominance of the British market—a factor which again affects both the general emphasis of agriculture and regional differences in production. Because of the small home market, the proximity of the large urban population of Britain and the political difficulties at present in obtaining access to other markets, farmers in Éire have had to gear much of their production to filling those gaps left to them in the British market, and this constraint has focused their efforts on the supply of store animals, particularly cattle, for fattening. Unlike farmers in Northern Ireland, those in the Republic have not had direct access to the stability of demand and the guaranteed prices for milk, beef and pig-mea that result from the British government's policies for its own agricultura industry; but British policies regarding prices have influenced conditions i the Republic indirectly, since the prices paid for fat cattle in Britain eventuall filter through to Irish farmers by influencing the amount they receive for stor

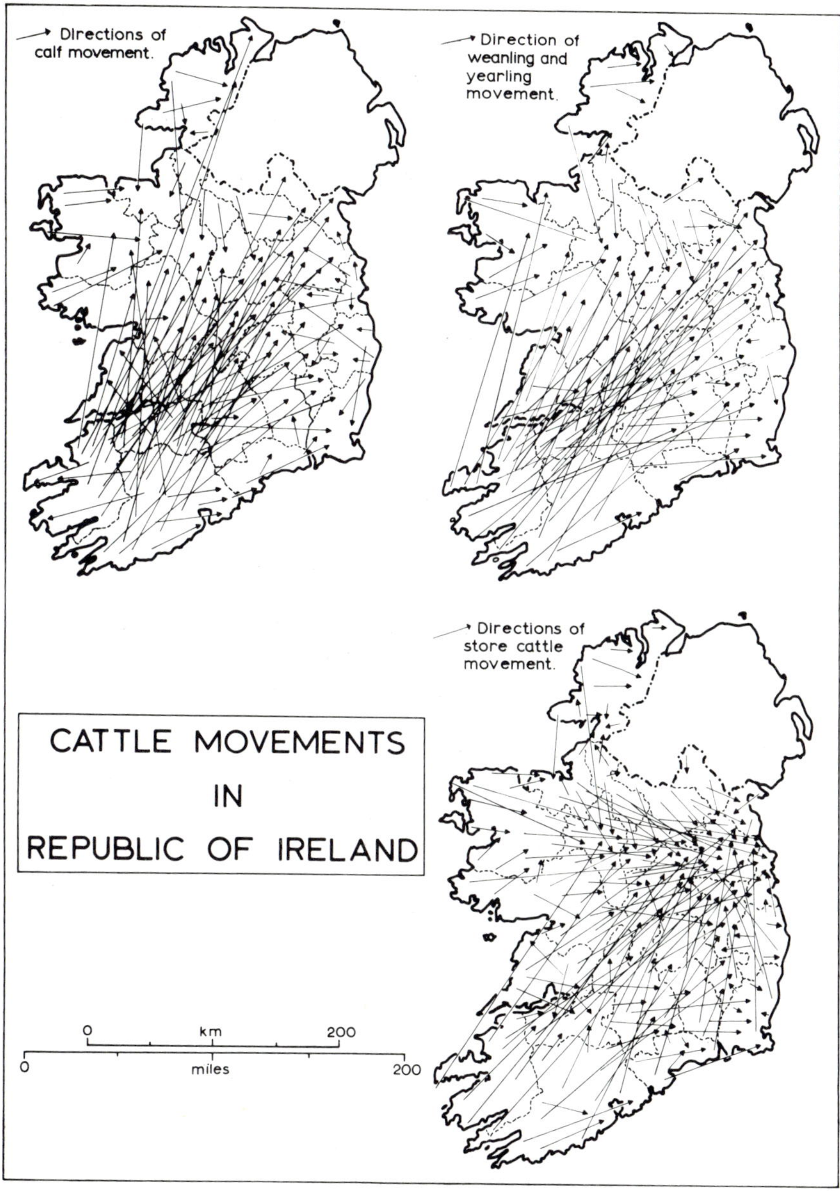

Fig 90 Republic of Ireland—Cattle Movements
Important movements of livestock take place within Ireland and reflect the supply of surplus cattle and the need for stock for fattening in the various agricultural regions of the country. In detail the movements that take place are complex, as this map, based on observations on sample farms, clearly indicates. The map presented here is a simplified version of work by D. A. Gillmor (1969).

cattle. Other agricultural products like butter and cheese are slowly establishing themselves in the modern British market as a result of recent relaxations in trading restrictions between the two countries, although the operation of a quota system has greatly limited the export of dairy products from Éire in the recent past. Paradoxically, the current price structure for butter and cheese in the British market means that they are currently being sold at a less than production cost, although the trade allows the disposal of surplus production and also gives a means of establishing a foothold in a market that is likely to become more profitable with the entry of both Britain and Éire into the E.E.C.

At present the supply of store cattle for the export market confirms the pastoral emphasis of Irish farming, traditionally encouraged by climatic conditions. Regional differences in farming are also produced by the manner in which the cattle trade operates. Dry cattle for rearing and fattening, surplus to the needs for replacement stock on the farm, are sold by the dairy farmers of the south-west. In addition, small farmers everywhere sell surplus store cattle, as they are unable to carry out efficiently the long-term process of fattening on their restricted holdings. As a result there is an annual readjustment in the distribution of the cattle population, with young cattle being sold from small to larger farms, and from dairying to stock-rearing farms (Fig. 90). Many of these movements take place on a local scale, but they also occur between regions because of the broad contrasts in farm sizes which have already been discussed, and because of the convenience of fattening cattle close to the east coast. Here the producers of finished animals have direct access to the dominant domestic market in Dublin and to the ports through which the animals will be exported to Britain.

The regional contrasts in Irish agriculture are thus the result of an amalgam of factors. The west coast is notable for its very small farms, a difficult environment for farming and remoteness from the major commercial markets. Together these factors have produced a region of 'cottage' farming, where the occupiers are rarely supported by the products of their holdings but depend on government assistance of various kinds and on remittances from relatives who have emigrated. In areas where commercial agriculture is more important, mixed farming is everywhere dominant, but there are regional differences in emphasis. Climate, tradition and the co-operative movement have combined to encourage milk production in the south-west as the dominant commercial activity. In the south-east, climatic conditions appear to have swung the balance towards cereals. Further north the cattle trade has focused on the good pastures north-west of Dublin, to produce a region where cattle fattening is a dominant activity. Close to Dublin, too, the production of vegetables and liquid milk, as well as marginal farming around the fringes of the Wicklow Mountains, have created a complex area with diverse types of agriculture on individual farms. Finally in the north and west of the Central Lowlands are two regions dominated by small, mixed farms. In the western region farmers tend to produce more store cattle and to rear sheep, while in the northern region the production of milk is somewhat more important. These regional contrasts are illustrated in Figure 91.

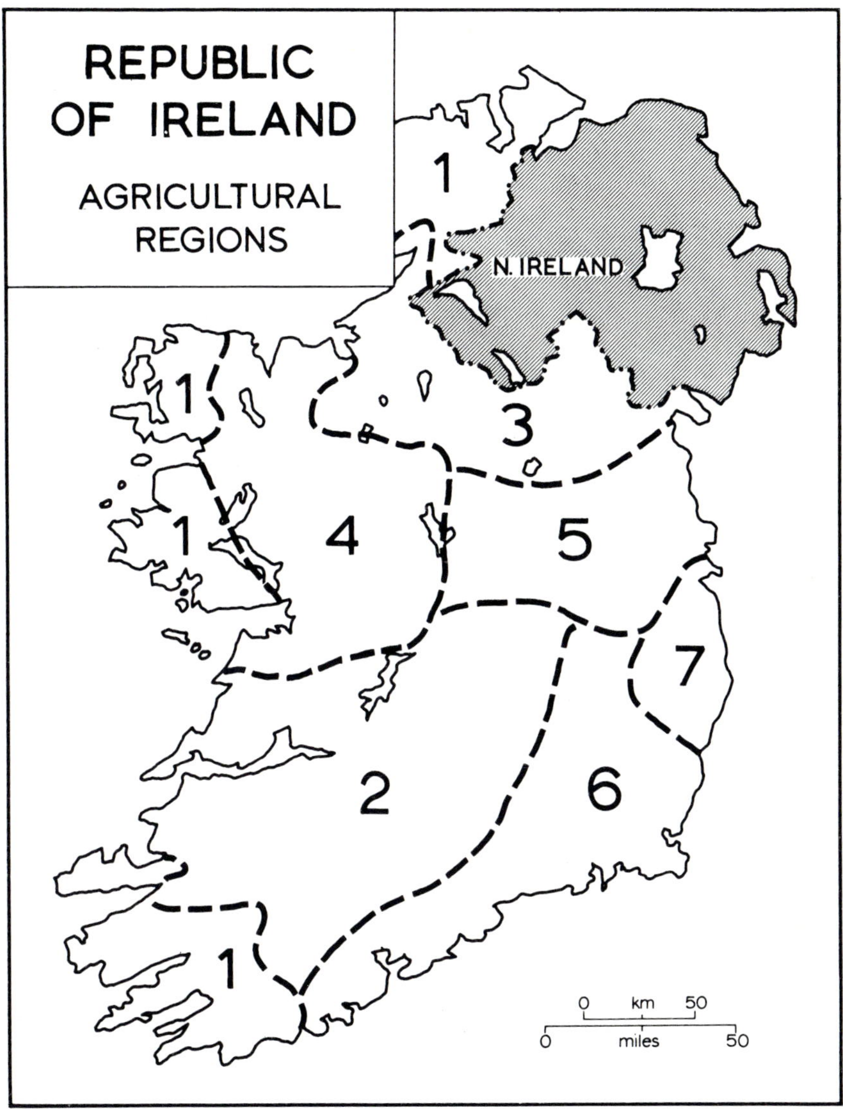

Fig 91 Republic of Ireland—Agricultural Regions

1. The Small 'Cottage' Farm Belt of the West Coast.
2. The south-western Dairying Area.
3. The Small Farm Belt, with some emphasis on milk production.
4. The Small Farm Belt, with some emphasis on store cattle and sheep.
5. The Eastern Cattle Fattening Region.
6. The south-eastern Arable Region.
7. The Dublin and North Wicklow Diversified Farming Area.

Industry

THE POLICY OF INDUSTRIAL PROTECTION

Agriculture remains the single most important occupation in terms of the number employed, but because of its relatively static output it is losing its predominant role in the Irish economy. By 1958 manufacturing had surpassed agriculture as the principal contributor to the gross national product; and since that date manufacturing has moved sharply ahead of the agricultural sector of the economy. This expansion was encouraged by the Éire government as long ago as the establishment of the Irish Free State in the 1920s by the erection of a tariff wall, which was designed to produce an economic environment where new manufacturing industries, aimed predominantly at the home market, could take root. The economies of scale and the industrial linkages that are often vital for the profitable operation of modern industrial plants in a competitive world were almost impossible to achieve at any distance from the environs of Dublin. Hence it was believed that protection would allow industry to flourish in smaller towns than would have been possible if the cold winds of international competition were blowing strongly.

This policy had a certain success: Irish industrialists proved able to manufacture goods like footwear, textiles and cutlery (to list but a few products) for the protected home market. Particularly in the larger port towns new industries were grafted on to the existing structure of industrial employment: in Limerick, for example, the manufacture of nails and cement was added to already-established local industries concerned with the processing of agricultural staples and with supplying such products as cattle feed to local farmers. In addition the State intervened in the establishment of larger industries like the Electricity Supply Board, Bord na Móna (the Peat Board), the Irish Sugar Company and in various transport undertakings, often with the aim of fully exploiting local resources. The electricity industry is a particularly good example of this policy, since, by the use of water-power and peat fuel for the generation of electricity, 80 per cent of the total output is now based on domestic resources. During this period of tariff protection, employment in manufacturing rose by just over 63 per cent from 164,000 in the 1920s to 268,000 in the early 1950s. The tertiary sector of the economy also expanded, but at a somewhat less dramatic rate.

This success appears less impressive, however, if judged in terms of the original goals of government policy. For one thing, not enough jobs were created to stop the decline in the total population of the State: in the 25 years from 1926 to 1951, for example, the total number of jobs merely increased by one per cent, so that the expansion of employment in industry and services just about balanced the fall in the agricultural labour force and, in turn, emigration approximately equalled the natural increase of population. The policy also failed to revitalize the small towns of Éire, particularly those in the most remote locations, since even those industries producing for the local Irish market often were unable to resist the pull of Dublin and of the largest towns. As a result the policy of industrial protection did nothing to counteract rural depopulation by providing alternative employment in the west and north-west of the Republic. It also did little to steer economic expansion away from the area in and around Dublin, which grew rapidly at the expense of the rest of the country.

This, however, was no new phenomenon in the human geography of Ireland. In 1801, when the Act of Union deprived Ireland of its own parliament, Dublin had already achieved the distinction of being the second largest city in the British Empire. The social brilliance and administrative importance of Dublin faded after the Union, but the growth of the city still continued steadily during the nineteenth century, if not at the spectacular rate of Belfast (see Chapter 18). Railway building confirmed the dominance of Dublin at the centre of the communications network of Ireland and although the city had few of the large-scale industries usually associated with nineteenth century economic expansion, some manufacturers were able to exploit the facilities of the port to expand into the British market as well as into the commercial economy that was becoming more widely established in Ireland itself during the second half of the nineteenth century. The most famous example of this

Plate 88 O'Connell Street, Dublin

After Irish independence Dublin resumed a more rapid rate of growth after a period of more stately expansion during the nineteenth century. O'Connell Street is one of the busiest shopping streets in the capital and represents a sector of the central business district of Dublin where popular shops dominate the urban scene.

process is provided by the firm of Guinness, which was operating the largest brewery in Europe at the end of the century.

After Irish independence Dublin became a capital once again, with the result that the city expanded rapidly through acquiring new functions in administration, education and commerce (Plate 88). The city also provided the most attractive location for manufacturing industry in the Republic of Ireland, since it contained a large and increasing proportion of the population, it lay at the point of maximum access to the rest of the country, and it was by far the largest port, providing direct access to Britain—the dominant source of imports and the destination of most agricultural and industrial exports.

THE NEED FOR A NEW EMPLOYMENT STRATEGY

By the 1950s the deficiencies of existing economic policies became inescapably apparent, since after a period of relative stability, emigration and population decline during this decade reached the highest levels that had been recorded since the dramatic flight from the land during the second half of the nineteenth century. That there was a limit to the effectiveness of the original policy was inevitable, since a total population of only 2·8 millions could only provide a restricted base for industrial expansion supported by the demands of the home market. As a result in the late 1950s a new strategy, in the form of a series of programmes for economic and social development, was adopted (Fig. 92). As has already been stressed, although the productivity of agriculture could be increased, no growth in the demand for labour could be expected from that sector of the economy. The tourist industry offered much greater opportunities in appropriate parts of the country, but the Irish tourist season is short and, at best, this type of employment could only provide a partial solution in some areas. As a result the most important element in the new policy was the aim of attracting manufacturing industry, producing for the export market. Suitable industrial investment was attracted from outside the country by the offer of very substantial tax concessions and capital grants. At the same time the Undeveloped Areas Act of 1952 attempted to steer more employment to the west and north-west of the Republic by offering much larger capital grants to industrialists willing to locate there.

An important recent stimulus to new industrial policies has been provided by the Anglo-Irish trade agreement of 1965 which abolished duty on Irish exports into the United Kingdom, where the Republic already enjoyed more favourable terms of trade than many foreign countries. As a result, one of the attractions for foreign firms to establish plants in Ireland has been the entry that this gave into the British market. In turn, and perhaps even more important, the trade agreement is involving the progressive removal of protective duties on Irish imports from Britain over a ten-year period giving free entry for British goods in 1976 but steadily reducing duties in the meantime. Entry into the European Common Market should stimulate trade even further.

In terms of the growth of exports the new policy must be reckoned a remarkable success. Industrial exports expanded from £28 million in 1958 to £184 million in 1968, an average growth of 19 per cent per annum. Industrial

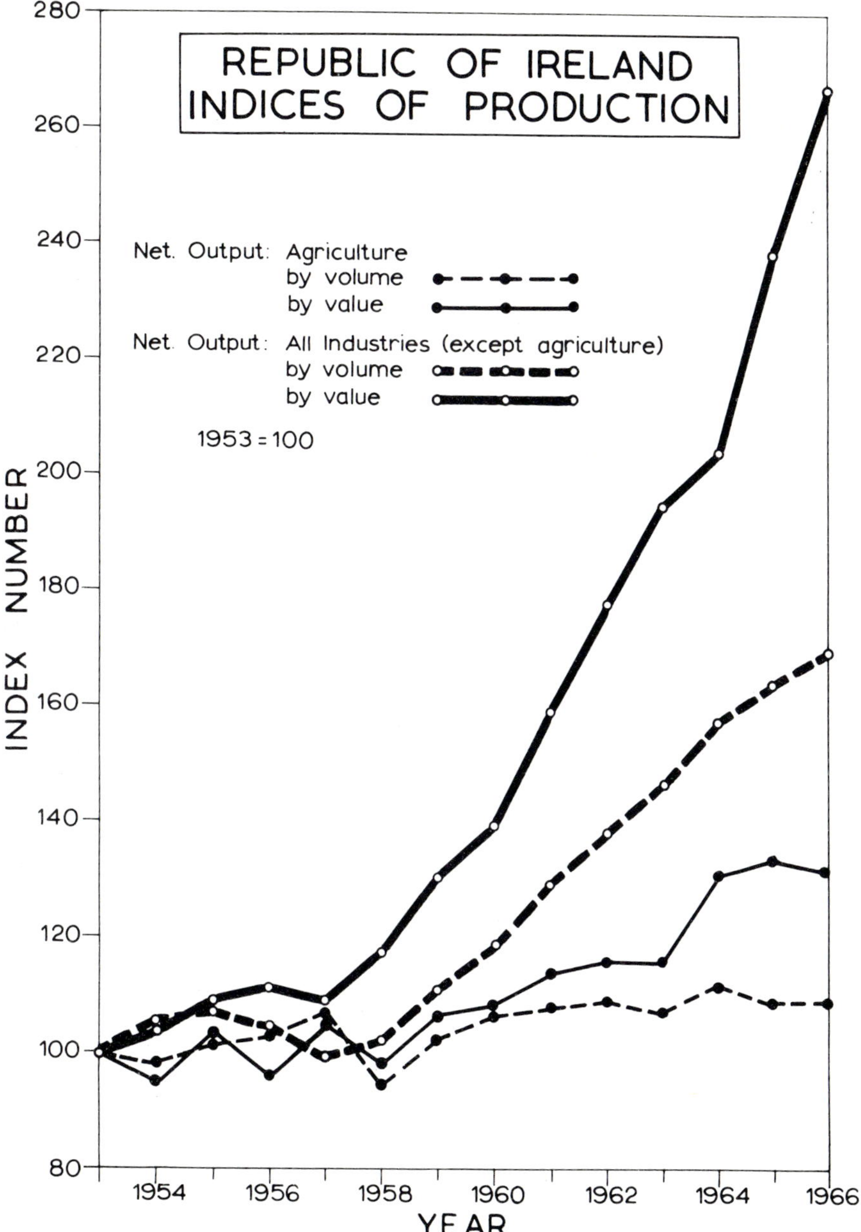

Fig 92 Republic of Ireland—Indices of Production

In the later 1950s a series of programmes for economic and social development was introduced by the Irish government. Little change was brought to the volume of agricultural output by these measures, but the effects on other types of employment have been more dramatic.

products only formed 25 per cent of total exports in 1958, but by 1969 they were over 50 per cent. In addition Irish manufactures have been successful in diversifying their markets: now 65 per cent of manufacturers are destined for Britain, compared with 80 per cent 10 years ago. The various programmes of economic development that were launched in 1958 have succeeded in increasing the gross national product by nearly 4 per cent per annum and in this achievement the growth of manufacturing industry played a dominant role. In terms of the number of jobs created success is less clear, although there is again substantial improvement in comparison with the past rate of growth. For example, from 1962 to 1968, the period of the second programme for economic and social development, industrial employment increased about 2 per cent and absorbed a growing share of the workers leaving agriculture. Unfortunately the labour requirements of new firms have been lower than expected, partly because of a rise in productivity per man. Yet at least the policy has checked the tide of emigration, if not halted it.

One difficulty of current industrial policies, however, is the continuing problem of bringing substantial expansion to the west, even with the help of

Plate 89 Galway Industrial Estate

Current thinking is to concentrate new manufacturing industry in a limited number of growth points, where industry can be backed by training facilities, effective communications and a reasonably large labour market. Galway is being looked upon as a regional growth centre and the photograph shows the new industrial estate in process of being built there. These factories will shortly be employing about 1,000 people, but, in comparison with what is possible near Dublin, there are considerable difficulties in generating dynamic industrial expansion in this western location.

substantial grants; if anything, with the new emphasis on exports, Dublin and the smaller towns immediately associated with it have had their attractiveness increased. Certainly some real success has been achieved in Sligo and, more particularly, in Galway. The new Galway industrial estate, for example, provides employment for 700 men and 300 women, but the total impact of this expansion, in what is probably the most favourable location in the whole Undeveloped Area, seems very modest in the light of the size of the surplus labour force still employed in local farming (Plate 89).

A much more dramatic success has been achieved by the new industrial estate attached to Shannon Airport, where about 5,000 workers are now employed, more than half of them men. Although this development is sometimes seen as an important contribution to economic growth in western Ireland, it should be noted that in fact the industrial estate lies just outside the designated Undeveloped Area and that the majority of its workers who travel in over a considerable distance every day do not come from the areas where rural unemployment is greatest. It is important also to record the special circumstances that exist here. This estate has the unique facilities of an international airport for the handling of air-freight and for the easy transit of visiting managers. It has also been made into a free trade area to reduce the complications of import and export—again a unique feature. Finally, it could be argued that a disproportionate amount of effort has been directed into making this estate a showpiece for current industrial policies. These advantages have attracted British, Japanese, South African, Dutch, American and German firms, producing goods as diverse as pianos and transistor radios; but it remains a matter of doubt whether this success can be repeated elsewhere in the west.

So far the only other area outside Shannon and the Dublin region that has been successful in attracting a substantial amount of new employment has been the city of Cork. Again there are local favourable conditions that are difficult to replicate elsewhere, since the city of Cork is the second largest urban settlement in the Republic, with 122,000 people in 1966, and hence can provide a substantial pool of labour by Irish standards. It has a good port with frequent services to Britain, and a local airport offering similar connections; it has good road and rail links with Dublin; and it has facilities for higher education and technical training. Hence it is not surprising that the city possesses a thriving industrial estate as well as a prosperous, Dutch-owned shipyard.

PROSPECTS FOR FUTURE DEVELOPMENT

Emigration still continues. Although the 1966 census registered the first important increase in population since 1841 (2·3 per cent between the 1961 and 1966 censuses), net emigration averaged 16,000 per annum between 1961 and 1966. Here lies the fundamental problem for future economic expansion, since new jobs are required to allow the necessary restructuring of agriculture as well as to absorb natural increase. Even the current Third Programme for Social and Economic Development (1969–72), which envisaged an increase in employment over its four-year period, still expects emigration to continue at 12–13,000 per annum. The basic problem is to create an economic environ-

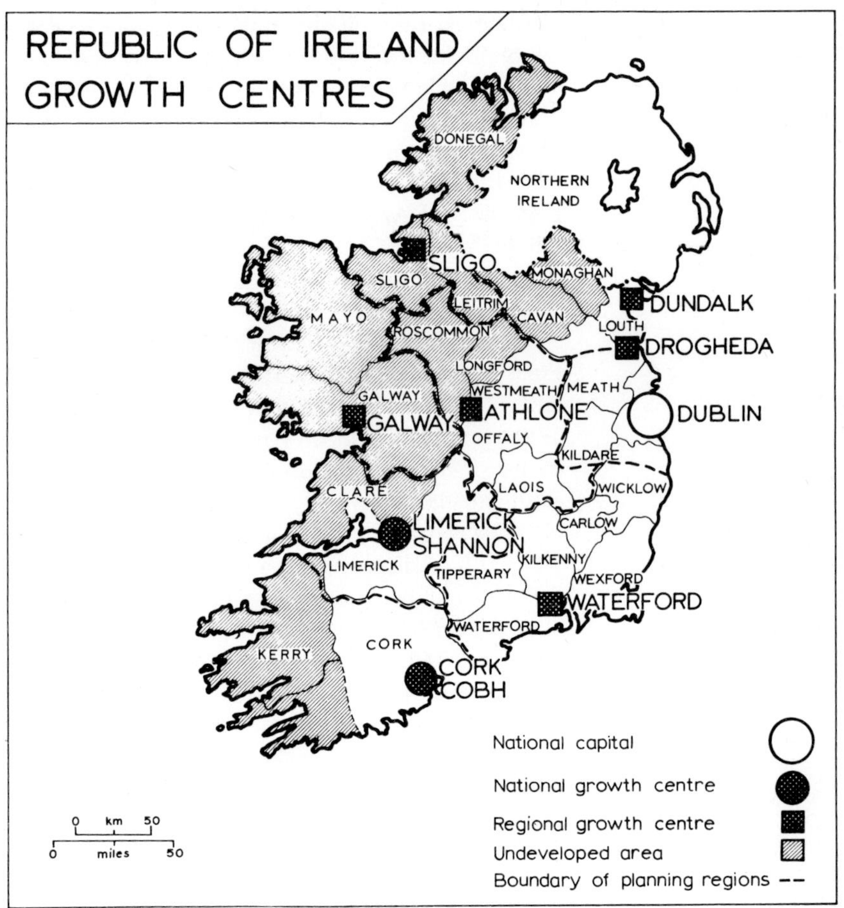

Fig 93 Republic of Ireland—Growth Centres
Since 1952 special capital grants have been given to industrialists willing to locate their factories in the so-called 'undeveloped' area of the north and west. A recent report has suggested that general economic expansion would be best encouraged by concentrating attention of a number of growth points. Current decisions now being made about industrial location seem to be moving towards the implementation of this advice. The planning regions into which the state has been divided are not the equivalent of the much more elaborate system found in Britain, but are probably better thought of as a working framework for the allocation of national financial resources.

ment which will attract increased employment. Here a difficulty is that industry cannot be attracted to Ireland by the offer of cheap labour, since wages must remain at a level not far below those obtainable in Great Britain. Irish workers can move freely to Britain, they are well aware of wage rates on the other side of the Irish Sea, and many young men and women accept emigration as a normal part of life.

The possible strategies that are open to the Éire government are thus quite limited. One extreme solution, given the need for as many well-paid jobs as possible and the more competitive economic climate that is developing with the growth of a wider free trade area, would be to concentrate all growth of employment in the Dublin region. Although this solution is economically valid, it is unacceptable politically or socially. The diametrically-opposed strategy of spreading new jobs in direct proportion to the level of emigration is economically impossible. By this criterion, for example, Donegal should get 17 per cent of all new jobs, a level five times higher than that found in the recent past in spite of efforts to steer industry to the west. In a more competitive future even the current level of industrial employment in these areas of high emigration may be difficult to maintain.

As a result a policy is evolving by which development may be steered to a limited number of growth centres, which are being designated in various parts of the country (Fig. 93). The idea is to concentrate most economic growth into towns where they can be backed by good training facilities, effective communications and a reasonably large labour market. The greater ease of movement that personal transport is bringing to the Irish countryside may make these schemes more viable, since these growth centres can develop extensive journey-to-work hinterlands around them. A report recently prepared for the Irish Government has suggested nine possible centres which could function in this way. Three of these centres already possess virile economic growth: Dublin, Cork and Limerick (which includes the Shannon airport estate); in some of the others factory estates have already been established and more new industries could be encouraged to locate there.

These proposals have been criticized from a number of points of view. Clearly they do not offer the possibility of creating the largest number of new jobs possible: that policy would demand concentration of effort on Dublin (and possibly Limerick and Cork). On the other hand the growth centre idea offers less hope for the future prosperity of some of the smallest Irish towns away from the east coast. Also, with the possible exception of Galway city, the centres chosen offer little prospect of increased prosperity in the areas where Irish survives as a native tongue; and the survival of these *Gaeltacht* areas is still a lively issue in Irish politics. Nevertheless it is a policy which is probably politically acceptable to the majority of the population and gives hope for future expansion in an economically more competitive world. Although these proposals are not yet official government policy, current decisions being made about industrial location in the Irish Republic seem to be moving towards their implementation.

FURTHER READING

E. E. Evans, *Irish Folkways* (London, 1957).

T. W. Freeman, *Ireland* (London, 1950).

D. A. Gillmor, Cattle Movement in the Republic of Ireland, *Transactions, Institute of British Geographers*, no. 46 (1969), 143–154.

J. H. Johnson, Population Changes in Ireland, 1951–1961, *Geographical Journal*, 129 (1963), 167–174.

J. H. Johnson, Population Change in Ireland, 1961–1966, *Irish Geography*, 5, no. 5 (1968), 470–477.

J. Meenan and D. A. Webb, *A View of Ireland* (British Association, Dublin, 1957).

N. Stephens and R. Glasscock (eds.), *Irish Geographical Studies in Honour of E. E. Evans* (Belfast, 1970).

The Island States

Of the many small islands of the British Isles only the Channel Islands and the Isle of Man have achieved and maintained a degree of autonomy and internal control sufficient to set them apart from the United Kingdom and the Republic of Ireland. The Channel Islands and the Isle of Man share a rather lonely island status, they share the distinction of having their own separate legal, social, and economic systems, they share an apprehension of the long-term effects of the Common Market upon their delicately balanced trading and financial positions, but they have little else in common.

The Channel Islands

Jersey, Guernsey, Alderney, and Sark, as the Introduction to this book made clear, are self-governing territories which may be regarded as dependencies of the British Crown. Their rather flexible constitutional position, combined with their geographical characteristics, have enabled them, in many senses, to enjoy both the penny and the bun. Their close association with the United Kingdom over the years has been of great benefit. Common citizenship has allowed the free movement of people to and from the Channel Islands, tourism is unimpeded by passport or other restrictions, local produce, particularly fruit, flowers and vegetables, has free entry into the British market, and the Channel Islands can make use of the many services, financial, social, and governmental, available on the mainland. At the same time, because the Islands have never been incorporated into the United Kingdom, they have retained a freedom of action, in such matters as taxation and company law, which has attracted high-income immigrants. These in turn have contributed to the prosperity of the Islands.

The physical characteristics of the Channel Islands are also contributory to their present economic development. They lie to the south of the remainder of the British Isles, nowhere closer than 90 kilometres (55 miles) to the coast of England. The climate is therefore warmer than is general in the United Kingdom, and no less maritime. Sunshine amounts are about 2 per cent higher than in the sunniest stations in England, but more important is that winters are remarkably mild, occasionally no frost at all being reported. The islands themselves are composed of igneous and Pre-Cambrian sedimentary and metamorphic rocks. Large, flat erosion surfaces give a flat-topped appearance to each island and, in practice, these level areas, often limon-covered, provide the most important agricultural tracts. Market gardening for British consumption is the dominating rural activity. In Jersey, for example, early potatoes,

Plate 90 Near St. Helier (Jersey)
Intensive farming to supply the markets of Britain is the dominant rural activity of the Channel Islands. Here, on the south coast of Jersey, is one of the most prosperous areas of market gardening. Also in evidence is the line of settlement—houses, hotels, and other tourist building—which has been attracted to the southern shoreline.

cauliflowers, tomatoes, and flowers together make up over 75 per cent of the value of agricultural production, and approaching 90 per cent of the value of agricultural exports.

The Channel Islands have a population of a little over 100,000 and in area amount to 195 square kilometres (75 square miles). The largest island is Jersey. It has a cliffed northern coastline, a deeply incised central plateau, and a southern coastal plain providing sites for urban development. Here the wide sandy beaches have stimulated growth and there is now an almost continuous line of settlement along the south coast, including St. Helier, the main town, seat of government, and major port of the island. Two-thirds of the island's population live in this southern coastal plain and almost all the tourists find accommodation there (Plate 90). Elsewhere agriculture predominates in a landscape which is almost classically bocage. Fields are small, sometimes tiny strips, and well above half the agricultural holdings are of less than 5 hectares (12·5 acres).

Guernsey, the second island in area and population, is equally dependent upon tourism and market gardening. Its economy, however, is more specialized than that of Jersey, the production of tomatoes dominating agricultural output. Greenhouses are much more evident than in Jersey and are particularly numerous in the north of the island, where a sandy lowland plain has given fertile light soils. St. Peter Port is the only main settlement and contains not only one-third of the total population, but almost all the economic activities other than tourism and agriculture.

Alderney and Sark, the two smaller islands, are in some respects subordinate to Guernsey in their constitutional status. Alderney is the northernmost of the Channel Islands, and also the closest to France. Quarrying, meat-packing, light-engineering, and flower growing are the main occupations. Sark, semi-feudal in its political organization, lies within sight of Guernsey, from which it attracts thousands of day visitors. Farming is the main occupation, though it is pursued less intensively than elsewhere in the Channel Islands.

The Isle of Man

Like the Channel Islands, the Isle of Man enjoys self government for internal affairs and is linked with the remainder of the United Kingdom through the Crown. It has an area of 570 square kilometres (220 square miles) and supports a population, now declining fairly sharply, of a little under 50,000. In its early history it was subjected to heavy Celtic and Scandinavian influence. More recently it is the English holiday visitor and the English tax-haven immigrant who have exerted more outside influence. The Manx language has virtually disappeared, though some of the traditional governmental institutions have survived the influx of tourists and residents.

Physically the Isle of Man consists of three major elements, two of which are very similar, though areally distinct. The southern one-third of the island is composed of a tightly-folded Manx slate upland, flanked by limited coastal lowlands, the most extensive lying in the south between Castletown and Port St. Mary. The area is defined to the north by a narrow trough of lowland extending from Douglas on the east coast to Peel on the west, lowland which has provided an important east–west routeway in the central part of the island. Immediately to the north is the second major physical element, another slate upland mass, rising to Snaefell at 620 metres (2,034 feet) above sea level. The northern part of the island is composed of a low-lying drift-covered plain, and

Plate 91 The Harbour, Douglas (Isle of Man)
A passenger ferry from England enters Douglas harbour and represents the major source of present prosperity in the Isle of Man as well as its potential point of economic difficulty as tourist numbers fall.

this constitutes the third physical element. It contrasts with the other two regions to the south not only in its lithology and elevation, but also in its farming landscape, which contains larger-scale, more productive, and certainly more prosperous farms than those of the uplands.

The population of the Isles of Man is peripherally distributed. Coastal towns and villages account for three-quarters of the total population and the southern and eastern coasts dominate. Douglas and Ramsey were already important ports and fishing harbours before the modern tourist development, but they flourished, together with their neighbours, particularly in the late nineteenth century following improvements in the means of sea transport to and from England. Steamer services into Douglas led to its rapid growth (Plate 91), but also eventually to the relative decline of other hitherto important industries such as fishing, mining, and manufacturing. Tourist traffic reached its peak in 1913, when nearly 650,000 summer visitors stayed on the island. Since then there has been a slow decline and today there are about 500,000 annual tourists, one-fifth of whom are day visitors only, travelling principally from Fleetwood and Liverpool. Most holidaymakers still arrive at Douglas, though air-traffic to Ronaldsway airport, near Castletown increases steadily. Most of the holiday visitors come from the industrial towns of northern England, and the season is limited to about 10 weeks. Neither the length of stay, nor the amount spent by the average visitor, matches the holiday-time and spending of the more affluent tourists who travel to the Channel Islands.

The improvements in transportation which introduced tourism, and killed the traditional industries of the Isle of Man have, of course, continued. The tourist industry itself is now threatened as it becomes easier and relatively cheaper to travel further to sunnier resorts in more southerly latitudes. To compensate, the Manx government has made strenuous efforts to introduce new employment opportunities to replace the old. In this it has achieved a certain amount of success, aided by low tax rates, and the numbers employed in the textile and light engineering industries have recently increased substantially. However, even greater efforts are needed to stem the increasing flow of younger Manx men and women who leave the island to seek employment in Great Britain.

FURTHER READING

J. W. Birch, The Economic Geography of the Isle of Man, *Geographical Journal*, 124 (1958), 494–513.

E. Davies, Treens and Quarterlands in the Isle of Man, *Transactions of the Institute of British Geographers*, 22 (1956), 97–117

R. H. Kinvig, *A History of the Isle of Man* (Liverpool, 1950).

D. C. Large and G. W. S. Robinson, The Channel Islands, in J. A. Steers (ed.), *Field Studies in the British Isles* (London, 1964).

Statistical Abstract

The regional statistics shown below are derived largely from Central Statistical Office, *Abstract of Regional Statistics* (H.M.S.O., 1970) and Central Statistics Office, *Statistical Abstract of Ireland* (Dublin, 1968), and refer mainly to the period 1965–1969. It should be noted that the figures for the Republic of Ireland are not always directly comparable with those for the United Kingdom either in date and method of collection, or in the precise definitions used. Such difficulties have made it impossible to give useful statistics for the Channel Islands or the Isle of Man.

AREA AND POPULATION

Region	*Area* (*thousand acres*)	*Area* (*thousand hectares*)	*Population* (*thousands*)	*Density* (*per acre*)	*Density* (*per hactare*)
South East	6,774	2,743	17,295	2·6	6·3
South West	5,846	2,368	3,730	0·6	1·6
East Anglia	3,105	1,258	1,657	0·5	1·3
East Midlands	3,014	1,221	3,349	1·1	2·7
West Midlands	3,216	1,302	5,145	1·6	4·0
Wales	5,130	2,078	2,724	0·5	1·3
Yorkshire and Humberside	3,503	1,419	4,810	1·4	3·4
North West	1,973	799	6,770	3·4	8·5
North	4,781	1,936	3,346	0·7	1·7
Scotland	19,465	7,883	5,195	0·3	0·7
Northern Ireland	3,489	1,413	1,512	0·4	1·1
Republic of Ireland	17,024	6,895	2,899	0·2	0·4

POPULATION OF MAJOR TOWNS AND CITIES
(over 200,000)

The figures shown are for administrative areas and do not necessarily refer to the whole urban agglomeration

(thousands)

Conurbations:	
Greater London	7,703
West Midlands	2,441
S.E. Lancashire	2,443
West Yorkshire	1,727
Merseyside	1,342
Tyneside	840
Boroughs and other urban areas:	
London Boroughs	7,699
Birmingham	1,085
Glasgow	928
Liverpool	677
Dublin	650
Manchester	594
Sheffield	529
Leeds	504
Edinburgh	465
Bristol	427
Teeside	394
Belfast	391
Coventry	336
Nottingham	303
Kingston upon Hull	293
Bradford	293
Cardiff	289
Lewisham	284
Leicester	283
Stoke-on-Trent	273
Wolverhampton	264
Newcastle upon Tyne	25[illegible]
Havering	25[illegible]
Plymouth	24[illegible]
Derby	22[illegible]
Sunderland	21[illegible]
Portsmouth	21[illegible]
Southampton	21[illegible]

POPULATION AGE STRUCTURE

(thousands)

Region	*0–4*	*5–14*	*15–44*	*45–64 (m)* *45–59 (f)*	*over 65 (m)* *60 (f)*
South East	1,435	2,499	6,806	3,753	2,802
South West	302	559	1,406	794	670
East Anglia	130	241	658	347	280
East Midlands	290	519	1,326	707	506
West Midlands	460	795	2,100	1,092	698
Wales	219	416	1,044	593	453
Yorkshire and Humberside	411	746	1,868	1,034	750
North West	588	1,073	2,587	1,454	1,077
North	273	540	1,314	709	510
Scotland	462	898	1,996	1,062	776
Northern Ireland	161	292	580	279	200
Republic of Ireland	316	584	1,058	602	323

EMPLOYEES IN MAJOR OCCUPATION GROUPS

(thousands)

Region	*Agriculture, Forestry, Fishing and Extractive*	*Manu-facturing*	*Service and Distribution*	*Activity Rate (per cent)*
South East	111	2,530	5,151	59·1
South West	56	416	832	46·5
East Anglia	55	208	369	49·9
East Midlands	119	631	645	55·9
West Midlands	60	1,216	1,002	59·5
Wales	73	336	533	46·7
Yorkshire and Humberside	126	873	1,002	56·0
North West	39	1,322	1,531	57·9
North	89	463	706	51·8
Scotland	105	746	1,247	56·6
Northern Ireland	12	182	291	49·1
Republic of Ireland	352	159	607	54·9

AGRICULTURAL LAND

Region	*Arable*		*Permanent Grass*		*Total in Improved Agriculture*		*Improved Agricul-ture as percentage of all Land*
	(thousand acres)	*(thousand hectares)*	*(thousand acres)*	*(thousand hectares)*	*(thousand acres)*	*(thousand hectares)*	
South East	2,980	1,207	1,203	487	4,183	1,694	62
South West	2,137	865	2,093	848	4,230	1,713	72
East Anglia	2,127	861	309	125	2,436	986	78
East Midlands	1,604	650	766	310	2,370	960	79
West Midlands	1,278	518	1,116	452	2,394	970	74
Wales	811	328	1,789	725	2,600	1,053	51
Yorkshire & Humberside	1,640	664	749	303	2,389	967	68
North West	413	167	660	267	1,073	434	54
North	1,201	486	1,215	492	2,416	978	51
Scotland	3,230	1,308	1,052	426	4,282	1,734	22
Northern Ireland	821	333	1,244	503	2,065	836	59
Republic of Ireland	1,302	527	10,517	4,259	11,819	4,786	70

SIZE DISTRIBUTION OF AGRICULTURAL HOLDINGS

Region	*0·25–4·75 acres* / *0·1–1·9 hectares*	*5–14·75 acres* / *2–5·9 hectares*	*15–49·75 acres* / *6–20·1 hectares*	*50–99·75 acres* / *20·2–40·3 hectares*	*100–149·75 acres* / *40·5–60·6 hectares*	*150–299·75 acres* / *60·8–121·4 hectares*	*300 acres and over* / *121·5 hectares and over*
South East	5,416	6,230	7,112	4,855	2,706	4,284	3,995
South West	4,042	6,539	10,525	9,702	5,387	5,892	2,435
East Anglia	3,684	3,639	4,082	2,779	1,472	2,233	2,293
East Midlands	2,364	2,920	4,508	3,456	2,034	2,805	1,962
West Midlands	2,244	4,744	6,309	4,307	2,594	3,676	1,631
Wales	1,570	6,220	11,999	9,895	4,487	3,330	569
Yorkshire & Humberside	2,129	3,160	4,947	3,949	2,216	2,791	1,936
North West	2,374	2,818	5,107	3,999	1,863	1,447	224
North	1,122	2,223	3,988	4,710	3,070	3,837	1,529
Scotland	10,518	12,266	8,623	7,250	4,880	6,264	3,135
Northern Ireland	4,377	15,172	29,857	9,836	1,681	631	123
Republic of Ireland	23,064	44,889	129,991	55,221	16,832	10,866	2,605

MANUFACTURING PRODUCTION
(£ million)

Region	*Number of Establishments*	*Total Sales*	*Net Output*	*Salaries and Wages*
South East	31,979	7,956	3,317	1,705
South West	4,033	1,286	482	252
East Anglia	1,809	529	207	104
East Midlands	5,837	1,725	682	365
West Midlands	10,644	3,626	1,454	826
Wales	2,328	1,298	434	219
Yorkshire and Humberside	9,729	2,667	1,025	550
North West	12,323	4,355	1,660	880
North	2,835	1,418	566	286
Scotland	6,569	2,219	850	433
Northern Ireland	1,863	621	174	93
Republic of Ireland	4,241	696	233	116

RETAIL DISTRIBUTION

Region	*Number of businesses*	*Turnover (£ million)*	*Numbers Employed (thousands)*
South East	149,459	4,075	871
South West	33,494	713	173
East Anglia	15,355	333	78
East Midlands	30,447	631	146
West Midlands	45,503	964	223
Wales	28,529	474	114
Yorkshire and Humberside	45,975	905	220
North West	80,780	1,376	330
North	26,413	596	144
Scotland	48,464	1,066	255
Northern Ireland	15,634	261	60
Republic of Ireland	29,750	243	110

ROAD TRANSPORT

Region	*Total surfaced road length* (*thousand miles*)	(*thousand kilometres*)	*Expenditure on roads* (£ *million*)	*Estimated Population per car*	*Goods Vehicles* (*thousands*)	*New Annual Registrations of all vehicles* (*thousands*)
South East	39·2	63·1	115·7	4·3	543	515
South West	27·9	44·9	33·7	3·9	118	94
East Anglia	11·6	18·7	9·7	4·0	60	52
East Midlands	13·8	22·2	33·8	4·5	110	89
West Midlands	16·5	26·6	34·8	4·6	157	161
Wales	20·5	33·0	30·0	4·9	70	53
Yorkshire and Humberside	15·8	25·4	42·0	5·8	137	119
North West	14·1	22·7	38·3	5·7	172	145
North	15·4	24·8	31·1	6·2	74	64
Scotland	29·0	46·7	49·5	6·2	121	110
Northern Ireland	14·0	22·5	18·7	5·5	41	34
Republic of Ireland	53·3	85·8	16·1	11·4	47	61

GROSS INCOME AND HOURS OF WORK
(adult males)

Region	*Manufacturing Earnings* (£ *per week*)		*Other Earnings* (£ *per week*)		*Average Working Week Manual Workers* (*hours*)
	Median	*Highest Decile*	*Median*	*Highest Decile*	
South East	25·1	35·7	22·0	34·0	46·2
South West	23·1	33·3	19·0	27·5	45·9
East Anglia	22·9	32·7	19·3	27·0	46·5
East Midlands	23·1	32·3	21·7	31·1	45·5
West Midlands	24·7	34·7	21·6	31·4	44·6
Wales	25·3	36·0	19·7	30·3	44·7
Yorkshire and Humberside	22·5	31·2	20·6	31·1	46·3
North West	23·5	33·9	20·8	32·8	46·1
North	23·6	33·9	20·5	30·1	45·9
Scotland	23·2	34·2	20·0	31·1	45·8
Northern Ireland	—	—	—	—	44·2
Republic of Ireland	15·4	—	14·6	—	45·3

Index

(Bold type indicates the more important references.)